THE ANCIENT NEAR EAST IN THE NINETEENTH CENTURY, I

Hebrew Bible Monographs, 67

Series Editors
David J.A. Clines and J. Cheryl Exum

Editorial Board
A. Graeme Auld, Marc Brettler, David M. Carr, Paul M. Joyce,
Francis Landy, Lena-Sofia Tiemeyer, Stuart D.E. Weeks

The Ancient Near East in the Nineteenth Century
Appreciations and Appropriations

I. Claiming and Conquering

Kevin M. McGeough

Sheffield Phoenix Press
2021

Copyright © 2015, 2021 Sheffield Phoenix Press
First published in hardback, 2015
First published in paperback, 2021
Published by Sheffield Phoenix Press
Sheffield Institute for Interdisciplinary Biblical Studies (SIIBS),
University of Sheffield, S3 7RA

www.sheffieldphoenix.com

All rights reserved.
No part of this publication may be reproduced or transmitted in any form or by any means, electronic or mechanical, including photocopying, recording or any information storage or retrieval system, without the publisher's permission in writing.

A CIP catalogue record for this book
is available from the British Library

Typeset by the HK Scriptorium

ISBN 978-1-909697-65-2 (hardback)
ISBN 978-1-910928-83-7 (paperback)
ISSN 1747-9614

For Elizabeth

CONTENTS

List of Illustrations	ix
Preface to Volume I	xv
Map of the Ancient Near East	xviii
INTRODUCTION TO VOLUME I	1
Part I: (Re)Discovering the Ancient Near East	27
Chapter 1 AFTER ABOUKIR: PARIS AS MEMPHIS AND THE PAST AS EMPIRE	28
Chapter 2 PRECONCEPTIONS: THE NEAR EAST IN THE BIBLE AND CLASSICAL LITERATURE	54
Chapter 3 THE STRONGMAN, THE GEOGRAPHER, AND THE DIPLOMAT: GIOVANNI BELZONI, EDWARD ROBINSON, AND AUSTEN HENRY LAYARD	83
Chapter 4 PROGRESS AND DECLINE; OR, HOW THE WHIGS AND THE ANTHROPOLOGISTS CLAIMED THE NEAR EAST	140
Chapter 5 VICTORIAN PERIODICALS AND THE BIRTH OF ARCHAEOLOGICAL JOURNALISM	184
Chapter 6 JOHN BULL AND HIS MOMMIES: THE ANCIENT NEAR EAST IN POLITICAL AND SOCIAL SATIRE	214
Part II: Exploring the Ancient Near East	275
Chapter 7 FROM TRAVELLER TO TOURIST IN THE NEAR EAST	276

Chapter 8
FROM TOURIST TO SCHOLAR: AMELIA EDWARDS AND
WOMEN TRAVELLERS   325

Chapter 9
SCIENCE IS MEASUREMENT: THE FIRST 'PYRAMIDIOTS'   350

Chapter 10
FROM GENTLEMAN SCHOLARS TO SCHOLARLY SOCIETIES: LEGITIMATING
THE SOCIALLY MARGINAL AND EXCLUDING MARGINAL READINGS   381

CONCLUSION TO VOLUME I   422

Bibliography for Volume I   431
Index of Biblical References and Other Ancient Texts   442
Index of Authors   443
Index of Subjects   446

LIST OF ILLUSTRATIONS

Map	The Near East: Marcus Dostie	xviii
1.1	August 10, 1793. The Festival of Unity at the Fountain of Regeneration on the ruins of the Bastille. Illustration by Bishop after Isidore Stanislas Helman's engraving, based on an original painting by Charles Monnet. Augustin Challamel, *Histoire-Musée de la République française*, I (Paris: Challamel, 1842), p. 333.	29
1.2	'Thebes–Ibis mummies', volume II, plate 52, in *Description de l'Égypte, ou recueil des observations et des recherches qui ont été faites en Égypte pendant l'expédition de l'armée française, publié par les ordres de sa majesté l'Empereur Napoléon le Grand* (Paris: Imprimerie Nationale, 1809–1829). Courtesy of the Thomas Fisher Rare Book Library, University of Toronto.	33
1.3	'Alexandria—View of the obelisk named Cleopatra's Needle and the so-called Roman Tower taken from the southwest', volume V, plate 32 in *Description de l'Égypte, ou recueil des observations et des recherches qui ont été faites en Égypte pendant l'expédition de l'armée française, publié par les ordres de sa majesté l'Empereur Napoléon le Grand* (Paris: Imprimerie Nationale, 1809–1829). Courtesy of the Thomas Fisher Rare Book Library, University of Toronto.	35
1.4	Library bookshelf designed for the *Description*. C. Percier and P.F.L. Fontaine, *Recueil de decorations interieures comprenant tout ce qui a rapport a l'ameublement* (Paris: Louvre, 1812), p. 107.	38
1.5	The Temple at Denderah, A, volume IV, plate 9, in *Description de l'Égypte, ou recueil des observations et des recherches qui ont été faites en Égypte pendant l'expédition de l'armée française, publié par les ordres de sa majesté l'empereur Napoléon le Grand*, folio 601. Beinecke Rare Book and Manuscript Library, Yale University, 1971.	46

1.6	Sphinx with Africanized nose. (A view of the sphinx at the pyramids at Gizeh, a Patera, charged with the portraits of Osiris and Isis, and sculptures of Egyptian musicians, Pompey's or Diocletian's Pillar, and Cleopatra's Needle.) Hand-coloured etching by Vivant Denon. © Victoria and Albert Museum, London. Purchased with the assistance of The Art Fund, the National Heritage Memorial Fund, Shell International and the Friends of the V&A.	47
1.7	*Blason de Paris* (coat of arms) from 1811. Wikimedia Commons.	52
3.1	Portrait of Belzoni as a strongman, by George Cruikshank, 1817. © Trustees of the British Museum	85
3.2	The Younger Memnon. © Trustees of the British Museum	86
3.3	View of the interior of the temple at Ybsambul [Abu Sumbul]. *Plates Illustrative of the Researches and Operations of G. Belzoni in Egypt and Nubia* (1820).	87
3.4	Section of the tomb of Samethis [Seti I] in Thebes. *Plates Illustrative of the Researches and Operations of G. Belzoni in Egypt and Nubia* (1820).	88
3.5	'Mode in which the young Memnon's head (now in the British Museum) was removed'. *Plates Illustrative of the Researches and Operations of G. Belzoni in Egypt and Nubia* (London: John Murray, 1822). Beinecke Rare Book and Manuscript Library, Yale University.	96
3.6	Forced passage into the second pyramid of Giza and Great Chamber in the second pyramid of Giza [Khafre's Pyramid]. Discovered by G. Belzoni, 1818 (pl. 12). *Plates Illustrative of the Researches and Operations of G. Belzoni in Egypt and Nubia* (1820).	97
3.7	Edward Robinson. Wikimedia Commons.	104
3.8	Portrait of Austen Henry Layard in Bakhtiari dress, by Amadea Preziosi (1843). © Trustees of the British Museum.	121
3.9	Excavations at Kuyunjik. From Austen Henry Layard, *Discoveries among the Ruins of Nineveh and Babylon with Travels in Armenia, Kurdistan, and the Desert: Being the Result of a Second Expedition* (New York: Harper & Bros., 1853), p. 88.	123
3.10	Lowering the bull. From Austen Henry Layard, *A Popular Account of Discoveries at Nineveh* (London: John Murray, 1851), frontispiece.	124

List of Illustrations   xi

3.11 'Human-headed and eagle-winged bull from Nimrud', *Illustrated London News*, October 26, 1850. 125

3.12 Colossal statue of a winged lion from the northwest palace of Ashurnasirpal II (Room B). © Trustees of the British Museum 126

3.13 Discovering the head. From Austen Henry Layard, *A Popular Account of Discoveries at Nineveh* (London: John Murray, 1851), p. 48. 130

3.14 'Baiting the Nineveh bull', *Punch* 28 (1855). 131

3.15 'The member for Nineveh digs out the British bull', *Punch* 28 (1855). 132

3.16 'Playing the Nineveh bull in the Stambul China-shop', *Punch*, March 2, 1878. 136

4.1 Here, Morton presents two mummified heads from his collection and compares them with an artistic depiction from Thebes. He classifies all three heads as those of 'idiots'. Samuel George Morton, *Crania Aegyptiaca; or, Observations on Egyptian Ethnography Derived from Anatomy, History and the Monuments* (Philadelphia: John Penington, 1844), p. 16. 153

4.2 Turquoise djed pillar amulet from the British Museum collection. Late Period (after 600 BCE). © Trustees of the British Museum. 169

4.3 Younger Memnon, Nineteenth Dynasty. © Trustees of the British Museum 180

5.1 'Nimrud sculptures just received at the British Museum (writing sample)', *Illustrated London News*, March 31, 1849. 192

5.2 'Nimrud sculptures: The siege and impalement of prisoners', *Illustrated London News*, December 16, 1948. 194

5.3 'The Nimrud sculptures: A domestic scene', *Illustrated London News*, March 2, 1850. 195

5.4 'Shipping the Great Bull from Nimrud', *Illustrated London News*, July 27, 1850. 199

5.5 'Cleopatra's Needle and Somerset House', from a watercolour by W.L. Wyllie. 205

5.6 'Proposed method for the removal of Cleopatra's Needle from Alexandria', *Illustrated London News*, March 10, 1877. 207

5.7 'Cleopatra's Needle. First night out: in the Bay of Biscay', *Illustrated London News*, January 26, 1878. 208

5.8	'Arrival of Cleopatra's Needle', *Illustrated London News,* January 26, 1878.	210
5.9	'Engineering methods for setting Needle on foundation', *Illustrated London News,* August 10, 1878.	211
6.1	'The Egyptian puzzle', from *The Egyptian Red Book* (London: William Blackwood & Sons, 1885).	221
6.2	'The mummy government', from *The Egyptian Red Book* (London: William Blackwood & Sons, 1885).	222
6.3	'Kicked out', from *The Egyptian Red Book* (London: William Blackwood & Sons, 1885).	223
6.4	'The sleeping beauties', from *The Egyptian Red Book* (London: William Blackwood & Sons, 1885).	223
6.5	'El Dar-Bé', *Punch* 92 (1887), p. 253.	239
6.6	'Golf is being played very much in Egypt', *Punch* 110 (February 1, 1896), p. 52.	240
6.7	'By tram to the pyramids', *Punch* 112 (February 13, 1897), p. 77.	240
6.8	'The ancient Egyptian Henley Regatta', *Punch* 113 (July 10, 1897), p. 12.	240
6.9	'The ancient Egyptian Lord Mayor's Show', *Punch* 117 (1899), p. 217.	241
6.10	'The <u>Valet</u> of the Nile', *Punch* 115 (November 12, 1898), p. 217.	241
6.11	'A fragment of the title-page of the ancient Egyptian *Punch*', *Punch* 114 (1898), p. 193.	241
6.12	'The earliest record of the appearance of the sea-serpent', *Punch* 111 (October 17, 1896), p. 181.	242
6.13	'Britannia discovering the source of the Nile', *Punch* 44 (June 6, 1863), p. 233.	243
6.14	'Turk the Sublime!', *Punch* 110 (March 7, 1896), p. 110.	243
6.15	'Egyptian Question in the time of King Krisis the Startler', *Punch* 83 (August 5, 1882), pp. 52-53.	244
6.16	'Embalmed—that they may keep until 1880—or longer. Mummy Hendricks to Mummy Tilden: "I am glad I am not so feeble as you"', by Thomas Nast; from *Harper's Magazine* (July 7, 1877). Beinecke Rare Book and Manuscript Library, Yale University.	245
6.17	'Disrael-I in triumph; or, the modern sphynx', *Punch* 52-53 (June 15, 1867), pp. 246-47.	247
6.18	'Mosé in Egitto!!!', *Punch* 68 (December 11, 1875), p. 246.	248

List of Illustrations

6.19	'The sphinx is silent', *Punch* 100-101 (July 15, 1876), p. 12 [28].	249
6.20	'The French sphinx, or the riddle of the present', *Punch* 35 (August 7, 1858), p. 38.	251
6.21	'The member for Nineveh digs out the British bull', *Punch* 27 (April 7, 1855), p. 135.	252
6.2	'Baiting the Nineveh bull', *Punch* 28-29 (May 12, 1855), p. 187.	254
6.23	'Joseph in Egypt', *Punch* 97 (1889), pp. 246-47.	256
6.24	'Israel and Egypt; or, turning the tables', *Punch* 95 (September 8, 1888), pp. 110-12.	258
6.25	'From Nile to Neva', *Punch* 99 (1890), pp. 67.	263
6.26	'Received with thanks', *Punch* 73 (1877), p. 159.	265
6.27	'Cleopatra's Needle-woman. (A sight of sites)', *Punch* 73 (1877), p. 194.	267
7.1	Drawing, Shepheard's Hotel Cairo, about 1860–1870, by Hercules Brabazon Brabazon. Purchased with the assistance of The Art Fund, the National Heritage Memorial Fund, Shell International and the Friends of the V&A. © Victoria and Albert Museum, London.	296
7.2	Shepheard's Hotel, *The Graphic,* September 30, 1882.	296
7.3	The *Skandria*, a *dahabiyya* used for the Prince and Princess of Wales' trip up the Nile. *The Illustrated London News,* February 27, 1869.	301
7.4	The Emperor of Austria being 'dragged' up the Great Pyramid. *The Illustrated London News,* December 25, 1869.	312
7.5	American women vandalizing the temple at Denderah. *The Graphic,* July 26, 1890.	315
8.1	Amelia Edwards. From Amelia Edwards, *A Thousand Miles up the Nile* (London: George Routledge & Sons, 1899 [1881]), frontispiece.	331
8.2	'The great rock-cut tomb of Nubia [Abu Simbel]'. From Amelia Edwards, *A Thousand Miles up the Nile* (London: George Routledge & Sons, 1899 [1881]), frontispiece.	333
8.3	'Floor plan of the Speos'. From Amelia Edwards, *A Thousand Miles up the Nile* (London: George Routledge & Sons, 1899 [1881]), p. 307.	334

9.1	The Great Pyramid in the centre of the world; Piazzi Smyth, *Our Inheritance in the Great Pyramid* (London: W. Ibister & Co., new and enlarged edn, 1874), plate V.	360
9.2	Ground plan of the Great Pyramid; Piazzi Smyth, *Our Inheritance in the Great Pyramid* (London: W. Ibister & Co., new and enlarged edn, 1874), plate II.	361
9.3	Various measurements including the sacred cubit and the pyramid inch; Piazzi Smyth, *Our Inheritance in the Great Pyramid* (London: W. Ibister & Co., new and enlarged edn, 1874), plate III.	362
9.4	Equality of areas demonstrating the sacred cubit; Piazzi Smyth, *Our Inheritance in the Great Pyramid* (London: W. Ibister & Co., new and enlarged edn, 1874), plate IV.	363
9.5	Section drawing of the Great Pyramid; Piazzi Smyth, *Our Inheritance in the Great Pyramid* (London: W. Ibister & Co., new and enlarged edn, 1874), plate I (frontispiece).	373
10.1	John Gardner Wilkinson. Wikimedia Commons.	384
10.2	George Smith in an 1875 engraving from *The Illustrated London News*. Wikimedia Commons.	393
10.3	Tablet XI of the Gilgamesh Epic. AN00372371_001. © Trustees of the British Museum.	394
10.4	Image of Gerald Massey, dated to 1856. Wikimedia Commons.	396
10.5	Samuel Birch. Wikimedia Commons.	412

Preface to Volume I

This is the first book in a three-volume series devoted to the study of the reception of the ancient Near East in the nineteenth century. It is not a history of the profession, except where it could not be avoided, so much as rumination on the various means through which people made sense of the new discoveries in that region. The study itself is organized more according to genre than anything else, with the three volumes dividing the subject into three larger thematic topics: travel, materiality and fantasy. Yet all three volumes are interrelated in a fugue-like structure, and, as is argued throughout, many of the same people, sites, concepts and understandings recur in different ways and in unexpected combinations. To facilitate some historical coherence, Great Britain has been taken as the central region of this study, although manifestations of ancient Near Eastern reception in the United States, France, Germany, Italy and other nations are shown consideration where appropriate throughout. Cross-references in the three books are designed to help readers follow arguments along different paths, and each indicates first the volume number and then the chapter number.

A rigid chronological constraint is somewhat artificial, and all three volumes take a very long view of the nineteenth century at times. The nineteenth century, however, is, it is argued throughout these books, central to the reception history of the ancient Near East for this is the period in which the rediscovery of the region by European and North American explorers began in earnest, and it is when Near Eastern studies came to be formalized as a distinct academic enterprise, separate from but related to the study of the Bible and classical literature. Not coincidentally, this is also a period that featured a tremendous explosion in literacy, in media production and mass transportation, all of which, as shall be shown, are entangled with the ways in which people began to think about Egypt, Mesopotamia and biblical Israel.

This project emerged very much out of my time first as a student and later as a faculty member at the University of Lethbridge. One of the most influential courses that I had the pleasure of taking as an undergraduate student was an advanced seminar on Victorian popular culture, led by Christopher Hosgood. Many of the ideas from that class stuck with me throughout my later graduate training in Near Eastern studies, and many of my graduate instructors (like Jeffrey Tigay and Holly Pittman at the University of

Pennsylvania) encouraged me to continue my studies of how the ancient Near East was made sense of within European intellectual traditions. When I returned to the University of Lethbridge as an instructor, I held a two-year appointment in the Liberal Education program, where I worked closely with my former instructor and now colleague D. Bruce MacKay. I had the good fortune to co-teach advanced seminars with Bruce, two of which encouraged me to return to the topic of Victorian popular culture: a seminar on 'Progress' and a seminar on 'Orientalism'. Although the material covered in those courses was only tangential to this project, the intellectual stimulation of working with Bruce and two very motivated and diverse groups of students inspired the purposeful multidisciplinarity of this project. After my two-year term was completed in the Liberal Education program, I was appointed to the Department of Geography, where archaeology is housed at the University of Lethbridge. That very nineteenth-century pairing of geography and archaeology further inspired this work, as did my interaction with colleagues who were conceptually related by problems of spatiality.

Numerous other colleagues at the University of Lethbridge are deserving of thanks for their conversations, assistance and encouragement of this project. Walter Aufrecht, a long-term mentor, shared his insight into academic genealogies, among other topics. I have taken great advantage of Malcolm Greenshields's expertise in European history and popular culture. Many friendly arguments were had with Jerimy Cunningham (to varying degrees of coherence) during long nights at the pub, usually followed by a sharing of bibliography from different fields of study. Christopher Epplett's encyclopaedic knowledge of popular culture made him an essential reference source. Janay Nugent offered information on specifically Scottish aspects of this work, and Christopher Burton gave advice more generally on the period. Maria Ng and Goldie Morgentaler in the Department of English advised on various issues relating to the nineteenth century, travel literature and imperialism. My partner in archaeological crime in the Geography Department, Shawn Bubel, is also deserving of thanks for her varieties of support over the course of this project. I would also like to thank the three departmental assistants that I had the pleasure to work with while writing these books: Bev Garnett, Charlene Sawatsky and Margaret Cook. The Department of History invited me to give a colloquium on this topic early on in its inception, and the feedback at the time was very useful. Similarly, members of the Department of Religious Studies also influenced my thinking on the topic. Jane Allen and Mary Butterfield in our Office of Research Services both helped me secure funding for this work, which included a Community of Research Excellence Development Opportunity (CREDO) Grant and a Research Dissemination Grant, both of which were essential to the completion of this study. This funding allowed me to hire student research assistants over the years, all of whom are now continuing their careers as graduate students: Darren Joblonkay, Dylan Johnson, Elsa Perry and Jeff Werner. Calvin Tams, while conducting his own doctoral research, was able to help me with some archival work as well. Marcus J. Dostie, a graduate student in Geography, drew the map printed in these books (pp. xviii-xix). I could not have done this project without Rosemary Howard and the interlibrary loan staff at the University of Lethbridge. Likewise, a semester-long study leave allowed me to finish these three books. Most of all, I must thank my wife, Elizabeth Galway, to whom these books are lovingly dedicated, who is in the Department of English and whose nineteenth-century knowledge and editorial talents have been, as always, tremendously helpful.

Many scholars outside of the University of Lethbridge are also deserving of thanks for their assistance in this project. Benjamin Porter of the University of California at Berkeley discussed many matters of disciplinary history with me. Matthew Rutz at Brown University was a constant source of new secondary literature and bibliographic ideas for the project. Bruce Routledge at the University of Liverpool was helpful in suggesting ways of drawing out some of the main arguments from the larger study. Steven Fine at Yeshiva University in New York shared with me an early version of his own work that was especially helpful for Volume III. Andrew Bond, Carol Davies, Charlotte Heath-Bullock and Stefan Lambert showed me great hospitality during my research trips to Europe, and were rarely puzzled by the often-bizarre demands to visit certain places. Representatives of many institutions facilitated my work and went above and beyond in offering me assistance or encouragement. Patricia Usick at the British Museum was very considerate in giving up her own time in order to allow me to peruse some of the correspondence in the Egyptian section. Felicity Cobbing at the Palestine Exploration Fund allowed me access to the archive and supplied me with high-resolution images of the Shapira forgeries in Volume II. Jonathan Schmitz of the Chautauqua Institution Archives, Oliver Archives Center answered questions about the institution and offered encouragement for the project. The nearly unbelievable access to images available from the British Museum and the Victoria & Albert Museum have also improved these volumes and made the illustrations financially feasible. Both are model institutions of scholarly access and are deserving of my thanks.

Finally, I would like to thank the people at Sheffield Phoenix Press for their work on this volume. Cheryl Exum initially invited me to consider submitting my work to their press, and David Clines graciously worked with me throughout the proposal and submission phase.

Kevin M. McGeough
Department of Geography (Archaeology)
University of Lethbridge
June 2014

CONSTANTINOPLE

TELL EL YAHÛDIEH
0 5 10 20
KILOMETERS

HELIOPOLIS
CAIRO
GIZA
SAQQARAH
HELWAN
MEMPHIS

BYBLOS
BEIRUT
SIDON
TYRE
AKKO/ACRE
GALILEE SEA

MEDITERRANEAN SEA

ROSETTA
SAIS
ALEXANDRIA
NAUKRATIS
CAIRO

JAFFA
JERUSALEM
ASHKELON

SHILOH
GIBEON
JERICHO
DIBON
DEAD SEA

JORDAN

LOWER EGYPT

SINAI DESERT

0 5 10 20
KILOMETERS

BAHARIYAH OASIS
BENI HASAN
AMARNA

EGYPT

DENDERAH

VALLEY OF THE KINGS
GOURNA
DEIR EL-MEDINA
THEBES/LUXOR
KARNAK

NILE

THEBES/LUXOR
EDFU
UPPER EGYPT
PHILAE
BERENICE

RED SEA

ABU SIMBEL

The Near East

0 100 200   400   600   800
Kilometers

Map credit: Marcus Dostie

Introduction to Volume I

And did those feet in ancient time
Walk upon England's mountains green:
And was the holy Lamb of God,
On England's pleasant pastures seen!

And did the Countenance Divine,
Shine forth upon our clouded hills?
And was Jerusalem builded here,
Among these dark Satanic Mills?

Bring me my Bow of burning gold;
Bring me my Arrows of desire:
Bring me my Spear: O clouds unfold!
Bring me my Chariot of fire!

I will not cease from Mental Fight,
Nor shall my Sword sleep in my hand:
Till we have built Jerusalem,
In England's green & pleasant Land.

From the preface to *Milton a Poem* by
William Blake (1804), better known today
as *Jerusalem*

William Blake's *Jerusalem* readily captures a perceived relationship between England and the Bible lands. Perhaps it is best known to twenty-first-century audiences as a unison song (treated variously as a patriotic anthem or hymn). Sir Hubert Parry brought this relatively forgotten poem to the centre of British consciousness when he set it to music in 1916. Robert Bridges, Britain's poet laureate at the time, had compiled it in an anthology (*The Spirit of Man*) as a means of inspiring the nation at war. Initially intended for the Fight for Right campaigns, the song was picked up more generally, especially in suffragette, socialist and other progressive contexts. King George V was said to have preferred it over 'God Save the King', and in some ways it grew to become an alternate anthem of Britain. Although not technically a hymn, the song is performed in English church services to this day. In this form, it reflects the merger of patriotism and Christianity that was typical of the early twentieth century.

As an anthem, it has been taken as an attack on the ecological destruction wrought by the industrial revolution or the conformity enforced by the Church of England (both potentially the 'dark Satanic mills'). Eitan Bar-Yosef suggests some of the different meanings that *Jerusalem* has for the British that heard/hear it: 'For some, dreaming of a lost Eden, the powerful pledge to rebuild Jerusalem offers a glimpse of heaven on earth . . . the fantasy of a socialist England . . . bitter-sweet memory of England's imperial greatness and the patriotic hope that glory is still within reach . . .'.[1] *Jerusalem*, as an anthem, however, is a greatly recontextualized version of Blake's poem, which was written as a prelude to his *Milton: A Poem*, and is placed after a diatribe against the influence of Graeco-Roman thought.[2] *Milton* is one of his prophetic books, which present his own vision of mythological history in poetic form. Here the lines of the poem should be treated almost literally, for Blake is suggesting that the origins of Christianity (and Judaism) can be found in England. This is not an argument about the universality of Christianity or the relationship between religion and the nineteenth-century state. This is a description of the universal religion that predated the flood, and he is asking if Christ ever actually walked in England.

The answer is given to some degree in his prophetic books and especially in his last, *Jerusalem: The Emanation of the Giant Albion*. There, Blake reinterprets the book of Genesis and argues that Britain was the original Holy Land and the Druids were the first patriarchs.[3] Some take this as a parody of Genesis, but Blake was sincere. True Druidism, and the universal religion that predated the flood (according to Blake), was preserved only by the Druid Abraham, and Zion was originally located near Paddington (as Blake argues in chap. 2 of *Jerusalem*, entitled 'To the Jews').[4] This was not just a flight of Blake's fancy but reflected more general views held by some contemporary English scholars.[5]

---

1. Eitan Bar-Yosef, *The Holy Land in English Culture 1799–1917: Palestine and the Question of Orientalism* (Oxford: Clarendon Press, 2005), p. 1.

2. The prologue begins as follows: 'The Stolen and Perverted Writings of Homer & Ovid.: of Plato & Cicero. which all Men ought to contemn.: are set up by artifice against the Sublime of the Bible . . .'. The condemnation of the classics is clear as is the celebration of biblical thought.

3. A.L. Owen, *The Famous Druids: A Survey of Three Centuries of English Literature on the Druids* (Westport, CT: Greenwood Press, 1962), p. 225.

4. Owen, *Famous Druids*, pp. 228-32.

5. Owen cites a number of these works, including the anonymous 1810 work *Complete History of the Druids . . . with an Inquiry into their Religion and its Coincidence with the Patriarchal* (*Famous Druids*, pp. 233-34).

This kind of mythologizing connection between Britain and the Near East was found not only in Blake's fantasy visions. For Irish and Scottish nationalists, ancient Egypt played a critical (but legendary) role in the formation of their states.[6] Tradition holds that Scota (or Scotia), the first queen of Scotland and founder of the Scots and Gaels, was the daughter of an Egyptian king. In some versions of the story, the king's name is Cingris, and he gave his daughter in marriage to a Babylonian language scholar named Niul. Their son was the first Gael, and he created the Gaelic language by combining the seventy-two best features of the known languages of the world. Another version has Scota marrying Geytholos (Gathelus) and encountering Moses before being exiled from Egypt. Whichever version was current at a given time, when Scottish kings were sworn in over the Stone of Destiny (Stone of Scone), their genealogy was recited all the way back to their presumed Egyptian origins. Blake, then, was operating from a well-established semi-scholarly tradition.

It is difficult to estimate the influence of Blake's thinking at the time, but *Jerusalem* does not seem to have been particularly well received initially. Yet as the nineteenth century progressed, there was something of a re-evaluation of Blake's writing and art, and while his literal arguments were not taken seriously by mainstream England (although they became tremendously important in esoteric circles) the symbolic meanings were embraced. As Bohlman and Davis write:

> William Blake's 'Jerusalem', in contrast [to the Jerusalem of diaspora Judaism], emerges from an England ravaged by the Industrial Revolution, with its devastation of traditional identities. Into the reality of that devastation, nonetheless, is fused myth, the poetic query of whether 'the Holy Lamb of God' might once have visited 'England's pleasant pastures'. The slippage that myth here allows is doubtless facilitated by the present in England—a belief which finds earlier expression, for example, in Arthurian legend. Yet the same slippage is surely made possible by an emerging Orientalism, in which timelessness and placelessness enter the time and place of history. The symbols that accrue to Blake's poem and Parry's song, with their fusion of biblical, classical and English pastoral imagery, thus acquire the fundamental attributes of an English Orientalist representation of Jerusalem. The song becomes anti-modernist, with England's future no less capable of idealizing the Garden of Eden in a new Jerusalem.[7]

---

6. See, for example, Edward J. Cowan, 'Myth and Identity in Early Medieval Scotland', *The Scottish Historical Review* 63, no. 176, part 2 (October 1984), pp. 111-35; William Matthews, 'The Egyptians in Scotland: The Political History of a Myth', *Viator* 1 (1970), pp. 289-306.

7. Philip V. Bohlman and Ruth F. Davis, '*Mizrakh*, Jewish Music and the Journey to the East', in *Music and Orientalism in the British Empire, 1780s–1940s: Portrayal of*

Archaeology and the exploration of the ancient Near East, which become prominent parts of British mass culture, facilitated and encouraged these readings. The relationship between progress and decline that these encounters produced, the triumph of British imperialism as manifest through intellectual exploration, and the implications of the colonial encounter for the understanding of the self helped the English claim the Holy Land as their own, even as these same positivist explorations proved that Blake's claims for a druidical patriarchal heritage could only be fantasy.

Yehoshua Ben-Arieh contrasts European exploration of the Holy Land with that of Africa, arguing that whereas Africa was virtually unknown, the Holy Land bore a spirit of familiarity due to its reception history.[8] As Bar-Yosef has argued, there was a British tradition, especially strong in the nineteenth century, of 'internalizing those central Biblical images . . . and applying them to England and the English'.[9] Bohlman and Davis write:

> A parallel symbolism arose in nineteenth-century industrial Britain, where Orientalist vocabularies of the arts and music came to occupy a liminal space, geographically and historically, with passage beyond that space equivalent to reaching the New Jerusalem. Transposed to rural England, this imaginary Jerusalem came to represent, for English artists and poets, an idealized vision of their country's future, while for social reformers it symbolized their concrete aspirations for its present. It was along the modern journey to that New Jerusalem that British Orientalism would thus appear as a series of political and cultural detours, and it is along that journey to Jerusalem that we first encounter the English nineteenth century.[10]

Jonathan Rose has similarly argued that the Sunday school tradition created a powerful sense of connection between the English and the Holy Land.[11] This tradition of internalizing the Bible was not new to the nineteenth century; for the English this can be traced back as early as the Crusades, but in the nineteenth century it became fused with a new experiential level of knowledge of the Holy Land through both elite and popular culture.

Yet Jerusalem was not the only frame through which England, and London in particular, was viewed. London came to be seen as the city in its essential form, and Babylon was the quintessential city of ancient times.[12] And so, London, as a whole and in part, was also Babylon. This could be

---

the East (ed. Martin Clayton and Bennett Zon; Music in 19th-Century Britain; Hampshire: Ashgate, 2007), pp. 95-125 (99).

8. Yehoshua Ben-Arieh, *The Rediscovery of the Holy Land in the Nineteenth Century* (Jerusalem: Sefer Ve Sefel Publishing, 2007 [1979]), p. 12.

9. Bar-Yosef, *Holy Land*, p. 4.

10. Bohlman and Davis, '*Mizrakh*', p. 97.

11. Jonathan Rose, *The Intellectual Life of the British Working Class* (New Haven, CT: Yale University Press, 2nd edn, 2010), pp. 350-51.

12. It should be noted that Rome often fulfilled the same semiotic role as Babylon.

a Babylon of urban progress, such as in the *Illustrated London News* story from December 31, 1842, quoted by Peter Sinnema, which celebrates the urban majesty of London's skyline ('the mighty congregation of buildings which forms the modern Babylon').[13] Or this could be the Babylon of the Old Testament prophets—a locus of vice, decadence and corruption, such as in 1794 prophecies of the Swedenborgian George Riebau.[14] Babylon was synonymous with the metropolis and with vice, and the metropolis itself came to be synonymous with vice. So London was also viewed from some perspectives as the decadent Babylon of the nineteenth century. These metaphorical views of London became entangled with and complicated by archaeological explorations of Jerusalem, Babylon and Egypt.

This use of an imagined relationship between a contemporary state and the ancient Near East was not unique to Britain. In the mid-nineteenth century, Napoleon III used Egypt as a reference point in the art celebrating his coronation. By the beginning of the twentieth century, the ancient Near East was still in use as a reference point for European political life. The Serbian colonel Dragutin Dimitrijević, for example (a member of the Black Hand Group who conspired in the assassination of Archduke Franz Ferdinand), used the codename 'Apis', after the ancient Egyptian god depicted as a bull. The archaeological site of Masada is a potent symbol of modern Israeli militarism and nationalism. Saddam Hussein's referencing of the Neo-Babylonian King Nebuchadnezzar in his own political propaganda is arguably the best-known recent example of this kind of overt use of the ancient Near East for political gain. This study, though, is primarily about Britain. It will look to Italy, Germany and especially France and the United States periodically, but British interpretations are the central concern. It seeks to look at how different groups made meaning out of ancient Near Eastern discoveries during the period when such explorations began in earnest—the nineteenth century.

Part of the inspiration for this study comes from Richard Jenkyns's *The Victorians and Ancient Greece*. In this important work, Jenkyns studies those institutions that the Victorians felt were Greek (but often were not) as well as Victorian interpretations of *Hellas*. Jenkyns's work is not a history of scholarship and does not spend much time on the analysis of the works of professional classicists. Instead, Jenkyns studies how ancient Greece was thought about by nonspecialists, how this thinking influenced understandings of ancient Greece and how it influenced Victorian society.

13. Peter W. Sinnema, *Dynamics of the Pictured Page: Representing the Nation in the* Illustrated London News (Aldershot: Ashgate, 1998), p. 25.
14. In these prophecies, Riebau argued that London, the spiritual Babylon, was to be destroyed. Swedenborgians, or members of 'the New Church' were part of new religious movements based on the prophecies of the Swedish scientist Emmanuel Swedenborg (1688–1722).

Given the extent of information available about the Victorian era, Jenkyns chose to 'take one element in the history of the period, to trace its diversity at different times and in different places, to hope that in this way a partial study may shed some light, however oblique and uncertain, upon a larger whole'.[15] Jenkyns approaches his study thematically as opposed to strictly chronologically or along disciplinary boundaries (i.e., literary criticism, art history) and does not force his observations into a larger thesis or argument. Rather, he explores persistent ideas in the Victorian era regarding the Greek world. This is the approach I have followed in this study.

While the approach and methods are similar, the subject matter is very different. Despite the fact that both the ancient Near East and ancient Greece are ancient cultures, the manners in which these cultures were manifest in the nineteenth century were markedly different. Much of Jenkyns's study involves politics, fine art, elite literature (such as poetry or 'respectable' novels) and language; whereas my work dwells more on popular matters. The study of the ancient Greeks (especially their language, literature and art) was part of a typical elite education, and knowledge of these subjects marked the knowledgeable as elite. Greece was seen as the basis of much that was considered good by the Victorians, and many classicists seemed to have wished to be as 'Greek' or 'Roman' as possible. As shall be explored here, the ancient Near East had a different entry into nineteenth-century society, and thinking about the Near East (while sharing some similarities to classical studies, especially in terms of biblical and Hebraic studies) played out in differing fashions. This study is particularly concerned with new discoveries in the nineteenth century and the new material engagement with the region, especially through archaeology and the discovery of new texts. It deals less directly with the many scholars who focused primarily on the textual analysis of the Bible. So while scholars like Julius Wellhausen made substantial contributions to Near Eastern studies at this time, they are rarely discussed here. Likewise, this three-volume study is not meant to be a professional history per se (numerous excellent works are already available), and so the choice of which scholars' works are discussed is selective and at times, representative of the nineteenth century but not necessarily representative of what, in retrospect, are seen as high points in Near Eastern studies. So, for example, E.A. Budge's suspect interpretations of Egyptian culture are discussed more thoroughly than W.F. Petrie's development of techniques in chronological seriation.

One of the goals of this study is to chart the different ways in which the study of the ancient Near East intersected and became absorbed into popular culture and how the academic study of this subject diverged from popu-

---

15. Richard Jenkyns, *The Victorians and Ancient Greece* (Oxford: Basil Blackwell, 1980).

lar dissemination of the results of these studies. The archaeology of Egypt and the Bible lands came to be increasingly adopted by mass culture, while the study of Mesopotamia has had only intermittent success in this venue. In the twenty-first century, these trends have continued to some degree. Mesopotamia (despite Iraq's prominence in geo-political events) is essentially ignored in popular culture, except, arguably, as the location of many 'firsts' in world history surveys. Meanwhile, biblical archaeology (to use a term that is used less frequently by twenty-first-century academics) still successfully interacts with popular audiences. Venues like the magazine *Biblical Archaeology Review* communicate legitimate (for the most part) academic research about the lands of the Bible to nonspecialist audiences. Of course the commodification of biblical archaeology still leads to the dissemination of much pseudo-scholarship, and debates about the boundaries of what is considered legitimate scholarship are commonplace.[16] Egypt's presence in twenty-first-century culture is bifurcated with very strict separation of the academic study of Egypt from popular explorations of Egypt. Indeed, the 'two Egypts' seem to be kept willfully separate as popular manifestations of Egyptology undermine the academic respectability of the scholarly discipline, and the scholarly discipline undermines the mystical and mysterious representation of Egypt that sells so well.

The roots of these different trajectories in mass consumption of the ancient Near East can be seen in the nineteenth century, influenced by a variety of changes in the development of popular culture. Peter Bailey, one of the pioneers of popular culture studies, offers an eloquent description of how the subject can be understood in a nineteenth-century context:

> Popular culture is conceived of here as a sprawling hybrid, a generically eclectic ensemble or repertoire of texts, sites, and practices that constitute a widely shared social and symbolic resource. . . . The constituency for popular culture fluctuates and recomposes; while not coterminous with any single class it is broadly democratic, answering both to the ritual promptings of an indigenous custom, old and newly forged, and the slicker formulations of mass or middlebrow commercial confection. It generates its own initiatives, while readily appropriating from other sources, including 'high' or elite culture. Its materials are put to specific and selective use

---

16. An extreme example of this type of conflict centres on Canadian film-maker Simcha Jacobovici's documentaries and books on biblical archaeology. Having no advanced degrees in Near Eastern studies, Jacobovici claimed to have discovered the tomb of Jesus' family and in his series *The Naked Archaeologist* argues for nonstandard interpretations of archaeological discoveries. Joe Zias wrote numerous articles and blog posts denouncing Jacobovici's work, criticisms that Jacobovici claims are libelous and Jacobovici has responded by suing Zias.

by its consumers, who variously embrace, modify, or resist its meanings under the particular conditions and relationships of its reception.[17]

This study shall explore some of the ways that the ancient Near East, which at the outset of the nineteenth century was best understood as a manifestation of elite culture, was adopted and revised in popular culture, how the scholarly significance of the ancient Near East was understood and adapted by producers and consumers of popular culture and how the growing popularity of this subject among the middle classes created new commercial prospects involving mummies, pyramids and biblical history.

But how popular was popular culture? Whose culture was this? Bernard Porter has, in the context of discussions of imperialism, warned against assuming that working-class values are reflected at all in the cultural productions of the elite.[18] What is of interest here are the various ways that the discoveries of Near Eastern exploration manifest in different types of media aimed at different audiences. In this study, the term 'popular' is used not in a Thompsonian sense but in opposition to 'specialist'; distinctions of class in this instance (not necessarily elsewhere) are less important than distinctions of degrees of fluency in the study of the Near East (and time devoted specifically to this enterprise).[19] Likewise, 'mass culture' refers more to mass-marketed materials as opposed to the working classes or masses. In some ways, the upper classes may have been more familiar with, for example, Rider Haggard's mass-marketed *She* than the working classes (although this point is problematized later in this study). As Patricia Anderson has noted, mass culture 'was never exclusively the experience of any one group or class, and for this reason "mass" must be understood to designate multiple social layers'.[20] The distinction between mass and high culture is taken here to be a distinction between inclusivity and exclusivity, which often manifested along class lines but should not be understood to always have correlated directly with those distinctions. Throughout the nineteenth century, the economic potential of mass culture eroded the influence of a more restricted high culture as patronage gave way to middle-class purchasing power as the means of financing cultural production.

It should also not be assumed that the production of knowledge moved in only one direction. The public consumption of the ancient Near East was

17. Peter Bailey, *Popular Culture and Performance in the Victorian City* (Cambridge: Cambridge University Press, 1998), pp. 10-11.

18. Bernard Porter, '"Empire, What Empire?" Or, Why 80% of Early- and Mid-Victorians Were Deliberately Kept in Ignorance of It', *Victorian Studies* 46, Papers from the Inaugural Conference of the North American Victorian Studies Association (2004), pp. 256-63 (257).

19. A Thompsonian approach equates 'popular' culture with 'working-class culture'.

20. Patricia Anderson, *The Printed Image and the Transformation of Popular Culture, 1790–1860* (Oxford: Clarendon Press, 1991), p. 11.

and is a partnership between those with the ideological sanction to engage in the academic work, those that distribute the knowledge and those that consume it. There is an entanglement here that has only recently begun to be acknowledged. Stephanie Moser has argued that popular/public representations and more typical academic products 'work together as active "partners" in the construction of knowledge'.[21] Moser notes that although much work has been done to understand how genres of representation produce new knowledge of the past, more work needs to be done. Benjamin Breed has called for an approach to reception history in biblical studies that embraces the constitutive effect of reception on the original text and that explores how a biblical text creates different effects in different times and places.[22] As this study shall show, the exploration of the ancient Near East and the reception of that exploration within the context of the nineteenth century together created new modes of thinking that were not just unidirectional.

In some ways this study may commit what Jonathan Rose has called the 'receptive fallacy'—where the text's message is examined through the study of its text rather than its audience's response.[23] It is not impossible to study the audience response to these forms, although a thorough examination would result in a considerably longer book. Circulation figures, ticket sales, and admissions records are all quantitative measures of reception and these are taken into account here. Critical reviews provide some insight into audience response, although the nineteenth-century critic represents a subsection of intellectual and cultural life of his (and sometimes her) own. Memoirs are also sources on reception, although museums and travel are discussed in more detail in diaries than memories of seeing pantomimes or reading horror fiction. These qualitative responses, as preserved, become part of the cultural production of the ancient Near East as well, informing and becoming the mass culture. In these cases, the boundaries of creation and reception become blurred. Following James Secord, it is assumed here that 'readers, watchers, and listeners actively engage with the media as a way of making sense of their own lives' and thus there are no truly 'typical' readers.[24] Just because something was printed does not mean that all agreed with it or understood it in the same manner.

21. Stephanie Moser, *Designing Antiquity: Owen Jones, Ancient Egypt and the Crystal Palace* (Paul Mellon Centre for Studies in British Art; New Haven, CT: Yale University Press, 2012), p. viii.

22. Benjamin Breed, 'Nomadology of the Bible: A Processual Approach to Biblical Reception History', *Biblical Reception* 1 (2012), pp. 299-322.

23. Rose, *Intellectual Life*, p. 4.

24. James A. Secord, *Victorian Sensation: The Extraordinary Publication, Reception, and Secret Authorship of* Vestiges of the Natural History of Creation (Chicago: University of Chicago Press, 2000), p. 519.

Despite the recognized importance of audience reaction, this is fundamentally a study of the presentation of the ancient Near East. In this, I follow Ralph O'Connor who has recognized the importance of spectacle and literature in the public presentation of the natural sciences in the nineteenth century.[25] As O'Connor has recognized for what will later be called biology and paleontology, there was less strict distinction between scientific writing and literature, and he views the presentation of scientific ideas from a literary perspective.[26] O'Connor argues that understanding the narrative strategy of science writers is important to understanding the science of the time and the public's reaction.[27] He argues that although some scholars may reject an approach that assumes that authorial intention is relevant, it is useful to approach scientific-literary works as having multiple meanings—multiple meanings intended by the author (as opposed to a single monolithic meaning) and readers who actively constructed multiple meanings from their encounters with the works.[28] For O'Connor then, his study is: 'a study of scientific projections'.[29] What follows, to some extent, is a study of archaeological and historical projections, especially as manifest through various forms of literature and spectacle.

It is not necessarily surprising that the ancient Near East was explored through nineteenth-century mass culture since this was a period in which mass culture exploded in commercial importance. Economically, the 1830s and 1840s were difficult times in England, and as economic hardships lessened in the 1850s, new economic patterns emerged. The emergence of the middle class led to a more urban population with a greater proportion of the population literate and with free time on their hands. Indeed, free time was an essential precondition for much of the economic growth that developed alongside of the middle class, since the new businesses required consumers; middle-class people needed money to consume with and free time in which to consume. Yet as Bailey has noted, the advent of leisure (and the consumption that was concomitant with it) created an awkward tension for a class whose 'root traditions had been determined by the imperatives of work' and had 'only an attenuated leisure culture to draw upon . . .'.[30] Thus leisure was almost dangerous space, since it was at odds with the Protestant work ethic that differentiated the middle class from the upper and lower classes, and perhaps more explicitly dangerously, provided both time and

---

25. Ralph O'Connor, *The Earth on Show: Fossils and the Poetics of Popular Science, 1802–1856* (Chicago: University of Chicago Press, 2007), pp. 1-2.
26. O'Connor, *Earth on Show*, pp. 13-14.
27. O'Connor, *Earth on Show*, p. 6.
28. O'Connor, *Earth on Show*, pp. 7-8.
29. O'Connor, *Earth on Show*, p. 8.
30. Bailey, *Popular Culture*, p. 19.

space in which the individual was free from the types of normative social controls that traditionally governed behavior.

The responses to this dangerous, but commercially necessary, free time, were to look for moral and religious justifications for its existence and moral and religious (and ideally consumer) activities to fill this time. The observance of the Sabbath acted as a model for the religious justification for leisure, or non-productive time. Increased productivity likewise justified leisure, and it came to be believed that workers needed time to 'recharge' and subsequently be more productive at work. As a subject of leisure, encounters with the ancient Near East were perfectly suited to alleviate Victorian concerns about moral or rational pastimes, since commercial or institutional encounters of these lands could always be understood as educational in terms of biblical literacy, in terms of world historical understanding (and especially the understanding of the place of the British empire in the grander scheme of things), and in terms of arts and aesthetics. Recent scholarship has emphasized the varied constituency of the middle class, and the 'billiard ball' view of monolithic and cohesive middle and working classes has been largely abandoned. Thus a variety of types of leisure experiences needs to be accounted for, and it must be assumed that individual tastes played a substantial role in the individual experiences of leisure activities.

The commercial successes of entertainment featuring Egypt and the Bible lands further encouraged the creation of avenues for delivery of ancient Near Eastern content in popular form. Bailey has noted that by the 1890s, the products of this mass culture were marketed by 'a new breed of entrepreneurs to appeal to the widest possible audience irrespective of class or other divisive market variables'.[31] This trend is observable in the changes of the mass delivery of information about the ancient Near East over the course of the century. As the presentations became less strictly educational, they required less 'work' on the part of the consumer to understand and relied more on stock images and genres that consumers were already literate in. Moreover, these processes should not merely be seen as a type of capitalist imposition on middle-class culture; the ways in which the ancient Near East were experienced in the nineteenth century were too varied for such a monolithic reading. There was something of a Gramscian consensus here; the consumers wanted experiences that they felt were educational, exotic, entertaining, morally conservative (but skirting the boundaries of the accepted) and easy to digest. The producers were happy to provide these experiences, given that they sold well, and the religious and moral authorities were happy that these experiences kept people away from what were considered more dubious types of activities.

---

31. Bailey, *Popular Culture*, p. 49.

Of course, representations of the ancient Near East in the nineteenth century cannot be solely understood as a commercial experience for the burgeoning middle class. The interest in ruins and long-vanished cultures reflect a Romantic interest where the past is glorified and celebrated through a sense of loss. As Gillen D'Arcy Wood describes it, 'the ancients "are what we were"', and just as nature reflects something that civilization has divorced us from, the past is another idealized space to which we cannot return but can hopefully visit.[32] The inhabitants of the Near East, and especially the Bedouin, presented a romantic alternative to industrial life, free from clocks, schedules and the pollution of urban life. Like the noble savage of the eighteenth century, the Bedouin provided a fantasy example of escaping from the rigors of everyday life, and their seemingly simple and unchanging lives were a romantic alternative to urban and industrial progress. The exotic East, more generally, presented fantasies of alternative social rules that were both more and less prescriptive than those of urban England. It was not a great leap to merge this kind of romanticism with biblical studies, and especially since Bedouin life was presumably changeless, as early as the eighteenth century, scholars such as Johann David Michaelis argued that the study of contemporary Palestine could shed light on ancient Israel. Other scholars would go so far as to argue that God had purposefully preserved Bedouin society to help later Christians better understand Scripture, and numerous scholarly works used this line of reasoning as the basis for ethnographic analogies between the Bible and the Bedouin.[33] These new understandings gradually replaced the traditional explanation for why Palestine was described as so fertile in the Bible and yet seemed to be such a wasteland to travellers. It had long been argued that the land was itself punished, or even perhaps cursed, for having been the location of Christ's crucifixion and the unfathomable crime of deicide.[34] Europeans seemed to have little difficulty embracing two mutually contradictory views of the Near East simultaneously: the Near East was utterly changeless, and the contemporary Near East represented a significant decline from the civilizations of antiquity.

This romantic sense is reflected in Frederick Bohrer's 2003 work *Orientalism and Visual Culture: Imagining Mesopotamia in Nineteenth-Century*

---

32. Gillen D'Arcy Wood, *The Shock of the Real: Romanticism and Visual Culture, 1760–1860* (New York: Palgrave, 2001), p. 121.

33. For more on nineteenth-century books that compared Bedouin and biblical customs, see Daniel Martin Varisco, 'Orientalism and Bibliolatry: Framing the Holy Land in Nineteenth-Century Protestant Bible Customs Texts', in *Orientalism Revisited: Art, Land and Voyage* (ed. Ian Richard Netton; New York: Routledge, 2013), pp. 187-204.

34. For more on this tradition, see Naomi Shepherd, *The Zealous Intruders: The Western Rediscovery of Palestine* (London: Collins, 1987), p. 14.

Europe.³⁵ There, Bohrer lays out an approach to studying the reception and generation of conceptualizations of Mesopotamia in the nineteenth century. Although his work is primarily focused on nineteenth-century visual culture, his approach and conclusions have wide-ranging ramifications for this project. Using 'dreams' as a metaphor for nineteenth-century approaches to the ancient Near East, Bohrer states:

> Rather than inherent values, the properties of ancient Mesopotamian artifacts as perceived by their nineteenth-century viewers are best approached as something like shared dreams: social projections situated in unique, discontinuous contexts (such as personal, communal, institutional, or national), applied to a relatively common repertory of objects.³⁶

For Bohrer, 'Mesopotamia' is a floating signifier, a word that is itself stable but a concept that is not.³⁷ Bohrer is not the first to understand the nineteenth-century experience of the ancient Near East through the metaphor of a dream. Victorian writers, especially those that travelled in the Near East, talk of the dream-like experience of the antiquities. Amelia Edwards, in her 1877 *A Thousand Miles up the Nile,* writes of her experiences of the great ruins in Thebes and Karnak: 'We rode back across the plain, silent and bewildered. Have I not said that it was like a dream?'³⁸ Martin Meisel has likewise read historical representations from the nineteenth century as dream-like in function: 'a process of assimilating the strange to the familiar, of integrating the old and the new, of eliminating anxiety'.³⁹

Building on this dream metaphor, Bohrer operates from a conceptual framework that blends together elements of art-historical reception theory (especially the works of Hans-Robert Hauss and Walter Benjamin) and postcolonial studies (especially the works of Edward Said and Homi Bhaba) to better understand how exoticism worked as a system for generating ideas about the ancient Near East. Bohrer uses the more generic term 'exoticism' as opposed to 'orientalism' in his analysis as a means of avoiding the binarisms that are implicit in discourse about orientalism.⁴⁰ For Bohrer, exoticism is an arrangement in which 'two distinct cultures' are 'separated by a palpable remoteness', and yet that remoteness is surmounted by a proximity between the cultures either through emulation or explicit reference

---

35. Frederick Bohrer, *Orientalism and Visual Culture: Imagining Mesopotamia in Nineteenth-Century Europe* (Cambridge: Cambridge University Press, 2003).
36. Bohrer, *Orientalism*, p. 3.
37. Bohrer, *Orientalism*, p. 5.
38. Amelia Edwards, *A Thousand Miles up the Nile* (London: George Routledge & Sons, 1899 [1881]), p. 154.
39. Martin Meisel, *Realizations: Narrative, Pictorial, and Theatrical Arts in Nineteenth-Century England* (Princeton, NJ: Princeton University Press, 1983), pp. 229-30.
40. Bohrer, *Orientalism*, p. 17.

to the other.⁴¹ Nineteenth-century archaeology is a worthwhile subject for this type of approach, given that archaeology brings a physical proximity to the exotic by removing artifacts from an original geographic and temporal setting and resituating them in a new context of the museum or, more abstractly, the academic study. Bohrer points out that 'remoteness' in exoticism is normally thought of in terms of geographical space but that temporal space is just as meaningful.⁴² This book seeks to build on Bohrer's work by further examining the nature of this recontextualization of Near Eastern antiquity in nineteenth-century England and the 'transformations' of both cultures within this exoticist arrangement.

As Bohrer points out in reference to visual culture, discoveries in Assyria (and I would extend this to discoveries throughout the Near East) destabilized the 'distinction between high and popular modes of visual perception'.⁴³ Unlike classical studies, which if anything, reified high and popular culture distinctions in the nineteenth century, the ancient Near East made this distinction difficult to sustain. On the one hand, the popular appeal of Assyrian reliefs in contrast to the popular disapproval of the Elgin Marbles (and concomitant elitist justifications of their acquisition and aesthetic value) points to a stable situating of the Near East within mass culture. On the other hand, the importance that the Near East played in the intellectual thought of the nineteenth century and the difficulties in making sense of archaeological artifacts without specialist mediation points to problems in conceiving of this material along a bifurcated elite–popular or high–low axis.

The prominence of the ancient Near East in nineteenth-century popular discourse is apparent in a number of media that will be explored in this study. Eitan Bar-Yosef has approached popular discourse about the Holy Land through two conceptual schema: vernacular biblical culture and vernacular orientalist culture.⁴⁴ These refer not to elite or scholarly understandings of the Bible and the Orient but to the understandings that a nonspecialist in the nineteenth century may have held. Bar-Yosef is particularly concerned here to distinguish his work from that of Said's, which concentrates on academic orientalism, but most certainly the elite–popular axis was very fluid, especially in this period before the professionalization of Near Eastern studies. Bar-Yosef, unlike Said, reads explorations of the Holy Land as explorations of the British self, not as explorations of the other. As he argues, the Bible provided the British with nostalgia and memories for ancient Palestine, feel-

---

41. Bohrer, *Orientalism*, p. 15.
42. Bohrer, *Orientalism*, p. 36.
43. Bohrer, *Orientalism*, p. 26.
44. Bar-Yosef, *Holy Land*, pp. 11-12.

ings of significant connectedness. Palestine and the Holy Land were more important for the British as metaphors than as part of the actual empire.[45]

John Davis has identified similar impulses in the United States' relationship to the Holy Land.[46] Beginning with the Puritan colonists, the settlement of the United States was understood through biblical metaphor, a metaphor that proved to be very flexible and relevant to a variety of differing political and social circumstances. The Bible was seen to provide a guide to the settlement of the new land and eventually the creation of a new nation (that was both secular and divinely inspired simultaneously).[47] Town names such as Canaan and Bethlehem perpetuated this view that North America was the new Holy Land, the settlers were the new Hebrews and Native Americans were Canaanites. There was a strong belief that the settlement of North America (especially the United States) by Europeans was divinely inspired, as had been the conquest of the Promised Land under Joshua. At times this view was taken quite seriously, as is the case with the Mormon movement (Chapter III.6). In such cases, the Anglo-Israel theories of old, similar to the myths about Scotia, were revived and revised. These theories held that lost tribes of Israel had made their way to Europe (or North America as would be argued in the nineteenth century) and that traces of this Hebraism were apparent in various traditions. As Davis has clarified, this imagined (but believed) genealogy connected nineteenth-century Protestants (mostly) with the ancient Hebrews but explicitly not modern Jews, circumventing the Semitic heritage of Christianity.[48] While this may have been an extreme revisionist approach to history, held by only marginal groups and thinkers, scholarship (especially archaeological and cartographical explorations) allowed North Americans and Europeans to exercise their relationship to the Holy Land through the mastery of its landscape.

It was not just the Holy Land that provided politically generative metaphors for the United States. Ancient Egypt provided complex and contradictory models for thinking about life in the new republic. In the nineteenth century in particular, issues of slavery and race were especially considered in relationship to the United States. On a literal 'scientific' level this manifested in the comparison of Egyptian craniums with African-American

45. Bar-Yosef, *Holy Land*, p. 301.
46. John Davis, 'Holy Land, Holy People? Photography, Semitic Wannabes, and Chautauqua's Palestine Park', *Prospects* 17 (1992), pp. 241-71; John Davis, *The Landscape of Belief: Encountering the Holy Land in Nineteenth-Century American Art and Culture* (Princeton, NJ: Princeton University Press, 1996), esp. pp. 3-26. See also Rachel Hallote, *Bible, Map, and Spade: The American Palestine Exploration Society, Frederick Jones Bliss, and the Forgotten Story of Early American Archaeology* (Piscataway, NJ: Gorgias Press, 2006), p. 8.
47. Davis, *Landscape*, pp. 13-16.
48. Davis, 'Holy Land, Holy People', p. 265.

craniums to identify the biological differences of race. Scott Trafton has shown that metaphorical uses of Egypt were more complex, however.[49] For if the Puritan settlers associated themselves with Joshua's Israelites settling the Holy Land, the post-Revolutionary government built its symbols of governance with Egyptian motifs. African-Americans also saw the new Republic in Egyptian terms, with themselves being the new Hebrews in bondage to pharaoh, finding hope in the story of the exodus for their own liberation. The North became their metaphorical Holy Land within the United States.[50] Perhaps contradictorily, although when speaking of metaphor there is no need to postulate a coherent monolithic sensibility, African-Americans also identified with pharaonic Egypt. The 'black orientalism' that would emerge as Afrocentrism in the twentieth century was rooted in this period. Nationalists such as Edward Wilmot Blyden (1832–1912) saw pharaonic Egypt as a black African society. Blyden, who moved to Liberia after being denied entrance to theological schools in the United States, connected black Africa with Egypt, using this to demonstrate connections with the Arab world of North Africa, while promoting Islam as the religion of Africa. These connections, as Trafton has shown, served a dual purpose, since they also provided a historical genealogy for pan-Africanism that gave black Africa cultural superiority over Arab North Africa.[51]

Bar-Yosef's, Davis's and Trafton's readings of these relationships to the Holy Land are part of a larger scholarly recognition that the Victorians were interested in the Orient as much for its affinities with them as for its differences. From an explicitly imperial context, David Cannadine writes:

> *pace* Edward Said and his 'Orientalist' followers, the British Empire was not exclusively (or even preponderantly) concerned with the creation of 'otherness' on the presumption that the imperial periphery was different from, and inferior to, the imperial metropolis: it was at least as much (perhaps more?) concerned with what has recently been called the 'construction of affinities' on the presumption that society on the periphery was the same as, or even on occasions superior to, society in the metropolis. Thus regarded, the British Empire was about the familiar and domestic, as well as the different and the exotic: indeed, it was in large part about the domestication of the exotic—the comprehending and the reordering of the foreign in parallel, analogous, equivalent, resemblant terms.[52]

This seems to naturally emerge from Said's conclusions, and it is not necessary to posit an either/or situation. Both similarities and differences

---

49. Scott Trafton, *Egypt Land: Race and Nineteenth-Century American Egyptomania* (Durham, NC: Duke University Press, 2004).
50. Davis, *Landscape,* pp. 22-23.
51. Trafton, *Egypt Land,* pp. 23-24.
52. David Cannadine, *Ornamentalism: How the British Saw their Empire* (Oxford: Oxford University Press, 2001), p. xix.

were emphasized—the systems of meanings were not necessarily coherent or stable. Difference could be emphasized in one context and smoothed over in another. As Steven Holloway has argued, individual orientalist viewpoints were very different (politically, socially, etc.), and it cannot be assumed that there was a monolithic orientalist perspective.[53]

Cannadine further argues that the hierarchical divisions of British society were so normative-seeming that these same structures were imagined for the rest of the empire (and by extension it could be argued they were understood for ancient civilizations). He explains:

> Far from seeing themselves as atomized individuals with no rooted sense of identity, or as collective classes coming into being and struggling with each other, or as equal citizens whose modernity engendered an unrivalled sense of progressive superiority, Britons generally conceived of themselves as belonging to an unequal society characterized by a seamless web of layered gradations, which were hallowed by time and precedent, which were sanctioned by tradition and religion, and which extended in a great chain of being from the monarch at the top to the humblest subject at the bottom. That was how they saw themselves, and it was from that starting point that they contemplated and tried to comprehend the distant realms and diverse society of their empire.[54]

Although perceptions of race should not be glossed over, Cannadine's basic point is sound—that class and the connectedness of class relationships within a web-like hierarchy were fundamental lenses through which the British observed the other. Working out and establishing hierarchy homogenized the empire and the exterior trappings of this (knights, peers, viceroys, etc.). What he calls ornamentalism were the performances of this homogenization.[55] This ornamentalism was (and is) embedded in anachronism, and thus the study of the past, and especially the perceived great civilizations that bore similar trappings (or at least cultural practices that could be read as such), also provided evidence that could be used to build this homogeneity.

One of the most immediate experiences where 'difference' or 'sameness' was mapped out was in the experience of tourism. Travel literature became one of the main media through which the general public experienced the ancient Near East in the nineteenth century. In the initial stages of establishing mechanisms of communicating scientific knowledge about other places, scholars relied on this genre of writing, which had become well established in the eighteenth century. The study of travel literature is a well-developed

---

53. Steven W. Holloway, 'Introduction: Orientalism, Assyriology, and the Bible', in *Orientalism, Assyriology and the Bible* (ed. Steven W. Holloway; Hebrew Bible Monographs, 10; Sheffield: Sheffield Phoenix Press, 2007), pp. 1-41 (31).
54. Cannadine, *Ornamentalism*, p. 4.
55. Cannadine, *Ornamentalism*, pp. 85, 122, 126.

discipline in its own right, and it is impossible to fully do justice to its theoretical developments here, but some points should be made at the outset, since they have a bearing on much of the rest of the discussion of this volume.[56]

Travel literature is the literature that emerges from the intersection of two or more cultures—that intersection is fundamental to the genre. Chloe Chard argues that travel writers need to perceive difference in order to have a subject matter, but at the same time, they need to be able to render the other into an understandable form through language.[57] Dennis Porter describes it as 'the way we conceptualize and represent the world, categorize its peoples according to a variety of overlapping schemas, affirm the relationships between them, and perceive our own (apparently central) place within this imaginary global geography'.[58] He continues:

> From the beginning, writers of travel have more or less unconsciously made it their purpose to take a fix on and thereby fix the world in which they found themselves; they are engaged in a form of cultural cartography that is impelled by an anxiety to map the globe, center it on a certain point, produce explanatory narratives, and assign fixed identities to regions and the races that inhabit them.[59]

That the early scholars of the ancient Near East should choose this medium through which to communicate their experiences should not be surprising. These should not be taken as straightforward accounts—these are the generative documents of the relationship between Europe and the rest of the globe, and between the nineteenth century and the past. Although one should not push the constructed nature of these relationships too far, this was the media for that initial construction, in which the major tropes were established.

If the basic premise of travel writing is an exploration of the interaction between self and other, then it cannot merely be the other that is reflected. Porter follows Foucault in arguing that the most interesting forms of the genre are those in which self-transformation, through those experiences, is apparent.[60] Rana Kabbani goes so far as to suggest that the other was

---

56. Travel literature relating to the Holy Land was extremely popular in the nineteenth century and this was no doubt one of the most important media for encountering the ancient Near East. Ben-Arieh estimates that at least five thousand items (books, articles, etc.) were published on the topic between 1800 and 1878 (Ben-Arieh, *Rediscovery*, p. 15). Ben-Arieh's book provides a useful overview of many of these travellers.

57. Chloe Chard, *Pleasure and Guilt on the Grand Tour: Travel Writing and Imaginative Geography 1600–1830* (Manchester: Manchester University Press, 1999), p. 3.

58. Dennis Porter, *Haunted Journeys: Desire and Transgression in European Travel Writing* (Princeton, NJ: Princeton University Press, 1991), p. 3.

59. Porter, *Haunted Journeys*, p. 20.

60. Porter, *Haunted Journeys*, p. 5.

only a 'backdrop' for the hero's journey.[61] In some instances this was surely the case, but with the early archaeological explorers, that 'backdrop' is so fundamental to the enterprise that it cannot be minimized so readily. Travel literature is also a literature of desire and of longing. Travel, as Porter has shown, is often driven by urges that cannot, for whatever reason, be satisfied at home.[62] It is, in his words, 'transgressive' as all borders can be. The results of these experiences, in their extremes, are either conservative or revolutionary. For either the traveler finds what he or she is looking for and realizes that his or her home and traditions are lacking, or the 'test of difference' has proven that home is truly superior to what is abroad.[63] In practice, at an individual level, travellers likely experienced a complex combination (and often contradictory combination) of feelings toward their travels, and so such clear-cut distinctions were never really straightforward. As Bar-Yosef cautions, 'one must recognize that denial, suppression, or simply ignorance were equally significant in defining the affinity between "here" and "there"', and perfect understanding of themselves or the other should by no means be posited for any of these travellers.[64] Chard offers another option: that travel literature, by identifying elements that *should* be seen as transgressive, keeps in check potentially destabilizing influences.[65] In this case, travel writing establishes boundaries regarding transgression; writers describe elements of the other in condemning tones, which allow the writers to participate in the experience but at the same time reifies the fact that it is or should be forbidden.[66] Similarly, danger is simultaneously to be avoided in travel but also provides the traveler with a sense of self-congratulation for having survived.[67]

At the same time that the location of travel becomes a place of escape and newness, the home is a location of duty. As Porter has shown, much of early travel literature reflects guilt felt toward the homeland, and the fulfilling of one's duty in relation to the home helps to sublimate the guilt of the traveler.[68] The travel writer then, as Kabbani has shown, 'feels compelled to note down his observations in the awareness of a particular audience: his fellow-countrymen in general, his professional colleagues, his patron, or his monarch'.[69] Archaeology and the collection of information about the

61. Rana Kabbani, *Europe's Myths of Orient* (Bloomington, IN: Indiana University Press, 1986), p. 7.
62. Porter, *Haunted Journeys*, p. 9.
63. Porter, *Haunted Journeys*, p. 28.
64. Bar-Yosef, *Holy Land*, p. 300.
65. Chard, *Pleasure and Guilt*, p. 11.
66. Chard, *Pleasure and Guilt*, p. 30.
67. Chard, *Pleasure and Guilt*, p. 213.
68. Porter, *Haunted Journeys*, p. 9.
69. Kabbani, *Europe's Myths*, p. 1.

ancient world are duty fulfilled through travel. Here is the exploration of the exotic engaged in as patriotic activity, as salvage, as a contribution to world knowledge. Curiosity, as Barbara Benedict has explored, is justified as a noble and moral behavior when the collection of objects, experiences or knowledge is enacted to educate those at home.[70] The anxiety for this type of traveler, then, is to make a contribution, to not merely repeat the experiences of previous travellers or find out information that is already known.[71] Long historical explanations and geographical descriptions were the enactment of this duty and formed the educational content of the accounts. Archaeology and historically meaningful observations were easily fit into what Chard has referred to as the fundamentally 'divagatory' nature of travel writing.[72] From a literary standpoint, archaeological observations justify digressions within a larger narrative.

The Near Eastern travel literature of the nineteenth-century contains both narratives of adventure and the dry cataloguing of scientific discoveries. A harrowing escape from bandits could be located, textually and semiotically, adjacent to a list of measurements of a monument. As Chard has noted, travel literature invokes two complementary claims: that the author is 'engaging in a form of imaginative seduction' while at the same time 'ordering knowledge'.[73] Porter's reading of Darwin's *The Voyage of the Beagle* is equally applicable to Giovanni Belzoni's or Austen Henry Layard's archaeological discoveries: '*The Voyage of the Beagle* invites an approach that relocates representation and the practice of science itself in the matrix of an individual as well as a collective history'.[74] However, in these cases, since description is the *point* of the work (or at least is appealed to as the point), the balance is shifted so that narrative supports description, the opposite of a fictional or purely autobiographical work.[75] Thus, to continue to follow Porter's reading of Darwin and apply it to the archaeologist: 'The naturalist, it turns out, is a traveler who trains the passionate intensity of his gaze. Darwin's natural history is a science of looking twice'.[76] So too is the archaeologist's science. Porter sees the travelogue replaced as a literary form for the academic enterprise with the rise of anthropology and ethnography.[77] For here is 'scientific' travel literature made professional. It is the domain of the trained anthropologist, a Malinowski or a Mead, not

---

70. Barbara M. Benedict, *Curiosity: A Cultural History of the Early Modern Period* (Chicago: University of Chicago Press, 2001), p. 203.
71. Porter, *Haunted Journeys*, p. 12.
72. Chard, *Pleasure and Guilt*, p. 6.
73. Chard, *Pleasure and Guilt*, p. 10.
74. Porter, *Haunted Journeys*, p. 147.
75. Porter, *Haunted Journeys*, p. 157.
76. Porter, *Haunted Journeys*, p. 163.
77. Porter, *Haunted Journeys*, p. 247.

the diplomat (Layard) or fortune hunter (Belzoni). Thus the archaeologist as hero traveler must recast him- or herself as the heroic scientist, and any narratives of adventure come to undermine the data, not enhance it.

Kabbani and others have asserted that travel writing is an essentially masculine venture, that despite the numerous female travel writers of the nineteenth century, this was essentially a patriarchal enterprise: 'for it fed on and ultimately served the hierarchies of power'.[78] That many of the female travel writers did put forward conservative views in their works is accurate. However, the situation is significantly more complex, and the sheer number of female archaeologists, especially toward the end of the nineteenth century, suggests that this was, from a gender perspective, an activity that helped subvert Victorian norms. There are many facets to the issue. For Gertrude Bell, who infamously hated the company of other women and did not support women's suffrage, Near Eastern archaeology seemed to provide an avenue into the patriarchy. However, women such as Amelia Edwards established new practices that revolutionized the field and subverted many of the patriarchal aspects of Near Eastern exploration. These, and other cases, challenge Kabbani's claims that Near Eastern studies was uniformly patriarchal.

As Edward Said has shown, the 'relationship between the Occident and Orient is a relationship of power, of domination, of varying degrees of a complex hegemony . . .'.[79] Said's conception of orient and occident should not be taken as 'stable' entities; for him they are a combination of empirical experience and imagination.[80] While this is not the place to summarize Said's work and the multiplicities of responses that emerged from it, it is important to acknowledge his demonstration of the relationship between the academic and nonacademic orientalism that is the subject of this book and the colonialist/imperialist power structures with which it was knowingly and unknowingly complicit. Kabbani adds to this argument in relation to travel literature:

> To write a literature of travel cannot but imply a colonial relationship. The claim is that one travels to learn, but really one travels to exercise power over land, women, peoples. It is a commonplace of Orientalism that the West knows more about the East than the East knows about itself.[81]

Archaeology is one instrument with which this power is exercised. The data produced was the 'better' knowledge that the West held over the

---

78. Kabbani, *Europe's Myths*, pp. 7, 86.

79. Edward Said, *Orientalism* (New York: Vintage Books, 25th anniversary edn, 2003 [1978]), p. 5.

80. See his comments on misreadings of his book in his 1994 afterword (Said, *Orientalism*, p. 331).

81. Kabbani, *Europe's Myths*, p. 10.

East, and the methods of archaeology were the acts of knowing that were unavailable to the East, except as mediated by the West. In his later *Culture and Imperialism*, Said writes that imperialism and colonialism are not just about physical control and possession. Rather, the imperialist-colonialist enterprises are informed by 'ideological formations that include notions that certain territories and people *require* and beseech domination'.[82] Later in the same book, Said explains that there was little resistance to the idea of empire from within the colonial powers since the idea that distant peoples needed to be subjugated was proven to be much more significant than just profit; the moral obligation for imperialism was a deeply held belief.[83] As shall be shown in later chapters, early archaeology cannot be disentangled from these ideological formulations, itself both informed by those ideologies and at the same time reifying them and creating new ones. Chapter I.3 shows that for Egypt, Palestine and Mesopotamia, early archaeological explorers spoke to and informed audiences about the need for European or North American domination, although the nature of the domination called for was highly variable.

For Said, Kabbani and many others, the dominant mode of relation between East and West in the nineteenth century was the imperial. As Kabbani has stated, 'If it could be suggested that Eastern people were slothful, preoccupied with sex, violent, and incapable of self-government, then the imperialist would feel himself justified in stepping in and ruling'.[84] The experiences of travellers such as Florence Nightingale, who was horrified by the animal-like life of the modern Egyptians squatting in the ruins of the ancient past, functioned as arguments for colonialism, rooted in ideas of progress.[85] As has been shown by many scholars and shall be further demonstrated throughout this book, the nineteenth-century argument for colonialism was made by juxtaposing the failure and decline of the Arab world with the glories of its past civilizations and its primacy as the original location of world civilization.[86] The question, then, of the relationship between ancient and modern Egyptian was a difficult one to answer, and,

---

82. Said, *Orientalism*, p. 9.
83. Said, *Orientalism*, p. 10.
84. Kabbani, *Europe's Myths*, p. 6.
85. For more on Nightingale, see John Barrell, 'Death on the Nile: Fantasy and the Literature of Tourism 1840–1860', *Essays in Criticism* 41.2 (1991), pp. 97-127 (107).
86. For example, one of the travelogues that greatly influenced early nineteenth-century thinking about Egypt, Comte de Volney's (Constantin François de Chassebœuf) 1787 *Voyage en Syrie et en Égypte pendant les années 1783, 1784, et 1785,* highlighted various problems in eighteenth-century Egyptian society in contrast to the glories of the past.

as John Barrell has argued, despite the various 'scientific' approaches that were employed, no clear resolution could be offered.[87]

Here then, is where the archaeologist comes in as imperialist and imperial facilitator. To continue Kabbani's description: 'The image of the European colonizer had to remain an honourable one: he did not come as exploiter but as enlightener. He was not seeking mere profit, but was fulfilling his duty to his Maker and his sovereign. . . .'[88] As neither soldier nor capitalist, the archaeologist provided the intellectual and moral authority of the responsible world citizen to the role of imperialist. Benedict has suggested that curiosity justified and legitimated the imperial enterprise, and what can be better seen as the material manifestation of curiosity than archaeology?[89]

Much has been written already about the relationship between colonialism and archaeology, and this does not need be repeated here. Colonial competition and national prestige play a great role in Near Eastern exploration, as motivating forces and justification for state support of the enterprise. These issues will come up intermittently throughout this study, but, no doubt, arguments about the importance of archaeology to colonialism will seem underdeveloped, partially because they are taken as a given. Here, my desire is to go beyond Said and the academy and explore how this colonially inspired knowledge is coopted by the commercial drives of entertaining the growing middle class. The focus, especially in Volumes II and III, will be on how these academic and politically motivated studies were and continue to be coopted by the entertainment industry and other industries of mass culture.

As Porter has argued, it cannot be presumed that issues of imperialism per se were of great interest to all classes, and the concept of imperialism should not be used as a simple causal explanatory framework.[90] Porter's argument that educational programs taught the obligations of various classes to one another (i.e., the elites were taught to rule and lead and the working classes to work hard and obey) more so than imperial pride seems upheld in many of the instances of mass-culture manifestations of ancient Near Eastern studies.[91] It was not pride in the nation state that was necessarily being taught; it was, to use Porter's term, the 'complementarity' of the different elements of British society that was being taught. The ancient Near East provided empirical evidence for the successes and failures of this kind of class complementarity.

87. Barrell, 'Death on the Nile', p. 118.
88. Kabbani, *Europe's Myths*, p. 6.
89. Benedict, *Curiosity*, p. 251.
90. Porter, 'Empire, What Empire?', p. 256.
91. Porter, 'Empire, What Empire?', p. 260.

Similarly, it is interesting to note that there is little direct connection between the archaeological exploration of Palestine in the nineteenth century and the Zionist movement in the region. Ben-Arieh and Shepherd point out that few of the early academic explorers of the region were Jews and that Jewish scientific study of the land did not come until much later.[92] Part of this must be due to the widespread and almost casual anti-Semitism that was typical of elite Victorian society (an issue that is worth further exploration in the context of Near Eastern reception but due to its complexity is only alluded to periodically throughout the following volumes). It may be the case, however, that the work of these nineteenth-century, mostly Christian, explorers, established the foundations for a view of the Near East that confirmed it as fundamentally European space that facilitated these later movements of people. As Ian Baucom has cogently argued, Englishness has long been associated with a specific locale, and the visibility of England's past as manifest in geography was fundamental to the constitution of English spatial identity.[93] The mapping out of Near Eastern space and identifying historical sites made the region into a European locale (or similarly American, French, German or Italian).

Regardless of these issues of cultural imperialism, it is assumed here that for the explorers of the ancient Near East themselves, an actual interest in their subject was really their main driving force. From an *emic* perspective, these scholars legitimately wanted to understand the past and to present those findings to other scholars. Their main motivations were intellectual curiosity and a desire to answer certain questions about the ancient Near East. That these motivations are not the main subject of my study should not be taken as an argument that academic motivations were not the most important motivations for this work on an individual level. Genuine interest is a real motivation for Near Eastern scholarship, but what is of interest here is how these interests are entangled with other modes of thinking.

These are some of the general theoretical underpinnings of this work. Given that each chapter deals with different types of materials and different areas of historical study, more specific theoretical underpinnings will be addressed throughout. A multifaceted approach is called for with this kind of subject and to attempt to apply a unitary framework to these different fragments of cultural production would miss the point. The field of film studies has to grapple with varieties of different types of cultural productions and unstable meaning, and so modeling an approach from that academic enterprise may be helpful. Victor Burgin has argued that rather than just study the narrative of an individual movie, film studies should seek to

---

92. Ben-Arieh, *Rediscovery*, pp. 232-33; Shepherd, *Zealous Intruders*, p. 235.

93. Ian Baucom, *Out of Place: Englishness, Empire, and the Locations of Identity* (Princeton, NJ: Princeton University Press, 1999), pp. 4-5.

study the space that surrounds the film—all of the different ways in which an audience could interact with a film (such as reviews, blurbs, posters, souvenirs, stills, etc.). The film, as approached in this way, is 'formed from all of the many places of transition between cinema and other images in and of everyday life'.[94] Following Burgin's model, rather than just looking at the production of academic works about the ancient Near East in the nineteenth century, this book approaches the points of contact between this academic study and the social world in which it emerged. This is not dissimilar from James Secord's approach to studying nineteenth-century reading where, rather than simply thinking about the words of the book, reading is treated as a social practice, and the results of reading are traced in a variety of manifestations.[95] For Secord, text is not just a standard edition of a work but any material manifestation related to that work.[96]

This is a book on British experiences of the ancient Near East, with some related comments on continental European (especially French) and American experiences, when warranted. The experiences of the nineteenth-century inhabitants of the Middle East in relation to the ancient Near East is a different question altogether and one that cannot be adequately addressed within the scope of this study. Numerous recent works have sought to address this question, particularly in regard to Egypt, and the interested readers should consult those works.[97] It is now no longer sufficient to read the products of orientalist projects entirely through the lens of colonial ideology (although this lens should not be disregarded). As will be shown throughout the book, the construction and reconstruction of the ancient Near East in nineteenth-century culture was not an enterprise that was driven solely by Europeans and Americans. That is to say, it was not the 'one-way street' that is so often emphasized in debates on the orientalism of the period. People living in the Near East helped frame the debate, from mediating the experiences of early travellers to showcasing their region's heritage through pavilions at world's fairs. Burgeoning nationalism and commercialism facilitated and encour-

---

94. Victor Burgin, *The Remembered Film* (London: Reaction, 2004), pp. 9-10. See also Victor Burgin, *In/Different Spaces: Place and Memory in Visual Culture* (Berkeley, CA: University of California Press, 1996).
    95. Secord, *Victorian Sensation*, p. 3.
    96. Secord, *Victorian Sensation*, p. 518.
    97. Elliott Colla, *Conflicted Antiquities: Egyptology, Egyptomania, Egyptian Modernity* (Durham, NC: Duke University Press, 2007); Jocelyn Hackford-Jones and Mary Roberts (eds.), *Edges of Empire: Orientalism and Visual Culture* (New Interventions in Art History; Malden, MA: Blackwell Publishing, 2005); Donald Malcolm Reid, *Whose Pharaohs?: Archaeology, Museums, and Egyptian National Identity from Napoleon to World War I* (Berkeley, CA: University of California Press, 2002); Neil Asher Silberman, *Between Past and Present: Archaeology, Ideology, and Nationalism in the Modern Middle East* (New York: Anchor Books, 1989).

aged these activities. It is also important to be cognizant that experiences of the ancient Near East were different for everyone. This study seeks to explore the varieties of ways that it could have been encountered and made sense of. At times, it would seem that there were contradictory approaches, and multiple meanings were derived from the same experiences. It is not problematic to assume that there were multiple ancient Near Easts, nor is it problematic to assume that there could have been multiple ancient Near Easts for any particular individual.*

---

* A volume that arrived on the author's desk too late for inclusion in this volume but is recommended is Shimon Gibson, Yoni Shapira and Rupert L. Chapman III, *Tourists, Travellers and Hotels in Nineteenth-Century Jerusalem* (PEF Annual, 11; Leeds: Maney Publishing, 2013).

Part I

(Re)Discovering the Ancient Near East

1

AFTER ABOUKIR: PARIS AS MEMPHIS AND THE PAST AS EMPIRE.

'The Sphinx Speaks'

CARVED by a mighty race whose vanished hands
Formed empires more destructible than I,
In sultry silence I forever lie,
Wrapped in the shifting garment of the sands.
Below me, Pharaoh's scintillating bands
With clashings of loud cymbals have passed by,
And the eternal reverence of the sky
Falls royally on me and all my lands.
The record of the future broods in me;
I have with worlds of blazing stars been crowned,
But none my subtle mystery hath known
Save one, who made his way through blood and sea,
The Corsican, prophetic and renowned,
To whom I spake, one awful night alone!
—Francis Saltus Saltus (1849–1889)

On August 10, 1793, a year after the French Revolution had begun and on the ruins of the Bastille, a cantata was sung to begin the Festival of Unity. Marie-Jean Hérault de Séchelles, the president of the National Convention, drank water that flowed into his cup from the breasts of a seated statue of the Egyptian goddess Isis. He then passed the cup on to a group of eighty-six elderly men, each representing one of the departments of France. As the men drank, the French state was reborn and regenerated (symbolically) by the 'breast-water' of Isis erected on the Parisian location were the Revolution had begun. The name of the statue—*Fontaine de la Régénération*—speaks to its perceived role in the festivals of the state (Fig. 1.1). That an Egyptian goddess was used to symbolize the birth of a new France is not surprising given the long-standing tradition that connected Paris with the

1. *After Aboukir* 29

Fig. 1.1. August 10, 1793. The Festival of Unity at the Fountain of Regeneration on the ruins of the Bastille. Illustration by Bishop after Isidore Stanislas Helman's engraving, based on an original painting by Charles Monnet; Augustin Challamel, *Histoire-Musée de la République française*, I (Paris: Challamel, 1842), p. 333.

cult of Isis and a long-standing use of Egyptian design in state art.[1] Isis's ancient worship was recast in the wake of the French Revolution as part of the Revolutionary Cult of Reason, which was intended to replace Christianity in the new Republic. In the revolutionary context, Isis was reimagined as an early, pre-Christian nature deity. As Mona Ozouf has argued, the celebrations of the Republic were calls to make a break with the recent past (the *ancien régime*) and to connect the Republic with a more ancient global history and the natural world.[2] Egyptian religion, with its seemingly anthropomorphized animal deities and its antique pedigree, provided a model for the revolutionaries of a highly civilized society that had not broken with nature. The sculptor of the statue—Jacques Louis David—used Egyptianizing ele-

---

1. Kevin McGeough, 'Imagining Ancient Egypt as the Idealized Self in 18th Century Europe', in *Eighteenth-Century Thing Theory in a Global Context: From Consumerism to Celebrity Culture* (ed. Christine Ionescu and Ileana Baird; Surrey: Ashgate Press, 2013), pp. 89-110.
2. Mona Ozouf, *Festivals and the French Revolution* (trans. Alan Sheridan; Cambridge, MA: Harvard University Press, 1988), p. 34.

ments typical of eighteenth-century continental design to indicate that this was supposed to be an Egyptian statue. Modeled in bronzed plaster, Isis sat upon a throne, wearing a *nemes*-headdress and Egyptian kilt. Her arms were crossed, and she grasped her breasts directing the flow of 'milk' from the fountain. While the sculpture did not survive very long, other Egyptianizing monuments, invoking iconography such as pyramids and obelisks, came to be popular secular and non-aristocratic symbols of the French state.

Egypt operated as a powerful rhetorical device in French statecraft long before Napoleon invaded North Africa. After, however, Egypt and France continued to be linked symbolically, but especially in the figure of the Corsican general. In most professional histories of Egyptology, the publication of the Napoleonic expedition to Egypt's research marks the beginning of the formal scientific study of Egypt.[3] When Napoleon invaded Egypt (part of his Mediterranean campaign) as a means of protecting French trade interests in the region and limiting British access to the east (especially India), he brought with him a parallel army of intellectuals. This was not the first of Napoleon's intellectual and artistic armies. As the French marched through Europe, the Government Commission for the Research of Artistic and Scientific Objects in Conquered Countries determined which artistic and cultural spoils of war should be sent back to France. Thus, the formation of a Scientific and Artistic Commission to follow Napoleon to Egypt was a continuation of policies that had already been enacted by the revolutionary government.[4] Yet the approach to Egypt was different in that this was a relatively unknown region. Whereas the European plundering took place in familiar territories and involved the looting of artistic treasures, the 'spoils' from Egypt were intellectual. It was knowledge that was acquired, and Egypt was transformed from a location of the unknown to a location of the known.

Scholars of postcolonialism, like Egyptologists, see the connection between Napoleon's military expedition to Egypt and his intellectual expedition. Edward Said well argued this point in his 1978 *Orientalism*, which explored the 'connection between British and French [intellectual] Orien-

---

3. Fewer scholars see this as the origin of biblical archaeology. However, Ben-Arieh points to the importance of the Napoleonic mapping of Palestine, rapidly enacted as it was, in shaping future explorations of the region (Ben-Arieh, *Rediscovery*, p. 21). That being said, the military exploits of Napoleon in Palestine led to greater destruction of monuments and little chance for his savants to conduct the kind of research that was possible in Egypt (Naomi Shepherd, *The Zealous Intruders: The Western Rediscovery of Palestine* [London: Collins, 1987], p. 16).

4. For a detailed account of the taking of spoils by the Napoleonic forces, see Dorothy Mackay Quynn, 'The Art Confiscations of the Napoleonic Wars', *The American Historical Review* 50 (1945), pp. 437-60.

talism' and 'the rise of an explicitly colonial-minded imperialism'.[5] The works of French and British scholars and writers were not neutral, in Said's view, and supported a larger program of political imperialism. Said argued that these scholars created and worked with an 'imaginative geography and history', and that this kind of poetic view of the past can 'help the mind to intensify its own sense of itself by dramatizing the distance and difference between what is close and what is far away'.[6] In other words, these writers, historians and ethnographers did not just deal with facts but supplemented what was known with what they could imagine about the orient and its past. For Said, 'the objective space . . . is far less important than what it is poetically endowed with', and so this poetic conceptual apparatus that emerged, surrounding seemingly objective academic work, is of prime interest.[7] The scholarly study of ancient Egypt, then, was an act of imagination (rooted in scholarship and perceptions of positivism) that were entangled with imperialist and colonialist viewpoints. The poetry of the work was activated so that the other could be conquered (and as shall be shown, the self), first intellectually and later politically and economically. Napoleon and his expedition are particularly good examples of this, since in that instance, the military and the scholarly operated in tandem, explicitly.

Napoleon fit within (or fit himself within) a typical eighteenth-century view that cultures were fundamentally coherent, independent units. Said discusses this in reference to Herder and other German orientalists (as well as musicians), and describes this view that 'all cultures were organically and internally coherent, bound together by a spirit, genius, *Klima*, or national idea which an outsider could penetrate only by an act of historical sympathy'.[8] Napoleon's expedition was one such act of historical sympathy. The work of the French scholars that he brought with him was an inspired attempt at historical sympathy through Enlightenment scientific methods. This historical sympathy went further than merely describing the past; it made sense of the present through historical analogue. Napoleon was the eighteenth-/nineteenth-century version of pharaoh, and France was the new Egypt.

Reading the Napoleonic Images

Scholars and antiquarians had long been familiar with the visual culture of ancient Egypt, which had never truly vanished from European intellectual

---

5. Edward Said, *Orientalism* (New York: Vintage Books, 25th anniversary edn, 2003 [1978]), p. 18.
  6. Said, *Orientalism*, p. 55.
  7. Said, *Orientalism*, p. 55.
  8. Said, *Orientalism*, p. 118.

life. Yet by the nineteenth century, the vision of Egypt had become mostly a vision mediated through classical and biblical sources or the smattering of Egyptian material culture in Italian collections. This changed dramatically in the aftermath of Napoleon's invasion. The publication of the results of Napoleon's scientific team, first as travel literature in Vivant Denon's best-selling *Voyage dans la Basse et la Haute Egypte* (1802) and second as the twenty-three-volume folio set *Description d'Egypte* (1809–1828), created a nearly universal (and empirically based) 'ancient Egyptian' visual culture, shared by Europeans and North Americans of all walks of life. It was these images, ancient Egyptian material culture mediated through the illustrative practices devised by the French team, that became the basis for the 'ancient Egypt' that was reproduced through other media and by the imaginations of nineteenth-century people. As Abigail Moore has shown, the French team translated Egyptian art and architecture into forms that were understandable for Enlightenment Europe through transcription into scientific illustrations.[9]

The Scientific and Artistic Commission that Napoleon brought with his invading force in 1798 had been aggressively recruited by Napoleon himself and the physicist Claude-Louis Berthollet. Many of the scientists (or savants as they were known) were in attendance at a meeting of the Institute of France, where Napoleon argued for the importance of the study of Egypt for French society. The group of savants that Napoleon recruited had diverse interests, but the scholars were generally the same age (mid-twenties) and shared Enlightenment ideals regarding the importance of a holistic-encyclopedic approach to knowledge. These savants were familiar with natural philosophy and the Enlightenment ideals of collection, and both of these provided the foundation for the application of techniques of natural science illustration to antiquarian pursuits.[10] The *Description* they created was one of many eighteenth-/nineteenth-century answers to Pliny's *Natural History*, which itself covered topics as diverse as anthropology, geography, zoology, botany and art.[11] The savants adopted Enlightenment artistic conventions and, by doing so, established the foundations for the conventionalization of archaeological illustration more broadly.

---

9. Abigail Harrison Moore, '*Voyage*: Dominique-Vivant Denon and the Transference of Images of Egypt', *Art History* 25 (2002), pp. 531-49 (534).

10. For more on the importance of the natural sciences in early archaeological illustration, see Joanne Pillsbury, 'Perspectives: Representing the Pre-Columbian Past', in *Past Presented: Archaeological Illustration and the Ancient Americas* (ed. Joanne Pillsbury; Washington, DC: Dumbarton Oaks, 2012), pp. 1-46 (12).

11. For more on the importance of Pliny to Enlightenment publications, see Byron Ellsworth Hamann, 'Drawing Glyphs Together', in *Past Presented: Archaeological Illustration and the Ancient Americas* (ed. Joanne Pillsbury; Washington, DC: Dumbarton Oaks, 2012), pp. 231-81 (245-46).

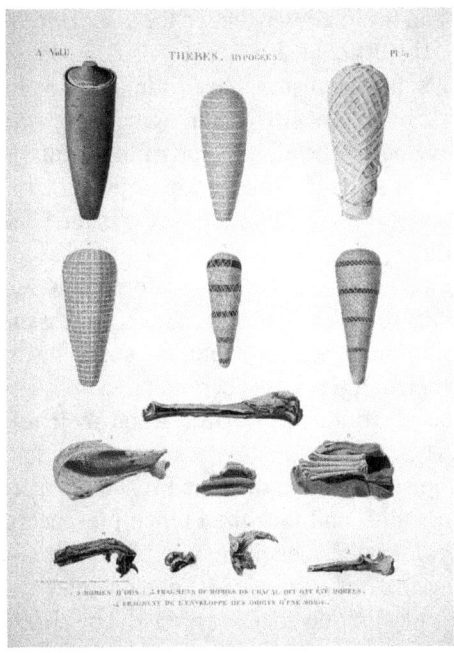

Fig. 1.2. 'Thebes–Ibis mummies', volume II, plate 52 in *Description de l'Égypte, ou recueil des observations et des recherches qui ont été faites en Égypte pendant l'expédition de l'armée française, publié par les ordres de sa majesté l'Empereur Napoléon le Grand* (Paris: Imprimerie Nationale, 1809–1829). Courtesy of the Thomas Fisher Rare Book Library, University of Toronto.

The images of Egypt collected in *Description d'Egypte* at first glance seem to capture two very different orientalist gazes. One gaze is the orientalist as Enlightenment scientist—the images are as accurate as two-dimensional renderings of three-dimensional objects could be (Fig. 1.2). Measurements are correct, and even though hieroglyphs could not be understood at the time, they have been reproduced faithfully—so much so that in many cases, twenty-first-century scholars can read from these images more readily than off the artifacts themselves. As Joanne Pillsbury has noted more generally about the rise of scientific illustration, what had been valued in visual depictions before was the ability to evoke and facilitate the exploration of different ideas and the imagination.[12] Scientific illustration, however, made visual fidelity the key goal of the artist. That is not to say that accuracy was fully achieved. Any line drawing is a representation, and line drawings as presented in a scholarly book decontextualize the original from its context.[13] Likewise, conventions require additions and omissions and perpetuate further omissions and judgments of importance.[14] Rather, it is

---

12. Pillsbury, 'Perspectives', p. 4.
13. For more on the issues of line drawings as representations, see Hamann, 'Drawing Glyphs', p. 267.
14. Stephen D. Houston, 'Telling It Slant: Imaginative Reconstructions of Classic Maya Life', in *Past Presented: Archaeological Illustration and the Ancient Americas*

that *veritas* is the goal of the artist and the quality by which the visualization is judged. As John Harvey argues, the difference between 'visual propositions' and 'scientific propositions' is that the visual 'have little by way of a fixed relation to knowledge', and 'cannot embody semantic meaning with any precision' since they are multivalent.[15] The elimination of this multivalency was, to some degree, the goal of scientific illustration as practiced in the late eighteenth century. The illustration, if truly scientific, was intended to have a fixed relation to knowledge.

The other gaze is that of the romantic orientalist—evocative landscape etchings featuring heroically posed French soldiers, abandoned ruins and indigenous people huddled in voluminous cloaks, reclining lazily in the shade (Fig. 1.3). The presence of human figures asks certain kinds of questions of the viewer in terms of the identities of the figures and their reasons for inclusion in the scene.[16] The *Description* answers these questions through the visual language of colonialism. Either only the French are there and the landscape is 'empty' or in 'ruins' and thus the French presence is justified (since there are no owners), or, the inhabitants are presented and their postures, clothing, etc., show that they are clearly not interested in or capable of handling the burden of curating their own past. The depiction of the French as physically present in the landscape also legitimizes their experiences and gives the French the authority of having actually been there. Images of the French climbing on the sphinx are also arguments for French possession of the sphinx.[17] These landscapes, however, should not be viewed solely through the lens of orientalism. It is a mistake to see in these landscapes only the political. The artists were genuinely attempting to communicate what they had seen. As Moore has shown, the landscapes share much in common with European picturesque landscape images, and thus the alien territory is made less alien when rendered in a familiar form.[18]

For Edward Said, the romantic and the objective gazes are one and the same. While the orientalist may wear many guises, at the heart of this endeavour is accumulation: accumulation of Egyptian territory for France as well as intellectual accumulation of the land. This intellectual accumulation of Egypt was really the long enduring 'success' of the French invasion. While French forces were rapidly forced out of Egypt, the encyclopedic scholarly production of the French team rendered the people (including dress, hairstyle and physiognomy), animals (including fish, birds and

(ed. Joanne Pillsbury; Washington, DC: Dumbarton Oaks, 2012), pp. 387-411 (391).

15. John Harvey, *The Bible as Visual Culture: When Text Becomes Image* (The Bible in the Modern World, 57; Sheffield: Sheffield Phoenix Press, 2013), p. 27.

16. For more on staffage, see Pillsbury, 'Perspectives', pp. 18-21; and Houston, 'Telling It Slant', p. 406.

17. Moore, '*Voyage*', p. 546.

18. Moore, '*Voyage*', p. 544.

Fig. 1.3. 'Alexandria—View of the obelisk named Cleopatra's Needle and the so-called Roman Tower taken from the southwest', volume V, plate 32, in *Description de l'Égypte, ou recueil des observations et des recherches qui ont été faites en Égypte pendant l'expédition de l'armée française, publié par les ordres de sa majesté l'Empereur Napoléon le Grand* (Paris: Imprimerie Nationale, 1809–1829). Courtesy of the Thomas Fisher Rare Book Library, University of Toronto.

insects), plants, geology, architecture and artifacts of Egypt into a form that simplified and circumscribed Egypt in a manner palatable to European audiences. Closer examination of Said's thesis and the images of the Napoleonic expedition demonstrate that the situation was/is perhaps more complex. Certainly Said is correct to argue that this expedition melded the political military act of imperialist conquest with the intellectual act of recording and observing Egypt and its people. From this point on, the intellectual goals of the Enlightenment and most especially those of France (with Diderot's compilation of the *Encyclopaedia* standing as perhaps the most important precursor) were melded with the imperialist expansion of the European powers. Beginning with France and Britain, followed later by Italy, the United States and Germany, the imperialist conqueror (each in its own manner) would bring along a host of academics to understand the new land in a way that the native (deprived of the benefits of the Western intellectual tradition) could not possibly hope to. Yet by creating a monolithic 'orientalist', Said engages in the kind of reductive smoothing over of difference that he lampoons the 'orientalist' for. The two very different types of images produced during Napoleon's campaign, while both aptly called orientalist, grew out of different intellectual traditions and developed into separate intellectual (and pseudo-intellectual) enterprises.

As Derek Gregory has explored, locating an 'other' in space is an important part of the imagined geography that is associated with the orientalist perspective.[19] The Napoleonic expedition brought with it the most advanced cartographic techniques since Roman times. Creating a map of Egypt created a tangible boundary and location for the Egyptian other, bringing the murky legendary Egypt into the domain of the fully understood French worldview. Now that Egypt had been mapped, its mysteries (and the powers derived from its mysteries) could be given up to France (and Europe)—Egypt became a known entity. So while the exploration of Egypt made the unknown known it also began a process of fixing boundaries of otherness. Now the Egyptian could be fixed in time and space and fully understood by the European. This grappling with and fixing of the other further complicates the issue, for as the relationship between France and Egypt came to be reconsidered in the light of the encounter with Egypt, Egypt and especially ancient Egypt came to be adopted as part of French identity.[20] The encounter between France and Egypt (or more broadly Europe and the Orient) was not as straightforward as two different selves encountering the 'other'; it was an entangled process that articulated, complicated and erased boundaries.

This material encounter with Egypt quickly involved Britain as well. In 1801, French forces in Egypt officially surrendered to the British, and the subsequent Treaty of Alexandria effectively put an end to the French scientific expedition of Egypt. The terms of the surrender were somewhat ambiguous. French troops were allowed to keep their personal items (including weapons), but larger weapons, such as cannons, were ceded to the British. The antiquities and specimens collected by the French team fit into neither category easily. The British felt that all of the scientific collections should be ceded into their hands. The French commander, General Abdallas Jacques-François de Menou, claimed the Rosetta Stone was his own private property, and thus, by the terms of surrender, he was at liberty to keep it. The French scientists argued that the specimen collections should remain intact and in their possession, threatening to destroy them if this was not the case. The British capitulated to most of these demands except that the Rosetta Stone and some of the larger Egyptian antiquities were to be turned over. Despite some French protests, the Rosetta Stone was sent to its perma-

---

19. Derek Gregory, *The Colonial Present: Afghanistan, Palestine, Iraq* (New York: Blackwell, 2004), p. 248.

20. For an argument on how ancient Egypt was made sense of within the context of European identity prior to and leading up to the Napoleonic period, see McGeough, 'Imagining Ancient Egypt'.

nent home, by decree of King George III, the British Museum.[21] The Rosetta Stone now bears the stenciled label 'Captured by the British Army in 1801; Presented by King George III'.

Nelson's defeat of the French navy marked an important turning point in the British public's perception of and interest in Egypt. Egypt was now in the news as part of the general media fervor for all things Napoleon. Since the French had seen fit to begin studying Egypt's ancient culture, this became an important (and legitimate) subject for British scholars as well.[22] News reports documenting the British defeat of the French in Egypt may have presented many English with their first visual impressions of ancient Egyptian material culture, outside of a biblical context. The newspaper accounts, which included both serious (but romanticized) documentation of the events as well as cartoons lampooning the French and other important personages, depicted the pyramids and other ancient structures as the setting for these events.[23] A century later, elements of ancient Egyptian material culture had become fully absorbed within Britain's own visual culture, and Egyptian style had become almost universally recognizable as such.

The academic result of the Napoleonic expedition was the twenty-three-volume *Description*. These were expensive volumes of significant heft, so much so that furniture makers built bookshelves expressly designed for holding and displaying the volumes (Fig. 1.4). The images were copperplate engravings, and some of the reasons for the expense of the set relate to the peculiarities of this kind of printing. Specialist engravers had to be hired to take the drawings by the savants and convert them into copperplate images. The copperplates allowed for significantly more detail than wood engravings, and the images could be reproduced on a much larger scale. Colour, however, had to be added in by hand, and there could be no text on the same page as the illustrations. The images themselves were arranged together in meaningful categories. Fragments of similar artifacts or designs were clustered together on the same page for easy comparison and reference, as this kind of comparative study was fundamental to Enlightenment science.[24] This was not, as has already been noted, a politically neutral set of scientific volumes. The underlying argument presents a cyclical view of history where Egypt rose and fell from the heights of global civilization and

---

21. For more on the British–French negotiations surrounding the fate of the antiquities, see Brian Fagan, *The Rape of the Nile: Tomb Robbers, Tourists, and Archaeologists in Egypt* (Cambridge, MA: Westview Press, rev. edn, 2004), pp. 53-55.

22. Alex Werner, 'Egypt in London—Public and Private Displays in the Nineteenth Century Metropolis', in *Imhotep Today: Egyptianizing Architecture* (ed. Jean-Marcel Humbert and Clifford Price; Encounters with Ancient Egypt; London: UCL Press, 2003), pp. 75-104 (76).

23. Werner, 'Egypt in London', p. 76.

24. Hamann, 'Drawing Glyphs', pp. 247-49.

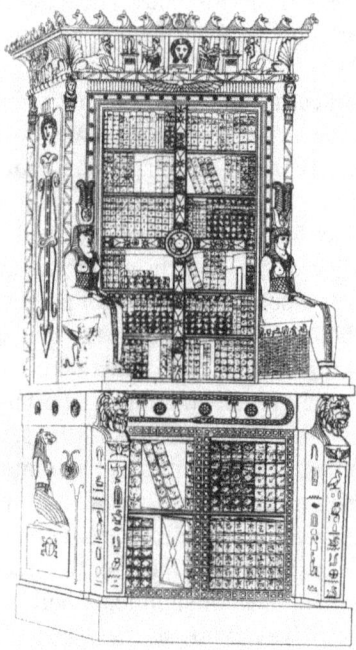

Fig. 1.4. Library bookshelf designed for the *Description*. C. Percier and P.F.L. Fontaine, *Recueil de decorations interieures comprenant tout ce qui a rapport a l'ameublement* (Paris: Louvre, 1812), p. 107.

now suffers under Ottoman rule. France is the leader of a new heroic age, and under France the glories of Egypt can be revived.[25] France is shown to be the heroic benefactor and protector of world culture.[26] As Edward Said notes, even the foreword to the volumes normalizes Napoleon's invasion of Egypt as part of a larger history of foreign conquest, listing the Corsican general among Egypt's past conquerors.[27]

Vivant Denon and his Voyage

While the elite public was perhaps most influenced by the *Description de l'Egypte*, it was sometime before this was actually published. A more affordable and easily digestible version of the French expedition to Egypt was available within the immediacy of popular excitement about the military conflict—*Voyage dans la Basse et la Haute Egypte*.[28] First published in

25. Moore, '*Voyage*', pp. 538-39.
26. Moore, '*Voyage*', p. 535.
27. Edward W. Said, *Culture and Imperialism* (New York: Vintage Books, 1993), p. 33.
28. As of 1826, George Smith, the English furniture maker, was crediting Denon's book, not the *Description*, with bringing Egyptian style to English design (see Chapter II.6). See also Moore, '*Voyage*', p. 53; and Eamonn Gearon, 'War and Peace and Travel and Writing: European Exploration in Egypt and the Sudan, 1798–1898', in *Souvenirs*

1802, this book was reproduced in numerous forms, sizes and prices. Written by Vivant Denon (1747–1825), *Voyage* presents the Napoleonic expedition to Egypt through the eyes of one individual adopting the genre of travel literature. Rather then presenting the scientific images of the Napoleonic expedition, *Voyage* provides an exciting narrative account of Denon's travels in Egypt, at the same time offering readers some of the first European accounts of the exploration of Egyptian antiquities. Essentially just a publication of Denon's journal, the story reads as an orientalist travel-adventure novel, with stories of dancing girls, snake charmers, crocodiles and famous battles. These romantic and adventurous elements, as well as the vogue for all things Napoleonic, made this book an immediate success in Western Europe. The *Edinburgh Review* commented on its popularity, saying, 'Few publications, we believe, have ever obtained so extensive a circulation in the same space of time as these travels'.[29]

Much of the success of *Voyage* is due to the personality of its author (and hero/narrator) who presents a story of high adventure and exploration that has as its goal the production of illustrations of Egyptian antiquities. Denon's life has been studied by numerous biographers, and in most accounts, Denon emerges as an exemplar of the ideal artist–scientist of the revolutionary era.[30] Trained in both the law and etching, Denon's background left him ideally suited to accompany the Napoleonic expedition to Egypt and to set some of the basic standards for the first scientific studies of Egyptian antiquities. Before the Revolution, under the patronage of King Louis XV, he was assigned the role of keeper of the cabinet of carved gems for Madame de Pompadour (the official *maîtresse-en-titre*—the chief mistress of the king of France). His legal background (which he had abandoned for the study of art and literature) and popularity at court led Louis XV to later bestow diplomatic roles upon him, and from 1772 to 1787 he worked as a French diplomat abroad. During this time he travelled to Sicily, and wrote about it in *Voyage en Sicile*, published in 1788. As his memoirs of Egypt would later, *Voyage en Sicile* included an account of his trip illustrated by various etchings he had made.

At the outbreak of the Revolution, he was living in Italy, sharpening his etching skills by drawing archaeological artifacts. Upon his return to Paris, like many who had been well established in courtly circles, he found that his fortunes had changed and his property confiscated. However, Denon

and New Ideas: Travel and Collecting in Egypt and the Near East (ed. Diane Fortenberry; Oxford: ASTENE and Oxbow Books, 2013), pp. 44-54 (48).

29. Quoted in Edward Ziter, *The Orient on the Victorian Stage* (Cambridge: Cambridge University Press, 2003), p. 31.

30. See, for example, Judith Nowhickey, *Baron Dominique Vivant Denon (1747–1825): Hedonist and Scholar in a Period of Transition* (Cranbury, NJ: Associated University Presses, 1970).

found favour with Jacques-Louis David (who had sculpted the *Fontaine de la Régénération*), one of the most influential revolutionary-era artists, and Denon's property and name were restored to the high status to which he was accustomed. Denon first began spelling his name as such upon his return to revolutionary France, to hide the aristocratic baggage of the original spelling (de Non).

It was not just Denon's relationship with David that allowed him to reclaim a position in Parisian society, for diplomacy and travel writing were not Denon's only sources of renown. He was infamous for his erotic art, to which his descriptive writing and drawing skills had already been put to good (and somewhat scandalous) use, especially in his *Point de lendemain: Conte dédiée à la reine*. Similar to other aristocratic stories (the most well know today being *Les liaisons dangereuses*), *Point de lendemain* presents the erotic adventures of a young man who transgresses the restrictions of societal etiquette in the pursuit of pleasure.[31] He also created numerous pornographic etchings, most famously a 1793 collection (*L'oeuvre priapique*) that purported to illustrate the sexual practices of the ancient Pompeians. His attention to artistic detail and accuracy made Denon's work popular among European audiences, much as these same traits would serve his analysis of Egyptian materials.

Finding favour with Robespierre, Denon was eventually introduced to Napoleon, who made Denon the commander-in-chief's advisor on artistic matters for his expedition to Egypt. Not formally a member of the Scientific and Artistic Commission, Napoleon's 'second army' of scientists and scholars, Denon had more freedom to travel in Egypt according to his whims, to some degree. However, given the dangerous conditions, he was unable to travel by himself. Denon travelled through Egypt with various divisions of the French army, and these travels are detailed in *Voyage*. He had the freedom to join various groups on various missions that would take him near sites of major antiquities. Throughout the book, Denon frequently laments the fact that he was never able to stay in one location for as long as he would have liked (acknowledging that it would be inappropriate for his work to hold up the military mission).

In *Voyage*, Denon describes his journeys throughout Egypt, beginning with the French arrival in Alexandria and continuing through his travels to Cairo and the pyramids, down to Thebes, to the cataracts, back up through Karnak and Luxor and his return to Cairo, where he learned that he was to return to France.[32] While at the Institute of Egypt, Denon met with the

---

31. In a later 1812 edition, the male protagonist is made into a naïve young man who is seduced by an older woman.

32. For a detailed commentary on Denon's travels, see Terrence M. Russel, *The Discovery of Egypt: Vivant Denon's Travels with Napoleon's Army* (Gloucestershire: Sutton Publishing, 2005).

savants of the Scientific and Artistic Commission and showed them his work. That team had not made it to Upper Egypt yet, so they were curious about what he had uncovered and consulted with Denon about their approach to exploring that region. Denon was given an audience with Napoleon, who was impressed with his work and encouraged him to publish his journal and etchings upon his return to Paris.

When Denon returned to Paris in October of 1799, he immediately set about following Napoleon's instructions and preparing his journal for publication. The results were two editions of the same two-volume work, one prepared on significantly finer paper than the other.[33] The success of *Voyage* inaugurated Denon's leadership in nineteenth-century aesthetics. Denon was appointed as the curator of the Louvre (Director of the Musée Central des Arts), where his ideas about what a museum should be and what it should showcase became formative for the modern museum. In postrevolutionary France, he played a role in the design and reconstruction of Paris, to which he brought an appreciation for Egyptian style and architecture. Similarly, he directly influenced design in porcelain and tapestry, incorporating Egyptian themes. As Humbert has stated, Denon became a 'quasi-dictator of the arts'.[34] Indirectly, his *Voyage* provided the basis for an Egyptian visual culture that was extremely prominent throughout the first half of the nineteenth century.

Denon's writings established some of the important ways that the ancient Near East came to be understood in relation to European civilization throughout the nineteenth century. This was the first non-classical account of Egyptian civilization that many read, and *Voyage* established some of the major conceptual frameworks through which ancient Egypt came to be understood. Denon's writing demonstrates the typical concerns of travel literature, such as the fetishization of difference and disjunction between the experiences of the traveler and those that he travels among. Yet, the goal of his explorations was to provide an accurate, scientific account of what he found. Thus for Denon's readers, the exoticization of Egypt and its ancient remains was accomplished through an Enlightenment-era approach to the world. It is both a military adventure account and a travel story of a journey to an exotic land, written in an appealing first-person prose. Denon can be aptly described as one of the fathers of modern Egyptology, and the themes that he established are worth further discussion.

---

33. For a description of the publication history of *Voyage* and the subscription raising efforts of Denon, see Russel, *Discovery*, pp. 254-56.

34. Jean-Marcel Humbert, 'Denon and the Discovery of Egypt', in *Egyptomania: Egypt in Western Art 1730–1930* (ed. Jean-Marcel Humbert *et al.*; Ottawa: National Gallery of Canada, 1994), pp. 202-49 (204).

Denon's description of the army's first view of Thebes reflects common features of nineteenth-century interactions with Egyptian antiquities. He writes:

> À neuf heures, en détournant la pointe d'une chaîne de montagnes qui forme un promontoire, nous découverîmes tout à coup l'emplacement de l'antique Thèbes dans tout son développement. . . . Décrite dans quelques pages dictées à Hérodoté par des prêtres égyptiens, et copiées depuis par tous les autres historiens . . . doctes et premiers monuments des arts, respectés par le temps; ce sanctuaire abandonné, isolé par la barbarie, et rendu au desert sur lequel il avait été conquis; cette cite enfin toujours enveloppée du voile du mystère par lequel les colosses meme sont agrandis; cette cite reléguée, que l'imagination, que l'armée, à l'aspect de ses ruines éparses, s'arrêta d'elle-même, et, par un mouvement spontanée, battit des mains, comme si l'occupation des restes de cette capitale eût été le but de ses glorieux travaux, eût complete la conquêtede l'Égypte.[35]

This first encounter with Thebes is presented as an exciting exploration narrative. Suddenly, Thebes appeared before the army in all of its glory. The breathtaking nature of the monuments is described in rapturous terms, emphasizing the 'veil of mystery and the obscurity of ages' that reflect the disjuncture between the past and the present and the most significant obstacle separating ancient Egypt and modern France. Immediately, Denon refers to classical descriptions of the site, a common starting point for nineteenth-century discussions of ancient Egypt and reflecting the most important prism through which ancient Egypt was initially viewed. The site is described as abandoned, and the culture that currently inhabits the space is described as *barbarie*, which in one clause distances nineteenth-century Egypt from ancient Egypt. An equation between viewing the ancient site and the conquering of Egypt is made explicit, and the reaction of the French

---

35. Dominique Vivant Denon, *Voyage dans la Basse et la Haute Égypte* (Paris: Éditions Gallimard, 1998 [1802]), pp. 193-94. Arthur Aiken's 1803 English translation (vol. II, pp. 48-49) reads: 'At nine o'clock, in making a sharp turn round the point of a projecting chain of mountains, we discovered all at once the site of the ancient Thebes in its whole extent . . . this illustrious city, described in a few pages dictated to Herodotus by Egyptian priests, that have been since copied by every historian . . . the first monuments of ancient learning which are still spared by the hand of time; this abandoned sanctuary, surrounded with barbarism, and again restored to the desert from which it had been drawn forth, enveloped in the veil of mystery, and the obscurity of ages, whereby even its own colossal monuments are magnified to the imagination, still impressed the mind with such gigantic phantoms, that the whole army, suddenly and with one accord, stood in amazement at the sight of its scattered ruins, and clapped their hands with delight, as if the end and object of their glorious toils, and the complete conquest of Egypt, were accomplished and secured by taking possession of the splendid remains of this ancient metropolis'.

troops to the site reflects how important this discovery was to the colonial enterprise.

The means through which ancient Egypt should be understood in relation to early-nineteenth-century French culture is established right at the outset of the book. *Voyages* is dedicated to Napoleon, and it is immediately apparent from this that Napoleon is understood to be part of a line of great historic leaders. It reads:

> À Bonaparte. Joindre l'éclat de votre nom à la splendeur des monuments d'Égypte, c'est rattacher les fastes glorieux de notre siècle aux temps fabuleux de l'histoire; c'est réchauffer les cendres des *Sésostris* et des *Mendès,* comme vous conquérants, comme vous bienfaiteurs.[36]

This is to become one of the major themes of nineteenth-century ancient Near Eastern studies—the equation of the great European powers with great ancient powers, especially Egypt and Mesopotamia. For Napoleon, Denon's work was excellent publicity, since it reframed what had been a military failure in the positive terms of a scientific success.[37]

The grandiosity of the Egyptian monuments is comparable to the grandiosity of the French Republic, in Denon's eyes. At times he sets ancient Egypt up as a rival of France. For example, in discussing the obelisks at Luxor Temple, he states:

> Il est sans doute glorieux pour les fastes de Thèbes [referring to the capital as one might refer to Paris as a synecdoche of France] que la plus grande et la plus riche des républiques ne se soit pas cru assez de superflu, non pour faire tailler, mais seulement pour tenter de transporter ces deux monuments, qui ne sont qu'un fragment d'un seul des nombreux edifices de cette étonnante ville.[38]

That French technological ingenuity (at least as much as Denon understands it) cannot rival ancient Egyptian is noteworthy and, to some extent, destabilizing. As shall be explored later in this volume, the act of the transportation of obelisks eventually comes to be symbolic of the successes of

---

36. Denon, *Voyage,* p. 27. Aiken's 1803 English translation (vol. I, p. iii) reads: 'To Bonaparte. To combine the luster of your Name with the splendour of the Monuments of Egypt, is to associate the glorious annals of our own time with the history of the heroic age; and to reanimate the dust of Sesostris and Mendes, like you Conquerors, like you Benefactors'.

37. Humbert, 'Denon', p. 204.

38. Denon, *Voyage,* p. 27. Aiken's 1803 English translation (vol. II, p. 149) reads: 'It is, without a doubt, flattering to the pomp of Thebes, that the richest and most powerful republic in the world should deem its means insufficient, not to hew out, but merely to transport these two monuments, which are no more than a fragment of one of the numerous edifices of that astonishing city'.

industrialism and modernization, despite the fact that people had been moving obelisks thousands of years earlier.

The comparison between past and present and especially the consideration of varying levels of technological skills also become a common trope in the consideration of Egypt in the nineteenth century. In a later publication of his engravings on Egypt, Denon offers the following revealing comments regarding Luxor:

> The entrance of the village of Luxor presents . . . a comparative scale of ancient and of modern times. . . . I returned several times to this place, to contrast the past with the present, to compare the buildings, that I might be enabled to compare their inhabitants. . . . The Sheikh of the village, once seeing me thus employed, asked me whether the French or the English had erected all those buildings.[39]

Denon's association of the great leaders of ancient Egypt with Napoleon is further argued through his treatment and discussion of the humble nature of the current inhabitants of Egypt that he encountered. Immediately following his acknowledgment that French engineering cannot rival the monumental construction skills of the ancient Egyptians at Luxor, he offers this comparison with the modern inhabitants of Luxor:

> Je fis malgré l'ardeur excessive d'un soleil du midi, un dessin de la porte du temple, qui est devenue celle du village de Luxor; rien de plus grand et de plus simple que le peu d'objets qui composent cette entrée; aucune ville connue n'est annoncée aussi fastueusement que ce miserable village, compose de deux à trois mille habitants, niches sur les combles, ou tapis sous les plates-formes de ce temple, sans cependant que cela lui donne l'air d'être habité.[40]

The nineteenth-century inhabitants of Luxor are described as squatters in contrast with the ancient builders. For Denon, the juxtaposition of the monumental entranceway to Luxor temple and the squalid modern village more generally reflected the relationship between ancient and modern in Egypt.

Similarly, the aesthetics of eighteenth-century Egypt left much to be desired, unlike the design of ancient Egypt, which had much to emulate. Denon's initial impression of Alexandria was unenthusiastic, and in par-

---

39. Dominique Vivant Denon, *Egypt Delineated* (London: Charles Taylor, 1819), p. 25.

40. Denon, *Voyage*, p. 261. Aiken's 1803 English translation (vol. II, p. 150) reads: 'Notwithstanding the excessive heat of the sun at mid-day, I made a drawing of the gate of the temple, which is now become that of the village of Luxor. Nothing can be more grand, and at the same time more simple, than the small number of objects of which this entrance is composed. No city whatever makes so proud a display at its approach as this wretched village, the population of which consists of two or three thousand souls, who have taken up their abodes on the roofs and beneath the galleries of this temple, which has, nevertheless, the air of being in a manner uninhabited.'

ticular, Denon seems to have been disturbed by the mixing of various eras in Ottoman architecture. Denon writes:

> Au reste ces constructions arabes et turques, ouvrages des besoins de la guerre, offrent une confusion d'époques et de différentes industries dont on ne voit peut-être nulle part ailleurs d'exemples plus frappants et plus rapprochés. Les Turcs surtout, ajoutant l'ineptie à la profanation, ont mêlé au granit non seulement la brique et la pierre calcaire, mais des madriers, et jusqu'à des planches, et de tous ces elements, si peu analogues et si étrangement amalgams, ont présenté l'assemblage monstrueux de la splendeur de l'industrie humaine, et de sa degradation.[41]

Here, the concern for antiquities is related to aesthetics, and the Ottomans are especially singled out as committing the stylistic crime of integrating the architectural tastes of various periods (a 'crime' that the French would later commit in their Egyptian displays at various *Expositions universelles* and through eclecticism in design). Denon's concern is that what would be examples of the 'splendour of human industry' are, when mixed together inappropriately, examples of its 'degradation'. This is in contrast to what he highlights of Egyptian style, which, given its 'splendid isolation' in antiquity, meant that it avoided culturally hybridized architecture, which to Denon, was a sign of degradation. On these lines, Denon writes about the Denderah:

> Rien de plus simple et de mieux calculé que le peu de lignes qui composent cette architecture. Les Égyptiens n'ayant rien emprunté des autres, ils n'ont ajouté aucun ornement étranger, aucune superfluité à ce qui était dicté par la nécessité: ordonance et simplicité ont été leurs principes; et ils ont élevé ces principes jusqu'à la sublimité. . . .[42]

In Denon's eyes, the aesthetic crimes committed in Ottoman Egypt are in direct opposition to the aesthetic achievements of ancient Egypt. Whereas Ottoman architecture, according to Denon, is characterized by the haphazard use of components from a variety of periods, the ancient Egyptians

---

41. Denon, *Voyage*, p. 63. Aiken's 1803 English translation (vol. I, pp. 101-102) reads: 'In short, these Arabian and Turkish buildings, the productions of the necessities of war, display a confusion of epochs, and of various industries, more striking and more approximated examples of which are no where else to be found. The Turks, more especially, adding absurdity to profanation, have not only blended with the granite, bricks and calcareous stones, but even logs and planks; and from these different elements, which have so little analogy to each other, and are so strangely united, have presented a monstrous assemblage of the splendour of human industry, and its degradation'.

42. Denon, *Voyage*, p. 186. Aiken's 1803 English translation (vol. II, pp. 38-39) reads: 'Nothing is more simple and better put together than the few lines which compose this architecture. The Egyptians borrowing nothing from the style of other nations, have here added no foreign ornament, no superfluity of materials: order and simplicity are the principles which they have followed, and they have carried them to sublimity.'

Fig. 1.5. The Temple at Denderah, A, volume IV, plate 9, in *Description de l'Égypte, ou recueil des observations et des recherches qui ont été faites en Égypte pendant l'expédition de l'armée française, publié par les ordres de sa majesté l'empereur Napoléon le Grand,* folio 601. Beinecke Rare Book and Manuscript Library, Yale University, 1971.

focused on simple designs without any foreign influences. The supposed unity of ancient Egyptian design is one of the aesthetic lessons that Denon later applied to France of the First Republic.

Of the sites Denon presents, Denderah (called Tentyra by Denon), was arguably the most influential in nineteenth-century aesthetics (Fig. 1.5). Denon describes the site of Denderah in rapturous terms, and this is very clearly one of the major sites that captured his imagination. In his discussion of the temple there, one can see how Enlightenment ideals were projected onto the past. He writes:

> Quelle constante puissance, quelle richesse, quelle abondance, quelle superfluité de moyens dans le gouvernement qui peut faire élever un tel edifice, et qui trouve dans la nation des hommes capables de le concevoir, de l'exécuter, de le décorer, de l'enricher de tout ce qui parle aux yeux et à l'esprit! [sic] jamais d'une manière plus rapprochée le travail des hommes ne me les avait présentés si anciens et si grands: dans les ruins de Tintyra [Denderah] les Égyptiens me parurent des géants.[43]

---

43. Denon, *Voyage,* p. 187. Aiken's 1803 English translation (vol. II, p. 40) reads: 'What unceasing power, what riches, what abundance, what superfluity of means must a government possess which could erect such an edifice, and find within itself artists capable of conceiving and executing the design, of decorating and enriching it with every thing that speaks to the eye and the understanding! Never did the labour of man shew me

Fig. 1.6. Sphinx with Africanized nose. (A view of the sphinx at the pyramids at Gizeh, a Patera, charged with the portraits of Osiris and Isis, and sculptures of Egyptian musicians, Pompey's or Diocletian's Pillar, and Cleopatra's Needle). Hand-coloured etching by Vivant Denon. © Victoria and Albert Museum, London. Purchased with the assistance of The Art Fund, the National Heritage Memorial Fund, Shell International and the Friends of the V&A.

In ancient Egypt, Denon has found a model of a society like that the revolutionaries of France had dreamed of—an Enlightenment fantasy of a society that supports artists in the construction of edifices that commemorate the best of the human spirit. His image of Denderah came to be one of the most replicated images of Egypt in the nineteenth-century and a synecdoche of ancient Egypt.

The temple of Denderah is not the only element of Egyptian visual culture that Europeans first encountered through *Voyage*. As Humbert has noted, one of the novel features of Denon's book was that he integrated his illustrations directly into the story.[44] The images of Egypt were not merely extraneous additions to make the book more appealing to readers. Rather, the discussion of the art and aesthetics of Egypt was central to his description, and the book needs his illustrations to move the narrative and his arguments. Because of the wide circulation of his book and its early release, many aspects of Egyptian visual culture that are thought to be informed by the more formal Napoleonic scientific volumes actually entered the European repertoire through Denon. These views of Egypt are not always as scientifically grounded as the images of the *Description*—the sphinx, for

the human race in such a splendid point of view: in the ruins of Tentyra the Egyptians appeared to me giants.'

44. Humbert, 'Denon', p. 204.

example, is presented in a form altered to better fit (at least as seen by Denon) within the context of late-eighteenth-century racial categories of African-ness (Fig. 1.6).

Denon's first encounter with Egyptian art was influenced by his knowledge of classical art, and comparison between the two is understandable given his background. Like many later art historians would argue, Egyptian art, in Denon's view, was of a less sophisticated nature than that of Greece and Rome. In this passage, regarding reliefs at the Temple of Amun at Luxor, he uses the metaphor of childhood to understand Egyptian art:

> cette sculpture [a relief on the entrance of Luxor temple] est de la composition la plus baroque, sans perspective, sans plan, sans distribution, et comme les premières conceptions de l'esprit humain qui a toujours la meme marche. J'ai vu à Pompéia des dessins faits par des soldats romains sur le stuc des murailles; ils ressemblaient entièrement aux dessins des nôtres, à ceux de tout enfant qui veut render ses premières idées, lorsqu'il n'a encore ni vu, ni compare, ni réfléchi. Ici le héros est gigantesque, et les ennemis qu'il combat sont vingt-cinq fois plus petites: si c'était déjà une flatterie des arts, elle était sans doute mal entendue, puisqu'il devait être honteux pour ce héros de n'avoir à combattre que des pygmées.[45]

In this instance, the reliefs of the Egyptians are equated with the untrained drawings of Roman soldiers. Denon's confusion about the uses of scale and perspective in Egyptian art are understandable given that these do not correspond with the realistic proportions that emerged in ancient Greece and were again in vogue in late-eighteenth-century France. Likewise, these are the first impressions of someone who has seen little Egyptian art, and, although Denon would be the one to introduce Egyptian aesthetics to Europe, these are his initial impressions. The metaphor of childhood for Near Eastern art would come to be commonplace in the nineteenth-century.

Denon (and the French) were not satisfied with merely bringing back illustrations and descriptions of Egyptian art. Throughout the journal, Denon notes objects that would be appropriate for transport to Europe. Near Luxor temple, he notes a colossal foot, which he believes could easily be removed to Europe to give a sense of scale regarding the size of the monu-

---

45. Denon, *Voyage*, p. 196. Aiken's 1803 English translation (vol. II, pp. 51-52) reads: 'This piece of sculpture is in the most irregular style of composition, without perspective, plan, or distribution, like the first conceptions of the unimproved human mind. I have seen at Pompeia [Pompeii] rude sketches done by Roman soldiers on the stucco of the walls; they entirely resembled in style those which I am now speaking of, which are like the first attempts of a child, before he has seen anything whereby to arrange his ideas. Here the hero is gigantic and the enemies whom he is overthrowing are twenty-five times smaller than himself; if this, however, could be meant for a piece of flattery in the arts, it was certainly ill-contrived, since the hero could gain no honour by fighting pygmies.'

ments and could be readily compared with colossal feet already present in Rome.[46] Similarly, on Philae, Denon suggests bringing the Kiosk of Trajan (mistaking it for an older edifice) back to France since its small size would have allowed easy transport but still give Europeans a sense of Egyptian temple architecture.[47] Perhaps most 'prophetic' (to use Russel's description) of Denon's comments about which objects should be sent back to Europe were his comments regarding Cleopatra's Needle (Fig. 1.3 and Chapter I.5).[48] Denon writes about the pair of obelisks (one of which was brought to England and set up on the Thames embankment and the other was set up in New York's Central Park):

> Ils pourraient facilement être embarqués, et devenir en France un trophée de la conquête, trophée très caractérisque, parce qu'ils sont à eux seuls un monument, et que les hieroglyphs dont ils sont couverts doivent les render préférables à la colonne de Pompée, qui n'est qu'une colonne un peu plus grande que celles qu'on trouve partout.[49]

Here, the rationale for sending the obelisks back to France is foremost to have a trophy of war. According to Denon's logic, since the object is already a 'monument', simply recontextualizing it in France will create a new type of monument. The fact that they are covered in hieroglyphs makes them preferable as trophies to Pompey's pillar since this means that they are of historical and aesthetic importance.

Elsewhere in the journal, Denon shows more concern for preserving antiquities than merely treating them as spoils of war. He reports on the conditions of the antiquities as parts of his general reports on what he has seen. For example, he reports about Karnak that 'à l'état present de cet edifice que sa destruction défigure une grande partie de son ensemble; tous les sphinx sont tronqués méchamment: fatiguée de détruire, la barbarie en a cependant negligee quelques-uns. . . .'[50] This concern would later be used first as justification for the removal of antiquities from Egypt altogether and

---

46. Denon, *Voyage,* p. 197.
47. Denon, *Voyage,* p. 229.
48. Russel, *Discovery,* p. 26.
49. Denon, *Voyage,* pp. 64-65. Aiken's 1803 English translation (vol. I, pp. 105-106) reads: 'They might be conveyed to France without difficulty, and would there become a trophy of conquest, and a very characteristic one, as they are in themselves a monument, and as the hieroglyphics with which they are covered render them preferable to Pompey's pillar, which is merely a column, somewhat larger indeed than is every-where to be found'.
50. Denon, *Voyage,* p. 260. Aiken's 1803 English translation (vol. II, p. 143) reads: 'a great part of the effect is lost by its very degraded state. The sphinxes have been wantonly mutilated, with few exceptions, which barbarism, wearied with destroying has spared. . . .'

later as a call for rethinking the treatment of antiquities more generally.⁵¹ Protecting art, as described here and elsewhere, functioned to justify the confiscation of art. Here, however, the ruined state of the finds is presented simply as a statement of fact, tinged with a value judgment that contemporary Egyptians could allow these monuments to fall into such ruin.

Although the academic aspects of Denon's book may have been of greatest interest to scholars, it is really the adventurous aspects of his book that captured the European public's imagination. Denon's narrative of his explorations of the Valley of the Kings reads like an adventure story and may very well have influenced the nineteenth-century writers in this genre (although this is merely speculation). He describes lighting a torch and crawling into a cramped tomb over decaying bodies. As one visitor was 'overcome' (presumably by the heat, smells and claustrophobic interior) the others saw the embalmed bodies resting in place and the bas-reliefs of the tombs.⁵² These exciting elements, the cheap price, and the timeliness of its publication (in the midst of the mania for Napoleon) gave this work an especially significant influence in the first part of the nineteenth century.

Egypt as French Culture

The Scientific and Artistic Commission that Napoleon brought with him remained in Egypt for two years longer than Denon. Denon was instrumental in establishing some of the principles that the team used for documenting antiquities, and he certainly excited the European public with news of the team's endeavors. The monumental *Description d'Egypte* that eventually presented the findings of the team to the world became a key reference source, providing academics and designers with trustworthy depictions of Egyptian monuments and artifacts. As Fagan has noted, the publication further exaggerated the wave of Egyptomania that had begun with Denon's best-seller.⁵³ This work eventually became the basis of the nineteenth-century visual culture of 'ancient' Egypt. However, Andrew Bednarski has convincingly shown that the *Description*'s influence on British academic Egyptology has been somewhat exaggerated for a variety of reasons. By comparing the distribution history of the *Description* with mentions in the periodical press, Bednarksi suggests that British Egyptology (especially as established by Wilkinson) had already taken firm root by the time copies of the *Description* were widely available in Britain.⁵⁴ Despite this, continental

51. Moore, '*Voyage*', p. 537.
52. Denon, *Voyage*, pp. 327-29 (Aiken's 1803 Eng. translation [vol. II, pp. 253-56]).
53. Fagan, *Rape of the Nile*, p. 56.
54. Andrew Bednarski, *Holding Egypt: Tracing the Reception of the* Description de l'Égypte *in Nineteenth Century Great Britain* (Egyptology, 3; London: Golden House Publication, 2005).

designers and painters had greater access to it (copies of individual images were available much earlier), and even though it may not have been cited directly, the visual tropes for conveying 'Egypt' were greatly influenced by this work, especially from the 1830s forward. In some ways the influence of the *Description* was felt more directly through popular culture and the works of professionals in other disciplines; it was (and still is, to some degree) underutilized by professional Egyptologists.

With the new wave of Egyptomania set off by the Napoleonic expedition, Denon's best-seller, and the nationalism of the war reporting of the Napoleonic era (with the battles between France and Britain in Egypt stirring tremendous interest), ancient Egypt became a forum for the discussion of national identity. Despite being a military loss, Napoleon's Egyptian campaign came to be seen as one of the highlights of the French empire.[55] For Parisians especially, Egypt took on direct importance in understanding the history of France, and earlier traditions about that relationship were revived. In the early nineteenth century, the belief that the cult of Isis had been instrumental in the founding of the city of Paris became widespread. Since the fifteenth century, scholars had speculated on the possible relationship between Isis and the city. Partially this was based on a number of false etymologies. The Egyptian *par*-Isis, meaning House of Isis or Temple of Isis, was reminiscent of 'Paris'. The name is better understood to be derived from *Parisii*, the name of a Gaulish tribe from that region; however, the problem with determining the origins of that name continues to inspire pseudo-scholars to postulate an ancient relationship between Isis and Paris. Thus for some, the name Parisii is a mispronunciation of the Latin bar-Isis. More likely, though, the faulty logic that led to the theory stems from the belief that Isis was worshipped at some of the older church locations (such as St Germain-des-Prés and Notre Dame) in the city.

However unlikely an Egyptian origin of the city of Paris is, this suggestion was taken seriously in the early nineteenth century, especially within the Egyptomania of the Napoleonic era. For example, during the Revolution, coats of arms had been banned along with the abolishment of the nobility. Prior to the Revolution, the Paris coat of arms simply depicted a ship. Napoleon believed that the ship on the coat of arms was related to a boat of Isis (although it is actually a symbol of the mediaeval *Marchands de l'eau*). Napoleon's commission deemed that there was a relationship between the boat and Isis. So, in 1811, when Napoleon restored coats of arms to cities, Isis, seated on the traditional ship, was added to the city's emblem (Fig. 1.7).

References to Egypt in Napoleonic and post-Napoleonic France were not just references to Paris's ancient pedigree. As I have argued elsewhere,

---

55. Moore, '*Voyage*', p. 539.

Fig. 1.7. *Blason de Paris* (coat of arms) from 1811. Wikimedia Commons.

ancient Egypt becomes a synecdoche for the Napoleonic empire as a whole.[56] Napoleon himself credited the Egyptian campaign as a formative period in the birth of the new empire since the men who became the important figures of his government were all present with him in Egypt.[57] Egyptian styles and designs created a new taste to be adopted by the new elite of France, a taste that was distinct from the tastes of the hated prerevolutionary aristocracy (see Chapter II.6).[58] Obelisks came to be used to glorify various military heroes, such as the monument to Louis Charles Antoine Desaix in Place Victoire and the monument to the Grande Armée on the Pont Neuf. Egyptianizing fountains (Fountain of Victory in the Place du Châtelet and the Fountain of the Fellah on rue de Sèvres, for example) are Egyptian-seeming monuments to Napoleonic France. The bonds of fraternity that developed during the Egyptian campaign were commemorated in funerary architecture as well, especially in the state tombs at Père Lachaise cemetery (founded by Napoleon in 1804). There, Egyptian symbols and design functioned as a material record of those who participated in the campaign. Even after the restoration of the monarchy, ancient Egypt remained a potent symbol of

---

56. McGeough, 'Imagining Egypt', pp. 104-105.

57. Thomas Gaehtgens, Jörg Ebeling and Ulrich Leben, 'Eugène de Beauharnais: *Honneur et fidélité* at the Hôtel Beauharnais', in *Symbols of Power: Napoleon and the Art of the Empire Style: 1800–1815* (ed. Odile Nouvel-Kammerer and Anne Dion-Tenenbaum; New York: Abrams, 2007), pp. 78-87 (79).

58. Moore, '*Voyage*', p. 537.

1. *After Aboukir*

French governance. When King Louis Philippe redid the coronation room at Versailles, he perpetuated the Napoleonic connection with Egypt. Named after the famous David painting in which Napoleon crowns himself, in Philippe's new context, it became part of the history of France. Egyptian symbols in the paintings hung in this room connect France's history to that of the ancient culture. Gros's 1799 *The Battle of Aboukir* demonstrates a literal connection, and Callet's 1801 *Allegory of 18 Brumaire* demonstrates a metaphorical connection (with Napolen's army symbolized by a barebreasted woman wearing a *nemes*-headdress).

Egypt came to be synonymous with a Paris-centred France as Jerusalem and the Holy Land were representative of London and England (in idealized or hoped-for form) respectively (see the Introduction).[59] Both Othmar Keel and Erik Hornung have noted that while French travellers to Egypt were reliant on classical sources to contextualize their encounters, British and American travellers were more likely to frame their experiences within a biblical perspective.[60] The Napoleonic campaigns, however, had interpretative implications far beyond the borders of the France. For these campaigns opened the Near East for a new era of exploration, especially archaeological and philological, and the impacts of this new access to raw data are the subject of the rest of the book.

---

59. Barbara Tuchman surveys the traditions of British connections to the Holy Land in Barbara W. Tuchman, *Bible and Sword: England and Palestine from the Bronze Age to Balfour* (New York: Ballantine Books, 1984 [1956]).

60. Erik Hornung, *The Secret Lore of Egypt: Its Impact on the West* (trans. D. Lorton; Ithaca, NY: Cornell University Press, 2001), p. 93.

2

Preconceptions: The Near East in the Bible and Classical Literature

> Still through Egypt's desert places
> Flows the lordly Nile,
> From its banks the great stone faces
> Gaze with patient smile.
> Still the pyramids imperious
> Pierce the cloudless skies,
> And the Sphinx stares with mysterious,
> Solemn, stony eyes.
>
> But where are the old Egyptian
> Demi-gods and kings?
> Nothing left but an inscription
> Graven on stones and rings.
> Where are Helios and Hephaestus,
> Gods of eldest eld?
> Where is Hermes Trismegistus,
> Who their secrets held?
>
> Where are now the many hundred
> Thousand books he wrote?
> By the Thaumaturgists plundered,
> Lost in lands remote;
> In oblivion sunk forever,
> As when o'er the land
> Blows a storm-wind, in the river
> Sinks the scattered sand.
>
> From 'Hermes Trismegistus' by Henry
> Wadsworth Longfellow (1807–1882)

Denon's *Voyage dans la Basse et la Haute Egypte* was the first new major source on ancient Egypt for Europeans in many years. Prior to the wave of

2. Preconceptions

Near Eastern exploration that was to begin in the aftermath of the Napoleonic campaigns, the European conception of ancient Near Eastern history was relatively stable and based on a few primary sources. The Bible provided the history of the Israelites and various peoples that the Israelites encountered, such as the Mesopotamian kingdoms, the Philistines, the Phoenicians and the Egyptians. Classical sources provided more direct historical accounts of the Mesopotamians and the Egyptians, and some of these sources (such as Josephus) added to Israelite history (although the Bible was the preferred source). There was another important literary source—hermetic literature—Graeco-Roman literature claiming to preserve the mystery traditions of Egypt. Mediaeval and Renaissance European scholarship on this literature was very robust, especially by scholars of alchemy and astrology. Emerging out of European reception of the hermetic corpus was *The Life of Sethos,* written by Jean Terrasson and published in English in 1732. By the nineteenth century, this fictional story of ancient Egypt had been mistaken by some as rooted in fact and played a curiously important role in conceptions of ancient Egypt. All of this would change with the decipherment of Egyptian and Mesopotamian scripts, but until those results were fully realized, ancient history remained based on these sources. The reliance on these biblical, classical and hermetic sources meant that the interested student of the ancient Near East had a very different view of ancient history at the beginning of the nineteenth century than at the end of the nineteenth century. Here then is a brief overview of the history of the Near East as it was understood before archaeological discoveries transformed the field.

The Biblical Egypt and the Near East

Given the widespread biblical literacy of the time, the importance of biblical accounts of the ancient Near East cannot be overestimated. In England, with its preponderance of churchgoers, even those with only a passing interest in the subject would have been familiar with the basics of the Bible's view of history. Children's Sunday school was, for the most part, non-denominational (or undenominational as Sarah Williams has argued) and practically universal.[1] Thomas Laqueur has observed that by the 1820s almost every working-class child outside of the major urban centres must have had some contact with Sunday schools, and this was a shared working-class experience.[2] The Bible was foundational for education, and before the advent of mandatory school in 1870, many children learned how to read at church,

---

1. S.C. Williams, *Religious Belief and Popular Culture in Southwark, c. 1830–1939* (Oxford: Oxford University Press, 1999), p. 141.
2. Thomas Laquer, *Religion and Respectability: Sunday Schools and Working-Class Culture, 1780–1850* (New Haven, CT: Yale University Press, 1976), p. xi.

through the Bible.³ Much of this education was through rote learning—the memorization of long biblical passages and other religious writings; but most Sunday schools also took advantage of the substantial number of textbooks and pamphlets aimed at children's education.⁴ Eitan Bar-Yosef argues that this childhood emphasis on the biblical lands created/creates a powerful sense of nostalgia for the ancient Near East and a kind of quasi-patriotism toward it.⁵ Jonathan Rose describes this as 'a kind of Anglo-Zionism, where children conflated contemporary England and ancient Israel to the point where they merged into a common homeland'.⁶ Even secular schools held the Bible as a basic text for developing reading skills, at an early stage, let alone for more advanced study. Biblical stories that lent themselves well to retelling, such as Jonah, would have made Assyrian cities such as Nineveh part of the imaginary geography of many. John Malcolm Russel has argued that St Jerome's commentaries on Jonah, Nahum and Zephaniah were particularly influential in nineteenth-century conceptions of Nineveh.⁷ Beyond the biblical text, Rose has suggested that the geography of the ancient Near East was taught in such detail that it was understood better than the geography of the contemporary world.⁸ Likewise, skepticism toward the veracity of these stories was not yet common, at least among popular audiences even though the chronological schema presented in the book of Genesis was coming to be seen as more and more problematic.

Curiously, despite the growth of German biblical criticism over the course of the nineteenth century and the widespread realization that the source-critical approach (which assumed that the Pentateuch was written by multiple authors) was essential to historical study of the Bible, these observations did not widely manifest in mass culture. For popular audiences, the basic outline of biblical history was relatively trustworthy, although there were varying degrees of faith in the early accounts of Genesis. The stories of the prophets were taken very seriously and treated as history—the books of Daniel and Jonah were used in thinking about the

---

3. Timothy Larsen, *The People of One Book: The Bible and the Victorians* (Oxford: Oxford University Press, 2011), p. 2.

4. Laquer, *Religion and Respectability: Sunday Schools and Working-Class Culture, 1780–1850* (New Haven, CT: Yale University Press, 1976), pp. 111, 113-19.

5. Eitan Bar-Yosef, *The Holy Land in English Culture 1799–1917: Palestine and the Question of Orientalism* (Oxford: Clarendon Press, 2005), p. 88.

6. Jonathan Rose, *The Intellectual Life of the British Working Class* (New Haven, CT: Yale University Press, 2nd edn, 2010), p. 350.

7. John Malcolm Russel, *From Nineveh to New York: The Strange Story of the Assyrian Reliefs in the Metropolitan Museum and the Hidden Masterpiece at Canford School* (with contributions by Judith McKenzie and Stephanie Dalley; in association with the Metropolitan Museum of Art; New Haven, CT: Yale University Press, 1997), p. 27.

8. Rose, *Intellectual Life*, pp. 350-51.

past in the same way that the books of Kings were. Thus, for the biblically literate nineteenth-century churchgoer, the history of the Israelites began with Abraham leaving Ur and settling in Palestine. The Hebrews left the land in drought conditions, were absorbed into Egyptian civilization and eventually enslaved until Moses liberated them and returned them to the Promised Land. After Joshua's military conquests, the United Monarchy (of Saul, David and Solomon) arose only to collapse into two separate kingdoms of Israel and Judah (the Divided Monarchy) after Solomon's death. Under Solomon, Israel reached its political, economic and geographic peak. Solomon constructed the Temple under Phoenician guidance and entertained foreign emissaries, most notably the Queen of Sheba, building a kingdom that was not just peripheral to world powers (like Egypt) but a major force in the region. Biblical and postbiblical tradition held that Solomon was the master of great wisdom, and for many later European mystics, the secret elements of this knowledge could be revealed through analysis of the biblical description of the Temple.[9] The Temple was itself thought to be an architectural manifestation of universal knowledge and the best-known building that had been designed by God himself. Renaissance magical texts, such as the *Clavicula Salomonis* (or 'Little Key of Solomon'), were attributed to him, and numerous pentagrams (drawings used in preparation for magical operations) were thought to allow the user to channel the powers of God. Egyptian hieroglyphs and 'Chaldaean' symbols were also used for magical purposes.[10]

After Solomon, the fortunes of Israel and Judah ebbed and flowed based on the theological behavior of their kings, sometimes pious (especially the kings of Judah) but often not. The prophets provide messages and commentary from God about the behaviour of the kings and the people of the land. During the period of the Divided Monarchy, Israel and Judah found themselves caught between Mesopotamia (first Assyria and then Babylon) and Egypt. Eventually Israel and then Judah succumbed to destruction by Mesopotamian hands. After the Neo-Babylonian king Nebuchadnezzar destroyed Jerusalem and the Temple, the people were exiled to Babylon, returning only after the Neo-Babylonian Empire was itself destroyed by the Persians.

The German biblical scholar Johann Gottfried Herder most clearly articulated the view of biblical history held at this time, seeing the period from Moses to Solomon as the high point of Old Testament history. Herder assumed that whenever God entered the narrative, the typical rules of

9. For more on this, see Paul Kléber Monad, *Solomon's Secret Arts: The Occult in the Age of Enlightenment* (New Haven, CT: Yale University Press, 2013), pp. 9, 161.

10. At this time Chaldaean symbols were completely imagined or based on Late Antique Aramaic traditions. Chaldaean also referred to Zoroastrian ideas and writings as well, in nineteenth-century usage. These were not based on Mesopotamian cuneiform script, which was not yet understood in Europe.

'history' were suspended and thus argued for a kind of biblical exceptionalism for Israelite history.[11] By the end of the nineteenth century, many academic scholars had begun to attempt to circumvent this kind of exceptionalism, and biblical history had started to be treated like any other type of history. For most British at the outset of the nineteenth century, the basic framework of divinely inspired ancient Near Eastern history was little questioned, merely accepted, much as the received histories of the Greeks and Romans were.

Unlike contemporary biblical archaeology, which tends to minimize any connection between Egypt and early biblical religion, scholars throughout the nineteenth century were keen to draw connections. The importance of Egypt in the biblical story was taken as evidence for the close relationship between the Hebrews and the people of the Nile. Especially since Egypt was thought to be the oldest civilization, it made sense to contextualize Israelite society (in its earlier periods) as having emerged in the shadow of (and potentially in antithesis to) the culture that built the pyramids. The pyramids themselves were thought by some to have been built through Hebrew slave labour (during the time of the exodus) despite the fact that no mention of this is made in the Bible.[12] Even atheist and anti-Christian writers were keen to make this argument. Charles Bradlaugh, for example, argued that the Egyptian origins of biblical religion undermined Judaism and the Old Testament. For Bradlaugh, the fact that Egyptian religion lent many of its practices to Hebrew practices discredited the possibility that Old Testament religion could have stemmed from divine revelation.[13]

The Classical View of Egypt and the Near East

Outside of the Bible, the other major sources of information available to the nineteenth-century European were the accounts preserved in Greek and Roman sources. Unlike the biblical accounts, these works cannot be presumed to have been familiar to everyone in nineteenth-century Britain. However, classical studies was an important element of an elite education, and those who went to school would have had a familiarity with Latin and Greek. Likewise, much of the classical heritage filtered into other avenues— theatre, the arts, and design all heavily referenced the Graeco-Roman world and, by extension, the Graeco-Roman world's view of the Near East. And

---

11. For more on Herder, see Suzanne L. Marchand, *German Orientalism in the Age of Empire: Religion, Race, and Scholarship* (Cambridge: Cambridge University Press, 2009), pp. 43-52, esp. 47.

12. Another much earlier European understanding of the relationship between the Hebrews and the pyramids was that the pyramids were actually the granaries of Joseph.

13. Larsen, *People of One Book*, p. 87.

like the Bible, the classical sources were treated with great reverence and not with the suspicion typical of modern historical-critical scholarship.

The history of the ancient Near East derived from classical sources was based on the accident of what survived in the transmission of this writing to later European society.[14] As such, important sources, such as Manetho's *Aegyptiaca,* were preserved only in fragmentary form in other works. These fragments were (and are) quite important. Manetho's work, for example, has provided the basis for the dynastic historical schema still used by Egyptologists today. Similarly, Berossos's Greek language *History of Mesopotamia* provided an outline of the Mesopotamian past from the perspective of a Mesopotamian priest, but it survives only in portions. There is no need to survey all of this material here.[15] However, in order to understand some of the more unusual nineteenth-century takes on the ancient Near East, it is important to be familiar with some of the classical traditions that were taken seriously then but are no longer considered historical. Ancient Near Eastern historical reconstructions, filtered first through a Graeco-Roman worldview, differed somewhat from those available at the end of the nineteenth century, after ancient Near Eastern studies had emerged as a formal discipline in tandem with discoveries in the region.

Herodotus's *Histories* (written c. 450–420 BCE) was one of the most important sources of classical knowledge on the ancient Near East and Egypt. His work was a conscious attempt to record information about the events and customs of peoples of, what was to him, the recent past. While Egypt, Mesopotamia and the biblical lands were not his major concern, his extended discussions of these cultures provided the basis for European knowledge of them for the next 2,400 years. This is not the place for an extended analysis of his presentation of the Near East, but it is useful to sketch an outline of what the nineteenth-century reader would have taken from Herodotus. The veracity of his account, the sources he used and his methods are not as important for this discussion as how the less critical nineteenth-century reader would have read Herodotus's book.

Herodotus's view of ancient Egypt is replete with outlandish stories, and the exotic view that the Greeks held of Egypt is key to understanding his discussion of the region and the messages that later readers would take from it. Of course, Egypt of the time was well familiar to the Greeks, who had trade colonies in the Delta and imported Egyptian luxuries. Tales of the

14. For an overview of these sources as related to Babylon, see I.L. Finkel and M.J. Seymour, eds., *Babylon: Myth and Reality* (London: British Museum Press, 2008), esp. pp. 102ff.

15. For an introductory account of Berossos and Manetho, see Gerald P. Verbrugghe and John M. Wickersham, *Berossos and Manetho, Introduced and Translated: Native Traditions in Ancient Mesopotamia and Egypt* (Ann Arbor, MI: University of Michigan Press, 1996).

inverted practices of other cultures were not atypical of Greek ethnographic accounts, and the more far-fetched tales Herodotus recorded were not taken seriously by most later readers. He states outright that the Egyptians do everything the opposite of the rest of the world (taking the Greeks as normative) and then lists these curious reversals (such as the fact that the women work outside of the home and the men stay at home and weave) (*Histories* 2.35). Herodotus (and other classical authors) were also very interested in queens who actually ruled people (instead of kings) and the men who bowed to female authority. Female leadership was not seen as merely an aberrant barbarian practice (like other customs described by Herodotus) but an issue for genuine consideration. The issue of women's participation in politics was, of course, of tremendous concern in the late-nineteenth century as well, and these classical stories became relevant for the times. Especially after the accession of Victoria, female leaders were of intense interest in British popular culture, and historical antecedents of Victoria and Albert became part of a larger political discussion.[16]

Readers took Herodotus's discussions of the religion of the Egyptians very seriously, understanding it to consist of trustworthy accounts of ancient cultic practices. Herodotus claims to have learned much from the priests of Egypt. The secret wisdom of the 'priests of Egypt' continues to be a font of claims about Egypt, and esoteric groups of the late-nineteenth century frequently claimed to be privy to similar sources. Herodotus establishes one of the major tropes for demonstrating authority by rooting it in supposed Egyptian knowledge. There are hints though, that unlike the nineteenth-century claimants, Herodotus must really have talked with Egyptian priests. For example, he describes mummification in great detail, and his account of this practice was fundamental for the twentieth-century physical anthropologists who reconstructed the practice.

Some of this secret priestly knowledge relates to Egypt's perceived position as one of the earliest civilizations. Herodotus's famous story of an experiment regarding Egypt's antiquity is found at the beginning of book 2. According to Herodotus, King Psammetichos wanted to test whether or not the common Egyptian claim to be the first civilization could be upheld. Thus, he ordered that two newborn babies be set apart from civilization and not spoken to. The first language spoken (once the children were old enough to speak) would be in the world's original language. The first words spoken, in this story were Phrygian, and thus it was proven that Egypt was not the oldest civilization (although Herodotus hints that he found this particular story to be implausible). Regardless of whether or not Herodotus viewed

---

16. Julia M. Asher-Greve, 'From "Semiramis of Babylon" to "Semiramis of Hammersmith", in *Orientalism, Assyriology and the Bible* (ed. Steven W. Holloway; Hebrew Bible Monographs, 10; Sheffield: Sheffield Phoenix Press, 2007), pp. 322-73 (346-47).

2. Preconceptions

Egypt as the oldest culture, he documents the various aspects of Greek society that emerged out of Egypt. Most important was religion. According to Herodotus, the gods and other aspects of Greek religious thought originated in Egypt, the source of sacred knowledge. Thus he perpetuates an approach to Egypt that continues throughout the nineteenth century until Sumer begins to be credited with the role of 'first inventor' of civilization.

Another theme in Herodotus's account that is picked up on in nineteenth-century studies is the Nilocentric nature of Egyptian society. Herodotus argues that Egyptian life was centred upon the Nile and that the society itself looked inward, uninterested in foreign influence. Much information is provided about the geography of Egypt and the relationship of that geography to various aspects of Egyptian life, and the geographic determinism that comes to typify some studies of Egyptian culture is prefigured by the Greek historian. The centrality of the Nile has continued to be a major theme in the presentation of Egypt to non-specialists. Victorian-era readers might have been particularly interested in Herodotus's theories about the source of the Nile, given the importance of this issue to nineteenth-century explorers and the periodical press, which celebrated their adventures. Nilocentrism also played a role in racial and cultural debates of the nineteenth century, with Egypt being paraded as an example of a closed culture (not susceptible to outside influence until its final years), for good or ill, depending on the argument being made.

The Victorians were also interested in (and sometimes horrified by) the Egyptian relationship to nature. Enlightenment ideas about nature worship (and to some extent pantheism) had established that religions revolving around nature were both primordial and appealing. For the French revolutionaries, this made Egypt exemplary. For others, it made Egypt a theological curiosity, an example of civilized heresy, or evidence that Christian beliefs were tangible evidence of progress. One of the main popular beliefs held about the Egyptians in Victorian times is that they worshipped animals, something heavily emphasized by Herodotus. His section on the embalming of animals (especially cats and dogs) was supported by archaeological finds in the nineteenth century, eliciting much popular interest. Ibises, discovered in mummified form by Napoleon's savants (see Fig. 1.2), were held in high esteem according to Herodotus, especially as they were helpful in killing winged serpents. The Victorians were particularly fascinated by the Apis bull, the animal form of the Egyptian god Apis. Many of the non-specialist accounts of ancient Egyptian religion focused on Apis worship in detail, partially because of its prominent mention in classical sources. Herodotus emphasizes the particularities of the treatment, sacrifice and worship of the bull. This seeming worship of an animal was generative for nineteenth-century scholars who were interested in the history of religion more generally. Despite the fact that the kind of Apis worship preserved in classical accounts reflects Graeco-Roman period traditions, scholars assumed that these practices were typical for much of Egypt's history.

Following his eyewitness accounts of Egypt's geography and customs, Herodotus offers an overview of Egyptian history as told to him by others. He begins Egypt's story with Min, who the priests told him was the first king of Egypt and founder of the city of Memphis. The priests provided him with a list of 330 names of the kings of Egypt who followed Min. Herodotus assumed that each generation lasted for about thirty to forty years, calculating three generations of men for every century. Thus Egyptian history, in Herodotus's view, spans 11,340 years (*Histories* 2.142). It is worth noting some of the curious stories about kings that Herodotus provided—those that have not been born out by historians but that were popular among the Victorians.

For example, Queen Nitokris (not to be confused with the Babylonian queen Herodotus describes of the same name) was the subject of popular historical fiction in the nineteenth century, given the particularly violent story of her reign (*Histories* 2.100).[17] Historically, she may have been the last queen of the Sixth Dynasty, although Egyptologists debate this. According to Herodotus, though, while reigning as king, her brother was murdered by a contingent of conspirators. As his next blood heir, Nitokris was installed as queen and preceded to enact vengeance against those that had killed her brother. She built a large underground chamber, invited the conspirators to a feast, and while they were eating, allowed the chamber to be flooded by the Nile through a secret chamber, killing all of the banqueters. Following this, she committed suicide by throwing herself into a chamber of ashes.

Some of the key plot devices of many of the archaeological adventure stories set in Egypt may originate in the story of the treasure of King Rhampsinitos (told in *Histories* 2.121), probably an amalgam of late Ramesside era kings. Rhampsinitos built an elaborate treasury to store the great wealth that he had amassed in his reign. It was accessible by a secret entrance—one of the stones could be removed by one or two men to allow access. Upon his death, one of his sons ascended to the throne but noticed that the treasury was gradually being depleted. The new king eventually realized that despite all of the seals being intact, someone was breaking in to steal treasure. The king thus ordered traps to be set to capture the thief, and, sure enough, one of the thieves was ensnared. In order to save his brother (who was one of the looters), the trapped thief told his brother to cut off his head and remove it from the chamber—that way, when the body was discovered the next morn-

---

17. Nitocris is also the heroine of some twentieth-century fiction, such as Lord Dunsany's *The Queen's Enemies*, and the Tennessee Williams short story 'The Vengeance of Nitocris. She also appears in H.P. Lovecraft stories. Her appearance in the stories of H.P. Lovecraft is discussed in Chapter III.10.

ing, the king would be unable to identify it and punish the thief's family. His brother did so, and the king was unable to identify the thief. The king ordered the body to be hung (and guarded over) so that when the family came to claim the body, the perpetrators would be revealed. The mother demanded that the thief's brother retrieve the body, so he came up with an elaborate plan. He filled some wineskins, tied them up on a donkey, and then led the donkey near the guards. Arranging for the wineskins to all begin leaking, he feigned rage as the guards rush out to drink it. After drinking their fill, the guards invited him to come join them. When they passed out from drinking too much, the brother took the body and then shaved the right cheek of each guard, as a humourous gesture, before fleeing. Upon hearing of this bold ploy, the king decided to set another trap, this time sending his daughter to work in a brothel. In order to lie with the king's daughter, the interested party had to confess the most impious or criminal act that they had ever committed. The thief's brother, deciding to commit another act of royal defiance, visited the king's daughter, but before doing so, he equipped himself with the arm from a corpse. He confessed his crimes truthfully, and when she reached out to grab him and catch him for the guards, the princess grabbed the corpse's arm instead and the brother was able to escape. The king was impressed by the continued daring of the brother, granted him a pardon and offered his daughter to him in marriage.

Herodotus's account of King Cheops's reign and the construction of the pyramids is similarly dramatic but is based on a real historical figure. He is clearly dependent on Egyptian traditions that Cheops (Khufu in Egyptian), the builder of the Great Pyramid of Giza, was a cruel and immoral king. Cheops is another king, according to Herodotus, who was willing to put his daughter into service in a brothel, in this case to earn funds for the construction of the pyramid. Herodotus claims that this led to the construction of what is now known to be Mycerinus's small pyramid on the Egyptian plateau.[18] According to Herodotus, however, Cheops's daughter requested that each client at the brothel give her a small stone for her own monument, and these were then used to construct that pyramid. Cheops's son, Khephron (Khafre), was also deemed to be a wicked and cruel king, and Herodotus reports that all Egyptians hate the memory of these kings of the pyramid age.

Herodotus makes a number of interesting, but inaccurate, points that influenced Victorian thought about Egypt. For example, the Greek historian believed that the pyramids were much younger than we now know. Another misconception is Herodotus's story that King Sesostris invaded Europe, a claim that for Victorian readers proved that there had been direct links

---

18. Despite the misattribution of Mycerinus's (Menkhaure's) pyramid, several stories are also told about this king (Herodotus, *Histories* 2.129-34).

between nineteenth-century European society and ancient Egypt. Stories about the Egyptian origins of Celtic culture are somewhat related to these traditions. Likewise, a labyrinth, greater than the pyramids, was said to have been built near Lake Moeris (*Histories* 2.148-49). Generally Herodotus was thought to be an untrustworthy source in the nineteenth century, but for his more plausible reports and his stories of different kings, it was difficult to sort out which elements were trustworthy until the decipherment of hieroglyphs.

Herodotus's take on Mesopotamian culture should be understood in the context of Greek relations with the Persians at the time. The Persians had been the enemies of the Greeks, and part of Herodotus's project was to understand the roots of this conflict. Accounting for how the East became Persian was part of this process. Thus there is a tendency to glorify the antiquity of Mesopotamia and to acknowledge the continuities of these glories. At the same time, Herodotus makes it clear that the current state of this worthy enemy's culture is one of decline, so the Greeks are seen to be battling an important but degenerate foe. Unlike Egypt, however, direct Greek experiences with Mesopotamia were not common, and this certainly played a role in the transmission of ideas about the region. In *Histories* 1.184, Herodotus makes mention of his history of Assyria, which he seems to have never had the chance to write.

An extended description of the city of Babylon is provided in *The Histories*. The urban districts, walls, moats and glazed bricks are described, all elements that were roughly confirmed through archaeological excavations. Given the details provided, nineteenth-century readers would have felt that they had a good sense of the city, and an accurate picture could be imagined. The resources of the city are described in opulent detail—gold, spices and other luxuries are listed in huge quantities, and the image that is formed is one of excess. The Hanging Gardens of Babylon were not mentioned by Herodotus, but were familiar enough to Victorian readers from other sources (see below) that they would have been included in their visions of this ancient city.

Herodotus describes two female queens of Babylon, Semiramis and Nitokris, who were important figures in the nineteenth-century reception of Mesopotamia. It is not clear if Nitokris (or Nitocris) has a historical antecedent, but Semiramis may have been based on Queen Shammuramat, wife of the Neo-Assyrian king Shamshi-Adad V and mother of Adad-Nirari III (for whom she acted as regent until he came of age).[19] Semiramis's promi-

---

19. For a discussion of the scholarly arguments about the 'historical' Semiramis, see Asher-Greve, 'Semiramis'. For an argument that traditions about Semiramis conflate three different historical queens, see Stephanie Dalley, 'Semiramis in History and Legend: A Case Study in Interpretation of an Assyriological Historical Tradition, with

nence in Herodotus's and Diodorus's accounts (all of which seem to be entirely legendary) made her an important figure in early reconstructions of Mesopotamian history, and many ideas were espoused in trying to identify her. For example, Alexander Hislop (1807–1865) believed that she ordered the construction of the Tower of Babel.[20] Herodotus is particularly interested in both queens' construction projects, especially their approaches to water management. Nitokris is described as the more clever queen. Herodotus tells of a decoy tomb that she created, with an inscription describing the luxuries within. Tomb robbers would then find a message of castigation, taunting them with the realization that the tomb was empty. Darius is said to have fallen for this trick. More stories about these queens were preserved by Diodorus (see below).

Some of the curious beliefs about Babylonian culture held by nineteenth-century scholars originate in Herodotus's accounts. Zeus-Belos was taken to be the equivalent of biblical Baal and the chief deity of Babylon. Herodotus describes Zeus-Belos's temples in detail, and Babylonian cultic practices were also of interest. Temple prostitution is described (still a point of contention among Assyriologists), and the sacred marriage rites are discussed, although Herodotus admits that these seem incredulous. For Herodotus, the most appalling Babylonian practice was that at least once in her life, every Babylonian woman had to have sexual intercourse with a stranger in the courtyard of the temple of Aphrodite. The woman had to wait until a man threw an amount of silver at her (any amount), which then became a temple donation. She could not refuse the man but had to wait until she was chosen. Herodotus notes that unattractive women could wait for up to three or four years.

Likewise, the story of the Babylonian marriage market is told in *Histories* 1.196. In a passage that appealed to nineteenth-century fantasies about the oriental harem, Herodotus describes how the Babylonians chose their wives. Once a year, a marriage market was held in every village, where all of the eligible women were auctioned off to their future husbands. This was, according to Herodotus, the only legal means of marriage. The most attractive women were auctioned off first, and then the proceeds from those sales were used to pay men to take the unattractive women as wives. Thus a misogynistic kind of social support system was enacted, one that Herodotus

---

Observations on Archetypes in Ancient Historiography, on Euhemerism before Euhemerus, and on the So-Called Greek Ethnographic Style', in *Cultural Borrowings and Ethnic Appropriations in Antiquity: Oriens et Occidens* (ed. Erich S. Gruen; Studien zu antiken Kulturkontakten und ihrem Nachleben, 8; Stuttgart: Franz Steiner Verlag, 2005), pp. 11-22.

20. John Harvey, *The Bible as Visual Culture: When Text Becomes Image* (The Bible in the Modern World, 57; Sheffield: Sheffield Phoenix Press, 2013), p. 86.

described as the finest Mesopotamian custom (and one no longer practiced after the Persian conquest).

Another key source for the study of the ancient Near East at the beginning of the nineteenth century was the *Bibliotheca historica,* written by Diodorus Siculus. This large work consisted of forty books; books 1-5 and 11-20 survive in their entirety, and fragments of the rest are preserved in other sources. Little is known of Diodorus's life, other than that he was born in Sicily and that he worked from about 60 to 30 BCE. Unlike Herodotus, Diodorus argues with certainty that the Egyptians were the first civilization, and *Bibliotheca historica* 1 is devoted to the subject of Egypt. In agreement with Herodotus, Diodorus establishes Egypt as a 'first inventor' culture and sees much of Graeco-Roman culture (and by proxy, civilization in general) as having originated along the banks of the Nile. As with Herodotus, Diodorus argues that Egyptian history spanned ten thousand years, from its origins until the arrival of Alexander the Great. The Egyptians were said to have established many colonies, and many Greek cities were claimed to have Egyptian foundations. The idea of Egypt spreading colonies throughout the world becomes an important element in fantasy and esoteric literature involving the ancient Near East (discussed in Volume III of this study). The Chaldeans, according to Herodotus, were Egyptian colonists, although he makes little mention of these most ancient of Babylonians.[21] However, he describes their divinatory practices in detail, especially their astrological practices. He credits the Egyptians with inventing the key concepts behind Chaldean astronomy.

Much information is provided about the geography of Egypt and about the Nile. The flooding of the Nile is explained in detail, and nineteenth-century Egyptologists used this information in their reconstructions of Egyptian agricultural practices. Diodorus provides some discussion of the origin of the Nile, but explains that no one has actually ever seen the source, so any ideas are merely conjecture. This was another important source for those nineteenth-century explorers concerned with the Nile and was of great interest to the Victorian public, frequently referenced in periodical culture.

Just as with geography, Diodorus was as interested in religion as Herodotus was. He presents an overview of Egyptian religion that attempts to make sense of its traditions within a Graeco-Roman framework and in tandem with Graeco-Roman deities. He provides a mythological history of early Egyptian civilization that became the basis for much of European thought

---

21. The Chaldeans are now understood to be a specific group of people who lived in the marshes of Mesopotamia and came to rule towards the end of the Neo-Babylonian period. The term became confused in Hellenistic times, and was used to refer to Mesopotamian culture more broadly. By the nineteenth century, the term Chaldean was used as a general term for Mesopotamian and especially Babylonian culture (in distinction to Assyrian). It was also commonly used to refer to the Aramaic language.

on the nature of Egyptian mythology until Egyptian hieroglyphs were translated. Hercules, Perseus and other heroes were born in Egypt, and Diodorus gives many Graeco-Roman figures a more ancient Egyptian pedigree. Osiris and Isis were among the first gods known to humans, although Diodorus provides divergent arguments on how they fit in the established pantheon. The relationship of the god Hermes to Osiris became quite important in later European traditions—Diodorus reported that Hermes was Osiris's sacred scribe.

One of the most important elements of Diodorus's account for nineteenth-century thinking about Egypt was his explanation of the death and subsequent immortality of Osiris. Osiris is said to have been murdered by Typhon (and many nineteenth-century writers refer to the murderer by the name Typhon as opposed to the name Seth, which would more accurately reflect the Egyptian tradition). The body of Osiris was then cut into twenty-six pieces and spread around Egypt. His sister-wife Isis gathered the pieces up again (except for the penis, which became symbolic for the nourishing powers of the Nile) and mummified the remains. His burial place, however, was kept a secret. In commemoration of Osiris, two sacred bulls (Apis and Mnevis) were consecrated, and these worship practices continued until Diodorus's time. These events were the basis of the Greek forms of the Egyptian mystery cults, according to Diodorus. The mystery cults preserved ancient Egyptian knowledge in a Greek context. Diodorus makes a few references to the secret wisdom held by the Egyptian priests (wisdom that was not shared with him), references that were treated with great interest in later European thought. Related, Diodorus discusses various famous wise men (such as Solon, Plato, Pythagoras, etc.) who travelled to Egypt to learn from its ancient traditions, a common theme of later searchers for Egypt's secret wisdom. Pythagoras's supposed journey to Egypt, where he learned geometry, arithmetic, and the secrets of the afterlife, was noteworthy to later readers.

Some of the customs that Diodorus ascribes to the Egyptians were also of interest to the nineteenth-century reader. Brothers and sisters were allowed to marry each other; Diodorus does not acknowledge that this was typically limited to royal marriages. Polygamy was common except among the Egyptian priests. Similarly, he describes gender roles that were inverted from those of the Greeks (and the Victorians). Queens have more power than kings, and in marriage, husbands have less legal authority than their wives. As already discussed in reference to Herodotus, ancient tales of powerful queens were particularly important within the Victorian political context, both in terms of understanding Queen Victoria and later in reference to the suffragette movement. Inverted gender roles were a typical means of expressing 'otherness' in Graeco-Roman writing, but nineteenth-century historians took these claims seriously as historical information about Egyptian customs.

After establishing some of the main features of Egyptian geography and its relation to the origins of human civilization, Diodorus launches into a discussion of Egyptian political history. As with Herodotus, he comments that the Egyptian priests have kept long records of the kings, and, as with Herodotus, the first of these kings was Menes. He also discusses the vast funerary sepulchers and the vast building projects of King Ozymandias. The exploits of King Sesostris are described in detail. The treatment of the pyramids and their construction reflects that Diodorus was less certain about their history than Herodotus. Having given a brief account of the main themes of Egyptian political history, Diodorus then turns to an account of their customs and practices. The governance of Egypt, including the nome system of administration, is laid out, and the class system explained.[22] Various legal practices are listed, and commentary is provided on how these compare to Greek law. The worship of animals is, as in Herodotus, discussed in depth with much curiosity. Diodorus also tries to explain the rationale for mummifying animals. An interesting claim is that red-headed people were sacrificed to Osiris, due to the fact that Typhon was a redhead.

Diodorus's treatment of Assyria begins with Ninus, whom he describes as the first Assyrian king recorded in history. Assyria emerges when Ninus makes an alliance with an Arabian king and conquers the province of Babylon. He eventually founds Nineveh, which, according to Diodorus, derives from the name Ninus. Thereupon he marries Semiramis, and her story is told in more detail than that given by Herodotus. Semiramis's story is a rags-to-riches story. It begins in Ashkelon (located on the coast of Israel), where, we are told by Diodorus, the Syrian goddess Derceto fell in love and became pregnant. She killed the father and exposed her newly born daughter to the elements. The daughter survived, having been nourished by a flock of pigeons, who fed her milk from their beaks, stolen from houses nearby. She was eventually adopted by the king's chief herdsman and named Semiramis, a name that according to Diodorus, is related to the ancient Syrian term for pigeon.

Semiramis grew into a beautiful woman, and she was noticed by Menon, a king's officer. He marries her and brings her back to Nineveh with him, and soon two sons are born. Ninus raises an army to fight the Bactrians, and Menon is forced to go to war. He becomes lovesick and sends for Semiramis to come to the soldier's camp. Semiramis covers herself in clothing that protects her from the elements and hides her identity (as a woman) and goes to Bactria. When she arrives, she notices a key tactical flaw in the enemy's plans and helps the Assyrian army conquer a Bactrian city. King Ninus, noticing her intelligence and beauty, asks Menon to give her to him. When Menon refuses, the king threatens him, and eventually Menon hangs

---

22. Nome is the Greek term for Egyptian administrative districts, or provinces.

himself, leaving Semiramis free to become queen of Assyria. Ninus and Semiramis have a son, Ninyas, and Ninus dies, leaving Semiramis regent of Babylon. As regent, Semiramis builds a magnificent capital, the city of Babylon. In the centre of Babylon, she builds a temple to Belus (taken to be the Assyrian version of Jupiter) upon which the Chaldean astrologers could make observations. Presumably this was the ziggurat. Diodorus describes her other building projects in depth (as well as the Hanging Gardens of Babylon, which he ascribes to a later period—under Prince Cyrus). Semiramis travels throughout the known world and eventually enquires about her future from the oracle of Jupiter Ammon in Libya (the Egyptian western desert). There, she learns that her son, Ninyas, is plotting against her. Eventually, after more military campaigns (extending as far as the Indian subcontinent), her son orders a eunuch to kill her. In response, rather than punishing him, she surrenders the throne to him and, according to some traditions, transforms herself into a dove and flies away. This, at least, is the story as told to Diodorus by Ctesias the Cnidian. Athenaeus's version is less elaborate, merely describing her as a beautiful woman who becomes the wife of the king of Assyria, and, through a banquet, convinces him to hand over his kingship to her.

Ninyas is not nearly as successful a leader as Semiramis. Diodorus describes him as spending most of his reign shut up in his palace, enjoying sensual pleasures. This sets the pattern for the next thirty generations of Assyrian kings, who proceeded in an uninterrupted line from Semiramis and culminate in Sardanapalus, the last king of Assyria. Diodorus preserves an account of King Sardanapalus of Assyria, also based on the now lost writings of Ctesias of Cnidus. However, as preserved by Diodorus, the story is very much a Roman story of self-indulgence, decadence and the calamitous events that occur as the result of these traits. The Roman moralizing made this a particularly appealing story for nineteenth-century readers, who appreciated its edifying qualities. According to Diodorus, the Assyrian empire falls as a direct result of Sardanapalus's self-indulgence and lack of sexual morals. The Romantics found this last king to be an interesting figure, exploring his character through art and verse. Indeed, even after the rediscovery and reconstruction of Assyrian history (which does not include a historical Sardanapalus), the figure remained an important component of popular and elite cultural reception of Mesopotamia. His character dominated nineteenth-century views of Assyria.

Sardanapalus was not a historical king, although it is possible that his name is a corruption of an Akkadian name (perhaps Ashurbanipal), and some of the elements of the story somewhat reflect events that occurred with the fall of the Neo-Assyrian Empire. Some have suggested that he may be associated with Sargon II, although the evidence for this is meager.[23] According to Diodorus, he was the embodiment of excess in all avenues of life. Engaging in transvestitism and dallying with his numerous male and female concubines, Sardanapalus epitomized Roman notions of sexual excess. Celebrations of drinking, eating and sex were common features of his palace. A rebellion arose against him, led by the Babylonians, Medes and Persians. After initial Assyrian successes, Sardanapalus and his troops renew their excessive lifestyles, the rebels renew their attacks and eventually Sardanapalus is surrounded in Nineveh. Once heavy rains breech one of the walls of Nineveh, he realizes he is doomed. The Assyrian king, not wanting to be captured, has a huge funeral pyre created for himself, with all of his treasures and concubines. He burns himself and all of his retainers to death, and thus the Assyrian Empire falls in a final act of gluttony. Following the collapse of Assyria, the Chaldeans (called as such by the Babylonians according to Diodorus) come to power in Mesopotamia. Here, Diodorus has confused the basic framework of Mesopotamian history. The biblical account preserved the final days of the Assyrian and Babylonian empires differently (and more accurately). However, the obvious disparity between these accounts meant that there was more than one outline of Mesopotamian history operative for much of the nineteenth century.

Herodotus and Diodorus were not the only classical sources on the Near East available to nineteenth-century scholars. Arguably the most important classical source on Egyptian religion is the essay by Plutarch (c. 46–c. 120 CE) contained in his collection *Moralia*. Much of what he offers is distilled from the writings of Herodotus and Diodorus. Other information may also be derived from his own conversations with Egyptian priests, perhaps held during his actual visit to Egypt but more likely with priests of Isis living in Greece. He was an initiate in the Apollo mysteries and was one of the senior priests of Apollo at Delphi so some of his interpretation of Egyptian religion may be coloured by his experiences in that tradition. Plutarch's account of Egyptian religion was arguably the most cited source on Egyptian religion for European scholars until the decipherment of hieroglyphs.

Plutarch provides an account of the Isis–Osiris–Horus myth and attempts to situate the Egyptian deities in relation to the Graeco-Roman pantheon. He describes Typhon's (Seth's) murder and dismemberment of Osiris, and Isis's subsequent protection of her son Horus and her gathering of her husband-brother's body parts. Horus grows up, training in warfare, and eventually avenges his father against Typhon. Plutarch describes the various locations that Egyptian priests have argued to be the locations of Osiris's

---

23. Rachel Hallote, *Bible, Map, and Spade: The American Palestine Exploration Society, Frederick Jones Bliss, and the Forgotten Story of Early American Archaeology* (Piscataway, NJ: Gorgias Press, 2006), p. 33 n. 5.

burial. These Egyptian divinities, are, according to Plutarch, neither gods nor men, but some creatures in between. They are also associated with various natural bodies (e.g. Osiris is related to the moon). Here is the evidence for Egyptian and animal and astral worship that would be of great interest to the Victorian scholars who studied the evolution of religion (see Chapter I.4). The activities of Egyptian priests are also preserved in Plutarch's essay. He details some of their cultic practices and provides a rationale for some of these activities. Much of this better reflects later practices of Egyptian religion, and much of Plutarch's discussion situates Egyptian religion within a Graeco-Roman framework. For example, he argues that earth, air and fire are the three 'first bodies' of creation and are thus fundamental elements. In this, and other cases, Plutarch's Greek take on Egyptian religion became the source of later interpretations of Egyptian religion and fit well within the Graeco-Roman context of hermetic writings on Egypt. It was not until the decipherment of hieroglyphs that older Egyptian religious traditions were accessible to scholars.

Plutarch's emphasis on the Egyptian mysteries was mirrored in other sources that European scholars used to reconstruct ancient beliefs. Very important in mediaeval and Renaissance scholarship was the set of writings known as the Hermetica, which include the *Corpus hermeticum* and *Asclepius*.[24] These are ancient writings, perhaps as old as the third century CE, that preserve dialogues between Hermes Trismegistus and others. Hermes Trismegistus (or 'thrice great' Hermes) is variously understood but is usually taken as a syncreticization of the Greek god Hermes and the Egyptian god Thoth (both gods associated with wisdom and writing). Thrice Great Hermes was understood to be one of the ancient pre-Christian sages and the bearer of the sacred lore of antediluvian times (which was also thought to be preserved physically in the temples of ancient Egypt). The hermetic writings are in dialogue form. Hermes Trismegistus discusses ancient wisdom with his son, with a deified form of the Egyptian architect Imhotep that is connected with the classical Asclepius, and with Isis and Horus. Hornung has argued that these writings are rooted in the ancient Near Eastern wisdom genre but in terms of content are more related to Gnosticism and Platonism.[25] It is not a unified philosophy, although there are consistent arguments that favour revelation (over Greek philosophical reasoning) as a better source of knowledge. This is primordial knowledge that must be protected even if it can no longer be understood.

---

24. For an overview of hermeticism from ancient times to the twentieth century, see Florian Ebeling, *The Secret History of Hermes Trismegistus: Hermeticism from Ancient to Modern Times* (trans. David Lorton; Ithaca, NY: Cornell University Press, 2007).

25. Erik Hornung, *The Secret Lore of Egypt: Its Impact on the West* (trans. D. Lorton; Ithaca, NY: Cornell University Press, 2001), pp. 51-52.

Early modern European scholars tended also to read a prefiguring of Christianity into this corpus.[26] This is apparent in the first translation, by Marsilio Ficino (1433–1499), who translated the text as though it made specific reference to Christ. Giordano Bruno (1548–1600), a Dominican monk who was greatly influenced by this translation, was expelled from his order for unorthodoxy and burnt at the stake for heresy. He argued that Christianity was actually a corruption of hermeticism.[27] After 1614, it was generally agreed that the Hermetica was not what it had been thought to be and not nearly as ancient. However, for alchemists, this was one of the most fundamentally important sources, and much early science is rooted in interactions with these dialogues.

By the nineteenth-century, scientists had long abandoned the hermetic corpus as a source of scientific or historical information, but many of the ideas that Egypt was the storehouse of ancient antediluvian knowledge remained accepted. Likewise, many still argued for a fundamental relationship between this timeless knowledge preserved by the Egyptians and the wisdom gained by the Hebrew patriarchs during their sojourns in Egypt. The principle that revelation is the best way to access this secret lore, preserved in the sands of Egypt, became an entry point for alternative readings of Near Eastern archaeology, since it encouraged the fruits of archaeological explorations to be understood through explicitly non-academic approaches. The hermetic corpus was also the basis for one of the most influential and misunderstood sources on Egyptian wisdom—*The Life of Sethos* (discussed below).

The 'Life' of Sethos

By the onset of the nineteenth century, one of the most influential works on ancient Egypt was *The Life of Sethos: Taken from Private Memoirs of the Ancient Egyptians, Translated from the Greek Manuscript into French*, a fictional work by Jean Terrasson (1670–1750). The Abbé Terrasson's book was first published in French in 1731 and in English in 1732.[28] It is the basis for a ballet (Jean-Philippe Rameau's *The Birth of Osiris,* 1751) and an opera (Johann Gottlieb Naumann's *Osiris,* 1781) and has been deeply influential in Freemasonry. *Sethos* is a historical fantasy of the life of Sethos (Seti in more contemporary usage), recounting his biography beginning with his

---

26. The hermetic tradition as preserved in mediaeval Arabic sources identifies three individual sages who had access to ancient primeval knowledge, given directly by God. See Ebeling, *Secret History,* pp. 44-47.

27. Mary Lefkowitz, *Not out of Africa: How Afrocentrism Became an Excuse to Teach Myth as History* (New York: BasicBooks, 1997), p. 107.

28. A German version also appeared in 1732 and an Italian translation appeared in 1734.

early education.²⁹ The book is strange to modern readers, as the genre of the work seems to shift, not remaining consistent throughout. At times, it is a typical story of courtly intrigue with the hero's stepmother working to undermine his succession to kingship. At other times it is an adventure narrative, following Sethos's exploits in warfare, sale into slavery, rise to influence among a Phoenician merchant fleet and explorations in Africa. There are long digressions on the history, monuments and geography of Egypt—most of the information seemingly coming from classical sources.³⁰ It is also a didactic work, instructing readers on Enlightenment virtues and making arguments about proper statecraft, education and other social institutions. It celebrates monastic life as the protagonist eventually renounces his kingship, takes a vow of celibacy and enters the priesthood. In fact, it is its detailed description of this priesthood that has had the longest lasting influence on readers, as it contains an extended account of a network of monotheistic Egyptian priests and their elaborate initiation rites. The book itself is an excellent example of how classical sources remained at the heart of interpretations of Egypt in different media.

For most readers it was probably difficult to distinguish between reality and fantasy in the book, that is to say, to differentiate between which descriptions of Egyptian culture were imagined by Terrasson and which were based on historical sources. This confusion of fact and fiction is purposeful and made clear right from the outset. In the Preface, Terrasson claims that this is a translation of a Greek manuscript, written in Alexandria during the reign of Marcus Aurelius.³¹ However, the location of the original Greek manuscript (other than that it is in the library of a foreign nation) cannot be revealed to the public, in this preface, because that particular nation is 'extremely jealous of this sort of treasure'.³² The events of the book are said to date to a much older period (one hundred years before the Trojan War) than the 'version' he has translated. Mimicking scholarly textual criticism, Terrasson writes that the ancient Alexandrian would have had access to far better sources about this era, and so the description of

---

29. The name Sethos is a historically plausible name. There is a New Kingdom king named Seti, who is well documented historically. According to Herodotus, a king named Sethos reigned at the time of Sennacherib, the Assyrian king (Sethos is said to have repelled the Assyrian advance on Egypt). This may be a mistake for King Shabataka, the king who actually did fight against Sennacherib's forces.

30. Terrasson was very familiar with these sources and in fact, he published a translation of Diodorus Siculus (one of the major sources for the vision of Egypt presented in *Sethos*).

31. Jean Terrasson, *The Life of Sethos: Taken from Private Memoirs of the Ancient Egyptians, Translated from the Greek Manuscript into French*, I (trans. Mr Lediard; London: J. Walthoe, 1732), p. i.

32. Terrasson, *Sethos*, p. i.

events in the copy can be trusted. Since Terrasson's scholarly authority as a translator was established, textual transmission issues were not unknown to him, and his fictional work is an accurate parody of this kind of work. Later in the preface, Terrasson compares the work to *Telemachus* (*Les aventures de Télémaque*, 1699, by François Fénelon) and *The Travels of Cyrus* (1727, by Andrew Michael Ramsay[33]), both didactic historic novels that would have been well known to eighteenth-century readers, and both works inspirational to Terrasson. During the Enlightenment, this was a relatively common conceit in fiction—to pretend that the work is actually much more ancient than it really is. It is unlikely that this would have confused most eighteenth-century readers. It is an almost postmodern approach to the novel, earnestly arguing for the authenticity of the book, knowing that this in fact signaled that it is not authentic. Later readers, however, not expecting this type of conceit, were taken in by the claims. Numerous later works in fact cite *Sethos* as a legitimate academic source on mystery religions.[34]

The book is clearly of Enlightenment provenience, exploring themes such as the legitimacy of princely power.[35] After explaining the 'origins' of the text, the author launches into a discussion of how valuable fiction can be and justifies the reading of fiction as a better source of moral instruction than the reading of history. History, to Terrasson, can only be 'a collection of facts, guided by providence, for ends generally unknown to us'.[36] In fiction, however, the author has the freedom to assign all possible virtue to his hero and place him in situations where he can demonstrate those virtues. Terrasson further apologizes for the fact that his hero is a pagan (and thus only capable of moral virtues, not Christian virtues), yet argues, in a manner common to Enlightenment-era church figures, 'that Christian virtues are in regard to moral virtues what faith is with respect to reason; superior, but never contradictory'.[37] Thus, what follows should be instructive, in terms of virtue, even though it does not involve a Christian hero. Furthermore, Terrasson argues, the book explains the actual customs of the ancient Egyptians, despite the fact that it is fiction. He writes, 'Many people have no other notion of the Greeks and Romans but what they have taken

---

33. Andrew Michael Ramsay was an early French Freemason. In print, he made the early connection between Masonry and the Crusades in his *Discourse Pronounced at the Reception of Freemasons by Monsieur de Ramsay, Grand Orator of the Order*.

34. Lefkowitz illustrates this with the writings of Alexandre Lenoir (1761–1839), who uses Sethos as evidence that Masonic rites were based on ancient Egyptian rites (Lefkowitz, *Not out of Africa*, p. 120). Future examples will be offered throughout this study.

35. James Stevens Curl, *The Art and Architecture of Freemasonry* (New York: Overlook Press, 1991), p. 137.

36. Terrasson, *Sethos*, p. iii.

37. Terrasson, *Sethos*, p. ix.

from Tragedy; and a certain principle, not very easy to define, teaches them to distinguish that which may be reasonably supposed to be true from what is probably the product of invention only'.[38] The later interpretative history of this work demonstrates that this is not the case.

The 'ancient book' begins with a cosmological history of Egypt that reads like a hybrid Graeco–Roman–Egyptian creation story, listing the gods as Vulcan, the Sun, Agathodemon, Saturn, Osiris, Isis and Typhon, with Vulcan referring to 'elementary fire'; Agathodemon a Roman *genius* and Typhon 'the evil principle'.[39] The hodge-podge of sources and ancient traditions continues as a secular history of Egypt, where reference is made to the 'Shepherd Kings, Mendes, Sesostris, Memnon, and Rameses'. Terrasson supplies footnotes, not breaking the conceit that this is a genuine ancient novel, interacting with scholarship from his time. For example, he writes, 'The preceding genealogies are conformable to those of Marham; but what follows seems to agree with the chronology of father Pezron'.[40] Thus, the work continues to masquerade as an ancient document with a critical apparatus. Most of Terrasson's history is cobbled together from classical sources (with occasional footnotes pointing to these sources) on Egypt, and the eighteenth-century reader may have felt like this was a legitimate introduction to ancient Egypt. And indeed, it likely was an attempt to provide a legitimate history of Egypt—heavily dependent on Diodorus and Herodotus.

Throughout the book, descriptions of Egypt, its monuments and history are provided as excursuses within the main narrative. In book V, for example, Amedes (an Egyptian priest) arranges for Sethos to travel through Egypt, accompanied by two priests of Isis. Terrasson imagines that priests were granted (as part of their religious authority) significant freedom of travel and that ancient networks linked them throughout the land. Sethos travels to various religious monuments within Egypt; descriptions of them based on classical sources are provided to the reader. Likewise, a discussion of the Nile River is inserted here, with the priestly companions instructing Sethos on its novelties. Sethos also spends some time in the Theban Temple of Jupiter, the location of an astronomical observatory and a related library. The practices of astronomy are described in detail, including a brief polemic against astrologers (interesting in an Enlightenment context in which astrology was a contested form of scholarship).

Journeys with priests and excursuses on elements of ancient science all reflect the general concern for the development of knowledge found throughout the book. Early in the novel, the narrative breaks into a general discussion of Egyptian education, as a means of informing the reader

38. Terrasson, *Sethos*, p. ix.
39. Terrasson, *Sethos*, pp. 1-2.
40. Terrasson, *Sethos*, p. 3.

about young Sethos's schooling. Here the Egyptian education is described as glorifying Enlightenment principles—cultivating interests in manners, civility and natural philosophy, including chemistry (especially the teachings of Hermes Trismegistus), anatomy, geometry, astronomy and botany (including the collection of specimens). All of these approaches (that were beloved by the eighteenth-century *philosophes*) were claimed to have been cultivated by the ancient priesthood. Physical education was likewise of concern to Terrasson's Egyptians, as it was to the eighteenth-century French. Terrasson offers a particularly Enlightenment-era comment on the wisdom of Egypt: 'The kings of Egypt had always been promoters of these academies, being convinc'd, that a love of the sciences, and the tranquility they requir'd, were alone sufficient to suppress all thoughts of revolt and sedition'.[41] Here is a description of the enlightened despot and the political value of an educated populace. The Egyptians are likewise depicted as having a sophisticated court culture, with Egyptian women conversing on educated subjects and freely with men. Fine literature was one of the main entertainments; musical concerts were held, and galleries at the palace at Memphis displayed sculptures and paintings. Here Memphis is an idealized version of Versailles.

Terrasson's descriptions of the parallels between ancient Egypt and eighteenth-century France have not been as influential as his descriptions of ancient religion. The longest lasting influence of *The Life of Sethos* has been in its vivid and detailed description of a monotheistic priesthood of Isis, highly advanced in its intellectual achievements and holding an elaborate series of initiation rites and secret initiation rituals. As Lefkowitz has demonstrated, this secret society bears more in common to a Greek mystery religion than to anything known from ancient Egypt.[42] And, as she notes, most of the initiation ceremony is actually based on a ritual in Apuleius's *The Golden Ass* merged with various ideas derived from Greek myth.[43] But the power of the elaborately detailed descriptions of the rites and practices has been enough to convince many subsequent readers that this reflects ancient Egyptian practices.

Some of the passages discussing the rites are worth discussing in detail, given that similar themes appear again in modified form in nineteenth-century literature. Sethos and Amedes enter the Great Pyramid and explore its secret passages. There, it is revealed to Sethos that every night priests and priestesses perform secret ceremonies within the Great Pyramid. Amedes informs Sethos that his youth is at an end and that it is now time for him to be initiated into the secrets of this priesthood. The initiation,

---

41. Terrasson, *Sethos*, p. 88.
42. Lefkowitz, *Not out of Africa*, pp. 92ff.
43. Lefkowitz, *Not out of Africa*, p. 114.

Amedes explains, will be quite rigorous, and the priests are under no obligation to admit him to their order. Amedes asks a series of questions to Sethos, who unwittingly answers while under the observation of the priests—his answers showing him to be a deserving initiate.

The actual initiation begins as Sethos walks through a passage, marked by an inscription reading:

> Whoever goes thro this passage alone, and without looking behind him, shall be purify'd by fire, by water, and by air; and if he can vanquish the fears of death, he shall return from the bowels of the earth, he shall see light again, and he shall be intitled to the privilege of preparing his mind for the revelation of the mysteries of the great goddess Isis.[44]

Sethos proceeds, walking through lanes of flames as the test of fire, swims across a canal as the test of water and operates a machine designed to lift him up as his test of air (also demonstrating his prowess in geometry and mechanics). That an initiate must be tested by fire, water and air may have been taken by Terrasson from Neo-Platonist writings, although Lefkowitz argues that it stems ultimately from the fifth-century philosophy of Empedocles.[45] Sethos then emerges in the presence of the Apis 'Ox' and is congratulated by the priests for his success at the trials, and he is initiated in a consecration ritual. Following this is a brief excursus on the Greek story of Orpheus in an Egyptian setting, demonstrating the supposed Egyptian origins of many Greek stories in the process.

The story returns to Sethos, who must now undergo a purification ritual involving invocation and instruction. Of particular interest is that Sethos is taught that there is only one God, who purposefully allowed the knowledge of his singularity to be hidden. Terrasson writes:

> But to comply with the frailty of mankind, they were allow'd to adore the different attributes of his essence, and the different effects of his goodness, under the symbols of the stars, as the sun and planets; of renowned personages, as Osiris, Jupiter, Mercury; and even of terrestrial bodies, as animals and plants. He added that the subaltern deities were likewise spirits, whose ministry the supreme God thought expedient to employ in the government of the universe. He did not forget that spirit, who was the temptor of men, and the disturber of nature, represented by Typhon, by the evil genius's and by pernicious animals and poisonous plants. . . . The Egyptians by this confus'd idea of unity in the divine being, and of multiplicity in his symbols, are the first authors of what has been the most sublime in philosophical opinions, and the most gross in popular superstitions.[46]

---

44. Terrasson, *Sethos*, p. 155.
45. Lefkowitz, *Not out of Africa*, p. 114.
46. Terrasson, *Sethos*, pp. 179-80.

Thus the priests of Egypt were the first monotheists, but they had confused the concept. For Terrasson, this may have been an important point, if one reads it in tandem with his comments from the preface. Here is evidence moral virtue can emerge separately from Christianity but not contradict it. Yet it also cannot replace Christianity.

In the last discourses of initiation, the personal nature of an initiate is spelled out. Sethos and the reader learn about the enlightened traits that an initiate should hold and learn that this priesthood was responsible for many of the advances in Egyptian civilization and in the peoples contacted by Egypt.[47] After this, Sethos is asked here questions, which he must ponder for nine days: 'What is the principal virtue of a hero? Does heroism consist in exceeding the bounds of duty? Is it heroick to sacrifice even one's honour to the interest of our country, or the general good of man?'[48] These questions may have been alien questions to an ancient Egyptian but were certainly important questions for an Enlightenment-era individual. Book III ends without Sethos offering answers to these questions, but with the arrival of a Carthaginian to Memphis, who had been sent to seek atonement for accidently killing his own brother in battle.

Book IV begins with a story of the origin of the city of Carthage, important, it turns out, because the Carthaginian visitor is Saphon, the son of Zoros, the founder. Saphon is tried by the priesthood; during the trial he tells the story that led him to this situation. Zoros had twin sons and, in order to decide which should rule after him, sent them off to demonstrate their merit. It was under these conditions that Saphon killed his brother. Sethos is called to speak in front of the tribunal about the teachings of the priests of Isis, and uses this as an opportunity to answer the three questions that he had been given to ponder. Here, Sethos explains that battle for the sake of battle is not worthy of a hero, thus demonstrating a change in character since book III when he secretly delighted at the prospects of battle with Thebes. After Sethos speaks, the priests of Isis laud his comments and then go on to render judgment, noting that 'The title of heir to a crown, or other paternal dignities, do not require those refin'd virtues which are inseparable from a hero: and it is even for the advantage and ease of the publick, that successions be rather dependent on the order of birth, than on the difficult and often dangerous estimate of personal merit'.[49] Saphon is then brought into the subterranean canal in which the initiates encountered the water trial and is stretched out on a wheeled contraption in order to be punished for his crimes (by being dunked under water and exposed to high heat). Thus, Terrasson writes, 'we see that the three parts of corporal atone-

---

47. Terrasson, *Sethos,* pp. 190-92.
48. Terrasson, *Sethos,* pp. 195-96.
49. Terrasson, *Sethos,* p. 223.

ment for criminals, answer'd exactly to the three trials of the purification of the body preparative to the initiation: but there was this difference, that these trials of candidates for the initiation were voluntary . . .'[50] After this, the expiatory sacrifices were offered, first to Typhon (noting that Typhon is who the Zoroastrians call Arimanus and quoting lines directly from Herodotus), then to the dead. Then the air was purified, and rituals taken directly from Plutarch were performed. After these rituals were performed, a new candidate appears, who, it turns out, is Typhon's supposedly dead brother, Giscon. It turns out that Giscon had not been killed at all, and after a number of moralizing speeches, the brothers embrace.

Sethos is now ready for the last stage of the initiation, a period of twelve days in which he is brought back to normal life, out of this liminal state of initiation. Various rituals are enacted such as offering obeisance in front of statues of Isis, Osiris and Horus and taking oaths. Sethos is then led into the subterranean passages that lay beneath the pyramids and temples of Memphis, where he encounters the wives and children of the priests who live underground. The underground society is described as similar to ancient Spartan society. Here, Terrasson describes an educational system where, at the age of eight, children are divided into those destined to learn the work of the mind and those destined to learn the work of the hand. The work of the mind branched into four courses of study: 'sacred or hieroglyphick literature, jurisprudence, experimental physics, and mathematics'.[51] Colour-coded robes distinguished pupils of different subject matters. 'The School of Language'—a 'publick school'—taught all issues relating to language, from pronunciation to eloquence and rhetoric. This was a self-contained society, and these students did not speak to outsiders until they had taken oaths of secrecy and spent their lives in service to the priesthood. Terrasson goes on to describe other elements of this subterranean society, including the punishment of criminals, exercise yards and theatrical performances. Some discussion is spent on how the Egyptians, so otherwise enlightened, were taken with divination, followed by a discussion of the various deities of the Egyptians. All of this constituted the mysteries of Isis. The priests and the wider community then celebrate Sethos's successful initiation. Processions through the streets of Memphis proclaim a new initiate. The initiate himself is introduced to the citizens of Memphis, dressed in a white tunic and veiled to hide his identity. Sethos is brought before the royals, Osoroth and Daluca, identity hidden, and kneels, offering his service to the king. Book IV ends with Sethos learning that he is to remain that day and evening in the college of the priests for a joyful reception.

50. Terrasson, *Sethos,* p. 229.
51. Terrasson, *Sethos,* p. 252.

What is perhaps most shocking about *The Life of Sethos* is how influential this book still remains. As Mary Lefkowitz has shown, in her excellent critique of Afrocentrism in the American academy, the supposed Egyptian mystery system described by Terrasson—based on his reading of classical sources—lies at the heart of this American pseudohistorical movement.[52] A relatively obscure work of dubious literary merit has been used as 'evidence' of Africa's intellectual primacy over the Greek world. That this view was held in the eighteenth century is certainly reasonable, as the classical writers were themselves convinced that Egypt was the first civilization and one that all others depended on. That this myth survives into the twenty-first century demonstrates that as the academic study of the Near East emerged in the nineteenth century, so too did alternative versions of that history. It is not just the Afrocentrists who have embraced *The Life of Sethos*. As will be explored throughout the rest of this study, alternative approaches to reconstructing ancient Near Eastern history relied heavily on this book's refracted version of classical accounts, and Terrasson's Enlightened Egypt is made into historical 'fact'.

The Decipherment of Ancient Near Eastern Languages

The most radical transformation in the nineteenth-century understanding of the ancient Near Eastern past came with the decipherment of Egyptian and Mesopotamian writing systems. Once ancient texts could be read, it was possible to challenge and supplement the classical view of the ancient Near East in ways that had not been possible for centuries. This was not an overnight transformation as it took years for the results of the translation of ancient texts to supplant the historical scheme provided by a classical education. Gradually, however, figures like Semiramis disappeared from scholarly historical accounts of the Near East.

As is well known, the key to the decipherment of Egyptian hieroglyphs was the Rosetta Stone, discovered by the Napoleonic expedition but handed over to the British as part of their victory settlement. The Rosetta Stone presented a trilingual version of a decree made by Egyptian priests in 196 BCE. This trilingualism was key since one of the languages was Greek and was readily translated. Once the Greek inscription was understood, the next step was to use that as a key to understand the Egyptian. In 1814 Thomas Young identified that the recurrent loop that surrounded the same sets of Egyptian characters throughout the text was an indicator of royal name (now called a cartouche). This allowed him to sort out the phonetic values of the Egyptian hieroglyphs within the cartouche; but believing that Egyptian was essentially a pictographic writing system, he was not convinced that

---

52. Lefkowitz, *Not out of Africa*, esp. chap. 4.

this approach could be used to understand the rest of the text. He believed that this was simply an Egyptian approach for rendering foreign words since the royal names on the Rosetta Stone were all Greek names. The next breakthrough came with the work of Jean-François Champollion. In 1822, looking at older cartouches, he realized that the phonetic approach also worked to read ancient, actual Egyptian (not Greek) names. Champollion then realized that earlier scholars had been correct in arguing that Coptic, the language of Egyptian Christians, was related. This still-living language provided him with source material to understand the basic structure of the hieroglyphic writing system. From that point on, it was a matter of refining knowledge of the language, but the basic problem that had beset would-be translators for the past 1,500 years had been overcome. Egyptian, written in both the hieroglyphic and hieratic script, could now be read.[53]

A trilingual inscription also facilitated the recovery of Mesopotamian languages. In 1835, Henry Rawlinson began to copy the Behistun Inscription, a large inscription in Persia made by the Persian king Darius (522–486 BCE). The inscription was in Old Persian, Akkadian and Elamite. Rawlinson was able to translate the phonetic Old Persian inscription. From that, other scholars were able to figure out the Akkadian inscription, and, as more texts were excavated by Paul Émile Botta, these were of assistance as well. While the exact process of deciphering Akkadian is more controversial than Egyptian (there are more issues relating to who should be credited with what), in 1857 an experiment proved that Akkadian could be read. The secretary of the Royal Asiatic Society gave four men who claimed to be able to read Akkadian a copy of a recently discovered inscription.[54] After the four men translated the text in isolation from one another, a jury compared the translations and determined that the results were close enough to show that Akkadian had been translated successfully.

Mesopotamian languages are written in a script called cuneiform (from the Latin meaning wedge-shaped). There are a number of different languages written with this type of script. The first to be translated was Akkadian (in the early nineteenth century referred to as Assyrian or Babylonian). This is a Semitic language, related to Hebrew, and was widely used in the ancient Near East until its replacement by Aramaic as a *lingua franca*. Sumerian is the oldest cuneiform language; its exact relationship to other language families is debated (it is a language isolate) but is now well understood by scholars and had begun to be so by the end of the nineteenth century.

---

53. Hieroglyphs are the more formal version of the Egyptian writing system. Hieratic is essentially the cursive form of Egyptian writing, using simpler shaped characters derived from the hieroglyphic forms.

54. These four men were Henry Rawlinson, Edward Hincks, Julius Oppert and William Henry Fox Talbot. As secretary of the Royal Asiatic Society, Edwin Norris conducted the test.

It was first recognized as being distinct from Akkadian by around 1850. Edward Hincks recognized that there was a non-Semitic language that predated Akkadian, and various names were used for it (including Akkadian and Scythic) until Sumerian was settled on in 1869. The term Chaldean was also used inconsistently in Mesopotamian studies (see n. 18 in this chapter). Numerous other languages were written using a cuneiform system, but Akkadian and later Sumerian were the languages that could read by the Victorians.

The decipherment of the Egyptian and cuneiform writings systems meant that scholars could use emic sources for ancient Near Eastern history, a development that completely transformed the field. Yet as shall be seen in what follows, classical and hermetic sources remained foundational for the popular presentations of Egypt and Mesopotamia throughout the nineteenth century. Challenges to the biblical account were and continue to be more complex than those to the Graeco-Roman writings, which is understandable given the complexity of biblical textual tradition. For nineteenth-century audiences, however, high biblical literacy was the normative framework through which early archaeological discoveries were understood. These early discoveries are the subject of the next chapter.

3

The Strongman, the Geographer, and the Diplomat: Giovanni Belzoni, Edward Robinson, and Austen Henry Layard

> The 'cheap excursions' that now open new sources of interest and information to the labouring classes are not confined to mere locomotion on the railroad or the river. Excursions of thought, not less useful, may be made by the artisan, without leaving his own fireside: there seated, in relaxation of physical toil, he may explore Egypt with Belzoni, and Nineveh with Layard, or perform pilgrimage to the Holy Land, as his fathers did in the old times before him.   —Eliot Warburton[1]

Early in the nineteenth century, it became easier for Europeans to travel to the Near East, for commercial, diplomatic and religious reasons. It was typical for these travellers to keep diaries and not very difficult to transform these diaries into travel monographs. At the same time, literacy increased dramatically in Europe and especially in Britain (see Chapter I.5), and technological improvements made the publication of long books more affordable.[2] For the first time, a significant proportion of the community could read new books very soon after their first publication. Publishers adapted to this growing audience by printing different versions of the same books aimed at different readership levels—expensive and extended versions for the serious reader and abridged and simplified versions to be read on the train or by the more casual reader. As a genre, the travel account could be modified in this manner very easily. The accounts of these journeys were, for the most part, narratives of the details of travel that linked descriptions of places and people and anecdotes about foreign encounters. Since the events

---

1. Eliot Warburton, 'Dedicatory Preface to the 8th edition', in *The Crescent and the Cross; or, Romance and Realities of Eastern Travel* (London: Hurst & Blackett Publishers, 16th edn, 1860 [1854]), pp. iii-iv.
2. For statistics on the considerable drop in price of books from 1800 to 1870, see James A. Secord, *Victorian Sensation: The Extraordinary Publication, Reception, and Secret Authorship of* Vestiges of the Natural History of Creation (Chicago: University of Chicago Press, 2000), pp. 30-31.

of the narrative were only loosely connected, sections could be removed or moved around easily, and there were no concerns about plot being disrupted or character motivation becoming confused. Thus these books were easily abridged or excerpted from and could be made suitable for readers of different literacy levels or with different levels of interest in the topic. The works of three authors in particular provided early-to-mid-nineteenth-century audiences with detailed accounts of the ancient Near East. These early best-selling authors were Giovanni Belzoni (the circus strongman who became an Egyptologist), Edward Robinson (the theologian who became a biblical geographer), and Austen Henry Layard (the diplomat–archaeologist who became an Assyriologist and a politician). Their books came to be some of the most popular full-length books of the first half of the nineteenth century.[3] Numerous biographies have been written on these men; what follows here is a discussion of their 'best-sellers' and how the form and contents of those works shaped ancient Near Eastern studies.[4] Later chapters shall return to these works, exploring how they (and their authors) were interacted with in other media.

The Strongman: Giovanni Belzoni

Of the numerous adventurers that participated in the early years of Egyptology, none had as much popular appeal as Giovanni Battista Belzoni (1778–1824). For twenty-first-century Egyptologists, the name Belzoni conjures up images of tomb robbing and the vandalism of archaeological sites; his signature is still emblazoned on a wall in Khafre's pyramid, reminding visi-

---

3. In terms of typical sales figures, a first-run book would typically have a print run of between 500 and 1,000 copies (and that does not indicate how many would actually have been sold). Austen Henry Layard's *Nineveh and its Remains* sold 8,000 copies in its first year of publication (1849). The abridged version, released in 1851, sold 14,000 copies. A typical first print run for works by Charles Dickens was 10,000. Assyriologists in the twenty-first century cannot even come close to these kinds of sales figures in absolute numbers. The contemporary equivalent would be for an Assyriologist to outsell Stephen King. Layard's sales figures are taken from Richard D. Altick, 'Nineteenth-Century English Best-Sellers: A Third List', *Studies in Bibliography* 39 (1986), pp. 235-41 (239).

4. The use of the term 'best-sellers' is somewhat anachronistic, since in the nineteenth-century the sales figures of books would not have been used for advertising. James Secord argues that any kind of emphasis on the sales of these books would have been perceived as vulgar (although that is not to say that this was not of primary interest to those involved in the book industry). Even though these books were aimed at 'middlebrow' audiences (to sell at a great enough scale to make a profit) it was important that the conversation about these books not be middlebrow so no reference to something as déclassé as sales would have been made in promotion (Secord, *Victorian Sensation*, p. 34).

3. *The Strongman, the Geographer, and the Diplomat*

Fig. 3.1. Portrait of Belzoni as a strongman, by George Cruikshank, 1817. © Trustees of the British Museum

tors of his somewhat destructive influence on archaeological materials (at least from today's perspective). In the early nineteenth century, his reputation was less controversial, or at least, controversial for different reasons. Europeans interested in Egyptology in the 1820s would likely have known much about Egypt from reading his book and visiting his exhibition; his works rivaled Denon's in this period for popularity and influence. His take on ancient Egypt was formative for the general public, and his accounts of his adventures were generative for adventure fiction (and especially any adventure fiction featuring archaeology).

Belzoni's success at the public presentation of Egyptological materials was in part due to his early experiences as a showman. Born in Padua, he came to London in 1803 and quickly became part of the theatre and carnival scene there (Fig. 3.1). His particular type of performance involved demonstrations of strength, especially through weight lifting and hydraulic machinery. The 'Patagonian Samson' (his stage moniker) toured the fair circuit in England and Scotland, and during this period he married Sarah Bane, who would accompany him on his adventures, write related accounts and keep his Egyptological work alive (to some extent) after Belzoni's death in 1824.

Belzoni's entrance into Egyptology seems somewhat accidental. In 1815, the Belzonis were travelling to Constantinople to take advantage of the thriving performance culture that was supported by the sultan. On their way, they stopped for an extended rest in Valletta, Malta. While there, the Belzonis met

Fig. 3.2. The Younger Memnon.
© Trustees of the British Museum

Captain Ishmael Gibraltar. Gibraltar was working for the pasha of Egypt, Muhammed Ali. Ali was working to modernize Egypt by recruiting talented Europeans to bring their innovations to Egypt. Gibraltar was a type of talent scout, charged with identifying skilled Europeans and convincing them to come to Egypt. When they met in Valletta, Belzoni had been thinking of other ways to make money off of his hydraulic skills and had come up with an idea for an advanced water wheel. Gibraltar convinced Belzoni to present this idea to the pasha, so the Belzonis travelled to Egypt, where Giovanni built a prototype of his water wheel. In the demonstration of his water wheel in Egypt, one of the people working it was severely injured, and Belzoni's device was deemed too unsafe and the project was scrapped.

With the failure of his water-wheel project, Belzoni had to look for other means of supporting himself and his wife. While in Cairo he had befriended the by-then famous orientalist Johann Ludwig Burckhardt (1784–1817).[5] Burckhardt told Belzoni about some of the impressive antiquities he had encountered in his travels up the Nile, including Abu Simbel and the statue fragment known as the 'Younger Memnon' (Fig. 3.2)—the head of a colossal

---

5. Burckhardt is an important figure in the early history of ancient Near Eastern studies. A Swiss explorer and orientalist (interested in the study of Arab and Islamic culture), Burckhardt is credited with rediscovering Petra in Jordan. Until his death in 1817, he was an important figure in orienting European travellers to Egypt and Palestine and, posthumously, his written works (the notes of which are kept at Cambridge University) provided guidance to these explorers.

3. The Strongman, the Geographer, and the Diplomat

Fig. 3.3. View of the interior of the temple at Ybsambul [Abu Sumbul]. *Plates Illustrative of the Researches and Operations of G. Belzoni in Egypt and Nubia* (1820).

statue of Ramses II in his mortuary temple (the Ramesseum).[6] The Younger Memnon was an impressive statue that the Napoleonic team had wanted to remove to France but had been unable to transport due to its vast weight. Other European travellers had similarly contemplated this venture but had been stumped as to how to go about doing so. Here, then, was an opportunity for Belzoni. Given his background in hydraulics and weight lifting (both freely and using levers), this was a perfect challenge for Belzoni's skills. Belzoni made a proposal to Henry Salt (the British consul-general in Cairo) that the British put up the money for the expenses to transport the Younger Memnon, and Belzoni would oversee the enterprise. Salt quickly agreed, and the two entered into the first of many business agreements in what was to become a rather tumultuous relationship.

Over the next four years, Belzoni travelled throughout Egypt, exploring sites and collecting antiquities. Sarah often accompanied him, but she had her own set of adventures, travelling to the Holy Land by herself.[7] On his first trip up the Nile, he was successful in transporting the Younger Memnon, and he began excavations at Abu Simbel (Fig. 3.3). He discovered the lost seaport of Berenice (on the Egyptian coast of the Red Sea). He managed to find an entrance into Khafre's pyramid and discovered the royal tomb

---

6. The statue came to be called 'The Younger Memnon' after it was brought to the British Museum. This reflects the classical name for the Rammassseum—the Memnonianum.

7. Sarah Belzoni set a new trend for European travellers to Jerusalem after she disguised herself in Ottomon garb to sneak on to the Temple Mount, and into the Al Aqsa mosque, to which entrance, at the time, was forbidden to non-Muslims. Her account encouraged others to try the same (Naomi Shepherd. *The Zealous Intruders: The Western Rediscovery of Palestine* [London: Collins, 1987], p. 37).

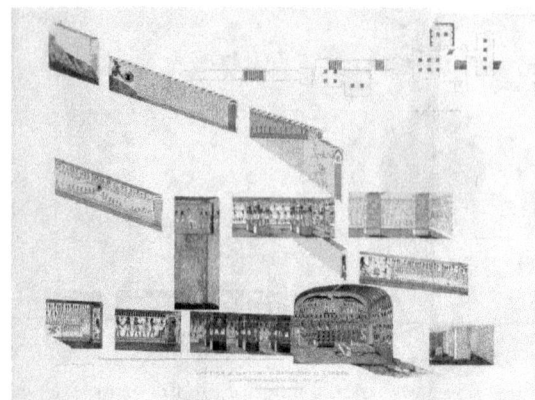

Fig. 3.4. Section of the tomb of Samethis [Seti I] in Thebes. *Plates Illustrative of the Researches and Operations of G. Belzoni in Egypt and Nubia* (1820).

of Seti I in the Valley of the Kings (Fig. 3.4)—what was to become (for him) his most commercially important discovery. Belzoni soon developed a reputation as a highly successful 'archaeologist', earning the animosity of his numerous competitors, who looked enviously upon his successes. Thus, much of his work was plagued with competition and rivalry. His charismatic personality seemed to have earned Belzoni as many enemies as it did friends.

Over the course of these adventures, Belzoni must have considered his long-term financial prospects. The collection of antiquities that he had gathered had become something of a sight to see for visitors to Cairo, and no doubt the commercial successes of travel literature about Egypt inspired him. Especially as he gathered his own personal collection of antiquities and worked on carefully recording what he found in Seti I's tomb, it is evident that he was imagining future public 'performances' of Egypt, clearly still inspired by his past as a performer in Britain. When he returned to England in 1819, he set out to do just that, eventually opening an exhibition of a reconstruction of Seti I's tomb (see Chapter II.2).

It was also apparent that a literary rendering of his adventures would be a commercial success. Upon his return to London, Belzoni arranged with John Murray to publish an account of his exploits, a book that came to bear the title *Narrative of the Operations and Recent Discoveries within the Pyramids, Temples, Tombs, and Excavations, in Egypt and Nubia; and of a Journey to the Coast of the Red Sea, in Search of Ancient Berenice; and Another to the Oasis of Jupiter Ammon.*[8] Publishing with John Murray was

---

8. The book is usually reprinted with the less wordy title: *Travels in Egypt and Nubia*.

quite a coup for Belzoni, as Murray's publishing house was one of the premier publishers of the time, and John Murray was especially skilled at promoting travel literature. Despite the book's many weaknesses, such as the awkward prose and blatant self-promotion, it received very good reviews and soon sold out of the first print run. A second run was quickly ordered, and the book was published in a number of different languages.

The book itself is written as a travel diary and is a straightforward chronological account of Belzoni's travels. It is divided into three sections (along with an apologetic preface), named 'First Journey', 'Second Journey', and 'Third Journey', each corresponding to a journey away from Cairo, although given the travels back and forth, this division is not as clear-cut as it may seem. The book also includes a work by Sarah Belzoni called 'Mrs. Belzoni's Trifling Account of the Women of Egypt, Nubia, and Syria', a section that is frequently omitted from reprints of the book. A number of colour plates also accompanied the early printings of this book.

By the time the Belzonis returned to England, they had already developed quite a reputation. *Quarterly Review* had reported especially favourably on his exploits, and *The Times* even printed an announcement of his return to London. His adventures had been widely reported in both the English and the French periodical press. Despite their warm reception in London and Parisian society, one of Belzoni's main reasons for writing is, he claims, to set the record straight about others' accounts of him and his work. He states:

> On my arrival in Europe, I found so many erroneous accounts had been given the public of my operations and discoveries in Egypt that it appeared to be my duty to publish a plain statement of the facts, and should anyone call its correctness in question, I hope they will do it openly that I may prove the truth of my assertions.[9]

His urge to 'correct' the record is apparent throughout the book, and this is how he justifies the fact that he himself has written the book. In the first paragraph of the book he apologizes, saying that:

> As I made my discoveries alone, I have been anxious to write my book by myself, though in so doing, the reader will consider me, and with great propriety, guilty of temerity, but the public will perhaps gain in the fidelity of my narrative, what it loses in elegance. I am not an Englishman, but I prefer that my readers should receive from myself, as well as I am able to describe them, an account of my proceedings in Egypt, in Nubia . . . rather than run the risk of having my meaning misrepresented by another.[10]

Right at the outset, Belzoni is making two pleas to the reader: a plea to the reader that this account is completely accurate (and that the proof of the

---

9. Giovanni Belzoni, *Travels in Egypt and Nubia* (Vercelli, Italy: White Star Publishers, 2007 [1820]), p. 10.
10. Belzoni, *Travels*, p. 7.

veracity comes from the roughness of the prose) and that he alone is responsible for all of the finds. Thus, this will be an account of his heroic adventures and discoveries. Throughout, Belzoni jokes with the reader through similar apologies, such as when he states, 'the old Sheik went to sleep, and so did I, but I hope my reader will not do the same'.[11] Asides such as these set a somewhat informal tone and signal the fact that this is not merely a travel diary that has been published but a self-consciously public account of his works.

Throughout Belzoni's book, he describes himself in heroic terms. He is the adventurer, the hero whom the reader cheers for as he pursues his goals. Belzoni is often credited as the inspiration for Indiana Jones, Allan Quatermain and other archaeological adventurers, and while direct inspiration is never so clear-cut, certainly Belzoni's *Travels in Egypt and Nubia* established many of the narrative conventions of the later archaeological adventure stories. The quest begins, in Belzoni's account, with Salt's contract 'for the purpose of raising the head of the statue of younger Memnon, and carrying it down the Nile', just as Indy's quest in *Raiders of the Lost Ark* begins with the request of the United States government for him to find the Ark of the Covenant.[12]

The body of the story involves the dangers that Belzoni faced and the difficulties he had in raising the Younger Memnon. Much of these troubles were caused by competition with his rival, Drovetti, working on behalf of the French. Thus, as in later archaeological adventure stories, the protagonist is faced with opponents working on their own behalf (or on behalf of an enemy government) in order to capture the artifacts first. Belzoni's account is filled with reference to the nefarious activities of Drovetti and his agents and the nationalist rivalries between the English and the French. The nationalist rivalries are most manifest as a race between opposing groups to get to and remove the antiquities first (a form of competition that was picked up by later fiction writers). Belzoni writes of the urgency to arrive in Thebes before Drovetti's agents:

> we learned that the two agents of Mr. Drouetti were making a forced march to Thebes, of their motives for which I was aware. They wished to arrive there before us and purchase all that had been accumulated by the Arabs in the preceding season so that we should have had no chance of buying anything on our arrival. It was not on this account however I was uneasy, but because the spot, where I had been digging and found the sphinxes and statues, was so evidently pregnant with objects worthy the risk of excavation that I had no doubt, if they reached Thebes before us, they would take possession of that ground and we should have no longer a right to explore it.[13]

11. Belzoni, *Travels*, p. 472.
12. Belzoni, *Travels*, p. 39.
13. Belzoni, *Travels*, pp. 168-69.

3. *The Strongman, the Geographer, and the Diplomat*

Thus it was imperative that Belzoni get to Thebes as quickly as possible. This was a race for treasure, typical of later adventure stories. Arguably this urgency is transformed in later professional archaeological accounts as a race to 'protect' or 'conserve' the artifacts.

Belzoni's account is filled with discussion of how Drovetti and his agents worked to sabotage the work of the English excavators. For example, Belzoni writes of how after getting the Younger Memnon to the bank of the Nile, his ability to ship the head was compromised by the machinations of Drovetti's agents. He writes:

> All my persuasions were useless and though I had a written agreement in my hands, they [the boat owners] signified to me that it was of no use; they would never take the stone on board. I had much to say to them, as may be imagined in such a case, for I was so circumstanced that if the present opportunity of transporting the bust were lost, the water in the Nile would have become much too low, and the conveyance could not have been effected till the next season. At the same time I was informed by my Janizary, whom I sent to Assouan in the same boat with the two agents of Mr. D—, that it was owing to them the owner would not take the stone on board, for they told him he would lose his boat, and never receive any recompense for it, and that the agreement I made with them was as good for nothing when in Cairo.[14]

This kind of meddling was a constant hindrance to Belzoni's work, according to the account in *Travels*. He describes many instances in which Drovetti compelled Egyptian officials and workers to block Belzoni's efforts. Sometimes this amounted to bans on selling antiquities to the English. In other instances, orders to stop excavating were presented and firmans revoked. Belzoni accuses the French of sabotaging the antiquities, such as at Philae, where a number of 'stones' were mutilated and the inscription *operation manqué* written in charcoal upon their remnants.[15]

In a few cases, the competition between the French and the English explorers reached near violence. Belzoni recounts an instance when Drovetti offered a thinly veiled threat:

> Mr. Drouetti told us a pleasant story of a man who was dressed like myself, and who was hidden among the ruins of the temple whom he, Mr. Drouetti, had great reason to believe was a person who wished to do him some injury, and that he had already acquainted the Camaikan [magistrate] of that place of the circumstance. I begged him to tell me what reason that man could have for assuming my appearance. He said that it was to make the people believe that it was myself who had done it. . . . The conclusion of all this was that, if I had happened to go among the ruins, which it was my constant practice to do, and some one had sent a ball at me [shot at

---

14. Belzoni, *Travels*, p. 147.
15. Belzoni, *Travels*, p. 283.

me], they could have said afterward that they mistook me for the person who had assumed my appearance in dress and figure.[16]

Although Drovetti insists to Belzoni that the imposter had been driven away from Thebes, not to return, Belzoni's telling of the story suggests that he at least still felt threatened by the encounter.

The competition between Drovetti's and Belzoni's teams reached their peak with guns drawn near Karnak. According to Belzoni's account, he was harassed by a man under Drovetti's employ named Lebolo, and, in the process, Lebolo drew a gun and pointed it at Belzoni's chest. The altercation stemmed from Drovetti's machinations to steal an obelisk, which the British had already claimed. Belzoni had ignored Drovetti's various attempts to prevent the removal of the obelisk and had begun transporting it. In the ensuing argument between the two teams of men, a gun was fired. Salt felt that Lebolo and the others who were involved should be tried for their actions by the French consul, since Lebolo's team was operating on behalf of the French. After a long process, the French determined that they had no jurisdiction over Lebolo and Drovetti, since the two were from Piedmont, and the case was dropped. Belzoni declined to pursue the matter further and returned to Europe. At the end of his account, Belzoni writes:

> At last, having put an end to all my affairs in Egypt, in the middle of September, 1819, we embarked, thank God! for Europe; not that I disliked the country I was in, for, on the contrary, I have reason to be grateful; nor do I complain of the Turks or Arabs in general, but of some Europeans who are in that country whose conduct and mode of thinking are a disgrace to human nature.[17]

The disenchantment with his fellow Europeans was not just confined to Drovetti and the French. Much of Belzoni's book seems to be a response to what he perceived as unfair accounts of him and his work by other Europeans. In particular, Belzoni was insistent to right the 'slanders' made against him by Count Forbin about his work at the pyramids.[18] Belzoni apologizes to the reader for bringing up the controversies, but insists that the indelicacy is necessary for the sake of establishing a truthful account.[19]

---

16. Belzoni, *Travels*, p. 394.
17. Belzoni, *Travels*, p. 494.
18. Belzoni, *Travels*, p. 289. Forbin was the director general of the French Royal Collections.
19. For example, Belzoni prefaces his remarks about the stand-off between his team and Drovetti's with: 'It is not agreeable to my wishes to insert in this volume these matters, which perhaps may cause a supposition of my inclination to expose, but such is the case that I cannot avoid mentioning it, as I have done many others; for if I was to conceal from the public what happened at that period, an advantage might be taken, and matters brought before them in any light but that of the truth' (Belzoni, *Travels*, pp. 394-95).

3. *The Strongman, the Geographer, and the Diplomat* 93

Belzoni's fall-out with Henry Salt also manifests in the story, and Belzoni goes to pains to reproduce Salt's letters in their entirety in order to make an argument regarding their financial dispute. Later adventure storywriters may have picked up on this kind of disenchantment between the 'hero' and the commissioner of the quest, since these kinds of fallings out (or dissatisfaction regarding the division of the loot) is common to these kinds of tales.

It is not just his European competitors that posed a threat to Belzoni. Egypt, in his account, was a dangerous place. Numerous narrative elements of Belzoni's book show marked similarities to later adventure tropes, involving descriptions of the violence and dangers implicit in the 'exotic' setting. For example, Belzoni describes the issue of eunuchs:

> This place [Egypt] is famous for the making of eunuchs. As soon as the operation is performed the boys are buried in the ground; all but the head and shoulders. Many who are not of strong constitutions die with the excruciating pain. It is calculated, that the operation—during its performance or afterwards—proves fatal to two out of three.[20]

Similar examples of Egyptian brutality are discussed in relation to the dispensing of 'justice'. Belzoni writes of an unfortunate individual who experienced a brutal judgment of guilt: 'This was the signal for taking him to a particular cannon, tied to the mouth of it, and then it was fired, loaded with a ball, so that the body was scattered about in pieces at a considerable distance'.[21] Belzoni describes another instance of barbaric punishment, in which two men were 'fastened to a pole like two rabbits on a spit, and roasted alive at a slow fire'.[22] Episodes such as these do not advance his narrative or particularly illuminate his autobiography, but they do add to the atmosphere of danger and exoticism. As an early archaeological report, it frames the excavation of antiquities as dangerous work, in a hostile and savage environment—a type of archaeological setting that was picked up by later adventure fiction writers.

Throughout his account, Belzoni informs the reader of the various hardships and dangers with which he was faced. Noteworthy among these problems is ophthalmia. Ophthalmia is an inflammation of the eye caused by excessive exposure to ultraviolet radiation, certainly a legitimate problem for European explorers in Egypt before the advent of sunglasses. The effects of the bright sun on Belzoni and his companions was to periodically afflict them with great pain for days at a time whenever they would open their eyes. Explicit descriptions of the hardships he faced establish an ethos of heroism.

20. Belzoni, *Travels*, p. 44.
21. Belzoni, *Travels*, p. 44.
22. Belzoni, *Travels*, p. 44.

Other incidents that Belzoni describes are not so much filled with danger as they are presentations of exotic, romantic and mysterious locations. His descriptions of venturing into darkened tombs filled with mummies best exemplify this tendency. In one instance, Belzoni juxtaposes what the typical traveler is satisfied to see in a tomb with what he is willing to endure:

> A traveler is generally satisfied when he has seen the large hall, the gallery, the staircase, and as far as he can conveniently go ... so that when he comes to a narrow and difficult passage, or to have to descend to the bottom of a well or cavity, he declines taking such trouble naturally supposing that he cannot see in these abysses anything so magnificent as what he sees above.[23]

Belzoni accurately describes the extent to which a casual traveler will encounter the tombs. Yet he continues, illustrating his own heroism and heightening the interest of his readers, by describing what happens if one does venture forth into the darkened abyss:

> Of some of these tombs many persons could not withstand the suffocating air, which often causes fainting. A vast quantity of dust rises, so fine that it enters into the throat and nostrils, and chokes the nose and mouth to such a degree that it requires great power of lungs to resist it and the strong effluvia of the mummies. This is not all: the entry or passage where the bodies are is roughly cut in the rocks, and the falling of the sand from the upper part or ceiling of the passage causes it to be nearly filled up. In some places there is not more than a vacancy of a foot left, which you must contrive to pass through in a creeping posture like a snail, on pointed and keen stones that cut like glass. After getting through these passages, some of them two or three hundred yards long, you generally find a more commodious place, perhaps high enough to sit. But what a place to rest! Surrounded by bodies, by heaps of mummies in all directions, which, previous to my being accustomed to the sight, impressed me with horror. The blackness of the wall, the faint light given by the candles or torches for want of air, the different objects that surrounded me, seeming to converse with each other, and the Arabs with the candles or torches in their hands, naked and covered with dust, themselves resembling living mummies, absolutely formed a scene that cannot be described. In such a situation I found myself several times, and often returned exhausted and fainting, till at last I became inured to it, and indifferent to what I suffered, except from the dust, which never failed to choke my throat.[24]

Belzoni's eerie description of a darkened tomb and the unpleasantness that is involved in venturing is provocative. He continues his account with an anecdote that horrifies professional archaeologists and interested lay people alike, but for drastically different reasons:

---

23. Belzoni, *Travels*, p. 181.
24. Belzoni, *Travels*, pp. 181-82.

3. *The Strongman, the Geographer, and the Diplomat*

> After the exertion of entering into such a place [a tomb] . . . I sought a resting-place, found one, and contrived to sit, but when my weight bore on the body of an Egyptian, it crushed it like a band-box. I naturally had recourse to my hands to sustain my weight, but they found no better support, so that I sunk altogether among the broken mummies, with a crash of bones, rags, and wooden cases, which raised such a dust as kept me motionless for a quarter of an hour waiting till it subsided again. I could not remove from the place, however, without increasing it, and every step I took I crushed a mummy in some part or another.[25]

Immediately following this, Belzoni describes another claustrophobic encounter with mummies:

> Once I was conducted from such a place to another resembling it, through a passage of about twenty feet in length, and no wider than that a body could be forced through. It was choked with mummies, and I could not pass without putting my face in contact with that of some decayed Egyptian, but as the passage inclined downwards, my own weight helped me on, however, I could not avoid being covered with bones, legs, arms, and heads rolling from above. Thus I proceeded from one cave to another, all full of mummies piled up in various ways, some standing, some lying, and some on their heads. The purpose of my researches was to rob the Egyptians of their papyri; of which I found a few hidden in their breasts, under their arms, in the space above the knees, or on the legs, and covered by the numerous folds of cloth that envelop the mummy.[26]

For professional archaeologists working today, Belzoni's account is horrifying, not because of the close quarters but rather due to the rampant destruction of remains. His lack of respect for the mummies, however, was by no means unusual for European explorations of the day.

Throughout, Belzoni presents himself as a modest hero (although the modesty is in no way convincing to the reader).[27] Elliott Colla assesses Belzoni's use of the first person as part of this heroic narrative, not just a function of the autobiographical nature of the writing. This is especially apparent in descriptions of excavations, where, despite the fact that Belzoni is not the one physically excavating, he still remains the grammatical subject of the sentences versus the agency-less grammatical treatment of his workers.[28] Colla writes, 'the labor of the Gurna peasants, which, lacking intent, is not fully active, not fully human'.[29] The physical act of excavating is a major element of Belzoni's 'heroism' that is made evident

---

25. Belzoni, *Travels*, pp. 182-83.
26. Belzoni, *Travels*, p. 183.
27. The fictional character Allan Quatermain displays similar character traits (see Chapter III.5).
28. Elliott Colla, *Conflicted Antiquities: Egyptology, Egyptomania, Egyptian Modernity* (Durham, NC: Duke University Press, 2007), pp. 36-37.
29. Colla, *Conflicted Antiquities*, p. 37.

Fig. 3.5. 'Mode in which the young Memnon's head (now in the British Museum) was removed'. *Plates Illustrative of the Researches and Operations of G. Belzoni in Egypt and Nubia* (London: John Murray, 1822). Beinecke Rare Book and Manuscript Library, Yale University.

through *Travels*. He goes to great lengths to present his brilliance at feats of engineering. This type of ingenuity was of interest to the nineteenth-century reader, and the ability of a European engineer to 'conquer' through the application of scientific approaches was of no small consequence. His removal of the colossal head of the Younger Memnon (Fig. 3.5) is presented as one of these feats (preceding Layard's similar accounts of the transport of the 'Nineveh' reliefs from Mesopotamia). He describes his own engineering techniques in juxtaposition with the wonder of the locals at his skills:

> The Fellahs of Gournou, who were familiar with Caphany, as they named the colossus, were persuaded that it could never be moved from the spot where it lay and when they saw it moved they all set up a shout. Though it was the effect of their own efforts, it was the devil, they said, that did it, and, as they saw me taking notes, they concluded that it was done by means of a charm. The mode I adopted to place it on the car was very simple, for work of no other description could be executed by these people, as their utmost sagacity reaches only to pulling a rope, or sitting on the extremity of a lever as a counterpoise. By means of four levers I raised the bust so as to leave a vacancy under it to introduce the car, and after it was slowly lodged on this, I had the car raised in front, with the bust on it so as to get one of the rollers underneath.[30]

Belzoni goes on to further describe how the head was lifted up in its entirety and then transported to the bank of the Nile, along with a description of

---

30. Belzoni, *Travels*, p. 58.

3. *The Strongman, the Geographer, and the Diplomat*

Fig. 3.6. Forced passage into the second pyramid of Giza and Great Chamber in the second pyramid of Giza [Khafre's Pyramid]. Discovered by G. Belzoni, 1818 (pl. 12). *Plates Illustrative of the Researches and Operations of G. Belzoni in Egypt and Nubia* (1820).

how ill he felt (from the heat and stomach ailments) the entire time he was engaged in this enterprise.

Another feat of Belzoni's engineering ingenuity that is presented in the narrative is his account of his penetration into Khafre's pyramid at Giza (Fig. 3.6). Part of Belzoni's motivation for writing about his 'work' at the pyramids was to dispel Count de Forbin's claims to have penetrated the interior of Khafre's pyramid.[31] He does so through his detailed description of how he found the passage and how earlier explorers clearly had not discovered it. In the book, Belzoni describes the deductive processes he used to identify the location of the entrance into the pyramid, based on his observations of the location of the entrance to Khufu's pyramid and observations about the accumulation of debris along the exterior of the pyramid.[32] After explaining how difficult it was to gain permission to work on Khafre's pyramid and to raise money for the venture, Belzoni describes the two large work teams he set up (on the north and east sides of the pyramid) consisting of forty adults each with uncounted numbers of children hauling away dirt. He describes cutting through the accumulated stone rubble (including parts of the attached mortuary temple) and removing some looser stones on the

31. Belzoni, *Travels*, p. 289.
32. Belzoni, *Travels*, p. 293.

exterior of the pyramid, which allowed him to work his way into the corridors of the pyramid through the interior.[33] This was not the main entrance to the pyramid, so Belzoni returned to Khufu's pyramid to compare the position of its entrance. When he returned to Khafre's pyramid, Belzoni noted marks positioned in a similar location on the exterior of that pyramid, which he states, 'gave me no little delight, and hope returned to cherish my pyramidical brains'.[34] Following this observation, Belzoni describes in detail the removal of stones to reveal the passage.

Belzoni's engineering ingenuity is clearly contrasted with the perceived lack of local engineering skill. In general, the nineteenth-century Egyptians are treated as just another type of obstacle in his quest. Belzoni is especially troubled by the disjuncture between what he perceives as the beauty of the antiquities and the ugliness of nineteenth-century life in Egypt, and this is a comparison that was made by scholars throughout the nineteenth and into the twentieth century.[35] After his exploration of the Ptolemaic-era Horus temple at Edfu, Belzoni writes:

> On looking at an edifice of such magnitude, workmanship, and antiquity, inhabited by a half-savage people whose huts are stuck against it, not unlike wasps' nests and to contrast their filthy clothes with these sacred images that once were so highly venerated makes one strongly feel the difference between the ancient and the modern state of Egypt.[36]

Belzoni, is of course, not the only European explorer to comment on this perceived juxtaposition between ancient and contemporary Egypt. With Belzoni's account of Egypt, however, this reading of the nineteenth-century Egyptian primitive is not as straightforward as in the writings of his contemporaries. Through numerous side comments peppered throughout the book, he emphasizes similarities between nineteenth-century Egyptians and Europeans, although usually these should be understood as criticisms of Europeans rather than a message of universalizing humanity. For example, he discusses how useful baksheesh was for motivating workers:

> Nothing has so much influence on the mind of an Arab as reasoning with him about his own interest, and showing him the right way to benefit himself. Anything else he seems not to understand. I must confess, at the same time that I found this mode of proceeding quite as efficacious in Europe.[37]

Comments like these that are meant to be disparaging of both Europeans and nineteenth-century Egyptians may signal a greater complexity to the

---

33. Belzoni, *Travels*, pp. 298-99.
34. Belzoni, *Travels*, p. 303.
35. Colla, *Conflicted Antiquities*, p. 40.
36. Belzoni, *Travels*, p. 73.
37. Belzoni, *Travels*, p. 296.

understanding of the other than is usually presumed. This should not be overstated, however, as it more likely reflects an attempt at humour based on drawing parallels between the supposed superior and the inferior.

One of the most consistent frustrations that Belzoni describes are his attempts to convince the locals that he was not looking for 'treasure' (meaning gold or precious gems) but merely 'stones'.[38] When Belzoni was unable to convince the locals that he was not looking for treasure, he often offered to split it with them—which led them to accompany him to the sites. The visit of a Turkish officer to the Seti I tomb reflected many of these encounters:

> Half an hour after they gave us the signal of their approach by firing several guns. I thought an armed force was sent to storm the tombs and rocks, as no other object could bring the Turks there; at last, when this mighty power reached us, I found it to be the well-known Hamed Aga of Kenneh, for some time commander of the eastern side of Thebes, and his followers. Accordingly I was at a loss to connive what he wanted there, as we were on the west, and under another ruler, but I suppose in case of a treasure being discovered, the first that hears of it seizes it as a matter of privilege. He smiled, and saluted me very cordially; indeed more so than usual, I presume for the sake of the treasure I had discovered, of which he was in great expectation. I caused as many lights to be brought as we could muster, and we descended into the tomb. What was on the walk of this extraordinary place did not attract his attention in the least; all the striking figures and lively paintings were lost on him; his views were directed to the treasure alone and his numerous followers were like hounds, searching in every hole and corner. Nothing, however, being found to satisfy their master or themselves, after a long and minute survey, the Aga at last ordered the soldiers to retire, and said to me, 'Pray where have you put the treasure?' 'What treasure?' 'The treasure you found in this place?' I could not help smiling at his question, which confirmed him in is supposition. I told him that we had found no treasure there. At this he laughed, and still continued to entreat that I would show it him. 'I have been told', he added, 'by a person to whom I can give credit that you have found in this place a large golden cock filled with diamonds and pearls. I must see it. Where is it?' I could scarcely keep myself from laughing, while I assured him that nothing of the kind had been found there. Seeming quite disappointed, he seated himself before the sarcophagus, and I was afraid he would take

---

38. It may be unfair to criticize Belzoni for these frustrations. I found in my own experiences excavating in Jordan that some Jordanians could not believe that I was not just looking for gold. One piece of advice that I was given was that the only way that I could find the 'gold' was to ask tribal elders for the spells that would reveal where it had been hidden by the *djinn*. For more on different valuations of heritage in Jordan, see Jennifer Jacobs and Benjamin Porter, 'Excavating *Turath*: Documenting Local and National Heritage Discourses in Jordan', in *Ethnographies and Archaeologies: Iterations of the Past* (ed. Lena Mortensen and Julie Hollowell; Gainesville, FL: University Press of Florida, 2009), pp. 71-88.

it into his head that this was the treasure, and break it to pieces to see whether it contained any gold; for their notions of treasure are confined to gold and jewels. At last he gave up the idea of the riches to be expected, and rose to go out of the tomb. I asked him what he thought of the beautiful figures painted all around. He just gave a glance at them, quite unconcerned, and said, 'This would be a good place for a harem, as the women would have something to look at'. At length, though only half persuaded there was no treasure, he set off with an appearance of much vexation.[39]

What is interesting here is that the humour for Belzoni lies in the Turkish commander's sense that what constitutes treasure is limited to only gold and jewels. It is not that the Turkish commander does not understand that the artifacts are valuable for their intellectual potential, rather that the Turk does not understand what can actually fetch a good price on the market. For Belzoni, the materials he excavated were little more than treasure to him, since he was selling these items for a profit, not studying them himself. His accounts of ransacking mummies to get papyrus and his hauling away of statues and artifacts reflect the same kind of treasure seeking as he, in this passage, mocks the Turkish commander for. The difference is that Belzoni has a greater knowledge of market values.

Despite the practical reality of Belzoni acting as a treasure hunter, he frequently makes pleas to his reader that this is not what he was doing. It is not that he did not sell the materials, but rather that he sold them for less than their value. For example, Belzoni writes about statues sold to Count de Forbin: 'What he paid me for them was not one fourth of their value, but I was fully satisfied, as I never was a dealer in statues in my life'.[40] Belzoni felt slandered by Forbin's later comments about him, so in some ways this particular passage is an argument against public comments made by Forbin. However, the nature of the defense is telling in itself, demonstrating an attempt on Belzoni's part to mask that his goals in this enterprise were the acquisition of private wealth. Here, in keeping with the values of European nobility, which spurned profit-making, Belzoni pretends that the acquisition of wealth is not of primary interest.

For Belzoni to profit from his activities, he needed to make certain that there was a market for Egyptian antiquities. This became somewhat problematic when the trustees of the British Museum denied the importance of Egyptian works as objects of art and were reluctant to acquire his pieces for the museum (see Chapter II.3). Thus, there was direct financial gain for him that was dependent upon his being able to convince British society to consider Egyptian art as part of the larger tradition of Western art. The

---

39. Belzoni, *Travels*, pp. 281-82.
40. Belzoni, *Travels*, p. 287.

exclusion of Egyptian art from the canon was preventing the purchase of his artifacts or at least lowering the prices he could fetch.

Colla interprets Belzoni's aesthetic evaluations of Egyptian antiquities within a broader framework of discourse on whether or not Egyptian antiquities constituted pieces of art.[41] To Colla, Belzoni's appreciation of the aesthetic quality of Egyptian pieces reflects a broadening of what constituted 'beautiful' (in artistic terms) beyond classical models and incorporating individual experiences and perceptions.[42] Belzoni explains to his European readers why ancient Egyptian art was technically sophisticated and worth consideration in the artistic canon. For example, he discusses their skills in perspective:

> The wonderful sculptures of the Egyptians are to be admired for the boldness of their execution. Their enormous arcs rendered it difficult for the artists to maintain their due proportions, which were according to the height of the figure. For instance, if a statue was of the natural size; if the statue were erected of the size of life, the head was of the natural size; if the statue were thirty feet high, the head was larger in proportion to the body, and if fifty feet high, the magnitude of the head was farther increased. Had it been otherwise in statues of so great height, the distance from the eyes of the spectator would have so much diminished the size that the head would have appeared too small in proportion to the legs.[43]

Here, then, Belzoni is explaining the mathematical sophistication that lay beneath Egyptian sculpture, certainly grounds for considering Egyptian materials as art. In other aspects of artistic achievement, Belzoni insists that Egyptian art be understood within its own context. For example, as regards painting, he acknowledges that Egyptian lack of knowledge of the use of shadow made their painting 'simple' but asserts that they must be given credit for their tasteful use of colours, stating, for example, 'There is great harmony even in the red and green, which do not always agree with us, and which they knew how to mingle so well that it produced a very splendid effect'.[44] Likewise, Egyptian architecture needed to be considered in terms of how well it was 'in conformity with their ideas'.[45] Their knowledge of the arch, to Belzoni, was evidence of their engineering sophistication. And in some instances, Belzoni asserts that their arts were of greater skill than those available in nineteenth-century Europe. Varnishing clay, for example, 'was in such perfection among them that I doubt whether it could be imitated at the present'.[46]

41. Colla, *Conflicted Antiquities*, p. 33.
42. Colla, *Conflicted Antiquities*, p. 33.
43. Belzoni, *Travels*, p. 207.
44. Belzoni, *Travels*, p. 202.
45. Belzoni, *Travels*, p. 203.
46. Belzoni, *Travels*, p. 202.

In apologizing for Egyptian art, Belzoni goes further though than to just state its merits. He argues that it should be seen in an evolutionary framework, as work that preceded Greek art, and that the Greeks learned from it and consciously imitated it. For Belzoni, the Egyptians were capable of 'invention', which makes them stand out as one of the great world civilizations. He compares their achievements to the Greeks: 'The Greeks may claim their having brought the art to great perfection, but it is well known that they took their principle hints from the Egyptians'.[47] He even goes so far as to suggest that contemporary designers could learn much from the study of ancient Egypt: 'The Egyptians were a primitive nation. They had to form everything without any model before them to imitate. Yet so fertile was their inventive faculty that to this day new orders of architecture might be extracted from their ruins.'[48] And that is precisely what happened with the wave of Egyptomania in architecture that took hold in the early part of the nineteenth century in Europe (see Volume II).

The comparison between Greek and Egyptian art points to Belzoni's more sophisticated understanding of classical sources than he is normally credited with. In fact, he seems to have adopted the mistrust of classical sources that gradually emerged throughout the nineteenth century. In particular, his use of Strabo and Herodotus is careful, and he does not take their accounts at face value. As he describes in reference to the Valley of the Kings, 'Having found by experience that the reports of ancient authors are not always to be depended upon, particularly when they speak from hearsay, I put them out of the account, and proceeded entirely on my own judgment to search for the tombs of the monarchs of Thebes'.[49] In other instances, he interacts more intensely with classical accounts, such as in his discussion of Egyptian burial customs. There, Belzoni quotes Herodotus's account and then explains in which areas he believes that Herodotus was incorrect. Then, Belzoni offers his own observations and conclusions, a mixture of factual observations and rampant speculation, as when he suggests that the Egyptians hung scarabs around their necks when they went to war, a conclusion that he admits is speculative.[50] On some occasions, Belzoni purposefully tests the descriptions provided in classical texts, such as his test of the water temperature at what he thought was the fountain of the Temple of Jupiter Ammon.[51] This particular instance, however, was fundamentally flawed in that Belzoni had been mistaken about the location of this temple—he never actually visited the temple or fountain discussed by Herodotus.[52]

47. Belzoni, *Travels*, p. 206.
48. Belzoni, *Travels*, p. 206.
49. Belzoni, *Travels*, p. 254.
50. Belzoni, *Travels*, p. 200.
51. Belzoni, *Travels*, p. 478.
52. Belzoni was actually investigating ruins at Wadi Bahariyah.

3. *The Strongman, the Geographer, and the Diplomat*

Much of what Belzoni writes about the antiquities he encounters is highly speculative. The popularity of this work in the nineteenth century meant that many of these speculative readings of sites and artifacts must have been taken seriously by his readers. Given the frequency with which he was quoted and the references made to him in various media, Belzoni's vision of ancient Egypt and Egyptology was absolutely formative, especially in popular culture. Chapter II.2 will deal with his contributions to museology and display practices, but suffice it to say that despite the negative retroactive evaluation of professional archaeologists (and this is not meant to be apologetic), Belzoni's book established many of the literary tropes of the field. Because of Belzoni, fictional accounts of archaeology involve violent competitive races against other Western adventurers to plunder antiquities, the sales of antiquities for great profits to museums, and a wilful disregard for the context in which the 'treasure' is found. His initial framing of archaeology within a context of danger, adventure and competition, as well as his arguments that Egyptian art should be considered part of the Western canon, set the foundations for the reception of Egyptian antiquities that would follow.

The Geographer: Edward Robinson

Edward Robinson's (Fig. 3.7) early work in biblical archaeology has held up better under later scholarly scrutiny than Belzoni's treasure hunting. Robinson (1794–1863) has been rightly called the 'Father of Biblical Geography' because of his pioneering work in that field, both in terms of establishing basic principles and methods and in terms of the results of his own investigations, especially as manifest in his *Biblical Researches in Palestine, Mount Sinai and Arabia Petræa: A Journal of Travels in the Year 1838* (1841). An American scholar who was partially trained in continental Europe, Robinson was widely respected and brought the theological tendencies of New England to British and continental biblical studies. The son of a Congregationalist minister, Robinson was first drawn to the classics and later to the academic study of the Bible. As professor extraordinary of sacred literature at Andover Theological Seminary (from 1830 to 1833) and later as professor of biblical literature at Union Theological Seminary (from 1837 on), he was immersed in the New England theological movements of the time where direct experiences of the divine and the divine mediated through nature were privileged. He was himself a conservative and wanted to demonstrate the literal truth of Scripture especially in response to the liberal attitudes of Unitarians.[53] As John Davis has noted, Robinson also

---

53. For more on Robinson's theological training and influences, see Neil Asher Silberman, *Digging for God and Country: Exploration, Archeology, and the Secret Struggle for the Holy Land 1799–1917* (New York: Alfred A. Knopf, 1982), pp. 38-39.

Fig. 3.7. Edward Robinson. Wikimedia Commons.

makes reference to his childhood and the childhoods of his fellow New Englanders, through which a kind of nostalgic view of the Holy Land had been inculcated, and thus the sojourn to the region became a self-reflective journey as well.[54] In retrospect, a new type of pilgrimage, in which the Holy Land was experienced in a scientific fashion (with measurement in various ways being the primary pilgrim activity), seems like an obvious outgrowth of New England intellectualism and the theology that emerged in response. This was Robinson's contribution, and his *Biblical Researches* became a best-seller throughout the United States and Europe. By the end of the nineteenth century, biblical geography would be established as not only a field of academic study but, especially for scholars from the United States, a means to experience revelation through a kind of natural theology, in which God's presence could be felt in the topography of the Holy Land.[55]

In *Biblical Researches*, Robinson writes of the experience of being in the physical location that was once inhabited by biblical individuals. He writes about one particular excursion, along the route to Jerusalem that Isaiah says was taken by the Neo-Assyrian king Sennacherib:

---

54. John Davis, *The Landscape of Belief: Encountering the Holy Land in Nineteenth-Century American Art and Culture* (Princeton, NJ: Princeton University Press, 1996), p. 16.

55. Burke O. Long, *Imagining the Holy Land: Maps, Models, and Fantasy Travels* (Bloomington, IN: Indiana University Press, 2003), pp. 97-98.

3. The Strongman, the Geographer, and the Diplomat

> This excursion was to us deeply interesting, and we returned from it highly gratified. It had led us through scenes associated with the names and historic incidents and deeds of Abraham and Jacob, of Samuel and Saul, of Jonathan and David and Solomon; and we had been able to trace out the places where they had lived and acted, and to tread almost in their very footsteps. True, in Jerusalem itself the associations of this kind are still more numerous and sacred; but they are so blended together, as to become in a measure indistinct and less impressive; while here in the country, they stand forth before the soul in all their original freshness and individuality. It was like communing with these holy men themselves, to visit the places where their feet had trod, and where many of them had held converse with the Most High. I hope that in this respect the visit was not without its proper influence upon our own minds; at any rate, it served to give us a deeper impression of the reality and vividness of the Bible-history, and to confirm our confidence in the truth and power of the sacred volume.[56]

Although referring to a specific excursion on their journey, what Robinson writes here well applies to many of the locations that they visited. Robinson's work implies that a direct experience of the Holy Land (even beyond Jerusalem) is helpful in interpreting the Bible; others agreed and his work became a fundamental text in the growing exploration of biblical-era material culture.

His *Biblical Researches in Palestine* was an academic work that reached a large audience beyond the academy in the mid-nineteenth century. By 1841 it was already a standard work used by most English-speaking travellers to the region, and by 1860 it had become a staple in seminaries.[57] The book was written by Robinson based on notes compiled by both him and his former student Eli Smith on their trip to the region in 1838. Smith was an American missionary, resident in Beirut, who was well versed in Arabic and knew the topography of Syria fairly well. The account of their 1838 visit provides a wealth of information on the region in a unique moment in time, when Palestine was under the direct control of the pasha of Egypt. They again visited Palestine in 1852, concentrating on areas that they had not been able to reach in their first visit. Although not the intention of the volume, Robinson's description of the unique situations in governance that this brought, along with descriptions of Egyptian policies (such as the quarantining of entire cities when threatened by plague), provides an interesting window into life in Palestine under the pasha's rule.

The book itself is divided into three volumes. Each volume contains appendices at the back on a variety of subjects, such as critiques of simi-

---

56. Edward Robinson, *Biblical Researches in Palestine, Mount Sinai and Arabia Petræa: A Journal of Travels in the Year 1838 by E. Robinson and E. Smith*, II (Boston: Crocker & Brewster, 1841), p. 148.

57. John James Moscrop, *Measuring Jerusalem: The Palestine Exploration Fund and British Interests in the Holy Land* (London: Leicester University Press, 2000), p. 20.

lar works and important Arabic phraseology. Large fold-out maps are also pasted into the back of each volume. The maps record Robinson's route and campsites, as well as ruins mentioned in the text and site identifications. The creation of these maps was one of the principal goals of Robinson and Smith and reflects an important scholarly contribution. About them, Robinson states, 'In the construction of the maps, it has been a main principle, to admit no name or position on mere conjecture, nor without some sufficient positive authority. Where a place is known to exist, though its position is not definitely ascertained, it is marked as uncertain.'[58] The importance of this approach is discussed below.

Robinson explains the motivation for writing the book at the outset: 'As here presented to the public, these volumes may therefore be said to exhibit an historical review of the Sacred Geography of Palestine, since the times of the New Testament...'[59] This was the literal truth of Scripture presented in cartographic and travel narrative form. At one point he suggests that the two had never intended their study of the region to be as extensive as it ended up being. Robinson explains:

> Palestine had for centuries been visited by many travellers; . . . and we could hope to add nothing to what . . . others had observed. Under the influence of these impressions, we carried with us no instruments, except an ordinary surveyor's and two pocket compasses, a thermometer, telescopes, and measuring-tapes; expecting to take only such bearings and measurements as might occur to us upon the road, without going out of our way to seek for them. But as we came to Sinai, and saw how much former travellers had left undescribed; and then crossed the great desert through a region hitherto almost unknown, and found the names and sites of long-forgotten cities; we became convinced that there 'yet remained much land to be possessed', and determined to do what we could with our limited means towards supplying the deficiency.[60]

Yet, the two had clearly intended to seriously research the region while travelling through, given the list of books that they had brought with them.[61]

---

58. Robinson, *Biblical Researches*, p. xii.
59. Robinson, *Biblical Researches*, p. ix.
60. Robinson, *Biblical Researches*, p. 47.
61. These included the following: Bibles in English, Hebrew and Greek; Reland's *Palæstina*—which Robinson describes as 'next to the Bible is the most important book for travellers in the Holy Land'; Raumer's *Palästina*; Burckhardt's *Travels in Syria and the Holy Land*; an English compilation of Laborde's *Voyage en Arabie Petrée*; and the *Modern Traveller in Arabia, Palestine, Syria*. In terms of maps, they had Laborde's map of Sinai and Arabia Petraea and Berghaus's map of Syria, which Robinson describes as 'the best undoubtedly up to the present time, but which was of little service to us in the parts of the country we visited'. Robinson laments that they did not bring with them a good history of the Crusades or Ritter's *Erdkunde* (Robinson, *Biblical Researches*, p. 48).

This was not atypical of cartography at the time, which combined detailed historical research of a variety of sources and on-the-ground measurements and observations.[62]

The book is written in diary format and in chronological order reflecting the actual journey that the two men took. He apologizes for the chronological structure in the preface, indicating that he would return to subjects over and over again in the narrative, as they came upon them in their travels, rather than grouping like subjects with like.[63] This structure makes the book more readable, on a popular level, than a mere discussion of various sites. It takes on the structure of a travel narrative and roughly follows many of the conventions typical of the genre in the mid-nineteenth century. The general 'plot' of the book, then, follows their journey to Egypt, and journey from Alexandria, to Cairo, to Thebes, and back to Cairo. The more academic work begins with their departure across the Sinai, attempting to track (and in some ways emulate) the route of the Israelites' exodus out of Egypt. The two eventually arrive in Jerusalem, which acts as the base for their journeys out into surrounding areas. Toward the end of their journey, they investigate the Galilee region and eventually travel up to Tyre, Sidon and Beirut. They depart the Near East from Beirut (taking a steamer back to Alexandria first since a Beirut–Europe run was not yet established). Yehoshua Ben-Arieh notes that they never retraced any route, except between Jerusalem and Bethlehem, so careful was their planning.[64]

Robinson apologizes that his book ended up taking on the form of travel writing, rather than just being an academic source for biblical scholarship. He justifies the choice:

> It was my original plan, to present to the public only the results of our researches in Palestine, without any reference to personal incidents. But the advice of my friends, whose judgment I could not but place above my own, was averse to such course. I have therefore everywhere interwoven the personal narrative; and have endeavoured so to do it, as to exhibit the manner in which the Promised Land unfolded itself to our eyes, and the processes by which we were led to the conclusions and opinions advanced in this work.[65]

---

62. Janet Starkey enumerates the variety of sources used by James Rennell in his posthumously published 1831 geography of western Asia, which include classical sources, European and Islamic travelogues, attesting to the command of languages and historical training necessary for Enlightenment-era geographers (Janet Starkey, 'James Rennell and his Scientific World of Observation', in *Knowledge Is Light: Travellers in the Near East* [Oxford: ASTENE and Oxbow Books, 2011], pp. 38-58 [42-43]).

63. Robinson, *Biblical Researches*, p. vi.

64. Yehoshua Ben-Arieh, *The Rediscovery of the Holy Land in the Nineteenth Century* (Jerusalem: Sefer Ve Sefel Publishing, 2007 [1979]), p. 154.

65. Robinson, *Biblical Researches*, p. v.

In the course of writing the book, he found that it became necessary to supply more than just his travel account. He explains:

> Another more important change of the original plan . . . I mean the introduction of historical illustrations, and the discussion of various points relating to the historical topography of the Holy Land. My first purpose was merely to describe what we saw, leaving the reader to make his own application of the facts. But as I proceeded, questions continually arose, which I could not pass over without at least satisfying my own mind; this sometimes led to long courses of investigation; and when I had thus arrived at satisfactory conclusions, it seemed almost like a neglect of duty towards the reader, not to embody them in the work.[66]

Thus the book becomes a fusion of genres. There is the framing narrative of Robinson and Smith's adventures travelling through Egyptian-controlled Palestine. There are excursuses throughout the text on the history of the main sites that they visited (often beginning with biblical times and including Hellenistic-Roman, Byzantine, Crusader and more recent periods). There are topographical descriptions that include measurements, coordinates, and prose accounts of locales. There are philological discussions of place names. And there is an interaction with ancient and contemporary authorities on the subject of biblical geography. Despite the length, the three volumes are an engrossing read, and it is easy to see why this large and unusual work was so popular in the nineteenth century and how it spurred the creation of an academic discipline.

Much of the manuscript involves attempts to identify specific place names mentioned in Scripture, and, concomitantly, identify locations that they came across with names mentioned in the biblical text. In some ways, his work was flawed from the outset since Robinson had no knowledge of tells and site formation and thus was unable to identify many of the major biblical cities.[67] The naming of sites is, as Derek Gregory and Eitan Bar-Yosef have argued, one strategy of dispossession common to imperialism.[68] By naming a site, 'space becomes a place' infused with history and political legitimation. A biblical geographer, then, was able to identify the 'real' names of the places of the Holy Land and restore them from the tyranny of tradition or decay. That being said, Robinson and Smith's work was enacted

---

66. Robinson, *Biblical Researches*, pp. vi-vii.
67. Ben-Arieh, *Rediscovery*, p. 90.
68. Derek Gregory, *The Colonial Present: Afghanistan, Palestine, and Iraq* (New York: Blackwell, 2004); Eitan Bar-Yosef, *The Holy Land in English Culture 1799–1917: Palestine and the Question of Orientalism* (Oxford: Clarendon Press, 2005), p. 89. It should be noted that Bar-Yosef agues for a more complex situation in relation to Palestine, most especially due to the a priori sense of ownership that the British felt toward the Holy Land. Regardless, the act of naming (or recovering names) is an act of intellectual–geographical transformation.

out of a genuine desire to relate geography and Scripture. The imperialist politics were not as important as their desire to demonstrate and experience the literal truth of the Bible. Yet as Silberman describes, Robinson was horrified by the present-day conditions of the Holy Land and wished to 'retrieve for the world the lovely vision of the Holy Land, so revered in his native New England, snatching it, if he must, from its present filth, degradation, and poverty'.[69]

A typical example of how Robinson and Smith went about identifying the sites is their evaluation of Shiloh. Robinson writes:

> The proofs that Seilûn is actually the site of the ancient Shiloh, lie within a small compass; and both the name and position are sufficiently decisive. The full form of the Hebrew name was apparently *Shilon*, as we find it in the gentile noun *Shilonite*; and Josephus writes it also both *Silo* and *Siloun*. The position of Shiloh is very definitely described in the book of Judges, as 'on the north side of Bethel, on the east side of the highway that goeth up from Bethel to Shechem, and on the south of Lebonah'. Eusebius and Jerome place it, one ten and the other twelve Roman miles from Neapolis, in the region of Acrabatene. With the exception of these confused and probably conjectural distances, all the other circumstances correspond exactly to Seilûn; for we were here on the East of the great road between Bethel and Shechem (Nâbulus), and in passing on towards the latter place, we came after an hour to the village of Lebonah, now el-Lubban.[70]

Along with the etymological discussion, Robinson provides a history of Shiloh, surveying biblical times until the present. He describes the geographic setting of Shiloh and discusses the biblical account of the city in light of that setting. For example, regarding a natural fountain near the city, he suggests that this was the setting described in Judg. 21:19-23, where the Benjaminites kidnapped the daughters of Shiloh who were dancing in their annual celebration. Robinson suggests, 'The scene of these dances may not improbably have been somewhere around the fountain above described'.[71] Thus, etymological arguments are used to identify the site, and the reader is then shown how the identification of the actual site can enhance their appreciation for the relevant Scriptures.

Throughout the three volumes, Robinson and Smith visit ancient ruins, and Robinson presents their initial impressions of these sites. At Wady er-Ruhaibeh, for example, Robinson and Smith came across the remains of an ancient city of which they had been otherwise unaware. Robinson provides a description of the ruins, in very general terms:

---

69. Silberman, *Digging*, p. 42.
70. Robinson, *Biblical Researches*, p. 87.
71. Robinson, *Biblical Researches*, p. 88.

> But on ascending the hill on the left of the valley, we were astonished to find ourselves amid the ruins of an ancient city. Here is a level tract of ten or twelve acres in extent, entirely and thickly covered over with confused heaps of stone, with just enough of their former order remaining, to show the foundations and form of the houses, and the course of some of the streets. The houses were mostly small, all solidly built of bluish limestone, squared and often hewn on the exterior surface. Many of the dwellings had each its cistern, cut in the solid rock; and these remain quite entire. . . . There seemed to have been no public square, and no important or large public buildings; nor could we trace with certainty any city walls. We sought also in vain for inscriptions. Once, as we judged upon the spot, this must have been a city of not less than twelve or fifteen thousand inhabitants. Now, it is a perfect field of ruins, a scene of unutterable desolation; across which the passing stranger can with difficulty find his way.[72]

Here Robinson is able to provide a basic description of the above-ground ruins, but their expedition is not prepared for an actual archaeological excavation and so only minimal conclusions can be drawn. The description of the ruins here is similar to other descriptions in the book, in that it notes observations about the general layout and appearance of the houses, construction materials used, the presence of cisterns, the presence or absence of public architecture and estimation of size. These descriptions of ancient sites would have filled readers with a sense of wonder that these two men (and their travelling party) had stumbled upon an ancient abandoned city, now utterly desolate.

Robinson and Smith used two main criteria to positively identify sites with their ancient place names. Of primary importance was that the site needed to reflect the topography as described in the biblical narrative and other historical documents. This is a similar methodology as that later used by Calvert and Schliemann to identify the lost city of Troy. The second criterion consisted of any noted linguistic similarity between the ancient place name and the modern place name. Beyond these two criteria, other evidence could be marshalled in the identification of the site, such as inscriptions. The use of these criteria in the identification of sites can be seen in Robinson's discussion of the ruins of Wady er-Ruhaibeh. Robinson writes:

> The place must anciently have been one of some note and importance; but what city could it have been? This is a question, which after long inquiry, and with the best aid from the light of European science, I am as yet unable to answer. The name er-Ruhaibeh naturally suggests the Hebrew *Rehoboth*, one of Isaac's wells in the vicinity of Gerar; but this appears to have been nothing but a well, and there is no mention in Scripture or elsewhere of any city connected with it. The position of the well too, would seem to have been much further North; and no town of this name is spoken of

---

72. Robinson, *Biblical Researches,* p. 290.

3. *The Strongman, the Geographer, and the Diplomat*

in all this region. The city probably bore some other name, now utterly forgotten.[73]

Here, then, it is apparent that the biblical description is more important than a possible linguistic connection, and the identification of the ruins at er-Ruhaibeh as Rehoboth is not accepted because the site deviates from what one would expect of the site based on the biblical account.

In identifying biblical sites, Robinson and Smith interacted with two thousand years of church and local traditions about the names of places and about the locations of biblical events. Working with these materials makes up a large portion of the book; Robinson writes, 'the attempt made to point out, in most cases, not only what is truth and what is merely legendary tradition, but also to show how far the latter reaches back'.[74] For Robinson, the trustworthiness of a tradition about a location's relationship to biblical history depended on how well that particular location matched the description given in the biblical text. Robinson makes this explicit in his account of their visit to Rachel's tomb: 'The general correctness of the tradition which has fixed upon this spot for the tomb of Rachel, cannot well be drawn in question; since it is fully supported by the circumstances of the Scriptural narrative'.[75] Here, Scripture itself is not questioned.

There are, however, instances when Robinson calls into question the accuracy of the scriptural description of locations. For example, he compares the geographic description given in 1 Sam. 14:4-5 with a location in the passage of Michmash: 'These would seem to be the two rocks mentioned in connexion with Jonathan's adventure; they are not indeed so "sharp" as the language of Scripture would seem to imply; but they are the only rocks of the kind in the vicinity'.[76] These challenges to Scripture are not usually substantial. Yet there are instances in which the experience of the topography of the land makes it difficult for Robinson to understand how biblical events could have unfolded the way that they did. For example, he writes while in the southern deserts:

> How in these wide deserts, this host of more than two million souls, having no traffic nor intercourse with the surrounding hordes, could find supplies of food and water sufficient for their support, without a constant miracle, I for one am unable to divine. Yet among them we read only of occasional longings and complaints; while the tribes that now roam over the same regions, although numbering scarcely as many thousands, are exposed to famine and privation of every kind; and at best, obtain only a meager and precarious subsistence.[77]

73. Robinson, *Biblical Researches*, p. 291.
74. Robinson, *Biblical Researches*, p. vii.
75. Robinson, *Biblical Researches*, p. 323.
76. Robinson, *Biblical Researches*, p. 116.
77. Robinson, *Biblical Researches*, p. 613.

This does not mean that he is actually questioning Scripture, however. For immediately prior to these words, Robinson explains how the itinerary given in the Bible for the Israelites' wandering could have worked.[78] His attempts to reinterpret Scripture are based on the realities he encountered while travelling. The physical experience helps lead one to a better understanding of the Bible, in Robinson's perspective, but does not undermine its authority. If anything, unexplainable circumstances simply emphasized the divine presence in scriptural events.

Throughout, Robinson's critical stance toward traditions is apparent.[79] For example, at one point, he writes, 'I must request the reader to bear in mind that for the lapse of more than fifteen centuries, Jerusalem has been the abode not only of mistaken piety, but also of credulous superstition, not unmingled with pious fraud'.[80] Part of this mistrust reflects Robinson's Protestant beliefs, for as he writes (here with the original italics and caps preserved): 'I would particularly direct the reader's attention,—that *all ecclesiastical tradition respecting the ancient places in and around Jerusalem and throughout Palestine,* IS OF NO VALUE, *except so far as it is supported by circumstances known to us from the Scriptures or from other contemporary testimony'*.[81] Robinson generally was unimpressed with the knowledge of Scripture held by local religious figures and was convinced that Christian pilgrimage was encouraged at shrines because of the revenue that it generated not because of any deeply held faith about the historicity of the identification.[82] Robinson's critical stance toward ecclesiastical tradition, especially in regard to the holy sites around Jerusalem, became points of controversy for the first readers of his book.[83]

---

78. Robinson writes: 'In this way, the scriptural account of the journeyings of the Israelites, becomes perfectly harmonious and intelligible. The eighteen stations mentioned only in the general list in the book of Numbers, as preceding the arrival at Kadesh, are then apparently to be referred to this eight and thirty years of wandering, during which the people of Ezion-geber, and afterwards returned northwards a second time to Kadesh, in the hope of passing directly through the land of Edom. Their wanderings extended doubtless over the western desert; although the stations named are probably only those head-quarters where the tabernacle was pitched, and where Moses and the elders and priests encamped; while the main body of the people was scattered in various directions' (Robinson, *Biblical Researches,* pp. 612-13).

79. For further comment on this, see Rachel Hallote, *Bible, Map, and Spade: The American Palestine Exploration Society, Frederick Jones Bliss, and the Forgotten Story of Early American Archaeology* (Piscataway, NJ: Gorgias Press, 2006), p. 12.

80. Robinson, *Biblical Researches,* p. 371.

81. Robinson, *Biblical Researches,* pp. 374-75.

82. For a discussion of Robinson's reaction to the Monastery of St. Catherine (the traditional location of Mt. Sinai) see Silberman, *Digging,* p. 41.

83. Ben-Arieh, *Rediscovery,* p. 133.

3. *The Strongman, the Geographer, and the Diplomat* 113

The especially distrustful approach to ecclesiastical authority consistent with Robinson's Protestant background is manifest in his evaluation of sources external to church traditions as being of more merit. For example, he writes:

> But there is in Palestine another kind of tradition, with which the monasteries have had nothing to do; and of which they have apparently in every age known little or nothing. I mean, *the preservation of the ancient names of places among the common people*. This is truly a national and native tradition; not derived from in any degree from the influence of foreign convents or masters; but drawn in by the peasant with his mother's milk, and deeply seated in the genius of the Semitic languages.[84]

This suggests that the locals have an almost primordial knowledge of biblical topography. Yet in other parts of the text, Robinson makes it quite clear that he also does not trust local informants' accounts of the locations of biblical sites. For example, he writes, 'A tolerably certain method of finding any place at will, is to ask an Arab if its name exists. He is sure to answer Yes; and to point out some spot at hand as its location.'[85] This contradiction is fundamental to how Robinson establishes an American 'claim' to the Holy Land, for he demonstrates that through his scientific method and command of Scripture, he understands the land better than the locals, whose understandings are confused at best.

The same skepticism is apparent in Robinson's accounts of his explorations of Jerusalem. Much of the three volumes of *Biblical Researches* is spent discussing Robinson and Smith's exploration of the city. The sections on Jerusalem are something of a hybrid between a typical nineteenth-century travel narrative, in which the various people met on the journey are described and their exploits recounted, and a more scientific discussion of the antiquities of Jerusalem. The scientific data is of primary importance, and Robinson describes their goals while there:

> The object of my journey to Jerusalem was not to visit friends, nor to inquire into the character of the present population, nor to investigate their political or moral state, except as incidental points. My one great object was the city itself, in its topographical and historical relations, its site, its hills, its dales, its remains of antiquity, the traces of its ancient population; in short, every thing connected with it that could have a bearing upon the illustration of the Scriptures.[86]

Robinson continues, with a description of the methodology of their investigations:

---

84. Robinson, *Biblical Researches*, pp. 375-76.
85. Robinson, *Biblical Researches*, p. 165.
86. Robinson, *Biblical Researches*, pp. 335-36.

> Time and again we visited the more important spots, and repeated our observations; comparing meanwhile what we had seen ourselves with the accounts of ancient writers and former travellers, until at length conjectures or opinions were ripened into conviction or gradually abandoned. Our motto was in the words, though not exactly in the sense of the Apostle: 'Prove all things; hold fast that which is good'. During the same interval, I also took many measurements both within and around the city.[87]

Robinson provides accounts of these visits, and explains the reasoning behind identifications of the sites or rejections of traditions about the sites. Inscriptions are copied and presented to the reader.

Robinson articulates a Protestant approach to the investigation of the land and its ancient sites, although he does not explicitly identify it as Protestant.[88] He writes:

> we early adopted two general principles, by which to govern ourselves in our examination of the Holy Land. The *first* was, to avoid as far as possible all contact with the convents and the authority of the monks; to examine everywhere for ourselves with the Scriptures in our hands; and to apply for information solely to the native Arab population. The *second* was, to leave as much as possible the beaten tack, and direct our journies and researches to those portions of the country which had been least visited. By acting upon these two principles, we were able to arrive at many results that to us were new and unexpected; and it is these results alone, which give a value (if any it have) to the present work.[89]

No doubt this approach did produce a work that was substantially different from the pilgrimage itineraries that had come before and marked a fundamental change in the approach to understanding the biblical lands. For here Robinson was creating new pilgrimage locations based on seemingly positivist criteria, as opposed to doctrine or tradition. Thus a Protestant approach to biblical geography was embedded within the academic program that continued to dominate biblical archaeology until the 1950s. Throughout his book, Robinson draws parallels between the ancient Jews and nineteenth-century Protestants, trying to link them across time and space.[90]

In Robinson's book, there is a clear connection between Israelite claims to the land in the Old Testament and the emotional claims of the land made by nineteenth-century Protestants. As Long has suggested, the act of mapping the Holy Land helped create an emotional connection to what was

---

87. Robinson, *Biblical Researches*, p. 336.
88. Rachel Hallote also points out the specifically puritanical concerns addressed by Robinson (Hallote, *Bible, Map, and Spade*, pp. 11-12).
89. Robinson, *Biblical Researches*, pp. 377-78.
90. Moscrop, *Measuring*, p. 20.

3. *The Strongman, the Geographer, and the Diplomat* 115

an otherwise alien-seeming Ottoman Empire through the biblical links.[91] This is embedded in Robinson's rhetorical approach. Much of Robinson's account consists of descriptions, almost an enumeration of the places of the Holy Land. Following a biblical style, Robinson describes the land in an essentially list-like manner. For example, near the cluster of mountains referred to generally in his time as Mt Sinai, Robinson writes:

> Taking our station on the highest part of the plain, or water-shed, and looking towards the convent, we found the general direction of the plain and valley of the convent to be S. E. ½ S. or more exactly S. 41° E. The mountain on the left or N.E. of the plain, called the Jebel el-Fureia', is long and high, with table-land on the top and pasturage for camels. It extends northward along the pass by which we ascended, and southwards to Wady Sheikh at the S.E. corner of the plain. South of this Wady, the mountain which overhangs the convent on the East, is called Jebel ed-Deir, and also Mountain of the Cross.[92]

The description goes on at length. Robinson does not just list topographic features. He also provides measurements directly in the narrative. Of the same plain, he writes:

> We measured across the plain, where we stood, along the water-shed, and found the breadth to be at that point 2700 English feet or 900 yards; though in some parts it is wider. The distance to the base of Horeb, measured in like manner, was 7000 feet, or 2333 yards. The northern slope of the plain, North of where we stood, we judged to be somewhat less than a mile in length by one third of a mile in breadth.[93]

This was useful information for geographers and other specialists attempting to make spatial and historical sense of the region at the time. However, the readers of *Biblical Researches* were much more varied, and it is interesting to think of what the seminary reader would have made of these detailed and numerous descriptions. No doubt many skipped through these sections, merely taking them as evidence of the scientific approach that Robinson used. As with other travel writing from the time, these sections are interwoven directly into the narrative and are part of the adventure. The description and measuring of the land are the heroic actions of the protagonists. Later on, Robinson justifies the necessity for presenting such detail in the midst of the narrative: 'The examination of this afternoon convinced us, that here was space enough to satisfy all the requisitions of the Scriptural narrative, so far as it relates to the assembling of the congregation to receive the law'.[94] So, the point of the detailed descriptions and measure-

---

91. Long, *Imagining*, pp. 133-34.
92. Robinson, *Biblical Researches,* p. 139.
93. Robinson, *Biblical Researches,* p. 140.
94. Robinson, *Biblical Researches,* p. 141.

ments in that section is to provide proof that this was the location where the biblical event occurred. This was scientific evidence related to one of the most important elements in biblical history. Similar explanations of the role of measurement are found scattered throughout the book.

Later in the account, Robinson presents a more romantic view of the same issue, and one that would have well resonated with his readers:

> Our conviction was strengthened, that here or on some one of the adjacent cliffs was the spot, where the Lord 'descended in fire' and proclaimed the law. Here lay the plain where the whole congregation might be assembled; here was the mount that could be approached and touched, if not forbidden; and here the mountain brow, where alone the lightnings and the thick cloud would be visible, and the thunders and the voice of the trump be heard, when the Lord 'came down in the sight of all the people upon Mount Sinai'. We gave ourselves up to the impressions of the awful scene; and read with a feeling that will never be forgotten, the sublime account of the transaction and the commandments there promulgated, in the original words as recorded by the great Hebrew legislator.[95]

Here was a narrative account of the direct experience of biblical history through travel in the Bible lands.

Robinson's analysis was critical of traditions surrounding biblical geography, but that does not mean that the work, in any way, attempts to undermine the veracity of the Bible. On the contrary, *Biblical Researches* provides a positivist confirmation of the legitimacy of the text, establishing a major theme in biblical archaeology (that still continues today in non-specialist and pseudo-scholarly forms of the discipline). This approach is well exemplified in his treatment of the exodus and the parting of the Red Sea. On the route of the exodus, Robinson takes the biblical account very literally and, using its veracity as a basic premise, tests various hypotheses about the route. The gravity with which he approaches the biblical text is apparent in this passage, where he rejects the possibility that the Israelites began their journey near Cairo or Heliopolis:

> We were quite satisfied from our own observations, that they could not have passed to the Red Sea from any point near Heliopolis or Cairo in three days, the longest interval which the language of the narrative allows. Both the distance and the want of water on all the routes, are fatal to such an hypothesis.[96]

Calculating the number of Israelites who would have been part of the exodus (basing his estimations on numbers given in the Bible, treating them literally) and comparing this with estimations of the typical distances traversed by modern armies per day, he determines that a march of this

---

95. Robinson, *Biblical Researches*, p. 158.
96. Robinson, *Biblical Researches*, pp. 74-75.

distance would take five days. Thus, since the biblical account suggests it was done in three days, he rejects this particular route.

Robinson similarly looks for a scientific explanation for the miracle of the parting of the Red Sea. He justifies this on the grounds that the Lord enacted this miracle through a strong east wind and thus:

> The miracle therefore is represented as mediate; not a direct suspension of, or interference with the laws of nature, but a miraculous adaptation of those laws to produce a required result. It was wrought by natural means supernaturally applied. For this reason we are here entitled to look only for the natural effects arising from the operation of such a cause.[97]

So Robinson justifies his desire to find a natural corollary of the parting of the Red Sea not as an attempt to understand the miraculous nature of God's action, but rather as looking for the physical manifestation of what is referred to as a natural process enacted through God's agency.

Nevertheless, Robinson is forced to emend the text somewhat (or at least offer a charitable reading) in order to make sense of there having been a naturally manifest east wind:

> In the somewhat indefinite phraseology of the Hebrew, an east wind means any wind from the eastern quarter; and would include the N.E. wind, which often prevails in this region. Now it will be obvious from the inspection of any good map of the Gulf, that a strong N.E. wind acting here upon the ebb tide, would necessarily have the effect to drive out the waters from the small arm of the sea which runs up by Suez, and also from the end of the Gulf itself, leaving the shallower portions dry; while the more northern part of the arm, which was anciently broader and deeper than at present, would still remain covered with water. Thus the waters would be divided, and be a wall (or defence) to the Israelites on the right hand and on the left.[98]

Robinson provides a natural, geographically based explanation that would have been convincing to his readers (though in reality scientifically unsound). His empirical explanation seemingly confirms the account of the parting of the Red Sea.

Robinson is pretty evenhanded in his presentation of various theories, as long as they could be harmonized with the Bible. If there was room for disagreement with his conclusions, he provides various possibilities and announces the divergent options to his readers. In terms of the location of the parting of the Red Sea, he is never able to come to any clear conclusions and is explicit about this:

> Our own observation on the spot, led both my companion and myself to incline to the other supposition, that the passage took place across the

---

97. Robinson, *Biblical Researches*, pp. 82-83.
98. Robinson, *Biblical Researches*, p. 83.

> shoals adjacent to Suez on the south and southwest. But among the many changes which have occurred here in the lapse of ages, it is of course impossible to decide with certainty as to the precise spot; nor is this necessary. Either of the above suppositions satisfies the conditions of the case; on either the deliverance of the Israelites was equally great, and the arm of Jehovah gloriously revealed.[99]

Regardless of where the event took place, Robinson asserts that it is a testament to the glory of God. Tacitly, there is a sense that his observations have confirmed that the parting of the Red Sea did take place, despite the fact that it is never claimed that this kind of proof was necessary nor is it actually proved by this evidence.

In their travels, even without miracles, Robinson and Smith felt that they were seeing Scripture lived out before them in the lives of the nineteenth-century inhabitants of Palestine. This was a corrupt form of scriptural life, as the people lived in squalor and ignorance (in Robinson's view), but their behaviours preserved ancient practices, in part due to what he saw as their lack of progress over the past two thousand years. The ethnographic analogies were especially apparent to Robinson in terms of agricultural practices and technologies. Upon seeing people gleaning in the fields near Bethlehem, he writes, 'Here indeed was the scene of the beautiful narrative of Ruth, gleaning in the fields of Boaz after his reapers; and it required no great stretch of imagination to call up again those transactions before our eyes'.[100] Similar practices elsewhere illuminated the New Testament (Mt. 22.11; Mk 2.23; and Lk. 6.1):

> The wheat was now ripening; and we had here a beautiful illustration of Scripture. Our Arabs 'were a hungered', and going into the fields, they 'plucked the ears of corn, and did eat, rubbing them in their hands'. On being questioned, they said this was an old custom, and no one would speak against it; they were supposed to be hungry, and it was allowed as a charity. We saw this afterwards in repeated instances.[101]

Food production equipment used in a nineteenth-century Bedouin camp appeared unchanged since biblical times: 'In another tent a woman was kneeling and grinding at the hand-mill. These mills are doubtless those of scriptural times, and are similar to Scottish *quern*.'[102] Perhaps more noteworthy were those practices that shed light on more obscure biblical passages, such as Deut. 11:10, which mentions 'watering with the foot'. Robinson notes the following practices at a well near 'Ajjur:

---

99. Robinson, *Biblical Researches*, p. 86.
100. Robinson, *Biblical Researches*, p. 161.
101. Robinson, *Biblical Researches*, p. 192.
102. Robinson, *Biblical Researches*, pp. 180-81.

> On the platform [of the well] was fixed a small reel for the rope, which a man seated on a level with the axis, wound up, by pulling the upper part of the reel towards him with his hands, while he at the same time pushed the lower part from him with the feet. This may not improbably have been the ancient Egyptian manner of 'watering with the foot'.[103]

These kinds of observations would come to be an important component of biblical archaeology as it emerged as its own discipline. By the end of the Victorian era, it was widely believed that God had preserved life as it was in scriptural times in the Palestine of the nineteenth century as a means of helping Christians better understand otherwise outdated references and practices mentioned in the Bible.[104]

More curious observations of similarities between past and present suggested the lingering effects of biblical events. These kinds of notices are not particularly common in the text, but when they do appear, Robinson's deviation from his more typically critical approach seems quite striking. This is most apparent in regards to comments made when the party was camped near Jericho. Robinson writes:

> At our encampment over 'Ain Terâbeh the night before we reached this place, we overheard our Arabs asking the Khatîb for a paper or written charm, to protect them from the women of Jericho; and from their conversation, it seemed that illicit intercourse between the latter and strangers who come here, is regarded as a matter of course. Strange, that the inhabitants of the valley should have retained this character from the earliest ages; and that the sins of Sodom and Gomorrah should still flourish upon the same accursed soil.[105]

It is hard to know what to make of this account, and one does not want to read too much into it, but it would seem that he believed that the sins of Sodom and Gomorrah have somehow stained the region permanently.

Robinson's studies established some of the main features of the early explorations of the Holy Land, although as Rachel Hallote has pointed out, the thoroughness of this work meant that little had to be replicated for many years.[106] It is remarkable that over the course of only five months (over two separate trips), Robinson was able to establish a field of study and produce a work of such foundational importance that Claude Condor, of the Palestine Exploration Fund (PEF), could claim that modern biblical research was based on what Robinson accomplished.[107] His emphasis on historical

---

103. Robinson, *Biblical Researches*, p. 351.
104. For more on this belief as expressed in the early twentieth century by Charles Foster Kent (who was Woolsey Professor of Biblical Literature at Yale College), see Long, *Imagining*, pp. 96-97.
105. Robinson, *Biblical Researches*, pp. 280-81.
106. Hallote, *Bible, Map, and Spade*, p. 13.
107. Ben-Arieh, *Rediscovery*, pp. 153-54.

geography was of tremendous influence. The professor extraordinary's basic approach, that the experience of the Holy Land and its material culture could help better understand Scripture, both intellectually and spiritually, influenced both archaeology and theology, and a number of similar works came out in the wake of Robinson's publishing success. What Robinson began was not a biblical archaeology in which Scripture may have been proven 'untrue'. This was a biblical archaeology that was enacted with the confidence that it would lead to material evidence of the Bible's veracity. Robinson's work was foundational for the kind of biblical archaeology later espoused by W.F. Albright, in which a positivist approach to verifying biblical history would not only verify the truth of Scripture but also make apparent God's presence through history. As Neil Silberman describes, Robinson saw a land where industry and agriculture were not present and the current inhabitants lived backward lives. Yet that same land held promise in the innumerable archaeological sites that were yet to be explored.[108] Robinson's contribution was to 'write' a map of these sites.

The Diplomat: Austen Henry Layard

Farther east, in what is now Iraq, lie the remains of the cities of the biblical enemies—the Assyrians and the Babylonians. As Britain and France established consulates in the Ottoman region, European officials had time on their hands to explore the ruins of these Mesopotamian cities, and in the 1840s, the field of Assyriology was truly born. The study of a region's history was seen as one of the explicit duties of the consulate.[109] On behalf of the British, Austen Henry Layard (Fig. 3.8) uncovered the amazing remains of an elaborate civilization, seemingly destroyed by its own success—a discovery that would help destabilize the confidence in unending progress held by the British. As Belzoni did, Layard managed to leverage his discoveries into celebrity, entangling the discoveries with his own personality. Yet unlike Belzoni, this celebrity was marshalled toward a political career rather than as a means of amassing wealth. Like Robinson, Layard would show how these finds helped illuminate Scripture, yet unlike Robinson, Layard did not do this out of a committed theological interest but as a mercenary attempt to excite public interest.

In the early part of 1849, Austen Henry Layard's *Nineveh and its Remains* was published to immediate critical acclaim and commercial success. As Seton Lloyd has stated, it is not the content of Layard's book nor its prose that captivates the reader so much as Layard's unbridled enthusiasm for the

---

108. Silberman, *Digging*, p. 45.
109. Deborah Manley and Peta Rée, *Henry Salt: Artist, Traveller, Diplomat, Egyptologist* (London: Libri, 2001), p. 130.

3. *The Strongman, the Geographer, and the Diplomat*

Fig. 3.8. Portrait of Austen Henry Layard in Bakhtiari dress, by Amadea Preziosi (1843). © Trustees of the British Museum.

adventure of it all.[110] Britain's reading public may have been introduced to the lost civilization of Assyria through some brief notices about Layard's excavations found in periodicals and perhaps through some of the materials associated with Paul Emile Botta's excavations, although given the political chaos of Paris in 1848, the French explorations were not as widely publicized. For almost all readers, this was their first encounter with Mesopotamian civilization beyond the accounts preserved in the Old Testament and in classical sources such as Herodotus and Berossus. For the next fifty years or so, the British public's experience of ancient Assyria was directly mediated through Layard's description of the culture and through the materials that he brought back with him to England.

Layard's road to Nineveh was more accidental than intentional.[111] Henry Austen Layard was born in Paris in 1817 and spent his early years in Italy, where his sickly father was compelled to live for health reasons. Later, the

---

110. Seton Lloyd, *Foundations in the Dust: The Story of Mesopotamian Exploration* (New York: Thames & Hudson, 1947), p. 87.

111. Much has been written about Layard, and the following treatment is not meant to be complete. To readers interested primarily in the history of the first excavations in Mesopotamia, Mogens Trolle Larsen's detailed account is recommended: *The Conquest of Assyria* (1996), written from the perspective of an Assyriologist. An older account of the origins of Assyriology is Seton Lloyd's *Foundations in the Dust: The Story of Mesopotamian Exploration* (New York: Thames & Hudson, 1947). Those interested in all of Layard's life are advised to consult Gordon Waterfield's 1963 biography *Layard of Nineveh*, although it should be mentioned that this work takes on an almost hagiographic tone as Waterfield was attempting to repair Layard's reputation (which had suffered after

Layards moved back to England because of the influence of Henry Austen's wealthy uncle, a man that wielded enough power to have Henry Austen switch the order of his names to Austen Henry. While living in England under his uncle's sphere of influence, Layard developed a love for things Eastern (especially orientalist travel literature), partly due to his encounters with a young Benjamin Disraeli, who at this time was living an extravagant life as a Byronesque travel writer and adventurer. For Layard, the excitement of adventures in the East were much more appealing to him than the monotony of life as a legal clerk, which was his first attempt at a profession. When his other uncle suggested that he start a legal business in Ceylon, he made earnest preparations to do so.

In 1839, accompanied by Charles Mitford, a more experienced traveler, Layard set out for Ceylon, a destination that he would never reach. By 1840, the two travellers had arrived in Mosul (in modern-day Iraq), where they spent two weeks exploring the Assyrian tells. This led to a two-month stay in the British residency at Baghdad, where Layard studied what was then known of Mesopotamian and Persian antiquities. It was then that Mitford and Layard parted ways as Mitford wanted to continue on to Ceylon; Layard had fallen in love with the Near East. Layard spent the next two years travelling around Mesopotamia and Persia, having numerous adventures—being robbed, beaten and narrowly escaping numerous life threatening encounters. By 1842, Layard was something of an expert on matters Eastern and was sent to brief the British consul in Constantinople, Sir Stratford Canning. On the way to see Canning, Layard stopped again in Mosul, where he met the French excavator Botta, who was digging at a nearby site. The two struck up a quick friendship, and it was then that Layard decided that he would also excavate one of the mounds.

Stratford Canning, however, was not immediately convinced of the need to send a British expedition to Mosul. He hired Layard as consular staff and eventually, under pressure from various prominent figures, including Henry Rawlinson (one of the key figures in the eventual deciphering of Akkadian—see Chapter I.2), allowed Layard to go survey the region so as to avoid a French monopoly on Assyrian antiquities. Shawn Malley has argued that this work was political from the outset and that Canning's authorization of the work was as much about creating a British diplomatic presence in the region as it was about excavating antiquities.[112] In 1845, Layard began digging. His friend Botta had been replaced by Rouet, who was less keen to work with the

---

his death). Layard's own accounts of his excavations and his various autobiographies are still quite interesting, and his popular prose still holds up today.

112. Shawn Malley, *From Archaeology to Spectacle in Victorian Britain* (Surrey: Ashgate, 2012), pp. 32-33. For a more thorough discussion of the political embeddedness of Layard's work, readers are advised to read Malley's account.

3. The Strongman, the Geographer, and the Diplomat   123

Fig. 3.9. Excavations at Kuyunjik. From Austen Henry Layard, *Discoveries among the Ruins of Nineveh and Babylon with Travels in Armenia, Kurdistan, and the Desert: Being the Result of a Second Expedition* (New York: Harper & Bros., 1853), p. 88.

Englishman in a collegial manner. Christian Rassam, the British vice-consul, was also a building contractor, so it was possible for Layard to put together an excavation team and equipment in secret. On his first day of digging, he discovered two palaces.[113] Layard's excavations did not long remain a secret, and soon he was forced to deal with the fluctuating attitude of the Turkish authorities to his digging (involving the granting and denying of the right to excavate) and competition with the French, who had claimed many of the Assyrian mounds as their own. Much of the funding for this project came from his family. He received relatively minor grants for the work from the Trustees of the British Museum, and his relationship with that institution was strained (and continued to be so for the rest of his life).

Despite the difficulties, Layard had great success in finding Assyrian treasures. As he was operating before the development of archaeological techniques, he used some of the approaches that had been developed at Pompeii and Herculaneum. Once he had identified a palace, he tunnelled through, until he found large statues or reliefs that were worth removing (Fig. 3.9). Once these were identified, he opened up the excavation area to remove them. Unlike Botta, Layard did not want to carve the monumental sculptures into smaller pieces so he developed techniques that involved leverage, pulleys, and much manpower to remove the statues from the palaces

---

113. These two palaces were the northwest palace of Ashurnasirpal II and the southwest palace of Esarhaddon, although it would be a long time yet before anyone knew this.

Fig. 3.10. Lowering the bull. From Austen Henry Layard, *A Popular Account of Discoveries at Nineveh* (London: John Murray, 1851), frontispiece.

(Fig. 3.10). As they were removed, the statues were crated up and made ready for transport back to Britain.

At this time, no one really understood what Layard was unearthing. The general tendency was to take these remains as reflecting the stories about Assyria preserved in classical accounts and to not associate them with the kings mentioned in the Old Testament (which in retrospect was a mistake). Part of the problem was that initially there was a reluctance to excavate anything that may have been construed as related to the Bible for fear of being sacrilegious. Layard also held some anticlerical values and was not intrinsically interested in looking for material remains of biblical times per se. However, Layard would eventually be convinced to use the Assyrian relationship to biblical times to promote his discoveries.

Much of the problem with understanding these materials came from the fact that nobody could read Akkadian yet. Rawlinson kept close tabs on Layard's excavations and on the inscriptions that were unearthed and was not particularly keen to share these inscriptions with other scholars working on the script. Unfortunately, Layard did not identify cuneiform as a type of writing system in his early excavations, merely thinking them to be curious pieces of pottery, and many tablets were not preserved in these excavations, despite Rawlinson's supervision.[114] Rawlinson himself suggested to Layard that the site that he was working on was the ancient city of Nineveh, a suggestion that was proven wrong after the initial publication of *Nineveh and its Remains* (it turned out that this was Nimrud). He continued to dig

---

114. Lloyd, *Foundations*, p. 125

Fig. 3.11. 'Human-headed and eagle-winged bull from Nimrud', *Illustrated London News,* October 26, 1850.

at Nimrud (thinking it Nineveh) until mid-May 1847, when he turned his attention to Kuyunjik, a mound that had first been excavated by Botta.

By the time Layard started work at Kuyunjik, his excavations were getting moderate notice at home in England. Occasional newspaper articles and longer feature stories by journalists suggested to the public that amazing discoveries were being made in Mesopotamia. *Athenaeum* wrote five articles on Layard throughout 1846, for example.[115] Layard had been aware of the importance of currying favour with the general public from very early on. Soon after his excavations began, he wrote to Stratford Canning explaining that the French government's support of Botta was based on the wide interest shown his work by the French public. Layard felt that the same strategy would work for his excavations, although he was unable to begin promoting his work until later.[116] On June 25, 1847, the first set of Assyrian antiquities was put on display by the British Museum, and shortly thereafter (Figs. 3.11 and 3.12), Layard returned to England a more famous man than when he had left.

Despite Layard's growing presence in British society, the Trustees of the British Museum and the government more generally were still not convinced of the importance of his work. In January of 1848, Layard was turned down for a five-year government grant to continue his excavations. He was

---

115. For example, see *Athenaeum*, October 10, 1846, pp. 1046-47.
116. Mogens Trolle Larsen, *The Conquest of Assyria* (New York: Routledge, 1996), p. 92.

Fig. 3.12. Colossal statue of a winged lion from the northwest palace of Ashurnasirpal II (Room B). © Trustees of the British Museum

permitted to write an account of his expedition to Nineveh, but to be written on his own, without support from the British Museum. After *Nineveh and its Remains* became a best-seller in 1849, the trustees were somewhat obliged to begin funding his work again, although the sums given him were insufficient for the work that they wanted done. The British Museum gave him £3000 to run an excavation and the Foreign office provided him with a salary of £250 a year. Layard's relationship with the British Museum was never good, and this relationship remained sour even after his 1866 appointment as a trustee, ironic since his name is intrinsically connected to that of the museum.

When Layard returned to the field to work, he concentrated his own efforts at Nimrud (which Rawlinson now thought was biblical Calah), and his assistant Horzmud Rassam supervised excavations at Kuyunjik. In 1850, Layard travelled south to excavate Babylon but was disappointed by the results and quickly abandoned that project. In January of 1851 he travelled farther south to Nippur (where he found only Parthian materials), and although he wanted to, he was not able to excavate at Uruk due to the political conditions there. By April of 1851, Layard was finished with life in Mesopotamia and in July returned to London, never to conduct an archaeological excavation again.

Despite his short time as an archaeologist, Layard's writings kept his name associated with archaeology for the rest of his life. The 1849 publication of *Nineveh and its Remains* was a watershed moment in the development of archaeology as a popular discipline, that is to say, as a discipline that the non-specialist public would come to hold widespread interest in and feel that they had some stake in. While classical archaeology and local British archaeology were well established as antiquarian pursuits, Layard's book was one of the first large-scale archaeological narratives aimed at the wide Victorian reading public, arguably the largest literate group that had existed up until that time. Unlike the *Description d'Egypte* or Botta's publication of his excavations, *Monuments de Ninive* (five volumes published between 1849 and 1850), *Nineveh and its Remains* was produced in a form that was accessible to a larger reading public, both in terms of content and in terms of price. The irony of Botta's publication is, as Larsen has noted, that neither Layard nor Rawlinson (arguably the two people who most needed these volumes) could afford to purchase them.[117] Rather than producing massive folio size tomes, as Botta did (although these had been delayed by France's political instability of 1848), working with the publisher John Murray, Layard produced a two-volume work that was printed on smaller-sized paper in a form that could be readily digested by those without any background in ancient studies.[118] In 1851, an abridged version was published, intended for the train stall market (in a series called *Murray's Reading for Rail*) that had about two-thirds less text but more illustrations. This was a major best-seller. This publication plan aimed at popular audiences was partly due to the fact that neither the British Museum nor the government were willing to subvent the publication costs in the way that the equivalent French institutions were willing to do for Botta. The popular publication strategy also reflected a genuine desire on the part of Layard for as many people as possible to have access to these works.

Part of what made *Nineveh and its Remains* (and its subsequent versions and reissues) a success was that this was not an archaeological report in the way that this genre has developed today. Layard was hardly ever on hand at the site and likely did not have enough information to even begin to approach the kind of detailed reporting that came to be expected of an archaeological excavation only a short time later. As Larsen has noted, unlike the academic

---

117. Larsen, *Conquest*, p. 154.

118. Paul Emile Botta's publication of his exploration of Mesopotamia met with only minimal circulation. His five-volume *Monument de Ninive* cost more to produce than his actual excavations but was supported by a large state subvention from the French monarchy in 1848. That same year, the monarchy was overthrown, and the volumes were not actually published until 1849, with a circulation of only about three hundred. So whereas anyone in England could pick up a copy of one of Layard's volumes almost no one had access to Botta's works, even in France.

fields of philology and literary studies archaeology was not an established discipline yet. As he states, 'its prestige was tied first of all to the discoveries themselves, great works of art or strange and interesting objects. It was therefore characteristically a popular interest which related to the reliefs and bulls . . . rather than the more academically oriented magazines and journals. . . .'[119]

Furthermore, as of 1849, cuneiform writing could not really be read so there was only minimal historical context in which to understand the Assyrian materials that he had uncovered. Layard needed to write this work quickly, so he wrote his report in one of his favourite genres—Eastern travel literature. The first part of the book could be any travel story from the time, featuring dangerous and frustrating encounters with the locals, experiences of new customs and exotic landscapes, culminating in the discovery of a long-lost ancient city. For the abbreviated 1851 version, the bulk of the text is the travel narrative, in which the excavations of artifacts are treated along with descriptions of customs of the lands and exciting stories of dangerous situations. Layard was well aware that writing the book as a travel narrative would appeal to the general public, and he states as much in an apologetic letter to Rawlinson.[120] The second part of the book is more academic. Although still centering on Layard's personal experiences, it explores how those experiences have shed light on an ancient Assyria. This second portion of the book was mostly omitted from the popular 1851 version, but parts appear again in the exhibition guide to the Nineveh Gallery at the Crystal Palace and in other formats throughout the nineteenth century. Layard's publisher, John Murray, also sought a market for *Nineveh and its Remains* in the United States. Murray was particularly convinced that the biblical connections that Assyria held would make Americans particularly interested in the work, and so Layard correlated his work as much as possible with the biblical accounts, despite his initial hesitation. The biblical connections were especially emphasized in the abridged 1851 edition, with these notes expanded upon there.

The reception of *Nineveh and its Remains* was widely positive, and most major periodicals reviewed the book. The review that was to appear in *The Times* was initially quite negative. However, Layard's publisher, John Murray, showed an advanced copy to Layard's Aunt Sarah. She quickly wrote a very positive review to replace the negative one, and Aunt Sarah's review appeared in the February 9, 1849, edition of *The Times*.[121] Since reviews were often unsigned, hardly anyone knew that this positive review was writ-

119. Larsen, *Conquest*, p. 147.
120. Larsen, *Conquest*, p. 155.
121. Gordon Waterfield, *Layard of Nineveh* (London: John Murray & Sons, 1963), pp. 192-93.

ten by his aunt (including Layard until after the fact). Frederick Bohrer has surveyed some of the major reviews of *Nineveh* and has found that while mostly positive the reviews are very different from one another, emphasizing different elements of the book depending on the political background of the periodical. *The Examiner*, a nationalist periodical, emphasized Layard's role as a British patriot, whereas *The Spectator* concentrated on Layard's perseverance without proper government support.[122] The political ambiguity of *Nineveh and its Remains* (despite Layard's liberal tendencies) made it appealing to a large British audience. Malley has argued that these reviews 'were crucial for lionizing Layard and raising interest in his finds through consistent reference to the three great themes of biblical history, cultural continuity, and imperial agency'.[123]

The political ramifications of Layard's books should be considered as this is one of the earliest loci where formal imperialist governance and archaeological practice are institutionalized. In this early instance, the relationships between the archaeologists and various governments were not yet clearly defined. Layard perpetuates the notion (established by Napoleon) that archaeology is a component of the imperialist enterprise (although there are numerous other ways that Layard's writing seems distinct from more typical Victorian accounts). Bohrer is correct to point out that in this work '[a]rchaeology emerges as a gesture of Western superiority'.[124] In many ways, *Nineveh and its Remains* continues the conventions established in *Description d'Egypte*, especially the visual conventions in which the locals are portrayed in subservient postures to the European travellers or juxtaposed with the 'more advanced' ancient cultures, which were thought by Europeans to have a stronger connection to Europe than contemporary Asia or Africa. Bohrer points out that these particular tropes are readily apparent in the illustrations of the transport of large artifacts, such as the bull. In one illustration, the backs of the locals are turned to the viewer, signifying to Bohrer the context from which these artifacts are being removed.[125] Malley makes similar comments, arguing that 'Archaeological value is measured by the immediacy and tangibility of Arab ignorance'.[126]

The depiction of archaeological knowledge as symptomatic of Western superiority is not only manifest in the illustrations—it is also apparent in

---

122. Frederick Bohrer, *Orientalism and Visual Culture: Imagining Mesopotamia in Nineteenth-Century Europe* (Cambridge: Cambridge University Press, 2003), p. 152.

123. Shawn Malley. *From Archaeology to Spectacle in Victorian Britain* (Surrey: Ashgate, 2012), p. 46. See also Shawn Malley, 'Austen Henry Layard and the Periodical Press: Middle Eastern Archaeology and the Excavation of Cultural Identity in Mid-Nineteenth Century England', *Victorian Review* 22 (1996), pp. 152-70.

124. Bohrer, *Orientalism*, p. 149.

125. Bohrer, *Orientalism*, p. 144.

126. Malley, *From Archaeology to Spectacle*, p. 52.

Fig. 3.13 Discovering the head. From Austen Henry Layard, *A Popular Account of Discoveries at Nineveh* (London: John Murray, 1851), p. 48.

episodes of Layard's encounter with locals. Most often the cultural superiority is conveyed in accounts of the reactions of the Arab workers to the discoveries of the artifacts. Layard uses these episodes almost as comic relief, such as when he describes the unwarranted terror on the part of the Arab workmen. For example, Layard writes about the discovery of a human-headed bull (Fig. 3.13):

> I was not surprised that the Arabs had been amazed and terrified at this apparition. It required no stretch of imagination to conjure up the most strange fancies. . . . One of the workmen on catching the first glimpse of the monster, had thrown down his basket and had run off towards Mosul as fast as his legs could carry him.[127]

Similarly, Layard seems to revel in Arab misinterpretation of the significance of the objects. He quotes Abd-ur-rahman's comments regarding the same human-headed bull that had so terrified the Arab workman:

> When they [Abd-ur-rahman and 'half his tribe'] beheld the head they all cried together, 'There is no God but God, and Mahommed is his Prophet!'

---

127. Austen Henry Layard, *Nineveh and its Remains*, I (London: John Murray, 1849), p. 66.

3. *The Strongman, the Geographer, and the Diplomat*

Fig. 3.14. 'Baiting the Nineveh bull', *Punch* 28 (1855).

> It was some time before the Sheikh could be prevailed upon to descend into the pit, and convince himself that the image he saw was of stone. 'This is not the work of men's hands', exclaimed he, 'but of those infidel giants of whom the Prophet, peace be with him! has said, that they were higher than the tallest date tree; this is one of the idols which Noah, peace be with him! cursed before the flood'. In this opinion, the result of a careful examination, all the bystanders concurred.[128]

Layard's dry wit is evident in his description of the 'careful examination' and the evaluation of the artifacts, indirectly demonstrating the importance of European analysis of these artifacts.

It is not just Layard's portrayal of Easterners that was influential; Layard came to play a major role in forming British imperial policy in the region. At the age of thirty-six, after having made some of the most important archaeological discoveries of all time, Layard retired from archaeological practice. Throughout the rest of his life, however, his archaeological fame was the foundation for his celebrity, and this celebrity (along with the political connections made during his work in the Foreign Office) led him to a career in politics. In Parliament, Layard was often jokingly referred to as the 'Member from Nineveh', and his relationship to Assyriology was never forgotten by the periodical press. His good friends called him 'Mr Bull', a play on both the Nineveh Bull he was famed for discovering and the cartoonish personification of Great Britain itself, John Bull (Fig. 3.14

---

128. Layard, *Nineveh*, I, pp. 66-67.

Fig. 3.15. 'The member for Nineveh digs out the British bull', *Punch* 28 (1855).

and 3.15).[129] Layard was often called upon to consult on archaeological matters, and other archaeological pioneers, such as Heinrich Schliemann, called upon him for advice. However, after his marriage, his interest in Assyriology waned and was replaced by an interest in Italian art.

Layard's postarchaeological political career began in January 1852 when he spent eleven days as the undersecretary to Lord Granville of the Foreign Office. When this government collapsed, he ran for office and became the liberal member for Aylesbury in Berkshire. From that point forward, he held a series of posts, the most noteworthy of which were the diplomatic posts he held in Spain (roughly 1869–1877) and Turkey (roughly 1877–1884). Throughout, his political career was marked by inconsistencies. He was well liked but quick to anger when confronted by his critics. His status as a liberal was often in jeopardy as he did not get along with William Gladstone, the most prominent liberal politician of the latter half of the nineteenth century. Yet he did get along quite well with a character from his youth, the writer–adventurer, now-Tory politician Benjamin Disraeli, a fact that often led to public criticisms of Layard by his own party. Of interest here is how his political career and his public reception were entangled with his celebrity as an archaeologist.

---

129. For more on *Punch*'s satirical cartoons of 'Layard the Bull' in the context of the Crimean War, see Malley, *From Archaeology to Spectacle,* pp. 119-24.

Upon his leaving the post of Commissioner of Works and Buildings to become ambassador to Spain, the periodical press commented on this through recourse to his Assyriological background. In an October 27, 1869, article, *The Times* editorialized that it was a disappointment that Layard would no longer be in charge of public works, stating, 'We had a man at the head of the Department of Works . . . who must be in a position to know that from the time of Nineveh no city of similar importance has been so ugly and has boasted so few fine buildings as London'. *Punch*, from its typical comedic view, published a poem and illustration commenting on this issue in November 6, 1869, issue. The illustration, captioned 'Don Layardos in Madrid', depicts Layard riding a bucking Nineveh Bull, saluting the crowd with his hat surrounded by excited toreadors. The accompanying poem of the same name (subtitled 'A Spanish Ballad') begins by mirroring *The Times*' sentiment: 'We had thought if any office could have kept thee from unrest, 'Twas the Aedileship[130] of London, arbiter of art confest: That if e'er peg fitted socket—round to round and square to square—Don Layardos and the Board of Works that peg and socket were'. The poem goes on to describe, in comic terms, the quarrelsome nature of Spanish internal politics at the time and the removal of the previous British ambassador from the post. It continues by questioning the wisdom of 'El Cid Gladstone's choice of Layard for a diplomatic post, given his reputation, writing about Layard, 'With the habit hot upon thee still of speaking out thy mind, And of punching heads whenever heads for punching thou canst find'. The 'ballad' concludes with a declaration by Layard: 'Saddle and from the Museum lead my Babylonian Bull, On his back, of Madrilenos I will face the *plaza*-full'. Despite *Punch*'s and other critics' misgivings, Layard's work in Spain was seen as generally successful, and his biographer, Waterfield, even credits him with preventing Spain from going to war with France and the United States.[131]

Yet for Layard, the post in Spain was something of an exile. He never loved Spain or the Spanish as he loved the East and his experiences there led him away from the type of liberalism espoused by Gladstone (who had been the one to post him there). Although as a young man in the Ottoman Empire, Layard had not been reticent about adopting local customs and dress, as a married diplomat in Spain, Layard embraced his 'English-ness' in response to what he perceived as the rudeness, immorality, and two-facedness of the Spanish upper classes.[132] He had begun to feel that Gladstone's desire to bring republican style governments to other countries was deeply flawed.

Layard found his way back to his beloved East by getting involved in the 'Eastern Question'. From the defeat of the Ottomans at the hands of the

---

130. An *aedile* was the ancient Roman official in charge of public works.
131. Waterfield, *Layard*, p. 356.
132. Waterfield, *Layard*, p. 321.

Russians in the Russo-Turkish War (1768–1774) until the final dissolution of the Ottoman Empire and its division among the Allied powers at the Treaty of Versailles (1919), the disintegration of the Ottoman Empire was one of the foremost concerns of European international diplomacy. As Malley has argued, Layard's own excavations in Assyria should be considered within the context of the Eastern Question, since they acted as 'a means of symbolic possession of Mesopotamia, a surveillance tactic in a region that assumed increasing strategic importance for Britain; protecting the overland route to India and deterring Russian expansion to the Black Sea'.[133] Here Malley follows Robert Aguirre's conceptualizations of informal imperialism to understand the strategic importance of Near Eastern archaeology, a strategic importance that still underpins archaeology in the region today.

Given that the lands of the ancient Near East were located within the Ottoman Empire, this meant that the Eastern Question was of significant concern to Near Eastern studies scholars at the time, and very often these scholars involved themselves in it. Paul Émile Botta, for example, was the French consul for Jerusalem when the Crimean War (1853–1856) broke out. The dispute began because of a conflict over the possession of Christian holy sites (the Church of the Nativity and the Church of the Holy Sepulchre) by the Roman Catholics (protected by France) and the Orthodox Christians (protected by Russia). The conflict escalated, despite attempts by Stratford Canning to smooth over the matter, and eventually France and England went to war with Russia. Although the Treaty of Paris (1856) brought the overt conflict to an end, hostilities surrounding Russia's expansion and the dissolution of the Ottoman Empire continued sporadically, exacerbated by the declining fortunes of the Ottoman Empire.

In 1875, rebellion against Ottoman authorities broke out in the Balkans, with a correspondingly violent reaction from the Ottoman sultan. In England, feelings were mixed about whether or not intervention by the Great Powers was essential. Gladstone published a pamphlet entitled *Bulgarian Horrors*, which encouraged anti-Turkish sentiments in England in the aftermath of the Turkish massacre of Christians in Bulgaria, especially creating fears that Christianity was in danger within the Ottoman Empire. In response to this pamphlet in particular (and what he thought of as a general anti-Turkish sentiment in England), Layard set his ambitions on gaining the post of ambassador to Constantinople. Layard was not convinced that Gladstone had any understanding of the East and worried that Gladstone's rhetoric and the passions of the English public would lead to a war with Turkey (that could result in Russian control of the Ottoman Empire). Layard advocated an end to the policy of diplomatic non-intervention in the Ottoman government that had been instituted by Gladstone's government and argued

---

133. Malley, *From Archaeology to Spectacle*, p. 7.

that the European powers should work to bring English-style governance to the Turks through diplomacy. In 1877, after much lobbying for the position, Layard, on the basis of his interventionist stance and knowledge of the region, was made ambassador to Constantinople.

Layard was quickly embroiled in this conflict, which became especially divisive in England. Gladstone, especially, was concerned that Layard would go too far in supporting English international interests. Gladstone was convinced that Layard was more interested in propping up the failing Ottoman Empire (as a means of preventing the expansion of Russia into this territory) than of preventing further massacres of minority groups within the Ottoman sphere of influence. During this crisis, he used British military support for Constantinople as leverage to allow archaeologists working for the British (especially Hormuzd Rassam) to remove Assyrian artifacts permanently to England (in contradiction of an 1874 law requiring artifacts to be given over to Turkish authorities).[134] In April of 1877, Russia declared war on the Ottoman Empire but quickly sued for peace after Disraeli negotiated an alliance against Russia with Austria and Germany to prevent the Russian seizure of Constantinople. On March 3, 1878, the Treaty of San Stefano was signed, which created an independent principality of Bulgaria and furthered Russian interests in the region. Throughout these events, Layard's credibility as a diplomat was called into question, especially by Gladstone's faction, and he was accused of war mongering. It was reported that Layard explained to a Turkish official: 'Do you think I, as a friend of Turkey, was sent here for nothing? Do you not see that it was to encourage you and offend Russia? Believe me; have courage. Make no peace. Fight to the End.'[135] Layard responded to these claims by a telegram, which was reported to satirical effect by *Punch* in the March 2, 1878, issue (the day before the signing of the Treaty of San Stefano). *Punch* begins by quoting his telegram: 'If sympathy for human suffering, a desire to uphold the interests and dignity of my country, and efforts to promote the cause of civil and religious liberty are considered offences, I confess to having been guilty of them'. *Punch* continues by mocking the lofty and defensive tone of Layard's grandstanding, stating, 'But as nobody has accused Mr. Layard of these 'offences', his denial is superfluous . . . what he is accused of—viz. playing the Nineveh Bull in the Stambul China-shop'. The note is accompanied by an illustration (Fig. 3.16) of the Nineveh Bull with Layard's head (and to prevent confusion, 'Layard' is written on the bull's wing). The bull

---

134. Julian E. Reade, 'Tablets at Babylon and the British Museum', in *Babylon: Myth and Reality* (ed. I.L. Finkel and M.J. Seymour; London: British Museum Press, 2008), pp. 74-80 (77).

135. Waterfield, *Layard*, p. 401.

Fig. 3.16. 'Playing the Nineveh bull in the Stambul China-shop', *Punch,* March 2, 1878.

is shown ploughing into an Eastern-looking China shop, knocking over vases with labels such as 'Caution', and 'Diplomatic Propriety'.

As evident from these popular representations of Layard as a politician, his pedigree as the 'member from Nineveh' authenticated his role in British public life at the same time that it left him open to criticism. Beyond the obvious artistic and creative pleasure that the Nineveh Bull provided political cartoonists at the time, his celebrity as an archaeologist was a key part of his public persona. References to his adventures at Nineveh reinforced notions that he was a keenly intelligent individual with extensive international experience and a civic character that compelled him to bring Assyrian treasures to his homeland in spite of a lack of assistance from his government and the British Museum. Yet with these references to Nineveh, usually having no substantial bearing on the issues at hand, there is a hint of contempt for his celebrity and non-normative background. There is no hint that Layard wanted to escape his reputation, and in fact he seems to have been complicit in perpetuating his identity as the 'member from Nineveh'. In an April 1855, speech upon his appointment as rector of Marischal College and University, Layard stated:

> I trust that even in the discharge of public duty, and in endeavoring to form my character as a public man, they [his excavations at Nimrud] will prove to me a continual warning, that the fate which befell Nineveh and Babylon may befall the mightiest of nations, when public virtue is no longer held

in honor, when great principles no longer guide its counsels, and when the public weal is sacrificed and made subservient to private interests.[136]

Here archaeology is marshalled to argue for public service, and Layard's direct experience of the decline of great cultures compels his own sense of duty.

Austen Henry Layard is remembered in a variety of ways, as one of the fathers of Assyriology and as a model for poor archaeological field practices. This is not the last mention that will be made of him in this study as he is fundamental to the construction of meaning surrounding the ancient Near East and its relationship to present-day times. In popular memory, the vision of Layard is perhaps most cogently captured in the verse of his friend, the poet Walter Savage Landor (1775–1864) who wrote:

> . . . My song shall rise,
> Altho' none heed or hear it; rise it shall,
> And swell along the wastes of Nineveh
> And Babylon, until it reach to thee,
> Layard! who raisest cities from the dust,
> Who driest Lethe up and her shades,
> And pourest a fresh stream on arid sands,
> And rescuest thrones and nations, fanes and gods
> From conquering Time; he sees thee and turns back.

Layard was and is a towering figure in Assyriology and ancient Near Eastern studies more broadly. Today his excavation techniques are seen as models of imperialist treasure hunting not scholarship. Yet, as shall be explored in the rest of this study, his interpretations of Mesopotamian culture and his promotion of Near Eastern studies were fundamental to the public reception of the field.

Although the motivations and personal characters of Belzoni, Robinson, and Layard were completely distinct from one another, all three were formative figures in ancient Near Eastern studies. All three wrote best-selling accounts of their work using the genre that was most suitable for the time—the travel account. This was before the 'site report' existed as a form and before scientific archaeology had become a desideratum. This was in keeping with trends of scientific writing at the time, which emphasized the individuality of the scholar, and typically biographical or autobiographical accounts sold better than data-heavy treatments.[137] As we shall see for Belzoni and Layard, their public personalities were very much a part of the

---

136. As quoted by Larsen, *Conquest,* p. 343.
137. Secord, *Victorian Sensation,* p. 43.

public reception of Egypt and Assyria. The same cannot be said for Robinson, who did not involve himself in public life to the same extent.

The works of these three scholars established many of the approaches that would come to distinguish their three academic fields: Egyptology, biblical archaeology and Assyriology. For Egyptology, much of the early work centred on the explorations of tombs, the collection of fine art and papyrus, and a race between European powers to collect as much as possible. Egyptological work did not need to be contextualized within biblical history in order to be supported. However, throughout the nineteenth century, biblical interpretations played a greater role in Egyptology than they would in the second half of the twentieth century when the fields diverged significantly. More important in this relationship, however, was how Egyptology would influence biblical interpretation throughout the nineteenth century, a theme that will be explored more fully through the rest of this study. Assyriologists similarly emphasized the collection of fine art (especially statues) and, once recognized as such, cuneiform tablets. For Assyriology, unlike Egyptology, the relationship between Mesopotamia and the Bible would become central to its emergence as a formal discipline and its popular reception. When Mesopotamian discoveries were not contextualized in relation to the Bible, popular interest waned. Later recognition that the civilization of Sumer predated Egypt would encourage interest in Mesopotamia as a place of 'firsts', but this would not be for some time. Biblical archaeology, as founded by Robinson, remained most stable throughout the nineteenth century, fundamentally oriented toward identifying the locations of biblical events, and presuming a level of 'sameness' in the cultures of Palestine from the Iron Age to the nineteenth century. A distrust of traditional and ecclesiastical knowledge about the land was assumed by most who engaged in the enterprise, but this same skepticism was not brought to bear on Scripture. Even when scholars claimed to be engaging in a positivist evaluation of the historicity of biblical events through archaeology, there was no expectation that the Bible would be proven wrong.

What connects these three 'best-sellers' of nineteenth-century archaeology is that they are framed in a form that came into being as a means of presenting experiences of the 'other'. The discovery of past is made into an experience of the other, mediated through encounters with an even more alien other—the nineteenth-century residents of the Near East. Throughout all three accounts, local lack of knowledge about antiquities provides 'evidence' for the disconnect between past and present. Thus, the past may be the 'other', but it is less 'other' to the Europeans and North Americans than to those under Ottoman rule. For Belzoni and Layard knew the 'true value' of the antiquities, and Robinson had a 'greater understanding' of Scripture than the patriarch of the Saint Catherine Monastery. Archaeology was a tool of possession, and familiarity with the land was the means through which a spiritual inheritance of the land could be manifest. Travel literature became the textual manifestation of the imperial gaze, sorting out what was of value and what was to be trivialized, depicting the current inhabitants of the land as children and using archaeology as a new means of ordering that space. These accounts present the European and North American reader with a duty to rescue the past from the present. It also suggests the tools that should be used to save the past—the technological and scientific mastery held by the West. Lifting, hauling and measuring are all acts of technological triumphalism that allow the heroic rescue of antiquity from the indolence of the Ottoman Empire. These messages were understood by nineteenth-century academics working in other fields. The next chapter shall explore the importance of these and other Near Eastern discoveries for thinking about progress and decline—two notions that were absolutely front and centre in Victorian intellectual life.

4

PROGRESS AND DECLINE; OR, HOW THE WHIGS AND THE ANTHROPOLOGISTS CLAIMED THE NEAR EAST

> These are vanities. Even these will pass away. And some day or other (but it will be after our time, thank goodness), Hyde Park Gardens will be no better known than the celebrated horticultural outskirts of Babylon . . .
> —W.M. Thackeray, *Vanity Fair*

> Progress is not an accident but a necessity. —Herbert Spencer

On December 3, 1873, George Smith presented a paper to the Society of Biblical Archaeology and in so doing articulated a vision of Mesopotamia that had been realized over the previous thirty years of scholarship. Smith, having worked years later than Layard, when scholars were now able to read cuneiform script, was in a position to make the following comments:

> This country the cradle of civilization, the birthplace of the arts and sciences, for 2,000 years has been in ruins; its literature, containing the most precious records of antiquity, is scarcely known to us, except from the texts the Assyrians copied, but beneath its mounds and ruined cities, now awaiting exploration, lay, together with older copies of this Deluge text, other legends and histories of the earliest civilization in the world.[1]

At first glance, there seems to be little of interest in these comments. Mesopotamia's literature had been long forgotten, and archaeology provided the means to retrieve it. Yet for a statement made in 1873, there are some very clear signs of transformations that had occurred over the past seventy or so years. There is recognition that the Assyrian texts found in Layard's excavations (and elsewhere) are copies of works from a much older literary heritage. This civilization is described as the oldest civilization in the world—Egypt had lost its position as the progenitor culture. The implications of this go beyond the history of textual transmission and

---

1. George Smith, 'The Chaldean Account of the Deluge', *Transactions of the Society of Biblical Archaeology* 2 (1873), pp. 213-34.

disciplinary competitiveness between Egyptologists and Assyriologists for the temporal primacy of their respective interests. For here, embedded in the rhetorical flourish, are some typically unquestioned conceptions of progress and decline. Mesopotamia is described as 'the cradle of civilization' and 'the birthplace of the arts and sciences', both epithets that are commonly employed by Assyriologists today but imply a teleological movement from barbarism to culture, and a link between Mesopotamia and Victorian England, itself the culmination of this teleology.

As an attempt at encouraging funding for further exploration in Mesopotamia, Smith played to two mutually connected Victorian impulses: the urge for archival collection and the urge to understand how great empires fell from glory. The second impulse was keenly felt throughout the Victorian intellectual community. Progress had become the dogma of the age; decline was its unwanted corollary, and both were most readily evident in the once-great civilizations of the ancient Near East. Whiggish views of history in which the past was a story of inevitable progress toward the contemporary British state were of the utmost importance in understanding the new world hierarchies. The discoveries of the ancient Near East provided the seeming proof of the whig belief in progress; but instead of increasing liberty, it was technological achievement that marked the steady improvement of humanity. That Prime Minister William Gladstone was in attendance when George Smith read his paper certainly added to the prestige and importance of the event. Gladstone, himself deeply interested in the classics and a keen supporter of ancient studies, was there for his own curiosity. His presence at meetings such as these was not atypical, and his influence on Near Eastern studies will be explored further. That a standing prime minister, however, should attend Smith's lecture no doubt signaled the importance of the event in British political life and Near Eastern studies' relevance for British society, both theologically and in terms of thinking about the British Empire's future.

By the beginning of the nineteenth century, notions of human progress had begun to infuse the study of the ancient Near East. By the end of the nineteenth century and the beginning of the twentieth, these notions had become fundamental to connecting the history of the Near Eastern and biblical worlds to the rest of human history and especially to the historical narrative of the rise of the West. Throughout the nineteenth century, notions of human progress were debated and argued over, and the outcomes of these debates are still apparent in twenty-first-century archaeological theory. Merging historical studies with evolutionary thinking (in the general sense, not just the biological sense), the study of the ancient Near East provided the seemingly empirical data for scholars in other disciplines to work with in articulating notions about the nature of progress and the creation of a vision of the Western tradition that included some cultures, excluded others, and stood as a monolith against a less fully articulated (by European historians) Eastern tradition and those regions of the world that 'lacked' a historical tradition altogether.

Creating 'World History' and Understanding Difference

Christian theology inspired a teleological view that humanity was moving toward perfection, and this had been influential in Enlightenment thinking, in a variety of guises. By the end of the nineteenth century, a conceptualization of the Western tradition within the field of history had been laid out and accepted within the academy. Within this schema, the ancient Near East came to play a privileged role as the location of the 'first civilizations' as well as the location of the origins of Judaism and Christianity. This is an incredibly powerful model for understanding the past and despite efforts at creating more inclusive world histories in recent years, the primacy of the Western tradition is difficult to escape. So how did Mesopotamia and Egypt come to play such a foundational role in this narrative (even if only as a prelude to the Greeks)? Why was the European tradition extended further back in time and beyond Europe itself? A combination of early nineteenth-century theological perspectives and the developments of social evolutionary and diffusion models helped fix the Near East in this privileged (yet problematic) position.

Antique Christian theology, which made the expulsion from the Garden of Eden a central point of human history, had long inspired Europeans to think of society as having degenerated from a perfect state. Classical notions of a Golden Age had helped inspire this and continued to reify this view well into the Enlightenment. The teleological movement toward perfection was taken, then, as a return to perfection. The evident social complexity of the ancient Near East gave proponents of the notion of 'degenerationism' an evidentiary non-biblical basis for their arguments that, coincidentally, could be related to the Tower of Babel narrative. Its collapse, as described in Genesis, led to the emergence of difference among people, symbolized especially through language. Some degenerationists followed a literal reading of the story of the Tower of Babel in which all humans had at one point enjoyed the benefits of civilization but no longer did. Thinkers such as Louis de Bonald and Martin Dobrizhoffer, in their attempts to understand the origins of language, came to the conclusion that only God could have created language and writing, and thus a culture's language was viewed as a gift of providence and a moral marker of God's degree of favor to a particular group.[2]

---

2. M. Dobrizhoffer, *An Account of the Abipones*, II (London: J. Murray, 1822 [1783]), p. 157. See also Louis de Bonald, *Sur les premiers objets des connaissances*

4. *Progress and Decline*

It was not just language, however, that provided proof of humanity's original *ur*-culture; it was all of the trappings of civilization that were becoming apparent with the exploration of the Near East. W. Cooke Taylor, one of the most vociferous proponents of degenerationism, explained, in 1840, how the creation accounts in Genesis, when harmonized with discoveries in the Near East, proved that God had fashioned these original cultures:

> Here we have it clearly stated, that man, instead of being placed upon the earth a helpless, untutored savage, was gifted with intelligence,—was taught the nature of the different beings by which he was surrounded,—was instructed in agriculture, one of the most important arts of life,—and was declared to be formed for society. To the truth of this statement, all the traditions of ancient nations, and all the investigations of modern science, bear concurrent testimony; they not only confirm the statement, but they deprive all other theories of the merit even of plausibility.[3]

The discoveries from the ancient Near East, even if not well understood by 1840, provided ample evidence for the kind of primordial complexity that Cooke and others needed as proof of degenerationism.

After the Tower of Babel was struck down, some societies degenerated into savagery—the evidence for these cultures being the 'primitives' in the South Pacific, pre-Columbian America and Africa, for example. The degenerationists believed that God provided assistance to some of these people, helping them achieve civilization. Thus, some parts of the world were thought to be progressing back toward the pre-Babel or pre-Fall state, while others lacked God's divine assistance and were stunted in a state of 'primitivity'. Thus, the degenerationists created a structure for privileging the ancient Near East) as a key element of the story of the West. The Ottoman Near East was excluded, however, except as a peripheral villain that loomed on the margins of Europe as a threat of a potential reversion to barbarism.

This privileged position for the ancient Near East was also perpetuated in a distinctly antitheological context, in the development of positivism. Although first coined by Claude Henri Saint-Simon, it was Auguste Comte who developed positivism into a coherent means of understanding the world. Comte's oft-quoted statement on 'his discovery' is perhaps the best means of explicating this theoretical system:

> I believe I have discovered a great fundamental law. This law is that each of our principle conceptions, each branch of our knowledge, passes

---

morales (Paris: D'Adrien Le Clere, 1826).

3. W. Cooke Taylor, *The Natural History of Society: The Barbarian and the Civilized State,* I (London: Orme, Brown, 1840), pp. 309-10.

through three different theoretical states: the theological or fictive state; the metaphysical or abstract; the scientific or positive.[4]

Thus Western Europe of the nineteenth century, according to Comte, was mostly operating in this positive state wherein scientific knowledge was granted a privileged position. These three different theoretical states of knowledge would come to have an important role in structuring understandings of the Near East, especially in understanding the differences between the Mesopotamian and the Greek world. Here, Comte had participated in the creation of a world-historical framework that privileged the Near East as formative and ignored other early civilizations. For Comte purposefully excluded other complex states, especially China and India, from his own analysis since these states developed independently yet had become stunted in their growth and had not played a role in world progress.[5] Indeed, for Comte, it was only the cultures that could be traced as ancestral to Europe that were worth consideration.

Similar exclusivity in the development of world history rooted in 'reason' can be seen in the works of Georg W.F. Hegel, who saw the history of the world as intrinsically goal oriented, moving toward 'the realization of the Idea of Spirit [Mind]' (or *Weltgeist* in the original German).[6] Hegel's *Weltgeist* was the dialectic of human history, a progressive force that inspired change and led to world improvement. As reason came to be more perfectly exercised, the *Weltgeist* reached ever-higher states and would eventually lead to the culmination of the human story. This was a worldwide teleology without recourse to the divine. The spirits of individual cultures could play a role in its development as could the actions of great men (*Volksgeister*). Hegel's notion of how this progress developed was through his model of the dialectic, where progress developed through the negation of the previous.[7] Like Comte, Hegel traces the development of world history, in this case the *Weltgeist*, only in those historical regions that could be seen as ancestral to Europe (and only state-level societies). Africa (excluding Egypt), the pre-Columbian Americas, India, China and elsewhere were explicitly not part of this development of the world spirit. India and China may have held historical interest in other ways, since like Babylonia, they developed some elements of civilization, but since Hegel did not believe that they partici-

---

4. Auguste Comte, *Cours de philosophie positive*, I (Paris: Bachelier, 1830–1842), p. 14.

5. Comte, *Cours de philosophie*, p. 5.

6. Georg W.F. Hegel, *The Philosophy of History* (trans. J. Sibee; London: Allen & Unwin, 1856 [1837]), p. 25.

7. The status quo is the 'thesis', which is then challenged by the 'antithesis'. The result of that conflict is the 'synthesis', which eventually becomes the status quo (the 'thesis'), and the cycle continues.

4. Progress and Decline

pated in maritime relations with other cultures, their impact on world affairs was minimal. Their participation in world history occurred only when other groups sought them out.[8] Hegel states that 'the history of the world travels from East to West, for Europe is absolutely the end of History, Asia the beginning'.[9] About anterior Asia, Hegel states, 'It presents the origination of all religious and political principles, but Europe has been the scene of their development'.[10] Thus his presentation of history begins with the 'Oriental World', continues with the Greeks and Romans and culminates in the 'German World' and 'Modern Times'.

Series of four were fundamental to Hegel's conception of history. As Hayden White has shown, these reflected four recurrent phases based on the analogy of human development: birth, childhood, adulthood and death.[11] As the Oriental World, coming after prehistory, was the second phase in Hegel's four-phase conception of world history, it reflected the childhood stage of world-historical development.[12] Hegel further subdivides the 'Oriental World' into another four separate 'theatres of history'. These were, in Hegel's order, China and the Mongols, the Indian subcontinent, Mesopotamia and Persia, and finally Egypt.[13] Hegel treats Phoenicia as being separate from (and Egypt as having a conflicted relationship with) Africa, a continent, which to him, played no part in the historical world:

> Historical movements in it—that is in its northern part—belong to the Asiatic or European World. Carthage displayed there an important transitionary phase of civilization; but, as a Phoenician colony, it belongs to Asia. Egypt will be considered in reference to the passage of the human mind from its Eastern to its Western phase, but it does not belong to the African spirit.[14]

Mesopotamia, Egypt and Syria–Palestine are all treated, in his larger discussion, as constituent elements of Persia, and thus all of their historical traits fall within a broader historical pattern of Persian practices, distinct from China and India. For Hegel, the geographic diversity of 'Persia' allowed it to play a part in world history in a way that China and India did not. It is worth quoting Hegel at length here to draw out how 'Persia' differed from the rest of the Oriental world, in the progress of history:

---

8. Hegel, *Philosophy of History*, p. 101.
9. Hegel, *Philosophy of History*, p. 103.
10. Hegel, *Philosophy of History*, p. 101.
11. Hayden White, *Metahistory: The Historical Imagination in Nineteenth Century Europe* (Baltimore: Johns Hopkins University Press, 1974), p. 123.
12. For further discussion of the childhood metaphor, see White, *Metahistory*, p. 126.
13. Hegel, *Philosophy of History*, p. 112.
14. Hegel, *Philosophy of History*, p. 99.

> The Persian Empire comprehends all the three geographical elements, which we classified as distinct. First, the Uplands of Persia and Media; next, the Valley-plains of the Euphrates and Tigris, whose inhabitants are found united in a developed form of civilization, with Egypt—the Valley-plain of the Nile—where agriculture, industrial arts and sciences flourished; and lastly a third element, viz. the nations who encounter the perils of the sea—the Syrians, the Phoenicians, the inhabitants of the Greek colonies and Greek Maritime States in Asia Minor. Persia thus united in itself the three natural principles, while China and India remained foreign to the sea. We find here neither that consolidated totality which China presents, nor that Hindoo life, in which an anarchy of caprice is prevalent everywhere. In Persia, the government, through joining all in a central unity, is but a combination of peoples—leaving each of them free. Thereby a stop is put to that barbarism and ferocity with which the nations had been wont to carry on their destructive feuds, and which the Book of Kings and the Book of Samuel sufficiently attest. The lamentations of the Prophets and their imprecations upon the state of things before the conquest, show the misery, wickedness and disorder that prevailed among them, and the happiness which Cyrus diffused over the region of Anterior Asia. It was not given to the Asiatics to unite self-dependence, freedom and substantial vigor of mind, with culture, *i.e.*, an interest for diverse pursuits and an acquaintance with the conveniences of life. Military valor among them is consistent only with barbarity of manners. It is not the calm courage of order; and when their mind opens to a sympathy with various interests, it immediately passes into effeminacy; allows its energies to sink, and makes men the slaves of an enervated sensuality.[15]

Most of Hegel's understanding of the Persians comes directly from Herodotus and the Bible. Based on these sources, Hegel understands Persia's place in world history as a location where a variety of historical practices co-existed neither totalizing (like China) or allowing anarchy to thrive (like in India) and thus allowing these cultures to play a part in world history.

Within the Persian historical theatre, Hegel finds the Phoenicians particularly noteworthy. Their maritime and commercial activities either signal or led to a cultural development beyond that found in Mesopotamia. Hegel discusses the results of Phoenician travels and trade:

> This opens to us an entirely new principle. Inactivity ceases, as also mere rude valor; in their place appears the activity of Industry, and that considerate courage which, while it dares the perils of the deep, rationally bethinks itself of the means of safety. Here everything depends on Man's activity, his courage. His intelligence; while the objects aimed at are also pursued in the interest of Man. Human will and activity here occupy the foreground, not Nature and its bounty. Babylonia had its determinate share of territory, and human subsistence was there dependent on the course of the sun and the process of Nature generally. But the sailor relies upon him-

---

15. Hegel, *Philosophy of History*, p. 188.

self amid the fluctuations of the waves, and eye and heart must always be open. In like manner the principle of Industry involves the very opposite of what is received from Nature; for natural objects are worked up for use and ornament. In Industry Man is an object to himself and treats Nature as something subject to him, on which he impresses the seal of his activity. Intelligence is the valor needed here, and ingenuity is better than mere natural courage. At this point we see the nations freed from the fear of Nature and its slavish bondage.[16]

Hegel describes industry as a liberating force, and the industriousness of the Phoenicians led them to evolve beyond the Babylonians, whom he sees as slaves to the natural world. Thus the Babylonians were passive and the Phoenicians active agents in their relationship to nature. Hegel similarly describes Phoenician religion as a step above Babylonian, which he characterizes as a 'rude, vulgar, sensual idolatry'.[17] While Phoenician religion could be characterized in this manner in principle, its adoption of Greek elements indicated (to Hegel) a higher level of theological sophistication.

Hegel next describes the people of Judaea, whose religion supersedes the Phoenician because it is completely free from the limitations of nature. Hegel describes it as 'the pure product of Thought'.[18] It is this divorcing of religion from nature that marks the separation between East and West, in Hegel's conception.[19] Hegel still points out what he saw as stunted features of Judaism, such as the lack of concern for the individual (and the soul) and the preponderance of miracles in historical accounts.[20] Thus for Hegel, the ancient Judaeans were not as advanced as the Greeks.

Although Hegel discusses Egypt within the context of the Persian theatre of history, his actual analysis suggests that it developed alongside of and in a similar fashion to Persia, rather than as a constituent element. His take on Egypt is exemplified by his discussion of the Great Sphinx at Giza:

> The Sphinx may be regarded as a symbol of the Egyptian Spirit. The human head looking out from the brute body, exhibits Spirit as it begins to emerge from the merely Natural—to tear itself loose therefrom and already to look more freely around it; without, however, entirely freeing itself from the fetters Nature had imposed. The innumerable edifices of the Egyptians are half below the ground, and half rise above it into the air.... Written language is still a hieroglyphic; and its basis is only the sensuous image, not the letter itself.[21]

---

16. Hegel, *Philosophy of History*, pp. 191-92.
17. Hegel, *Philosophy of History*, p. 192.
18. Hegel, *Philosophy of History*, p. 195.
19. Hegel, *Philosophy of History*, pp. 195-96.
20. Hegel, *Philosophy of History*, p. 197.
21. Hegel, *Philosophy of History*, p. 199.

For Hegel, the Egyptians possessed that Spirit, which allowed participation in world history. Yet, they were held back. He states, 'It is that African imprisonment of ideas combined with the infinite impulse of the spirit to realize itself objectively, which we find here'.[22] One of the most noteworthy ways in which the Egyptians were stunted by 'African' influence, in Hegel's view, was through their 'zoolatry', the worship of 'brutes', which he takes as a fundamental part of Egyptian religion (based mostly on Herodotus's treatment)—'a most stupid and non-human superstition'.[23] Hegel determines that it is the static contradiction between 'Spirit sunk in Nature' and the 'impulse to liberate it [Spirit]' that defines Egypt within world history.[24] After Egypt is conquered by the Persians, and then under the influence of the Greeks, Spirit is finally liberated in the Greek World and the Oriental World passes out of the progress of Hegel's history.

Hegel's approach to understanding world history through the concept of the *Weltgeist* was tremendously influential. That individual cultures had their own *Geist* seemed to make sense within the context of the new globalism that had emerged in the eighteenth century. It also seemed to explain why some cultures seemed to have been isolated, some were very influential but are no longer, and why some have a more important role to play in the present. Other nineteenth-century conceptualizations of 'progressive' cultures were less teleologically oriented, that is to say, they did not assume a goal of progress per se, rather just the relative ability for the culture to progress at all. For example, Gustav Klemm's ten-volume history of humanity merely divided cultures into 'active' or 'passive' categories.[25] The ancient Egyptians, for example, were categorized as passive. Eduard Meyer's *Geschichte des Altertums* was a survey of world history, seen as the history of states (which became gradually more complex) and of those individuals who played a major role in human events. The story began with the Near East (and Meyer's own dissertation was on ancient Egypt); but, in Meyer's view, the Near East did not have the same kind of impact on world civilization as the classical world, and the individual was too invisible in the Oriental cultures to be of great interest to the world historian.[26] By the mid-twentieth century, these sorts of progressive narratives of world history, beginning in the ancient Near East, had become widely accepted. H.G. Wells, in his 1920 *The Outline of History* (released serially in 1919),

22. Hegel, *Philosophy of History*, p. 207.
23. Hegel, *Philosophy of History*, pp. 211-12.
24. Hegel, *Philosophy of History*, p. 218.
25. Gustav Klemm, *Allgemeine Cultur-Geschichte der Menschheit* (Leipzig: Leubner, 1843).
26. For more on Meyer's work within the context of German academia, see Suzanne L. Marchand, *German Orientalism in the Age of Empire: Religion, Race, and Scholarship* (Cambridge: Cambridge University Press, 2009), pp. 206-11.

4. *Progress and Decline*

argues for a world history with a common purpose (eventually) leading to a near-utopian state. Egypt and Mesopotamia were the first civilizations (although Wells remained uncertain about which was the first), and their histories were marked by a dialectical antagonism between the city and the nomads who would periodically destroy the city. Oswald Spengler's 1918 *The Decline of the West* (*Der Untergang des Abendlandes*) is less optimistic. In it, he argues that all civilizations eventually decline, having a limited life span. Arnold Toynbee's twelve-volume *Study of History* (finished in 1961) created a master narrative of world history that explained historical change in terms akin to a biological life cycle and larger historical patterns on analogy with a cycling wheel (hence the truism associated with Toynbee that those that don't know the past are doomed to repeat it). He saw civilizations developing through life stages: birth, growth, maturity and death. Yet each time one culture died, it left humanity at a higher point of spiritual growth. New and more developed cultures are born out of the decayed matter of the older cultures.[27]

Wells, Spengler and Toynbee, now criticized for their views on race and valuations of different cultures, were still markedly different from the nineteenth-century philosophers in terms of thinking about the biological foundations of humanity. The issue of the race(s) of the people of the ancient Near East was dealt with in a variety of ways in the nineteenth century. One particular stream of thought was polygenesis, a belief that God had created more than one species of human being. Polygenesis seems to have developed in the seventeenth and eighteenth centuries, in particular among scholars who rejected a literal reading of the book of Genesis. Thus, while not disputing God's key role as creator, polygenesists did dispute the idea that God's creation of Adam was a unique event. One of the clearest articulations of this notion was presented by Isaac La Peyrère, who claimed that the Jews were the ancestors of Adam whereas the Egyptians and Chaldeans were the descendants of an individual who was older than Adam and not mentioned in the biblical accounts.[28] La Peyrère was particularly influenced by extrabiblical historical records, those of the 'Caldeans, Egyptians, Scythians, and Chinensians', which suggested that the biblical account of the creation of humanity left out some of the other races of humans.[29] These records, taken with New Testament exegesis, allowed La Peyrère to argue against the standard biblical reading of Genesis and argue that other humans

---

27. For more on Toynbee, see Bruce Kuklick, *Puritans in Babylon: The Ancient Near East and American Intellectual Life 1890–1930* (Princeton, NJ: Princeton University Press, 1996), p. 191.

28. See Isaac La Peyrère, *Praeadamitae* ('Men before Adam') 1655.

29. David Livingstone, *Adam's Ancestors: Race, Religion, and the Politics of Human Origins* (Baltimore: Johns Hopkins University Press, 2008), pp. 34-35.

existed before Adam.³⁰ Thus the practice of reading the Bible within the context of other ancient texts was fundamental to the study of biology at the time, and the two fields were interrelated.

Pre-Adamite and polygenesis notions were inconsistently influential in the nineteenth century but are apparent in discussions of race and slavery in the United States. The case of the American doctor Samuel George Morton (1799–1851) is one instance where archaeological finds from Egypt inspired the further development of ideas of polygenesis and justified nineteenth-century racism. Morton's initial work on modern crania identified a number of races that constituted distinct species but that could have descended from one initial creator.³¹ While the bulk of his research presented in this 1839 work consists of measurements of skulls of native North Americans, he does present a discussion of world races in the introduction to his work where he described the 'families' ('Nilotic', 'Libyan' and 'Arabian') within the 'Caucasian Race'. Morton writes:

> From remote ages the inhabitants of every extended locality have been marked by certain physical and moral peculiarities, common among themselves, and serving to distinguish them from all other people. The Arabians are at this time precisely what they were in the days of the patriarchs....
> In like manner the characteristic features of the Jews may be recognized in the sculpture of the temples of Luxor and Karnak, in Egypt, where they have been depicted for nearly thirty centuries.³²

Here Morton cites the *Description de l'Egypte*, clearly inspired by the Napoleonic imagery. Morton believes that God would have created the human being already adapted to the 'physical' and 'moral' circumstances of his dwelling place on earth.³³ Since one race could not have successfully adapted to all of the diverse regions of earth after the biblical flood, God must have created races that were adapted to their 'peculiar local destination' from the beginning.³⁴

Morton then goes on to describe the characteristics peculiar to each of the families, both physical characteristics and behavioral ones. He sees the Arabian Family as disposed toward migration; he gives the example of a

---

30. Livingstone, *Adam's Ancestors*, pp. 33-34. La Peyrère especially considered Paul's statement in Romans that sin existed before God gave humans the law. He argues that Adam was given 'law' by God, and since sin existed before God did this, and thus before Adam's time, sinners must also have existed before Adam. This kind of supplementing of the biblical text was not unusual in early modern biblical interpretation.

31. Samuel George Morton, *Crania Americana; or, A Comparative View of the Skulls of Various Aboriginal Nations of North and South America* (Philadelphia: J. Dobson, 1839).

32. Morton, *Crania Americana*, pp. 1-2.

33. Morton, *Crania Americana*, pp. 2-3.

34. Morton, *Crania Americana*, p. 3.

supposed Canaanite migration to Africa (after being expelled from the land by Joshua) as evidence of this Arabian tendency in history.[35] Originally pastoral, the Jews or Hebrews, according to Morton, have subsequently adapted themselves to city life and are dispersed throughout the world (although they retain their original physical characteristics and 'undeviating form of worship').[36] Morton argues that the Hebrews are descendants of the Chaldeans (here following the biblical story of Abraham) and that the Idumeans or Edomites (whom he credits with having built Petra) are also of this family.[37] 'Wandering', as one of the characteristics of the Arabian Family, is also evident with the Phoenicians, according to Morton, since they 'roved upon the ocean as the cognate tribes did upon the land'.[38]

The Egyptian Family consists of only two 'cognate nations'—the Egyptians and the Nubians, who 'though dwindled and degenerate, appear to constitute a family distinct from the rest of mankind'.[39] Morton follows Hermann Niebuhr and Denon in asserting that the modern Copts are the racial descendants of the ancient Egyptians, just as the Coptic language is the modern survival of ancient Egyptian.[40] However, the vast majority of people living in nineteenth-century Egypt were taken to be a mixed racial population.[41] Morton relies on Madden's reports in *Travels in Egypt* for evidence on the skull shapes and sizes of the ancient Egyptians as well as evidence from ancient Egyptian art. After his main discussion of the Egyptian Family, Morton provides a three-page excursus '*On the Supposed Affinity between the Egyptians and Negroes*'—an affinity that he rejects using classical sources (such as Herodotus and Diodorus Siculus), reports of the physical characteristics of mummies, and Egyptian art (as reported by Belzoni, Denon and Wilkinson).[42] Morton asserts that Volney was wrong in taking the 'negro' features of the sphinx as evidence that 'the Egyptians were real Negroes', since, according to him, Buddhists also 'represent their principal god with Negro features and hair'.[43] He also reminds the reader that there is 'no absolute proof' that the sphinx was an Egyptian shrine, suggesting that it could perhaps have been a 'shrine of the Negro population of Egypt'.[44] Morton also quotes Georges Cuvier who states, 'It is easy to prove, that *whatever may have been the hue of their skin* [original italics], they belonged to the

---

35. Morton, *Crania Americana*, p. 19.
36. Morton, *Crania Americana*, p. 21.
37. Morton, *Crania Americana*, p. 21.
38. Morton, *Crania Americana*, p. 22.
39. Morton, *Crania Americana*, p. 24.
40. Morton, *Crania Americana*, p. 25.
41. Morton, *Crania Americana*, p. 25.
42. Morton, *Crania Americana*, pp. 29-31.
43. Morton, *Crania Americana*, p. 29.
44. Morton, *Crania Americana*, p. 29.

same race with ourselves'.[45] Morton further adds, assuming that Egypt was the birthplace of human civilization, 'if science, art and literature, had their origin with a Negro tribe on the skirts of Africa, how does it happen that the stream of knowledge has never flowed into, but always from that country?'.[46]

This was not the last statement of Dr Morton in regards to ancient Egyptian physiognomy. In 1844, *Ancient Egypt*, by George Gliddon (1809–1857), the vice-consul in Egypt, was published, in which it was asserted that races had already been fixed much earlier than Morton thought. Gliddon argued against the idea that the environment was 'the agent of racial differentiation'.[47] Gliddon and Morton had already been corresponding, leading Morton to rethink the problem. Gliddon supplied Morton with more than one hundred Egyptian skulls, giving Morton access to a substantial sample for a study devoted to ancient Egypt.[48] Ancient Egyptian skulls were widely sold by Cairene antiquities' agents, and because the price they fetched was high, there was ample incentive for tomb robbing.[49] In 1844, Morton published *Crania Egyptica*, a study of the skulls and racial features of various individuals dating from, presumably, pharaonic times (Fig. 4.1). When Morton had learned of the relatively recent date of ancient Egyptian civilization and saw tomb paintings depicting both 'Negroid' and 'Caucasoid' individuals, he became convinced that not enough time had elapsed since the pharaonic era to allow these separate racial species to have developed on their own.[50] So, in *Crania Egyptica*, Morton put forward his argument for polygenesis based on the evidence from numerous Egyptian skulls sent him. Morton's argument includes discussions and conclusions on the varying intellectual and moral capacity of the races, in which African-Americans and Native Americans are found lacking. For Gliddon,

45. Morton, *Crania Americana*, p. 31.
46. Morton, *Crania Americana*, p. 31.
47. Livingstone, *Adam's Ancestors*, pp. 174-75.
48. Ann Fabian, 'The Curious Cabinet of Dr. Morton', in *Acts of Possession: Collecting in America* (ed. Leah Dilworth; New Brunswick, NJ: Rutgers University Press, 2003), pp. 112-37 (118).
49. For contemporary comments on the skull trade in Cairo, see Charles Piazzi Smyth, *Life and Work at the Great Pyramid; during the Months of January, February, March, and April, A.D. 1865; with a Discussion of the Facts Ascertained*, I (Edinburgh: Edmonston & Douglas, 1867), p. 312.
50. In 1854, George Gliddon published another work comparing the art of the ancient world with cranial features through a racist doctrine. Co-authored with a medical doctor named Josiah Clark Knott, *Types of Mankind; or, Ethnological Researches, Based upon the Ancient Monuments, Paintings, Sculptures, and Crania of Races, and upon their Natural, Geographical, Philological, and Biblical History* presented profile line-drawing of Egyptian faces to explain the features that proved their 'Caucasian' heritage. For more on this work, see Scott Trafton, *Egypt Land: Race and Nineteenth-Century American Egyptomania* (Durham, NC: Duke University Press, 2004), pp. 45-54.

16   OBSERVATIONS ON EGYPTIAN ETHNOGRAPHY,

TWO HEADS OF LUNATICS, FROM THEBES.

Wood-cut 1. (Cat. 841.) An elongated head, with a very receding forehead, long, aquiline nose, and large, ponderous jaws, which project so as to reduce the facial angle to about 65°. This person has been embalmed with evident care, but with the mouth open, the tongue protruded, and the eyelids raised, giving a frightfully vacant expression to the whole countenance, and leaving no reasonable doubt that this is the head of an idiot. A little hair remains, which is remarkably fine, and encroaches on the eyebrows.

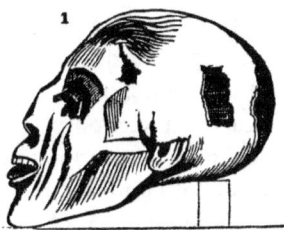

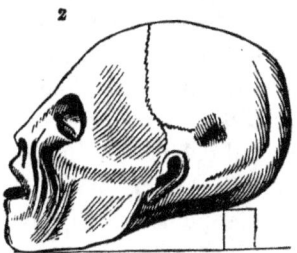

Wood-cut 2. (Cat. 863.) Another idiotic head, embalmed also with the mouth open and the tongue partially protruded. The cranium is long, the forehead low and receding, the face remarkably prominent, and the whole expression, as in the former instance, to the last degree vacant and repulsive. I presume that no one accustomed to comparisons of this nature can examine these heads, without agreeing with me in opinion as to their position in the intellectual scale. It may appear, and, indeed, is surprising, that two idiotic heads should be found among one hundred taken at random from the catacombs; and I can only explain the fact by supposing that a particular tomb was reserved for this unfortunate class of persons; and that the Arab servant employed by Mr. Gliddon, in his explorations at Thebes, invaded by chance this very sanctum. It is well known that idiotic persons have, in all ages, been regarded with a certain degree of veneration in the East; and hence their remains would be likely, in Egypt, to be carefully preserved after death. In examining Professor Rosellini's plates, I find a solitary example of an idiot, whose head is represented in the annexed diagram; and it is curious to remark, that the sagacity of the Egyptian artist has admirably adapted this man's vocation to his intellectual developments, for he is employed in stirring the fire of a blacksmith's shop. This singular effigy is seen at Thebes.

NEGROID HEADS.

In addition to the two heads of this class from Maabdeh and one from Memphis, I subjoin descriptions and outline drawings of five others from Thebes, which are here grouped for the advantage of more ready comparison.

Fig. 4.1. Here, Morton presents two mummified heads from his collection and compares them with an artistic depiction from Thebes. He classifies all three heads as those of 'idiots'. Samuel George Morton, *Crania Aegyptiaca; or, Observations on Egyptian Ethnography Derived from Anatomy, History and the Monuments* (Philadelphia: John Penington, 1844), p. 16.

this research was an important argument in support of American slavery.[51] Couched in pseudoscience and falsified data (as Stephen Jay Gould has demonstrated), the works of Morton and Gliddon show the complex ways in which the study of the ancient Near East was utilized in tandem with biology to justify racial policies in the United States.[52]

Yet it was the rejection of polygenesis more than its embrace that made the study of the ancient Near East so important for nineteenth-century scholars. This meant that alternative explanations needed to be offered to explain the diversity of world cultures at the same time that European dominance was assumed. It was the peculiar combination of biological and historical thinking that led to some of the most important nineteenth-century explanations for world diversity. Prior to the nineteenth century, the same individuals that worked on what are now known as the natural sciences also studied humans and society (what were then called the artificial sciences). These two arenas of thought had not yet become entirely divorced from each other. Although academics may have specialized in one or the other of these fields of inquiry, the elite men of letters, untrained but with time and wealth on their hands, still dabbled in multiple fields. Thus, it was not unusual to bring the theoretical advances of the natural sciences to the study of what are now thought of as humanist pursuits: history, art-history, literature, etc., and vice versa.

This was certainly the case with Charles Darwin and Alfred Wallace, who were both inspired by the writings of Thomas Malthus in the development of their notions of 'natural selection' and 'survival of the fittest'. Darwinian ideas became tremendously important in making sense of the history of humanity. Regardless of how *directly* influential Darwin was on the scholars of antiquity (and how mangled his ideas became in their translation into historical thinking), throughout the 1860s and continuing on until the beginning of the twentieth century, many scholars of world history continued to work from a similar conceptual framework to what had been in place since the 1760s—the notion that the story of humanity was a story of progress and perfectibility. Whereas the eighteenth-century historians were working from a primarily theological perspective, the scholars of the 1860s began describing 'progress' and 'perfectibility' in evolutionary terms. So rather than there being a spiritual or teleological end point to social evolution, in a semi-Darwinian fashion, certain cultures survive and adapt and certain cultures do not. Thus it was seemingly objective fact that some cultures were at a higher level of advancement than other cultures.

51. Livingstone, *Adam's Ancestors*, p. 180.
52. Livingstone, *Adam's Ancestors*, p. 175. See also Stephen Jay Gould, 'Morton's Ranking of Races by Cranial Capacity: Unconscious Manipulation of Data May Be a Scientific Norm', *Science* 200 (1978), pp. 503-509.

It was archaeology that in many ways provided the impetus for the collapse of the degenerationist and other theologically oriented approaches to understanding the world. In particular, the discovery of the Paleolithic and Neolithic Periods and especially the publication of Charles Lyell's *Antiquity of Man* (1863)—a volume that combined archaeological, geological, and linguistic evidence in an attempt to situate humanity within a geological time schema—made it difficult to take degenerationist ideas seriously. Until the publication of Lyell's work, it was possible to harmonize a roughly six-thousand-year-old Earth with a Golden Age of Egyptian and Mesopotamian civilization and prehistoric Europe. Proponents of this viewpoint simply took European prehistory as a 'degraded epilogue' to the civilizations of the Near East.[53] One particularly noteworthy harmonization of the Bible and geology came from William Francis Lynch (1801–1865), who led an American geological survey of the Dead Sea in 1847. In disagreement with the earth scientists from his expedition, Lynch argued that he had proven the general accuracy of the biblical narrative and that the geology of this region provided ample evidence for Scripture.[54] It is likely that many others attempted to reconcile geology and the Bible by not really considering the issues too deeply. When Lyell extended the time frame of the Earth's (and humanity's) existence, this kind of harmonization was more difficult. Now the cultures of the Near East could no longer be thought of as the high point from which humanity had descended. Thus the work of Lyell ushered in a new approach to world history, made possible by an extended chronology. In many ways, the embrace of this new chronology led to a return to previous (non-degenerationist) ways of thinking about human progress. For the eighteenth-century philosophers had assumed that humanity must have progressed through particular stages; they merely lacked the evidence to prove it. Now, archaeology was able to provide the evidence for these stages.[55] Anthropologists, interacting with this data as well as ethnographic evidence from still-living 'primitive' cultures, developed a conceptual framework for understanding these stages that came to be known as unilinear cultural evolution.

Edward Tylor's 1865 work *Researches into the Early History of Mankind* was profoundly important in merging Lyell's new geological-based chronology with the growing acceptance of stages of cultural development. For

---

53. Marvin Harris, *The Rise of Anthropological Theory* (Walnut Creek, CA: Altamira Press, updated edn, 2001), p. 147.

54. Naomi Shepherd, *The Zealous Intruders: The Western Rediscovery of Palestine* (London: Collins, 1987), p. 87. For more on the Lynch expedition, also see Rachel Hallote, *Bible, Map, and Spade: The American Palestine Exploration Society, Frederick Jones Bliss, and the Forgotten Story of Early American Archaeology* (Piscataway, NJ: Gorgias Press, 2006).

55. Harris, *Rise of Anthropological Theory*, p. 145.

Tylor, the cultures of the Near East where not the high point that humanity subsequently fell from. Rather, these cultures developed from Stone Age cultures, much as Europe seemed to have.[56] Tylor's two-volume *Primitive Culture* (1871) demonstrates the importance of education on social evolution; this is the trait that differentiates cultures at different stages, not a biological difference. Tylor's reliance on evidence to back his analysis seems obvious today, but as David Katz has argued, 'he helped turn armchair ethnographers into encyclopaedists of culture'.[57] Rather than making broad generalizations about the development of various cultures, scholars were forced to go out in the field and gather evidence on their own. In many ways, this moved the issue of the comparative study of cultures away from the philosophers and into the purview of fieldworkers. Thus archaeological evidence, gathered to address these issues, became primary sources of data. Despite this, in *Primitive Culture* most references to the ancient Near East relate to its religious practices, and Tylor relied mostly on classical and biblical sources to illustrate how Egyptian and Syro-Palestinian cultures fit within his evolutionary schema.

Herbert Spencer also promoted evidence-based comparative research on social evolution. Spencer's *Descriptive Sociology* was published in fifteen volumes from 1873 to 1934 (only eight were published by 1881 and the rest after his death). The extended study was based on Spencer's general research with three assistants who read aloud various source materials. As the students read the books and articles, Spencer took notes about the cultures and organized these notes into comparative tables.[58] The tables were organized into a series of headings, underneath a twofold division of 'structural' or 'functional', each successively broken down into smaller units.[59] These notes were initially just intended as notes, but once Spencer recognized that he had summarized the major features of many world cultures in an easy to digest format, he set about publishing his cultural synopses with the assistance of various scholars. Individual volumes were dedicated to specific cultures. Spencer and Scheppig released volume VII, *Hebrews and Phoenicians,* in 1880. Financial problems prevented Spencer from releasing later volumes, yet he insured their publication after his death through a bequest in his will. Volume XI, *Ancient Egyptians,* was released in 1925

56. Harris, *Rise of Anthropological Theory*, p. 149.
57. David Katz, *God's Last Words: Reading the English Bible from the Reformation to Fundamentalism* (New Haven, CT: Yale University Press, 2004), p. 290.
58. David Duncan was the first hired and was responsible for different 'uncivilized' cultures. After Duncan left his employ, Spencer hired two other helpers: James Collier was responsible for researching contemporary 'civilized' cultures, and a German named Richard Scheppig was in charge of ancient civilizations.
59. An overview of the categories is presented in Jay Rumney, *Herbert Spencer's Sociology* (New York: Atherton Books, 1966), p. ix.

(compiled by Sir W.F. Petrie), and volume XIII, *Mesopotamia*, in 1929 (compiled by Reuben Levy). By then both were very out of date, and Petrie himself acknowledged that the lack of illustrations in any of the volumes is problematic.[60]

Spencer explains that the goal of the series is to 'supply the student of Social Science with data standing towards his conclusions in a relation like that in which accounts of the structures and functions of different types of animals stand to the conclusions of the Biologist'.[61] Material is presented in tabular form so that the reader can quickly see the relations between the different constituent elements. To accommodate information about cultural change over time, the charts are organized vertically as well, with the oldest aspects of a culture at the top and the most recent at the bottom of the page. The tables on the Hebrews are divided into three: the Pre-Egyptian and Egyptian Period; the Periods of the Judges, of the Monarchy, and of the Two Kingdoms; and Exilic, Persian, Greek, Asmonean, Roman Periods. Each volume is quite large—designed to make the detailed charts within legible. The charts categorize the elements of each culture into two large groups: structural and functional. Within these categories, cultural elements are further divided into regulative and operative categories. Those are then further subdivided into the categories of political, ecclesiastical, ceremonial, sentiments, ideas, language, processes, products, division of labour and regulation of labour. These categories are subdivided again under headings such as bodily mutilations, laws of intercourse, language, implements, aesthetic products, etc. At the smallest unit of division, brief summaries are given. For example, the entry on 'Habitations' for the Hebrews in the Pre-Egyptian and Egyptian Periods reads simply, 'Dwelt in tents of black goats' hair'.[62] Under 'Clothing' in the same table, the entry reads, 'Wore one garment with a girdle. The richer people wore two garments. Probably head-dresses after the fashion of Bedouin *Keffiah.*'[63] Some entries were longer, but the basic style remained the same for each. The charts were intended for quick reference, but each volume also consists of expanded sections describing each of these 'groups of sociological facts' in detail. The extended treatments consist of excerpts on the topic of interest from major secondary

60. Flinders Petrie, *Descriptive Sociology; or, Groups of Facts, Classified and Arranged by Herbert Spencer: Ancient Egyptians*, XI (London: Williams & Norgate, 1925), p. i.
61. Herbert Spencer, 'Provisional Preface', in *Descriptive Sociology; or, Groups of Facts, Classified and Arranged by Herbert Spencer: Hebrews and Phoenicians*, VII (ed. Richard Scheppig; London: Williams & Norgate, 1880), pp. i-ii (i).
62. Richard Scheppig, ed., *Descriptive Sociology; or, Groups of Facts, Classified and Arranged by Herbert Spencer: Hebrews and Phoenicians*, VII (London: Williams & Norgate, 1880), table I.
63. Scheppig, ed., *Descriptive Sociology*, table I.

sources. The amount of extra synthesis added varies depending on the individual editor. Levy offers little commentary beyond what he quotes from the secondary literature. Petrie's treatment includes his own discussion, and, as he acknowledges in the preface, he published two other 'more generally accessible' works that were 'based on this material, but with a more personal treatment'.[64] Each culture is treated uniformly in the volumes, so as to facilitate easy comparison between volumes of different cultures. In theory, someone using the volumes for comparative purposes could quickly find out the 'sociological facts' about each culture and get references to the scholarly authorities on the subject.

Spencer was never able to complete the work in which all of the different cultures were compared according to specific cultural subsections (such as political or ceremonial).[65] His work was not a critical success at the time, and reviewers disliked the application of a social-science approach to the study of world cultures (perhaps if it had been released in the 1960s the reaction would have been different).[66] Furthermore, criticisms of the lack of historical methods in his research and his seeming lack of interest in writing a more typical history of each culture were levied at the works. It is clear that Spencer accumulated a vast amount of historical material; what he sought to do with that material was to generalize from it and identify what traits are common to all of humanity. Yet Carneiro points to the profound misunderstanding that many critics held toward Spencer's view of cultural evolution.[67] Although later taken as a proponent of unilinear cultural evolution, the work of his *Descriptive Sociology* and his later arguments suggest that he was in fact arguing for a model of classifying cultures based on divergence and redivergence (explicitly based on biological models), and that this was explicitly non-linear.[68] Spencer was, however, convinced that 'progress' was a key feature of this cultural evolution and that humanity was constantly improving, and this optimism may have translated into unilinear models for some of his readers. Regardless, Spencer's supposed unilinear arguments influenced a generation of anthropologists.

---

64. Petrie, *Descriptive Sociology*, p. i. The two other books were *Social Life in Ancient Egypt* and *Religious Life in Ancient Egypt*.

65. Harris, *Rise of Anthropological Theory*, p. 159.

66. Robert L. Carneiro, 'Herbert Spencer as an Anthropologist', *Journal of Libertarian Studies* 5 (1981), pp. 153-210 (163-64).

67. Carneiro, 'Herbert Spencer', p. 187.

68. Spencer's reliance on biology is apparent in the following statement he made on the nature of social evolution: 'A social organism is like an individual organism, it grows; in growing it becomes more complex; its parts acquire increasing dependence; its life is immense in length compared with the lives of its component units. Increasing integration is accompanied by increasing heterogeneity and increasing definiteness' (quoted in the introduction to Rumney, *Herbert Spencer's Sociology*, p. vii.

4. Progress and Decline

Spencer's version of social evolution was widely debated, and Lewis Henry Morgan was one of the influential sociologists who offered an alternative view. In his 1877 *Ancient Society*, Morgan laid out three major 'ethnical periods' that humans developed through. These periods were savagery, barbarism and civilization, and each could be further subdivided into lower, middle and upper (based upon certain technological achievements). Corresponding with these technologically based ethnical periods were a number of developmental models for various components of culture such as sociopolitical organization and kinship terminology. One of the most influential of Morgan's observations for scholars of the Near East was his observation that Hebrew (as well as Roman) culture organized family structure on a patriarchal model in which supreme authority was held by the patriarch of the household. This idea would later be taken up by Max Weber and has had a resurgence in twenty-first-century Near Eastern studies.

The work of Tylor, Spencer and Morgan led to the widespread acceptance of unilinear models of cultural evolution. These models (best exemplified by Tylor and Morgan, less so Spencer) posited that societies had life cycles much as humans do: they are born, develop through childhood, peak in adulthood, decline in old age and eventually die out. This mode of thinking was heavily dependent on Hegelian theory and evolutionary theory. It readily explained the radical cultural differences around the world (especially technological) and justified imperialism in a paternalistic fashion, for the 'adult' cultures had a responsibility to care for the child-like cultures. Marvin Harris has argued that nineteenth-century unilinear evolutionary models have been mischaracterized and that these scholars did not argue that every culture had to go through every stage of development.[69] Harris suggests that these scholars seemed to have argued this because they concentrated on shared elements of culture as they were attempting to write a universal history. Areas of cultural divergence were less relevant (or less interesting) since they were not thought to shed light on the universality of humanity. The categories of similarity were also not intended to be as rigid as they seemed to be to later scholars.

While models of unilinear cultural evolution were extremely influential in the nineteenth century, there was another prominent and contradictory model for explaining why change happened and how change occurs: diffusion.[70] Proponents of diffusion presume that acts of inventions (technological, intellectual, etc.) occur in historically discrete instances. Once something is invented, it spreads to other cultures through a variety of

---

69. See Harris, *Rise of Anthropological Theory*, pp. 171-73, for his discussion of this and especially his refutation of Julian Steward's interpretation of these scholars.

70. In retrospect Spencer's ideas are probably more closely related to diffusionist thought, but this is not how they were understood in the Victorian era.

mechanisms, such as trade or colonization. So diffusionists will attempt to trace the movements of one 'thing', like agriculture, through its transmissions between various cultures. Whereas unilinear evolution provides for the same types of changes at the same relative stages of development, diffusion necessitates cultural contact to explain change. The introduction of metal and farming into Europe from the Near East were important diffusionist arguments that linked the two regions for nineteenth-century thinkers, with the Phoenicians typically seen as the intermediary.[71] Diffusion, then, became a mechanism through which the ancient Near Eastern world could be directly linked to (and claimed for) European prehistory.

There were, of course, world historians in the nineteenth century who could be categorized neither as evolutionists nor as diffusionists. The diversity of other approaches to understanding the past makes it impossible to survey them all here, but the Swiss historian Jacob Burckhardt is an interesting example of a social conservative who used historical evidence to champion the freedom of the individual and warn of liberal democracy's potentials for despotism. His type of history was an evaluative type, not an objective type, and fundamentally, Burckhardt's arguments about the past were arguments about the present. For Burckhardt, history was best understood not as a series of gradual improvements; to him, this was the propaganda of the nineteenth century. Rather, he studied history by identifying key issues of concern for all civilizations and comparing how these concerns were balanced in relation to one another. His universal history, then, was not a history of the entire world but a history that identified examples of societies that had developed different types of equilibrium in regards to these key concerns.[72] The ancient Near East, to Burckhardt, exemplified a particular type of despotism, one in which the state had complete control over cultural production, creating a kind of long-term stasis.[73] The Egyptians maintained state control by framing art and science as sacred, and thus inviolable.[74] He was less clear about Mesopotamian cultures but argued that similar approaches prevented the emergence of individual liberty in those cultures as well.[75] The first hints of the breakdown of this kind of Near Eastern despotism are apparent in ancient Hebrew poetry, and as each societal

---

71. For an example of this kind of discussion in relation to bronze, see John Lubbock, *Prehistoric Times, as Illustrated by Ancient Remains, and the Manners and Customs of Modern Savages* (London: Williams & Norgate, 1865), pp. 31-59.

72. For a more in-depth discussion of Burckhardt's conception of history, see Nichols's introduction in Jacob Burckhardt, *Force and Freedom: Reflections on History* (ed. James Hastings Nichols; Boston: Beacon Press, 1943), pp. 60-62.

73. Burckhardt, *Force*, p. 170.

74. Burckhardt, *Force*, pp. 172, 192.

75. Burckhardt, *Force*, p. 172.

concern gradually detached itself from sacrality and state control, the despotism of the Near East gave way to the classical era.

Burckhardt's approach reflected his own fears about European society and especially disenchantment with the oppression that emerges after revolutionary action. His fellow scholars of universal history were less clearly positioned on the side of the conservative order, especially those who worked from evolutionary frameworks, in which the 'newer' reflected progress. The widespread acceptance of evolutionism among nineteenth-century scholars was simultaneously conservative and subversive. On the one hand, these scholars saw Victorian-era England as the culmination of human progress so far. Darwinian notions of survival of the fittest, when applied to European society, could easily be made to show that Europe was the 'fittest' society, and thus a sort of natural law underpinned European supremacy. On the other hand, as Harris has pointed out, this was a fundamentally destabilizing concept for it demonstrated that the major institutions that made up European life (such as family and private property) were not intrinsic to being human.[76] It meant that other alternatives to life were possible and that these institutions were not necessarily divinely inspired. Perhaps this was the most destabilizing element—that these unilinear models removed God as the causal force behind the development of humanity. The primacy of the Christian God was still easily justified through these evolutionary models, but God's participation was perceived as less visible.

Within this context of post-Darwinian and post-Lyellian scholarship, which used the study of the ancient Near East to generate knowledge about humanity more broadly, were the works of Karl Marx and Friedrich Engels. Marx and Engels were clearly inspired by the writings of Darwin (with Engels claiming at Marx's memorial that Marx had discovered the law of evolution in human history much as Darwin had discovered it in biology) and saw history as a progress narrative toward a potentially utopian future. Early civilizations were important to their reconstruction of history but not central, which was predicated on a Hegelian dialectic, with struggles between classes substituted for struggles between ideas. Their work has been influential in twentieth-century studies of the Near East, especially that which has come out of Eastern Europe and more recently Italy.[77] Its influence on nineteenth-century thinking about the ancient Near East is less apparent, but some consideration here is warranted. For Marx, societies had progressed in a specific order, much as the archaeologists and anthropologists had demonstrated. This was consistent with his understanding of

---

76. Harris, *Rise of Anthropological Theory*, p. 210.
77. For a discussion of Marxist approaches to the ancient Near East, see Kevin M. McGeough, *Exchange Relationships at Ugarit* (Ancient Near Eastern Studies Supplement, 26; Leuven: Peeters, 2007), pp. 49-60.

culture having a materialist base, dependent on technology. Since technological development is incremental and requires certain discoveries before others can occur, a set evolutionary pattern can be expected. The writings of Marx and Engels show a dynamic understanding of this evolutionary pattern, and changes to their thinking are evident in different works. It is not possible to do justice to the variations in their approaches, but some general themes can be considered here.

Of greatest obvious influence on Near Eastern studies was the specific framework, somewhat articulated by Marx and Engels, that has come to be known as the Asiatic Mode of Production. Given their obvious interest in economic behavior and their belief that understanding economic relationships is fundamental to understanding any society, it should not be surprising that the Asiatic Mode of Production reflects the structure of economic relationships. Marx and Engels identify one key principle that differentiates the Asiatic Mode of Production from other modes, and that is the lack of private property in terms of landholding.[78] Marx and Engels were not the first to identify the Near East as a locus for a different type of economic situation than that of Western feudalism. John Stuart Mill described a situation akin to 'oriental despotism' in which the climate of Asia required massive amounts of state intervention in order to allow for irrigation agriculture.[79] Marx picked up on this, and the control over irrigation works becomes a key component of the Asiatic Mode of Production, for in his view, the vast requirements for irrigation and the peculiarities of the Asian climate necessitated direct state intervention at an early stage. For these reasons, in Asia, the state was the only landowner, in real terms.

The centralization of land ownership and control over irrigation is fundamental to the oriental state, which Marx and Engels come to see as one stage in world historical development. In *The German Ideology* (1846), Marx and Engels set out these specific stages. The second stage is germane to the Near East, as this is when the states of the Near East came into being. Cities were formed (on both a voluntary and coercive basis) by the merging of different tribal groups. As cities (and state-level polities) formed, notions of private property developed, and what was once communally owned came to be owned by the state. The culmination of these developments came with the rise of the Graeco-Roman city-states. In *The Critique of Political Economy* (1859) and the posthumously published notes (originally written from 1857–1858) for this work, now called *Outlines of a Critique of Political Economy* (1939–1941), Marx set out different evolutionary stages and

---

78. Ralph Miliband, 'Marx and the State', *The Socialist Register* 1965, pp. 278-96 (accessed at https://www.marxists.org/archive/miliband/1965/xx/state.htm).

79. Karl A. Wittfogel, *Oriental Despotism: A Comparative Study of Total Power* (New Haven, CT: Yale University Press, 1957), pp. 372-73.

here separated the ancient Near East from the classical world (differentiating between Asiatic and Ancient stages). In the Asiatic stage, the primitive communalism that underpinned the birth of cities lasted longer than had been previously understood. This became a key feature of twentieth-century Marxist thinking on Near Eastern studies. Much of the focus there has been on the conflict between primitive communalism and the landholding power of the state, especially in Mesopotamia.

Marxist thinking about oriental despotism is much in line with the perceptions about the Ottoman economic conduct toward Palestine (especially) held by late eighteenth- and early-nineteenth-century travellers. Naomi Shepherd has identified a number of these travellers who were particularly important in articulating a connection between Ottoman misrule and the poor economic development of Palestine. Count Volney was one of the most influential early travellers who argued that Ottoman financial mismanagement was much of the reason for the lack of productivity in Palestine, which otherwise should have been a productive region for agriculture and maritime resources.[80] Edward Clarke, who first arrived in Acre in 1801, later argued that Ottoman taxation levels were too punitive to encourage the people of the region to engage in any significant agricultural production, and fears of property confiscation led to actions like the superficial mutilation of animals (cropping ears, for example) in order to make that property less appealing to tax collectors.[81] Burckhardt even saw these practices as the root of the semi-nomadic lifestyle in Palestine, with people preferring to move and not plant fields in order to avoid taxation.[82] Furthermore, the Ottoman approach to security in the region, allowing the Bedouin tribes to compete and war with one another, meant that pillaging and violence were almost formalized elements of governance. Evidence such as this, mixed with orientalist notions that the region never changed, made it easy for Marxist scholars to project Ottoman practices into their reconstructions of ancient economic life.

Marx's understanding of the material basis of society seems, at first glance, to be readily compatible with archaeological work, as archaeologists find and study the material remains of a society. As archaeology emerged as an almost mature discipline, new methods of classifying the stages of society based on their material remains were developed. And with the Near East increasingly considered the progenitor of civilization, early technology and objects were tangible evidence for progress and decline. In the nineteenth century, typological analysis came to be essential to archaeology, in which the life cycles of types of objects could be traced from their original inven-

---

80. Shepherd, *Zealous Intruders*, p. 15.
81. For more on Clarke's evaluation of these practices, see Shepherd, *Zealous Intruders*, p. 22.
82. Shepherd, *Zealous Intruders*, p. 55.

tion, through their rise in popularity, then their decline in quality and their final abandonment in use. Without a doubt, C.J. Thomsen's (1788–1865) development of the Three Age System as a means of ordering the artifacts in the Museum of Northern Antiquities in Copenhagen (now the National Museum of Denmark) was of paramount importance. Influenced by classical traditions (especially the Ages of Man discussed by Hesiod), Thomsen identified a temporal relationship among the European artifacts in the museum's collection. Stone artifacts were oldest, followed by bronze and then iron. These observations made sense in terms of technological sophistication, and so it made sense to think of the Stone Age, followed by the Bronze Age and then the Iron Age. This system was readily adopted for use in the ancient Near East, for it was essentially based on the technological ability to work metals (which further relates to increasing skill with pyrotechnology) and is still the main chronological scheme used in biblical archaeology.

By the end of the nineteenth century, evolutionary models for understanding materials were used by proponents of unilinear cultural evolution and diffusionists; typology and seriation worked/work equally well for either perspective. Yet Thomsen's original schema reflects a longer Enlightenment tradition of collecting; it is a system of ordering rooted entirely in the logic of the collector, grouping like artifacts with like to construct meaning and reveal relationships. The different purposes and approaches to collecting antiquities were early manifestations of considerations of progress and diversity. This was really a tension that should be understood as part of the Enlightenment, and in particular the work of natural philosophers to 'order' the world. Luke Syson has recognized that this negotiation (and of the eventual dominance of progress over diversity) reflected a 'substantial epistemological shift'.[83] This shift had pronounced effects on how we have come to understand the Near East.

The attempt to understand the history of the human spirit through its materials became a fundamental conceit of the museum as an institution, where objects are fetishized, taken out of their original contexts and placed within this new context as an icon or symbol of certain aspects or moments of human history. Even in the absence of a strict chronological framework, different elements of this universal progress narrative could be explored in an unsystematic (though seemingly systematic) fashion. Syson describes this approach to universal history as 'founded on a scheme of the succession of world empires, which could be related to the concept of passing on, or

---

83. Luke Syson, 'The Ordering of the Artificial World: Collecting, Classification, and Progress', in *Enlightenment: Discovering the World in the Eighteenth Century* (ed. K. Sloan; London: British Museum Press, 2003), pp. 108-21 (113).

4. *Progress and Decline*

"translations" of the arts and learning—the notion of progress from barbarism to civilization'.[84]

The consideration of the ancient Near East and Egypt led numerous philosophers, historians, anthropologists and natural scientists to consider the nature of difference throughout the world in both time and space. While a diversity of approaches to reconciling the experience of difference emerged, most reflect an underlying faith in the idea of progress and a fear of decline. The ancient Near East in particular provided empirical data of both progress and decline since both the achievements of the societies and their decay are readily evident archaeologically. In particular, the evaluation of the people of the nineteenth-century Near East as stunted in comparison to the grandeur of the past encouraged fears that progress could always be reversed. In fact, progress, while the ideal situation, was by no means the only possibility for the European future, as was apparent from the remnants of the collapsed (and formerly great) societies of Egypt and Mesopotamia. As shall be shown, theologians (especially Protestants) came to believe that God had created a living museum out of the Holy Land in order to instruct later Christians on the context of the Bible. The opposite message could also be read into the seeming decline of the nineteenth-century Egyptian and Holy Land populations—a romantic belief that people like the Bedouin engage in a lifestyle that can be an alternative to the increasing horrors of industrialization.

Beyond the societal scale of evolutionary thinking, the ancient Near East was particularly useful for considering the evolution of religion and the evolution of objects (and especially style). Monotheism, if not Christianity itself, was understood to be the culmination of the cultural-evolutionary process. John Barrell has argued that many Victorians saw the Greeks as 'closet monotheists' (in order to explain their advanced polytheistic civilization), and the same was true for the Egyptians, as shall be explored throughout this study.[85] Marvin Harris has noted that Tylor (although others may also be included in this) seemed to have developed a separate evolutionary path for religion.[86] That is to say, the unilinear evolutionary models for culture did not tend to include religion within the various stages of development, and in many ways religion was taken to be distinct from culture in a way that economy, politics and family were not.

The Evolution of Religion

Victorian evolutionary views of the origins and development of religion were, in large part, based on Enlightenment-era approaches to understand-

---

84. Syson, 'Ordering', p. 117.
85. John Barrell, 'Death on the Nile: Fantasy and the Literature of Tourism 1840-1860', *Essays in Criticism* 41 (1991), pp. 97-127 (97).
86. Harris, *Rise of Anthropological Theory*, p. 204.

ing religion, which generally understood religion as a negative or restraining force on human achievement. The new sources of data, derived from archaeology and ethnological studies, tended to be interpreted through the theoretical frameworks of the late eighteenth century. For Enlightenment thinkers such as John Locke and David Hume, it seemed that ancient and/or primitive people were incapable of abstract reasoning and that primitive religion reflected an early stage of intellectual evolution. As Katz has stated, 'the *philosophes* of the Enlightenment were often the silent partners of nineteenth-century anthropological discussion'.[87] He identifies Charles Dupuis and Giambattista Vico as typical.[88] Charles Dupuis applied this directly to the ancient Egyptians, arguing that the Egyptian masses were unable to understand the nearly scientific reasoning of the Egyptian intellectual elites and instead worshipped anthropomorphized and zoomorphized forms of these ideas as idols or fetishes. Giambattista Vico took these ideas even further, arguing that religion was the poetic form that primitive peoples used to describe their world. For Vico, every culture evolved in roughly the same way, inventing religion out of fear (the fear of thunder in most cases), followed by a greater interest in heroes and then humans. With Vico, one of the main theses underlying the nineteenth-century comparative approach to religion emerged: similarities between ancient religions did not stem from the diffusion of ideas; rather, the primitive mind worked within a fairly set framework with limited room for deviation.

Whereas diffusionism readily supported models of religious change based on literal biblical interpretation, evolutionary models led to new ways of thinking about biblical religion. Rather than identifying a historical moment of revelation (like the covenant with Abraham or the theophany at Sinai), the emergence of monotheism was seen as a type of intellectual and spiritual progress. This new approach to religion can be seen in Tylor's *Primitive Culture,* where he blends ethnographic evidence, Enlightenment ideas about religion and his own theories of social evolution.[89] Much of *Primitive Culture* is devoted to exploring the evolutionary development of religion, gradually from animism, to polytheism, and eventually to monotheism, although he never formulates a rigid system of rules for when these developments occur.

Within this evolutionary context of the study of religion came W. Robertson Smith's 1889 work *Religion of the Semites*, which attempted to uncover the social functions of various religious phenomena in the Bible. What distinguished his work from prior studies of biblical religion is that he treated the subject much as nineteenth-century scholars of religion studied non-

---

87. Katz, *God's Last Words,* p. 287.
88. Katz, *God's Last Words,* pp. 285-86.
89. Lubbock, *Primitive Culture,* p. 422.

biblical cultures.⁹⁰ Using an evolutionary approach to the study of religion, Smith argued against, to some degree, the novelty of Mosaic faith. Rather, he attempted to reduce biblical religion to its most basic forms in order to identify the evolutionary traits common to societies in general. Smith's conclusions (in very simplified form) were that myth arises out of ritual practice and that sacrifice was the most important component of religious practice since it was the primary means through which ancient communities interacted with their deities.

One of Smith's good friends (and most apt pupils), James Frazer, played an even more important role in the development of late-nineteenth- and early-twentieth-century views on comparative religion. In 1890, the first edition of Sir James Frazer's *The Golden Bough* was released, which, for the most part, followed Tylor's model of the evolution of religion, but with less emphasis on sociology and anthropology and more emphasis on literature.⁹¹ Frazer broke with Smith's understanding of the importance of the social role of religion in binding a group together.⁹² Primitive religion was not so much a tool of group solidarity and identity formation for Frazer, but rather was a philosophical system sanctioned by divine or supernatural authority. The underlying theme of *The Golden Bough* is that the oldest religions were essentially fertility cults centred on the worship (and sometimes sacrifice of) a sacred king. The book was particularly scandalous in that Christianity was included in this schema, seeing Jesus as one of many dying-and-rising gods. For Frazer, ancient (and contemporary undeveloped) cultures did not see human and divine powers as profoundly different, so the possibility of semi-divine humans was easily adopted within ancient worldviews.⁹³ In Frazer's evolutionary schema, sympathetic magic was an important component of this stage of religious development, in part because, as he states, 'the savage, whether European or otherwise, fails to recognize those limitations to his power over nature which seem so obvious to us'.⁹⁴ The sacred king, then, was more than just an intercessor between humans and the gods but had divine powers himself and was expected to

---

90. See Katz, *God's Last Words*, p. 294.

91. The name *The Golden Bough* refers to a section of *The Aeneid*, where Aeneas and the Sibyl give the golden bough to the gatekeeper of Hades to be allowed to pass through the gates. The second and third editions (published in 1900 and 1911–1915 respectively) differ significantly from the initial publication. It is the first edition that is of concern here (since this is a study of nineteenth-century reception), in terms of how Frazer used ancient Egypt and Syro-Palestinian religions in his comparative approach.

92. Katz, *God's Last Words*, p. 301.

93. James Frazer, *The Golden Bough: A Study in Comparative Religion*, I (London: Macmillan, 1894), pp. 31-32.

94. Frazer, *Golden Bough*, p. 30. Frazer's view of sympathetic magic was that it was predicated on a belief that like could influence like and that something could be

control the natural world, especially through sympathetic magic. As gods came to be understood as more powerful, Frazer believed that prayer and sacrifice came to be seen as more efficacious approaches to influencing the deities than sympathetic magic.

Frazer's take on Egyptian kingship was one element of the comparative evidence that he used to justify his interpretation of the development of sacred kingship in primitive religion. As he states:

> From this survey of the religious position occupied by the king in rude societies we may infer that the claim to divine and supernatural powers put forward by the monarchs of great historical empires like those of Egypt, Mexico, and Peru, was not simply the outcome of inflated vanity or the empty expression of a groveling adulation; it was merely a survival and extension of the old savage apotheosis of living kings.[95]

In Frazer's reading, that sacred kingship is found outside of the classical civilizations (Greece and Rome) is indicative of the fact that this 'is a common feature of societies at all stages from barbarism to civilisation'.[96] Thus, Frazer reads the Egyptian evidence in a manner that emphasizes similarities with other cultures. He emphasizes the importance of divine kingship and reads the mortuary temples of the Egyptian kings as equivalent to the temple complexes of the gods, a reading that is generally in keeping with late-nineteenth-century understandings of these Egyptian practices. Frazer further emphasizes the sympathetic powers of Egyptian kings, with observations such as, 'The King of Egypt seems to have shared with the sacred animals the blame of any failure of the crops'.[97] Frazer also slightly misreads comments made by the Egyptologist C.P. Tiele in a manner that suits his comparative framework. Frazer quotes Tiele's discussion of how after death, 'every good man... became Osiris' and how thus it was understandable how the king could also be placed on the same level as the divine. Frazer pushes Tiele's argument beyond a mortuary context and argues that every Egyptian claimed divine powers for himself and the only real difference between the powers of the king and the powers of the commoner were in scale (which is far different from what Tiele argues).[98]

Frazer also used ancient Egyptian religion as comparative evidence for his related arguments about the importance of dying-and-rising gods. The Egyptian deity Osiris is an obvious candidate for this kind of analysis. Interestingly, Frazer goes out of his way to demonstrate that the roots of Osirian

manipulated through the manipulation of something else that looked similar or had been previously been in contact with the intended object of the magic.
   95. Frazer, *Golden Bough*, p. 48.
   96. Frazer, *Golden Bough*, p. 51.
   97. Frazer, *Golden Bough*, p. 50.
   98. Frazer, *Golden Bough*, p. 50.

4. Progress and Decline

Fig. 4.2. Turquoise djed pillar amulet from the British Museum collection. Late Period (after 600 BCE). © Trustees of the British Museum.

worship lay not in astral or solar phenomenon (*contra* Tiele, Renouf and other nineteenth-century Egyptologists). Rather, Osiris was first a tree spirit and then a corn (wheat, not maize) deity.[99] This analysis of the Osirian cult is somewhat difficult to justify. Frazer explains that the Egyptian tendency to assimilate various deities has obscured Osiris's true origins, but, at heart, Plutarch's account of the Osiris–Isis–Seth–Horus myth reflects an interest in agriculture; his body parts being scattered across Egypt reflects a 'mythical way of expressing either the sowing or the winnowing of the grain'.[100] Other classical sources suggest that the Egyptians believed that Osiris had taught them agriculture, further proof to Frazer that Osiris was 'a deity of vegetation'.[101] Frazer explains (referencing classical literature not Egyptian) how Osiris was even earlier associated with pine trees. Frazer also uses some Egyptian evidence to support this. Most notably, he understands the Egyptian djed-pillar symbol (Fig. 4.2) as 'a conventional representation of a tree stripped of its leaves' (acknowledging the typical Egyptological reading of this pillar as a stylized rendering of Osiris's spine).[102] So, while Frazer is interacting with ancient Egyptian evidence, his analysis transforms that evidence in a manner that more readily fits his comparative-evolutionary schema.

99. Frazer, *Golden Bough*, pp. 307, 316-18.
100. Frazer, *Golden Bough*, p. 306.
101. Frazer, *Golden Bough*, p. 305.
102. Frazer, *Golden Bough*, p. 304.

Part of the problem with Frazer's take on ancient Egypt may lie in his reliance on classical sources. Despite how well established Egyptology was as a discipline in 1890, there are only a few Egyptological authors that Frazer cites.[103] He is mostly reliant on Plutarch, Diodorus, Herodotus and others for the primary evidence on which he builds his arguments. Although Frazer does treat these sources critically, his heavy usage of them suggests a somewhat tautological framework, in that Egypt probably should not be understood as independent from the classical traditions if Egypt is primarily approached through the classical sources. This tautological approach is inherent in his discussion of 'the death and resurrection of vegetation', where he argues that the ceremonies in Egypt and western Asia 'appear to have been most widely celebrated with ceremonies like those of modern Europe'.[104] Since he has previously used these European rituals as analogues with which to reconstruct Egyptian practices, his line of reasoning is suspect, for he is not arguing that these traditions are historically related. Rather, their similarities derive from a universal evolutionary progress.

Frazer's readings of Syrian practices and their associations with Adonis were more in line with what was believed by specialists in the late-nineteenth century. He argues that the Greek god Adonis was originally a Syrian deity (based on the etymology of Adonis as derived from the Semitic word *adôn*—meaning lord). Aphrodite took on the role of the Semitic goddess Astarte, and so Frazer sees the celebration of the dying and rising of Adonis as a ceremony of Syrian origin.[105] Frazer explains how this tradition makes sense within the geographical context of the Syrian city of Byblos, how in the spring, as red earth washes down from the mountains, the river nearby takes on a blood-red hue. Within this discussion, Frazer references Sayce's translation of the Babylonian story of Ishtar and Tammuz, which has noteworthy similarities to the Adonis myth and can just as easily be associated with the rebirth of vegetation in the spring.[106]

Elsewhere throughout *The Golden Bough*, Frazer compares ancient Near Eastern practices with those of other cultures around the world in order to build up his argument about the evolution of religion. For example, Phoenician, Moabite and biblical practices of child sacrifice, as reported in the Bible and classical sources, are said to reflect practices that Frazer describes as 'not peculiarly Semitic', since cultures around the world also engaged in child sacrifice.[107] He compares the reports of these practices with cultures in Wales, Florida and Africa. Maspero's translation of the Egyptian story nor-

---

103. Roughly in order of frequency of citation (omitting some), he most commonly references Tiele, Erman, Brugsch, Wilkinson, and Maspero.
104. Frazer, *Golden Bough*, p. 278.
105. Frazer, *Golden Bough*, pp. 280-81.
106. Frazer, *Golden Bough*, p. 287.
107. Frazer, *Golden Bough*, pp. 235-36.

mally referred to by scholars as 'The Tale of Two Brothers' is paraphrased and read as evidence of the near universal belief that the soul can be kept safely outside of the body.[108] Victorian interest in the seeming reverence with which the ancient Egyptians were believed to have treated their animals led Frazer to posit what he calls 'a sacrament of the Egyptian type'.[109] Frazer compares what he believes to be the Egyptian's abhorrence of pig, the special treatment of the Apis bulls, and the relationship between rams and the cult of Amun at Thebes to argue that the Egyptians would give particular animals special treatment at most times of the year but would sacrifice them in specific, solemn ceremonies.[110] Relatedly, Frazer discusses Plutarch's confusion regarding the Jewish aversion to pork, and concludes (in tandem with something of a misreading of Isa. 65:3-4, 66:3, 17) that the Jews originally held the pig as a sacred animal.[111]

In general, Frazer privileges classical accounts of Egyptian and Near Eastern religion over the works of nineteenth-century scholars. It is clear that even this late in the nineteenth century, those sources were still the most useful for scholars working on mythology. Even when specialist studies are cited, the classical accounts remain the basis of Frazer's arguments, meaning that Frazer's study of the Near East is better thought of as a study of Graeco-Roman perceptions of the Near East than an analysis of Near Eastern thought directly. The immediate influence of this work was profound, and non-specialists who worked through it would have found a seeming academic perpetuation of classical views of the Near East, confusing the study of mythology for some time to come. What emerges from *The Golden Bough* in popular usage is a kind of generic and interchangeable ancient mythology, easily transformed in its details but sharing the same basic underlying principles. The book provided an 'evidentiary' basis for Jung's treatment of archetypes and later variations of archetypal criticism and thinking. It also provided inspiration for non-academic uses of ancient mythology, perhaps most influentially in Baden-Powell's Boy Scout initiation ceremonies, which were modeled on aspects of initiation rites that were common cross-culturally.[112]

That scholars and non-specialists readily accepted a kind of generic ancient, polytheistic religion is not surprising given the scorn held for

---

108. Frazer, *Golden Bough*, pp. 315-18. This is an important element of Frazer's larger argument, in that it helps justify his explanation that primitive peoples felt that they could keep the divine soul alive after having killed the host body and that that soul was believed to be transferable to another host.
109. Frazer, *Golden Bough*, p. 136.
110. Frazer, *Golden Bough*, pp. 50-93 (*passim*).
111. Frazer, *Golden Bough*, pp. 51-52.
112. Rani Kabbani, *Europe's Myths of Orient* (Bloomington, IN: Indiana University Press, 1986), p. 8.

non-Christian religion. Degenerationist ideas survived the longest among scholars studying religion for it was easy for Christian scholars to accept monotheism as a gift presented to the ancient Israelites by God that did not develop out of earlier forms of religion. To some, it was distasteful to find the origins of Christianity in the superstitions of primitive people. These notions are not necessarily dissimilar to the *Bibel-und-Babel* controversies that allowed for a Mesopotamian (as opposed to Jewish) background for Christianity, and would be especially influential in later German scholarship (discussed later in this chapter).

Not all of the scholarship on ancient religion reflected unilinear evolutionary models. Diffusion was equally useful in attempts to explain the apparent similarities between traditions. A noteworthy attack on Tylor's notions of the origins of religion among primitive cultures was offered by Andrew Lang in his 1898 volume *The Making of Religion*. There, Lang argues that God and gods could not be understood as developing out of the type of animism described by Tylor.[113] Lang was not the only example. One of the longer lasting diffusionist arguments about religion was the solarism theory presented by Max Müller. Most noted for starting the fifty-volume series *The Sacred Books of the East*, which translated the major works of Eastern religions into English, Müller noted that most Indo-European religious traditions centred on deities that manifested the powers of the sun. Myth reflected a deficiency in primitive languages. Lacking abstract terminology, myths were the ancient language for expressing abstract ideas. Eventually the scientific reasoning that lay behind the myths was forgotten, and the stories were preserved as archaic vestiges.[114]

Especially after Smith's discovery that there was a demonstrable relationship between Mesopotamian and biblical literature, the ancient Near East became an important locus for the consideration of progress and decline in terms of religion. Given that monotheism appeared later than polytheism and that Christianity eventually emerged as the dominant religion in Europe, replacing polytheistic traditions (for the most part), models of progress appeared to be born out by the evidence. The Old Testament itself provides a narrative of religious history that harmonizes well with this. Decline could also be identified in a number of ways. The decline of Egyptian and Mesopotamian civilization was seen in relation to the failure to reject the idolatries of polytheism. Or, the decline could be situated much later—for Protestants in the movement of the Catholic tradition away from the purer traditions of the early church or for Catholics in the degeneration of the authority of Rome. One of the clearest manifestations of this is in the

---

113. Harris, *Rise of Anthropological Theory*, p. 207. Lang makes this argument forcefully in chap. 11 of his *The Making of Religion*.

114. Katz, *God's Last Words*, p. 284.

4. *Progress and Decline*

burgeoning understanding of the Near Eastern context of the Bible. Thus the flood story, which George Smith described in his 1873 address, fit this schema perfectly as a literary account that had been adapted, revised and improved upon by the Israelites.

The evaluation of which society was more progressive, Mesopotamian or Israelite, lay at the heart of the so-called *Bibel-und-Babel* controversy. The uncomfortable question that emerged from George Smith's discovery, and that had been lurking at the edges of Assyriology, was what to make of the differences that were apparent in Mesopotamian literary accounts that were otherwise similar to those found in the Old Testament? Did the appearance of these stories in both contexts prove that the Flood actually happened or that a baby was discovered in a reed basket (like Moses or Sargon)? If so, the situation could easily be explained through recourse to Abraham's origins in Ur—he brought Mesopotamian accounts with him, only his were divinely inspired. Or, removing Abraham from the explanation, the Mesopotamian and biblical narratives were just accounts of the same events but told from different perspectives, and again, primacy could be given to the biblical versions as divinely inspired. By 1902, these issues could no longer be ignored and erupted as the *Bibel-und-Babel* controversy, signaled by Friedrich Delitzsch's lectures at the German Oriental Society in the presence of Kaiser Wilhelm II.[115] These lectures were what Arnold and Weisberg have called 'a kind of "command performance" of German élites (business, government and military leaders) to co-opt academics' (who were willing participants) into a larger vision of growing German world power.[116] Printed copies of the first lecture sold out quickly, and by 1905, over 60,000 had been sold.[117] Responses were numerous, and over 1,650 articles were written over the next couple of years by people from all walks of life.[118] Delitzsch's talk had become a cultural phenomenon within Germany.[119]

---

115. Friedrich Delitzsch, *Babel and Bible: Three Lectures on the Significance of Assyriological Research for Religion, Embodying the Most Important Criticisms and the Author's Replies* (Chicago: Open Court Publishing Company, 1906).

116. Bill T. Arnold and David Weisberg, 'Delitzch in Context', in *God's Word for our World, Volume II: Theological and Cultural Studies in Honor of Simon John De Vries* (ed. J. Harold Ellens, Deborah L. Ellens, Rolf P. Knierim and Isaac Kalimi; Journal for the Study of the Old Testament Supplement Series, 389; Sheffield: JSOT Press, 2004), pp. 37-45 (38).

117. Marchand, *German Orientalism*, p. 244.

118. Marchand, *German Orientalism*, p. 245.

119. Rachel Hallote has argued that since so many American scholars took their degrees in Germany (before the establishment of programs in the United States) Delitzch's views were quite influential for early American biblical archaeology. See Rachel Hallote, 'Jacob H. Schiff and the Beginning of Biblical Archaeology in the United States', *American Jewish History* 95 (2009), pp. 225-47.

Delitzsch's arguments became more explicit and assured over time, but, beginning in 1902, Delitzsch articulated a view that the Bible was not divinely inspired and that similarities with Mesopotamian literature proved that there had been human error in the transmission of the text. For Delitzsch, then, the goal of fusing Assyriology and biblical studies was to identify fact from fiction from the Old Testament and highlight the non-Semitic aspects of early Christianity.[120] Here though, Delitzch's views should not be seen as merging evolutionary and diffusionist conceptualizations (but rather as solely diffusionist), for they are rooted in the thinking of the pan-Babylonian movement, which saw all human religion as originally rooted in Mesopotamia.[121] Thus the older the religion, the more 'pure' it was, with Christianity marking a major evolutionary step forward from this *ur*-religion. As Delitzsch's thinking on the subject progressed, his views became more explicitly anti-Semitic, and by the 1920s he was arguing that Assyriology was unearthing the dangers of Jewish thinking. He would go so far as to argue that Christians should completely abandon the Old Testament.[122] Although his scholarship would come to be virtually ignored by the academy (and even his third lecture on the topic did not arouse nearly the same level of interest as the previous two), his ideas would hold popular sway in Germany for some time.[123] That this debate would first emerge in Germany is not surprising in retrospect. A number of German scholars, led by Hugo Winckler (who excavated the Hittite capital at Boghazkoi) had begun arguing for the historical primacy of Mesopotamian culture in the ancient Near East.[124] Germany had been the centre of critical biblical scholarship for many years, and so scholars were well prepared to think of the Bible as a document that had been curated by a number of hands over a number of years and that it contained material derived from earlier sources. This tendency was further fueled by Kaiser Wilhelm II's interest in Near Eastern studies, both academic (he actually published on the subject during

---

120. Eckart Frahm has shown that to prove the non-Semitic nature of Assyria Delitzsch was forced to make recourse to reconstructions of Mesopotamian civilization from before cuneiform could be read, for example, reviving older arguments that images of Assurbanipal's wife showed her to be blonde. See Eckart Frahm, 'Images of Assyria in Nineteenth- and Twentieth-Century Western Scholarship', in *Orientalism, Assyriology and the Bible* (ed. Steven W. Holloway; Hebrew Bible Monographs, 10; Sheffield: Sheffield Phoenix Press, 2007), pp. 74-93 (84).

121. Steven W. Holloway, 'Introduction: Orientalism, Assyriology, and the Bible', in *Orientalism, Assyriology and the Bible* (ed. Steven W. Holloway; Hebrew Bible Monographs, 10; Sheffield: Sheffield Phoenix Press, 2007), pp. 1-41 (19); Marchand, *German Orientalism*, p. 199.

122. Frahm, 'Images of Assyria', pp. 82-85.

123. Marchand, *German Orientalism*, p. 246.

124. Marchand, *German Orientalism*, pp. 237-51.

4. *Progress and Decline*

his exile after World War I) and imperialistic (he saw archaeological work in the Near East as both an imperial responsibility of the European powers and a marker of German international maturity). Exacerbated by rising German anti-Semitism, the goal of eliminating the Semitic elements that had leaked into Christianity was easily fused with an evolutionary model of religion that placed Judaic national/ethic monotheism and Mesopotamian polytheism on one level and Christian universal monotheism at the highest level.[125]

Evolutionary and diffusionist models of religion did not disappear with the Victorians. The corollary response to the *Bibel-und-Babel* issues may be seen in the growth of Semitic studies in the United States, especially as manifest at the outset of the twentieth century at Johns Hopkins, Harvard and the University of Pennsylvania. In this academic context, biblical archaeology came to involve multidisciplinary approaches (especially archaeology, philology and ethnology) to studying the Mediterranean broadly, where the Iron Age stood as the central concern of the enterprise.[126] Jerusalem was the centre of this pan-biblical–Mediterranean culture, and rather than divorcing Judaism from Christianity, early manifestations of Hebraic culture were seen as foundational for the Western tradition. At the 1903 opening of the Semitic Museum at Harvard, Cyrus Adler, for example, explained that such a museum was necessary because 'in everything which makes for the higher life the modern man derived directly from a few groups of people that lived about the Mediterranean, and that knowledge of their civilization is essential to an understanding of the higher history of human thought'.[127] Well into the twentieth century, evolutionary models of religion were adopted by Near Eastern studies scholars to explain the emergence of Christianity, especially by scholars working in the United States. W.F. Albright's monumental *From the Stone Age to Christianity: Monotheism and the Historical Process* articulated a vision of Syro-Palestinian archaeology that was distinctly teleological.[128] This work, which would set the tone for twentieth-century North American biblical archaeology, provided a means through which scientific archaeology could demonstrate the triumph

---

125. For an introduction (including bibliography) to the Bible *and* Babel question, see Mogens Trolle Larsen, 'The "Babel/Bible" Controversy and its Aftermath', in *Civilizations of the Ancient Near East*, I (ed. Jack M. Sasson, Peabody, MA: Hendrickson Publishers, 2000 [1995]), pp. 95-106.

126. Barbara Kirschenblatt-Gimblett, 'A Place in the World: Jews and the Holy Land at World's Fairs', in *Encounters with the 'Holy Land': Place, Past, and Future in American Jewish Culture* (ed. Jeffrey Shandler and Beth S. Wenger; Hanover, NH: University Press of New England, 1997), pp. 60-82 (66-67).

127. As quoted in Kirschenblatt-Gimblett, 'Place in the World', p. 68.

128. W.F. Albright, *From the Stone Age to Christianity: Monotheism and the Historical Process* (Baltimore, MD: Johns Hopkins University Press, 1940).

of Scripture. For many scholars working from a faith-based perspective in the field of Syro-Palestinian archaeology, there is a tendency to tone down the overt Christian triumphalism, but the nineteenth-century evolutionary framework still informs their research. This was not just the case for biblical archaeology; evolutionary models continued to be used to understand Mesopotamian religion. Following a more Frazerian approach, Thorkild Jacobsen's *The Treasures of Darkness*, for example, explained the development of Sumerian religion through a distinctly evolutionary framework, where a more abstract form of polytheism (centred on political power and later the individual) developed out of a simple animistic nature religion.[129]

The Decline and the Collapse of the British Empire

While this chapter has concentrated on academic thinking about progress and decline, these concerns were not limited to the Ivory Tower in the Victorian era. The rediscovery of the grand civilizations was a truly destabilizing notion for the nineteenth-century British. The evidence of the highly advanced societies that had collapsed and vanished centuries ago triggered feelings of insecurity vis-à-vis the perceived dominance of the British Empire. For popular writers, this acted as a 'hook' to excite readers and to promote introspection on the nature of English society. In an unofficial guide to the British Museum from 1852, the writer suggests that the visitor think about possible ramifications for English society after a visit to the Egyptian galleries:

> It is well, however, to pause upon the threshold, and before dismissing these interesting glimpses into the life, long since scattered as dust, upon the soil of Egypt, to call to mind the prominent points of the impressive story that may be read in the room he is about to quit. He may wander back through the histories of ages upon ages.... So silently, for us of the present hour, time rolled by in those days, that we fail to grasp the measure of the distance which separates our fret and toil of the nineteenth century, from that busy valley of the Nile.... Curious thoughts crowd in every busy brain, before these strange relics. Lost in the depths of the past, the mind, with a leap, often grasps at the future; and men will be found seriously saying to themselves, as they notice how we depend for our knowledge of ancient Egyptian fabrics upon the shrouds of ancient Egyptians,—what, if we looked forward, and in the remote centuries that are rolling toward us, see all our vast and busy Lancashire some layers underground, and archaeologists busy with our winding sheet [burial shroud]! Well, at the least, these thoughts are not idle. It does all of us good to think often of what has been, and to dream of the future to which we are driving 'down the ringing grooves of time'—to think sometimes of the fine people who had their

---

129. Thorkild Jacobsen, *The Treasures of Darkness: A History of Mesopotamian Religion* (New Haven, CT: Yale University Press, 1976); p. 21.

glorious days, when London was distributed, untouched by human hands, in clayey strata, and remote stone quarries; and hereabouts, to the minds of the Greeks, lay the islands of the blessed.[130]

These somewhat long-winded ruminations (here shortened considerably) are indicative of the kind of thinking about the present and the future that these encounters with the past may have inspired.

That the civilizations of Egypt and Mesopotamia were now in a state of collapse was readily apparent to the nineteenth-century thinker in the apparent lack of contemporary civilization in those regions. Striking evidence of progress and potential decline was this juxtaposition of the present and past states of civilization in the Near East. As presented by Victorian travellers and Victorian media, the glory of Egypt, Assyria and Judah was long gone, replaced by a stagnant culture paralyzed by archaic practices. For example, take this comment on Egypt's showing at London's Great Exhibition in 1851:

> Egypt, once the renowned of all nations, made but an insignificant display on this occasion, her former dignity and industrial position being remembered.... It was evident that all the glory of this country had departed, and that a feeble race occupied the position once held by the most mighty, wise and industrious population of the globe.[131]

Here the perceived disjuncture between past and present is made clear. The site of the once most 'industrious population' has become the home of a 'feeble race'. The nineteenth-century inhabitants of the Near East dwell within the ruins of its former glory.

For some, the ruins of the Near East were evidence of the proof of Scripture. The reverend Alexander Keith's journeys to the Holy Land inspired in him a belief that all of the biblical prophecies about the destruction of ancient Near Eastern societies had come true. Believing that this kind of evidence would be sufficient to convince non-believers of the truth of Christianity, the Scottish clergyman wrote an extremely popular book detailing this evidence, *Evidence of the Truth of the Christian Religion Derived from the Literal Fulfilment of Prophecy; Particularly as Illustrated by the History of the Jews, and by the Discoveries of Recent Travellers*. First published in 1826 and reprinted in many editions, Keith

---

130. W. Blanchard Jerrold, *How to See the British Museum in Four Visits* (London: Project Gutenberg E-Book, 2004 [1852]).

131. N.A., *The Industry of Nations, as Exemplified in the Great Exhibition of 1851: The Materials of Industry* (London: Society for Promoting Christian Knowledge, 1852), p. 232. See also Eileen Gillooly, 'Historical Remedies for Taxonomic Troubles: Reading the Great Exhibition', in *Victorian Prism: Refractions of the Crystal Palace* (ed. J. Buzzard, J. Childers and E. Gillolly; Charlottesville, VA: University of Virginia Press, 2007), pp. 23-39 (32).

describes biblical prophecies about the destruction of Jerusalem, the Jews, the cities of Judaea, Samaria, Ammon, Moab, Edom, Philistia, Lebanon, Nineveh, Babylon, Tyre, Egypt, and the Arabs. His logic is simple. The Bible foretold the destruction of these places; he and other visitors to the region have seen that they were destroyed, so, the Christian religion is itself proven. Despite the length of the book, this is really the only argument. For example, Keith summarizes:

> On a review of the prophecies relative to Nineveh, Babylon, Tyre, and Egypt, may we not, by the plainest induction from indisputable facts, conclude that the fate of these cities and countries, as well as the land of Judea and the adjoining territories, demonstrates the truth of the prophecies respecting them?[132]

It is doubtful that this kind of logic was very convincing to non-believers, but given its strong sales, the book was popular. Keith's argument points to how many non-specialists must have understood the ruins of the ancient Near East, as evidence that biblical prophecies of destruction had come true and that Christianity's survival was evidence of its veracity.

In nineteenth-century literary-poetic and scientific accounts of the ancient Near East, the motif of 'ruins' provided a means of thinking about the location of the past. As Elliott Colla has noted, 'More than a pile of rubble but less than a monument whose original use has been preserved, the ruin evokes a peculiar sense of historical time, namely, that there is an absolute break between the ancient past and the modern present'.[133] For the romantics and the scientifically minded, the ruin was a liminal space where the ancient past was still physically present; its decrepit nature physically signifying the difference that the passage of time makes. As will be explored throughout this study, the ruin was rendered into both scientific and artistic form. Archaeological works treat the ruin as a specimen to be examined. The landscapes of Roberts and others (see Chapter III.1) use the collapsed temples and monumental buildings of the Near East as romantic symbols of time past and civilizations vanished. The very act of destruction was presented in dramatic form in the very popular paintings of John Martin, which gave the viewer an impression of destruction as it was happening, from the fall of Nineveh to the destruction of Pompeii.

---

132. Alexander Keith, *Evidence of the Truth of the Christian Religion Derived from the Literal Fulfilment of Prophecy; Particularly as Illustrated by the History of the Jews, and by the Discoveries of Recent Travellers* (New York: Harper & Brothers, 6th edn, 1850), p. 246.

133. Elliott Colla, *Conflicted Antiquities: Egyptology, Egyptomania, Egyptian Modernity* (Durham, NC: Duke University Press, 2007), p. 34.

4. *Progress and Decline*

Arguably the best-known nineteenth-century poem about Egypt is 'Ozymandias' by Percy Bysshe Shelley. At its heart is a discourse on progress and decline. First published in January 1818 in *The Examiner* (under the pseudonym Gilrastes), it is a powerful commentary on the eventual collapse of empire and leadership. One of the most anthologized poems in English, readers have undoubtedly encountered Shelley's sonnet at some point, but it is worth reprinting in this context:

> I met a traveller from an antique land
> Who said: Two vast and trunkless legs of stone
> Stand in the desert. Near them, on the sand,
> Half sunk, a shattered visage lies, whose frown
> And wrinkled lip, and sneer of cold command
> Tell that its sculptor well those passions read
> Which yet survive, stamped on these lifeless things,
> The hand that mocked them and the heart that fed.
> And on the pedestal these words appear:
> 'My name is Ozymandias, king of kings:
> Look on my works, ye Mighty, and despair!'
> Nothing beside remains. Round the decay
> Of that colossal wreck, boundless and bare
> The lone and level sands stretch far away.

The poem interacts directly with ancient Egyptian materials and the fruits of European exploration there. Ozymandias is a Greek rendering of a throne name of Ramses II. Much ink has been spilled discussing which particular statue inspired Shelley, and no answer is entirely satisfactory, and to a great degree, this question does not really matter. Most seem to agree that the so-called Younger Memnon statue, acquired by Belzoni and now displayed in the British Museum, was the inspiration (Fig. 4.3). However, it should be pointed out that the statue itself was not on display at the British Museum in 1817 (when the sonnet was written), and its physical appearance deviates from the description in the poem. Despite this, given how widely reported the existence of this statue was in England in the first twenty years of the nineteenth century (both through Napoleon's attempted acquisition of it and Belzoni's exploits), it is likely that this was the inspiration. The differences in physical appearance suggest that Shelley only knew of it from these reports. He may even be alluding to the fact that he had never seen it by the first two lines in the poem, which indicate that his description is based on hearsay. The inscription quoted in the poem (and often misquoted), 'My name is Ozymandias, king of kings: Look on my works, ye Mighty, and despair!', may be based on a classical source. In his *Bibliotheca historica*, Diodorus Siculus records an inscription of Ramses II: 'King of Kings am I, Osymandias. If anyone would know how great I am and where I lie, let him

Fig. 4.3. Younger Memnon, Nineteenth Dynasty. © Trustees of the British Museum

surpass one of my works'.¹³⁴ Regardless, Shelley's 'inscription' captures the boldness and conceit of a typical inscription of Ramses II, and works well in juxtaposition with the description of the current state of Ramses' works.

'Ozymandias' was actually written in competition with Horace Smith, whose poem deals with similar themes and first appeared in print one month after Shelley's, in a February 1818 issue of *The Examiner*.¹³⁵ Smith made his fortune as a stockbroker (and in fact managed Shelley's finances) and was also a relatively well-acclaimed writer at the time, although his works have mostly been forgotten. His 'Ozymandias or on a Stupendous Leg of Granite, Discovered Standing by Itself in the Deserts of Egypt, with the Inscription Inserted Below' deals with the same theme as Shelley's sonnet but in a bit more of a pedestrian manner. In the first half, the statue of Ramses is used as a vehicle for discussing the eventual collapse of empires; the second half explicitly describes a future in which the same fate has befallen London, and one of its monuments is found in desolation. Smith writes:

---

134. Diodorus Siculus, *Library of History* (trans. C.H. Oldfather; Loeb Classical Library, 303; Cambridge, MA: Harvard University Press, 1961), p. 47. This was suggested by the editors of the University of Toronto website 'Representative Poetry Online'.

135. These types of friendly poetry contests were not uncommon in the nineteenth century. In February of 1818 Shelley had another Egyptian-themed poetry contest, this time with John Keats and Leigh Hunt on the subject of the Nile. Keats and Shelley both titled their poems 'To the Nile'; Hunt's poem was simply 'The Nile'.

> In Egypt's sandy silence, all alone,
> Stands a gigantic Leg, which far off throws
> The only shadow that the Desert knows:
> 'I am great Ozymandias', saith the stone,
> 'The King of Kings; this mighty City shows
> 'The wonders of my hand'. The City's gone,
> Nought but the Leg remaining to disclose
> The site of this forgotten Babylon.
> We wonder, and some Hunter may express
> Wonder like ours, when thro' the wilderness
> Where London stood, holding the Wolf in chace,
> He meets some fragment huge, and stops to guess
> What powerful but unrecorded race
> Once dwelt in that annihilated place.

Both Smith and Shelley deal with the problem of progress and collapse that the encounter with past great civilizations inspired in nineteenth-century Europeans. Perhaps these poems in turn inspired some of the more academic figures already discussed in this chapter to use ancient Egypt as a means of exploring the possible future decline of the British Empire.

Mary Elizabeth Coleridge (1861–1907) offers a somewhat less gloomy take on the ruinous state of ancient civilizations. In her poem 'Egypt's Might Is Tumbled Down', Coleridge writes:

> Egypt's might is tumbled down
>   Down a-down the deeps of thought;
> Greece is fallen and Troy town,
> Glorious Rome hath lost her crown,
>   Venice' pride is nought.
>
> But the dreams their children dreamed
>   Fleeting, unsubstantial, vain,
> Shadowy as the shadows seemed,
> Airy nothing, as they deemed,
>   These remain.

As Coleridge's verse suggests, the fear of becoming ruined was not the most important message derived from the exploration of the ancient Near East. For her, something akin to Hegel's Spirit outlives all of these once mighty societies. For the romantic, the spirit of the dead civilization resides in its ruins, in its material remnants. There is a lasting spirit (or *Geist*) that survives from antiquity that can be revived in the present. The ghosts that haunt the ruins are not quite dead. The radical nature of archaeology in terms of potentially undermining teleological views of Victorian superiority was made less radical through these various models of progress and decline that naturalized hierarchies.

Fundamentally, the professionalization of Near Eastern studies required that the destabilizing messages about decline and the political implication that Great Britain was not exceptional needed to be transformed into something more conservative. Professional history, as a university-based discipline, provided this conservatism since it could naturalize present-day institutions through long-term historical narratives. As 'history' (especially British history) emerged as a professional academic discipline within the context of the university in the mid-nineteenth century, it was essentially conservative. As Phillipa Levine writes, 'The identification of past events with current structures and their use as a justification for an explanation of those structures, was a means of establishing not just a common consensus but a sense of both individual and collective purpose'.[136] History became part of the curriculum not necessarily to better understand the roots of British institutions but rather to justify British institutions through reference to the past. The mediaeval period became romanticized, especially as a society where *noblesse oblige* provided a moral ordering principle, justifying the authority of the landed gentry for nineteenth-century audiences who were becoming increasingly aware of the erosion of wealth and power of the aristocracy. Critical thinking about history was not so much about debating the values of the past but about identifying practical lessons for citizens, and when 'history' was established at Cambridge, it was established as a 'seminary of politicians'.[137] The program of history was to indoctrinate with certain values, not 'to encourage individual discovery or reevaluation'.[138] The work for Near Eastern studies scholars was to imagine how their subject could be used in a similar fashion. In the United States, proof of Christianity's superiority was the dominant theme. The British and French, however, seemed more concerned with issues of empire.

For the British of the nineteenth century, the consideration of the ancient Near East was rooted in a consideration of broader historical issues and the creation of universal models for understanding humanity. By crafting a Western tradition, the British were able to connect themselves to a longer scheme of human history, of which their society was the most recent manifestation and so far the highest achievement of the *Weltgeist*. The origins of contemporary institutions were rooted in the past, and this, by the curious logic of historical narrative, justified their present-day forms. Diffu-

---

136. Phillipa Levine, *The Amateur and the Professional: Antiquarians, Historians, and Archaeologists in Victorian England, 1838–1886* (Cambridge: Cambridge University Press, 1986), p. 84.
137. Levine, *Amateur*, p. 160.
138. Levine, *Amateur*, p. 161.

sion explained the movement of technologies and ideas. Unilinear cultural evolution explained difference and technological superiority and provided a moral justification for the expansion of empire and the development of world economic systems. The ancient Near East also provided a frightening glimpse of the future, and the potential for societal collapse was an impetus for reformers (and later the reforming historians of the twentieth century, such as H.G. Wells). The ancient Near East was the beginning of both progress and decline and was the first step in the history of Britain when contextualized within a world historical schema. These ideas may have been most cogently articulated by philosophers, historians and anthropologists in the nineteenth century, but, as shall be shown in the next chapter, these same kinds of concerns were worked through in the periodical and popular presses as well.

5

VICTORIAN PERIODICALS AND
THE BIRTH OF ARCHAEOLOGICAL JOURNALISM

> Every act of reading is an act of forgetting: the experience of reading is a palimpsest, in which each text partially covers those that came before.
> —James Secord[1]

In the twenty-first century, archaeological journalism (in magazines, newspapers, and especially documentaries) is the primary means through which non-specialists are informed about archaeological discoveries. It is striking how similar twenty-first-century archaeological reporting is to that of the nineteenth century, and upon close examination it is evident that many of the tropes, themes and journalistic framing mechanisms that are in common use today originated in Victorian times. Many of these articles emphasize the same issues and use the same kinds of approaches to simplify complex subjects in terms that are easily digestible to a wide readership. For many readers, journalists provide the first introduction to ancient cultures, and this was even more so in the nineteenth century; newspaper accounts of Assyriological discoveries especially provided the first public framework for understanding that culture outside of a church setting. Still, these media accounts taught audiences to understand Mesopotamia (and to a lesser extent Egypt) in reference to the Bible and the more established field of classics. In fact, it was the role that Near Eastern archaeology could play in illuminating these fields that justified the excavations, at least according to some journalists. That the newspapers reported on Assyriology legitimized the enterprise for the public, and media calls for the funding of excavations established archaeology as a type of enterprise worthy of patronage. Yet not all of these messages are messages that archaeologists are comfortable with today. Most

---

1. James A. Secord, *Victorian Sensation: The Extraordinary Publication, Reception, and Secret Authorship of* Vestiges of the Natural History of Creation (Chicago: University of Chicago Press, 2000), p. 515.

are fine with celebrations of technology and science (transportation technology was especially newsworthy in Victorian times). Political messages, and especially messages that celebrate empire and the relative value of different civilizations, however, trouble archaeologists, yet they still appear in popular accounts of the ancient Near East. It is worth considering archaeological journalism as a genre and attempting to understand how some of these explanatory and interpretive frameworks were established.

One of the hallmarks of the Victorian era in England was the rise to prominence of the periodical press.[2] This was directly related to a fundamental shift in literacy rates that marked a major change in cultural life—a rapid rise of literacy among most segments of the Victorian public. The degree to which any particular individual may have been literate varied dramatically, and there are cases of individuals who had once learned to read but had subsequently forgotten. Regardless of degrees of literacy, for the working classes some level of literacy became possible in ways that it had never been before. Richard Altick has shown that as early as the 1790s the notion that a literate working class was dangerous began to be replaced by a belief that literacy was an important part of the improvement of the lower classes.[3] The expanding urban middle class saw an increase in the importance of literacy in their work, as clerk and copy jobs in London used up a greater proportion of the workforce. As more readers emerged, periodical publication made better commercial sense, and as more periodicals were published, the popularity of reading increased.[4] While lower-class reading materials had typically consisted of astrological manuals, chapbooks, biblical materials and pamphlets, a new focus on more general education emerged.[5] Illustrated periodicals were particularly successful (based on circulation and sales figures) in reaching audiences with divergent degrees of literacy as the illustrations supplemented or replaced the text depending on the needs/interests of the reader.[6]

---

2. The study of Victorian periodicals is a discipline in its own right. A study that specifically focuses on archaeology in Victorian periodicals that is recommended is James Phillips, *The Past and the Public: Archaeology and the Periodical Press in Nineteenth Century Britain* (PhD thesis, University of Southampton, 2004). Although not devoted solely to the presentation of the ancient Near East, Phillips's thesis surveys a number of different periodicals and topics that are of interest here.

3. Richard D. Altick, *The English Common Reader: A Social History of the Mass Reading Public, 1800–1900* (Chicago: University of Chicago Press, 1957), pp. 7, 66. For more on the periodical press and the reform movement, see Phillips, *Past and the Public,* pp. 64-65.

4. Of course, the situation was far more complex than this, but these basic trends are clear. See Altick, *English Common Reader,* p. 318.

5. Secord, *Victorian Sensation,* p. 67.

6. For more on this, see Patricia Anderson, *The Printed Image and the Transformation of Popular Culture, 1790–1860* (Oxford: Clarendon Press, 1991), pp. 2-3.

Periodicals were financially far less risky than books; they were cheaper to produce, easier to print, made of cheaper materials and had more room for advertisements. By 1830, technological advances (in printing and the transportation of printed works) and reductions in taxes related to paper products made the production of periodicals significantly cheaper than ever before.[7] Periodicals were easier to distribute than books, and therefore it was much easier to find new audiences. The quick turn-around for periodicals also meant that the producers of these publications had a greater ability to quickly respond to the public's interest (or lack of interest) in various subjects. Magazines also had much larger readerships than circulation and sales records indicate. Altick has noted that in the late eighteenth century, a single copy of a periodical provided in a coffee house would have been read (or at least perused) by numerous readers over a course of a few months.[8] Similarly, one periodical in a home could have been read by all members of the household, including domestic servants (of whom there were over one million in England by 1861).[9] Circulation figures also do not take into account the practice of reading periodicals aloud to larger groups. As Jonathan Rose argues, pubs, coffee shops, Chartist meetings, Methodist gatherings, workshops and the home were all locations where reading aloud was a major form of communication, education and entertainment.[10] By the 1840s, circulating libraries had started to become commonplace in London and provincial towns.[11]

The ability to read and the ability to get access to periodicals were not enough. Readers needed to have enough time to read. For many, this time was found on Sundays, when other forms of leisure were restricted. Altick has argued that religion may have had a similarly influential force in driving people to read on other days since, according to new religious sensibilities, many other types of leisure were now deemed inappropriate.[12] Middle-class women grew into an especially large reading class as it became common practice to hire domestic servants, and limitations on work outside of the home generated more leisure time that needed to be filled with 'productive' activities.

The English periodical press was of profound importance in educating the general public about the ancient Near East. This was not as much the case in France where ancient Near Eastern studies remained a relatively elitist enterprise confined to a relatively small group of antiquaries. Yet, as

7. Anderson, *Printed Image*, p. 1; Secord, *Victorian Sensation*, pp. 32-34.
8. Altick, *English Common Reader*, p. 47.
9. Altick, *English Common Reader*, p. 83.
10. Jonathan Rose, *The Intellectual Life of the British Working Class* (New Haven, CT: Yale University Press, 2nd edn, 2010), p. 84.
11. Secord, *Victorian Sensation*, p. 139.
12. Altick, *English Common Reader*, p. 86.

Patricia Anderson has argued (and exaggerates for effect), this periodical culture reflected the emergence of a 'global village' since news from Britain, western Europe and the United States was all reported together.[13] News from farther abroad arrived in London with some delay, but now events in Mesopotamia, Egypt and Palestine were part of the cultural life of the English reader. The reading public as a whole was able to interact with the ancient Near East and its antiquities and participate, to some degree, in its reconstruction and reimagining. Barbara Benedict maintains that periodicals help to define what should and should not be studied.[14] So news stories about Near Eastern explorations affirmed that Near Eastern studies was a subject that *should* be known about.

Anderson has explored how the relationship between the periodical press and its readership was not just a top–down perpetuation of elite values nor was it merely a form of social control masquerading as improvement.[15] That is not to say that the privileged position of the elites did not play a role. Rather, her Gramscian analysis suggests that the success of these periodicals lay in their conformity to readers' pre-existing values and interests and their willing interest in looking for informal models of 'social, moral, and intellectual leadership'.[16] The relationship was still unequal, as the editors of these periodicals were in a better financial situation than the majority of their readership, but there had to be willingness on the part of the consumers. Given the speed with which periodicals were produced and the market-driven principles through which their production was financed (where mass sales were imperative), content was negotiated between authors and consumers. Those periodicals that were widely commercially successful often reached a number of different groups within society, and this economy of scale was one of the fundamental transformations of the Victorian age.[17]

The News in Pictures

Of particular relevance for a discussion of the ancient Near East and Egypt in nineteenth-century journalism is *The Illustrated London News* (*ILN*).[18] This was a weekly general newspaper (large folio size), but the novelty of its approach was to include images in each issue. It was purposefully miscellaneous, in order to appeal to as wide a readership as possible; and,

---

13. Anderson, *Printed Image,* p. 194.
14. Barbara M. Benedict, *Curiosity: A Cultural History of the Early Modern Period* (Chicago: University of Chicago Press, 2001).
15. Anderson, *Printed Image,* pp. 5, 78-79, 129.
16. Anderson, *Printed Image,* p. 5.
17. Anderson, *Printed Image,* p. 176.
18. For an account of the history of *The Illustrated London News,* see Phillips, *Past and the Public,* pp. 101-14 (101-103 esp.).

as Peter Sinnema notes, it blended a diverse variety of seemingly contradictory but fundamentally conservative viewpoints.[19] Given the importance of visual culture in the study of the ancient Near East, an illustrated periodical was a particularly important means of disseminating the results of archaeological activities, and given its sales figures the *ILN* was one of the most important sources of archaeological news for the Victorian general public. Artists in London drew most of the illustrations; reporters in distant locals would create rough hand sketches and send these back to the London offices to be transformed into more formal graphics.[20] In the 1890s, photographs began appearing, but graphic art continued in use through World War I. With reading material reaching the working classes, Anderson explains, 'the printed image more than the word represented a cultural break with the past, for it demanded neither formal education nor even basic literacy. The new inexpensive printed image thus became the first medium of regular, ongoing, mass communication.'[21] The first issue appeared in 1841, and it ran as a weekly until 1971. The sales records show a steady growth from its initial issue until 1863, when it sold over 300,000 issues every week (significantly greater sales than any other British newspaper of the time).[22] Phillips has argued, that in comparison with Austen Henry Layard's 'bestselling' monograph about his discoveries in Assyria, at least twelve times as many people would have read about his discoveries as presented in the *ILN*.[23] Although the *ILN* may have been more ephemeral (as opposed to the book, which has remained on library and bookstore shelves to the present day), the impact of this periodical should not be underestimated.

The *ILN* was a unique publication, since its wide audience superseded the boundaries of the working and middle classes (although its cost may have been somewhat prohibitive for working-class readers). The breadth of its audience was related to the breadth of its content and its illustrations. Despite this broad audience, the text of the articles often presumed a high level of intellectual engagement from its readers. As already noted, it was the illustrations that allowed all levels of readers to engage with the pub-

---

19. Peter W. Sinnema, *Dynamics of the Pictured Page: Representing the Nation in the* Illustrated London News (Aldershot: Ashgate, 1998), p. 11.

20. For a description of the technical approaches to illustration in the *ILN*, see Nicholas Warner (ed.), *An Egyptian Panorama: Reports from the 19th Century British Press* (Cairo: Zeitouna, 1994), pp. xx-xxiv.

21. Anderson, *Printed Image*, p. 3.

22. For contrast, in 1861, *The Times* had a circulation of 70,000 (at most), the *Daily News* sold 6,000 copies, and the *Morning Post* sold 4,500 copies (Christopher Hibbert, *The Illustrated London News: Social History of Victorian Britain* [London: Angus & Robertson Publishers, 1975], pp. 13-14). For more on *ILN* sales figures, see Phillips, *Past and the Public*, p. 101.

23. Phillips, *Past and the Public*, p. 109.

lication. Frederick Bohrer has described the illustration as 'a substitution, a self-sufficient, simulacral realm presenting its reader/viewer things he or she had little opportunity to obtain otherwise'.[24] The widespread viewing of images of ancient Near Eastern art helped this art become a recognized component of nineteenth-century visual culture. Bohrer has convincingly shown that the periodical was one of the most important media through which Assyrian art was 'approved' as legitimate art, and it can be argued more broadly that these kinds of reports also legitimated the academic study of the ancient Near East.[25] Interpretations provided by the paper need be taken seriously in reconstructing how the Victorians understood the ancient Near East. For the simulation not only allows the reader to experience the otherwise 'unexperienceable', but it also entangles the viewer in the story. Peter Sinnema has argued that the pictured page creates a perspective that puts the viewer at the centre of this pictured world. He writes, 'As a simulacrum of the world on paper or canvas, perspective is the centering praxis. It allows the viewer to believe that the scene exists for him or her, that the visual convergence of lines and shapes depicted in the image is a reality made subject to the viewer'.[26] Thus the reader of the illustrated periodical becomes central to the story, entangled with the image presented. The simulated version cannot be separated from the viewer, although the viewer is likely not cognizant of this. The illustration obscures this constructed relationship through an ethos of material fact or, in Sinnema's words, 'seems to transform the *appearance* of reality into objective fact'.[27]

Bohrer has argued that the presentation of antiquities in the *ILN* is in many ways antithetical to a construction of meaning through narrative.[28] In his analysis of the full-page spreads that often presented information on Assyrian antiquities, Bohrer notes that the organization of images is at odds with the otherwise narrative-driven text that accompanied them. Bohrer sees this as an implicit attack on the British Museum's presentation of the materials. Whether or not this can be upheld, the lack of narrativity in articles about the ancient Near East may have been one of the most successful means of conveying the ancient Near East to the general public. Certainly the lack of narrativity was appealing to newspaper copy-editors who could cut articles at will for layout needs. Especially given the lack of historical context that is typical of new discoveries, often the only narrative that is accessible to the journalist is the narrative of excavation. Thus images of artifactual discoveries seem to float outside of context, especially apparent

24. Frederick Bohrer, *Orientalism and Visual Culture: Imagining Mesopotamia in Nineteenth-Century Europe* (Cambridge: Cambridge University Press, 2003), p. 133.
25. Bohrer, *Orientalism and Visual Culture*, pp. 138-39.
26. Sinnema, *Dynamics*, p. 22.
27. Sinnema, *Dynamics*, p. 31.
28. Bohrer, *Orientalism and Visual Culture*, pp. 135-37.

when not contextualized within an institution like a museum but rather contextualized by stories of other current events.

Presenting Ancient Objects

Patricia Anderson's discussion of the depiction of ancient art within *The Penny Magazine* can be extended to help understand how readers interpreted Near Eastern artifacts presented in the *ILN*. Taking as an example an article on 'The Dying Gladiator' (a piece of classical art dating to the third century BCE), Anderson argues that three messages are presented: the illustration of the statue; the written caption and full-length article about the piece; and 'the interaction of the first two *and* their socially and culturally symbolic context'.[29] Here is the narrative that Bohrer argues is missing, supplied by the context of the artifact as 'news', which provides the frame for understanding what was reported. This object is presented as something that the citizen should know about and interact with, and the necessary tools and guidelines for interacting with it are provided in the written description. Here is how, in Anderson's understanding, the guided presentation of illustrations worked to 'civilize' the reader: by presenting the artifacts in a manner in which the reader could emulate the elite activities surrounding the appreciation of the artifact. This was instruction without the appearance of instruction.

Of course, the idea that amazing treasures of a long-lost culture were emerging from the ground in a distant land was (and is) intrinsically interesting to viewers. The lure of the artifacts themselves was strong, so one does not need to exaggerate the deconstruction of the presentation of these finds. Phillips contextualizes Layard's discoveries with stories of the California Gold Rush, which was a news story that was an even greater media sensation.[30] So it is not surprising that the *ILN* would capitalize on the excitement for buried treasure and provide illustrations of Assyrian 'treasure'.

Many of the feature stories in the *ILN* were substantial articles in their own right, more like short magazine or journal entries. Occasionally, digests of scholarly papers are presented, as was the case in the March 22, 1873, issue, which presents a digest of Thomas Morgan's paper on Ephesus given at a British Archaeological Association meeting.[31] Articles in *ILN* typically involved extended descriptions of archaeological artifacts along with illustrations. This is not surprising given the explicitly visual orientation of this periodical. That text should so closely replicate what was already presented

---

29. Anderson, *Printed Image*, p. 58.
30. Phillips, *Past and the Public*, p. 105.
31. 'Ephesus', *ILN*, March 22, 1873.

through image reflects the Victorian belief that prose was better suited to eliciting understanding; it was thought that the mental image produced through words was more useful than that produced by an illustration.[32] It may simply be that given the intentionally varied audience of the *ILN*, the dual presentation of image and text was suitable for two different levels of readership: the text was intended for the advanced reader and the image for all levels.

The justification for providing detailed copies of artifacts in the periodical, however, is not usually that it is an attempt to reach different audiences or to sell copy through exciting illustrations. Rather, justification is more often framed in terms of the scientific contributions that publishing illustrations and descriptions offer. For example, explicit justification is provided in an article on 'the Nimroud Sculptures' dating to March 31, 1849. Illustrations of Neo-Assyrian reliefs are provided along with a description of the writing (referred to as 'arrow-head characters') and the iconography (Fig. 5.1). The author of the article states:

> Although we ourselves are unable to construe this inscription, there are so many now engaged in studying this division of cuneiform writing, that we do not hesitate to insert it here, as it will thus meet the eye of many who may not be able to obtain a correct copy of the original without difficulty; and may excite curiosity and induce examination and comparison in others who, perhaps, would never, otherwise, have turned their attention to the subject. We vouch for the perfect accuracy of our copy and merely add that the erasure in the eighth line is no error of ours, but exists in the original; the repetition of the same combination of characters being evidently a mistake, thus erased on revision by the sculptor.[33]

It is not likely that many readers of *ILN* would have attempted to grapple with translations of the cuneiform script, although it is likely that this would have been a good source for those few who did (often though cuneiform and hieroglyphs are depicted as illegible scribbles if the article was not discussing the monument's text). Within this justification, there is an appeal to the reader that *ILN* is contributing to scientific knowledge and working to cultivate interest in the subject among the larger British community. It is also interesting to note the appeal that is made to the readers regarding the accuracy of their copy, even going so far as to predict possible queries, for it presumes an expectation of genuine intellectual engagement with the illustration.

---

32. Ralph O'Connor, *The Earth on Show: Fossils and the Poetics of Popular Science, 1802–1856* (Chicago: University of Chicago Press, 2007), pp. 3-4.

33. 'The Nimroud Sculptures Just Received at the British Museum', *ILN*. March 31, 1849.

Fig. 5.1. 'Nimrud sculptures just received at the British Museum (writing sample)', *Illustrated London News,* March 31, 1849.

The detailed descriptions of artifacts were quite extensive, and careful readers of *ILN* could learn much from them, depending on the artist. Drawings of varying accuracy were presented alongside detailed description of what those images represent and what can be inferred from them. Most often, these inferences seem to be the inferences of non-specialists, but, given the infancy of Assyriological studies at this time, this is difficult to evaluate. For example, a March 31, 1849, article argues that the beardless figures in Neo-Assyrian art were eunuchs, an argument that may reflect a supposition of the journalist or an academic argument. Another example of an article about Neo-Assyrian palace reliefs depicting the Assyrian siege of the Judahite city of Lachish illustrates the sophistication of non-specialist interpretations:

> The next relievo . . . [Fig. 5.2] . . . is a continuation of the attack and most interestingly indicates that the military operations of this early period closely resemble those of the present day, for the assailants are fighting in ranks under cover of a moveable wicker breastwork, and immediately before the troops is a war-engine on wheels, and covered by a hanging. The engine is impelled against the walls up a leveled roadway on the rocky ascent on which the city is built; and the two spears attached have already effected a breach in a tower, upon the top of which a man stands with hands extended, as if asking for a truce. In front of the walls, and in view of the citizens are three men impaled, as a warning to the besieged; and below, as if fallen from the walls, are a dying man and a headless body, the head having doubtless been removed for the purpose of numbering the slain, as in modern eastern warfare.[34]

In contrast to the minimal notices available at the British Museum (although guidebooks fulfilled this function later), the periodical reporting frames the reader's understanding of this ancient visual culture. It describes what is pictured but also explains to the reader how this should be understood. The writing is both descriptive and explanatory and the author has attempted to make the material seem less alien to the reader by drawing parallels with contemporary life (even if these connections seem a bit stretched). This is significantly more interpretive 'public outreach' then what would have been available at the British Museum at the time. And in fact, the *ILN* claimed that it acted as a guide for readers who were unable to actually visit the museum.[35] The article quoted above is not unusual and this is how much information about the ancient Near East was presented to the Victorian public—this is the kind of intellectual context in which these discoveries were framed.

---

34. 'The Nimroud Sculptures Lately Received at the British Museum', *ILN*, December 16, 1848.
35. *ILN*, June 26, 1847, p. 412.

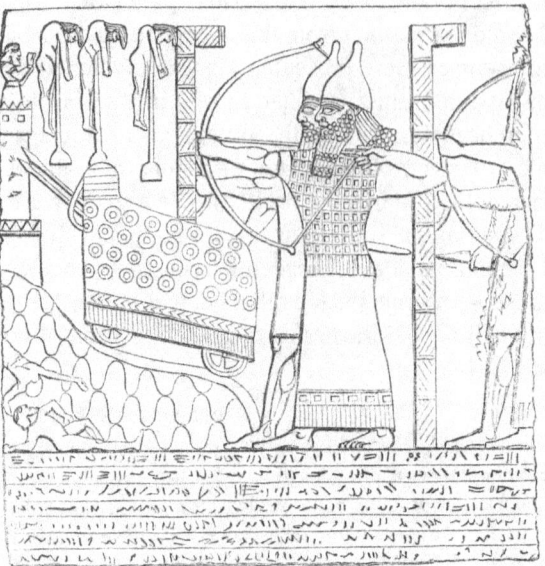

Fig. 5.2. 'Nimrud sculptures: The siege and impalement of prisoners', *Illustrated London News,* December 16, 1948.

Archaeology in Victorian Society

It is striking that many of the articles in *ILN* assume a fairly broad understanding of history and art history. The analysis of the ancient Near East often takes place through references and comparisons to other, better understood times and places. Analysis through analogy is not surprising, but perhaps the extent to which this took place in the popular periodical press (as opposed to academic settings) is. For example, in a discussion of a Nimroud sculpture depicting domestic scenes (Fig. 5.3), the following comparison is made: 'This group, altogether, bears a remarkable resemblance to the grotesques which are depicted in manuscripts of the Middle Ages. Below these mummers, as they may be called . . .'[36] The high degree of literacy and historical knowledge that is presumed is striking, but, as postulated earlier, much of this was likely aspirational. That is to say, the tone of the *ILN* was that less educated readers could feel as though they were participating in elite culture, and so some level of complexity in presentation was preserved.

36. *ILN,* March 2, 1850.

Fig. 5.3. 'The Nimrud sculptures: A domestic scene', *Illustrated London News,* March 2, 1850.

Status was of great interest in Victorian society, and this was readily signaled in the *ILN* in a number of ways. One of the topics frequently reported on in relation to ancient Near Eastern explorations regards who funded the excavation or acquisition of artifacts. The Victorian press lauded those prominent individuals who, for whatever reasons, funded projects related to the ancient world that were thought to be of benefit to public life. Often these notes are relatively minor, such as in an *ILN* article dated November 16, 1878, in which it is mentioned that the British Museum and the proprietors of the *Daily Telegraph* funded Rassam's excavations at Balawat. These are important signs, nonetheless, of how the press shaped public understandings of value and encouraged support of archaeology as an emergent enterprise. Sometimes editorial comments are made alongside the discussion of patronage, which illuminate to some extent the feelings of non-specialists toward this type of community contribution. For example, an article printed in the June 26, 1847, edition of *ILN* called 'The Nimroud Sculptures' applauds the funders of Layard's research and comments on the British government's lack of support. The article reads:

> We are indebted for such remains as have hitherto come to light to the indefatigable labours of M. Botta, the French Consul at Mossal, and to our own countryman, Mr. Layard; and it is no more than justice to indicate to the latter to remark that he was the *first* to indicate the probability of these ruins, though his suggestions were coldly received by our Government that he was left to pursue his researches unaided, excepting by the private resources of Sir Stratford Canning. The French Government, however, with its accustomed liberal sympathy in the cause of science, stepped in and most nobly assisted M. Botta, who was thus able to precede Mr. Layard in discoveries of sculptures, etc., etc., at Khorsobad, which have, some time since, been forwarded to Paris. The prompt liberality of our neighbors has, at length, had some effect upon ourselves, as we are

informed that some pecuniary assistance has been transmitted to Mr. L., though, certainly, somewhat at the eleventh hour; for he has energetically worked, regardless of obstacles, and succeeded in forwarding to this country some of his important discoveries, which have within the last few days arrived safely at the British Museum.[37]

This is a rather extensive note about the private funding that Sir Stratford Canning provided for Layard's work that appears in the introduction to the first article about the Nimroud sculptures in *ILN*. What is interesting here is how the paper calls for support of Layard's venture by appealing to nationalism. The notice contrasts the cold reception of the British government toward requests for support with the 'accustomed liberal sympathy' of the French government. The tone here does not suggest that the writer truly wants to laud the French government but rather to point out deficiencies in the British. This is a call for direct government support of archaeology.

Other articles present a different view of England, more impressed with the country's growing participation in archaeological accumulation; there was no coherent editorial stance on this matter. For example, comments from an 1850 article about Layard's discoveries read:

It is gratifying that England has not only rendered herself the first of the nations by those sterling qualities which so strongly characterise her natives—that she is not only distinguished by her arms and commerce, but that she uses these means to extend and disseminate the wealth, and comfort, and advantages produced by the arts of civilisation, at the same time that she administers happiness and contentment by inculcating the tenets of a pure religion.[38]

The comments here appear to be somewhat *non sequitur* in the context of an article about shipping Assyrian sculpture back to England. However, they illustrate the growing sense of archaeology as a heroic enterprise and that the acquisition of antiquities reflects an imperial enterprise that goes beyond mere military and monetary gain. Here is a moral justification for imperialism, in that the use of military and economic force is enacted in tandem with cultural activities and missionary work. This kind of message was not uncommon in illustrated periodicals, for as Anderson has pointed out in her study of the genre, articles on technology were mechanisms through which: 'the reader learned that English civilization was technologically and culturally superior to all others, that its continued existence required an ordered and harmonious society, and that both civilization and order depended on

37. 'The Nimroud Sculptures', *ILN*, June 26, 1847.
38. 'The Nimroud Sculptures Afloat', *ILN*, July 27, 1850.

the moral improvement of the English worker'.[39] These are not, therefore, just articles about how sculptures were transported.

The periodicals of Victorian times did not hesitate to endorse projects or organizations that they deemed worthy. The *Daily Telegraph* actually paid for some Assyriological expeditions (discussed in Chapter I.10). The *ILN*, with its large distribution and high readership levels was in a position to lobby for policy changes regarding antiquities and their collection. More often, the kinds of lobbying that newspapers engaged in crafted public opinion by signaling whether or not a project was a worthwhile enterprise. For example, in an extended article from 1869, 'The Underground Survey of Jerusalem', the *ILN* recommends the efforts of the newly formed Palestine Exploration Fund (PEF), discussed in greater detail in Chapter I.10:

> The fund is raised by a society whose objects are the accurate and systematic investigation of the archaeology and topography, the geology and physical geography, and the manners and customs of the Holy Land; with a view to Biblical illustration, but with a view no less to the general interests of historical and scientific inquiry. Its undertaking is therefore one that deserves the aid of persons of the most diverse religious opinions, associating their efforts in the common pursuit of that knowledge which is desired by every intelligent mind. We have great pleasure in recommending this enterprise to the liberality of our readers, and in setting before them a few Illustrations . . . furnished by our Special Artist, of some of the underground explorations at Jerusalem, conducted by Lieutenant Warren, the more detailed accounts of which are printed in the society's tracts. . . .[40]

There are a number of features of this testimonial that make it exemplary of the kind of endorsement that a Victorian-era periodical might offer. The society is valuable because of its scientific approach to the exploration of the Holy Land. This information will, in the eyes of this reporter, be useful for understanding the Bible but will also be appreciated for more general interests, outside of the religious sphere. There is a rhetorical appeal here that undermines possible objections from differing religious perspectives, suggesting that no matter what religious principles are held, the 'common pursuit of knowledge' is a goal that all can agree on. Here then, is a hopeful and positivistic forecast of the possibilities that supporting the PEF can bring. Other stakeholders were also able to use the public interest aroused by the newspaper in order to gain leverage in disputes over the value of the antiquities. Shawn Malley notes, for example, that Layard and the keepers of the Near Eastern section of the British Museum used the public interest in his research to pressure the trustees of the museum and Parliament to

---

39. Anderson, *Printed Image*, p. 54.
40. 'The Underground Survey of Jerusalem', *ILN,* April 24, 1869.

allocate funds and space for the study of Mesopotamia.[41] These were conscious efforts to craft public interest in the field by its practitioners.

Celebrations of Empire and Technology

Often the reports regarding Near Eastern antiquities presented in the *ILN* narrate the great feats of transportation between England and the far-off reaches of her empire. For example, a story printed in the July 27, 1850, edition was called 'The Nimroud Sculptures Afloat' and reported pretty much that. It informs readers that 'the Great Bull and upwards of a hundred tons of sculpture, excavated by our enterprising countryman, Dr. Layard, are now on their way to England, and may be expected in the course of next September'.[42] Accompanying this notice is an illustration of a ship anchored beside a large mudbrick building (Fig. 5.4). Numerous people pulling a rope can be discerned, apparently loading the Great Bull onto the ship. In the foreground, a number of people in turbans and robes watch the activities involving the ship, suggesting locals marveling at the same subject that is being reported on. The illustration is explained in the article: 'It represents the action of shipping the Great Bull on board the *Apprentice*, at Marghill, on the right bank of the Euphrates, about three miles above the old city of Busrah'.[43] Malley finds an explicitly nationalistic message in this image by comparing the empty flagpole on the foreign shore with the Union Jack displayed so prominently on the ship.[44] Bohrer's reading is similar but rooted in an analysis of orientalist art, comparing the juxtaposition of the small Arab canoe with the large British ship and the loss of the artifacts for the people of Mesopotamia with the concomitant gain of the artifacts for the English.[45]

Malley sees the narrative presentation (especially visual presentation) of the transportation of Assyrian antiquities as part of an important set of discursive tools between Britain and Assyria that served a variety of cultural purposes. The presentation helped work out internal debates within the British Museum about the nature of the institution, and they provided a forum for Layard's own self-promotion. Of interest here is how the narratives of transporting these antiquities were understood by the larger non-specialist public. Malley states, 'Superficially, the images of archaeological mastery

---

41. Shawn Malley, *From Archaeology to Spectacle in Victorian Britain* (Surrey: Ashgate, 2012), pp. 63-64.
42. 'The Nimroud Sculptures Afloat', *ILN,* July 27, 1850.
43. 'The Nimroud Sculptures Afloat', *ILN,* July 27, 1850.
44. Shawn Malley, 'Austen Henry Layard and the Periodical Press: Middle Eastern Archaeology and the Excavation of Cultural Identity in Mid-Nineteenth Century Britain', *Victorian Review* 22 (1996), pp. 152-70 (161-62).
45. Bohrer, *Orientalism and Visual Culture*, p. 140.

Fig. 5.4. 'Shipping the Great Bull from Nimrud', *Illustrated London News*, July 27, 1850.

and material possession in 'Shipping the Bull' naturalize Britain's cultural and political will in the Ottoman Near East'.[46] No doubt, consistently seeing images of British adventurers and engineers transporting artifacts such as these helped familiarize the public with the idea that this foreign other was a possession of Britain's and that their country had the technological prowess to master foreign regions—as demonstrated through the transportation of these massive objects.

Reporting Religion through Archaeology

Beyond nationalism, archaeology was seen to have great potential for religious benefit. Throughout the *ILN*'s accounts of Near Eastern archaeology are explanations of how these artifacts and finds can help to illuminate the biblical text. As in other media at this time, the periodical press used the Bible as a point of context for the readers and as a means of justifying the value of the enterprise. As Malley argues, this was a deliberate strategy for selling Assyria to the public that was purposefully employed by Layard, Rawlinson and their publishers.[47] Perhaps the clearest evidence of the cynicism of this approach is the following statement of Sir Charles Alison, the Oriental Secretary at Britain's Embassy in Constantinople. Alison urged

---

46. Shawn Malley, 'Shipping the Bull: Staging Assyria in the British Museum', *Nineteenth-Century Contexts* 26 (2004), pp. 1-27 (2).

47. Malley, 'Layard and the Periodical Press', pp. 152-70 (157-58).

Layard to 'fish up old legends and anecdotes, and if you can by any means humbug people into the belief that you have established any points in the Bible, you are a made man'.[48] In the first report of Layard's and Botta's work in Assyria, the *ILN* writes:

> The extent and magnificence, however of the two palaces described by Mr. Layard and of that discovered by M. Botta at Khorsobad, as well as the elaborate detail of the sculptures, lead us to the conclusion that they are of such remote antiquity as to afford evidence of that primitive civilization of the human race, so abundantly proved in the books of the Old Testament.[49]

Here, the justification for the study of Assyria is that it can shed light on people discussed in the Bible.

Another approach to the Bible through Mesopotamia that is still somewhat common in the field today is the use of artifacts to understand specific verses or expressions in the Bible. The author of an 1851 article called 'The Nimroud Sculptures at the British Museum' perhaps stretched this approach when he attempted to interpret a sculpture featuring tribute bearers approaching the Assyrian king. The reporter writes:

> These two slabs . . . are not only interesting because they are of the finest Assyrian sculpture that has yet arrived in this country and because they are in a high state of preservation, but more particularly because they embody a metaphor frequently used in Psalms, and other of the sacred Books of the Old Testament, expressive of the interference of the Divinity in human affairs. Thus, in the 16th Psalm it is said, 'The Lord is the portion of mine inheritance and of *my cup*: thou maintanest my lot.' And again in the 23rd Psalm, 'Thou preparest a table before me in the presence of mine enemies: thou anointest mine head with oil; *my cup* runneth over'.[50]

The connection here seems to be merely that one of the slabs has a cup depicted on it and that both of these verses mention cups. While not a particularly noteworthy observation, the author reveals the naïve approach to biblical illustration presumed at the time. Archaeology was thought to allow simple correlations between artifact and text.

The *ILN* did not hesitate to disagree with others' evaluations of the biblical implications of various finds. For example, an 1873 story rejects the notion that biblical Ophir had been found in Zimbabwe, stating, 'Recent examination, however, throws the cold shade of doubt over this pretty romance'.[51] The 'find' was made by a lion hunter and a German explorer who visited a region of recently opened gold fields where locals had supposedly been to afraid to go. The 'cold shade of doubt' stems from geo-

---

48. Malley, 'Layard and the Periodical Press', pp. 157-58.
49. 'The Nimroud Sculptures', *ILN,* June 26, 1847.
50. 'The Nimroud Sculptures at the British Museum', *ILN,* December 21, 1850.
51. 'The Ophir of Scripture', *ILN,* January 11, 1873.

logical analysis of what had been, in the field, taken to be architectural fragments, but once sent back to Britain were found to be calcareous deposits on shale. It is suggestive of a type of approach to biblical exploration of the time: non-specialists in historical matters explored the new colonies and sent back what they took to be evidence of biblical times for analysis by specialists. As shall be discussed in Chapter III.5, the Bible helped situate the edges of empire, and if an area of Africa could be proven to have a biblical connection, European expansion there was justified. In this example, the *ILN* is participating in this kind of border construction.

It can be assumed that interpretation of periodical reporting was not just unidirectional, from reporter to passive and uncritical reader, fully absorbing exactly what was written. Some evidence for multidirectional interpretation is apparent in the letters of readers printed in the periodical itself. Readers of the *ILN* drew parallels between the Assyrian artifacts that they were seeing in the periodical and the Bible. A letter to the editor dating from 1850 (signed only A.M. in the publication) offers the following suggestions about the winged lion and bull iconography that the writer had noticed in Assyrian art:

> Now I find, in the 7th chapter of the prophecies of Daniel, that the Babylonian Kingdom (which was a part of the Assyrian Empire) was represented under this very figure of a lion with eagle's wings. Might not this be used justly as a strong argument for the antiquity of Daniel's prophecies, and that they were written at a time when the Assyrian Empire was remembered, or the Babylonian Empire (its most important part) was known by this figure. Allow me to refer your readers to the whole of the 7th chapter, and to the 2nd chapter also, in which (under the figure of an image of divers metals) the same successive empires are spoken of. On this point all writers are agreed. I write only a first impression.[52]

Assuming that this letter was not just concocted by the editors, it may be somewhat unusual in that the individual in question has clearly thought about Assyrian iconography and its possible ramifications. Although most readers would not have taken their perusal of the Assyrian sculptures this seriously, it does suggest the types of conclusions that were being made about the ancient Near East with little scholarly mediation other than perhaps the newspaper's general suggestion that these artifacts will shed light on the Bible. It also shows that the media was an important forum for this kind of interpretative work.

In less explicitly secular periodicals, the religious importance of Mesopotamian discovery was at the forefront of discussion. Malley identifies a number of religious publications, of a variety of faiths and perspectives, that all agree on the importance of Layard's discoveries for verifying the

---

52. 'Letter to the Editor', *ILN*, December 28, 1850.

truth of Scripture.[53] Most of the articles in these periodicals suggest that Layard's discoveries confirm the truth of Scripture and act as a scientific verification of the Bible's veracity. Not all of these religious writers followed the archaeologists' conclusions about the religious significance of their finds, and the religious controversies of the time often spilled into discussions of Near Eastern explorations. Malley notes a Catholic response to Layard's book, particularly to his 'overt Protestant sympathies'.[54] Layard makes a number of comments in his publications about the Christian Nestorians (he calls them Chaldeans) whom he met while travelling in Mesopotamia and how their practices seemed more akin to Protestantism than Catholicism. Layard's tone is not neutral. For example, he states about the Nestorians, 'ignorance of the superstitions of the church of Rome, and their simple observances and ceremonies, may be clearly traced to a primitive form of Christianity received by them before its corruption'.[55] Malley notes George Crolly's response in *The Dublin Review*, where Crolley suggests that Layard 'would have acted much more wisely for his fame although perhaps not so prudently for his pocket, if he had not discovered the fossil remains of Protestantism amid the rubbish of Assyria'.[56] Crolley asserts that Catholics also should look to Assyria for the roots of their religion.[57]

Romantic Ruins and Origin Stories

It is not just the Bible that can be better understood by Near Eastern explorations, according to the *ILN*, there is also potential to better understand the classical world (an enterprise that in the nineteenth century needed no justification). The study of Assyrian and Egyptian art was argued to inform the study of classical art. About the Neo-Assyrian reliefs from Nimroud, the *ILN* writes:

> In short, for comparative purposes, independently of their value to the history of art, these Marbles are of the greatest importance; whatever may be their real antiquity [note that at this time there was some uncertainty of the dating of these artifacts], they are probably of an earlier date than the first scintillations of Grecian genius, and, therefore, may be reasonably supposed to have exercised some influence over the conceptions and works of the Ionian colonists at least.[58]

---

53. Malley, 'Layard and the Periodical Press', p. 157.
54. Malley, 'Layard and the Periodical Press', p. 158.
55. As cited in Malley, 'Layard and the Periodical Press', p. 158.
56. As cited in Malley, 'Layard and the Periodical Press', p. 158. Original citation from George Crolley, 'Review of *Nineveh and its Remains*, by Austen Henry Layard', *Dublin Review* 28 (1850), pp. 354-98.
57. As cited in Malley, 'Layard and the Periodical Press', p. 158.
58. *ILN*, March 2, 1850.

In this view, there are two justifications for the study of Assyrian art. It is valuable in its own right as a kind of encyclopaedic exemplar of all world art. But it is also valuable since it predates Greek art and may have been foundational for the artists of a culture whose art was thought to exemplify the highest point of human achievement. The art of the ancient Near East was considered important from an evolutionary perspective, as insight into more primitive forms of artistic display.

That Greek art had origins in the Near East was one of the arguments that was made in constructing a new linear Western historical tradition. The periodicals reporting the finds in Assyria and Egypt saw the ancient Near East as the source(s) of Western history just as the excavators did. They participated in the construction of a linked narrative of 'world' history that began in the Near East, continued through Greece and Rome, entered mediaeval Europe and culminated in nineteenth-century western Europe. Malley understands this form of progress as linked to tradition and loaded with moral baggage.[59] He sees the creation of this type of Western tradition as 'an appropriation of a foreign past into its [Britain's] own historical self'.[60] Certainly this is true, and this linear progress-based history was constructed in the periodical press much in the same way that it was constructed in academic literature.

Some periodical writers were inspired by these ruins to imagine what future progress will look like. Malley cites a comment from the *ILN*'s review of Layard's *Discoveries in the Ruins of Nineveh and Babylon*, which explicitly considers the conceptual relationship between nineteenth-century Britain and the ancient Near East:

> Independently of the indisputable fact, that our moral and material civilization is more worthy to be preserved in human remembrance than is the most perfect development ever attained by idolatrous Egypt, or by idolatrous Ashur, there is another fact equally certain—that our times will be thus preserved. . . . It is impossible—and impossible physically as well as morally—that, after any lapse of ages five times as numerous as those which separate the present era from the era of Ninus, the same shadows should develop the memory of Victoria.[61]

Here, the Victorian writer has imagined that his own culture is exceptional and cannot collapse like Assyria, and he bases this on two foundations. First, the physical remains of Victorian England are so impressive—the technology, the buildings, the material culture—that they will not be able to be obliterated and buried like those at Nineveh. Second, the moral superiority

---

59. Malley, 'Layard and the Periodical Press', p. 161.
60. Malley, 'Layard and the Periodical Press', p. 161.
61. 'Review of *Discoveries in the Ruins of Nineveh and Babylon*, by Austen Henry Layard', *ILN*, April 2, 1853.

of Victorian England is such that future cultures will be dependent on those achievements in building their own cultures. The progress that has been made between ancient Near Eastern times, in the mind of this reviewer, is improved technology and the abandonment of idolatry. These predictions about the archaeological future of Victorian Britain point to the kinds of thinking that Assyrian discoveries inspired. The tangible evidence of 'collapse' encouraged people to think about their own futures and how their cultures fit in the larger scheme of history. Unlike the mediaeval period, and to some extent Roman times, there was a seemingly clear-cut material break between the ancient Near Eastern cultures and the Victorians. In some ways, this kind of disconnectedness was more destabilizing. As shall be shown throughout this study, however, much effort was expended by nineteenth-century scholars to prove that in fact Britain was still connected to ancient Mesopotamia.

Other than the finds themselves, similar kinds of approaches to archaeological reporting can be found in twenty-first-century news accounts about the discoveries of the ancient Near East. Technology and the scientists who use technology are still described in heroic terms and, more often than not, newspaper accounts focus on these elements of the discovery rather than the historical context of the discovery or the actual knowledge deficit that the discovery fills. The archaeologist is described in heroic terms as 'rescuing' the past, through the technological advances of European or North American academia, from the dangers of the region (whether they be warfare, looting or environmental risks). There is less of an emphasis on donors, and the periodical press does not play as large a role in leveraging archaeological funding for demonstrations of status (and no doubt this also relates to the transformations in funding strategies that have occurred since Victorian times).

As in the nineteenth century, the media of the twenty-first century participates in the construction of a shared culture through the reporting of news. As Sinnema has noted, 'The *ILN* makes the world, fabricating an English identity for its nineteenth-century readers, by contributing to such solidifying ideologies as those of national superiority, limitless technological progress, and bourgeois solidarity'.[62] Archaeology provides the framework for making 'history' news and allows historical debates to enter into public discussion about the present. The stories about the ancient Near East presented similar arguments then as now, and these kinds of ideological underpinnings continue to be present in archaeological reporting in the twenty-first century. This ideological apparatus is markedly apparent in the sensationalism surrounding Cleopatra's Needle, and an analysis of the reporting surrounding this object makes transparent the ideological messages embedded in archaeological journalism.

62. Sinnema, *Dynamics*, p. 31.

Fig. 5.5. 'Cleopatra's Needle and Somerset House', from a watercolour by W.L. Wyllie.

Cleopatra's Needle: A Periodical Sensation

Now an established feature of London's embankment, Cleopatra's Needle was the subject of much debate and discussion in nineteenth-century London, and the story of how it came to stand by the Thames was one of the great news sensations of the Victorian period (Fig. 5.5). The needle has nothing to do with Cleopatra. It is actually one of two obelisks erected during New Kingdom times by King Thutmoses III in Heliopolis (its partner was moved to New York City from Egypt). Ancient Romans had previously moved the obelisk to Alexandria (around 12 BCE), where it had eventually been toppled and partially buried (Fig. 1.3). It came into British possession in 1819 when Muhammed Ali presented it in commemoration of Nelson's and Abercromby's victories in Egypt against the French. The English had actually first prepared to remove it to Europe in 1802 after the defeat of the French but were unable. The British government, thereafter, declined to pay the expenses of transporting Muhammed Ali's gift even after methods of removal were identified, and it remained in Alexandria for years.

In 1877, Sir James Erasmus Wilson, a wealthy surgeon, offered to pay for the transport of the Needle to London. The expense was quite significant (£10,000). Wilson's charity was acknowledged in the periodical press:

> The expenses of bringing the Obelisk to England, it is well known, are defrayed by the splendid liberality of Mr. Erasmus Wilson, the eminent surgeon, to whom some token of royal favour, or some other public testimonial, should presently be offered. He has received from the Princess

of Wales, a gracious message in recognition of his generous gift to the country.⁶³

Here the press urges the reward and acknowledgment of Wilson's philanthropy, which itself would have been something of an award in status conscious Victorian London.⁶⁴ In an earlier article, the British government's lack of financial support for the transport of Cleopatra's Needle to London is also noted with derision:

> Its removal [Cleopatra's Needle] has been considered a matter of such great expense that the British Government has not felt justified in undertaking it and, had it not been for the private generosity of Dr. Erasmus Wilson, and the ingenuity of the engineer, it would most likely have remained to form the foundations of the new houses leading to the Alexandria Railway Station.⁶⁵

This comment comes at the beginning of an article that introduces London readers to Cleopatra's Needle. The implication that the obelisk needed to be removed to London in order to insure its preservation is not convincing now, but likely would have been to Victorian readers. And here again, the government's lack of funding for this enterprise is not viewed positively by the periodical. The periodical here actively cultivates public interest in the collection of antiquities.

Like the tales of transport of the large Assyrian sculptures, the periodical press thrilled readers with heroic transportation narratives about the shipping of Cleopatra's Needle. Certainly much of the interest came from the reports of misadventures in attempting to transport it as well as debates regarding what should be done with it when it arrived in London. Even before it was shipped, discussion of how it would be transported was newsworthy. In a March 10, 1877, story ('Cleopatra's Needle'), an extremely detailed report of the plans made for transporting it over water is presented along with illustrations documenting its position before, during and after as well as depicting sections of the iron pontoon on which it was placed (Fig. 5.6). The pontoon was a 28-metre-long iron cylinder, outfitted with a rudder, keels, mast, and deckhouse. Called 'Cleopatra', it was to be towed to London by ship (the steamship *Olga*).⁶⁶

---

63. 'Arrival of Cleopatra's Needle', *ILN,* January 26, 1878.

64. Waynman Dixon and his brother are not acknowledged, even though they were the masterminds behind the transport of the obelisk and incurred substantial out-of-pocket costs themselves. See Ian Pearce, 'Waynman Dixon: In the Shadow of the Needle', in *Souvenirs and New Ideas: Travel and Collecting in Egypt and the Near East* (ed. Diane Fortenberry; Oxford: ASTENE and Oxbow Books, 2013), pp. 129-41.

65. 'Cleopatra's Needle', *ILN,* March 10, 1877.

66. For a more recent account of the transport of the obelisk along with photographs of the 'Cleopatra', see Pearce, 'Waynman Dixon', pp. 134-37.

Fig. 5.6. 'Proposed method for the removal of Cleopatra's Needle from Alexandria', *Illustrated London News,* March 10, 1877.

Stories of the Needle's abandonment at sea (in its floating pontoon) because of a storm and subsequent recovery were newsworthy and exciting (Fig. 5.7). In October, the Cleopatra encountered a storm in the Bay of Biscay. Six men who piloted a rescue boat from the steamship towing the pontoon drowned attempting to save others who were on the vessel carrying the Needle.[67] Eventually the captain had to give up the Cleopatra as lost, assuming it had been sunk, and the *Olga* docked at Falmouth. Four days later, Spanish boats found the Cleopatra floating, and arrangements were made for it to be towed to a Spanish port for repair. It remained in a Spanish port awaiting carriage to London until payment for transportation could be negotiated.[68] Images of the Needle being tossed by the sea's waves and heroic stories of the sailors involved made for good copy. As Sinnema has noted, stories of shipwrecks were extremely common in the *ILN*, and he has demonstrated how rail accidents were used as markers of ever-present, uncontrollable and unpredictable disaster.[69] Accidents, especially ones that led to death, involving the new technologies of the transportation era showed just

---

67. Their names are now commemorated on a plaque on the obelisk's base.
68. George Burrel and his son salvaged the obelisk; their salvage charges were disputed in court, and eventually John Dixon was forced to pay them over £9000 (Pearce, 'Waynman Dixon', p. 137).
69. Sinnema, *Dynamics,* pp. 6-8.

Fig. 5.7. 'Cleopatra's Needle. First night out: in the Bay of Biscay', *Illustrated London News,* January 26, 1878.

how frightening these new changes could be. Sinnema's reading is applicable in the treatment of the disaster that befell the *Olga*, celebrated only days before as an example of the triumph of British industry. For here is the other side of progress, the implicit danger that progress brings; this is one of the reasons why the purveyors of progress are framed as heroes.

Cleopatra's Needle's arrival in London was equally noteworthy for the periodicals. The masts of the ship carrying the Needle had to be taken down to get past the bridges on the Thames. It is reported that the ship's captain flew the Union Jack, and a procession of other ships followed the Needle up the Thames. Cast in glowing, triumphant language, the story of the Needle had become a story of British ingenuity and heroism; the series of misadventures only heightened the significance of the achievement. Here was a story of heroic transportation, one of the signs of the power of the British Empire. Despite all odds, British industrial transportation technology managed to succeed in procuring the massive obelisk and 'rescuing' it from its resting place in the Egyptian sand. This was an impressive achievement, despite the fact that the Romans had made similar accomplishments thousands of years ago.

Controversy also surrounded the question of where Cleopatra's Needle should be erected in London (a controversy that was encouraged by the press). The trustees of the British Museum, for example, argued that it should be erected near the museum, whereas the Crystal Palace Company claimed that Sydenham, and especially the Egyptian Court there, was a more appropriate location.[70] The *ILN* chimes in on this issue through a story, the relevant portions reading:

> The controversy about the best site for it in London has not yet been ended. Mr. Erasmus Wilson has proposed the centre of the ornamental garden, adjacent to Old Palace-yard and to St. Margaret's-churchyard, Westminster, sometimes called Parliament-square, where a wooden model of the obelisk, equal to it in size, has been erected to show the effect. The view . . . presented in the Engraving which forms our Extra Supplement, including portions of the Abbey north front and of the Houses of Parliament, will be acceptable to readers at a distance from London.[71]

The text of the article indicates that the periodical is performing a public service by presenting information to those readers who cannot come to London to view the test model for themselves. The large engraving in the Extra Supplement depicting the obelisk in its proposed position seems to present more of an argument (Fig. 5.8). In the illustration, the obelisk towers over Westminster, looking appropriately majestic in the moonlit scene. Groups of well-dressed people (and one dog) surround the obelisk; all are gazing up at it in awe. This must have been a powerful argument for the Needle's erection in Westminster, helping readers imagine an idealized situation. The spot in Westminster was argued to be suitable because it linked a monument of ancient governance with present-day governance, but, conversely, to be unsuitable because an icon of foreign governance should not be associated with British Parliament. Regardless, the site was abandoned because an underground railway tunnel posed engineering difficulties.[72]

On September 12, 1878, the obelisk was erected on the Victorian embankment, where it stands today. A time capsule was installed in the front of the pedestal, containing various items symbolic of Victorian life, including an account of the transportation of the obelisk itself and a length of cable used to lift it—signifying the importance of the event for the Victorians.[73] The same kinds of celebrations of technology are apparent in the stories of the lifting and erection of the obelisk itself. Like many archaeological stories today, the press concentrated on explaining how the engineers used technol-

---

70. Ian Jenkins, *Archaeologists and Aesthetes in the Sculpture Galleries of the British Museum 1800–1939* (London: British Museum Press, 1992), p. 117.

71. 'Arrival of Cleopatra's Needle', *ILN,* January 26, 1878.

72. Phillips, *Past and the Public,* pp. 169-70.

73. Other objects in the time capsule include hairpins, smoking paraphernalia, imperial weights, children's toys and equipment, a hydraulic jack, coins, a rupee, a portrait of Queen Victoria and photos of the 12 'most beautiful' women of London, Bibles, newspapers, other typical books of London, and a model of the monument. For more discussion on the contents of the time capsule, and especially the industrial connotations, see Phillips, *Past and the Public,* p. 172.

Fig. 5.8. 'Arrival of Cleopatra's Needle', *Illustrated London News*, January 26, 1878.

ogy to move the obelisk rather than discussing the historical relevance of the artifact itself. The cranes and leverage systems are described in great detail; the engineers are cast in heroic terms, rescuing the obelisk on behalf of the London public (Fig. 5.9). Two modern sphinxes (in Egyptian style) were cast out of bronze to flank the Needle. Against Egyptian custom, the sphinxes were oriented so as to look at the obelisk rather than guard it. However, the inscriptions on the sphinxes recognize the obelisk's relationship to Thutmoses III (not Cleopatra), and, translated, they read, 'the good god Thutmoses III given life'. Since its erection, London's embankment has had further Egyptianizing decorations added, such as benches with sphinxes set along the footpath.

A penny pamphlet was circulated in tandem with the erection of the obelisk titled *Complete History of the Romantic Life and Tragic Death of the Beautiful Egyptian Queen Cleopatra; and All about her Needle, 3,000 Years Old! And the Events That Led to its Arrival in England; with an Interpretation of its Curious Hieroglyphic Inscriptions*.[74] The title gives an accurate sense of its contents, illustrating how the press still emphasized the fallacious connection with Cleopatra. The pamphlet ends on a curious (and

---

74. N.A., *Complete History of the Romantic Life and Tragic Death of the Beautiful Egyptian Queen Cleopatra; and All about her Needle, 3,000 Years Old! And the Events That Led to its Arrival in England; with an Interpretation of its Curious Hieroglyphic Inscriptions* (London: W. Sutton, 1878).

Fig. 5.9. 'Engineering methods for setting Needle on foundation', *Illustrated London News*, August 10, 1878.

chronologically problematic) note, emphasizing possible connections with biblical figures. It suggests that the obelisk, when it was standing in its original position in Heliopolis, may have been seen by Abraham, Joseph, and 'Jerhemiah' [sic]. It ends with a statement on the collapse of the idolatrous empire:

> Moses lived among them about the same time, prophesied against the powerful Egyptian Monarchy, and led the exodus of the Israelites when they were dwelling under it as a horde of slaves. Ezekial, Isaiah, and Jeremiah uttered similar predictions of its downfall, which have been fulfilled. The glory of its greatness has departed forever.[75]

For readers of the penny pamphlet, the obelisk was a marker of the end of the idolatrous Egyptian Empire and the supremacy of the technologically sophisticated British Empire.

The recontextualization of obelisks outside of Egypt was recognized by some as odd, and the anachronism of an ancient Egyptian object coming to symbolize British progress was not lost on all. The poet and German translator Mathilde Blind (1841–1896) wrote a poem empathizing with Cleopatra's Needle, 'To the Obelisk during the Great Frost, 1881', sug-

---

75. N.A., *Queen Cleopatra*, p. 8.

gesting that the cold English climate must have come as a shock to it. The poem reads:

> Thou sign-post of the Desert! Obelisk,
> Once fronting in thy monumental pride
> Egypt's fierce sun, that blazing far and wide,
> Sheared her of tree and herb, till like a disk
> Her waste stretched shadowless, and fraught with risk
> To those who with their beasts of burden hied
> Across the seas of sand until they spied
> Thy pillar, and their flagging hearts grew brisk:
>
> Now reared beside our Thames so wintry grey,
> Where blocks of ice drift with the drifting stream,
> Thou risest o'er the alien prospect! Say,
> Yon dull, blear, rayless orb whose lurid gleam
> Tinges the snow-draped ships and writhing steam,
> Is this the sun which fired thine orient day?

Here Blind explores the strangeness of the obelisk's new setting. Its companion piece, which was erected in New York, also received poetic treatment. The imperialist ramifications of the erections of obelisks taken from Egypt are explicitly acknowledged in the poem 'The Obelisk', written by the American Civil War veteran Richard Watson Gilder (1844–1909). In 'The Obelisk', Gilder celebrates the arrival of an obelisk in New York and reflects on a rising American supremacy over other colonial powers. Gilder writes:

> Beneath a stone wrenched from Egyptian sands
> Six rivers run through six imperial lands;
> Nile, Bosphorus, Tiber, Seine, and Thames, till now
> The Hudson wears the jewel on her brow.
> Land that we love! O be thou, by this sign,
> Tho' last, the noblest of the mighty line.

Here, Gilder offers a nationalistic message that even though the Americans may not have gotten an obelisk until after the Egyptians, the Turks, the Italians, the French and the British, the United States is 'the noblest' of all of these powers.

As Phillips has noted, the discussion of archaeology within the context of current events in the periodical press, and especially in the *ILN*, meant that archaeological finds were considered 'news'.[76] Near Eastern discoveries were not just academically peripheral events but the kinds of events that people needed to be made aware of in the context of world news. In part, it may have been that archaeology was already functioning as a kind of infotainment—lighter stories of interest that increased the appeal of the periodical to a wider audience. However, this cannot be the full story. The journalistic reports of nineteenth-century archaeological discoveries in the ancient Near East were often as much about Victorian England as they were about antiquity. Through these articles, the Victorian reading public made sense of their own place in the world, both chronologically and geographically; and, most often, the conservative nature of the reports reified their own positions as normative within a global framework. Not all periodical publications were as conservative, however, and the next chapter deals with how the ancient Near East was leveraged for satirical purposes, as a means of criticizing Victorian England within the periodical press.

---

76. Phillips, *Past and the Public*, p. 102.

6

JOHN BULL AND HIS MOMMIES:
THE ANCIENT NEAR EAST IN POLITICAL AND SOCIAL SATIRE

An Egyptian Haul (From the Old Saws of the Nile)

The following curious question and answer, throwing a strong light upon the social habits of the subjects of the Pharaohs, has been translated from some lately discovered hieroglyphics. The question is—Why is an Egyptian Son remarkable for his filial affection? To which is appended the answer,—Because after the decease of his Pappy, he takes such care of his mummy. —*Punch* [1]

For the Victorian press, Cleopatra's Needle had all of the makings of a good story—an exotic artifact of historical interest, distant travel, innovative transportation technologies, deaths at sea, surprise rescues, engineering marvels and public debates on its new location in London. Responses to the Needle reflected the polyvalence of late-Victorian society and touched on issues that lurked beneath the surface of public life. It is not surprising that the satirical press also built on the Needle's popularity and, in particular, used it as inspiration for comedies of manners, in which the values of different classes of people are understood through humour. *Mrs. Brown on Cleopatra's Needle* (1878), written in the year of the obelisk's erection on the Thames, imagines how an elderly Cockney woman would have misunderstood the accounts of the transport of Cleopatra's Needle found in the periodical press and the public debates about what should be done with the obelisk. Using this as a basic theme, the book also mocks how the lower middle class would understand (or misunderstand) Shakespeare, the arts and the acquisition of antiquities.

---

1. 'An Egyptian Haul (*From the Old Saws of the Nile*)', *Punch* 44 (1863), p. 258.

In total, there were thirty-two *Mrs. Brown* volumes published in Victorian times, each based on the same conceit, that of an old, unintelligent lower-middle-class woman (perhaps inspired by Dickens's Mrs Gamp) offering her comments on major topics in the news. This was a new form of the *commedia dell'arte*'s stock character of *la Ruffiana*—the old woman who was the village gossip—here made the centre of the story rather than a side character. The books were written from a first-person perspective, all in a simulated Cockney accent, with purposeful misspellings indicating Mrs Brown's confusion about the world around her. The stories centre on Martha Brown's conversations with various people, but mostly these amount to long, nearly stream-of-consciousness soliloquies (in which she recounts conversations she's had), mocking not only major news items and public figures but how the lower middle classes would have understood those events. Each book takes a central news item or location as its main theme and uses that as a platform for joking about other issues, such as taxation, politics and politicians (especially Gladstone and Disraeli), religion, teatotaling, the royals (especially Queen Wictorier as she is called), the poor, labour relations, international relations, and different ethnic and racial groups.

These were the works of George Rose, who wrote and performed them under the pseudonym Arthur Sketchley. According to promotional materials from the nineteenth century, Sketchley performed these soliloquies all over the world. Presumably, then, people would have purchased the books and/or seen them performed in person. These were intrinsically conservative works, and the audience found them humorous and reassuring, as they proved that the readers were of a class who could understand the world, in a way that Mrs Brown could not. One of these volumes presents Mrs Brown's reaction to Cleopatra's Needle, *Mrs. Brown on Cleopatra's Needle*.

Puns based on Mrs Brown's presumed illiteracy or unintelligence are one of the many comedic elements throughout the work and are often used as a narrative means of moving the discussion to topics other than Cleopatra's Needle. After the preface, the first discussion of the Needle comes with Mrs Brown's confusion about what the Needle is. The main section of the book opens with the following:

> As to Clearpatrer's Needle bein' found, I were a-sayin' to Mrs. Padwick, a-settin' at work, did ever you 'ear sich rubbish in your life a-tryin' for to make anyone believe sich foolishness, as if it was easy for any one to find their own needle, let alone any one's elses, at the bottom of the sea, as there ain't a chance arter 'avin' been dropped all them years ago in the sand; for I'm sure if you only jest drops your needle, a settin' at your own fireside, why, it's ten to one as you ever finds it agin, unless it should

'appen to run into any one's foot as is walkin' about with no slippers, or in a pair of them purnellers, or be dropped on a chair or sofy.[2]

Evidently, the humour here is that Mrs Brown thinks that Cleopatra's Needle is a sewing needle. Discovering that this needle has no eye, Mrs Brown becomes particularly concerned about shipping this needle across the sea:

So I says never, why it might come in collusion with a wessel, and run into it that sharp as would sink the Dook of Edinburrer 'isself, let alone the royal yott. Cos, in course, a needle will run into any one as comes in contract [sic] with it, partikler this one, thro' not 'avin' of no eye to see where it's-a-goin' to.[3]

This type of humour may reflect the stage origins of the Mrs Brown series as this kind of punning plays better when spoken to an audience than when read silently.

Punning is used in the Mrs Brown stories as a means of mocking (in an obviously exaggerated manner) lower-middle-class misunderstandings of society. In *Cleopatra's Needle*, a section of the book, for example, illustrates how confusing the theatre could have been for this class. This is established when Mrs Brown reports, 'Miss Pilkington she says as she doats on the play, not as ever she can tell you wot it's all about. In my opinion she don't really care for the play, but, like a great many more, goes jest for a outin' . . . '[4] The reader already has a sense that Miss Pilkington and Mrs Brown do not understand Shakespeare, after Mrs Brown describes the reactions to a performance of *Antony and Cleopatra*:

as she'd [Miss Pilkington] been out and got out of a play as she'd see acted two or three years ago, as made out as Cleopatrer were found in a pirrymid, where she 'ad been berried alive arter as she'd been and poisoned 'erself ou the top of it, to get away from the Romans, thro' a-suckin' asses' milk out of a basket of figs, as is certing death when took together, and as a party in the name of Anterny, as loved 'er, he took and climbed up arter 'er and died on the spot, thro' them same asses a-takin' and bitin' on 'im to death.[5]

The confusion between 'asps' and 'asses' is brought up again later, when 'asses' is corrected to 'hasps' by Miss Biber. Mrs Brown recounts the correction and her reaction to it:

'No', says Miss Biber, 'not asses, but hasps, as was fastened on 'er breast'.
'Law!' I says, 'wot agny! And I'm sure if them hasps shet 'arf as tight as

---

2. Arthur Sketchely, *Mrs. Brown on Cleopatra's Needle* (London: George Routledge & Sons, 1878), p. 27.
3. Sketchely, *Mrs. Brown on Cleopatra's Needle*, p. 32.
4. Sketchely, *Mrs. Brown on Cleopatra's Needle*, p. 38.
5. Sketchely, *Mrs. Brown on Cleopatra's Needle*, pp. 37-38.

6. *John Bull and his Mommies* 217

them as we 'ave put new to our winder, it must 'ave been a hagonizin' death, as bad as them thum'-screws as old Betsy were so fond on.'[6]

The punning of asps comes to a climax immediately following this as Mrs Brown recounts Miss Biber's reaction:

Miss Biber she ain't one to answer you, but only stares with a toss of the 'ead; not as I cares whether it's asses or hasps as that there fieldmale died on, and no wonder somethink bit'er, for she wasn't 'arf clothed, and she'd only a needle jest for curiosity, for she couldn't never 'ave 'ad no use for it, as seemed to me to be dressed up in wails and them loose things, as was all a-slippin' off 'er back.[7]

The confusion about asps culminates with a return to the theme of Mrs Brown's mistaken notion that Cleopatra's Needle is a sewing needle. These are fairly typical jokes regarding the drop of the 'h' (and replacement with a glottal stop) in Cockney speech.

Yet at various points in the narrative (which in this genre has no need to remain consistent), Mrs Brown understands what the Needle is. At one point she states that it is 'a old ainshent nobbylisk, the same as they been and set up in Paris, for to show the spot where they cut off the king's and queen's 'ead . . .', referring here to the obelisk in Place de la Concorde (see Chapter II.5).[8] Mrs Brown is similarly worldly enough to recognize that a 'nobbylisk' was erected in front of St Peter's Basilica in Vatican City.

Further puns are utilized by the author to demonstrate Mrs Brown's confusion about the issues surrounding the transport of Cleopatra's Needle. Miss Pilkinton is once again talked about with scorn, when Mrs Brown believes that she has 'talked a lot of rubbish about fairies a-carryin' that Needle'.[9] Beyond puns, Mrs Brown adds her own two cents to the public discourse surrounding the proper transport of the Needle. She rambles:

'But', I says, 'I do 'ope as they won't go a-rollin' this 'ere hobbylisk thro' the streets, as might crush' em all in, jest as the new main drains 'as been laid down, as would cut off the gas and water, and be for all the world like a hearthquake, a-breakin' out and swallerin' up everybody all round, as is preaps why it were left so many years a-stickin' in the sands of Egyp', thro' a-breakin' down the cart as were a-movin' it, along with that Clearpatrer's other goods, and 'er a-settin' on the top on a bundle of beddin', as is 'ow Mrs. Weldin got tipped into the Surrey Canal . . .'[10]

The monologue continues on with the comedy building as Mrs Brown uses local gossip to 'understand' the problems of moving the Needle. The

---

6. Sketchely, *Mrs. Brown on Cleopatra's Needle*, p. 121.
7. Sketchely, *Mrs. Brown on Cleopatra's Needle*, p. 121.
8. Sketchely, *Mrs. Brown on Cleopatra's Needle*, p. 29.
9. Sketchely, *Mrs. Brown on Cleopatra's Needle*, p. 109.
10. Sketchely, *Mrs. Brown on Cleopatra's Needle*, p. 107.

absurdity of the analogues would have been evident to the reader who would have laughed at the 'un-worldliness' of Mrs Brown.

Despite her confusion about the world around her, Mrs Brown discusses the plans she made to go see the Needle being floated on the 'Tems' and about the penny steamers that could be hired to take one to view this spectacle.[11] She discusses an episode involving a waterman taking a few of her friends aboard a boat to see it and the problems that arose due to the weight of one of the passengers and their propensity to stand up and shift the boat off balance.[12]

Even though she considers going to see it, Mrs Brown is not convinced of the importance of the Needle. She does not trust the translations of the hieroglyphs since in her words 'suppose they was to stuff us up with a lot of rubbish, who is to say as it ain't truth'.[13] Miss Pilkington tries to explain the historical value of the obelisk, although her take on it is a bit off:

> 'Oh!' says Miss Pilkington, 'but think of the light as it may throw on things, as perhaps some of them Iryglyphics might be 'rote by Moses 'isself.' 'Law bless you', I says, 'you don't think as the Jews would 'ave left it behind, if it 'ad been, besides I says, Clearpatrer weren't no 'Ebrew.' 'Well', she says, 'it may be a Moerbite stone, and 'ave all the 'istory of the world rote on it.'[14]

The literature available about Cleopatra's Needle tended to emphasize fallacious biblical connections, so these comments are not as divergent from Victorian readings of the monument as they may seem. Her knowledge of the Moabite Stone also reflects widespread familiarity with this sensational find (see Chapter II.1). Yet it becomes clear where they have heard of the Moabite Stone and where they expect to learn of the historical value of Cleopatra's Needle, when Miss Pilkington is quoted as saying, 'I'm sure as our minister will make all out, and will preach about it'.[15]

Religion is also parodied in Sketchley's book through the conversations of various characters. Miss Biber and Mrs Yellman discuss whether or not Joseph could have married a daughter of an Egyptian priest, arguing about whether or not priests could marry. Mrs Yellman points out that this a Catholic practice, or in her words, 'that's Popery, as is the wust of all idolatry. . . .'[16] Concerns about the erection of the obelisk as a kind of idolatry are also brought up and satirized. The religious figure of Mrs Yellman, who is depicted as consistently quoting Scripture, is described as characterizing

---

11. Sketchely, *Mrs. Brown on Cleopatra's Needle*, p. 105.
12. Sketchely, *Mrs. Brown on Cleopatra's Needle*, pp. 125-27.
13. Sketchely, *Mrs. Brown on Cleopatra's Needle*, p. 109.
14. Sketchely, *Mrs. Brown on Cleopatra's Needle*, p. 75.
15. Sketchely, *Mrs. Brown on Cleopatra's Needle*, p. 76.
16. Sketchely, *Mrs. Brown on Cleopatra's Needle*, p. 125.

the obelisk as 'a gross idol as were set up for to 'oner the sun, and if we was to put it up agin it would bring a judgement, as might be a hearthquake or a pestilence'.[17] Mrs Brown rejects this concern, stating, 'I'm sure nobody won't be sich a ass as to think of settin' up on the Tems Embankmint to 'oner the sun this time of year, when he ain't out for days together'.[18]

Cleopatra's Needle is used as a means of mocking political figures as well. In one side comment, Mrs Brown dismisses it as one of 'Dizzy's fads', referring to Disraeli.[19] She also displays concerns that the transport of the Needle has been a parliamentary ruse to get money out of an unsuspecting population (when she misunderstands her husband's warning not to join the crowds on Westminster Bridge since from that vantage point there is 'nothink to see arter all'.[20] Taking this to mean that there is literally nothing to see, Mrs Brown launches into a complaint about the six million pounds the British government was trying to raise in case of a fight with the Russians (in relation to the Russo-Turkish War) and thinking that the Needle would be paid for out of this.[21]

It is not just domestic political affairs that Mrs Brown chimes in on in this book, but international affairs as well, even affairs concerning antiquities. She demonstrates a confused interest in the fact that the 'Kurdive' had given the obelisk to the English and rejects the notion that the sultan was the one with the authority. Her rejection is based on her belief that this is a matter that the sultan and 'Kurdive' should deal with between themselves and that if the 'Kurdive' was in the wrong, he should 'get the sack for 'is pains'.[22] Mrs Brown also echoes her husband's sentiment that the English should sack Egypt to take what they want (as the king of Italy has done with things that 'didn't belong to 'im').[23] Were the English to do so, Mrs Brown suggests that 'we shouldn't want no more Clearpatrer's Needles, nor yet 'ave them Pirrymids floated over 'ere; cos we could go there and look at 'em'.[24] As became apparent after the Anglo-Egyptian War of 1882, when Egypt became a protectorate of Britain, the Browns' outlook on colonial politics mirrored the state's outlook.

Mrs. Brown on Cleopatra's Needle ends in a manner that foresees later discussions about artifact preservation and repatriation. She offers her final thoughts about where the Needle should be placed, saying:

---

17. Sketchely, *Mrs. Brown on Cleopatra's Needle*, p. 125.
18. Sketchely, *Mrs. Brown on Cleopatra's Needle*, p. 125.
19. Sketchely, *Mrs. Brown on Cleopatra's Needle*, p. 52.
20. Sketchely, *Mrs. Brown on Cleopatra's Needle*, p. 109.
21. Sketchely, *Mrs. Brown on Cleopatra's Needle*, p. 110.
22. Sketchely, *Mrs. Brown on Cleopatra's Needle*, p. 144.
23. Sketchely, *Mrs. Brown on Cleopatra's Needle*, p. 115.
24. Sketchely, *Mrs. Brown on Cleopatra's Needle*, p. 115.

But as to where to put the Needle, I can't say, not as I believes in no judgements a-follerin' of it, so long as it ain't put too near the footpath, as might topple over on to them as was passin' by, . . . and if left too near the river, might rust and break off short, as it's a pity it weren't left like a oyster in its native sanded bed, where it wasn't in nobody's ways . . . as will be werry out of place in a November fog, and be werry soon begrimed with London sut, as it will pretty soon tarnish it, tho' it may be a deal more anshent than the British Iles themselves.[25]

With the Mrs Brown series, knowledge about and familiarity with Egypt and Egyptian travel had become a marker of a knowledgeable and educated citizen. Perhaps this cultural familiarity with the 'other' did not quite constitute a status symbol, but in the kind of class humour that Mrs Brown represented, facility in discussion about Egypt and events relating to ancient Egypt could at least be aspirational.

For the most part, the treatment of Cleopatra's Needle by the press was celebratory, and so a comedy of manners like *Mrs. Brown* was a suitable form of satire. Tragedies and deep-seated public disagreements, however, were better suited for political satire, and one of the acts of empire that divided the late-Victorian populace surrounded British support (or lack thereof) of General 'Chinese' Gordon and his garrison during the 1884–1885 siege of Khartoum. The Sudan had been facing a Mahdi revolt, a revolt of Muslim forces against the Egyptian administration of the Sudan. Although Egypt was Britain's protectorate at this time, Gladstone felt that the Sudanese affair was best left as an internal Egyptian matter and ordered the evacuation of all Egyptian outposts. Gordon feared that the Mahdists had aspirations to take over all of North Africa and argued that Britain needed to take an aggressive stance against this army. Despite their disagreements, Gordon (himself a hugely popular figure in Victorian Britain) agreed to go to the Sudan to oversee the evacuation and made a very public showing of his departure. However, when Gordon arrived in Khartoum he did not begin the evacuation immediately. Rather, he began to reorganize the administration of the city and ordered controversial changes to the city's legal system, including the legalization of slavery (as a means of appeasing local elites). Actions such as these polarized public opinion in Britain, and Gladstone's government began rejecting calls for aid from Gordon. As the Mahdists approached Khartoum, Gordon reinforced the city. Supplies were cut off from the city, but communications remained open, meaning that the British press were able to keep the public informed of events as they happened. Gladstone recalled Gordon, but he refused to abandon the city. Eventually Khartoum was overrun, and Gordon was killed by Mahdist forces.

25. Sketchely, *Mrs. Brown on Cleopatra's Needle*, p. 154.

6. *John Bull and his Mommies*

Fig. 6.1. 'The Egyptian puzzle', from *The Egyptian Red Book* (London: William Blackwood & Sons, 1885).

Gordon's controversial action and Gladstone's controversial inaction were widely debated in the media, and satire was one of the approaches through which opinions on Khartoum were expressed. One such volume, *The Egyptian Red Book*, criticizes the lack of government support for Gordon and clearly sides with Gordon in his public dispute about British policy in the Sudan with then Prime Minister Gladstone. *The Egyptian Red Book* was published by William Blackwood & Sons, known for its occasional humorous volumes satirizing political events through the juxtaposition of political cartoons with actual quotes from politicians of the day. These illustrated magazines cost six pence and were typically slanted to argue one particular point consistently throughout. *The Egyptian Red Book* uses Egyptian imagery and styles to complain that the government's lack of action led to Gordon's heroic but tragic death. The book collects political cartoons that use Egyptian references in their illustrations in a fairly consistent fashion. Images are drawn in the ancient Egyptian style, as though they were found on ancient tomb walls. The illustration facing the title page is captioned 'The Egyptian Puzzle' (Fig. 6.1) and depicts the main political figures in the saga in Egyptian profile postures, in a scene evoking a temple wall. Pharaoh astride his chariot holds a bow and arrow and tramples over his enemies,

Fig. 6.2. 'The mummy government', from *The Egyptian Red Book* (London: William Blackwood & Sons, 1885).

although here Pharaoh wears the British Royal Navy hat, not the blue military crown. Numerous snails, made to look like an Egyptian artist drew them, reflect the illustrator's belief that the British government was too slow in action. Lord Granville is depicted with a snail's body. Another cartoon, labeled 'The Mummy Government' (Fig. 6.2), depicts the leaders of Gladstone's government as stylized sarcophagi. The final image in the book (Fig. 6.3) depicts an Egyptian-style Gladstone being kicked out of office. In stylized faux hieroglyphs, the liberal party slogan 'Peace, Retrenchment, Reform' is parodied. 'Peace' and 'Retrenchment' are written right behind Gladstone's head, labeled as Egyptian figures often were. But 'Reform' is used to label the politician who is kicking Gladstone from behind, and written beside are the dates of the government (1880–1885), reflecting the reform that comes with the fall of the government.

The other cartoons are in more contemporary style. Egyptian monuments are reshaped to bear the faces of British politicians or British politicians are depicted in action in front of the monuments. In one (Fig. 6.4), the colossi at Abu Simbel are depicted with the faces of key politicians, including Gladstone and Granville. A broken and missing statue bears a sign 'Notice— J. Bright Resigned', referencing a party member who had quit. The caption

Fig. 6.3. 'Kicked out', from *The Egyptian Red Book* (London: William Blackwood & Sons, 1885).

Fig. 6.4. 'The sleeping beauties', from *The Egyptian Red Book* (London: William Blackwood & Sons, 1885).

refers to them as 'The Sleeping Beauties', using the cartoon trope of sleepy Egyptian monuments to criticize their perceived inaction. Another cartoon shows Granville and Gladstone hauling a rowboat named 'Egyptian Policy' (filled with bills with government members' names) through the Egyptian desert as the sphinx dozes behind them.

The anger toward Gladstone's policies and the sense of helplessness surrounding the death of Gordon are readily apparent in *The Egyptian Red Book*. By 1898, the British public supported Kitchener's absolute decimation of Mahdist forces at the Battle of Omdurman, as much in revenge for Gordon as in reconquering the Sudan. *The Egyptian Red Book* offered topical humour in a subversive manner that called for changes in policy and changes in government and offered a particular vision of British colonialism. For the political cartoonists whose works were collected in the *Red Book*, Egypt's visual culture was by this point familiar enough to facilitate multiple different kinds of uses in visual parody. Tomb paintings offered the opportunity for narrativity in a single scene. Egypt's monuments and material culture could imply outdated policy or bumbling governance. For a book like this to be effective, people had to be able to understand the cartoons with little explanation. Fundamentally, Egyptian visual references were used because Gordon had died in the region. But it was neither Ottoman Egypt's nor the Sudan's visual culture that was used for the satire. Egypt's ancient past provided the preferred semiotic system through which ideas about the siege of Khartoum could be articulated.

Punch *and the Ancient Near Eastern Charivari*

With all of these satirical approaches to the ancient Near East, from the light-hearted *Mrs. Brown* to the partisan *Red Book*, the ancient Near East was mimetic of Victorian Britain. Once ancient Near Eastern material culture and history became sufficiently familiar to periodical readers, it could be enlisted as a means of commenting on the news of the day. In particular, political satire and political cartoons used the juxtaposition of antiquity and contemporary political figures for comic effect. To be successful, the allusions had to be sufficiently well understood by a large enough group so this kind of satire provides strong evidence for the general level of familiarity with antiquity. More interestingly, these comics can also shed light on how the ancient Near East could be used by the Victorians to better understand the self. Arguably the most popular source of topical comedy in Victorian England was *Punch, or the London Charivari*. *Punch* was a weekly satirical news magazine, launched in 1841, which played a significant role in public discourse throughout the period. 'Punch' refers to the character of Mr Punch from the traditional (and satirical) glove puppet Punch-and-Judy shows. *The London Charivari* is a nod to an early French periodical, itself named for older socially leveling folk customs. These customs were outlets for social criticism, especially aimed at figures of authority, and *Punch* fulfilled this same role in periodical form.

At first the periodical was not much of a success, but its conservative stances and lack of crude humour meant that it was more widely acceptable in mid-Victorian society than other satirical publications. Brian Maidment has argued that once the radicalism of the periodical was replaced by a softer type of comedy of manners, *Punch* was able to reach and sustain a wider audience.[26] It also assumed the voice of a middle-class audience and reified the values of that class and thus the aspirations of its largest readership.[27] The satirical periodical had a large circulation throughout the empire and was widely imitated in other national settings. Some of its individual comics reached a much wider audience when more mainstream newspapers (like *The Times*) began using its illustrations as column fillers, thereby also instituting the tradition of political cartoons embedded within straight news accounts. In fact, the term 'cartoon' was first used by *Punch* to refer to its particular brand of illustrated comic in 1843; the word had until then referred to preliminary sketches, not necessarily humorous images, with captions. In *Punch*, the juxtaposition of image and text was often the location of humour, and this was often why ancient Near Eastern visual culture was employed in the periodical.[28]

Within the pages of *Punch*, readers found linguistic word play (especially verbal–visual puns), political satire and comedies of manners. Specific public figures were mocked, and caricatures were used to criticize certain types of public figures. As a source of gentle subversion, *Punch* took aim at any figure of authority, and 'history', as an authoritative view of the past, was treated in a similar mocking fashion. Any genre in print was subject to *Punch*'s parody, and so any of these genres through which the ancient Near East was presented may also have been lampooned.[29] *Punch*'s humour was particularly visual and poetic, and the ancient Near East appears sporadically throughout its run, especially in relation to news events of the Middle East. What is of interest to this study is that *Punch* explicitly uses the results of ancient Near Eastern explorations in order to highlight issues within nineteenth-century Britain. Whereas sociologists and anthropolo-

---

26. Brian Maidment, 'The Presence of *Punch* in the Nineteenth Century', in *Asian Punches: A Transcultural Affair* (ed. Hans Harder and Barbara Mittler; Heidelberg: Springer, 2013), pp. 15-44 (44).

27. Maidment, 'Presence of *Punch*', p. 31.

28. For more on the nature of *Punch*'s visual humour, see Hans Harder, 'Prologue: Late Nineteenth and Twentieth Century Asian *Punch* Versions and Related Satirical Journals', in *Asian Punches: A Transcultural Affair* (ed. Hans Harder and Barbara Mittler; Heidelberg: Springer, 2013), pp. 1-11 (9-10).

29. Maidment, 'Presence of *Punch*', p. 25.

gists used the ancient Near East to draw conclusions about the nature of humanity and global history, and journalists used the ancient Near East to celebrate empire and technology, political satirists used ancient Near Eastern discoveries to highlight social and political problems (rarely offering solutions, however). The satirical periodical's use of the ancient Near East in its discourse reflects a very direct use of history to understand the present. Even though the specific references to the ancient Near East may have been relatively shallow, the fact that it was used points to how historical settings were (and are) safe locations for social commentary. The following examples also highlight how the past as 'other' was invoked to understand the 'self'. Marilyn Booth's comment about *Punch*'s treatment of nineteenth-century Egypt is just as relevant for its treatment about ancient Egypt. She writes, 'in *Punch* Egypt is but a mirror reflecting the self-interested preoccupations of those at the centre [of the colonial relationship]'.[30]

Like mummy/mommy jokes, some of *Punch*'s humour is just based on word play and does not require much of its readers other than a recognition of archaeological terminology. It is not clear when puns on mummies and mommies started becoming tired, but this kind of joke appears in *Punch* periodically and continues to plague Egyptology in innumerable iterations. The same kind of word play appears in *Punch*'s jokes that play on class differences, where 'hieroglyphics' frequently signal the incomprehensibility of working-class speech and regional dialects. In an illustrated caption titled 'Modern Hieroglyphics' the incomprehensibility of lower class speech is gently mocked:

> 'I say Bill, 'ave you send Wotdyecallum?'
> 'Wot, do you mean Wots 'isname?'
> 'O no, not 'im,—that 'ere tother.'
> 'O, ah! I seed 'im fast enuff.'[31]

Here the joke is the slang dialect mixed with the confusion caused by making reference to an individual without using his name. Essentially though, this kind of joke reflects little of the Near East—it is merely making fun of different levels of incomprehensibility.

Another approach to merging word play with the juxtaposition of antiquity and modernity was to substitute modern terms for similar sounding technical vocabulary about the ancient world. For example, in 'An Egyptian Find', *Punch* reports the discovery of a fragment of dialogue from an ancient restaurant scene, while punning on Egyptian sounding dining terms:

30. Marilyn Booth, 'Insistent Localism in a Satiric World: Shaykh Naggār's "Reed-Pipe" in the 1890s Cairene Press', in *Asian Punches: A Transcultural Affair* (ed. Hans Harder and Barbara Mittler; Heidelberg: Springer, 2013), pp. 187-218 (210).
31. 'Modern Hieroglyphics', *Punch* 9 (1845), p. 192.

Dear Mr. Punch,

I Fear this is rather an ambiguous title, and might cast unjust reflections on the Egyptians. Find means a discovery—not that a son of Khem has been amerced by the Magistrat. However, this is what I have discovered in a copper cylinder in a hidden chamber in a forgotten pyramid in a sanded-up desert. It is a fragment of a dialogue, and runs as follows:—

'Isis, Sir?'

'Yes; and Osiris, if you have any.' 'Very sorry, Sir; Osiris is off.' 'Waiter, a papyrus roll.' 'Yes, Sir.' 'And butter.' 'D'rec'ly, Sir.'

'And a Lybian dessert to follow.'

Here, unfortunately, the fragment ends, though I can just decipher something which looks like Cigarcoffagus. The fragment is apparently from a familiar work, either of the great Mur-ra, or of the Ta-bel DotabDus, of the so-called Three-and-sixpenny Dynasty. I found it myself in the Kaf-feh Restaur—On Chamber of the Pyramid of Chops, near Cowey Steaks, on the Pelasgic branch of the Nile. It has given me six months' work, and the translation of it has nearly killed me; but it will, like Mr. Rider Haggard's *Cleopatra* MS., drive every Egyptologist in Europe mad with envy.

Yours, severely, The Yen. Thomas, Q.T., I.O.U., &c. *Knippin Court, St. Neots.*[32]

This is a fairly common type of *Punch* joke. The humour is rooted in homophonic word shifts. The numerous puns here require a certain fluency in Egyptological terminology to be understood: 'Chops' for King Cheops or 'Cigarcoffagus' for sarcophagus. Also of comic interest here is the implication that some of the 'finds' from the ancient world are of dubious interest. It plays on the idea that many Egyptological finds are merely remnants of ancient everyday life, perhaps of little significance in antiquity, let alone in the nineteenth century.

Punching the Sphinx and Unrolling the Mummies

More directly related to the ancient Near East are the numerous references that are made to the Great Sphinx in *Punch*. The sphinx becomes an icon, in the Peircian sense, of a set of behavioural and characteristic attributes, related to but slightly different from what it had referenced for millennia. Through the satirical press, this ancient symbol was revised and transformed in such a way that its presentation in a comic immediately brought to mind set characteristics. Egyptian and Greek sphinxes are not distinguished in satirical usage, but visually are almost always depicted in Egyptian styles.[33]

---

32. 'An Egyptian Find', *Punch* 97 (1889), p. 9.

33. Egyptian sphinxes are male and usually wear a *nemes*-headdress, like that worn by the Great Sphinx at Giza. Greek sphinxes are usually based on the female sphinx that Oedipus encounters, usually depicted with wings and often some type of militaristic helmet.

The sphinx, in a fashion that has been typical since Greek times, is invoked as a riddler in *Punch*.[34] Or, likewise, it is invoked as mysterious architecture, as is the case in the 1842 article 'The Modern Sphinx', which puzzles over the identity and function of a tarp-covered monument erected at Charing Cross.[35] The idea that the sphinx is symbolic of silence emerges from the long-standing folk tradition that the sphinx rarely reveals its secrets, and the expression 'sphinx-like' still has this connotation today.

In the 1891 poem 'The Sphinx and the Stick', *Punch* lampoons James Crichton-Browne's comments on the reserve of the British people. Crichton-Browne (1840–1938), a psychiatrist, was Lord Chancellor's Visitor in a Lunacy, a government position that also allowed him to give numerous public addresses on issues of public mental health. Punch responds to one of these addresses, first by quoting Crichton-Browne's actual statement:

A song wherein is suggested a suitable subject for an Ibsenite Tragedy.

[Sir JAMES CRICHTON-BROWNE thinks that 'the reserve and suppression of emotional movement which is observed in English people' will probably result in all the women becoming sphinxes, and all the men sticks.]

'If you'll only indulge in a shrug and some winks,
You'll perhaps set *me* off', said the Stick to the Sphinx.
'Nay, long "inhibition"', the Sphinx made reply,
'Has imparted rigidity, love, to my eye.'
'"Emotional movement" no longer is mine',
Sighed the Stick to the Sphinx; 'though I greatly incline
To a dig in your ribs, or a slap on your back
(As a sign of my love), all my muscles are slack.
My poor "motor-centres" are all out of gear,
And I can't even "chuck' your soft chin, sweet, I fear.
I'm sure such a stolid inflexible "stick" you'll hate,
But, though I adore you, I *cannot* gesticulate—'
'My case is as bad', sighed the Sphinx to the Stick,
'For I cannot "bridle"—no more than a brick.'
Said the Stick to the Sphinx, 'Ah, we once knew what love meant!
But, thanks to the loss of "emotional movement",
We can't give it "graceful and chastened expression",
And so it seems slipping fast out of possession.
Heigho! we had far better die, darling, quick!
Since you are a Sphinx, love, and I'm but a Stick!'[36]

---

34. For example, 'The Sphinx's Latest Riddle', *Punch* 113 (1897), p. 17.
35. 'The Modern Sphinx', *Punch* 3 (1842), p. 100.
36. 'The Sphinx and the Stick', *Punch* 101 (1891), p. 273.

6. *John Bull and his Mommies*

Here, as is common in *Punch*, is the invocation of the sphinx as silent and reserved. Again, this is a typical *Punch*-style joke, where a public figure's statement is imagined to be taken quite literally. This was relatively safe political humour, since it commented on the word uses of public figures, not their actual policies.

In another instance, the sphinx is treated as a type of society woman, and the article, titled 'The Minx—A Poem in Prose', uses the sphinx to mock society paper interviews:

> Poet. It's so good of you to see me. I merely wished to ask one or two questions as to your career. You must have led a most interesting: life.
> Sphinx. You are very inquisitive and extremely indiscreet, and I have always carefully avoided being interviewed. However, go on.
> Poet. I believe you can read hieroglyphs?
> Sphinx. Oh yes; I can, fluently. But I never do. I assure you they are not in the least amusing.
> Poet. No doubt you have talked with hippogriffs and basilisks?
> Sphinx (modestly). I certainly was in rather a smart set at one time. As they say, I have 'known better days'.
> Poet. Did you ever have any conversation with Thoth?
> Sphinx (loftily). Oh, dear no! (Mimicking.) Thoth he wath not conthidered quite a nice perthon. I would not allowhnim to be introduced to me.
> Poet. You were very particular?
> Sphinx. One has to be careful The world is so censorious.
> Poet. I wonder, would you give me the pleasure of singing to me? 'Adrian's Gilded Barge', for instance?
> Sphinx. You must really excuse me. I am not in good Voice. By the way, the 'Gilded Barge', as you call it, was merely a shabby sort of pant. It would have had no effect whatever at the Henley Regatta,
> Poet. Dear me! Is it true you played golf among the Pyramids ?
> Sphinx (emphatically). Perfectly untrue. You see what absurd reports get about!
> Poet (softly). They do. What was that story about the Tynan?
> Sphinx. Merely gossip. There was nothing in it, I assure you.
> Poet. And Apis?
> Sphinx. Oh, he sent me some flowers, and there were paragraphs about it—in hieroglyphs—in the society papers. That was all. But they were contradicted.
> Poet. You knew Ammon very well, I believe ?
> Sphinx (frankly). Ammon and I were great pals. I used to see a good deal of him. He came in to tea very often—he was quite interesting. But I have not seen him for a long time. He had one fault— he would smoke in the drawing-room. And though I hope I am not too conventional, I really could not allow that.
> Poet. How pleased they would all be to see you again! Why do you not go over to Egypt for the winter?
> Sphinx. The hotels at Cairo are so dreadfully expensive.
> Poet. Is it true you went tunny-fishing with Antony?

Sphinx. One must draw the line somewhere! Cleopatra was so cross. She was horribly jealous, and not nearly so handsome as you might suppose, though she was photographed as a ' type of Egyptian Beauty'!
Poet. I must thank you very much for the courteous way in which you have replied to my questions. And now will you forgive me if I make an observation? In my opinion you are not a Sphinx at all.
Sphinx (indignantly). What am I, then ?
Poet. A Minx. [37]

The 'poem' is not really about ancient Egypt but uses a variety of Egyptian references to emphasize the uniformity of these kinds of interviews (recognizable in the twenty-first century) and of the public figure disparagingly known as a 'minx'. Here Egypt is a useful means to safely criticize contemporary society. The sphinx's aristocratic background and Egypt's generalized association with luxury and decadence by the late nineteenth-century make it an easy substitution for a vapid society lady and her interview in a gossip paper.

It is not only the sphinx that is referenced in this manner. A Philistine is not an enemy of David but a boorish, rude and uneducated person following Matthew Arnold's (1822–1888) recoining of the descriptor. References to contemporary excesses often invoked 'Babylon', such as an 1888 poem, inspired by Shelley's *Oedipus tyrannus,* about boar hunting.[38] In most cases, however, the referents do not enter into popular parlance but are rather one-off references in individual articles. For example, in this 1894 note, *Punch* references Lynn Linton (1822–1898) and Henry Drummond (1851–1897). Linton was a social critic and author, whose first book was the historical romance *Azeth, the Egyptian; Amymone* (1848). She was famously outspoken, especially against feminism and the New Woman. Drummond was a theologian who pioneered natural theology, and his book, *Ascent of Man,* consists of a series of lectures about the role of altruism in natural selection. Linton wrote a particularly scathing review of the book. In the following short poem, *Punch* makes reference to Drummond and Linton, the book of Isaiah's Assyrians and the battle of music between Apollo and Marsyas, writing:

> When Drummond wrote of the Ascent of Man,
>   He did not think of the Descent of Woman
> Upon his poor doomed head. The Assyrian
>   Did not 'come down' with wrath more superhuman,
> Or more like a fierce wolf upon the fold:
> Mrs. Lynn Linton, sweetest mannered scold
> That ever heresy to judgment summoned,

---

37. 'The Minx—A Poem in Prose', *Punch* 107 (1894), p. 33.
38. 'The Babylonian Boar-Hunt', *Punch* 95 (1888), p. 27.

> Hath! had her dainty will, and drummed out Drummond!
> Give us a gentle lady, without bias,
> To play Apollo to a new Marsyas![39]

This is the type of satirical use of the ancient Near East that is most frequent. Satire through substitution was extremely common in Victorian poetry and prose. Though this poem says little of the ancient Near East directly, the fluency of the references to biblical and classical literature illuminate the background of the readership, and the general comments about Assyrians reflect popular conceptions of them. This and other examples show how much the ancient Near East was part of a shared Victorian cultural canon.

In the mid-to-late 1850s, when the Nineveh bulls were still news stories of interest to the British public, *Punch* occasionally made plays on these winged bulls and the anthropomorphized character of the British nation—John Bull. In a poem titled 'The Winged Bull', which appeared in 1856, the new practice of the 'vacation' and the related seasonal international exploits of the British people are explored through the allegory of the Nimrud finds. The poem opens as follows:

> Bull, three-fourths of each year the sedatest of mortals,
>   Desk-chained, as the slave to his oar at the galleys is,
> With Autumn, grows like those Winged Bulls at the portals
>   Of Kouyunjik's or Nimroud's mysterious palaces.
> From his two breeches-pockets shoot wide-spreading pinions,
>   Composed of bank-paper or circular notes,
> With which he soars forth from the British Dominions,
>   And through land and o'er ocean, ubiquitous floats![40]

Here, 'John Bull' is described as transforming into the winged bull every autumn as he sets out in quest of wealth, distinction and leisure abroad. The rest of the poem describes the 'Brit abroad' stereotype, mocking the new middle-class tourist who uses a visit to another country as an excuse to reject the staid behaviour expected at home. What is of interest here, though, is how ancient Assyrian sculpture can now be used to stand in for the British public at large and be comprehensible to *Punch*'s wide audience.

Punch also made direct comparison between the ancient Near East and Victorian Britain. One of these reflections on the two cultures is an 1862 poem called 'The Prince and the Pyramid', which was inspired by Prince Edward's 1862 visit to Egypt. The poem describes Prince Edward's amazement at the sites of Egypt:

---

39. 'The Professor of the Period', *Punch* 107 (1894), p. 153.
40. 'Winged Bull', *Punch* 31 (1856), p. 104.

> Now Sol from yonder grey horizon winks,
> And Albert Edward rises near the Sphynx,
> He leaves the tent the Pasha's care had raised,
> And looks upon the desert quite amazed.
> Gaze on, brave Prince, the thought must surely strike
> That in your country there is nothing like
> Unto that Pyramid whose curious pile
> Has stood so many years beside the Nile,
> Or like the sand that makes the thought occur,
> How fast our sands of life are fleeting, Sir.

Here, a difference between Egypt and Britain is highlighted, for Britain has nothing in its history to compare to the Great Pyramid. Egypt's sand evokes a sense of how much time separates the two cultures. The poem continues:

> You now are far from Windsor's hoary towers,
> Saint James's brick, and Osborne's beauteous bowers,
> And on your mind must come this feeling high,
> That land and sea 'twixt you and England lie.
> And yet what is it practically, sire?
> (I should say, Sir) with that electric wire?
> O, when the Pharaohs swayed this region fine;
> Or Cleopatra dropped that fishing line;
> Or the young Memnon by Achilles' hands
> Fell, though his bust in the Museum stands;
> Or when Amenophis, the fierce and brave,
> With all his chariots sank beneath the wave,
> (Here let me scorn the Essays and Reviews,
> That seek to steal that victory from the Jews).
> Or when in later times stern Mehemet
> Slaughtered the Mamelukes, ungrateful set,
> There was small thought, O Prince of England, then,
> That lightning e'er should write with iron pen.
> 'Tis sweet to think that standing on these sands
> You can send messages to distant lands;
> And while they go, can muse, on Shakspeare's plan,
> And say, 'O what a piece of work is man!'

Here the achievements of modern technology are celebrated through the invocation of past times. Despite the numerous achievements of the Egyptian kings and the many historical events that are still remembered and celebrated, the electrical telegraph was unimaginable in those ancient days. In the nineteenth century, the geographical distance between London and Cairo was meaningless, and since the ancients could not imagine this, the British future was equally unimaginable.

> But up, young Prince, before the hour is late,
> Behold yon string of dromedaries wait,

> The matutinal meal discussed and done,
> Now for the Pyramid, and meet the Sun.
> many suns have shone since that was built,
> And shone, alas, on many scenes of guilt.
> We reach the base; ascend as well you may,
> That corner's broken stones present the way.

Prince Edward is now set to climb the pyramid, and, unusual for the time, as described in the next stanza, he chooses to climb on his own, not to be dragged up the side of the pyramid as was typical practice at the time (see Chapter I.7).

> For youth like yours exertion hath its charms,
> And you repulse those Arabs' dingy arms,
> You climb alone, and swift the height you gain,
> Your panting suite toil after you in vain;
> And now upon the apex, Sir, you stand,
> And rapidly survey old Egypt's land:
> Yonder is Cairo, as you may suppose,
> And at your feet the Nilus river flows.
> No English Heir Apparent to the Crown
> Ever before upon that scene looked down.
> Omens are heathen things, but O permit
> A thought from Poet-lip not all unfit.
> Even as the platform on that mighty block
> Bests on a basis firm as any rock,
> So may the Throne of England long endure,
> Built on foundations solid and secure.
> Come back, my muse, and wear a sober brow,
> That dazzling flight of Fancy's over now.

Now Prince Edward has done something that has never been done before—an English monarch gazes from atop the pyramid. His youthful vigour allowed him to climb the pyramid easily, in comparison to the others, whose stamina was less impressive. Now, from his vantage atop the pyramid, the hope is expressed that his throne will prove to be as stable as the ancient monument.

> Paid is the visit. On yon loftiest stone
> Names are cut deep—our Prince has cut his own,
> Or modestly (lest he might seem to claim
> What's Abbas Pasha's, by his full-writ name)
> Cuts his initials—Vowels—then descends
> Accompanied by his respectful friends.
> And so to Cairo. On his princely way
> What thoughts arose 'tis not for me to say,
> But for myself, delighted and amused,
> The story of his journey I perused,
> Cried, 'Might I join his party—would I could!

> A proverb now and then might do him good.'
> But circumstance o'er which I've no control
> Prohibits what I wish with all my soul,
> (Not that I'd seek, of course, with envious teeth
> To tear a leaf from Canon Stanley's wreath[41]),
> 'No', I exclaimed, 'but I shall do no wrong
> If I embalm the tale in deathless song,
> And 'neath a Prince's Vowels bid folks see
> A Poet's Consonants, his M.F.C.'[42]

Conceptually this poem fulfills the same role that the Napoleonic expedition's images of the Corsican contemplating the sphinx fulfill. Both normalize the current political status quo and draw connections between the ancient fallen empire and the current world power. The shared gaze between the contemporary leader and the ancient statue fixes the two figures conceptually through time and space. The vigour of the prince and the splendours of technology are celebrated, and the juxtaposition of the ancient with the modern reflects a hope for a stable future England.

Prince Edward's visit to Egypt was a media sensation at the time, the kind of royal event that still sells copy in the twenty-first century. The journalistic culture that could manufacture excited responses to this kind of event was already well established by mid-century and could itself be satirized. Many *Punch* jokes represented self-referential commentary on journalism and news stories. As a genre of writing that was just emerging, the form of short journalistic stories was still being worked out. The following seems to be a relatively straightforward notice (unusual for *Punch*) reporting on a relatively amusing fact about alcohol. Simply titled 'Anglo-Egyptian', the notice reads:

> A Statistical account of Beer, by M. Vögel, contains some interesting particulars relative to that invigorating liquor. Among these is the statement that in Egypt, where beer was first brewed at Pelusium, 'in the year 2017 [BCE]', it continues to be brewed still, and is called 'booza'. What a pretty instance of analogy between the popular dialect of one of the 'Indo-European' races, and the Egyptian language![43]

Here, *Punch* makes reference to an actual book from 1874, *On Beer: A Statistical Account,* by M. Vögel.[44] Here, though, the joke is based not only

---

41. This is a reference to Canon Arthur Stanley's (1815–1881) well-known book, *Sinai and Palestine in Connection with their History*, detailing his trip through the region and the implications that his observations had for understanding the Bible.

42. 'The Prince and the Pyramid', *Punch* 42 (1862), p. 123.

43. 'Anglo-Egyptian', *Punch* 66 (1874), p. 115.

44. The passage that *Punch* refers to here reads: 'In the dimmest ages of antiquity we find traces of beer, and the Greek historian, Diodorus of Sicily, informs us that the art of brewing beer was brought to Egypt by her god or king Osiris, who in the year

on the observation of a seeming cognate term (booze-*booza*) in two different languages but also on the kind of minor observation that was used to fill newspapers.

Specific reports from other, more serious publications were frequently mocked in *Punch*. In these cases, *Punch* satirizes not only the subject of the stories but the approach to reporting as well. In the mid-nineteenth century, a shortage of paper in the United States led to various calls for different sources of paper. At the time, paper was more commonly made from a pulp of cotton and linen rags than from trees, so one idea that seems to have been floated was that the rags of mummies be used.[45] In 1847, *Punch* quoted an Italian periodical that reported that Muhammed Ali had made this proposal and calculated that '420,000,000 must be deposited in the pits of Egypt'.[46] That the Italian public may have been worried about this makes sense given that at the time, Italy was the largest supplier of the linen pulp for paper production, so such an enterprise would, in theory, have put Egypt into conflict with one of Italy's major industries.[47] *Punch*'s musings on the subject are fascinating, both as commentary on the potential industrial uses of ancient human remains and as satire of this kind of media sensation. *Punch* writes:

> Oh, shade of Memnon!
> Cheops and Rameses, shake in your cere-cloths!
> Save smoke-dried pashas of true Eastern phlegm, none
> Can read, unmoved, the end of all your glory,
> Announced in the Grand Cairo *Spettatore*;
>   How, in the place of mere cloths
>   Of woollen, linen, cotton,
>   More or less rotten,
> As made at Manchester, and sold by every draper,
> They're going to take the bier-cloths
> That wrap the sons and daughters of old Nile,
> From gilded kings to rough-dressed rank and file,
>   And turn them into paper![48]

2017 brewed it first in the city of Pelusium. The same author speaks of two descriptions of beer brewed by the Egyptians: Zythos a strong, and Cunni a weaker beer. The art of brewing appears to have continued down to our days in Egypt, and they brew a kind of beer called Room; but it is bad, says Grasse' (M. Vögel, *On Beer: A Statistical Account* [London: Trübner & Co., 1874], p. 1).

45. For an overview of this issue and a collection of news articles on the subject of the industrial use of mummies, see S.J. Wolfe with Robert Singerman, *Mummies in Nineteenth Century America* (Jefferson, NC: McFarland & Co., 2009), pp. 173-200.

46. 'Musings on Mummy-Paper', *Punch* 12 (1847), p. 224.

47. After the United States cotton industry collapsed in the aftermath of the civil war, similar discussions of alternative uses of mummies re-emerged.

48. 'Musings on Mummy-Paper', *Punch* 12 (1847), p. 224.

In the first stanza, the author juxtaposes the industrial production of Manchester with the kings of the Egyptian past—Memnon, Cheops and Ramses. That the dead are not left to their rest but instead must have their burial garb donated to manufacturing, basically mined from the Egyptian desert, points to the dehumanization of the new manufacturing economy.

> We're not told, in the Egyptian Spectator,
> What daring speculator
> Conceived the notion; but I'd make a bet he grew
> Up to the thought from watching Dr. Pettigrew,
>   At some *soirée* or *conversazione*,
> Midst talk of Young, Champollion, or Belzoni,
> And such hieroglyphic twaddle,
> Unwinding nimbly, swaddle after swaddle,
>   The wrappings aromatic
>   Of some aristocratic
> Dandy, of hundred-gated Thebes or Heliopolis,
> Consigned to our mushroom of a metropolis
> Per last Peninsular and Oriental packet;
> And from the hush of his Necropolis—
>   So deep and drear—
> Tumbled ashore, midst the unholy racket
>   Of the Southampton pier.

Dr Pettigrew was famous for his mummy unrolling performances (see Chapter II.2), and the author of the poem suggests that public mummy unwrappings inspired this idea. The poet describes the removal of bodies from their ancient resting place and their unceremonious treatment in London.

> Heaven only knows what acreage of mummy-hood
> Is resting in its thousand-year-old dummy hood
>   Under the desert sands;
> Nor what miles upon miles of linen bands
> Are rotting in the bosom of the lands
>   Which Mehemet commands.
> But these are times when not e'en mummies
> Can longer rest as dummies;
> And as the grains of wheat found at their side
> Were sown, have grown, and now grow far and wide,
> So must old Egypt's gentlemen and ladies,
> To the disgust of each old-fashioned ghost,
> Give up their cerements to the hand whose trade is
> To turn them into foolscap or Bath-post,
>   To fly round all creation,
>   In tongues of every nation,
> Spreading (at least we'll hope it) useful information.

6. *John Bull and his Mommies*

The poet is clearly disturbed at the possibility that human remains can be mined in this fashion and converted into products of everyday use. The new industrial economy has made new demands on the suppliers of raw materials, and even the dead cannot be exempted from this.

> But yet, methinks, the venerable sheets,
>   In which have slept, their long, millennial night,
> Those who once trod Theban, or Memphian streets,
> Should not receive the vulgar black and white,
> Impressed by common types on common reams;
> No—mummy-paper should record the dreams
>   Of those who'd have society rolled back
>   Into the track
> Which the world left five hundred years ago—
> The lovers of the stony *statu quo*—
> 'Standers in the old ways', whom nothing stirs,
> To whom 'the wisdom of our ancestors'
> Is wisdom yesterday, to-day, forever;
> Who, midst a world of change, boast, blind, of changing never.
>
> On mummy-paper a Lord George might find
> Fit place for utterance of his 'stable mind';
> On mummy-paper Gladstone should dilate
> On old-world theories of church and state;
> Let mummy-paper bear our penal laws
> 'Gainst those who hold a different faith or cause
> On mummy-paper print the outworn story,
> And useless Shibboleths of Whig and Tory—
> Watch-words that rouse no cry—exploded shams—
> 'Our glorious constitution', and such flams;
> In short, print on it (we'll lend aid most hearty)
> A Library for next year's 'Country Party'[49].

The poem ends with a tongue-in-cheek suggestion for the appropriate use of mummy paper, not for common newspapers but for the writings of those public figures who look to the past for inspiration. In some ways, the sentiments here prefigure later urges toward the conservation of antiquities, and the author is clearly horrified at the possibility of actually converting human remains into industrial products. The issue of the commodification

---

49. The Country Party was a non-partisan coalition of Tories and Whigs who claimed to argue on behalf of the entire 'country' as opposed to the 'court' of London politicians, who enacted patronage appointments and worked only for their own gain. The reference here is somewhat historical, as this movement was prominent in the eighteenth century and was especially inspirational in the United States on the eve of revolution. The outdated reference makes sense within the context of the poem.

of the ancient Near Eastern past is the subject of volume II, and the potential industrial uses of mummies are discussed in Chapter II.1.

The Ancient Near East in Political Cartoons

Although satirical poetry like 'Musings on Mummy-Paper' was one of the most common forms of *Punch*'s comedy, it is better remembered today for its political cartoons. In the late nineteenth century, a number of issues featured comic illustrations in a distinctly Egyptianizing style. In these cases, commentary on everyday life is provided through anachronistic depiction of nineteenth-century activities in ancient styles. The May 28, 1887, issue printed a comic drawn in an Egyptian tomb style depicting a Derby in the nineteenth century (Fig. 6.5). The caption reads, 'El Dar-Bé: Hieroglyph Excavated from among the Tuffite Remains. Supposed to Represent Some Annual Sports in Honour, Probably, of Hoss-Iris.'[50] The February 1, 1896, issue features an image of golfers (dressed more like Assyrians than Egyptians) in poses mocking Egyptian tomb paintings (Fig. 6.6). The caption reads, 'Golf Is Being Played Very Much in Egypt'. The Egyptians also look more like Assyrians in the February 13, 1897, issue, in an image and caption called 'By Tram to the Pyramids', which reprints a notice from the *Daily Telegraph* reporting the construction of a new tramline to the pyramids from Cairo (Fig. 6.7). *Punch*, through the illustration of a mash-up of a nineteenth-century train cart and an ancient Assyrian chariot, offers a suggestion for the style.[51] The Assyrian-looking Egyptians also attended the 'The Ancient Egyptian Henley Regatta' (Fig. 6.8) in the July 10, 1897, issue and 'The Ancient Egyptian Lord Mayor's Show' (Fig. 6.9) in an 1899 issue.[52] 'The Valet of the Nile' appears in the November 12, 1898, issue (who is 'much talked about, but very seldom seen!'), dressed in nineteenth-century butler garb but wearing an ancient Egyptian headdress (Fig. 6.10).[53] He is attending a sleeping Egyptian, and faux hieroglyphs are drawn on the upper- and lower-left corners of the comic. An ancient edition of *Punch* itself appears in an 1898 issue (Fig. 6.11).[54] The image is filled with Assyrian-looking Egyptianizing images, with an artist painting a portrait of a cat and the cover of an issue of *Punch* made up in faux hieroglyphs. A procession of ancient revellers marches past on the bottom register. The

---

50. 'El Dar-Bé', *Punch* 92 (1887), p. 253.
51. 'By Tram to the Pyramids', *Punch* 112 (1897), p. 77.
52. 'The Ancient Egyptian Henley Regatta', *Punch* 113 (1897), p. 12; and 'The Ancient Egyptian Lord Mayor's Show', *Punch* 117 (1899), p. 217.
53. 'The Valet of the Nile', *Punch* 115 (1898), p. 217.
54. 'A Fragment of the Title-Page of the Ancient Egyptian *Punch*', *Punch* 114 (1898), p. 193.

Fig. 6.5. 'El Dar-Bé', *Punch* 92 (1887), p. 253.

Fig. 6.6. 'Golf is being played very much in Egypt', *Punch* 110 (February 1, 1896), p. 52.

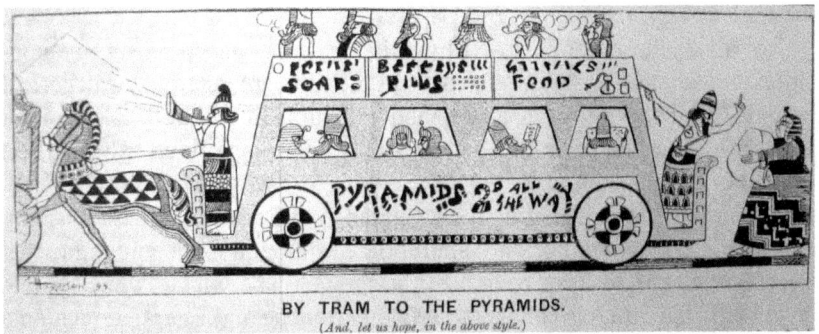

Fig. 6.7. 'By tram to the pyramids', *Punch* 112 (February 13, 1897), p. 77.

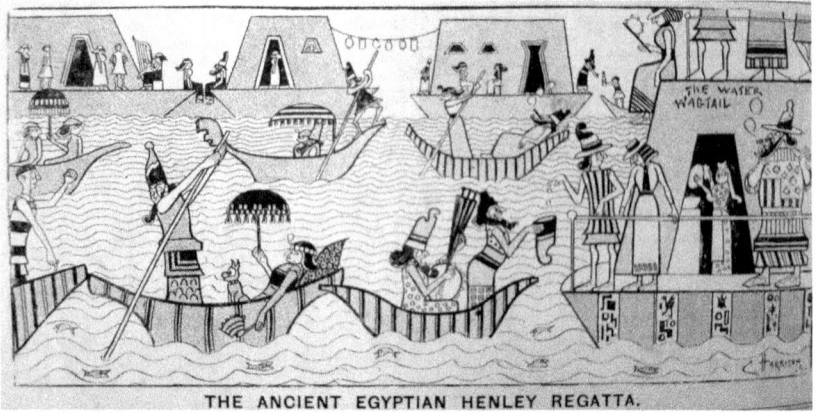

Fig. 6.8. 'The ancient Egyptian Henley Regatta', *Punch* 113 (July 10, 1897), p. 12.

Fig. 6.9. 'The ancient Egyptian Lord Mayor's Show', *Punch* 117 (1899), p. 217.

caption indicates that this is in reference to a report in the *Daily News* 'that the ancient Egyptians had comic papers'.

Not all of these comics used Egyptian style for anachronistic juxtaposition. Occasionally, *Punch*'s artists imitated the conventions of historical periods to suitably illustrate a story about the time in question. The October 17, 1896, issue, for example, has an article and image titled 'The Earliest Record of the Appearance of the Sea-Serpent'.[55] The text consists of a selection from Herodotus detailing the appearance of a sea-serpent at Pelusium, and so ancient conventions are appropriate (although one could argue that Greek styles would have been a better choice). The image is in Egyptian style, with faux hieroglyphs in a pseudo-cartouche and Egyptian men on a

---

55. 'The earliest record of the appearance of the sea-serpent', *Punch* 111 (1896), p. 181.

Fig. 6.10. 'The Valet of the Nile', *Punch* 115 (November 12, 1898), p. 217.

Fig. 6.11. 'A fragment of the title-page of the ancient Egyptian *Punch*', *Punch* 114 (1898), p. 193.

boat encountering a sea serpent, with fish in the water, all drawn in the strict two-dimensionality of Egyptian art (Fig. 6.12).

Egyptian styles and archaeological imagery were also used to create anthropomorphized representations of the state of Egypt. The state of Egypt was often caricatured personified in Egyptian garb, as in a cover comic (Fig. 6.13) depicting 'Britannia Discovering the Source of the Nile'.[56] In that comic, 'Mr Nilus' is depicted wearing a *nemes*-headdress and a cartouche-like armband while smoking a pipe. Similarly, rulers of Egypt are referred to as Pharaoh, as in an 1868 poem called 'Welcome, Viceroy of Egypt'.[57] An 1868 editorial titled 'Popping the Pyramid' parodies Egypt's development plans by claiming to be a report that the pasha of Egypt has sold the pyramids and associated structures.[58] It was at this time that Egypt's monumental debt to European banks (for development projects and especially the construction of the Suez Canal) was becoming apparent to the world, and this issue, in particular, was commented upon through ancient Egyptian references.

56. 'Britannia Discovering the Source of the Nile', *Punch* 44 (1863), p. 233.
57. 'Welcome, Viceroy of Egypt', *Punch* 56 (1869), p. 269.
58. 'Popping the Pyramid', *Punch* 54 (1868), p. 266.

Fig. 6.12. 'The earliest record of the appearance of the sea-serpent', *Punch* 111 (October 17, 1896), p. 181.

British involvement in the governance of Egypt was heavily debated in the periodical press, and *Punch* picked up on these discussions. The annexation of 1882 and the later protectorate status were controversial issues for the British public and within the shifting governments of the late-Victorian era. Surprisingly, *Punch*'s treatment of nineteenth-century Egyptians is more sensitive than in the other media that have been examined so far in this study. Marilyn Booth characterizes the representations as 'quietly sympathetic, recognising the dignity of colonised peoples (or at least some of them), while skewering the British paternalistic discourse that hardly concealed imperial ambition'.[59] A few examples of cartoons commenting on this topic give a sense of the nature of the debate. The March 7, 1896, issue of *Punch* features a cartoon titled 'Turk the Sublime!' (Fig. 6.14), with an image of John Bull in full desert military dress standing in front of the sphinx, holding a woman dressed in Arabian robes (and a hat labeled Egypt) in his right arm. Before him, a Turkish man (labeled Sultan) stands in a pose of supplication asking, 'Now, Mr. Bull, You have been Miss Egypt's guardian long enough, so I invite you to consider whether the time has not yet now arrived for her to return to the arms of her loving Uncle'.[60] In other instances, John Bull was related to the Egyptian Apis bull, as in a February 3, 1883, notice in which 'Bull-Apis' explains his invasion of Egypt: 'I must have my trade-ways unblocked, but god Fellahs [Egyptian peasants]

---

59. Booth, 'Insistent Localism', p. 208.
60. 'Turk the Sublime!', *Punch* 110 (1896), p. 110.

6. *John Bull and his Mommies*

Fig. 6.13. 'Britannia discovering the source of the Nile', *Punch* 44 (June 6, 1863), p. 233.

Fig. 6.14. 'Turk the Sublime!', *Punch* 110 (March 7, 1896), p. 110.

Fig. 6.15. 'Egyptian Question in the time of King Krisis the Startler', *Punch* 83 (August 5, 1882), pp. 52-53.

from me need not fear, King Bull-Apis fights not for booty; he means only kindness and good'.[61] Ancient Egyptian (or Egyptianizing) visual culture was often parodied in tandem with Anglo-Egyptian relations. An August 5, 1882, article titled 'The Essence of Parliament' depicts British politicians in a scene made to look like it came from an ancient Egyptian tomb wall (Fig. 6.15).[62] The caption reads, 'Egyptian Question in the time of King Krisis the Startler', and portrays the various politicians involved in the debate as ancient Egyptian figures.

The British were not the only ones to depict their politicians as ancient Egyptian figures. The German-born American cartoonist Thomas Nast (the creator of Uncle Sam), most associated with *Harper's Weekly*, was one such artist. In the catalogue for an Egyptomania exhibit at the Hillwood Art Museum (1992), Bob Brier traces how Nast used mummy motifs to lampoon the notoriously corrupt Democratic presidential candidate Samuel J. Tilden throughout his political career in the 1870s and 80s (Fig. 6.16). Brier demonstrates how Nast skilfully uses mummy and sarcophagus imagery (with hieroglyph-inspired text and pictures) to mock Tilden's corrupt activities in a way that would have been immediately apparent to an American reading audience.[63]

---

61. 'How Bull-Apis Went up against Tel-el-Kebir: Fragments of an Epic from Modern Egypt', *Punch* (1883), p. 53.

62. 'Essence of Parliament. Extracted from the Diary of Toby, M.P.', *Punch* 83 (1882), pp. 52-53.

63. Bob Brier, *Egyptomania* (Middlesex, NJ: Hillwood Art Museum, 1992), pp. 9-15.

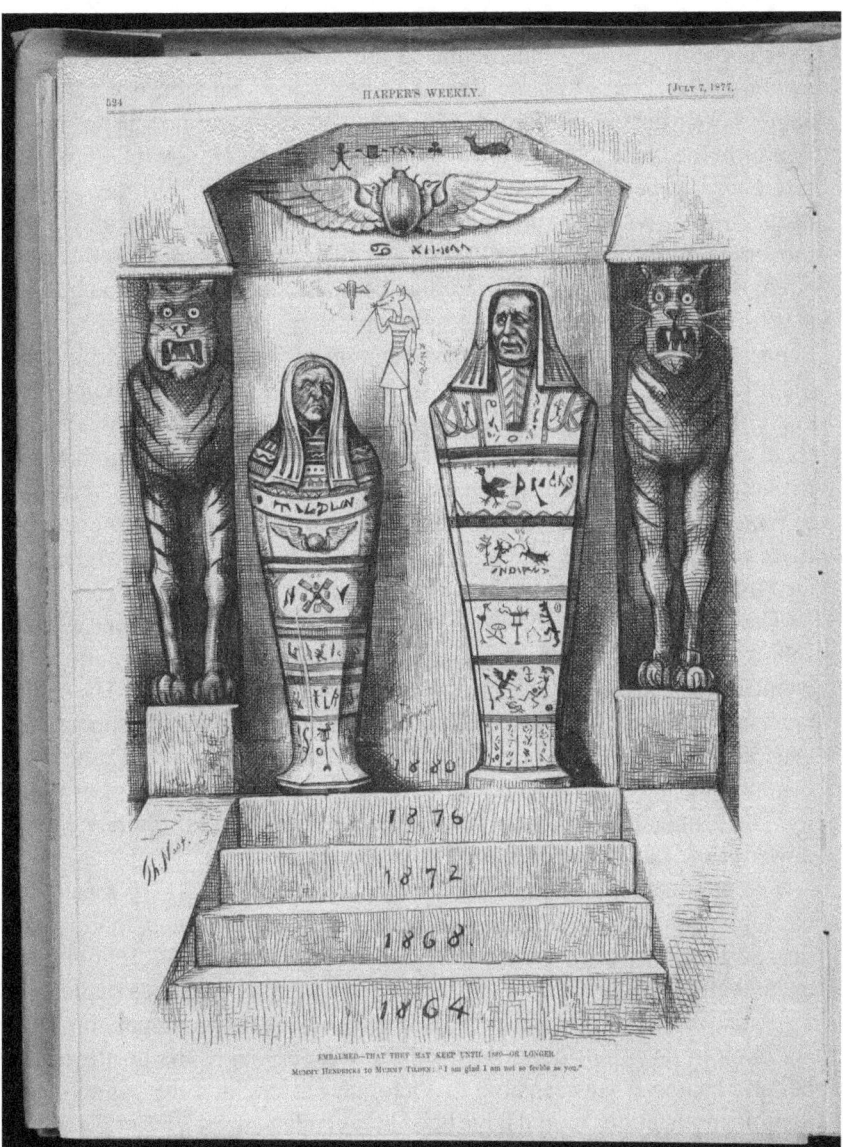

Fig. 6.16. 'Embalmed—that they may keep until 1880—or longer. Mummy Hendricks to Mummy Tilden: "I am glad I am not so feeble as you"', by Thomas Nast; from *Harper's Magazine* (July 7, 1877). Beinecke Rare Book and Manuscript Library, Yale University.

Nast's satirical cartoons were often aimed at specific politicians, and their depictions were fundamental to the humour and the political commentary. This kind of comic was one of the most common ways that the ancient Near East was referenced in *Punch*, by representing various public figures in the guise of ancient personages. Various Near Eastern kings were referenced, especially those with a biblical connection, and that biblical connection provides the meaning behind the reference. For example, the movement to repeal the Corn Laws (laws that protected grain producers in Great Britain and Ireland from foreign competition) led *Punch* to compose a narrative poem recounting the parliamentary intrigues, titled 'A New Sennacherib'.[64] There is no further mention of Assyria in the article, but the title here refers to Prime Minister Robert Peel, one of the major players in the debate and the 'New Sennacherib' of the title. Biblical accounts (later confirmed by Assyrian historical texts) relate that Sennacherib failed to capture Jerusalem and was murdered by his own sons. Peel, according to *Punch*, was like Sennacherib because, even though he championed free trade aggressively, he voted against repealing the corn laws when he realized that he lacked party backing.

The most common ancient Near Eastern referent, however, was the sphinx. This ancient monument was ubiquitous in British visual culture and would have been easily recognizable to almost any *Punch* reader. The sphinx represented silence and inscrutability. In political cartoons the sphinx, as a general reference to Egypt, also signified imperialism. This became more common as the Great Sphinx came to be synecdochal for Egypt as a polity. The connotations of imperialism emerge from the clear reference to the power of the Egyptian kings and Egypt's ancient empire.

The connotations of inscrutability and imperialist yearning meant that the sphinx was well suited for referencing Benjamin Disraeli and his politics. So Disraeli's purposeful public depictions of himself as an imperialist made their way into *Punch*'s satire. Usually when Disraeli was depicted as a sphinx, it was in reference to his silence on particular issues, but there are often implications about Disraeli's Jewish heritage. His portrayal as a Semitic character was sensible to Victorian readers, and the vaguely anti-Semitic implications would have been acceptable to most Victorian readers. As shall be discussed further, *Punch* occasionally inverted Old Testament roles in its comics by depicting Jewish public figures as Egyptian slave drivers. This is explicit in the June 15, 1867, issue, in an image entitled 'Disrael-I in Triumph; or, the Modern Sphynx [*sic*]' (Fig. 6.17). It is noted that this image is 'suggested by Mr. Poynter's admirable picture of "Israel in Egypt"'. Poynter's original painting (see Chapter III.1) is a depiction of Exod. 1:7-11, and shows Israelite slaves pulling a red granite lion statue in

---

64. 'A New Sennacherib', *Punch* 9 (1845), p. 262.

6. *John Bull and his Mommies* 247

Fig. 6.17. 'Disrael-I in triumph; or, the modern sphynx', *Punch* 52-53 (June 15, 1867), pp. 246-47.

front of an Egyptian building (created from a hodge-podge of Egyptian architectural features known at the time). *Punch*'s depiction replaces Israelite slaves with members of Parliament, and the red granite lion is replaced with a Disraeli sphinx. The comic image is lampooning Disraeli's success in introducing the Reform Bill of 1867 (signalled by the word 'reform' printed on the Egyptian façade in the background), which was a strategic political action that was thought would lead to a Disraeli-led conservative majority government the following year (it did not) by extending the franchise significantly. Lord Derby (Disraeli's partner in enacting the bill) whips the slaves from atop the cart, himself shaded by John Bright (a radical MP that held large public meetings to support the bill). Lord Cranborne, a member of the conservative party who spoke out against the bill and subsequently resigned from the party, lies crouching in the left-hand corner in the pose and costume of the old seer from Greek metopes.

Disraeli's portrayal as a sphinx increased greatly after the 1875 public discovery that he had purchased shares in the Suez Canal. This was not an issue of corruption; rather, the Khedive of Egypt had gone bankrupt, and sold shares as a means of generating revenue. Fearing that the French would gain control of the canal (and British access to India), Disraeli purchased the shares without bringing the issue to Parliament (receiving financial assistance from the Rothschild family instead). Gladstone's public accusations that Disraeli had subverted parliamentary procedure, however, created a media firestorm, and the secret nature of dealings with Egypt made the sphinx an obvious comic reference. From that point on, the on-again off-

Fig. 6.18. 'Mosé in Egitto!!!', *Punch* 68 (December 11, 1875), p. 246.

again prime minister was frequently depicted as the sphinx, with his own face replacing that of Khufu's. In a December 11, 1875, cartoon, titled 'Mosé in Egitto!!!' (referencing the opera), Disraeli stands near the sphinx, sharing a conspiratorial look with the ancient statue, who is winking back at him (Fig. 6.18). Disraeli, dressed in a suit and turban (implying connections to the Middle East and India), holds a large key that is labeled 'Suez Canal, the Key of India'. No doubt this cartoon is poking fun at Disraeli's various machinations to gain control of shares of the Suez Canal for Britain. Disraeli's stance on the Eastern Question further encouraged Egyptian comparison. In the July 15, 1876, issue, the Disraeli sphinx looks on stoically as a crowd of gentlemen clamour below him demanding that he speak (Fig. 6.19). Behind him, the words 'Eastern Questi . . .' imply that the subject of interest is the Eastern Question (the general term used to refer to the political issues that emerged with the disintegration of the Ottoman Empire). The caption, which reads 'The Sphinx Is Silent', indicates that Disraeli is not speaking on the issue.

Disraeli's characterization as the sphinx was not just in cartoons. He was often referred to as the sphinx in other sections of *Punch*. In a March 20, 1870, poem, for example, *Punch* writes:

Fig. 6.19. 'The sphinx is silent', *Punch* 100-101 (July 15, 1876), p. 12 [28].

THE RIDDLE OF THE SPHINX;
or, an Enigmatical Career.
He took
'A Leap in the Dark'
being
DIZZY,
is now
Earl of Beaconsfield
LUX ET DUX
Of the Conservative Party,
and as a
'Man of Light and Leading',
confident in his power
to keep his following in the dark,
looks forward to
DISSOLUTION
to
Retard the Decomposition of the
Empire,
Revive the vigour of the Constitution,
and secure The reattainment of his own Majority![65]

---

65. 'The Riddle of the Sphinx', *Punch* 78 (1880), p. 122.

Here, *Punch* is lampooning the upcoming General Election, which ran from March 31 to April 27, 1880, in which Disraeli's conservatives would go on to lose to Gladstone's liberals and Gladstone would be elected prime minister for the second time.

An 1878 dialogue ('The Sphinx and the Obelisk') was inspired by Disraeli's visit to Cleopatra's Needle. In it, Disraeli (the sphinx) ponders the obelisk 'as a tribute paid by East to West', and is visited by the shades of Antony and Cleopatra.[66] The three discuss empire and love and compare Antony and Cleopatra's fall to Disraeli's present courtship of Egypt. The classical story of Euro-Egyptian romance was frequently invoked as a means of thinking through British–Egyptian relations and is especially apparent in the aftermath of the British annexation of Egypt. The protectorate relationship seemed to well mirror the situation in Cleopatra's days. A May 13, 1893, comic draws these parallels explicitly. In a comic simply titled 'Antony and Cleopatra', the role of Cleopatra is said to be played by Egypt and the role of Antony by John Bull. Cleopatra is depicted as a beautiful semi-nude olive-skinned woman in Egyptian dress, and John Bull poses beside her in Roman garb.[67] A quote from *Antony and Cleopatra* Act II, Scene 2 is adapted and printed beneath the image. The quote is an aside in which Mecaenas tells Enobarbus (played by Gladstone) that Antony must leave Cleopatra and Enorbarbus responds, 'Never; He will not . . . At least, not yet.'[68] Here, the play is recontextualized as a statement about 1893.

Disraeli and the British were not the sole subjects of Egyptianizing satirical comment. Napoleon III was also depicted as the sphinx, in a large, foldout cartoon in the August 7, 1858, issue (Fig. 6.20). There, the reasons for doing so were many. Similar to its commentaries on Disraeli, *Punch* uses the sphinx to highlight the secretive and mysterious policies of Napoleon III. In this case, the title of the comic is explicit: it is named: 'The French Sphinx, or the Riddle of the Present'. In 1858, Napoleon III opened the Cherbourg–Paris railway line, and accompanying this he erected an equestrian statue celebrating his uncle, inscribed with his uncle's famous statement: 'I have resolved to restore at Cherbourg the marvels of Egypt'. The inclusion of this imperialist statement and the fact that the statue seemed to point toward England (this was unintentional) worried some British critics at the time about potential French hostilities. A related article in the August 21, 1858, issue offers similar sentiment of confusion regarding Napoleon III's motives: 'The French Sphinx, it is known, delights to be mysterious; but the deepest of his mysteries are invariably fathomable by the British

---

66. 'The Sphinx and the Obelisk', *Punch* 75 (1878), p. 93.
67. 'Antony and Cleopatra', *Punch* 104 (1893), p. 203.
68. 'Antony and Cleopatra', *Punch* 104 (1893), p. 203.

Fig. 6.20. 'The French sphinx, or the riddle of the present', *Punch* 35 (August 7, 1858), p. 38.

Punch'.[69] *Punch* comically attempts to deconstruct Napoleon III's motives behind his plans to erect a 'pyramid of peace' at Cherbourg to commemorate Queen Victoria's visit to France.[70] Cherbourg, given its location in Normandy, had been heavily fortified during the Napoleonic Wars to protect against a British invasion.

Of course, the most obvious political figure to satirize through ancient Near Eastern references was Austen Henry Layard. Once Layard left archaeology for politics, it did not take long for his ancient Near Eastern credentials to be used for humorous purposes.[71] After his election in 1852, Layard was an open critic of the ruling government and was especially noted for his criticism of British conduct in the Crimean War and for his refusal to accept a government appointment not related to foreign affairs (since he did not hold expertise in the area of appointment). This led Layard to complain through a resolution in Parliament (on June 15, 1855) that appointments were no longer based on merit but on patronage. Layard's outspokenness was lampooned in *Punch* (although generally in a favourable manner), usually in tandem with his Assyriological background. One of *Punch*'s responses to the controversy over Layard's refusal of appointment was an April 7, 1855, comic (Fig. 6.21) that bears the caption 'The Member for Nineveh Digs Out the British Bull'. It references Layard's association

69. 'The Pyramid of Peace', *Punch* 35 (1858), p. 85.
70. 'The French Sphinx', *Punch* 35 (1858), p. 55.
71. For an alternate but complementary discussion of these cartoons, see Malley, *From Archaeology to Spectacle,* pp. 119-25.

Fig. 6.21. 'The member for Nineveh digs out the British bull', *Punch* 27 (April 7, 1855), p. 135.

with Nineveh, his work as an archaeologist, the famed Nineveh bulls, which he brought to the British Museum, and the personification of Britain—John Bull. John Bull, depicted with his usual head and torso, bears the body of a Nineveh bull and is buried in a heap of dirt. The dirt is covered with the following words: routine, jobbery, incompetence, muddle, patronage and red tape. Malley also sees this as playing on Victorian fears that a fate similar to Nineveh's would eventually befall Britain.[72] In this case, however, it is political/bureaucratic problems that will sink the country, not the sensuous and idolatrous vices of biblical Nineveh.

There were other responses to Layard's refusal of an appointment that he did not feel that his experience warranted. *Punch* comically chastised him in a lengthy letter, poking fun at what could constitute fitness for office in British politics. The introduction of the letter speaks to his experiences in Assyria and the British public's appreciation of his work there:

> This will never do. In the aromatic, flowery meads of Mesopotamia, you may be quite at home: you may delight in the fullness of your sagacity in a Nineveh mound: you may know all the political subtleties of a Sheikh—but you really know nothing of the means by which men rise to fame and fortune in the public service. You had better take ship for the East, and again betake yourself to the ' ship of the desert', the old, Biblical camel—

---

72. Malley, *From Archaeology to Spectacle*, p. 123.

6. *John Bull and his Mommies*

unless, indeed, you amend the simplicity of your ways, and become commonly astute among the official sons of men.

We have a great respect for you: we thank you, spiritually, when we look upon your bulls: bulls, that in any other country—(but here we prefer golden calves)—would have been as animals drawing you in a car of triumph—but here it is otherwise; we are a practical, hardheaded and soft-hearted, and soft-headed and hard-hearted people. We wish to speak plainly to you, Mr. Layard; and we tell you that you have presumptuously flown in the face of office.[73]

His expertise on the mound of Nineveh is comically contrasted with what is described as behaviour atypical of a British politician.

Similar sentiments are echoed in an 'Ode to Mr. Layard'. There his outspokenness against the ill treatment given to British soldiers in the Crimean War and his refusal of patronage appointments are lauded. And, as in the 'Word to Mr. Layard', the remarks are prefaced with comments on his Assyriological work:

Layard, whose energy and perseverance
   From Nimroud's human-headed bulls with wings,
Did of the sand of ages make a clearance:
Those giant-idols of Assyrian kings;
   Those monuments of sacred story, which,
Britain's Museum, thanks to thee, enrich,
Whereat a peep were not an ill-judged boon
To working men on Sunday afternoon.
As in unearthing Ninevite antiquities
   Thou strovest manfully, thou now dost strive
From mess and mire of blunders and iniquities
   The British Bull to extricate alive;
John Bull to disinter, and disencumber
His shoulders of official lumber.[74]

Again, the favour he has done for the 'working man' by giving something to view on a Sunday (in the British Museum) is favourably contrasted with Layard's political work as public service.

The May 12, 1855, issue comments on the furor evoked in the House of Lords when Layard's letter detailing improper promotion practices within the army was read. A comic labeled 'Baiting the Nineveh Bull' features Layard's torso attached to a living version of the winged Nineveh bull, standing in a posture of defense against a group of angry animals dressed in the clothing of parliamentarians (Fig. 6.22). The previous page features a poem called 'The Den Down upon Layard', which reads:

---

73. 'A Word to Mr. Layard', *Punch* 28 (1855), p. 97.
74. 'Ode to Mr. Layard', *Punch* 28 (1855), p. 138.

Fig. 6.22. 'Baiting the Nineveh bull', *Punch* 28-29 (May 12, 1855), p. 187.

What may that frantic uproar mean; groans, hootings, shrieks, and howls,
The snarl and bark of angry curs, the screams of carrion fowls?
What makes St. Stephen's walls resound with cries more dire and dread,
Than you ever hear in the Regent's Park when the animals are fed?

Layard in eager zeal the mask from jobbery to strip.
Mistaken on a point of fact, has chanced to make a slip,
So down the vultures swoop on him, the ravens, and the crows,
The wolves, jackals, and poodle dogs of state that are his foes.

The little foxes snap at him for showing up the Whigs;
In angry chorus round him grunt and squeak official pigs:
With threatening horns and bullying roar the stalled placeman-ox
Assails him; Berkeley groans at him, and bellows Colonel Knox.
'He's down: and now set on him; at him Lindsay, at him Byng;
Before the public teach him names of gentlemen to bring;
Give it him well: pitch into him; to lesson other snobs
In caution how they venture on exposing army-jobs.

'Down, down upon him, Palmerston, with final crushing stroke!
His is a mouth that must be stopped; a voice that you must choke,
Take we the opportunity that Fortune kindly sends,
Kick him, and nit him hard; he has among ourselves no friends!'

'Friends!' to the yell within the House an echo from without
Repeats, and thrice ten millions 'Friends' unanimously shout;
'Hit Layard? hit him if ye dare! avast, dishonest crew,
Humbugs, get out and make room for a better man than you!'[75]

75. 'The Den upon Layard', *Punch* 28 (1855), p. 186.

Here then, *Punch* chastens Layard's fellow parliamentarians for their attacks against him on a minor point of error, especially in this case where *Punch* believed that Layard held the moral high ground. When Layard returned to politics, *Punch* endorsed him as a candidate for Southwark. In an 1860 editorial ('Hooray for Nineveh!'), *Punch* offers a threat to Southwarkians: 'Return Mr. Austen Henry Layard, or what Nineveh is now, you shall be at Christmas 1861'.[76]

Biblical Comedy

While politicians like Layard were fair game, biblical issues were rarely mocked in *Punch*, which is to be expected for the time period and the conservative populist stance of the weekly. However, the assumed biblical literacy of readers seems to have been quite high, and biblical allusions are made quite frequently. For example, an 1877 article called 'Solomon at Fault for Once' juxtaposes the wisdom of King Solomon with a criticism in *The Times* about the lack of seats in the Painted Hall at Greenwich—the seats had been removed by the keeper, Mr Solomon Hart. Thus, 'the wisdom of Solomon appeared to have failed him'.[77] From the 1870s onward, the term Philistine is used extensively, and numerous jokes play on the contemporary implications of the term and the biblical connection. An 1889 article references the Joseph story in Genesis in order to poke fun at the Septennial Act (of 1715), which set the maximum length of a Parliament at seven years (meaning that an election had to be called within seven years).[78] The speaker, a nineteenth-century 'Joseph' (Joseph Chamberlain, who at the time was the MP of the Birmingham West constituency) foresees seven years of lean following the current 'Seven years of Conservative fatness'. Chamberlain is caricatured on the next page as a Colossus of Memnon, pointing to the Joseph story's Egyptian setting (Fig. 6.23).

One way in which the Bible could be treated comically was through the humour of childish misunderstandings of the biblical text. An 1869 cartoon, labeled 'A Young Philistine', features a Sunday school teacher asking a group of students who the strongest man was and a pupil 'addicted to light literature' answers 'Jack the Giant-Killer, Teacher!!'.[79] An 1875 comic depicts a little girl asking why Adam and Eve where expelled from paradise, and a little boy (the squire's son) answering, 'P'raps they shot a fox!'.[80] Another comic from 1875 involves a mother telling her three girls about

---

76. 'Hooray for Nineveh!', *Punch* 39 (1860), p. 220.
77. 'Solomon at Fault for Once', *Punch* 73 (1877), p. 59.
78. 'Joseph in Egypt', *Punch* 97 (1889), pp. 246-47.
79. 'A Young Philistine', *Punch* 56 (1869), p. 13.
80. 'Bring Up a Child', *Punch* 68 (1875), p. 63.

Fig. 6.23. 'Joseph in Egypt', *Punch* 97 (1889), pp. 246-47.

Pharaoh's order that all male children should be killed. One of the daughters answers, 'But mamma! Didn't *any* of their mothers say they was girls?'.[81] A more precocious child appears in an 1876 cartoon. Master Tommy has been naughty and has subsequently been 'amusing himself with his scripture prints'. He exclaims, 'Here's Daniel in the Lion's Den!', and when mother asks why Daniel was cast into the den, Tommy responds (with triumph it is noted), 'Cause he was good!'.[82] More political is an 1878 comic in which a mother and child have entered a toyshop asking for a 'Noah's Ark'. The clerk responds, 'No, mum; we've given up keeping them since the school boards come in, you see, they was too denominational'.[83] Noah's Ark is also the subject of an 1843 article, which describes the purchase of the Ark and its contents for one shilling.[84] The mixing of commercial and religious practices is also the subject of satire in an 1846 notice titled 'The River Jordan Company', which reads as a straightforward announcement of plans to start importing water from the river so that 'no christening in high life will now be considered complete without the article the Company has been formed to import'.[85]

    81. 'A Happy Thought That Never Occurred', *Punch* 69 (1875), p. 198.
    82. 'Master Tommy's View of It', *Punch* 71 (1876), p. 143.
    83. 'Toys and their Teaching', *Punch* 75 (1878), p. 235.
    84. 'Works and Objects of Art. (Written with an Eye towards the Patronage of the Society for the Diffusion of Useful Knowledge)', *Punch* 4 (1843), pp. 181-82.
    85. 'The River Jordan Company', *Punch* 11 (1846), p. 56.

Less archaeologically oriented, although somewhat informed by it, was the use of the book of Exodus in discussions about nineteenth-century labour conditions. Almost always, these articles are fundamentally anti-Semitic in outlook, contrasting the slavery of the Hebrews in biblical times with perceptions of Jewish financial practices in the Victorian age. Anti-Semitic commentaries about Jewish banking practices became quite prominent in response to the growing Egyptian financial crisis, rooted in the Khedive's debt to European banks. These trends are all apparent in *Punch*'s 1879 comparison of the current Egyptian economy with ancient economic conditions in 'Egyptian Bonds and Bondsmen':

> The peasantry of the land of Egypt appear to be in a state of destitution perfectly disgraceful to their Misruler. Extortion, leaving them scarcely the means of subsistence, threatens to reduce the 'Nile Population' to *nil*—at least, *Ex Nilo nihil fit.* Such Nihilism is even worse than that of the Russians. Talk of the flesh-pots of Egypt, when these poor Egyptian Fellahs have scarcely bread to eat, much less flesh! The peasantry of Egypt are in suffering, in more senses than one, under Egyptian bondage. The modern Egyptians may envy their forefathers beneath whose Pharaohs it was the Jews, and not the Egyptians themselves, who groaned under Egyptian bondage. The Egyptians of to-day, *for the interest* of the Jews, who rule the money-market, are in bitter bondage to their own Pharaoh.[86]

Here, of course, reference is made to the Old Testament story of the bondage of the Hebrews in Egypt before the exodus with the casual anti-Semitism typical of Victorian public life.

A similar argument that the roles have been reversed since the days of the exodus (in terms of Jewish financial practices) is expressed in the September 8, 1888, issue, in an article titled 'Israel and Egypt; or, Turning the Tables'. The article begins with a near-full-page illustration (Fig. 6.24) labeled 'Egyptian Taskmaster and Jew Sweater'.[87] It depicts an Egyptian pharaoh holding a flail and looking nervously to his right. There, a 'Jew sweater' dressed as a leering dandy gazes back at the pharaoh with a look of triumph. He has a paper copy of the evidence of the committee on sweating rolled up in his pocket, and he points to the wall behind him. There, on the wall, is a hieroglyphic scene of Egyptian taskmasters flailing slaves (presumably Hebrews) who are making bricks. A poem extends through the next two pages, explicating the image, introduced by quotations from a history book and a newspaper to contextualize the parody. The impetus for this poem was the appointment of a committee by the House of Lords to investigate the 'sweating system' in the tailor industry. By the time this committee

---

86. 'Egyptian Bonds and Bondsmen', *Punch* 76 (1879), p. 153.

87. Here the term 'sweater' refers to an employer who works an employee in particularly harsh conditions, for minimal pay. In other words, a 'slave driver'. It is the nineteenth-century colloquialism from which 'sweatshop' is derived.

Fig. 6.24. 'Israel and Egypt; or, turning the tables', *Punch* 95 (September 8, 1888), pp. 110-12.

was formed, sweating was most associated with factories in East London, often employing unskilled immigrants in dismal working conditions. Here, *Punch* plays on the stories of the exodus and the widespread myth that the Hebrew slaves built the pyramids to argue that the Jewish sweaters are the nineteenth-century slave masters. Archaeological and biblical references have been employed as commentary on labour relations.

> 'The Children of Israel multiplied so as to excite the jealous fears of the Egyptians. . . . They were therefore organised into gangs under taskmasters, as we see in the vivid pictures of the monuments, to work upon the public edifices. "And the Egyptians made the Children of Israel to serve with rigour. And they made their lives bitter with hard bondage in mortar and in brick, and in all manner of service in the field."'—*Smith's Ancient History*. 'The Sweater is probably a Jew, and, if so, he has the gift of organisation, and an extraordinary power of subordinating everything—humanity, it may be, included—to the great end of getting on. . . . The conditions of life in East London ruin the Christian labourer, and leave the Jewish labourer unharmed.'— '*Spectator*' on '*Sweaters and Jews*'.'

Punch begins the poem by juxtaposing a quotation from a contemporary school textbook on ancient history with an editorial from the *Spectator* blaming Jewish overseers for difficult working conditions. The poem begins:

> The screed of the Shade of the Poet Pentaour, to Punchiss that came,
> Even Pentaour Bard unto Pharaoh, the singer whose song was as flame:
> The pupil of mild Ameneman, he painted the lot of the poor
>   In the far distant days of Rameses, who shut on sweet Mercy the door.

6. *John Bull and his Mommies*

> The form was the form of the Pharaoh, as Wilkinson shows him he
> > stood,—The pose was exceedingly proud, the perspective, per-
> > chance, was not good,—
> And he looked in the face of the Hebrew, the changeless, the oily, the
> > fat, Whether crowned with the cap of the Copt, or the Saxon's
> > cylindrical hat.
> He stood, and he stared, and he spake: 'O! thou Oleaginous One,
> Whose tresses so reek of the oil-pot, whose finger-rings flash in the sun,
> I. Pharaoh the Pyramid-builder, the slayer of Hittites, the King Whom
> > Pentaour magnified greatly—*my* Laureate knew how to sing;—
> I, mighty one named by Manetho, right well to Herodotus known,
> I, pictured in wall-paintings many, and chiselled on acres of stone,
> I, I was the scourge of the Semites, the Hyksos, the Hebrews, my foes,
> The swart-bearded sons of the shepherds, the slaves of the aquiline nose.

The poem proper begins with a notice that the screed that follows (acknowledging that it is long and tedious) was inspired by Pentaour, an Egyptian poet whose epic celebration of Ramses II is preserved in Papyrus Sallier in the British Museum. 'Punchiss' references John Gardner Wilkinson, the British Egyptologist whose accounts of Egypt were among the most popular of the period (see Chapter I.10), as well as two of the major classical sources on Egyptian history (see Chapter I.2). It continues:

> Behold on this rock you perceive them, my heel on their neck, and my
> > scourge
> On the hides of them; look at the sticks of my taskmasters, eager to urge
> The staggering slaves to their toil in their agonised thousands, so loth,
> Yet helpless as rogues before Ra, or as fools in the presence of Thoth.
> I made them shape bricks without straw, and the mouths of them scantily
> > fed
> With radishes, onions, and garlic, with scraps of affliction's black bread.
> Read the ideographical Coptic around them in characters hewn,
> And you'll see that their life was a curse, that the coming of death was a
> > boon.
> When I rose in my might like to Mentu, and lifted like Horus the flail,
> Then the heart of the Hebrew would melt, and the cheek of the Hebrew
> > would pale;
> And now—' Then a chuckle forth crackled, a nasal but jubilant sound,
> And a whiff of tobacco and patchouli mingled was wafted around.
> A hat took a knowinger rake, and there brake on the sight of the King
> The wave of an adipose hand, and the flash of a glittering ring.
> A sound 'twixt a creak and a snuffle from lips like an Ethiop's dropt—
> All unlike the calm smile of the King, all unlike the clear tone of the
> > Copt—
> 'Ha! ha! Mr. Pyramid-builder, at present you're out of the hunt.
> Yes, you once gave the Semite the stick, but the Semite now gives you
> > the shunt;

> Ask Tewfik, or good Mr. Goschen! Old Cheops, if that's your dashed name—
> Sesostris, Rameses, or what not,—a change *has* come over the game.
> Your 'name is a noise' and no more. Yes, the Gentile once 'sweated' the Jew,
> But the Hebrew has now turned the tables; Dunraven will tell you that's true.
> You worked us, and whipped us, and starved us; you robbed us of shekels and joy;

Punch describes the typical scene of Old Testament bondage, marked with references derived from Egyptological scholarship, that while perhaps were not understood by most, at least signalled the Egyptian flavour of the piece. Some of the contemporary figures in Egyptian politics are juxtaposed with ancient kings, like Cheops. Tewfik Pasha, Khedive Ismail's eldest son, was the ruler of Egypt, but basically in name only from 1879 to 1892. Real power had been ceded to people like George Goschen (1831–1907), who became the representative of the British holders of Egyptian bonds in the 1876 establishment of 'dual control' between British and French agents over Egyptian state finances. Here then, the bondage is moved from the factory floor to global finance, referencing the financial industry's control over Egypt. The *SS Dunraven*, a ship that hit a reef and sunk in the Red Sea in 1876, is called upon to attest to the reversal in power between the Egyptians and the Jews from ancient times to the present.[88] The nineteenth-century factory is described:

> But now it's *our* turn, and we've bettered your ancient instruction. old boy.
> Look here!—' Then there shaped through the shadows a sordid and sorrowful scene—
> There were men pinched, and pallid, and bowed, there were women dishevelled and lean;
> And the stress of their toiling was harsh, and the strain of their torture was fierce,
> And the splendour of day might not pass, and the sunlight of hope might not pierce
> Through the darkness and damp of the den where they crouched to the Sweater's stern nod,
> As Pharaoh's own scourge without pity, and harsh as his task-master's rod.
> The thong-marshalled gang of the sand-wastes were hardly so servile as these,
> So helplessly vassals to Mammon—so hopeless of health or of ease.

Mammon, the New Testament personification of greed, is the real ruler of the factory, which is described in terms evocative of slavery under Pharaoh.

---

88. The crew survived and the ship is now a scuba-diving site for Red Sea tourists.

In the next stanza, the 'Hebrew' goads Pharaoh by asking how he would feel if the new Egyptian bondage was depicted on a temple wall, like the art of Egypt.

> 'That cuts the Copt record, I reckon; makes Mummydom sing rather small.
> How would *that* look I paint on a temple, or chipped on a ruined church wall,
> Three thousand years hence, Mr. Pharaoh?' So sniggered the Hebrew and shook.
> The soul-sweated gold in his pocket. And lo! an unspeakable look
> Was seen on the face of the Pharaoh. And I, Poet Pentaour, I saw
> That the cycles of time bring no change to the merciless Mammonite maw.
>
> I sang the Rameseid, I, when Orontes beheld the great King
> Wield the sword unresisted of Ra; but I also betook me to sing
> The pitiful life of the peasant, the prey of the locusts and rats
> And men-vermin more merciless yet who took tithe of his barns and his vats.
> And, behold, though the Sun-God is silent, the Son of the Sun-God still asleep.
> Merciless Mammon is master, the slaves of the Gold-God still weep;
> Be his ministers Hebrew or Gentile, his worship is cruelty still;
> Still the worker must sweat 'neath the scourge that the stores of the tyrant may fill.[89]

The poem ends by arguing that Mammon, the 'Gold-God', is really responsible for this kind of misery. The actual 'sweaters' change over time, but the motivation for inflicting suffering remains the same.

Not all of *Punch*'s evocations of the Hebrew experience in Egypt are anti-Semitic. An 1890 article called 'From Nile to Neva' was inspired by news that the Russian government had legalized the persecution of Jews within its empire. This was in the period of the Russian pogroms that occurred in the aftermath of the assassination of Tsar Alexander II, which was blamed on the Jews. By 1890 the pogroms had wound down, but Russian Jews were still living under the restrictions set out by the May Laws. For Jews living in and out of Russia, there was a very real fear that pogroms would be enacted again (which they eventually were in 1903). *Punch*, in verse, warns the Russians of what happened to Pharaoh when he persecuted the Jews in biblical times.[90] The poem begins with a biblical verse and excerpt from *The Times* to provide context and is very similar in structure to 'Israel and Egypt; or, Turning the Tables', even being credited again to Pentaour:

---

89. 'Israel and Egypt', *Punch* 95 (1888), pp. 110-12.
90. 'From Nile to Neva', *Punch* 99 (1890), pp. 66-67.

> ['And the Egyptians made the children of Israel to serve with rigour.
> And they made their Urea bitter with hard bondage.'—Exodus.
> 'The Russian Government, by the new edicts, legalises persecution, and
> openly declares war against the Jews of the Empire.'—Times.]
>
> 'Beware' 'Tis a voice from the shades, from the dark of three thousand
> long years,
> But it falls like the red blade of Ra, and should echo in Tyranny's ears
> With the terror of overhead thunder; from Nile to the Neva it thrills,
> And it speaks of the judgment of wrong, of the doom of imperious wills.
> When Pentaour sang of the Pharaoh, alone by Orontes, at bay,
> By the chariots compassed about of the foe who were fierce for the fray,
> He sang of the dauntless oppressor, of Rameses, conquering king;
> But were there such voice by the Neva to-day, of what now should he
> sing?
> Of tyranny born out of time, of oppression belated and vain?
> Put up the old weapon, O despot, slack hand from the scourge and the
> chain;
> For the days of the Pharaohs are done, and the laureates of tyranny mute,
> And the whistle of falchion and flail are no set to the chords of the lute.

Here, *Punch* argues almost the opposite of what was argued in 'Israel and Egypt', for the message is that the world has changed from ancient times. There is no place for a tyrant, like those of old, in the nineteenth century. While being a despot may have been worth celebrating in the ancient world, it is no longer. The poem continues:

> True, the Hebrew, who bowed to the lash of the Pyramid-builders, bows
> still,
> For a time, to the knout of the Tsar, to the Muscovite's merciless will;
> But four millions of Israel's children are not to be crushed in the path
> Of a Tsar, like the Hittites of old, when great Ramses flamed in his wrath
> Alone through their numberless hosts. No, the days of the Titans of Wrong
> Are past, for the Truth is a torch, and the voice of the peoples is strong.

The poem continues in a similar vein for a few lines until it changes focus. The rest is not so much an argument that the world has changed but a warning to the Tsar that what happened to Pharaoh in the story of the exodus may happen once again:

> And—one hears the mad rush of the wheels that the fierce Red Sea billow
> pursues!
> O Muscovite, blind in your wrath, with your heel on the Israelite's neck,
> And your hand on that baleful old blade, persecution, 'twere wisdom to
> reck
> The Pharaoh's calm warning. Beware! Lo, the Pyramids pierce the grey
> gloom
> Of a desert that is but a waste, by a river that is but a tomb,

6. *John Bull and his Mommies* 263

Fig. 6.25. 'From Nile to Neva', *Punch* 99 (1890), pp. 67.

FROM THE NILE TO THE NEVA.

Shade of Pharaoh. "FORBEAR! THAT WEAPON ALWAYS WOUNDS THE HAND THAT WIELDS IT."

> Yet the Hebrew abides and is strong. Ameneman is gone to the ghosts,
> He the prince of the Coptic police who so harried the Israelite hosts
> When their lives with hard-bondage were bitter. And now bitter bandage you'd try.
> Proscription, and exile, and stern deprivation. Beware, Sire! Put by
> That blade in its blood-rusted scabbard. The Pharaohs, the Caesars have found
> That it wounds him who wields it; and you, though your victim there, prone on the ground,
> Look helpless and hopeless, you also shall find Persecution a bane
> Which shall lead to a Red Sea of blood to o'erwhelm selfish Tyranny's train.
> 'Beware!' Tis the shade of Meneptah that whispers the warning from far.
> Concerning that sword there's a lesson the Pharaoh may teach to the Tsar![91]

Here, *Punch* blends biblical tradition with contemporary Egyptological knowledge to make sense of nineteenth-century Russian anti-Semitism. An accompanying illustration (Fig. 6.25) shows the Tsar in military regalia, preparing to draw his sword (inscribed with the word 'persecution'), stand-

---

91. 'From Nile to Neva', *Punch* 99 (1890), pp. 66-67.

ing with his foot on the neck of a bound Russian Jew. The shade of Pharaoh stands behind him and offers the following warning: 'Forebear! That weapon always wounds the hand that wields it.'[92] *Punch*'s efforts to make sense of the world and offer suggestions for political action are exemplified by the article 'From Nile to Neva'. There, *Punch* blends historical and literary references, poetry and illustration to create a larger argument about the news of the day. This topicality, rooted in a variety of cultural references, makes *Punch* a useful source for this investigation of how the Victorians used the ancient Near East to make sense of their own lives. The ancient Near East could be employed in satire to comment on the issues of the day.

Cleopatra's Needle according to Punch

It should be of little surprise, then, that the issues surrounding one of the media sensations of the Victorian age, Cleopatra's Needle, made their way into *Punch* given their prominence in the *ILN* and other serious periodicals (see Chapter I.5). Many of the gags play on the seemingly strange use of the term 'needle' to describe the obelisk. An 1851 article simply makes puns on the name given to the obelisk:

> There seems some difficulty in getting the public to have an eye to Cleopatra's needle, which is, nevertheless, valuable, on account of its connexion with the thread of history. A recent writer in the *Times* suggests that the needle should be allowed to remain sticking in the mud of Memphis, in order that we may bring over from the same spot a statue of Rameses, the Sesostris of the Greeks, who only wants a new head-dress and a new pair of legs to place him on a footing with the most respectable pieces of sculpture. We, by no means, coincide with the suggestion to leave Cleopatra's needle behind; for considering the tremendous piece of work she was always getting up, the needle of Cleopatra must always be an object of interest.[93]

This was a fairly common joke to make about Cleopatra's Needle (as already seen with Mrs Brown). In comic imagery, the obelisk is sometimes depicted with a needle's eye (Fig. 6.26).[94] More substantially, articles in *Punch* parodied the real discussions that were being carried out in the periodical press—debates on where the obelisk should be located in London and concerns about how the obelisk would be erected. A similar punning approach is taken to the debate on where the obelisk should be erected in London. 'The Shade of Champollion' offers a suggestion:

---

92. 'From Nile to Neva', *Punch* 99 (1890), p. 67.
93. 'Cleopatra's Needle', *Punch* 21 (1851), p. 160.
94. See 'Received with Thanks', *Punch* 73 (1877), p. 159.

6. *John Bull and his Mommies*

Fig. 6.26. 'Received with thanks', *Punch* 73 (1877), p. 159.

To Mr. Punch.

Venerable Punch,

The true site for this great monument has not been yet suggested. I suggest it now. I do so through your columns, of course, as to them the world looks for final judgment on all things under the Sun— and indeed over it—'*usque ad cerium*'.

Let the obelisk be erected in front of the Royal Exchange. The associations of the spot leave nothing to be desired. Threadneedle Street adjoins it. The adjacent Bank of England will recall the banks of the Nile. Capel Court is in the immediate neighbourhood, and the dealers in Egyptian Bonds there may daily pass this great memorial which looked down, so many centuries back, on Egyptian bonds which their victims found not less hard to get off their hands. There, too, Moses may still be found amongst the Bull-rushes, as in the days of Pharaoh. Nor will the site be without its moral uses; for revellers going to Lord Mayors' dinners with Aldermanic appetites may be reminded by it of the Skeleton at the Feast.

The Shade Of Champollion.

P.S.—At the same time my own countrymen might advantageously remove their obelisk of Luxor from its present inappropriate site to the Place de la Bourse.[95]

---

95. '*The* Site for Cleopatra's Needle', *Punch* 73 (1877), p. 205.

The Place de la Bourse is a square in Bordeaux that, by 1877, had seen numerous monuments erected and removed, mirroring the instability of French politics, and the final comment is a joke about the similar debates that had been ongoing in France.

The sheer volume of ink spilled in the public debate over where the obelisk should be placed was also worth satirizing:

> Sites for Cleopatra's Needle.
> On the Pedestal of the Guards' Memorial, Waterloo Place, in lieu of the objects already there.
> On the top of the Marble Arch, Hyde Park.
> On the apex of the Dome of the Albert Hall.
> On Fish Street Hill, to match the Monument.
> In the Old Bailey.
> In Ely Place, Holborn.
> In Bolt Court, Fleet Street.
> On a thousand other spots, equally suitable, and daily suggested by casual correspondents.[96]

Clearly, for this writer, the debate had become tiresome. Various possible locales are also caricatured and anthropomorphized in another comic in the 1877 issue (Fig. 6.27).[97]

A long article from 1877 records the visit of Cleopatra to Mr Punch's home in a dream.[98] There she discusses the various issues surrounding the Needle. As a queen, she objects to her name being associated with a 'housewife's humble implement'. When Mr Punch explains that this is just a nickname, she responds that 'nicknames are the Nemesis of greatness'. She goes on to ask why it should be removed from Caesar's temple, to which Mr Punch responds that in Roman times it had been removed from the temple of the god Tum (perhaps referring to Atum). She then urges him to make sure that her gift is well taken care of, and with that, Mr Punch awakens.

Punch also received a letter from a jealous obelisk in an 1877 issue. In that letter, titled 'Why Cleopatra's Needle?', the obelisk in Ramsgate Harbour asks why another obelisk is needed.[99] This obelisk had been constructed in 1822 and unveiled in 1823, commemorating the king's visit to the harbour. It was known as 'the royal toothpick'. The poor, mistreated obelisk is especially upset at Erasmus Wilson (who paid for the Needle to be shipped to London), since Wilson lives so close to Ramsgate Harbour and never visits.

---

96. 'Sites for Cleopatra's Needle', *Punch* 73 (1877), p. 155.
97. 'Cleopatra's Needle-Woman. (A Sight of Sites)', *Punch* 73 (1877), p. 194.
98. 'From Nile to Thames', *Punch* 72 (1877), pp. 88-89.
99. 'Why Cleopatra's Needle?', *Punch* 73 (1877), p. 217.

Fig. 6.27. 'Cleopatra's Needle-woman. (A sight of sites)', *Punch* 73 (1877), p. 194.

Punch followed the travels of Cleopatra's Needle as did the rest of England. A poem commemorates its second to last stop, when it is safely moored but not yet erected:

> 'Your Obelisk's ne'er drawn such crowds, it declares,
> As now that it's moored off Adelphi new stairs;
> Since a derelict over from Ferrol it came,
> In the Cylinder-ship, *Cleopatra* by name!
> Says Wilson to Dixon,[100] "We've done it, by gum!"
> Says Dixon to Wilson, "The *crux* is to come".
> Says Wilson to Dixon, "Two hundred tons weight".
> Says Dixon to Wilson, "To lift, and set straight!"
> Says Wilson to Dixon, "If *you* can do *that*".
> Says Dixon to Wilson, "Or else crush me flat".
> Says Wilson to Dixon, "Our stone if we show",
> Says Dixon to Wilson, "O'er Paris we'll crow".
> Says Wilson to Dixon, "Lux*or* theirs they call",
> Says Dixon to Wilson, "And we ours Luck's all".'[101]

The nervousness about the prospects of actually being able to erect the obelisk is presented in the latter half of the poem. After the obelisk was erected,

---

100. Erasmus Wilson and Waynman Dixon were the men responsible for financing and organizing the Needle's transport to Britain (see Chapter I.5).
101. 'The Obelisk's Last Move but One', *Punch* 74 (1878), p. 263.

Punch published a cartoon of a contented obelisk seated within a throne. At the base of the throne is an inscription reading 'Metropolitan Board of Works' and beside it is a contented hydraulic pump, smoking a pipe and flexing its muscles.[102]

Punch's take on the ancient Near East, is, as should be expected from a topical humour magazine, mostly concerned with how ancient discoveries can be used to satirize the present. The typical issues that were satirized through *Punch*'s archaeological articles were commentaries on class, political events and political figures. The typical forms that these satirical observations took was to substitute something from contemporary life with a humorous ancient analogue or to make direct comparisons between ancient and modern, either to show that little has changed since ancient times, that things have gotten worse, or that situations have become reversed. These direct comparisons took the form of textual presentations that mimicked various genres or, more frequently, as comic illustrations. Puns and jokes about misunderstandings (especially linguistic) were also commonly presented through reference to archaeology. So why was the ancient Near East invoked? In part, the visual culture of the region, especially Egypt, made for creative and interesting illustrations. By the 1890s, enough daily life scenes from Egyptian tombs had been published that comic illustrators could easily parody them. Biblical references were references that the writers could safely assume that most readers would understand. Some figures like Layard, and to a lesser extent Disraeli, were obvious choices to be parodied through Assyrian or Egyptian forms. The ancient world also provided a safe medium through which a conservative but seemingly subversive humour magazine could criticize the present. Rather than risk losing readers through pointed and partisan humour, a publication like *Punch* needed safe mechanisms with which to entertain the wide middle-class readership but without deeply challenging them.

Mrs Brown's Trip to Egypt

Punch's middle-class readership was not just familiar with Near Eastern visual culture through media representations. Many of its readers had the opportunity to experience Egypt directly through the new tourism that emerged. Returning to the comedy of manners that the Mrs Brown stories provided, similar types of satire were evoked to understand middle-class British experiences abroad. *Mrs. Brown up the Nile* (1869) pokes fun at and imagines how a lower-middle-class dotty old lady would make sense of and react to a trip to Egypt, like those offered by Thomas Cook (see Chapter I.7). The humour here, for the Victorian reader or audience member, would

---

102. 'At Last', *Punch* 75 (1878), p. 121.

6. *John Bull and his Mommies* 269

be in seeing how someone of Mrs Brown's age and class was ill-prepared for an experience as safe as a guided tour, let alone the experience of a foreign culture. As these tours were all the rage, the volume itself would have been topical, and even for readers who had not experienced Egypt themselves, Sketchley presumes a high level of familiarity with Egyptian travel.

Mrs Brown's lack of understanding is the general conceit of this particular work. The central joke of the book is that this elderly lower-class woman has had the opportunity to travel to Egypt but lacks the intellectual and social skills to understand what she has encountered. This is made clear in the introductory remarks to the book, presented as a letter to Mr Sketchley from Mrs Brown herself:

> Sir,—As to you're a-askin' me what I've seed and 'eard in Egyp', you might as well ask the babe unborn, as the sayin' is, for I'm that confused in my 'ead as I don't know whether I ain't been a-walkin' on it all thro' them pirrymids and over the place, and that knock'd and pulled about by Turkeys, as did used to flock about me for black sheep, as is their 'abits.[103]

In this first paragraph of the book, some of the main jokes that run throughout the book are presented, which are based on the misunderstandings of various words related to Egyptian travel. Perhaps the most common in the book is the reference to Turks as Turkeys. Similarly, pirrymids appears over and over. Other commonly misspelled words are 'Gypshuns (for Egyptians) and drummyderries (for dromedary camels). Mistaking baksheesh for black sheep is less frequent, but the joke is interesting in that it implies that an 1869 English audience would understand the reference.

Later in her story, Mrs Brown explains 'black sheep' a bit more:

> Talk of the plagues of Egyp', I do think as them waggerbone boys is the werry wust, and a parcel of lazy fellers as was a-showin' you things as you didn't want to see, and askin' for 'black sheep', or somethink like that, as is what they calls money; and I'm sure the way as them boys would drive their donkeys full butt ag'in you a-walkin' peaceful, and not 'avin' eyes behind, of course couldn't see 'em a-comin', and then a-'owlin' like mad 'cos some rubbishin' old pots as was made of raw herth, I should say, got knocked off by me unawares.[104]

Mrs. Brown up the Nile is peppered with descriptions like these. Brief narratives are rooted in language gags that mock typical features of Egyptian travel, demonstrating how well known some of these aspects of Egyptian travel would have been to a mid-nineteenth-century audience. Puns, such as Mrs Brown's explanation of the etymology of 'daggerman' (for dragoman, a type of guide—see Chapter I.7) as deriving from him 'a-keepin' a sharp

---

103. Arthur Sketchely, *Mrs. Brown up the Nile* (London: George Routledge & Sons, 1869), p. 3.
104. Sketchely, *Mrs. Brown up the Nile*, p. 49.

look out', hint that Egyptian tourist infrastructure would have been well known.

Mrs Brown's trip to Egypt is merely the framing narrative for her comic soliloquy, which for the most part does not deal with Egypt. But the framing narrative reflects a typical trip to Egypt from England, with stops in Malta, then a stay in Alexandria before travel down to Cairo and visits to the pyramids. So while a critique of Egyptian tourism is not the point of the story, this theme crops up throughout, allowing her to make crotchety observations about travel. For example, she resists visiting the pyramids, but, as she explains, finally concedes to going since this is, she is told, the point of going to Egypt:

> 'Well', I says, 'I don't seem to care about them pirrymids, as is old ancient places, no doubt, but I don't seem to fancy them myself'. 'Oh', says the others 'do come', . . . they says, 'it's downright ridic'lous for you to come all the way from Mile End to Egyp' and not see them pirrymids, as is for all the world like a-goin' to the pump and not getting no water'.[105]

Not all of her reactions to travel reflect poorly on her specifically. At times, Sketchley uses her to mock travellers and travel culture, through her habit of saying things as she sees them. For example, she complains about her companion's use of a guidebook:

> Miss Pullock she made me that savage with 'er ridic'lous ways, as 'ad a guide-book as she was a-readin' constant on the sly, and then a comin' out with things as if she'd know'd all about 'em, a-standin' me out as the Nile did ought to overflow for the sake of the rices as grow'd in it.[106]

Although Mrs Brown is somewhat missing the point of the guidebook, she accurately characterizes how a particularly keen companion with a guidebook may come across as annoying.

Mrs Brown's trip to the pyramids is one of the longer narrative elements of the story.[107] She describes how stifling it felt to go inside a pyramid, how cramped and dark it was, and how claustrophobic she felt, all reactions that are fairly common among travellers to the pyramids. She describes how she would have turned back but was forced forward by the press of tourists behind her. When she arrived at the King's Chamber in the Great Pyramid, she demonstrates that she does not understand that it was intended as a burial. She comments that 'I thought would be well worth seeing thro' bein' that awful grand as them kings of Egyp' always was'.[108] Yet as she states later, 'You never see such a place for kings to live in as

---

105. Sketchely, *Mrs. Brown up the Nile*, p. 64.
106. Sketchely, *Mrs. Brown up the Nile*, p. 71.
107. Sketchely, *Mrs. Brown up the Nile*, pp. 73-78.
108. Sketchely, *Mrs. Brown up the Nile*, p. 74.

that pirrymid, as is big as St. Paul, and no daylight'.[109] She is then invited to continue to tour inside the pyramid. Outside of the pyramid, she continues her typical nineteenth-century tour by being literally dragged up the side of the pyramid (as was the practice) and afterward runs into the Prince of Wales who is also touring Egypt (whose visit, as parodied by *Punch*, was discussed above).

Early on in the book, Mrs Brown seems to question the ethics of archaeological work. Sketchley writes:

> I [Mrs Brown] says, 'And I'm sure no one don't want to [build a pyramid today]'; and as to them mummies, as in my opinion never was alive, a-layin' in their coffins in the British Museum, and frightened Lizzy Wilkins pretty nigh into fits, and isn't a place where a child did ought to be look, partickler for pleasure; and I considers it's a shame as they don't give'em Christshun berryin', if ever there was 'uman bein's, as of course, would come on the parish, thro' not 'avin' no friends, and didn't ought to have been disturbed in their graves as is sacred to their memories, for a tombstone is a tombstone all the world over, tho' 'owever, they could bring themselves to put over old Gruston, as he lived respected and died lamented, I can't think, as was a downright old thief, and ground the poor to hashes like a overseer, and robbed 'em of their burial-club money.[110]

Although it may seem that Mrs Brown is offering a relatively modern reading of the ethics of repatriation and the treatment of the archaeological dead, Sketchley's goal here is humorous. Thus, the view that the mummies should be treated like the Christian dead is not meant to be sophisticated; rather, it is here presented as the ravings of an unintelligent lower-class woman, who is weighing in on issues that are beyond her social place. That being said, the ambiguity of the voice makes it difficult to know if Sketchley would have shared Mrs Brown's view that archaeologists were basically grave robbers.

Much of the book, though, deals with Mrs Brown's encounters with the people of Egypt rather than its antiquities. There is quite an emphasis on polygamy and harems (Mrs Brown visits one), and she offers her thoughts on the practice of wearing veils. The issue of slavery also appears in the book, as Mrs Brown comments to a missionary, 'You're werry fond of 'owlin' over them black niggers bein' slaves, as is all they're fit for, but don't do nothink for poor Christshun gals, as is stole from their parents and sold to these filthy Turkeys'.[111] The missionary responds to Mrs Brown that in Egypt, girls are sold into slavery by their parents and that Queen Victoria's official response is to not interfere. No doubt, this would have been one of the topical issues that made Sketchley's humour of interest at the time.

---

109. Sketchely, *Mrs. Brown up the Nile*, p. 75.
110. Sketchely, *Mrs. Brown up the Nile*, p. 11.
111. Sketchely, *Mrs. Brown up the Nile*, p. 28.

In other parts of the monologue, Mrs Brown presents various details and evaluations of ancient Egyptian society. She argues that hieroglyphs are meaningless and states that there is no way of knowing what the Egyptians had or had not in their day, since they did not leave anything.[112] She comments about how ugly mummies are: 'As to them mummies, I ain't a-goin' to speak ag'in the dead, but, oh, my gracious, they must 'ave been uncommon 'omely in life to look like that when berried'.[113] About the sphinx, she offers, 'There's the spinx too, as is a reg'lar monster with a flat nose, as looks for all the world like a negro black, tho' I 'ave know'd parties as 'ad their noses quite as flat as negroes'.[114] Despite the comments that reflect nineteenth-century attempts to identify the race of the ancient Egyptians (here suggesting that they were not black Africans), the joke seems to be that Mrs Brown does not realize that the nose of the sphinx has been damaged. She expresses the common misidentification that the Hebrews built the pyramids, saying, 'Of all the waste of time as it was to set 'em to build them pirrymids, as couldn't never 'ave been of no use, and was only built for to keep them children out of mischief, as we all knows will get at it if idle; and I'm sure them young Israels as I know'd a-livin' up by Great Prescott Street. . . .'[115] Mrs Brown is likewise unimpressed with Egyptian religion, stating that she doesn't want to visit any temples since 'it's downright disgraceful to leave a place of worship in that state'.[116] She also complains about ancient Egyptian religion, both its idolatry and its antagonism toward Mosaic religion, as presented in the Bible. She explains, 'whatever can you espect from them 'Gypshuns, as considers a cat is a sacred edifice, and wusships a cow, as Miss Pulbrook was a-tellin' me about; and then the way as they treated them children of Israel, we all knows about'.[117]

All in all, Mrs. Brown's evaluation of Egypt and its antiquities is negative. In her 'introductory remarks to Mr Sketchely' she comments:

> [I] shall never want to go there no more, as is 'ighly interestin' no doubt; but Margate's quite sands enough for me, and there's the British Museum for mummies, as I'm a-goin' to spend the day there soon, and shall feel quite at 'ome among 'em ag'in, a-considerin' on 'em old friends like, thro' 'avin' seed 'em in their native pirrymids.[118]

Mrs Brown may not have wanted to go back, but Victorian travel to Egypt and the Holy Land only increased throughout the late Victorian

---

112. Sketchely, *Mrs. Brown up the Nile*, p. 71.
113. Sketchely, *Mrs. Brown up the Nile*, p. 48.
114. Sketchely, *Mrs. Brown up the Nile*, p. 48.
115. Sketchely, *Mrs. Brown up the Nile*, p. 47.
116. Sketchely, *Mrs. Brown up the Nile*, p. 47.
117. Sketchely, *Mrs. Brown up the Nile*, p. 47.
118. Sketchely, *Mrs. Brown up the Nile*, p. viii.

period. The fact that someone like Mrs Brown could have gone to Egypt reflects a fundamental change in global life, facilitated by improved transportation technology and the commodification of the new leisure time that emerged in tandem with urban and industrial life. Whether or not someone of Mrs Brown's status could have afforded to go is a bit questionable, but certainly the stereotype of the middle-class 'Brit abroad' that emerged at this time (and that Mrs Brown represents) was rooted in the new opportunities for tourism that emerged. The latter half of the nineteenth century saw the beginning of temporary population movements on a scale that had never appeared before. The changing nature of this travel is the subject of the next chapter.

Part II

Exploring the Ancient Near East

7

FROM TRAVELLER TO TOURIST IN THE NEAR EAST

> Approaching Jaffa from the sea, the traveller will be struck with the singular beauty of the scene upon which he gazes, and will experience what so many travellers have expressed—the strange sensation of gazing upon a land sacred above any earthly place.
> —From *Cook's Tourist Handbook for Palestine and Syria* (1876)

> Ampère has put Egypt in an epigram. 'A donkey-ride and a boating-trip interspersed with ruins' does, in fact, sum up in a single line the whole experience of the Nile traveller. Àpropos of these three things—the donkeys, the boat, and the ruins—it may be said that a good English saddle and a comfortable dahabeeyah add very considerably to the pleasure of the journey; and that the more one knows about the past history of the country, the more one enjoys the ruins.
> —Amelia Edwards in the preface to the first edition of *A Thousand Miles up the Nile*

> I had come to Jerusalem with a far different purpose from that of forming the acquaintance of men and women. My desire was to shake hands with *David*; to greet *Solomon* face to face; . . . in short, to identify myself as much as possible with *the past*.
> —Robert Morris[1]

In 1845, *Punch* published a series of articles titled 'Punch in the East' reporting on the travels in the East of their 'fat contributor'. The fat contributor was actually William Thackeray, and his satirical wit shows through.[2] He parodies, in great detail, the travel accounts of British tourist expeditions to the East, describing the voyage through the Mediterranean with the typi-

---

1. Robert Morris, *Freemasonry in the Holy Land. Or, Handmarks of Hiram's Builders: Embracing Notes Made during a Series of Masonic Researches, in 1868, in Asia Minor, Syria, Palestine, Egypt and Europe, and the Results of Much Correspondence with Freemasons in Those Countries* (Chicago: Knight & Leonard Printers, 10th edn, 1876), p. 289.
2. A few years later, Thackeray commented in *Vanity Fair* on how tired accounts of Eastern travel are (see Chapter II.2).

cal stops on such a journey (Greece, Malta, etc.) and accounts of ship life. Installment II ('On the Prospects of Punch in the East') describes disembarkation at Alexandria and satirizes the various organizational necessities of arriving in Egypt.[3] Installment III continues with the fat contributor's comments about Athens and Greece.

Installment IV, 'Punch at the Pyramids', begins with the fat contributor reporting the date (using faux calendars mocking those of the Near East) and comparing the pyramids' age with that of Waterloo Bridge in London, noting that the London monument shall not hold up nearly as well.[4] The fat contributor experiences a typical imperialist adventure at the pyramids. He pastes placards on the pyramids, proving that *Punch* was there, and the narrative mocks the solemnity with which tourists treated such acts of vandalism. The account then backtracks to the beginning of the journey and parodies the typical reports of travel writers—the listing and description of supplies, the hiring of guides, and the harrowing travel to the pyramids (including fording rivers 'on the shoulders of abominable Arabs').[5] He quotes the notes of his journey from his pocketbook, which actually does read much like some early nineteenth-century travel accounts:

> —Cairo—Gardens—Mosquitoes—Women dressed in blue—Children dressed in nothing—Old Cairo—Nile, dirty water, ferry-boat—Town—Palm-trees, ferry-boat, canal, palm-trees, town—Rice-fields—Maize-fields—Fellows on dromedaries—Donkey down—Over his head—Pick up pieces—More palm-trees—More rice-fields—water-courses—Howling Arabs—Donkey tumble down again—Inundations—herons or cranes—Broken bridges—Sands—Pyramids.[6]

Cleary by 1845 the tropes of travel writing were standardized enough to be parodied very accurately.

The account of 'Punch at the Pyramids' is concluded in a later issue that same year.[7] It picks up with the fat correspondent waking up after spending a night beneath the shadow of the pyramid. He comments that he 'thought to have had some tremendous visions . . . Pharaoh or Cleopatra, I thought, might appear to me in a dream'.[8] However, he goes on to complain that he was not able to sleep at all. The fat correspondent then describes the morning preparations and his ascent up the side of the pyramid, comically recalling being dragged up, as was typical of the time. After this struggle, the cor-

---

3. 'On the Prospects of Punch in the East', *Punch* 8 (1845), pp. 35-36.
4. 'Punch in the East. IV. Punch at the Pyramids', *Punch* 8 (1845), p. 61.
5. 'Punch in the East. IV. Punch at the Pyramids', *Punch* 8 (1845), p. 61.
6. 'Punch in the East. IV. Punch at the Pyramids', *Punch* 8 (1845), p. 61.
7. 'Punch in the East. IV. Punch at the Pyramids-(Concluded)', *Punch* 8 (1845), p. 75.
8. 'Punch in the East. IV. Punch at the Pyramids-(Concluded)', *Punch* 8 (1845), p. 75.

respondent concludes by discussing whether or not it is worth climbing the pyramids: 'And if, my dear Sir, you ask me whether it is worth a man's while to mount up these enormous stones, I will say in confidence that thousands of people went to see the Bottle Conjuror, and that we hear of gentlemen becoming Free-Masons every day'.[9] So, in the view of the fat correspondent, there are many useless things that people do to entertain themselves.

Thackeray was not the only writer to lampoon Near Eastern travel in the pages of *Punch*. In 1848, travel to Egypt was becoming significantly more feasible for greater numbers of people. *Punch* writes, in an article titled 'Nobility at the Pyramids', of these changes in transportation technology:

> The season for continental tripping and touring being happily rather remote at the present period of the year, there is just a chance that, by the time the autumn comes round, the state of Europe will be sufficiently tranquil to allow one to entertain the notion of going, for pleasure, to France or Italy. Unless a change does take place, the Pyramids will be the only perfect substitute for Baden-Baden, and the port of Ascalon will be the recognized apology for Boulogne, as a foreign bathing-place.
>
> We shall be hearing of a *table-d'hôte* on the shelving precipices of Palmyra, and a boarding-house started on the Libyan sands, with water laid on from the grand African Junction and Friendly Nile Association, for the supply of genuine Nile on equitable principles. The means of rapid locomotion are so very numerous, that the journey to these remote places will be almost as easy as it used to be formerly to visit France or Italy; and, as peace and quiet are indispensable to the full enjoyment of a holiday, nothing nearer than the Pyramids can be thought of, at present, by travellers for pleasure.[10]

Here, *Punch* notes the problem inherent with tourist development—that it facilitates the travel of greater numbers of tourists. The main theme of this chapter is the transformation of Egypt and Palestine from places visited by travellers to places visited by tourists.

Travellers or Tourists?

Increased globalization is truly one of the remarkable changes that occurred in the nineteenth century and lies at the heart of this study of Britain's new encounter with the Near East. Victorian intellectuals framed the encounters of globalization through models of progress and decline, making sense of Britain's and France's (and later Germany's and the United States') roles in a hierarchical world—a hierarchy that was extended through time and space. By the end of the nineteenth century though, travel to the Near East

---

9. 'Punch in the East. IV. Punch at the Pyramids-(Concluded)', *Punch* 8 (1845), p. 75.

10. 'Nobility at the Pyramids', *Punch* 14 (1848), p. 169.

was no longer restricted to the elites (be they economic, political, or intellectual elites) or to people of dogged religious determination who defied social norms in order to go on pilgrimages. Transportation and industrial advances meant that the middle-classes of Europe and North America were no longer confined to their own borders, and so the intellectual models of progress and decline were experienced directly by a wide swath of the population as more people travelled for leisure than ever had before. A commodified tourist trade emerged, reflecting the dramatically increased ability of Europeans and North Americans to experience other locales. At the same time, the tropes for mediating and understanding those experiences were established.[11] Critical theorists working on tourism studies tend to distinguish between travellers and tourists. Daniel Boorstin classifies travellers as active participants in the exploration of new lands, whereas tourists are passive voyeurs, witnesses to difference through the safety of familiar mediators (like professional tourist guides and European-style hotels).[12] For Boorstin, this is a distinction related to the alienation of modern American life, but it also works here, distinguishing the mass tourism that emerges from early nineteenth-century travel. As tourism became commodified, it was framed as an end in itself; it is something that one fills one's leisure time with, for reasons that, while, perhaps, not fully conscious, are framed as virtuous regardless.[13] Similarly, James Buzard (following Paul Fussel) also sees the tourist as a more passive consumer than the traveler; the tourist is directed by an external authority (usually industry) and provides a conservative experience by reaffirming the values of home and helping experience the other in conventional or familiar ways.[14] Inderpal Grewal likewise notes that the use of the term 'travel' is decidedly political and hegemonic, normalizing Eurocentric types of mobility and obscuring other forms.[15] The latter half of the nineteenth century sees the emergence of a normative mode of global travel based on commercial, imperialist and exoticizing foundations. Movement itself, in Grewal's perspective became

11. This chapter cannot do justice to the many volumes of work that have been produced on the subject of nineteenth-century travel to the Near East. Those that wish to pursue this topic further are advised to begin with the series of books published by the Association for the Study of Travel in Egypt and the Near East (ASTENE). ASTENE publications are filled with a variety of scholarship on issues dealing with travel in the Near East, from very specific accounts of particular travels to broader theoretical discussions.

12. Daniel Boorstin, *The Image or What Happened to the American Dream* (London: Penguin Books, 1961).

13. Dennis Porter, *Haunted Journeys: Desire and Transgression in European Travel Writing* (Princeton, NJ: Princeton University Press, 1991), p. 11.

14. James Buzard, *The Beaten Track: European Tourism, Literature, and the Ways to Culture, 1800–1918* (Oxford: Clarendon Press, 1993), p. 3.

15. Inderpal Grewal, *Home and Harem: Nation, Gender, Empire and the Cultures of Travel* (London: Duke University Press, 1996), p. 2.

'ideologically inscribed', and this movement helped to 'construct home and away or empire and nation at various sites in the colonial period through gendered bodies'.[16] The construction of new modes of travel experiences were equally significant for making sense of relations once the tourists had returned home. As Buzard has argued, following Dean MacCannel, leisure came to play a central role in articulating late-nineteenth-century social arrangements (even more so than employment did), and given the importance of tourism as an organized form of leisure, the study of this kind of travel is fundamental to understanding new forms of postindustrial social organization.[17] The study of ancient Near Eastern tourism is central to understanding how the ancient world was understood and employed within nineteenth-century society more broadly and was central in helping nineteenth-century Europeans and North Americans make sense of the changes that their own societies were experiencing.

At the beginning of the nineteenth century, travel for Europeans was still exploration, and the early part of this period saw travellers motivated by colonial conquest. By the end of the nineteenth century, the impulses for conquest were less part of the conscious motivations of mass tourists, even though the successes of colonial conquest provided the basis of the infrastructure of tourism to the Near East. Rather, these tourists were engaging on journeys of self-exploration and self-discovery. Late-nineteenth-century tourists emulated the practices of earlier explorers, but the real discovery was a discovery of nostalgia and otherness that came from visiting the exotic and ancient East. This type of personal exploration is prefigured in the Grand Tour, which from roughly 1600 to 1800 acted as a sort of cosmopolitanizing rite of passage for elite Europeans. The Napoleonic wars interrupted this kind of voyage, and industrialized transportation advances democratized it. Complicating this picture of Near Eastern tourism, however, were issues of religion. The Holy Land had long been a site of pilgrimage, and now pilgrims had greater access to the Promised Land than they had for many years. Christians visiting the region could walk in the footsteps of Jesus; Jews visiting the region could see a future where the land was reclaimed. For both sets of visitors, the seeming stagnancy of the region in the nineteenth century inspired an urgency to revive the land, to transform it again into a land of biblical promise.[18] In the twenty-first century, Egyptian tourism does not rely much on perceived biblical connections, but for many nineteenth-century travellers, the visit to Egypt was also

16. Grewal, *Home and Harem*, p. 4.
17. Buzard, *Beaten Track*, p. 5.
18. Jeffrey Shandler and Beth S. Wenger, '"The Site of Paradise": The Holy Land in American Jewish Imagination', in *Encounters with the 'Holy Land': Place, Past, and Future in American Jewish Culture* (ed. Jeffrey Shandler and Beth S. Wenger; Hanover, NH: University Press of New England, 1997), pp. 11-40 (19).

a biblical journey. Emmet Jackson has, for example, studied Lady Harriet Kavanaugh's 1846 visit to Egypt (and her attempt to follow the path of the Israelites across the Sinai), identifying the deeply held religious convictions that motivated the trip.[19] Kavanaugh's motivations were not unique, and pilgrimage impulses should be considered along with imperialist, class and recreational motivations for travel.

Issues of domination and colonialism were (and are) thoroughly imbued in the tourist experience of the Near East. However, for most mass tourists, these issues were probably not as readily apparent as the tourist's personal experience of difference. Billie Melman has argued that the scholarly emphasis on travel as a type of domination over the other has obscured the important role that travel played in facilitating the comparison of oneself with the other experienced while travelling.[20] In regards to women travellers, Melman asserts:

> Travel and encounter with systems of behaviour, manners, and morals . . . resulted in analogy between the polygamous Orient and the travelling women's own monogamous society. And analogy led to self-criticism rather than cultural smugness and sometimes resulted in an identification with the other that cut across the barriers of religion, culture, and ethnicity.[21]

While certainly true of women travellers, Melman's analysis can be extended to male travellers as well. With the rise in middle-class travel after 1870, it is likely that these travellers, who were not directly involved in the political or intellectual endeavors of imperialism, reacted in a multiplicity of manners to their encounter with Egypt and/or the Bible lands and their inhabitants. Still, Grewal's argument (following John Mackenzie) that there was an imperial vision tied intrinsically to nineteenth-century patriotism suggests that colonial values would have been manifest, in some degree, in visitors of all classes and backgrounds.[22] The experiences would have been filtered through the lens of European imperialism but would also have provided potentially destabilizing experiences of something other than the Victorian normative construct. However, as managed through tourist package companies, the Victorian normative construct was, more often than not, actually reified by the encounter with the other wherein tourists 'learned' that their own culture was superior.

---

19. Emmet Jackson, 'An Irish Woman in Egypt: The Travels of Lady Harriett Kavanagh', in *Souvenirs and New Ideas: Travel and Collecting in Egypt and the Near East* (ed. Diane Fortenberry; Oxford: ASTENE and Oxbow Books, 2013), pp. 55-67 (esp. 56-59).

20. Billie Melman, *Women's Orients: English Women and the Middle East, 1718–1918* (London: Macmillan, 1992), p. 9.

21. Melman, *Women's Orients*, pp. 7-8.

22. Grewal, *Home and Harem*, p. 86.

For both travellers and tourists to Egypt and (less often) the Near East, the exotic Orient provided an instructive contrast to home but a contrast itself filled with contradiction. Hussein Fahim rightly argues that the Egypt of travellers (and this may be extended to the rest of the Near East as well) was an Egypt of two contrasting cultures, both of which reified evolutionary models that justified European superiority.[23] There was the exotic ancient civilization, now in ruins, that evoked glorious images of the past, and there was the contemporary culture, which the European visitor constructed as paralyzed in a morass of mediaeval backwardness. The simultaneous experience of these two cultures was already framed in terms of progress and decline before the tourist ever encountered the 'evidence' of this dichotomous relationship. These and other messages about the region were reified by package tourism, in which there were commercial motivations for showing the tourist the land that they had already imagined the Near East to be. As Nadia el Kholy states, '[t]ravellers to Egypt had a tendency to perceive in the reality the world that legend had painted'.[24] This is not a feature of tourism that is necessarily unique to Egypt and the Near East. Timothy Mitchell has argued that there is a tension between wanting to be separate from the place that one travels to and the urge to fully immerse oneself in that locale—and that this becomes problematic in locations that were not designed with this contradiction in mind.[25] The experience of antiquities, however, easily bridges this contradiction by allowing the tourist to physically experience the past through its material culture and at the same time remain aloof from the surrounding culture, engaging in the performance of tourism. For Egypt and the rest of the Near East, ancient cultures played a specific role in the construction of that hyperreal experience.

The emergence of the hyperreal in travel can be seen as concomitant with the gradual shift toward the romantic and personal experience of travel that accompanied the beginning of the nineteenth century. Enlightenment-era travellers who attempted to enlarge their understanding of 'Man and Things' had participated in an earnest collection of data and objects, while attempting to eliminate the subjective from their experiences of the other.[26] The Napoleonic expedition may have been the pinnacle of this type of enterprise,

---

23. Hussein M. Fahim, 'European Travellers in Egypt: The Representation of the Host Culture', in *Travellers in Egypt* (ed. Paul Starkey and Janet Starkey; London: I.B. Tauris Publishers, 1998), pp. 7-11 (10).

24. Nadia el Kholy, 'Romances and Realities of Travellers', in *Unfolding the Orient: Travellers in Egypt and the Near East* (ed. Paul Starkey and Janet Starkey; Reading: Ithaca Press, 2001), pp. 261-75 (261).

25. Timothy Mitchell, *Colonising Egypt* (Cambridge: Cambridge University Press, 1988), p. 27.

26. Anita Damiani, *Enlightened Observers: British Travellers to the Near East, 1715–1850* (Lebanon: American University of Beirut, 1978), p. 171.

although certainly these urges are resurrected with the positivist approaches to the past that are gradually adopted in archaeology. Yet much of the experience of the nineteenth-century traveler needs to be understood as part of a romantic reaction that valued the personal experience over an objective reality. From Kinglake to Lawrence, travellers and travel writers valued emotional truth and impressions over strictly factual accounts. While these issues may have been thoroughly thought through by the intelligentsia as they wandered the antiques of Egypt or the sacred sites of Scripture, the less reflective traveler was probably quite content to be provided with a romantic, hyperreal and eventually commoditized encounter with the other.

The origins of the now heavily commoditized Egyptian and Israeli tourist industries are readily apparent in the 1870s. Despite the hyperreal practices of travel, the desire for the experience of authenticity drove tourists as it does today. From the 1870s to the early 1900s, the forms in which this authenticity was staged were sorted out and established. As tourists paid for 'authentic' experiences of nostalgia and otherness, the meanings of these experiences were assigned exchange values, and thus, for the host cultures, local relationships to ancient things became commercial relationships. This is a well-documented process in tourism studies, and the Near East is no different—experiences were structured through the values of commodity and profit.[27] The 'authentic' becomes staged in easy-to-access formats. A five-minute ride on a camel at Giza, costing a few shillings, becomes a synecdochal authentic experience of Bedouin and ancient Egyptian life for the tourist, despite the fact that this would have been an alien encounter to both ancient Egyptians and nineteenth-century Bedouin (at least before the arrival of European tourists). This kind of commoditization of 'authentic' experiences has been shown to be potentially harmful to the host culture as their cultural practices are transformed from events of cultural significance to events of economic significance. Generally, for antiquities, the process is initially positive, at least in terms of preservation. However, these benefits are often overshadowed by the problems associated with overdevelopment.

The Motivations of Near Eastern Travellers

For elites and aristocrats, travel had long been a part of the cultured life. Many elite men (and later women) of the eighteenth century experienced two to three years of travel centred on Italy, but also involving Austria, Greece and at times the Ottoman Empire—an experience that was known as the Grand Tour. The tour was to be partly educational, familiarizing upper-

---

27. For more on the general process of commoditization in tourism, see Sine Heitmann, 'Authenticity in Tourism', in *Research Themes for Tourism* (ed. Peter Robinson, Sine Heitmann and Peter U.C. Dieke; Oxfordshire: CABI, 2011), pp. 45-58.

class youth with the cultures of the region, and giving them a familiarity in art, history and literature that came with travel through Italy and neighbouring locales. In part, this expatriate dislocation forced elites to mingle, helping to cultivate a sense of internationalism among Europe's ruling class. As Dennis Porter has described it, the Grand Tour was 'undertaken to the center of a self-confident cultural tradition for the purposes of self-cultivation and the reaffirmation of a common civilized heritage'.[28] For Porter, there was a paradox implicit in the Grand Tour, for it 'was both a form of higher education and an instrument of social reproduction that required an extended absence from paternal surveillance and an exposure to temptation that risked subverting the institutional goals'.[29]

The Near East was peripheral but also proximal to this common European 'civilized heritage'. By the eighteenth century, European relations with the Ottoman Empire, while not always peaceful, were normalized enough to often facilitate travel through the urban areas of the empire and some of the neighbouring hinterlands. The more remote parts of the empire were not very accessible and still provided dangers for European travellers, even to those travelling in great luxury. Constantinople, though, acted as a centre of European eastern travel, with the embassies there functioning, as Philip Mansel states, as 'miniature courts and centres of news, protection, and entertainment'.[30] However, accessibility does not necessarily motivate travel. For many travellers of the eighteenth century, the point of travel was, in Porter's words, 'to move up on the scale of civilization, not down, to go from a land where artistic creativity and the arts of social living were less developed to one where they were more so'.[31] Enlightenment romances of the 'primitive' may have been intellectual trends, but these did not motivate mass travel, as experiences of high culture were more appealing in the context of the Grand Tour. However, not all travellers were the same, and some did seek out the primitive and return to Europe with novel tales of their encounters. Sex and drug tourism was also available in Egypt; Europeans could and did purchase slave girls, visit brothels (most notably Flaubert), and frequent opium dens.[32] That these unhealthy diversions were available in the Near East was well known in Europe, although most European accounts of the nineteenth century cast scorn on these aspects of life in Cairo since travel was framed as an activity of 'betterment'. So what

28. Porter, *Haunted Journeys*, p. 19.
29. Porter, *Haunted Journeys*, p. 51.
30. Philip Mansel, 'The Grand Tour in the Ottoman Empire, 1699–1826', in *Unfolding the Orient: Travellers in Egypt and the Near East* (ed. Paul Starkey and Janet Starkey; Reading: Ithaca Press, 2001), pp. 41-64 (43).
31. Porter, *Haunted Journeys*, p. 164.
32. Piers Brendon, *Thomas Cook: 150 Years of Popular Tourism* (London: Secker & Warburg, 1991), p. 134.

encouraged the betterment of the self through travel to places that would have seemed lower on the scale of civilization? Just as in Greece, experiencing the materiality of ancient greatness justified the visit to what was otherwise framed as a cultural backwater. Antiquities provided the material evidence that ancient Egypt had been the first great civilization (in the eyes of Europeans), and so the experience of antiquity was desirable and a means of personal improvement. Again, here is where progress narratives played a role; the juxtaposition of the past and the present was a powerful means of making sense of perceived European superiority.

As travel became easier, port cities became cosmopolitan hubs, and the kind of cosmopolitan mixing that had been centred in Italy during the eighteenth century came to be replicated at the numerous ports of call on the established travel routes. For the Near East, there were two main routes: through Constantinople or through Alexandria. As already noted, Constantinople replicated a European court on a smaller scale. The route through Alexandria was less courtly in form, but elites were brought together in a liminal space of travel in specific stations (stopping for quarantine at Crete, Corfu, Malta or other locations on the way). In each locale, European travellers were gradually introduced to one another but also to the otherness that they were hoping to experience in Egypt. By the time they reached Alexandria, communities of European travellers had come to know one another and were prepared for the destabilizing encounter with life that was very different from what they had previously experienced. Robinson writes about his embarkation at the Alexandria customhouse:

> We found ourselves in the midst of a dense crowd, through which we made our way with difficulty,—Egyptians, Turks, Arabs, Copts, Negroes, Franks; complexions of white, black, olive, bronze, brown, and almost all other colours; long beards and no beards; all costumes and no costume; silks and rags; wide robes and no robes; women muffled in shapeless black mantles, their faces wholly covered except peep-holes for the eyes; endless confusion, and a clatter and medley of tongues, Arabic, Turkish, Greek, Italian, French, German, and English, as the case might be; strings of huge camels in single file with high loads; little donkies, bridled and saddled, each guided by a sore-eyed Arab boy with a few words of Sailor-English, who thrusts his little animal *nolens volens* almost between your legs;—such is a faint picture of the scene in which we found ourselves on landing in Alexandria.[33]

The truly cosmopolitan nature of the city must have seemed very strange, even to dwellers of such diverse locales as New York, London, Paris and Vienna.

---

33. Edward Robinson, *Biblical Researches in Palestine, Mount Sinai and Arabia Petræa: A Journal of Travels in the Year 1838 by E. Robinson and E. Smith,* I (Boston: Crocker & Brewster, 1841), p. 20.

As the European expatriate presence increased in the region, Egypt especially came to have the same informal networks of British and French residents that Italy and Greece had. Throughout the nineteenth century, British expatriate communities especially grew in prominence throughout Egypt and the Near East. There were a variety of work-related reasons to justify a semi-permanent resettlement in the Near East. Archaeologists, of course, if they could fund their projects, either through an external grant or through their own private resources, resided in the region for long stretches of time. Missionaries established permanent houses from which to proselytize. Even in Palestine, where it was illegal to try to convert Muslims, missionaries still worked, explicitly aiming their message at the Jewish population.[34] In Jerusalem, new centres of religious faith were established or revived, such as the 1847 reinstitution of the Latin patriarchate.[35] Diplomatic posts and work in the foreign service, although interrupted by trips back to England, led to long residencies in the region. Engineers and other highly skilled Europeans were in great demand by the Ottoman Empire and often grew to know the region well. Businessmen of all stripes, from bankers to investors, found the Near East offered opportunity for commercial ventures. With all of these people, families were often brought along, depending on the type of post and the location of residence.

Of course, there were other, less tangible motives for Europeans to adopt the expatriate lifestyle. It was possible to have a high quality of life for considerably cheaper in the Holy Land and Egypt than it was in England. The trappings of Victorian success—land, servants and leisure—could be had with considerably fewer funds. The obvious embarrassments of dwindling wealth could be hidden much more successfully abroad (without looking as though this was intentional). Likewise, those who did not feel that they fit into the rigid hierarchies of Victorian society could establish an alternative lifestyle for themselves abroad, without risking public condemnation. Women, especially, were freed from the obligations of house and motherhood. Gertrude Bell, for instance, who never felt comfortable in the company of women, was able to become a prominent public figure in Mesopotamia, where she was able to keep mostly male company (see Chapter I.8).

Ill health also made Egypt a desirable location for those fleeing the cold, damp climate of the British isles. In the nineteenth century there were

---

34. Sarah Searight, *The British in the Middle East* (London: East–West Publications, 1979), p. 222.

35. For more on these types of institutions and the complex role they played in the nineteenth century, see Paolo Maggiolini, 'Studies and Souvenirs of Palestine and Transjordan: The Revival of the Latin Patriarchate of Jerusalem and the Rediscovery of the Holy Land during the Nineteenth Century', in *Orientalism Revisited: Art, Land and Voyage* (ed. Ian Richard Netton; New York: Routledge, 2013), pp. 165-75.

numerous supposed health benefits of the Near Eastern climate, especially for tuberculosis, which was known to have been exasperated by the coal-polluted air of London. Bronchial problems, congestive diseases, abdominal issues and heart problems were all thought to be alleviated in Mediterranean climates. Many unhealthy individuals set up homes in Egypt and spent their final years as expatriates. In 1858, the sulfur springs at Helwan opened as a health resort for European travellers who wanted relief from a variety of physical and emotional ailments. One of the most memorable of these resident invalids was Lucie Duff Gordon, who made a home for herself in Luxor Temple from 1863 until 1870.[36] After her death, Luxor's role as a health resort became firmly established. In 1876, the travel firm Thomas Cook & Son established a hotel with a full-time physician there, partially inspired by the popularity of Lady Duff's letters, which, as Sarah Searight has described, provided the romance 'of a young woman dying in a strange and exciting land which few of her readers had visited'.[37]

Travel to the Orient posed its own health concerns for European travellers, and digestive upsets were very common (as they still can be). The steamship (and the railroad), which allowed much more rapid transit around the world, brought cholera to the Near East.[38] A cholera epidemic ravaged Egypt in 1831 and 1832, and many succumbed to this illness. Prior to 1844, the Black Plague was also still present in Egypt, thus necessitating periods of quarantine while in transit. Most travellers would not have noticed this as they moved between Egypt and Europe since the quarantine period was spent on the steamship between the locales. As tourist travel increased to the region, especially in Palestine, camp sites became increasingly polluted, and insect infestations more common. Piers Brendon has pointed out that the Victorian dress that was recommended for travellers (especially tweeds and wools) may have increased the problem of sunstroke.[39]

Travel in the Near East was generally not easy at the beginning of the nineteenth century, and those that voyaged there for academic, health or commercial reasons needed to be dedicated. Edward Robinson writes about some of the inherent problems:

> But travelling in Egypt and Syria, is quite a different thing [from travelling in America or Europe]. Here are neither roads, nor public conveyances, nor public houses; and the traveler is thrown back wholly upon his own resources. In Egypt he must hire a boat for himself unless he can find a

---

36. Her letters were published in 1865 and have since been re-issued (Lucie Duff Gordon, *Letters from Egypt* [London: Virago Press, 1983]).

37. Searight, *British in the Middle East*, p. 228.

38. For a thorough account on how steam-powered technology changed nineteenth-century travel, see Sarah Searight, *Steaming East: The Forging of Steamship and Rail Links between Europe and Asia* (London: Bodley Head, 1991).

39. Brendon, *Thomas Cook*, p. 133.

companion to share it with him; he must provide his own bed and cooking-utensils, and also provisions for the journey, except such as he can procure at the villages along the Nile; and withal and above all he must have a servant, who can at the same time act as cook, purveyor, and interpreter. He will soon find himself very much in the power of this important personage, who will usually be able neither to read nor write; and the discomforts and vexations of this relation of dependence will probably continue more and more to press upon him, until he has learned something of the Arabic language....[40]

It was not until the advent of the package tour, though, that travel to the Near East became a viable option for the middle classes and the less adventurous. By the 1870s the package tour had become prominent, and the site of coddled European tourists being guided through archaeological ruins had become commonplace.[41]

Mass Tourism and Package Tours for the Middle Classes

Most often, visitors to the Near East and Egypt were only temporary visitors—not the informal migrants of health-seekers, scholars and Zionists. However, until the 1870s most were members of the upper classes of Europe. The Grand Tour, and its class-closedness, was gradually supplanted as a cultural institution throughout the nineteenth century as infrastructure devoted to tourism became more readily available, and the idea that those other than the upper classes should travel came into vogue. In terms of technology, advances in railways and steamer passage made it possible for large groups of people to travel longer distances for considerably less cost in relative safety.[42] New ideas about health mixed with a Protestant work ethic led to a belief

---

40. Robinson, *Biblical Researches,* p. 23.

41. In Palestine the development of the package tour also occurred in tandem with permanent migrations of Europeans into the region (the German *Templegesellschaft* and Zionist movements being the most influential for the development of tourism). See Yehoshua Ben-Arieh, *The Rediscovery of the Holy Land in the Nineteenth Century* (Jerusalem: Sefer Ve Sefel Publishing, 2007 [1979]), p. 12.

42. Robinson had predicted that this would be the case, and believed that tourism would bring positive development to the Holy Land. Writing about the benefits of these technologies for the Near East, he suggested: 'The introduction of steam-navigation in the Levant and on the Nile and Black Sea, is bringing the power of European civilization into still closer contact with the East, and cannot but augment its influence a thousandfold. Already the oriental churches are in parts beginning to awake from their slumber; and the whole fabric of Muhammedan prejudice and superstition is sapped and tottering to its fall. In all human probability, the coming generation will behold changes and revolutions in the oriental world, of which few now have any conception. Then may the Egyptian people be freed from the oppressions under which they now groan,—a bondage more galling than that inflicted by their ancestors upon the Israelites of old; then

that travel could be used as a means of recharging oneself so as to become a more productive worker and Christian. The idea that a vacation could be considered morally sound encouraged people of all classes to travel.

Thomas Cook was especially important in creating the types of mass tourism that became common by the end of the nineteenth century. By purchasing advance train and steamer tickets (and reselling them to tourists), billeting travellers in hostels with clean amenities, and selling promissory notes that could be used as funds (the precursors of Thomas Cook travellers checks), Thomas Cook made travel at least seem like less of an ordeal. Because the climate allowed tours to be run year round, by 1872, excursions to Egypt and Palestine were Thomas Cook's most important sources of revenue, and so travel to the region was promoted quite heavily.[43] The influence of his particular approach to mass tourism in the latter half of the nineteenth century cannot be overestimated. According to Ruth Kark, for example, four-fifths of all American and British tourists to the Holy Land between 1881 and 1883 had their travel facilitated by a Thomas Cook agency.[44] Kark provides other figures that provide a similar sense of the transformation that these tours brought to the region: 'The annual total [of tourists to the Holy Land] rose from between 2,000 to 3,000 in the first half of the century to around 7,000 in the 1870s and around 30,000 on the eve of World War I'.[45] Not all of these 30,000 travellers were travelling through Cook agencies, since by World War I a number of competitors had arisen, but the basic approach to travel was modeled on Cook's. This was primarily a middle- and upper-middle-class phenomenon and meant that a very different group of people was now visiting the Near East. The temporary but continuous mass infusion of a relatively homogenous group of Europeans and North Americans suggests a quite substantial change in the relationship between the West and the East.[46]

Although Thomas Cook had been arranging tours since the 1840s, he did not organize mass tours to the East until the late 1860s. Much of this, according to Kark, was due to his personal desire to travel the route first, and he was unable to spare the time to do so until his son joined the firm.[47]

---

may Egypt cease to be, what she so long has been, 'the basest of kingdoms' (Robinson, *Biblical Researches,* pp. 45-46).

43. Brendon, *Thomas Cook,* p. 129.

44. Ruth Kark, 'From Pilgrimage to Budding Tourism: The Role of Thomas Cook in the Rediscovery of the Holy Land in the Nineteenth Century', in *Travellers in the Levant: Voyagers and Visionaries* (ed. Sarah Searight and Malcolm Wagstaff; Durham: University of Durham, 2001), pp. 155-74 (157).

45. Kark, 'From Pilgrimage', p. 165.

46. Eitan Bar-Yosef, *The Holy Land in English Culture 1799–1917: Palestine and the Question of Orientalism* (Oxford: Clarendon Press, 2005), p. 65.

47. Kark, 'From Pilgrimage', pp. 160-61.

Upon travelling to the Orient himself, Cook was able to help establish accommodations for his tours, arrange for trustworthy guides, and insure that food was up to the hygienic standards of his mostly middle-class North American and British clientele. Prior to Cook's work, pilgrimages had been popular means of mass tourism to the Holy Land, but that infrastructure could not accommodate the much larger groups that Cook's tours (and subsequent tour operators) brought in. Previously, pilgrims had been billeted in monasteries or stayed in camps outside the city; throughout the 1870s, Cook and others opened hotels in Jaffa, Jerusalem and elsewhere to accommodate an English-speaking clientele (discussed below). In 1873, Cook opened permanent headquarters in both Jaffa and Cairo in order to better facilitate his tours. The tours themselves cost roughly thirty-one shillings a day, all-inclusive, and so were an expensive pastime (but similar in price to what it would cost in the twenty-first century, when adjusted for inflation).[48] There were a variety of itineraries that tourists could take through the Holy Land with Thomas Cook & Son. The shorter routes tended to begin at Jaffa and travel around Jerusalem's environs, down to the Dead Sea and back up to Galilee. Longer excursions started in Beirut or continued into Moab. These involved visits to places mentioned in Scripture; guidebooks were supplemented with Bibles, and a religious tone was maintained throughout the tours. Cook himself had been a missionary, and he adapted what he had learned from those experiences to the organization of the tours.

Egypt had been seen as a safe and comfortable place for British visitors as early as the 1830s, well before the Levant was. Cook, and his competitor Henry Gaze, established the Nile cruise as a comfortable means to see Egypt and its monuments, mixed with a longer stay in Cairo to enjoy the sites and bazaars of that metropolis. Thomas Cook organized his first tours to Egypt in 1860 and soon gained a monopoly on Egyptian tourism, being appointed the official Egyptian government agent for tourism in 1870. By the 1870s, his son, John Mason Cook, had begun to play formal administrative roles in the region, acting as a government agent for Nilotic passenger traffic and later took full control of the delivery of mail and the passage of steamers on the river.[49] In 1887, Cook had constructed a luxury hotel in Luxor, so tourists would stay in Cairo, Luxor, and on steamships in between. A three-month Cook tour of Egypt cost £120 in 1873 (which was three times the annual wage of a typical manservant).[50] After the British occupation of Egypt began in 1882, Cook spent most of his winters in Egypt, conducting the day-to-day operating of his tours. He also assisted the British military

---

48. Kark, 'From Pilgrimage', p. 164.
49. Buzard, *Beaten Track*, p. 136.
50. Trevor Mostyn, *Egypt's belle epoque: Cairo 1869–1952* (London: Quartet Books, 1989), p. 127.

in a number of manners, ranging from the provision of pleasure cruises to off-duty soldiers to actually transporting military officials and contingents up and down the Nile.[51] It was Cook that transported General Gordon down to the Sudan for the ill-fated siege of Khartoum (1884–1885), and Cook continued to supply the transportation needs for the British military operation throughout the conflict (see Chapter I.5).[52] Although there were numerous disputes between Cook and the British military over costs, the agency gained significant publicity for their patriotic participation in a very popular cause. Thomas Cook & Son did not have the same level of formalized government position in Palestine, but it was certainly important there. The fact that John Cook himself guided Kaiser Wilhelm II through Jerusalem on his 1898 visit speaks to Cook's quasi-diplomatic influence.[53]

Not all nineteenth-century travellers were enamored of Cook's tours, and the same kinds of complaints that are made by 'more experienced' travellers regarding these types of guided tours were made in the nineteenth century. In her 1877 *A Thousand Miles up the Nile*, Amelia Edwards complains about the tourists that take luxury cruises up the Nile instead of in the smaller rental boats (known as *dahabiyyas*).[54] Later in the volume, Edwards further mocks Cook's tourists by suggesting that a brief camel ride at Aswan that bears no real resemblance to true desert travel 'figures as the crowning achievement of every Cook's tourist'.[55] Robert Morris, a Freemason who travelled through the Holy Land to report back to his society, goes even further in criticizing the 'tourist'. Upon reading a letter in a Cincinnati newspaper, which he characterizes as 'effeminate', Morris responded to the letter, which he clearly understood to have been written by this type of tourist:

> The writer's opinion [referring to the Cincinnati letter writer] was that of a man accustomed to a quiet, studious life, dyspeptic in his internal arrangements, to whom a prancing horse is a terror, and the cry of a jackal at midnight as a voice from the dead. Now look at the other side. Take a person who knows how to mount a horse from the left side, and to load and fire a pistol, one who is in the habit of sleeping soundly after a hearty supper, and every 'adventure' described by the reverend gentleman in his twenty-seventh letter is but the commonest frolic.[56]

---

51. Brendon, *Thomas Cook*, p. 189.
52. Brendon, *Thomas Cook*, pp. 189-200; Donald Malcolm Reid, *Whose Pharaohs? Archaeology, Museums, and Egyptian National Identity from Napoleon to World War I* (Berkeley, CA: University of California Press, 2002), p. 91.
53. Brendon, *Thomas Cook*, p. 140.
54. Amelia Edwards, *A Thousand Miles up the Nile* (London: George Routledge & Sons, 1899 [1881]), p. 36.
55. Edwards, *Thousand Miles*, pp. 185-86.
56. Morris, *Freemasonry*, p. 476.

Morris goes on to explain that the expenses of travel to the Holy Land are exaggerated. The costs, he claims, come from the use of guides and the excessive luxuries that are provided. The elaborate tents, the massive feasts and the controlled environment are all what make tourism expensive. Without these, Morris argues, the expenses are minimal, and the traveler can go where he likes, when he likes, in a completely safe manner.[57]

The Infrastructure of Travel

Outside of formal tour packages, infrastructure gradually became available for the semi-independent tourist. The British public was long used to travelling to India, a region with a well-established infrastructure for tourism. As Louisa Vaczek and Gail Buckland have noted, the long history of British colonial rule over India had facilitated the creation of institutions that separated the European tourist and expatriate from the local South Asian population.[58] The same could not be said for the British tourist to Egypt or the Holy Land; British influence in Egypt gradually developed throughout the nineteenth century but was not entrenched to the same formal degree as in India (although explicitly formal colonial mechanisms were enacted after the British occupation in 1882). Thus a British tourist of the nineteenth century would have been kept less separate from the locals. Amelia Edwards discusses this difference:

> In Europe, and indeed in most parts of the East, one sees too little of the people to be able to form an opinion about them; but it is not so on the Nile. Cut off from hotels, from railways, from Europeanised cities, you are brought into continual intercourse with natives. The sick who come to you for medicines, the country gentlemen and government officials who visit you on board your boat and entertain you on shore, your guides, your donkey-boys, the very dealers who live by cheating you, furnish you endless studies of character, and teach you more of Egyptian life than all the books of Nile-travel that were written.[59]

Despite her 'continual intercourse with natives', Edwards's summation of the character of Arab Egyptians does not differ much from the Orientalist stereotype. On the same page, she describes the Fellah (an Egyptian peasant) as 'half a savage', and someone who is:

> easily amused, easily deceived, easily angered, easily pacified. He steals a little, cheats a little, lies a great deal; but on the other hand he is patient, hospitable, affectionate, trustful. He suspects no malice, and bears none.

---

57. Morris, *Freemasonry*, pp. 477-78.
58. Louisa Vaczek and Gail Buckland, *Travelers in Ancient Lands: A Portrait of the Middle East, 1839–1919* (Boston: New York Graphic Company, 1981), p. 169.
59. Edwards, *Thousand Miles*, p. 166.

> He commits no great crimes. He is incapable of revenge. In short, his good points outnumber his bad ones; and what man or nation need hope for a much better character?[60]

Edwards's Fellah is basically a child. So despite the more extensive interaction that a British traveler would have had with an Egyptian (as opposed to an Indian), the understanding of that encounter (from the traveler's perspective) was still conceptualized through hierarchies and perhaps even cultural evolutionary models. Even with the lack of infrastructure to keep locals separate from tourists, after 1882, Trevor Mostyn has characterized Cairo as an 'Englishman's playground', with British society recreated in microcosm.[61] While language barriers encouraged these divisions, it is possible to see here the beginnings of the polarization between host culture and tourist that is a typical impact of mass tourism.[62] By the nineteenth century this was well established for India, and it became so for Egypt as tourists became increasingly separated from their hosts, experiencing only enclaves of tourist culture.

For most English tourists to the Near East and Egypt, the experience was mediated through a dragoman.[63] Essentially a tour guide, this was a local resident or European expatriate who commanded at least English and Arabic (and possibly French, German, Italian and Turkish as well, especially in the first half of the nineteenth century). The dragoman dealt with the basic travel needs that the group may have encountered and explained the sites that were visited. In the early part of the nineteenth century, many dragomans were British or French veterans of the Napoleonic wars. The basic costume was a set of blue robes with a velvet jacket, identifying a dragoman visually as a resource for visitors and distinguishing them from the population at large.[64] Most tourists would have been unable to arrange the basic necessities of food, lodging and travel, nor would they have been able to understand the sites that they were encountering. The dragoman was the essential linguistic, cultural and historical source for the tour group and had a very significant impact on the experience of the visitor. The dragoman's interests, however, were not historical so much as economic. As Edwards cynically relates, 'He [referring to dragomans in general] cannot

---

60. Edwards, *Thousand Miles*, p. 166.

61. Mostyn provides an interesting account of the various British social institutions established in Cairo during (and immediately prior to) the British occupation (Mostyn, *Egypt's belle epoque*, pp. 129-40).

62. For more on these processes in general, see Duncan Marson, 'From Mass Tourism to Niche Tourism', in *Research Themes for Tourism* (ed. Peter Robinson, Sine Heitmann and Peter U.C. Dieke; Oxfordshire: CABI, 2011), pp. 1-15.

63. The term is related to the Semitic *targum*, which bears the general semantic range of 'interpretation'.

64. Brendon, *Thomas Cook*, p. 122.

quite understand why travellers come so far and spend so much money to look at them [ancient sites]; but he sets it down to a habit of harmless curiosity—by which he profits'.[65] Baedeker's *Egypt: Handbook for Travellers* also recommends the use of a dragoman but notes a number of typical faults, explaining that 'most of the dragomans are fond of assuming a patronising manner towards their employers, while they generally treat their own countrymen with an air of vast superiority'.[66] Generally, larger parties would hire dragomans for extended tours; otherwise, tourists may have paid the hotel to arrange for a guide for the day (the cost of which was about five to ten francs). The importance of the dragoman in facilitating tourism lessened with the advent of the Cook tour, so much so that in 1874 a group of them wrote a letter of complaint against Thomas Cook to the *Times*.[67]

Before the Cook tour, travel was facilitated through informal networks. Letters of introduction allowed elites access to the foreign residencies, and upon presentation of such qualifications, they would be provided with living quarters in the major cities.[68] From these travel bases, it was possible to arrange for travel to more distant locations, to places where there were no established residencies. Travellers in the early part of the nineteenth century needed to meet with their foreign consul in Egypt and arrange for an audience with Muhammed Ali (or his representative) to acquire a firman for travel. This practiced was discontinued in 1847, and after the British occupation, British citizens did not even need a passport to enter the country. These informal networks were insufficient to support larger numbers of tourists and easily broke down, given the slow communication technologies of the era.

In the 1830s, hotels designed for European tastes began opening in Egypt. Numerous luxury hotels were established in Cairo with full hotel staff ready to assist wealthy European travellers in navigating an Egyptian visit. The Hotel du Nil was founded in 1836 and hosted Gustave Flaubert on his journey to Egypt. The British first stayed at Hill's Hôtel de l'Europe (later called Rey's Hôtel de l'Europe), but the 1846 opening of the Hôtel

---

65. Edwards, *Thousand Miles*, p. 70.

66. Karl Baedeker, *Egypt: Handbook for Travellers. Part 1* (Leipzig: Karl Baedeker, 2nd edn, 1885), p. 14.

67. Brendon, *Thomas Cook*, p. 122; Naomi Shepherd, *The Zealous Intruders: The Western Rediscovery of Palestine* (London: Collins, 1987), p. 177.

68. For example, Edward Robinson writes that upon arrival at Alexandria, he first 'paid respects to Mr. Gliddon [see Chapters II.2], Consul of the United States, to whom I had an official letter; and he immediately sent his Kawaaâz or Janizary to procure us lodgings, and to pass our luggage at the custom-house' (Robinson, *Biblical Researches*, p. 21). Later, he describes arriving in Cairo and having a difficult time because nobody to whom he had letters of introduction was available to see him (Robinson, *Biblical Researches*, p. 25).

de l'Orient (referred to by most as Shepheard's, named after the English owner) eventually supplanted Hill's as the centre of British cultural life in Cairo. Shepheard's Hotel (Figs. 7.1 and 7.2) tried to present an atmosphere reminiscent of London or Paris high society, but contemporary evaluations were mixed, with Mark Twain going so far as to call it the second worst hotel in the world.[69] French travellers were more inclined toward Coulomb's Hôtel de l'Orient. A night's stay at any of these hotels ran between forty and fifty piastres a day (the equivalent of about 1£).[70] The 1885 Baedeker's guide warns that hotel rooms should be reserved before tourists depart from Alexandria as they are frequently full.[71] Travellers would take the train from Cairo and be met at the hotel by a hotel commissioner, who would handle the rest of the transportation for a fee. At all of these hotels, dragomans vied for the attention of European tourists and would take care of their main needs on the journey.[72]

These European enclaves soon developed their own distinctive expatriate cultures. By the 1870s, Shepheard's was, at least from a literary perspective, the place to be for British and American tourists in Egypt. Amelia Edwards opens her 1877 book *A Thousand Miles up the Nile* with a discussion of whom she finds at Shepheard's:

> It is the traveller's lot to dine at many table-d'hôtes in the course of many wanderings; but it seldom befalls him to make one of a more miscellaneous gathering than that which overfills the great dining-room at Shepheard's Hotel in Cairo during the beginning and height of the regular Egyptian season. Here assemble daily some two to three hundred persons of all ranks, nationalities, and pursuits; half of whom are Anglo-Indians homeward or outward bound, European residents, or visitors established in Cairo for the winter. The other half, it may be taken for granted, are going up the Nile. So composite and incongruous is this body of Nile-goers, young and old, well-dressed and ill-dressed, learned and unlearned, that the new-comer's first impulse is to inquire from what motives so many persons of dissimilar tastes and training can be led to embark upon an expedition which is, to say the least of it, very tedious, very costly, and of an altogether exceptional interest.[73]
>
> His curiosity, however, is soon gratified. Before two days are over, he knows everybody's name and everybody's business; distinguishes at first

---

69. For a summary of other reviews of Shepheards, see Brendon, *Thomas Cook*, p. 121.

70. The 1885 Baedeker's guide suggests that a day's board and lodging would cost between 15 and 25 francs a day (Baedeker, *Egypt: Handbook*, p. 3). Baedeker's also gives the equivalence of 100 Egyptian piastres for 26 French francs.

71. Baedeker, *Egypt: Handbook*, p. 231.

72. For a vivid discussion of these two hotels, see Mostyn, *Egypt's belle epoque*, pp. 149-59.

73. Edwards, *Thousand Miles*, p. 1.

Fig. 7.1. Drawing, Shepheard's Hotel Cairo, about 1860–1870, by Hercules Brabazon Brabazon. Purchased with the assistance of The Art Fund, the National Heritage Memorial Fund, Shell International and the Friends of the V&A. © Victoria and Albert Museum, London.

Fig. 7.2. Shepheard's Hotel, *The Graphic,* September 30, 1882.

> sight between a Cook's tourist and an independent traveller; and has discovered that nine-tenths of those whom he is likely to meet up the river are English or American. The rest will be mostly German, with a sprinkling of Belgian and French. So far *en bloc*; but the details are more heterogeneous still. Here are invalids in search of health; artists in search of subjects; sportsmen keen upon crocodiles; statesmen out for a holiday; special correspondents alert for gossip; collectors on the scent of papyri and mummies; men of science with only scientific ends in view; and the usual surplus of idlers who travel for the mere love of travel, or the satisfaction of a purposeless curiosity.[74]

This was a liminal space, where an international crowd was mixed and brought together in a small space, all devoted to roughly the same enterprise—the experience of Egypt.

It is not just the company that made the travel experience so liminal. The whole setting was very different from what was encountered at home. Edwards describes the exotic feeling of waking up at Shepheard's after a night of travel:

> It was dark last night, and I had no idea that my room overlooked an enchanted garden, far-reaching and solitary, peopled with stately giants beneath whose tufted crowns hung rich clusters of maroon and amber dates. It was a still, warm morning. Grave grey and black crows flew heavily from tree to tree, or perched, cawing meditatively, upon the topmost branches. Yonder, between the pillared stems, rose the minaret of a very distant mosque; and here where the garden was bounded by a high wall and a windowless house, I saw a veiled lady walking on the terraced roof in the midst of a cloud of pigeons. Nothing could be more simple than the scene and its accessories; nothing at the same time more Eastern, strange, and unreal.[75]

In Edwards's account of her first morning at Shepheard's, she refers to typical orientalist tropes of Egypt—it is Eastern, strange and unreal. Despite what to the twenty-first-century reader must feel like an uncomfortable conflation of the East with the mysterious, this no doubt well reflects the feelings that a nineteenth-century British traveler would have had upon waking up in an urban environment very different from London, Paris or a small English village.

Despite the hotels established by Cook and others in the urban centres, the accommodations available in Palestine were less established. In keeping with the kinds of sites visited, they were a cross between campsite and what one might except from reading *Arabian Nights*. The camps, as arranged on a Cook tour by their own dragomans and the tents, at least as described, must have seemed inviting. Each was, according to Cook's promotional material,

---

74. Edwards, *Thousand Miles*, pp. 1-2.
75. Edwards, *Thousand Miles*, p. 3.

> designed to accommodate two or three persons, and is well furnished . . . has an inner lining of chintz, which gives it a gay and inviting appearance, and Turkey [sic] or Persian carpets are laid over the floor; it is fitted up with neat iron bedsteads, with the cleanest of clean linen, and good comfortable beds; round or against the tent-pole is a table, with washing basin; and on the bole are strapped pegs for holding clothes. . . .[76]

Pictures that survive of the tents show that they were not as luxurious as described, but certainly a far cry from 'roughing it'. For many travellers, the portable camp may have been more appealing than the dubious inns available for let, and the organization of the Cook tour meant that Victorian propriety could be upheld (such as through gender segregated bathing areas).[77] At every stop the dragomans pitched the same tent for the same guests (marked by a number or symbol) and placed their luggage within. A makeshift 'saloon' was located in the centre of the camp for communal events. As already mentioned, the accommodation situation was different while in Jerusalem, as of 1876. By that time, Cook tours put the travellers up in the Mediterranean Hotel or the Hotel d'Europe rather than having them camp outside of Jaffa Gate as had been prior practice.[78]

Days followed a set routine, beginning with the wake-up call from the dragomans (through whistles or bell ringing or other types of noise making), and the tourists were given half an hour to dress and pack. Most were likely exhausted, especially the middle-class tourists who were not accustomed to riding horses.[79] A large breakfast was served (while the dragoman broke down camp), which, according to Cook's guide started with 'tea, coffee, and milk, with boiled eggs or omelette'; then next was 'a course of hot chicken, and another of cutlets'.[80] The journey began after breakfast with a stop for lunch consisting of 'hard-boiled eggs, cold chicken and lamb, sardines, bread and cheese, and a plentiful supply of oranges'.[81] Lunch lasted for about two hours, during which the travellers could nap or read up on the sites they were to visit. Sightseeing was normally finished by six or seven; dinner consisted of 'soup, fish, mutton, lamb, goose or wild boar, chicken, turkey, a capital pudding, and dessert'.[82] As the guide explains, 'the general aspect of the social board is such as might be expected in the

---

76. *Cook's Tourist Handbook for Palestine and Syria* (London: Thomas Cook & Son, 1876), p. 7.
77. Shepherd, *The Zealous Intruders*, p. 177.
78. *Cook's Tourist Handbook for Palestine*, p. 101.
79. For a discussion of the various difficulties involved in tourist travel on horseback, see Shepherd, *Zealous Intruders*, pp. 178-79.
80. *Cook's Tourist Handbook for Palestine*, p. 8.
81. *Cook's Tourist Handbook for Palestine*, p. 8.
82. *Cook's Tourist Handbook for Palestine*, p. 8.

neighborhood of the Italian Lakes, but not in the wilds of Syria'.[83] All this provided the Cook traveler with the comforts of Europe and minimized the 'need' to experience things Eastern. Of course, these are the descriptions of the Cook guide, designed to entice the prospective tourist, and the reality of the meals was far less enticing, given the numerous accounts of illness among the tourists.

The 1830s were a transformative period in terms of tourist access to Egypt. The guidebooks from the first half of the decade still recommended that visitors wear local dress to avoid harassment, but by 1836 began to advise against this kind of behaviour.[84] The change in advice relates to changes in the safety of the visitor and the fact that a European presence in the region was becoming less novel. That did not mean that travel through Egypt was entirely without peril. As Edwards, a particularly adventurous traveler, wrote, 'Never to go on shore without an escort is one of the rules of Nile life'.[85] She goes on to describe her constant escort (who is otherwise mostly unmentioned in her book) who follows her around, helping to facilitate her travels and makes sure that no dangers befall her. The possible perils varied, although more were related to unfamiliarity with geography and customs rather than experiences of petty crime. For example, Edwards provides an account of a time that her party dallied too late and found it incredibly hard to find their way back to their accommodations in the pitch blackness of the Egyptian night.[86]

Reid charts how amateur research diverged from tourist interests from 1830 to 1870 through changes in instructions in guidebooks.[87] The first guidebooks recommend travellers bring surveying equipment (such as sextants and tape measures with them). Lists of academic topics in need of further research were also presented in guidebooks until the 1870s. When tourism emerged as a distinct category of travel, different from the kinds of travel made by gentlemen scholars, these academic aspirations were abandoned and more generalized academic 'work' is recommended. Explaining that 'it is always desirable . . . to dispense with unnecessary luggage',

---

83. *Cook's Tourist Handbook for Palestine*, p. 8.

84. Reid, *Whose Pharaohs?*, p. 74. The issue of Europeans wearing orientalizing costumes is particularly controversial. The postcolonial argument that the disguise was merely an adornment of colonial power is well explained in Kabbani, *Europe's Myths*, pp. 90-92. For an overview of the debates about the significance of this issue and an argument for how local costuming was, at times, more of an issue of practical safety than colonial subterfuge, see John Rodenbeck, 'Dressing Native', in *Unfolding the Orient: Travellers in Egypt and the Near East* (ed. Paul Starkey and Janet Starkey; Durham: Ithaca Press, 2001), pp. 65-100.

85. Edwards, *Thousand Miles*, p. 163.

86. Edwards, *Thousand Miles*, p. 130.

87. Reid, *Whose Pharaohs?*, pp. 81-82.

an 1876 guide for travellers to Palestine suggests bringing botanical cases (for specimens), sketching books, and other hobby equipment that will be otherwise unobtainable in Palestine.[88] Reid notes that by the 1870s, most of the materials that guides had previously listed as unavailable in Egypt could now be purchased in Cairo or Alexandria.[89] The European or American traveler typically engaged in hobbies such as painting and collecting while touring; these quasi-scientific enterprises, documenting and recording, were part of the performance of tourism. These tasks also helped tourists feel as though they were being productive, and thus the leisure time was not time wasted. The vast number of illustrations and paintings produced by nineteenth-century travellers to the region is indicative of the importance of this kind of 'work' before photography was readily available to amateur enthusiasts.

Throughout the nineteenth century, travel throughout Egypt became significantly easier, due to changes in transportation technology. Early travellers to Egypt cruised down the Nile in houseboat-like vehicles called *dahabiyya* (Fig. 7.3). These were two-masted, flat-bottomed vessels that were sailed or rowed. The sizes of the boats varied but typically carried between two and four passengers with crews (including dragomans and other types of servants) of up to ten. The largest *dahabiyyas* carried crews of twelve or thirteen, servants, and the captain (the *reis*) and perhaps six to eight passengers. There would be two to three cabins (located on deck) for passengers along with bath facilities. Depending on the vessel, there could be separate decks for male and female passengers. This was possible because the cabins were usually located on the fore and aft-decks, with the middle of the vessel used for the kitchen (a small shed with charcoal stove) and other locations of crew work. Usually the crew's quarters (if there were any) were in another part of the ship, most often the hold, located below deck. The crew provided meals mostly cooked on board; bread, however, was baked by the crew in communal stoves located in most port cities while the tourists were visiting sites. The quality of each vessel varied considerably. Jackson notes that the *dahabiyyas* often became so infested by vermin that they would have to be scuttled.[90]

In 1858, according to Reid, a large and furnished *dahabiyya* cost between £50 and £79 a month.[91] Reid lists other variations in prices, depending on how long the voyage lasted and how far the boat travelled, but generally one could expect a forty-day round-trip voyage from Cairo to Luxor to

---

88. *Cook's Tourist Handbook for Palestine*, pp. 3-4.
89. Reid, *Whose Pharaohs?*, p. 80.
90. Jackson, 'An Irish Woman in Egypt', p. 59.
91. Reid, *Whose Pharaohs?*, p. 84.

Fig. 7.3. The *Skandria*, a *dahabiyya* used for the Prince and Princess of Wales' trip up the Nile. *The Illustrated London News*, February 27, 1869.

cost £110 and a fifty-day round-trip voyage as far as Aswan to cost £150.[92] Letting a *dahabiyya* could be an onerous task, one that Edwards compares with 'house-hunting' but 'more bewildering and more fatiguing'.[93] Travellers would go to the Bulak district in Cairo (also the location of the Bulak Museum) and go to the section of the Nile where between two hundred and three hundred of these vessels would be moored, awaiting rental. The *reis* of each ship would attempt to convince potential renters to hire his boat, using the reference letters of past travellers as evidence of the quality of the experience. The Baedeker's guide for Egypt warns (in reference to dragomans) that travellers are often tempted to provide better recommendations than deserved at the end of a voyage ('from motives of good nature'), and this was likely the case with letters of this type for any kind of service provided.[94] Although generally similar, the renters would have to decide on the conditions of the future voyage at that moment—how much room was required, how far down the Nile they wanted to voyage, and the quality and quantity of meals provided, for example.

Reid documents the changes in travel times and costs as the *dahabiyya* is gradually replaced by the steamer (available as of 1858) and finally by railroad as of 1900.[95] The differences in travel by steamer versus travel by *dahabiyya* were profound. In the preface to *A Thousand Miles up the Nile*, Edwards characterizes these differences:

92. Reid, *Whose Pharaohs?*, p. 84.
93. Edwards, *Thousand Miles*, p. 11.
94. Baedeker, *Egypt: Handbook*, p. 14.
95. Reid, *Whose Pharaohs?*, pp. 84-86.

> The choice between dahabeeyah and steamer is like the choice between travelling with post-horses and travelling by rail. The one is expensive, leisurely, delightful; the other is cheap, swift, and comparatively comfortless. Those who are content to snatch but a glimpse of the Nile will doubtless prefer the steamer.[96]

Despite Edwards's obvious scorn for steamer travel, the steamer did greatly facilitate the ability of tourists to travel the Nile, both in terms of cost and time. Transit on the twenty-day Cairo–Aswan voyage (available on an on-demand basis) cost £20 per person and £10 for accompanying servants.[97] In 1880, according to Reid, a steamer would stop at Luxor for three days, allowing passengers to sightsee in the vicinity, and would spend about a day and a half in Aswan.[98] The changing nature of transportation over the course of the nineteenth century had implications for the length of the entire trip as well. In the mid-nineteenth century, a relatively quick trip to Egypt from London would have taken about three months, but by 1880, travel time could be cut to as low as six weeks. Ideal trips were more leisurely, and these are more often the subject of the travel literature produced in the period, perhaps making the average trip seem longer than it really was.

Guidebooks for Near Eastern Tourism

Beginning in the eighteenth century and lasting through the nineteenth century, a process emerged in which the genres of 'autobiographical' travel writing and 'factual/objective' travel writing became thought of as distinct from each other. This genre tension can be seen somewhat in Layard's writing, which presents in the same work his own heroic archaeological adventures alongside objective-style descriptions of Mesopotamian history. Stand-alone guidebooks represent a logical culmination of this process, in which narrative voice is almost completely subsumed by a non-personal instructive voice. Although there is a narrator to some extent in a guidebook, that narrative voice is devised as a non-personal, authoritative, and nearly scientific expert. In some ways, this narrative voice has always existed in travel literature, since along with the autobiographical references in travel accounts there are usually 'objective statements of fact' that the reader presumes do not reflect the personal voice of the narrator. What changes with the guidebook is what is removed: personal experiences and narratives of specific events that befell the traveler. The guidebook provides the tourist with a fully formed conceptual framework through which to understand

---

96. Edwards, *Thousand Miles*, p. x.
97. Reid, *Whose Pharaohs?*, p. 85.
98. Reid, *Whose Pharaohs?*, p. 85.

what he or she will experience. It clearly outlines, in Inderpal Grewal's words, 'a travelling subject as consumer and the sight as commodities'.[99]

The tourist handbook is ready made, easily digestible and ideal for the middle-class tourist. The tour group and the guidebook are easily criticized by the 'traveler', who claims to directly experience the 'authentic' exotic as opposed to those that need this to be mediated or explained to them.[100] That there was or is anything more 'authentic' in any one tourist experience over another is obviously debatable, but the performance of one's own culture in the midst of the other became fundamental to the middle-class tourist experience. As Grewal argues, the guidebook itself becomes part of the costume of the tourist.[101] More will be said on costume shortly, but the costume sets the tourist apart from the local, signaling out-of-placeness, keeps the tourist separate from his or her surroundings, allowing the home to be replicated to some degree abroad. For Grewal, the tourist who uses the guidebook does so not to explore exotic locales but to

> authenticate foreign territory as a known, social space. This space would have its living and moving arrangements all mapped out within the guidebooks in a familiar taxonomy that replicated the domestic, English space; even the mysterious would become familiar, when placed within a known aesthetic geography. The exotic would be domesticated, suggesting the ways in which English culture in this period would be receptive to creating colonies, to making other familiar spaces far from their own homes.[102]

As James Buzard has observed, there is a fundamental irony to guidebooks.[103] They were created to help visitors travel independently and to make areas more accessible, but, by doing so, these guides actually proscribed itineraries and bureaucratized the travel experience.

Since guidebooks were such an important means of making the Near East (and its antiquities) available for European and North American consumption and adaptation, they are worth further examination. In the early part of the nineteenth century, there were few if any guidebooks to help tourists understand what they were visiting or how to go about visiting. Patricia Usick notes accounts such as those of William John Bankes, who explains how he received various types of advice from explorers and diplomats who made up the expatriate community, and it is likely that this type of ad hoc advice was particularly common.[104] Usick also presents a 'question-and-

---

99. Grewal, *Home and Harem*, p. 95.
100. Grewal, *Home and Harem*, p. 95.
101. Grewal, *Home and Harem*, p. 96.
102. Grewal, *Home and Harem*, p. 103.
103. Buzard, *Beaten Track*, p. 47.
104. Patricia Usick, 'The Reverend Joliffe's Advice to Travellers', in *Unfolding the Orient: Travellers in Egypt and the Near East* (ed. Paul Starkey and Janet Starkey; Reading: Ithaca Press, 2001), pp. 219-24 (220).

answer appendix' from Reverend Joliffe's account of his travels in the Near East (1820) in which he provides advice to prospective tourists on what to do about baggage, what kind of bed to request while travelling, what charges to expect in various situations, how to get lodgings, what routes to take and what kinds of permissions were needed.[105] The first formal guidebooks (of the genre tourists still use in the twenty-first century) were John Murray's, which began publication in 1836. Grewal traces some of the history of these early guides, noting that since Murray was Lord Byron's publisher, Byron's travel accounts became a model, to some extent, for the genre.[106] By the end of the nineteenth century, Murray, Baedeker and Cook had institutionalized and formalized the genre; and although the authority of the books as guides was rooted in these men's personal reputations, the utility of the guides was based on their standardization.[107] A closer look at two examples, *Cook's Tourist Handbook for Palestine and Syria* (1876) and *Baedeker's Egypt: Handbook for Travellers* (1885), illustrates some of the main features of these kinds of guides in relation to Near Eastern antiquity.

The preface to the 1876 edition of *Cook's Tourist Handbook for Palestine and Syria* begins by describing the general nature of tourism in Palestine at the time: 'Travellers in Palestine pass through the land in the saddle, and by night sleep in the tent'.[108] This is a far cry from the comforts that were available for Egyptian travel at the same time. The discomforts of travel in Palestine are the motivating factors of the guide, which, it is said, was written

> as to be read without difficulty, either on horseback or in the dim light of the tent; shall be arranged in such a manner, that in a moment any information may be ascertained; and shall contain the full text of Scripture references, so as to avoid the inconvenience of having to turn to the passage in the Bible.[109]

The Cook tourist to Palestine, then, was expecting a rugged expedition that would illuminate Scripture. The preface further goes on to explain that the book is a substitute for the entire library a traveler would want with him, and provides the insights made by Robinson, Warren and others in their expeditions.[110]

Travellers to Palestine are encouraged to not go alone, but travel in a larger party (no doubt an encouragement to partake in a Cook tour). In the 1830s, books such as *Murray*'s had insisted that local Bedouin needed to be

---

105. Usick, 'Reverend Joliffe's Advice', pp. 221-23.
106. Grewal, *Home and Harem*, p. 102.
107. For more on this, see Buzard, *Beaten Track*, p. 65.
108. *Cook's Tourist Handbook for Palestine*, p. iii.
109. *Cook's Tourist Handbook for Palestine*, p. iii.
110. *Cook's Tourist Handbook for Palestine*, p. iv.

hired as guides and for security, but by the 1870s, as already mentioned, Palestine had been made less dangerous for the tourist.[111] After 1839 there was a British consul in Jerusalem who was also able to assist travellers in need.[112] Still, there were advantages to travelling as a group. The guide explains, 'there is no doubt that in no other country is the pleasure of a tour so much enhanced by being associated with a party of friends and acquaintances, or even of strangers with no other bond than that of being fellow-tourists in strange and novel scenes, than in Palestine'.[113] The guide continues, noting the exceptionalism of Palestine, 'In no other country in the world are there so many associations which link together those who visit it; and in no other country, perhaps, is the tourist so dependent for the pleasure of a tour on fellow-travellers'.[114] The emphasis on fellowship is interesting and would have been convincing for travellers interested in exploring the geography usually discussed in a church setting.

Since travellers would be spending most of their time at a campsite or on horseback, the guide recommends clothing that would not be all that out of place in Victorian country life:

> For gentlemen, light tweed suits, and a flannel suit, with a suit of darker material for wearing on particular occasions; this latter is of course not absolutely necessary, but some prefer when attending divine service, or making any special visit, to wear garments of this kind. Woolen stockings and strong boots, flannel or cotton shirts; slippers, and light shoes, a mackintosh suit, white umbrella lined with green, felt hats, or 'helmets' with puggeries. Ladies are recommended to take a good woolen costume, not heavy; one or two of light texture; and a serviceable dark silk.[115]

The costume of the Cook tourist is one that sets the tourist apart from the locals, explicitly. That these individuals travelled in groups and were marked as different was part of the hierarchy of tourism.[116] It set the tourist apart from the community, helped create English (or American or French, etc.) space within the foreign land. By wearing clothes that were similar to but slightly different from the clothes of everyday life, the liminality of the tourist's current state is emphasized. He or she is not labouring but engaged in leisure (marked by tweed in the British case), although that leisure may be seen as productive or improving.

What further sets the tourist apart from the people of the region is the commercial relationship. The guide affirms a tension between the tourist

---

111. Brendon, *Thomas Cook*, pp. 138-39.
112. Searight, *British in the Middle East*, p. 222.
113. *Cook's Tourist Handbook for Palestine*, p. 2.
114. *Cook's Tourist Handbook for Palestine*, p. 2.
115. *Cook's Tourist Handbook for Palestine*, p. 4.
116. Grewal, *Home and Harem*, p. 94.

who wants to spend as little as possible and the local who wants to get as much money from the tourist as possible. The relationship is cast in moral terms by the guide, which, while acknowledging the commercial realities that lay beneath the relationship, casts the local in a negative light. The guidebook's instructions on the issue of baksheesh is instructive:

> Everywhere from morning till night, the traveller will be tormented with applications for backsheesh, which has been called the alpha and omega of Eastern travel. It is the first word an infant is taught to lisp; it will probably be the first Arabic word the traveller will hear on arriving in Palestine, and the last as he leaves it. The word simply means 'a gift', but is applied generally by the naked children who swarm around the traveler when he arrives in a village, then by the enlightened officials of the Custom House, or other public institutions.[117]

The ubiquity of requests for baksheesh is complained about frequently in the travel literature of the time.

Guides did not just provide practical information for the tourist; they also provided context for what was to be seen. The historical introduction offered in the guidebook first paraphrases the Old Testament's historical accounts and is then followed by a political history from the Persian period onward. Also peppering the account are important events in Judaism (such as the Maccabean revolt) and the history of Christian pilgrimage (which the traveler might have imagined themselves to now be included in). Yet the guide explains that it is not history that brings the visitor to Palestine, quoting a 'modern traveller':

> Phoenician fleets once covered those silent waters; wealthy cities once fringed those lonely shores; and during three thousand years, war has led all the nations of the earth in terrible procession along these historic plains. Yet it is not mere history that thrills the pilgrim to the Holy Land with such feelings as no other spot on the wide earth inspires; but the belief that on yonder earth the Creator once trod with human feet, bowed down with human suffering, linked to humanity by the Divinest sympathy—that of sorrow; bedewing our tombs with his tears, and consecrating our world with his blood. Such thoughts will influence the most thoughtless traveller on his first view of Palestine, and convert the most reckless wanderer into a pilgrim for the time; even the Infidel, in his lonely and desecrated heart, must feel a reverence for the *human* character of one who lived and died like Him of Nazareth.'[118]

Thus history took a backseat to the religious experience of the Holy Land, accommodated by the Thomas Cook agency.

For each major site on a Cook's itinerary, the guide provides information about that location from a variety of sources, although Scripture is by far the

---

117. *Cook's Tourist Handbook for Palestine*, p. 6.
118. *Cook's Tourist Handbook for Palestine*, p. 48.

7. *From Traveller to Tourist in the Near East* 307

most quoted authority on these matters. For example, on the section regarding Siloam, the guide references (in the following order) the books of Luke (13.4), Isaiah (8.6), John (9.6-7) and Nehemiah (3.5), as well as Milton and Josephus.[119] Following the lead set by Robinson, the guide also points to historical associations that may not be trustworthy. In many instances, the works of important scholars are made reference to (a bibliography of which can be found on page 461 of the guide), although often these notices make more mention of the personages involved than the actual results of their investigations. For example, almost two pages are spent discussing the excavations of Jerusalem by Wilson, Warren and Condor (see Chapters I.10 and III.7). Here, what is mentioned is that they dug through the centuries of 'rubbish' that had accumulated and that each layer of rubbish reflected a successive era of the city. The tourist would have simply been convinced that they were walking upon centuries of history but would have had no way of understanding this further. References to specific archaeological finds are made throughout the section on Jerusalem, in association with the Cook itinerary, and this would have allowed the Cook tourist to make sense of those discoveries (otherwise reported in a variety of media) while standing among or near them. For example, the guide quotes James Fergusson and others in detail regarding the different classes of tombs that are excavated in Palestine, providing information about construction, dating and cultural affiliations.[120] Of more interest to the writer of the guidebook were the hardships faced by the excavators, and their work is described in near-heroic terms:

> Among many other difficulties which the Explorers have had to encounter may be mentioned the looseness of the *débris*, causing much danger to the excavators; the impure state of the soil, saturated with the sewage of ages; the opposition of the Muslims, the interference of the Pasha and local authorities, the indolence of Oriental workmen—notwithstanding all this, the results have been most satisfactory....[121]

Here are the various 'dangers' that frame the European or North American archaeologist as 'heroic' and in the case of excavations in Jerusalem (or of other holy sites) as scientific Christian crusaders. The archaeologist has become the savior of the past by the time this guide was written.

A series of guides that surpassed Cook's in popularity were those of the German publisher Baedeker. They were so ubiquitous, in fact, that the word 'Baedeker' came to stand for a travel guide in general. The books all shared the same form. They were pocket sized with a distinct 'limp' cover (yellow

---

119. *Cook's Tourist Handbook for Palestine*, p. 168.
120. *Cook's Tourist Handbook for Palestine*, pp. 179-82.
121. *Cook's Tourist Handbook for Palestine*, p. 115.

first and then by the late 1850s red with gilt letters).[122] Each volume is sized to fit the palm of the hand, yet is over five hundred pages. The print is very small, and there are numerous, detailed maps pasted into pages that fold out to about legal paper size. The layout of a Baedeker was consistent no matter what the subject, and readers familiar with a guide for one location could easily use a guide for another.

The 1885 edition of *Egypt: Handbook for Travellers*, edited by Karl Baedeker, is divided into two separate parts (each its own volume), the first part detailing Lower Egypt and the Faiyum and the second explicating Upper Egypt and Nubia as far as the Second Cataract.[123] The second edition is based upon the first, which was written mostly by Georg Ebers.[124] The second edition, however, was compiled by Karl Baedeker himself, based on his own travels, in consultation with various Egyptological authorities.[125]

The first thirty pages of part I offer general information that would be helpful to a tourist before embarking on a journey, such as the types of tobacco one can expect to find in Egypt. A noteworthy section is titled 'Intercourse with Orientals', in which Baedeker notes, 'Orientals reproach Europeans with doing everything the wrong way, such as writing from left to right, while they do the reverse, and uncovering the head on entering a room, while they remove their shoes, but keep their heads covered'.[126] The section goes on to explain some of the practices that Europeans should avoid, such as asking about a Muslim's wife, on account of 'his relations to the fair sex being sedulously veiled from the public'.[127] The tourist is advised that petty crime is rare and that one need not be too cautious since 'many of the natives with whom he comes in contact are mere children, whose waywardness should excite compassion rather than anger, and who often display a touching simplicity and kindliness of disposition'.[128] The next 170 pages or so are filled with a variety of detailed information about Egypt's geography as well as its past and present. The past dealt with is mostly the ancient past; the present is mostly discussed in terms of Islam. Fourteen pages are spent giving tourists information about hieroglyphs (including replicas of the most common cartouches) in a section written

---

122. A 'limp' cover is a semi-hard cover that is stronger than a typical paperback cover but is still pliable enough to be kept in a pocket.

123. Karl Baedeker, *Egypt: Handbook for Travellers* (Leipzig: Karl Baedeker, 2nd edn, 1885).

124. Georg Ebers (1837–1898) was a German Egyptologist whose name is now associated with the Ebers Medical Papyrus (which he discovered). For German readers, he was also famous for his series of ancient Egyptian historical fiction.

125. Baedeker, *Egypt: Handbook*, p. v.

126. Baedeker, *Egypt: Handbook*, p. 25.

127. Baedeker, *Egypt: Handbook*, p. 26.

128. Baedeker, *Egypt: Handbook*, p. 27.

by Georg Ebers. It may be noteworthy that only twelve pages are spent discussing Arabic, suggesting that the spoken language of the country was of less interest than a dead one.

The remainder of both volumes is designed mostly to give site-by-site information about what to see and what infrastructure is available. Various itineraries are offered, the excavation history of archaeological sites is provided (if relevant) and images and detailed maps and floor plans are provided to assist the tourist. Most of the descriptions are written from the perspective of someone following the itinerary, and thus readers would have had to orient themselves accordingly. For example, in the section on Giza, it is explained that 'In the valley before us, to the right, rises a projecting ridge of rock containing tombs of no interest.... To the left of the trees rises a kind of truncated *Tower*....'[129] Although not the clearest directions, the conceptualization underpinning the Baedeker guide is that the tourist will slavishly follow the route set out in the book. Interpretation of what is to be seen is mediated directly through the instructions of the guidebook.

The Act of Tourism

Guidebooks helped identify and standardize what the tourist was supposed to 'do' and see while touring. Part of the hyperreality of tourism is the virtual checklist that many travellers operate with to prioritize what is to be visited and to provide some focus of accomplishment for the otherwise 'unproductive' act of travel. In the nineteenth century, this kind of hyperreality became entrenched in the corporatism and consumerism of travel to the Near East. Tourists would visit important sites and purchase souvenirs to commemorate the fact that they had visited the site. Buying souvenirs provided them with an activity at the site and helped them communicate those experiences to others when they returned home. Flaubert finds his visit to the pyramids utterly boring, not because of the pyramids per se, but because by visiting them, one is doing what one is expected to do, not what one wants to do.[130]

One of the most important souvenirs to purchase or tasks to achieve while 'checking sites off of the list' is the visual documentation of the site. At the beginning of the nineteenth century, tourists had to be content with purchasing a watercolour or drawing of the site, or, more fulfilling, making their own. With the advent of photography, it became easier to document one's physical presence in the location, and the practice of being photographed in front of a monument became entrenched almost as soon as photography came into existence. Visitors to Egypt who did not own a camera

---

129. Baedeker, *Egypt: Handbook*, p. 369.
130. Cited in Porter, *Haunted Journeys*, pp. 171-72.

could purchase photographs from local studios after 1862.[131] For John Urry, photography organizes expectations of what tourists will see, provides them with activities to engage in while travelling and constructs their memories of the tourist event long after.[132] Here Urry offers a Foucauldian conception of the 'tourist's gaze', arguing that there was an emphasis on 'looking' in travel encounters and that 'looking' became a primary action, next to shopping, in mass tourism.

Other goods and services were hawked by local vendors who would mob tourists (as they do at Near Eastern tourist sites today). Guidebooks from the nineteenth century warn about this kind of inconvenience and recommended that any purchases be mediated through a dragoman off site.[133] As early as 1830, Rifaud's guidebook warns about the purchase of fake antiquities from these and other types of vendors.[134] However, not every traveler's experience of the vendors who worked at the pyramids was negative. Amelia Edwards describes her taking leave of them after her first encounter with them:

> 'You come again!' said they. 'Good Arab show you everything. You see nothing this time!' . . . The Pyramid Bedouins have been plentifully abused by travellers and guide-books but we found no reason to complain of them now or afterwards. They neither crowded round us, nor followed us, nor importuned us in any way. They are naturally vivacious and very talkative; yet the gentle fellows were dumb as mutes when they found we wished for silence. And they were satisfied with a very moderate bakhshish at parting.[135]

Here, Edwards tries to correct the negative impression of these vendors held by the guidebooks. However, her patronizing tone is obvious, and the image of the 'Pyramid Bedouin' merely replaces one negative stereotype with another. Later in the same volume, Edwards describes the unavoidable outcome of these encounters:

> Every traveller on the Nile brings away a handful of the smaller scarabs, genuine or otherwise. Some may not particularly care to possess them; yet none can help buying them, if only because other people do so, or to get rid of a troublesome dealer, or to give to friends at home.[136]

---

131. John Urry, *The Tourist Gaze* (London: Sage, 1990), pp. 136-40.
132. Urry, *Tourist Gaze*, p. 140.
133. See, for example, Karl Baedeker, *Egypt: Handbook for Travellers. Part 1* (Leipzig: Karl Baedeker, 2nd edn, 1885), p. 13.
134. See Reid, *Whose Pharaohs?*, pp. 77.
135. Edwards, *Thousand Miles*, p. 17.
136. Edwards, *Thousand Miles*, p. 97.

It was as rare then as it is now for a tourist to leave Egypt without these kinds of baubles.[137]

Having something 'to do' at the sites was an important part of the travel experience. This need was met not just through shopping and taking photographs. In the nineteenth century, more active endeavors were encouraged of tourists. Concerns about physical contact with antiquities were not yet prominent, and restrictions on touching were not easily policed (see below). Graffiti from the nineteenth century is especially apparent on Egyptian monuments, where the act of writing one's name on an ancient object gave the traveler a feeling of connection to the past as well as the satisfying (if illusory) feeling of colonial conquest.

Climbing atop the monuments was also a satisfying activity. In his 1869 *The Innocents Abroad*, Mark Twain humorously describes his experiences clambering up the steps of a pyramid at Giza. He writes:

> Each step being full as high as a dinner table; there being very, very many of the steps; an Arab having hold of each of our arms and springing upward from step to step and snatching us with them, forcing us to lift our feet as high as our breasts every time, and do it rapidly and keep it up till we were ready to faint—who shall say it is not lively, exhilarating, lacerating, muscle-straining, bone-wrenching and perfectly excruciating and exhausting pastime climbing the pyramids? ... Twice, for one minute, they let me rest while they extorted baksheesh, and then continued their maniac flight up the pyramid. They wished to beat the other parties.[138]

Elsewhere, Twain humorously plays on the term dragoman, referring to the Arabs who helped the Europeans up the side of the pyramid as 'draggers' (Fig. 7.4).

The descent from the pyramids was perhaps even more exhausting, as described by H.J. Ross (1820–1901), who had worked in the British consular service and with Layard at Nineveh. No stranger to the Near East, Ross writes:

> I clutched my two Arabs with most earnest grasp, for one descends with one's back to the Pyramid, and the idea of being precipitated headlong down its side was by no means pleasant. All I know is that when I did get

---

137. Edwards describes the production of new souvenir scarabs in more detail: 'Both [Copts and Arabs] sell more forgeries than genuine antiquities. Be the demand what it may, they are prepared to meet it. Thothmes is not too heavy, nor Cleopatra too light, for them. Their carvings in old sycamore wood, their porcelain statuettes, their heiroglyphed limestone tablets, are executed with a skill that almost defies detection. As for genuine scarabs of the highest antiquity, they are turned out by the gross every season. Engraved, glazed, and administered to the turkeys [marks] in the form of boluses, they acquire by the simple process of digestion a degree of venerableness that is really charming' (Edwards, *Thousand Miles,* p. 410).

138. As quoted in Vaczek and Buckland, *Travelers in Ancient Lands,* p. 169.

Fig. 7.4. The Emperor of Austria being 'dragged' up the Great Pyramid. *The Illustrated London News,* December 25, 1869.

down, my knees were powerless, and I had great difficulty in walking. I was never so tired in my life.[139]

Here, concerns to avoid certain kinds of physical exertion probably made a difficult task even more unpleasant, but at least provided heroic stories with which to regale those at home.[140]

Tombs provided another activity for travellers at a site; today in Egypt, tombs open for tourists are well lit and easy to gain access to. For a nineteenth-century tourist, this was less the case. Edwards describes her experience:

> We went in [to a tomb at Saqqarah]. A hot, heavy atmosphere met us on the threshold; the door fell to with a dull clang, the echoes of which went wandering away as if into the central recesses of the earth; the Arab [tomb

---

139. H.J. Ross, *Letters to the East* (1902); as reprinted in Deborah Manley and Sahar Abdel-Hakim (eds.), *Egypt through Writers' Eyes* (London: Eland, 2007), p. 79.

140. Piazzi Smyth describes many elements of pyramid tourism that he observed while working at Giza over the course of a few months in 1865. Of particular note is a similar, though not as intentionally humorous as Twain's description, of European tourists being dragged through the candle-lit interior of the pyramids, while being clutched around the waist by Arab guides (Charles Piazzi Smyth, *Life and Work at the Great Pyramid; during the Months of January, February, March, and April, A.D. 1865; with a Discussion of the Facts Ascertained,* I [Edinburgh: Edmonston & Douglas, 1867], p. 307).

> guard] chattered and gesticulated. He was telling us that we were now in the great vestibule, and that it measured ever so many feet in this and that direction; but we could see nothing—neither the vaulted roof overhead, nor the walls on any side, nor even the ground beneath our feet. It was like the darkness of infinite space. A lighted candle was given to each person, and the Arab led the way. He went dreadfully fast, and it seemed at every step as if one were on the brink of some frightful chasm. Gradually, however, our eyes became accustomed to the gloom, and we found that we had passed out of the vestibule into the first great corridor. All was vague, mysterious, shadowy. A dim perspective loomed out of the darkness. The lights twinkled and flitted, like wandering sparks of stars. The Arab held his lantern to the walls here and there. . . . So we went on, going every moment deeper into the solid rock, and farther from the open air and the sunshine. Thinking it would be cold underground, we had brought warm wraps in plenty; but the heat, on the contrary, was intense, and the atmosphere stifling. We had not calculated on the dryness of the place, nor had we remembered that ordinary mines and tunnels are cold because they are damp.[141]

Descending into a tomb, while perhaps not offering much visual sensation, provided an adventurous activity for those who arranged to enter one. Lucky visitors may even have been able to watch excavators at work. After the establishment of the Bulak Museum, small groups of untrained excavators worked at various sites to excavate tombs. Tombs would be opened and the mummies and other major artifacts would be sent back to the museum. Visitors were able to watch the spectacle of work gangs hauling these treasures from the ground.[142]

Various other types of activities, more reflecting orientalist ideas rather than ancient Egyptian realities, were provided near antiquities sites. Brief camel rides became ubiquitous in the nineteenth century; camels were brought to tourist sites expressly for this purpose. Edwards describes both the appeal and lack of authenticity in the experience:

> Taken from this honest calling [the actual transport work that camels were used for] to perform in an absurd little drama got up essentially for the entertainment of tourists, it is no wonder if the beasts are more than commonly ill-tempered. . . . The ride, nevertheless, has its advantages; not the least being that it enables one to realise the kind of work involved in any of the regular desert expeditions. At all events, it entitles one to claim acquaintance with the ship of the desert. . . .[143]

No doubt many Victorian tourists returned home to regale their friends with 'the adventure' of riding a camel near the pyramids. Less adventurous, but

141. Edwards, *Thousand Miles*, p. 56.
142. Edwards writes of her own experience watching an excavation at Thebes (*Thousand Miles*, pp. 412-15).
143. Edwards, *Thousand Miles*, p. 186.

arguably better reflecting the realities of life in Upper Egypt, were the donkey rides also offered at sites.[144]

Museums became a tourist destination in the nineteenth century.[145] When Auguste Mariette opened the Egyptian Museum in Bulak, European travellers were one of his main intended audiences (although he also wanted Egyptians themselves to have access to the antiquities).[146] Mariette wanted tourists to have easy access to the museum, initially suggesting that Alexandria was the best location for it. However, given the speed of rail travel between Cairo and Alexandria, he changed his mind and arranged for it to be located near the hotels of Cairo.[147] By 1877, Amelia Edwards could write, 'if there was nothing else to tempt the traveler to Cairo, the Bulak Museum would alone be worth the journey from Europe'.[148] Admission was free, and guidebooks and photographs of the exhibits were available for a small fee. The building itself was too small for the exhibits, and in 1878 the Nile flooded the museum. The exhibits were saved, but it had become apparent that the Bulak Museum was insufficient.[149] It would take until 1902, however, for the new building to be completed. By that point, Mariette had been dead for over twenty years. His body was exhumed from its tomb and reburied in the garden of the new museum.

Vandalism and Concern for the Destruction of Antiquities

The act of defacing archaeological monuments in Egypt may have been common in the nineteenth century, but at the same time, awareness of the negative effects of this kind of vandalism mounted. An 1890 cartoon in *Graphic* (July 26) shows three British women among ancient Egyptian pylons covered in hieroglyphs (Fig. 7.5). One woman holds a parasol; the other two are carving (presumably their names) onto the face of one of the pylons. As early as 1841, the American vice-consul (in Egypt), George Gliddon, wrote a treatise called *An Appeal to the Antiquaries of Europe on*

---

144. For Edwards's description of the donkey vendors, see Edwards, *Thousand Miles*, p. 135.

145. For an overview of museological practices in Egypt, see Wendy Doyon, 'The Poetics of Egyptian Museum Practice', *British Museum Studies in Ancient Egypt and Sudan* 10 (2008), pp. 1-37.

146. Reid, *Whose Pharaohs?*, pp. 105-106.

147. Reid, *Whose Pharaohs?*, p. 104.

148. Edwards, *Thousand Miles*, p. 487.

149. For a description of the exhibition space at the Bulak Museum, see Elaine Altman Evans, *Scholars, Scoundrels, and the Sphinx: A Photographic and Archaeological Adventure up the Nile* (Knoxville, TN: University of Tennessee Press, Frank H. Clung Museum, 2000), pp. 73-74.

Fig. 7.5. American women vandalizing the temple at Denderah. *The Graphic,* July 26, 1890.

the Destruction of the Monuments of Egypt.[150] This work is an impassioned plea to stop the destruction of Egyptian monuments, especially by the hands of Muhammad Ali. Yet as Colla has noted, embedded within this plea are various messages about the inadequacies of Muhammad Ali's government and negative sentiments against Muslims in general.[151] Gliddons's aim in the work was to encourage European governments to support conservation efforts and put pressure on the Egyptian government to preserve the ancient monuments. In biblical terms, he describes Egypt as the 'house of bondage' and implies that the four great powers can provide a Moses-like salvation to the endangered antiquities.[152] In 1888, the Society for the Preservation of the Monuments of Ancient Egypt (SPMAE) was formed in London. Its main goals were to lobby the British colonial administration to protect antiquities and sites and provide better conditions at the Bulak Museum.

The impulse to take antiquities from sites is often too strong for tourists to resist, and the idea that this should not be done was unimaginable until the very end of the nineteenth century. Even Amelia Edwards (who would later go on to advocate for the protection of Egyptian antiquities) writes

150. It is ironic that Gliddon's later career involved the public unrolling of mummies for entertainment, another form of destruction of Egyptian antiquities (see Chapter II.2).

151. Elliott Colla, *Conflicted Antiquities: Egyptology, Egyptomania, Egyptian Modernity* (Durham, NC: Duke University Press, 2007), pp. 109-13.

152. Colla, *Conflicted Antiquities*, p. 113.

about her experiences collecting artifacts from sites and the mania for gathering objects that sets in: 'Presently some one picks up a little noseless head of one of the common blue-ware funereal statuettes, and immediately we all fall to work, grubbing for treasure'.[153] The issue of collecting is further dealt with in Chapter II.1.

Creation of Icons and the Sacralization of Sites

In the nineteenth century, some of the important archaeological sites of the Near East came to be icons, signifying not only the ancient culture that created them but the experience of exotic travel. Dean MacCannell has called this general process 'site sacralization', in which a space is transformed into a tourist location.[154] The process is generally similar in most tourist settings. The site is named, and the borders of what constitutes the site are established. It is separated from other space within the host community, sometimes physically through walls and entrance kiosks but more importantly through the presentation of the site as space to be visited by the tourist (and in some instances avoided by the host culture). The site is presented in tourist brochures, posters, etc., in forms that signify it as a tourist site; it is reproduced in souvenir form (i.e., miniature models of pyramids for purchase) and in the naming and iconography of associated tourist infrastructure (gift shops, hotels, restaurants, etc.). The site then becomes a sight—part of the itinerary of a tour of the region.[155]

Arguably, Egypt's most prominent icons were the sphinx and pyramids at Giza. That the sphinx had been activated as an icon of the nation-state of Egypt is apparent in the fact that all Egyptian postage stamps issued from 1867 to 1914 bore an image of the monument.[156] State symbols are easily transformed into spectacles for the tourist's gaze. Photographs taken in the latter part of the nineteenth century and the beginning of the twentieth century are quite captivating, as the sphinx, at this time, was still buried almost up to its shoulders in sand, and, unlike today, visitors were able to climb all over the ancient monument.[157] Thus the pictures depict men and women,

---

153. Edwards, *Thousand Miles*, p. 51.

154. Dean MacCannell. *The Tourist: A New Theory of the Leisure Class* (Berkeley, CA: University of California Press, 1999), pp. 43-48.

155. For more on sites and reactions against them, see Chloe Chard, *Pleasure and Guilt on the Grand Tour: Travel Writing and Imaginative Geography 1600–1830* (Manchester: Manchester University Press, 1999), pp. 18-20.

156. Steven W. Holloway, 'Introduction: Orientalism, Assyriology, and the Bible', in *Orientalism, Assyriology and the Bible,* (ed. Steven W. Holloway; Hebrew Bible Monographs, 10; Sheffield: Sheffield Phoenix Press, 2007), pp. 1-41 (13).

157. Vaczek and Buckland have compiled a few travel photographs taken of visitors to the sphinx (Vaczek and Buckland,*Travelers in Ancient Lands,* pp. 165-67).

often in heavy formal clothing or Victorian era 'safari-gear', posing on various parts of the sphinx, assisted by local Egyptians. Most of the photos are taken from such a distance that the actual features of the individuals in question are unidentifiable, but the head of the sphinx and at least one pyramid (depending on the angle) are visible in the frame.

If the sacralizing experience has worked, the visitor expects to feel a quasi-religious sense of wonder. Flaubert describes this of his approach to Thebes (despite the fact that he found the pyramids and monuments generally boring): 'I felt rise within me a sense of solemn happiness which went forward to meet the spectacle, and I thanked God in my heart for having made me capable of taking pleasure (*jouir*) in such a way'.[158] It is important, as Buzard has shown, that the signs (in the semiotic sense) of the place of travel match what the visitors actually see, which allows them to feel as though they have 'made meaningful contact with what these places essentially were'.[159]

The transformation of travel into hyperreal commodified experiences was both encouraged by and perpetuated through the kind of bland experience tourists often complain of when encountering a travel icon that has been reproduced in other formats too frequently. By the end of the nineteenth century, visitors to Egypt had perhaps become overfamiliar with the main icons of ancient Egypt. Amelia Edwards writes about the first views one gets of the pyramids at Giza: 'The well-known triangular forms look small and shadowy, and are too familiar to be in any way startling'.[160] That being said, Edwards does state that the experience is more interesting when 'the Great Pyramid in all its unexpected bulk and majesty towers close above one's head, the effect is as sudden as it is overwhelming. It shuts out the sky and the horizon. It shuts out all the other Pyramids. It shuts out everything but the sense of awe and wonder.'[161] This sense of awe and wonder is what tourists hope to experience and what tourism vendors hope to sell. Yet, of course, that is quite difficult to prepackage. Edwards goes on to discuss how her experience of the pyramids deviated from that suggested by her guidebook, and one gets the sense that it is the unexpected and unusual that most captures her imagination.

In his poem 'Egypt Unvisited (Suggested by Mr David Roberts' Egyptian Sketches)', Aleric Alexander Watts (1797–1864) explores the fact that he still longs to visit Egypt despite the fact that science has robbed the earth of mystery and poetry. He writes:

> The poetry of earth is fading fast;
> It hath no region it can call its own;

---

158. As cited in Porter, *Haunted Journeys*, p. 175.
159. Buzard, *Beaten Track*, p. 10.
160. Edwards, *Thousand Miles*, p. 13.
161. Edwards, *Thousand Miles*, p. 14.

> The dim, religious light of old that cast
>   Mysterious beauty on its haunts hath flown!
>
> Science, with eye of microscopic power,
>   And disenchanting lamp, from land to land,
> With railroad speed continues still to scour,
>   Till scarce a spot on earth remains unscanned.
>
> Even the vast Pyramid hath now become
>   A thing whose secrets all are known too well;
> The Harp of Memnon is for ever dumb;
>   And even the Sphinx hath nothing left to tell!
>
> The Nile, so long a river of the heart,
>   Hath now no mystic problem to unveil;
> And its drear desert, once a thing apart
>   From common roads, we soon may cross by rail!
>
> No green oasis now enchants the eye,
>   With its tall palms and fountains bubbling o'er;
> The desert ship we loved in days gone by,
>   Is but a camel now, 'and nothing more!'
>
> Then why through Egypt should I seek to roam,
>   Fancy to feed with scenes that will but mock it;
> With graphic Roberts for my guide (at home),
>   And Murray's trusty 'Hand-Book' in my pocket.

Watts's poem captures one of the attractions that Egypt held for a European or American in the latter half of the nineteenth century. In the wake of positivism and the seeming mastery of the earth through the physical sciences and technology, Egypt offered the possibility for romance and mystery. For Watts, though, the development of the region for tourism has robbed it of its aura.

Anthony Trollope on Egyptian Tourism

The novelist Anthony Trollope spent two months of 1858 in Egypt, negotiating a postal treaty on behalf of the British General Post Office.[162] As Nadia Gindy notes, his experiences in Egypt are hardly mentioned in his *Autobiography* or in any of his travel writings, and unlike many English travellers, he does not seem to have been greatly influenced by his visit to Egypt.[163] However, Trollope did write two short stories lampooning the

---

162. Trollope, although a successful writer from the 1850s onward, remained an employee of the post office until 1868, when he resigned in order to run for public office (an election he lost).

163. Nadia Gindy, "'While I was in Egypt, I finished *Dr. Thorne*'", in *Interpreting the Orient: Travellers in Egypt and the Near East* (ed. Paul and Janet Starkey; Reading: Ithaca Press, 2001), pp. 139-51 (139).

British tourist experience of Egypt—'George Walker at Suez' (1861) and 'An Unprotected Female at the Pyramids' (1860). Gindy suggests that the two stories share a common theme:

> Through placing the English traveller in an Egyptian setting and exposing him or her as being almost completely impervious to the traditional icons of Egypt, Trollope achieves a dual purpose: he deflates the stereotyped notion of the exotic Orient and he ridicules the ordinary British travellers, both en masse and as individuals abroad.[164]

In particular, 'An Unprotected Female at the Pyramids' criticizes the British experience of Egyptian antiquities and is worth further discussion in this context. Indeed, Trollope's descriptions of travel in Egypt are so vivid (and scathing) that they furnish a very detailed image of what it would have been like to travel through Egypt in this era. The story reflects Trollope's own frustrations with both European tourists and Egyptians involved in the tourist industry, and neither group comes across in a particularly favorable light. He purposefully stereotypes all of the characters, but, of course, read in the twenty-first century, his depictions of Egyptians and women are problematic (although likely accurately reflect the feelings of Trollope's contemporaries).

Trollope begins the story with an acknowledgment of the orientalist fantasy of what Egypt should be and mourns its loss, brought on by increased European tourism. The story begins, 'In the happy days when we were young, no description conveyed to us so complete an idea of mysterious reality as that of an Oriental city. We knew it was actually there, but had such vague notions of its ways and looks!'[165] Yet, by mid-century, this is no longer the case. Trollope continues:

> But the route to India and Australia has changed all this. Men from all countries going to the East, now pass through Cairo, and its streets and costumes are no longer strange to us. It has become also a resort for invalids, or rather for those who fear that they may become invalids if they remain in a cold climate during the winter months. And thus at Cairo there is always to be found a considerable population of French, Americans, and of English. Oriental life is brought home to us, dreadfully diluted by western customs, and the delights of the 'Arabian Nights' are shorn of half their value. When we have seen a thing it is never so magnificent to us as when it was half unknown.[166]

---

164. Gindy, 'While I was in Egypt', p. 141.
165. Anthony Trollope, 'An Unprotected Female at the Pyramids' (1860); originally published in *Cassell's Illustrated Family Paper*, 1860; Project Gutenberg edition released February 2003.
166. Trollope, 'Unprotected Female'.

Here, Trollope describes a cosmopolitan Egypt, a type of cosmpolitanism that is tempered by the particular constituency of the traveler to Egypt—the invalid. For Trollope, actually visiting Egypt is a disappointment, not out of any particular issue presented by Egypt itself, but because of the disjuncture between imaginary geography and tourist space. There cannot be anything but disappointment when one expects to find the Arabian Nights and one actually finds a convalescent resort.

Trollope makes a similar point in regards to the actual experience of antiquities in person (or any iconic destination for that matter):

> It is astonishing how such things lose their great charm as men find themselves in their close neighbourhood. To one living in New York or London, how ecstatic is the interest inspired by these huge structures. One feels that no price would be too high to pay for seeing them as long as time and distance, and the world's inexorable task-work, forbid such a visit. How intense would be the delight of climbing over the wondrous handiwork of those wondrous architects so long since dead; how thrilling the awe with which one would penetrate down into their interior caves—those caves in which lay buried the bones of ancient kings, whose very names seem to have come to us almost from another world! But all these feelings become strangely dim, their acute edges wonderfully worn, as the subjects which inspired them are brought near to us. 'Ah! so those are the Pyramids, are they?' says the traveller, when the first glimpse of them is shown to him from the window of a railway carriage. 'Dear me; they don't look so very high, do they? For Heaven's sake put the blind down, or we shall be destroyed by the dust.' And then the ecstasy and keen delight of the Pyramids has vanished for ever.[167]

According to Trollope's observations, being in the physical presence of the icon acts to undermine the imaginative power of that icon.

Trollope continues, describing the hub of British life in Cairo—Shepheard's Hotel:

> A quarter of the town has in this way become inhabited by men wearing coats and waistcoats, and by women who are without veils; but the English tongue in Egypt finds its centre at Shepheard's Hotel. It is here that people congregate who are looking out for parties to visit with them the Upper Nile, and who are generally all smiles and courtesy; and here also are to be found they who have just returned from this journey, and who are often in a frame of mind towards their companions that is much less amiable. From hence, during the winter, a cortege proceeds almost daily to the pyramids, or to Memphis, or to the petrified forest, or to the City of the Sun.[168]

Trollope's description of Shepheard's is that of a colonial outpost, acting as a hub for the tourist to make incursions to a predetermined series of stock

---

167. Trollope, 'Unprotected Female'.
168. Trollope, 'Unprotected Female'.

7. *From Traveller to Tourist in the Near East*

locales. He proceeds with the story describing the organization of one such day trip to the pyramids, consisting of a group of travellers, having met at Shepheard's, deciding to visit the pyramids as a group. Trollope's description of the tourist group well reflects the experience of most such groups at this time:

> And now the donkeys, and the donkey boys, and the dragomans were all standing at the steps of Shepheard's Hotel. To each donkey there was a donkey-boy, and to each gentleman there was a dragoman, so that a goodly cortege was assembled, and a goodly noise was made. It may here be remarked, perhaps with some little pride, that not half the noise is given in Egypt to persons speaking any other language that is bestowed on those whose vocabulary is English. This lasted for half an hour. Had the party been French the donkeys would have arrived only fifteen minutes before the appointed time.

The conspicuousness of the group undertaking a visit to the pyramids is comically described here and probably without much exaggeration.

The characters of this group, as sketched by Trollope, reflect the stereotypical travellers one might meet in Egypt at this time: the middle-class British family (with pretensions of upper-class status); the nationalist rival—the Frenchman—arguing about the futility of the Suez Canal project; the American travelling the entire world in one trip ('as American gentlemen so often do'); and Miss Dawkins—the unprotected woman of the title—a woman who has abandoned society obligations and the quest for a husband so as to follow her own whims. Trollope describes a tour where the visit to the pyramids is the explicit goal but in fact takes second place to the social interactions of the tourists. In fact, the actual arrival at the pyramids hardly interrupts them. Throughout the story, there are numerous side comments about the awkward manners that the men display in attempting to act as gentlemen to the 'unprotected woman'—by remaining both attentive and distant simultaneously. The contemporary reader likely best identifies with the 'unprotected lady', but Trollope's description of her becomes more and more negative throughout the course of the story; and, as Gindy has argued, the story must be seen, to some extent, as something of a critique of the independent woman, who, despite her positive qualities, has made the fatal error of not finding a husband or remaining under male protection.[169] Much of the point of the story seems to be to juxtapose the 'unprotected woman's' superiority of response to travel with her social failure. Trollope's own take on this matter is somewhat ambiguous in this story. It may anticipate later critiques of the 'New Woman' (see Chapter III.4), but Trollope's female protagonists are usually lively women who test expected boundaries.

---

169. Gindy, 'While I was in Egypt', p. 148.

The first stop in their journey occurs on the banks of the Nile, where negotiations for water travel drag on:

> Here they were kept half an hour while their dragomans made a bargain with the ferryman, a stately reis, or captain of a boat, who declared with much dignity that he could not carry them over for a sum less than six times the amount to which he was justly entitled; while the dragomans, with great energy on behalf of their masters, offered him only five times that sum. As far as the reis was concerned, the contest might soon have been at an end, for the man was not without a conscience; and would have been content with five times and a half; but then the three dragomans quarrelled among themselves as to which should have the paying of the money, and the affair became very tedious.[170]

The reactions of the Europeans (and the American) are mixed. Some find the whole affair 'odious' while others praise the dragomans for their hard work on behalf of their employers.

Upon arrival at the pyramids, Miss Dawkins gets into a mild argument with the American traveler (Mr Ingram):

> 'Enormous! What a grand idea!—eh, Mr. Ingram? The human race does not create such things as those nowadays!'
>
> 'No, indeed', he answered; 'but perhaps we create better things'.
>
> 'Better! You do not mean to say, Mr. Ingram, that you are an utilitarian. I do, in truth, hope better things of you than that. Yes! steam mills are better, no doubt, and mechanics' institutes and penny newspapers. But is nothing to be valued but what is useful?' And Miss Dawkins, in the height of her enthusiasm, switched her donkey severely over the shoulder.
>
> 'I might, perhaps, have said also that we create more beautiful things', said Mr. Ingram.
>
> 'But we cannot create older things'.
>
> 'No, certainly; we cannot do that'.
>
> 'Nor can we imbue what we do create with the grand associations which environ those piles with so intense an interest. Think of the mighty dead, Mr. Ingram, and of their great homes when living. Think of the hands which it took to raise those huge blocks—'
>
> 'And of the lives which it cost'.
>
> 'Doubtless. The tyranny and invincible power of the royal architects add to the grandeur of the idea. One would not wish to have back the kings of Egypt'.
>
> 'Well, no; they would be neither useful nor beautiful.'
>
> 'Perhaps not; and I do not wish to be picturesque at the expense of my fellow-creatures'.[171]

Here, the Victorian argument between the relative merits of aesthetics and utility is played out through a discussion of the worth of the pyramids. The

---

170. Trollope, 'Unprotected Female'.
171. Trollope, 'Unprotected Female'.

argument continues to the topic of the rights of woman until Mr Ingram manages to extricate himself from the discussion.

Whether or not the pyramids had a utilitarian value in the past, Trollope describes their utilitarian value, as revenue generators, in his time. The typical reception one would have (and still does) at the base of the pyramids is described:

> And now at last they were on the sand, in the absolute desert, making their way up to the very foot of the most northern of the two Pyramids. They were by this time surrounded by a crowd of Arab guides, or Arabs professing to be guides, who had already ascertained that Mr. Damer was the chief of the party, and were accordingly driving him almost to madness by the offers of their services, and their assurance that he could not possibly see the outside or the inside of either structure, or even remain alive upon the ground, unless he at once accepted their offers made at their own prices.[172]

Trollope's treatment of the harassed feelings of the travelling party probably reflects feelings from his own visit. He depicts the locals in a particularly unfavorable light, at one point comparing them to flies and rendering their broken English in the conversations.

Once the group arrives at the pyramids, the itinerary for what is to be 'done' at the pyramids is laid out:

> And now they had reached the very foot of the Pyramids and proceeded to dismount from their donkeys. Their intention was first to ascend to the top, then to come down to their banquet, and after that to penetrate into the interior. And all this would seem to be easy of performance. The Pyramid is undoubtedly high, but it is so constructed as to admit of climbing without difficulty. A lady mounting it would undoubtedly need some assistance, but any man possessed of moderate activity would require no aid at all.[173]

Trollope illustrates how this activity is commodified by the locals:

> But our friends were at once imbued with the tremendous nature of the task before them. A sheikh of the Arabs came forth, who communicated with them through Abdallah. The work could be done, no doubt, he said; but a great many men would be wanted to assist. Each lady must have four Arabs, and each gentlemen three; and then, seeing that the work would be peculiarly severe on this special day, each of these numerous Arabs must be remunerated by some very large number of piastres.[174]

Pictures of forays up the pyramids such as these taken in the nineteenth century show that there is not much exaggeration in Trollope's description.

---

172. Trollope, 'Unprotected Female'.
173. Trollope, 'Unprotected Female'.
174. Trollope, 'Unprotected Female'.

After ascending the Great Pyramid and having lunch, the next task on the itinerary was to enter the pyramid. Trollope describes the motivations that compelled the tired tourists to continue:

> And then the interior of the building had to be visited. To tell the truth none of the party would have cared to perform this feat had it not been for the honour of the thing. To have come from Paris, New York, or London, to the Pyramids, and then not to have visited the very tomb of Cheops, would have shown on the part of all of them an indifference to subjects of interest which would have been altogether fatal to their character as travellers. And so a party for the interior was made up. . . . This entrance into the Pyramids is a terrible task, which should be undertaken by no lady. Those who perform it have to creep down, and then to be dragged up, through infinite dirt, foul smells, and bad air; and when they have done it, they see nothing. But they do earn the gratification of saying that they have been inside a Pyramid.[175]

Trollope cannot help but offer his own critique on this 'terrible task', performed for the sake of social performance, not out of actual desire for the experience. Indeed, the picture that Trollope paints of visiting the antiquities of Egypt is that this is something that is done because it aught to be done (socially) rather than because it is a rewarding experience.

Trollope's particularly scathing critique of Egyptian tourism does not necessarily reflect the impressions of Egypt that a typical middle-class tourist would have had. Certainly the descriptions of the places and the infrastructure are accurate, but it is unlikely that the average middle-class tourist would have been so self-aware of their experience of antiquities. Yet undoubtedly Trollope is correct in pointing to how the imagined icon is never as rewarding as one imagines it will be. No doubt this reality of travel motivates much of the current hyperreality that masquerades as the authentic in modern travel, and concomitantly this same feeling of disappointment propels travellers (who consider themselves more aware than mere tourists) in their quest for the 'authentic'. It is not random that Trollope chose to use Near Eastern travel (and visits to archaeological sites) as a setting for thinking through issues of women's independence. For, as is the subject of the next chapter, these issues were entangled in the latter half of the nineteenth century.

175. Trollope, 'Unprotected Female'.

8

From Tourist to Scholar:
Amelia Edwards and Women Travellers

The issue of women travellers in the Victorian era is well studied, and, as many scholars have noted, travel provided Victorian women with a means of experiencing life beyond the narrow confines of patriarchal England. Women (particularly elite women) used travel as an opportunity to gain access to public space and escape the normative frameworks imposed upon them by British society. Many scholars of women travel writers describe these women as exceptional and read their travel accounts as attempts at liberation from the oppressive culture of Victorian life. However, recent scholarship has argued for a more complex view of these travellers. Sarah Mills has shown that the desire to produce coherent and stable readings of these women travel writers has, in fact, skewed our understanding of these texts and the culture in which they were written.[1] In particular, Mills argues that scholars of women travellers tend to ignore any element of their writing that 'doesn't support meta-narrative of personal struggle against society's constraining forces'.[2] Billie Melman likewise suggests that the focus on the issues of domination and power relating to travel have obscured the importance of travel for the consideration of the self and especially women's selves.[3] And, as Patricia O'Neill has pointed out, travel itself cannot necessarily be taken as a critique of patriarchy.[4] This chapter will investigate these themes in relation to one of Egyptology's foundational figures, Amelia Edwards, a woman who first experienced Egypt as a traveler and

---

1. Sarah Mills, *Discourses of Differences: An Analysis of Women's Travel Writing and Colonialism* (London: Routledge, 1991), p. 5.

2. Mills, *Discourses of Differences*, pp. 34-35.

3. Billie Melman, *Women's Orients: English Women and the Middle East, 1718–1918* (London: Macmillan, 1992), p. 9.

4. Patricia O'Neill, 'Amelia Edwards: From Novelist to Egyptologist', in *Interpreting the Orient: Travellers in Egypt and the Near East* (ed. Paul Starkey and Janet Starkey; Reading: Ithaca Press, 2001), pp. 165-73 (166). Gertrude Bell is a particularly good example of a woman traveler who actively worked to preserve the patriarchy, fighting against suffragette causes.

later helped develop the standards for professional scholarly investigation of the ancient Near East.

Debating Women Travellers

Indeed there are significant complexities in applying a postcolonial critique to women travellers. Masculine discourse tends to situate women travellers as markers of home and femininity, although, as shall be shown, this does not necessarily reflect the emic perspectives of women travellers.[5] As most nineteenth-century women travel writers were middle class and outside of the empowered elite, their relationship to power and authority was ambiguous. They were both symptomatic of colonial power and themselves marginalized by it. They replicated some of the power structures as they travelled but also worked around some of those power structures through the very act of travel. Clothing, as an example, is often privileged in women's travel writing. For the twenty-first-century reader early travel accounts seem to dwell to an excessive degree on detailed descriptions of the physical appearances and functions of different types of clothing. For a nineteenth-century reader, however, these excursuses were part of larger arguments about clothing reform.[6]

According to Sarah Mills, part of what makes these women's stories more palatable to twenty-first-century readers than male travel writing of the same period (and potentially subversive of patriarchy) is that there are fewer overarching comments about race and fewer blanket critiques of 'otherness'—these tends to be framed at the individual level.[7] Many of these female travellers express sympathy with the colonial 'other' that they encounter, but, as Mills cautions, this should not be read as a belief in the equality of the 'other'.[8] As we shall see, Amelia Edwards brings to bear the 'scientifically' founded racial ideas of the nineteenth century to make sense of the different peoples of the Near East in a manner that does not suggest an interest in equality for all. All of these issues lead to the larger question that Mills asks: Does writing about subverting norms actually enforce and stabilize those norms?[9] The answer seems to be both yes and no.

---

5. Mills, *Discourses of Differences*, p. 3.
6. Mills, *Discourses of Differences*, p. 105. Clothing was also an important object marker of civilization and Christianity. In missionary discourse, especially, the clothing of the 'other' was symptomatic of moral and spiritual issues and worth discussing in detail. See Erin Hasinoff, 'Faith in Objects: American Indian Object Lessons of the World in Boston', in *Archaeologies of Materiality* (Malden, MA: Blackwell, 2005), pp. 96-125 (104).
7. Mills, *Discourses of Differences*, p. 3.
8. Mills, *Discourses of Differences*, p. 97.
9. Mills, *Discourses of Differences*, p. 119.

Often, biographers emphasize the personalities of these women over their writing, and the label of 'eccentric' allows women who did undermine normative gender and cultural roles to be understood in a manner that better reflects pre-existing expectations of Victorian women.[10] Mills argues that the label 'eccentric' usually means that the woman deviates from feminine expectations.[11] Certainly Amelia Edwards has been the victim of this kind of marginalizing (despite her popularity among feminist scholars and historians of Egyptology) as her forceful personality is very often at the forefront of accounts about her. The 'atypicality' of Edwards's experiences of Egypt are emphasized in biographies, despite the fact that many women (such as Gertrude Bell) could be considered semi-professional adventurers. Yet at the same time, it is important not to fall into the trap that Gerda Lerner has identified, in simply making history involving women into descriptions of women that did things like men did.[12] The formative role of women in the development of ancient Near Eastern studies in the latter half of the nineteenth century was important and evident beyond merely mirroring established male approaches, and much of how the field has developed (in distinction from other forms of regional studies) may be due to this early and influential participation of many different women.

Near Eastern studies was a 'useful occupation' with which to fill one's time and, as it stood for most of the nineteenth century, required little in the way of formal university training (it was not even taught outside of a theological context, see Chapter I.10). Travel was a non-institutional outlet for engagement with the Near East and facilitated participation in historical, archaeological, geographic and anthropological work in an informal manner.[13] By the end of the nineteenth century, with the establishment of middle-class tourism to the region, women were able to make major contributions to the field since they could easily gain access to the region. Amelia Edwards was one such figure who played a tremendous role in the establishment of professional Egyptology, and she shall be discussed in detail here.

---

10. In some cases, the use of adjectives like 'eccentric' may be appropriate. It is hard to consider the choices of Lady Hester Stanhope, for example, who believed that she had received omens that she would become the bride of the messiah and engaged in a treasure hunt at Ashkelon, as other than eccentric. Yet even in cases like this, the ability of designations like 'eccentric' to mask non-normative behavior (and skew historical readings) should be considered. Lady Hester is discussed in further detail later in the chapter.

11. Mills, *Discourses of Differences*, p. 96.

12. For a discussion of applying Lerner's arguments in the context of Near Eastern studies, see Julia M. Asher-Greve, 'From "Semiramis of Babylon" to "Semiramis of Hammersmith"', in *Orientalism, Assyriology and the Bible* (ed. Steven W. Holloway; Hebrew Bible Monographs, 10; Sheffield: Sheffield Phoenix Press, 2007), pp. 322-73 (324).

13. Melman, *Women's Orients*, p. 9.

Similarly, Gertrude Bell (1868–1925) was a pioneer in the archaeology of Iraq and a driving force behind the establishment of the Baghdad Museum and the borders of the modern Middle East. Bell was a woman who did not like the company of other women (she was an anti-suffragette) and found that she could better escape her proscribed gender roles in the Near East. However, her participation in Near Eastern studies is better situated within the twentieth century and outside the confines of this study.

Travel writing was arguably the most evident 'product' of the informal work of travel. Some of the constraints of women's participation are evident in the constraints on genre. Whereas male travel narratives (like those of Belzoni and Layard) were framed as adventures, women's stories were not. For Mills this reflects a 'double-bind situation'—women's writing was deemed either trivial (dealing with issues of interest only to women) or inappropriately masculine.[14] The framing of anecdotes of women's adventures needed to be as comic 'larks', not as heroic encounters with danger.[15] Or, dangerous events were purposefully downplayed. Belzoni's wife, Sarah, for example, wrote 'Mrs. Belzoni's Trifling Account of the Women of Egypt, Nubia, and Syria', which was printed with her husband's *Travels in Egypt and Nubia*, and which is more of an ethnographic account of women's lives than the adventure story her husband wrote (despite the fact that she travelled with him through much of his journey and travelled by herself to Palestine). Sometimes, however, women were privileged with experiences unavailable to men travelling in the region—access to the *harem* was perhaps the most sensationalized of these kinds of licenses, allowing women writers to present erotically charged and embellished accounts (framed as ethnographic descriptions) that Victorian audiences craved.[16]

Lady Hester, the Queen of the Jews

Yet even before tourism to the Middle East had become common, women were able to play a role in the development of the field. One of the most interesting of these figures, who played a dubious role in the development of Syro-Palestinian archaeology, was Lady Hester Stanhope (1776–1839). She can be said to have conducted the first archaeological excavation in what is now Israel at the coastal site of Ashkelon.[17] Lady Hester was the

---

14. Mills, *Discourses of Differences*, p. 118.
15. Mills, *Discourses of Differences*, p. 105.
16. Emmet Jackson, 'An Irish Woman in Egypt: The Travels of Lady Harriett Kavangh', in *Souvenirs and New Ideas: Travel and Collecting in Egypt and the Near East* (ed. Diane Fortenberry; Oxford: ASTENE and Oxbow Books, 2013), pp. 55-67 (60).
17. Lady Hester is the subject of numerous biographies. See, for example, Kirsten Ellis, *Star of the Morning: The Extraordinary Life of Lady Hester Stanhope* (New York:

granddaughter of William Pitt the Elder and the niece of William Pitt the Younger, who held the office of prime minister twice. As an unmarried man, Pitt needed a hostess for his household, so his niece moved in with him to assume those duties during his second term in office (1804–1806). After his death, she received a pension from the British government, which provided her with some degree of independence. Silberman notes that her personality made her numerous enemies while head of Pitt's household, and, after his death, she found herself without supporters in London society.[18] Romantic disappointment and the death of her brother in the Napoleonic wars further led her to give up London and move to Asia Minor.

Lady Hester's travels to Syria–Palestine are extremely interesting, and her unusual encounters cannot really be taken as normative for the period, other than to point to the eclectic nature of Near Eastern travel before the advent of middle-class tourism. According to Silberman, she was inspired to visit the Holy Land by an inmate of the insane asylum of Bedlam, who told her that he had seen her future as the queen of the Jews, and that she would lead the Jews back to the Holy Land.[19] En route to the Orient, at Athens, she visited Lord Byron. Her ship wrecked in Rhodes, where she was forced to borrow Turkish clothing, and it was at that point that she started wearing the clothing of Ottoman men (specifically choosing not to borrow typical Ottoman women's clothing). This remained her standard practice while in the Middle East. Once in the Holy Land, she met Burckhardt in Nazareth, who convinced her to further explore the region.

After visiting Palmyra, a location that had been thought too dangerous for Europeans to visit, Lady Hester gained the affection of local Bedouin. She settled on the coast of Syria, where all sorts of visitors came to see her. Among these visitors were Franciscan monks who gave her what was purported to be a mediaeval map indicating the location of buried gold at the site of Ashkelon. Lady Hester travelled to Ashkelon, having gotten permission to excavate the site from the sultan in Constantinople. Once at Ashkelon, and accompanied by a representative of the sultan, she commenced her excavations. There she did not find gold but did find a seven-foot-tall Roman statue in marble. Once it became clear that there was no gold, rather than collect the antiquities, she had the statue destroyed and cast into the sea. Silberman explains that this rather curious choice was

---

HarperPress, 2008); and Lorna Gibb, *Lady Hester: Queen of the East* (London: Faber & Faber, 2005). Chapter 8 of Kinglake's classic provides a contemporary's account of Lady Hester (A.W. Kinglake, *Eothen: Traces of Travel Brought Home from the East* [London: J. Oliver, 1844]).

18. Neil Asher Silberman, *Digging for God and Country: Exploration, Archeology, and the Secret Struggle for the Holy Land 1799–1917* (New York: Alfred A. Knopf, 1982), p. 24.

19. Silberman, *Digging for God and Country,* p. 24.

rooted in her desire not to encourage the plundering of Holy Land sites by Europeans in order to fill museums.[20] Having visited Athens and aware of the controversy associated with the Elgin Marbles, Lady Hester, who by this time was quite quick to temper and on bad terms with the British consulate, chose to make her public statement about European antiquities collecting through this act of vandalism. Thus ended the first excavation in Palestine and Lady Hester's archaeological career. She spent the last twenty years of her life in seclusion in Lebanon, although Tuchman notes that Lady Hester became something of a tourist attraction herself for European travellers.[21]

Amelia Edwards and her First Trip to Egypt

A more constructive figure in the development of Near Eastern archaeology was Amelia Edwards (Fig. 8.1). Throughout the previous chapter, Amelia Edwards's book *A Thousand Miles up the Nile* has been frequently cited as a source on travel to Egypt. She is a nineteenth-century individual worth discussing in significantly more detail in the context of popular understandings of Egypt. In some ways, she is unique in that she had a profound influence on the shape of modern Egyptology. Yet emphasizing her 'uniqueness' masks the ways in which she well represents some of the major issues in the experience of the ancient Near East by Europeans in the nineteenth century. She had no formal training in Egyptology but taught herself after a trip. She was the driving force behind the creation of a scholarly society devoted to the study of Egypt (the Egypt Exploration Fund). She wrote a semi-scholarly (but accessible) discussion of ancient Egypt, explored through the framing narrative of the travel genre, and she wrote numerous articles (signed and unsigned) in the periodical press. She collected antiquities and became deeply concerned for the destruction of Egypt's cultural heritage. Edwards was also interested in issues of race and progress and approached world history through a unilinear cultural evolutionary framework.

For Amelia Edwards, one trip to Egypt in 1873, at the age of forty-two, changed the course of her life. Edwards was a gifted writer, who, by the time she first visited Egypt, had written numerous novels and articles for various periodicals, many of which she illustrated herself.[22] Never having married and not having any family money, she made her living as a pro-

---

20. Silberman, *Digging for God and Country*, 26.

21. Barbara W. Tuchman, *Bible and Sword: England and Palestine from the Bronze Age to Balfour* (New York: Ballantine Books, 1984 [1956]), p. 168.

22. Much has been written on Edwards, but to those desiring an extended treatment of her life the following are recommended: For those interested in a detailed account of her life, see Brenda Moon, *More Usefully Employed: Amelia B. Edwards, Writer, Traveller, and Campaigner for Ancient Egypt* (Egypt Exploration Society Occasional Publication, 15; London: Egypt Exploration Society, 2006); for those preferring a thorough

8. *From Tourist to Scholar*

Fig. 8.1. Amelia Edwards. From Amelia Edwards, *A Thousand Miles up the Nile* (London: George Routledge & Sons, 1899 [1881]), frontispiece.

fessional writer, and the decision to transform herself into an Egyptologist could not have been made lightly. Edwards's first contribution to Egyptology was a travel novel called *A Thousand Miles up the Nile* (1877), which is still read today, although in general her works, unlike those of many of her contemporaries, have not survived in the popular literary consciousness.

Like many Europeans and North Americans do on their first visit to Egypt, Edwards claimed to have felt at home immediately upon arrival. She writes that Wilkinson's *Manners and Customs of the Ancient Egyptians* (see Chapter I.10) had inspired her at a very young age.[23] Remarking on her familiarity with the art in the tombs at Thebes, Edwards writes, referring to Wilkinson's book:

> I had read every line of the old six-volume edition over and over again. I knew every one of the six hundred illustrations by heart. Now I suddenly found myself in the midst of old and half-forgotten friends. Every subject

discussion of Edwards's literary production, see Joan Rees, *Amelia Edwards: Traveller, Novelist and Egyptologist* (London: Rubicon Press, 1998).

23. Amelia Edwards, *A Thousand Miles up the Nile* (London: George Routledge & Sons, 1899 [1881]), p. 415. Rees argues that this directly contradicts Edwards's earlier claims in the books to have come to Egypt almost accidentally, attempting to escape bad weather in Europe. See Joan Rees, 'Preparing to be an Egyptologist: Amelia Edwards Before 1873', in *Egypt through the Eyes of Travellers* (ed. Paul Starkey and Nadia el Kholy; Durham: ASTENE, 2002), pp. 39-44 (41). See also Moon, *More Usefully Employed*, pp. 112-14, 117, about Edwards's long-term planning for the trip (despite Edwards's seeming claims to the contrary in *Thousand Miles*).

> on these walls was already familiar to me. . . . It seemed to me that I had met all these kindly brown people years and years ago—perhaps in some previous stage of existence; that I had walked with them in their gardens; listened to the music of their lutes and tambourines; pledged them at their feasts.[24]

This is a different reaction to Egypt than could have been expected even thirty years earlier. By the 1870s, ancient Egypt had entered into the common knowledge of educated and semi-educated Europeans, and although most would not have had the level of familiarity that Edwards claims, undoubtedly, the Egyptian materials would no longer have seemed so alien.

On this trip 'up the Nile', Edwards was accompanied by a number of companions, including the English painter Andrew MacCallum and his friends, and the twenty-five-member party journeyed to Abu Simbel by *dahabiyya*. Rather than take the short three-week trip offered through Cook's tours, Edwards and her companions proceeded slowly, with her attempting to visit the ancient monuments in as close to chronological order as possible, despite this not being the most geographically convenient route.[25] Biographers are able to reconstruct her route through comparison of *A Thousand Miles* with diaries and letters, and other material written by those who accompanied her. The diary of her maid, Jenny Lane, has been especially useful in reconstructing Edwards's otherwise undocumented trip through Palestine immediately following the Egyptian journey.[26] Given that no mention is made of this trip in Edwards's writing, one must conclude that she found the Holy Land far less inspirational.

Of particular note is the group's visit to Abu Simbel (Fig. 8.2), which lasted a few weeks (interspersed by a journey farther south), where McCullum discovered a previously unknown sanctuary, the existence of which he reported in a letter to *The Times* (printed as an appendix to the book). The account of this amateur archaeological investigation is one of the longest in the book, and provides a break in the narrative of travelling up and down the Nile. Edwards provides an account of McCullum's initial discovery, the excitement inspired in the party, and the first attempts by the group to excavate the site (referred to as the *speos* throughout). Once it becomes clear that they cannot excavate the full site by themselves, the group hires locals to assist them (and the issues surrounding the negotiations of salary are described with good humour). The party is said to have inscribed their names on the wall in typical Victorian fashion but atypical

---

24. Edwards, *Thousand Miles*, p. 415.
25. Edwards explains her rationale for this with the analogy that Egypt is a book and that visiting monuments out of historical order is like reading a book backward (*Thousand Miles*, pp. 69-70).
26. Moon, *More Usefully Employed*, pp. 131-32.

Fig. 8.2. 'The great rock-cut tomb of Nubia [Abu Simbel]'. From Amelia Edwards, *A Thousand Miles up the Nile* (London: George Routledge & Sons, 1899 [1881]), frontispiece.

of Edwards's usual approach to the antiquities (suggesting that Edwards's later concern for this type of vandalism had not yet been fully realized). Edwards provides more than just a narrative of their excavation adventure. She provides a detailed description of the site, including a floor plan (Fig. 8.3) and measurements as well as a description of the artistic program in the complex. Her illustrations of some of the hieroglyphs are accurate and accompanied by a translation by the Keeper of Egyptian Antiquities at the British Museum, Samuel Birch (modified by E.A. Budge, his successor, in the second edition). Thus in the middle of this travel novel intended for popular audiences is something more resembling a preliminary site report.

The fusion of different genres is not unique to her book and, as has been discussed, is typical of the early semi-scholarly works on the ancient Near East (such as Belzoni's, Robinson's and Layard's; see Chapter I.3). *A Thousand Miles* is a purposeful blend of genres, mixing a traditional travel narrative with information derived from then-current scholarly reports on the antiquities of Egypt. Moon suggests that Edwards likely had not intended to produce as complicated a work in her initial travels to Egypt, but while in Egypt, had been moved to write a book that would inspire people to make an effort to help preserve Egyptian antiquities.[27] To do so successfully required significantly more research on her part, and Edwards began an informal process of mastering the scholarly literature on Egypt and corre-

---

27. Moon, *More Usefully Employed*, p. 135.

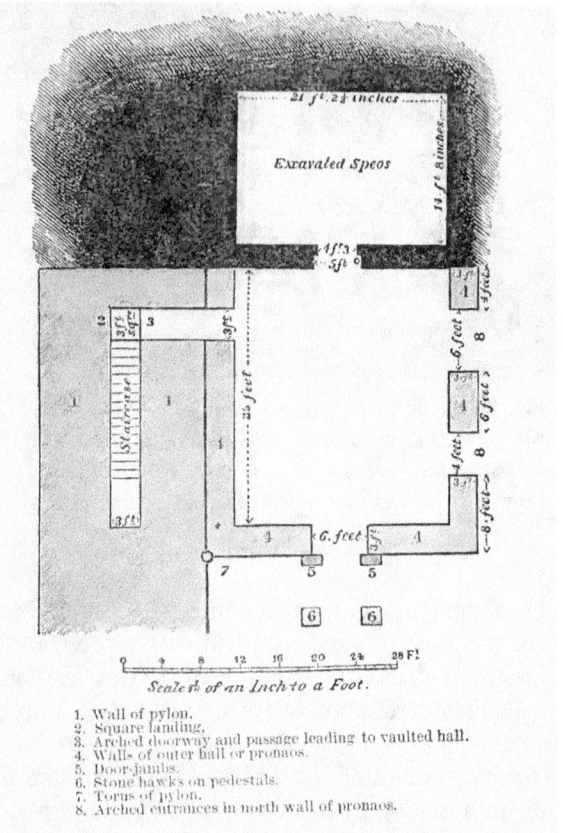

Fig. 8.3. 'Floor plan of the Speos'. From Amelia Edwards, *A Thousand Miles up the Nile* (London: George Routledge & Sons, 1899 [1881]), p. 307.

sponding with the leading figures of the time (such as Gaston Maspero and Samuel Birch).[28]

The blend of academic and popular approaches to writing is arguably most apparent in her discussion near the beginning of the book of the Serapeum at Saqqarah.[29] In this section, Edwards discusses the excavation of the site by Mariette and references to the temple made by Strabo. She describes

---

28. For an amusing (and telling) discussion of Edwards's correspondence with Birch (documenting her somewhat forward queries and his less-than-friendly replies), see Moon, *More Usefully Employed*, pp. 136-39, 140-41.

29. The Serapeum at Saqqara was the site of the burial of the Apis bulls, sacred bulls related to the god Ptah (and Osiris from the Hellenistic period onward). Edwards's discussion of the complex can be found in Edwards, *Thousand Miles*, pp. 53-59.

the layout of the temple and its present condition. She also writes about some of the finds made there, referring the reader to the museum in Vienna, to which some of the artifacts had been removed. She includes a discussion of Egyptian chronology and provides historical notes as well as bibliography for further reading. Interested readers would have enough information to continue their studies of this temple, but those who were less keen would not find the presentation of the information off-putting.

Edwards's treatment of the tomb of Ti at Saqqarah is similarly interesting, although it takes a slightly different form.[30] Along with a description of his tomb and its contents (or at least what had been its contents), Edwards paraphrases the scenes of daily life found in the tomb. For example:

> He was fond of fishing and fowling, and used sometimes to go after crocodiles and hippopotamuses, which came down as low as Memphis in his time. He was a kind husband too, and a good father, and loved to share his pleasures with his family. Here we see him sitting in state with his wife and children, while professional singers and dancers perform before them. Yonder they walk out together and look on while the farm-servants are at work and watch the coming in of the boats that bring home the produce of Ti's more distant lands.[31]

Although such a literal reading of scenes of daily life from Old Kingdom tombs would no longer be held by scholars, Edwards provides a vivid (if rather too idyllic) view of Old Kingdom life as known through its art.

The discussion of historical figures in *A Thousand Miles* is mostly interspersed throughout the narrative, but there is one chapter (chap. 15) that is devoted to Ramses the Great. Given the preponderance of monuments erected by Ramses, it makes sense for her to provide a relatively long excursus on this figure. As Edwards puts it, 'The interest that one takes in Ramses II begins at Memphis, and goes on increasing all the way up the river'.[32] She compares him to other historical personages, such as Pericles, Lorenzo the Magnificent, Henry VIII and Louis XIV and explains that the accounts of Ramses II found in guidebooks are insufficient. She writes:

> the traveller is ill equipped who goes through Egypt without something more than a mere guide-book knowledge of Ramses II. He is, as it were, content to read the Argument and miss the Poem. In the desolation of Memphis, in the shattered splendour of Thebes, he sees only the ordinary pathos of ordinary ruins. As for Abou Simbel, the most stupendous historical record ever transmitted from the past to the present, it tells him a but half-intelligible story. Holding to the nearest thread of explanation, he wanders from hall to hall, lacking altogether that potent charm of foregone asso-

---

30. Also first excavated by Mariette, this is a mastaba tomb from Dynasty V of the Old Kingdom.
31. Edwards, *Thousand Miles,* p. 60.
32. Edwards, *Thousand Miles,* p. 262.

ciation which no Murray can furnish. Your average Frenchman straying helplessly through Westminster Abbey under the conduct of the verger has about as vague a conception of the historical import of the things he sees.[33]

With this as justification, Edwards presents much information about Ramses to supplement guidebook accounts. She explains the different cartouches of Ramses the Great (with transliterations and translations), provides different scholars' suggestions as to the dates of Ramses II's birth and death, gives a basic account of what was known of his life (making reference to the pertinent sources), supplies extensive footnotes discussing different scholarly works on Ramses, makes reference to relevant artifacts in the British Museum and elsewhere and offers a discussion of his possible relationship to the pharaoh of the exodus. At the end of the book, Edwards also provides appendices that readers can use as a reference source for ancient Egypt, including sections on religion (that enumerate the different deities), a section on chronology and extended quotations of relevance from other academic works on Egypt.

Including its scholarly asides, Edwards's book is best understood as typical nineteenth-century travel literature. The travel-writing genre provided a number of possibilities for an intelligent, talented, middle-class woman writer. O'Neill argues that the travel genre provided Edwards with more writing freedom than was typical of Victorian woman novelists. Edwards did not have to worry about character and plot (as she would have had to in a novel), and she did not have to hide the instructive elements of her work.[34] As opposed to more typical travel narratives, which emphasize personal experiences, O'Neill notes that Edwards's book concentrates on scientific descriptions and discussions of the important ancient sites in different regions.[35] Melman notes that the reader learns little about the personal Edwards in the over-five-hundred pages of the book.[36] In order to encourage visitors to Egypt, Edwards purposefully omitted discussions of the discomforts of travel (almost exactly the opposite of the narrative choices made by Belzoni, Robinson and Layard).[37] This omission supports Sarah Mills's argument that women authors 'feminized' their accounts by removing references to travel difficulties since it was not lady-like to have dangerous adventures. For Edwards then, the travel genre is merely a framing mechanism for a discussion of ancient Egypt in a popular tone. After the successful reception of *A Thousand Miles up the Nile*, Edwards had established her reputation as a serious authority on Egypt and was able to dispense with this

---

33. Edwards, *Thousand Miles*, p. 263.
34. O'Neill, 'From Novelist to Egyptologist', p. 166.
35. O'Neill, 'From Novelist to Egyptologist', pp. 167-68.
36. Melman, *Women's Orients*, p. 259.
37. Rees, *Traveller, Novelist and Egyptologist*, p. 40.

framing narrative and write as a journalist, reporting the major Egyptological discoveries of her time. Her writing, likewise, was by this stage well beyond the level of an amateur. As Mills has shown, women's writing, at the time, was expected to be 'amateurish', and so women writers often used the strategy of avoiding scientific or authoritative tones in their work in order to gain acceptance.[38] Yet Melman characterizes Edwards's use of the word 'science' as 'compulsive', reflecting her desire to emphasize her intellectual authority.[39] This freedom to write in a scientific and authoritative manner differs substantially from the experiences of many other Victorian women travel writers. Edwards's undeniable knowledge of the subject eventually facilitated her widespread acceptance, and 'official' acknowledgment came later, with her receiving three honorary degrees.

Despite *A Thousand Miles* being relatively positively reviewed, Brenda Moon has shown that some male reviewers still responded to it in a gendered manner. For example, the review in *The World* describes this as a 'delightful gossiping book', and *The Saturday Review* characterizes her writing as 'easy, good-natured, chatty'.[40] Other gendered elements of the reviews were more problematic. As Mills has shown, one of the legitimate concerns that women travel writers had to face in regards to the reception of their work was that it would be questioned as untruthful. As Mills states, 'women writers are caught in a double-bind situation: if they tend towards the discourses of femininity in their work they are regarded as trivial, and if they draw on the more adventure hero type narratives their work is questioned'.[41] Edwards's works are clearly more set in the adventurous and scientific mode, and the veracity of her earlier works had been questioned by reviewers.[42]

From Professional Writer to Almost Professional Egyptologist

Joan Rees has argued that Edwards's skills as a professional writer were of great use to her in transitioning from being a novelist to an Egyptologist. Rees says that Edwards's understanding of the role of the novel was 'to record life as it is in the author's own time and thereby leave for the future an authentic account of life as the author has directly observed or experienced it'.[43] This belief in the importance of accurately documenting

---

38. Mills, *Discourses of Differences*, p. 83.
39. Melman, *Women's Orients*, p. 261.
40. As cited in Moon, *More Usefully Employed*, p. 141.
41. Mills, *Discourses of Differences*, p. 118.
42. For examples of reviews of Edwards's earlier books in which she is accused of lying, see Moon, *More Usefully Employed*, pp. 109-10.
43. Joan Rees, 'Preparing to Be an Egyptologist: Amelia Edwards before 1873', in *Egypt through the Eyes of Travellers* (ed. Paul Starkey and Nadia el Kholy; Durham: ASTENE, 2002), pp. 39-44 (41).

life was merged with an interest in imaginatively documenting life through prose, which sets her work apart from her contemporaries. Rees cites, as an example, her article on Petrie's expedition to Tanis that appeared in an 1886 issue of *Harper's New Monthly Magazine* in which she describes an imaginary visit of Ramses II to the site as a means of reconstructing the city in the minds of her readers.[44]

Edwards's literary playfulness goes a long way to making *A Thousand Miles* enjoyable for readers, when, in terms of narrative, it is really almost a listing and description of places visited. The pacing of the book and the blending of the academic with the anecdotal facilitate an effortless read. Despite a structure that is relatively repetitive, she alters her approach to the descriptions of the sites in a way that makes them never seem pedantic. For example, she transforms the historical inscriptions of Ramses III at Medinet Habu into a present tense battle scene (providing actual translations of the text in quotation marks):

> Again the king goes forth in his might, followed by the flower of Egyptian chivalry. 'His horsemen are heroes; his foot soldiers are as lions that roar in the mountains'. The king himself flames 'like Mentu in his hour of wrath'. He falls upon the foe 'with the swiftness of a meteor'. Here, crowded in rude bullock-trunks, they seek safety in flight. Yonder their galleys are sunk; their warriors are slain, drowned, captured, scathed as it were, in a devouring fire. 'Never again will they sow seed or reap harvest on the fair face of the earth'.[45]

Immediately following this action-packed narrative, she writes from Ramses III's perspective:

> 'Behold!' says the Pharaoh, 'Behold, I have taken their frontiers for my frontiers! I have devastated their towns, burned their crops, trampled their people under foot. Rejoice, O Egypt! Exalt thy voice to the heavens; for behold! I reign over all the lands of the barbarians! I, King of Upper and Lower Egypt, Ramses III!'[46]

The reader is caught up in Ramses III's narrative in a way that no one likely had been since ancient times. Edwards makes the story come alive, using legitimate translations of the inscriptions and fairly accurate paraphrasing.

She uses a slightly different approach in describing her visit to the Temple of Hathor at Denderah. Using a reader-inclusive first-person plural, Edwards describes a walk through the temple as though she and the reader are walking along with the ancient king and priests. She writes:

---

44. Amelia Edwards, 'The Story of Tanis', *Harper's New Monthly Magazine* 73 (1886).
45. Edwards, *Thousand Miles,* p. 432.
46. Edwards, *Thousand Miles,* p. 432.

> We have hitherto been tracing in their order all the preparations for a great religious ceremony. We have seen the King enter the Temple; undergo the symbolical purification; receive the twofold crown; and say his prayer to each divinity in turn. We have followed him into the laboratories, the oratories, the holy of holies. All that he has yet done, however, is preliminary. The procession is yet to come, and here we have it.[47]

In the next sentence, it is clear that Edwards has been describing the reliefs on the temple walls, and her description continues in a vivid manner that conjures their image better than a mere discussion of the lines of the sculpture:

> Here, sculptured on the walls of this dark staircase, the crowning ceremony of Egypt is brought before our eyes in all its details. Here, one by one, we have the standard-bearers, the hierophants with the offerings, the priests, the whole long, wonderful procession, with the King marching at its head. Fresh and uninjured as if they had but just left the hand of the sculptor, these figures—each in his habit as he lived, each with his foot upon the step—mount with us as we mount, and go beside us all the way. Their attitudes are so natural, their forms so roundly cut that one could almost fancy them in motion as the lights flicker by. Surely there must be some one weird night in the year when they step out from their places, and take up the next verse of their chanted hymn, and, to the sound of instruments long mute and songs long silent, pace the moonlit roof in ghostly order![48]

Her evocation of a ghostly night when the ancient Egyptians live again would never be found in an academic text, yet writing about these reliefs describes without describing in a manner that readers still find powerful more than a hundred years later.

Edwards's writing is far different from the academic writing of other Egyptologists working at the end of the nineteenth century. Her prose has much more in common with Layard and Belzoni than the archaeologists whose work she was writing about. Rees quote a section of a letter in which Edwards explains the differences between her writing and those of her Egyptological contemporaries:

> I study style like a poet; calculating even the play of the vowel sounds and the music of periods. Style is an instrument which I have practiced assiduously, and which I can now play upon. But our Egyptologists . . . what do they know of that subtle harmony? They have never flung themselves into the life of love of imaginary men and women; they have never studied the landscape painting of scenery in words; they have no notion of the art, the dexterity, the ear required for musical English; they have no time for such

---

47. Edwards, *Thousand Miles,* pp. 129-30.
48. Edwards, *Thousand Miles,* p. 130.

things. It is not their vocation. I am the only romanticist in the world who is also an Egyptologist.⁴⁹

Only a few years earlier, Edwards would not have been able to make this claim because Belzoni, Layard and others were nothing if not romantics. Yet by the time Edwards had begun working, the gulf between popular approaches to the ancient Near East and academic approaches had grown dramatically. O'Neill argues that Edwards's use of the genre of travel writing as the medium for her exploration of ancient Egypt enabled her to 'assert her authority in the field of scientific exploration' yet still write in a popular genre.⁵⁰ This is consistent with how the travel genre was used by both Belzoni and Layard in their publications of their 'excavations'. Neither had any particular training in the ancient Near East, and by framing their accounts as travel adventure stories, they were able to side step their lack of scholarly pedigrees.

Feminist readings of travel writing, like those of Sara Mills, emphasize the difference in voice, especially in terms of colonialism, between the writings of men and of women.⁵¹ Mills demonstrates that the discursive positions of male and female writers in the nineteenth century were different enough to impact both the production and reception of their writing. For many women, the Victorian expectation that they should write about family life and manners influenced the subject matter of their travel accounts. Some scholars have been surprised that this does not seem to have been the case in Edwards's writing, particularly in her seeming lack of interest in Egyptian domestic life.⁵² Melman convincingly argues that Edwards's lack of interest in this subject may reflect an attempt to 'degender' her narrative.⁵³ However, it is just as likely that this subject did not interest her.

The Protection of Antiquities, the Establishment of the Egypt Exploration Fund, and the Lecture Circuit

Writing was not Edwards's only contribution to Egyptology. She was one of the co-founders of the Egypt Exploration Fund (EEF; known today as the Egypt Exploration Society), in which she served as honorary joint secretary for the remainder of her life. The fund began officially in 1882. It had

---

49. As quoted in Rees, 'Preparing to be an Egyptologist', p. 43. The letter was originally published in William Copley Winslow, 'The Queen of Egyptology', *The American Antiquarian* 14 (1892).

50. O'Neill, 'From Novelist to Egyptologist', p. 165.

51. Mills, *Discourses of Differences*.

52. See, for example, Melman, *Women's Orients*, p. 262.

53. Melman, *Women's Orients*, p. 263. O'Neill follows this reading; see O'Neill, 'From Novelist to Egyptologist', p. 169.

originated as an idea of hers in correspondence with Gaston Maspero while checking details for *A Thousand Miles up the Nile*. Samuel Birch of the British Museum was not particularly supportive of the organization, but others were; and by 1883 she had begun selling memberships in the United States as well.[54] Under her, William Flinders Petrie was supported by the EEF. He was not necessarily popular with other members but made foundational contributions to the field, and Edwards's support was instrumental in his success.

One of Edwards's great concerns was the impact of tourism and development on Egyptian antiquities. The preservation of ancient Egypt's material remains in the face of these threats is a dominant trend in contemporary Egyptology, and this is in no small part due to the concern that she showed for this issue, acting as an advocate for the monuments. By popularizing these issues and attracting interest in the science of conservation, Edwards made a lasting impression on the field. This concern is evident in, for example, how she worries about the ravages of time and other destructive forces at the Temple of Hathor at Denderah, noting significant changes since Ampère visited thirty years earlier.[55] Edwards's approach was new in that it recognized that European valuation of antiquities was, ironically, driving the destruction of those same antiquities. Earlier archaeologists had justified their removal of antiquities from the countries of origin through arguments of protection, but with little hint of recognition that their actions perpetuated this destruction.

One of Edwards's most successful methods of advocacy for Egyptian antiquities was through her popular reports in the periodical press, which were quite prolific. Moon has quantified these contributions; between 1877 and 1891, Edwards wrote over one hundred signed articles for *The Academy* (and numerous unsigned ones), seventy-four unsigned articles to *The Times*, as well as sporadic articles in other publications.[56] In 1886, Edwards gave her first public lecture on Egyptological matters, at the Orientalists' Congress in Vienna. From this point forward, she recognized the public lecture as a less onerous means than writing for disseminating Egyptological

---

54. As has already been commented on, Birch was hostile toward the EEF, due to its inclusivity of amateurs and the prominence of a female founder. It may also have been due to his frustration with the growing trend of antiquities being given to the Egyptian Museum at Boulak (instead of the British Museum). So Birch's unfriendly relationship with Mariette may also have been part of the problem. In a letter to Edwards, he writes: 'The first step towards a successful advocacy is to ascertain that the results of the excavations will be sent to the British Museum not that of Boulaq, the ultimate destiny of which is not clear. A public subscription in these bad times would be quite inadequate and better days must be waited for' (as cited in Moon, *More Usefully Employed*, p. 161).

55. Amelia Edwards, *Pharaohs, Fellâhs, and Explorers* (London: Harper & Brothers, 1891), p. 123.

56. Moon, *More Usefully Employed*, p. 182.

information to the public. Arguably, her greatest popular success at this was in her tour of the United States, begun in 1889. Rees describes the response to Edwards in America: 'She was to receive recognition and acclaim in America unmatched at any other time in her career and the tour, which lasted through into 1890, became nothing short of a triumphal progress'.[57] Modified versions of these lectures are collected in *Pharaohs, Fellâhs, and Explorers* (1891).

Edwards's lectures were surprisingly detailed, given that they were aimed at popular audiences; however, they are written in a lively conversational style that, despite their academic subject matter, makes them quite easy to follow. The lectures preserved in *Pharaohs* consist of a general introduction to exploration in Egypt, a more detailed report on the results of the EEF-funded excavations in Egypt (by Naville and Petrie), three lectures on Egyptian art, a lecture on literature and religion, a lecture on Hatshepsut and a lecture on the hieroglyphic writing system. The lecture on hieroglyphs is surprisingly complex; Edwards provides an overview of the basic grammatical structure of Middle Egyptian (as it was understood at the time) and works through the meaning of a number of signs, showing how they can be combined into meaningful words.

Edwards explicates the specific skills that an Egyptian explorer (she does not use the term Egyptologist) required, skills such as trigonometry, which allowed for accurate surveying.[58] Similarly, Egyptian explorers, in Edwards's description, needed to have a good scholarly knowledge of all of the ancient cultures that interacted with Egypt, since, as she describes, an archaeologist could come across a cache of cuneiform tablets (as at Amarna), a 'Jewish' cemetery (as at Tell el Yahûdieh), or Greek materials (as at Naukratis).[59] None of these skills enumerated by Edwards may seem strange now, but this reflects a profound change in the understanding of who should be involved in work in Egypt. The recognition that an Egyptologist required specific academic skills (if not specific types of university-based training per se) reflects a fundamental shift from the earlier part of the nineteenth century and the backgrounds of individuals like Belzoni.

Besides these kinds of academic skills, Egyptian explorers needed other personal traits: 'In the first place, the explorer in Egypt must have a fair knowledge of colloquial Arabic, no small share of diplomatic tact, a strong will, an equable temper, and a good constitution'.[60] Indeed, as Edwards describes, there is still a heroic element to Egyptology, and the traits needed to be successful are not traits that can necessarily be learned in the classroom. She describes:

57. Rees, *Traveller, Novelist and Egyptologist*, p. 61.
58. Edwards, *Pharaohs*, p. 23.
59. Edwards, *Pharaohs*, p. 22.
60. Edwards, *Pharaohs*, p. 22.

After this, it must I think be admitted that the explorer, like the poet, is 'born, not made'. The wonder perhaps is that he should ever be born at all. Fortunately, however, for the cause of knowledge, this phenomenal individual does from time to time make his appearance upon earth; and according to the form he assumes under different *avatars*, he proceeds to excavate Troy, Curium, Halicarnassus, Nineveh, Bubastis, or Naukratis.[61]

This statement is very interesting, even though it was probably written as a kind of off-hand conclusion to the lecture. The heroic nature of archaeology is made explicit here, with archaeologists being afforded a near semi-divine status by her use of the Hindu term *avatar* (since it obviously would not yet have had the cyber-culture connotations that it took on in the 1980s). Archaeologists such as Schliemann, Layard and Petrie were a manifestation of brilliance deserving of celebration.

By her 1890 tour, Edwards could argue that archaeology had become a specialized discipline. It was no longer a merely antiquarian enterprise nor was it just an approach to history that uses material culture instead of documents. Rather, at least in Edwards's description, it has taken on the features of a multidisciplinary social science. She writes:

It must be remembered, first of all, what that science is, or rather that aggregate of sciences, which goes by the name of Archaeology. Were I asked to define it, I should reply that archaeology is that science which enables us to register and classify our knowledge of the sum of man's achievement in those arts and handicrafts whereby he has, in time past, signalized his passage from barbarism to civilization.[62]

In this description of archaeology, she makes reference to registration and classification, and although not explicitly stating as much, is referring to the new approach to the handling of antiquities, especially as manifest in the work of her protégé, Flinders Petrie. Similarly, archaeology's role in anthropology is articulated, and its ability to make sense of past cultures within the framework of unilinear cultural evolution is referenced.

Indeed, much of the analysis presented in her popular lectures reflects a concern to make sense of human cultures (and races) through the perspective of unilinear cultural evolution and progress. Throughout her lectures, Edwards emphasizes the 'sameness' of different cultures at certain stages of evolution. For example, about art, she explains:

The beginnings of pictorial art in all nations, at all periods, are curiously alike. The archaic tyro tries his 'prentice hand' on the same subjects; he encounters the same difficulties; he meets those difficulties in the same way; he commits the same blunders. Egyptian, Assyrian, Etruscan, Greek, repeat one another. They all draw the face in profile, and the eye as if seen

---

61. Edwards, *Pharaohs*, p. 26.
62. Edwards, *Pharaohs*, p. 24.

from the front. They all represent the feet planted on precisely the same line. They all color in flat tints, and are alike ignorant of light and shade, of foreshortening and perspective.[63]

Here, early art is described not in terms of having style in its own right but rather as not having developed techniques and skills yet. Likewise, she devotes an entire lecture to illustrating what the Greeks learned from the Egyptians. This type of evolutionary approach is manifest even when she discusses Egypt without cross-cultural reference. On the Egyptian language she writes, 'The Egyptian grammar is of most elementary barrenness. Its structure, as compared with the grammar of other languages, is like the structure of the polyp as compared with the complex organism of the higher animals.'[64] About tomb art found at Giza, she says, 'The heads of all these Fourth Dynasty personages are marked by that child-like simplicity which distinguishes the archaic school. . . .'[65] Here the analogy that cultures move through developmental stages as humans do is made explicit, and despite the fact that the Fourth Dynasty was the period of the construction of the pyramids at Giza, the work of the artists is still described as child-like.

Edwards continues her statement about the child-like simplicity of the Giza artists by commenting on how this art can help one understand the race of the Egyptians. According to Edwards, the artistic heads of the Fourth Dynasty personages 'place before us with much fidelity the ethnological type of the earliest Egyptians. There is not a drop of negro blood in this race. Their noses are slightly arched; their lips are full and well turned; their chins are short; their jaws are delicate; their heads high, and well rounded.'[66] Throughout the lectures, Edwards attempts to make sense of ancient Egyptian materials through nineteenth-century racial categories. This is perhaps most evident in her discussion of Fayûm mummy portraits, in which she categorizes the mummies into these groups based on physical attributes. For example, she describes one individual (named in the Greek label as Diogenes of the Flute of Arsinoe) as follows: 'The hair is very thick and curly, and the features are distinctly Jewish in type. That he should be a Jew would be quite in accordance with his profession for the gift of music has ever been an inheritance of the children of Israel.'[67] Elsewhere in her lectures, Edwards uses suspect biological reasons to explain perceived physical differences between ancient and nineteenth-century Egyptians: 'Long

63. Edwards, *Pharaohs*, pp. 73-74.
64. Edwards, *Pharaohs*, pp. 259-60. She follows this with a humorous aside, stating: 'It must not be supposed for a moment that the rudimentary character of the Egyptian grammar helps to make it one jot easier. On the contrary, it would be a great deal easier if it were a little more difficult.'
65. Edwards, *Pharaohs*, p. 137.
66. Edwards, *Pharaohs*, p. 137.
67. Edwards, *Pharaohs*, p. 105.

admixture with Asiatic blood has so thinned down the race that a fat native is now one of the rarest of Egyptian curiosities; but elderly men of very comfortable proportions are frequently represented in the sculptures of the early school'.[68] Hints of her acceptance of nineteenth-century views on race and biology can be found in *A Thousand Miles* as well, where she makes the claim that foreigners cannot successfully breed in Egypt.[69]

While Edwards did not work from the kind of racially superior standpoint as people like Morton, who attempted the same type of categorization, she still demonstrates the urge to create hierarchies of races and world cultures. Indeed, her 'anthropological' analysis of the Fayûm portraits ends with a comment on how these ancient racial types relate to those (thought-to-be) present in the nineteenth century:

> One very striking feature of the Fayûm portraits is the modern character of the heads. There is not a face in the whole series which we may not meet any day in the streets of London or New York. There is nothing to surprise us in this fact. . . . The truth probably is that as regards features, stature, and complexion, the ancient Egyptians differed very little, if at all, from the Copts of the present day; and that the Greeks and the Romans of the classic period were actually more like the people of northern Europe than are their modern descendants. Hadrian, Marcus Aurelius, Lucius Verus, and many other noble Roman who yet lives in marble and bronze, far more nearly resembles the type of modern Englishman than that of the modern Italian. Seneca, Germanicus, and Julius Caesar might pass for typical Americans. Past or present, we are in truth but members of one great family . . . the paintings of the four races of men in the tombs of the kings at Thebes. And in these we see depicted racial types which survive unchanged to the present day in Nubia and Palestine.[70]

Here, then, Edwards repeats to popular audiences the kinds of equations between ancient and modern cultures that were *au courant* in Britain in the nineteenth century. The Romans were not racially Italians, according

---

68. Edwards, *Pharaohs*, p. 139.

69. Edwards writes: 'Subdued again and again by invading hordes; intermixed for centuries together with Phoenician, Persian, Greek, Roman, and Arab blood, it fuses these heterogeneous elements in one common mould, reverts persistently to the early type, and remains Egyptian to the last. So strange is the tyranny of natural forces. The sun and soil of Egypt demand one special breed of men, and will tolerate no other. Foreign residents cannot rear children in the country. In the Isthmus of Suez, which is considered the healthiest part of Egypt, an alien population of twenty thousand persons failed in the course of ten years to rear one infant born upon the soil. Children of an alien father and an Egyptian mother will die off in the same way in early infancy, unless brought up in the simple native fashion. And it is affirmed of the descendants of mixed marriages, that after the third generation the foreign blood seems to be eliminated, while the traits of the race are restored in their original purity' (Edwards, *Pharaohs*, p. 104).

70. Edwards, *Pharaohs*, p. 112.

to this viewpoint; rather, they were more closely aligned to the British and northern Europeans who colonized the United States. The ancient Egyptians, however, were an exotic other, preserved as the modern-day Coptic community in Egypt (but not, at least racially, in the Muslim inhabitants of Egypt).[71] Nubians and people of Palestine have remained unchanged since ancient times.

Edwards's sense of cultural evolution presents a framework for understanding the Egyptians. This is most evident when she uses ethnological comparison to understand Egypt's prehistoric past. For example, when she discusses the history of Egyptian religion, she says:

> As a matter of fact, the barbarian origin of the Egyptians is more distinctly traceable than the barbarian origin of any other highly civilized nation of antiquity. It is traceable in their laws, in their customs, and even in their costumes. Above all, it is traceable in their religion. We have but to turn our eyes to the far West of America in order to discover the living solution of some of our most puzzling Egyptian problems. Just as the northern half of that great continent was originally possessed by tribes of Indians, so the land of Egypt, in the ages before history, was divided into many small territories, each territory peopled by an independent clan. The red man had, and has, his 'totems', or clan crests; these 'totems' being sometimes animals, as the bear, the wolf, the beaver, the deer; and sometimes birds, as the snipe, the hawk, the heron. So, in like manner, the prehistoric tribes of ancient Egypt will have had their 'totems', taken from the familiar beasts, birds, and reptiles of the Nile Valley—the jackal, the crocodile, the ibis, and so forth.[72]

Despite the distance in time and space, prehistoric Egypt is understood through analogy with Native American culture. This 'totemism' is understood as an early stage in the evolution of Egyptian religion. However, in Edwards's mind, the evolution of Egyptian religion is traceable historically. She discusses:

> But, having started from totemism, animal worship, and polytheism, did they not rise at last to higher things—to monotheism, pure and simple? Yes; they did rise to monotheism; but not, I think, to monotheism pure and

---

71. She makes similar comments in *A Thousand Miles*. She writes: 'And this is a Copt; a descendent of the true Egyptian stock; one of those whose remote ancestors exchanged the worship of the old gods for Christianity under the rule of Theodosius some fifteen hundred years ago, and whose blood is to be purer of Mohammedan intermixture than any in Egypt. Remembering these things, it is impossible to look at him without a feeling of profound interest. It may be only fancy, yet I think I see in him a different type to that of the Arab—a something, however slight, which recalls the sculptured figures in the tomb of Ti' (Edwards, *Pharaohs*, p. 80).

72. Edwards, *Pharaohs*, p. 229.

simple. Their monotheism was not exactly our monotheism: it was a monotheism based upon, and evolved from, the polytheism of earlier ages.[73]

Edwards picks up on this nineteenth-century notion that an advanced culture is one that embraces monotheism. Yet she is clear to differentiate Egyptian monotheism from Christianity. She states:

> In a word, it is certain—absolutely certain—that every great local deity was worshipped as the 'one God' of his own city or province; and it is also certain that, to whatever extent these gods were identified one with another, the Egyptians never agreed to abolish their Pantheon in favor of one, and only one, supreme deity.[74]

Thus the Egyptians, while advanced, were not as advanced in their evolution as Christians. Yet she does credit them as the first culture to identify the immortality of the soul and speaks highly of their ethics. Based on her analysis of the *Book of the Dead*, she explains:

> It gives the measure of their standard of morality. The teachers who established that standard, and the people who endeavored faithfully to live up to it, may have had very childish and fantastic notions on many points; they may in one place have put gold rings in the ears of their sacred crocodiles; they may have shaved their eyebrows when their cats died; but as regards uprightness, charity, justice, and mercy, they would not, I think, have much to learn from us, if they were living to this day beside the pleasant waters of the Nile.[75]

Thus the ancient Egyptians were both child-like and advanced, a step on the way to civilization but primitive nonetheless.

Edwards does not really present a coherent comparison of the relative level of advancement of ancient Egypt to modern Egypt. In the preface to the first edition of her *A Thousand Miles up the Nile*, she argues that Egypt has remained relatively unchanged since ancient times:

> I must, however, add that I brought home with me an impression that things and people are much less changed in Egypt than we of the present day are wont to suppose. I believe that the physique and life of the modern Fellâh is almost identical with the physique and life of that ancient Egyptian labourer we know so well in the wall-paintings of the tombs.[76]

Despite her comments elsewhere about the racial differences between ancient and modern Egyptians, here she suggests that the society is so unchanging that it preserves even the physical features of the inhabitants. Both of these societies are dramatically different from nineteenth-century

---

73. Edwards, *Pharaohs*, p. 230.
74. Edwards, *Pharaohs*, p. 231.
75. Edwards, *Pharaohs*, p. 233.
76. Edwards, *Pharaohs*, p. xii.

European society, and that difference is marked mostly by the degree of modern complexity. She argues that these differences make it difficult to understand ancient society. She writes, 'Our own habits of life and thought are so complex that they shut us off from the simplicity of that early world'.[77] For the twenty-first-century reader, Edwards's off-hand discussions of race and progress reflect quite a disjuncture from the rest of her lectures, which concentrate on close analyses of specific artifacts. Yet these two distinct subjects were fully entangled in her thinking about antiquities, and fundamentally, her calls for the preservation of Egypt's past cannot be separated from her cultural-evolutionary beliefs about race.

Edwards's presentations of Egyptological discoveries to popular audiences often provided means for understanding those discoveries within the context of British society. For example, in an unpublished lecture on 'The Social and Political Roles of Women in Ancient Egypt', Edwards uses the opportunity of lecturing on ancient women to comment on contemporary women's issues. Over the course of that lecture, she explored the relative backwardness of English law over property rights in marriage in comparison to ancient Egyptian law, vis-à-vis the rights of women.[78] Likewise, Edwards's lecture on Queen Hatshepsut (rendered Hatasu in the lecture) has been understood as a commentary on women's roles in nineteenth-century Britain. Melman argues that Edwards's discussion of Queen Hatshepsut would have been particularly controversial to Victorian audiences.[79] However, this does not take into account the fact that the Victorians were particularly used to the notion of a female monarch (with Victoria as their uncontested sovereign), despite the fact that women were otherwise marginalized in political life. Indeed, Edwards describes Hatshepsut as 'the Queen Elizabeth of Egyptian history'.[80]

Edwards the Collector

Edwards's private collection of Egyptian antiquities was also in keeping with the time.[81] An 1891 autobiographical article called 'My Home Life' (published in *The Arena*) describes the various ancient Egyptian body parts in her home, including two heads that she kept in her bedroom. After her death, Flinders Petrie and her friend Kate Bradbury sorted through her belongings and found Egyptian artifacts squirreled away in every nook of

---

77. Edwards, *Pharaohs*, p. xiv.
78. Both O'Neill and Melman have commented on this particular lecture (O'Neill, 'From Novelist to Egyptologist', p. 171; Melman, *Women's Orients*, pp. 264-69).
79. Melman, *Women's Orients*, p. 266.
80. Edwards, *Pharaohs*, p. 261.
81. Her collection now is held by the Petrie Museum at University College London.

her home.⁸² Despite the lack of display and study space for the objects, her collecting began, at least, as a serious attempt at developing a scholarly collection.⁸³ The beginnings of her impulse toward collecting things Egyptian is already evident in *A Thousand Miles*, where she describes numerous instances of artifact acquisition. For example, in their visit to Elephantine, Edwards and her companions noticed numerous ostraca, clearly written in Greek, strewn about. Unfortunately, in Edwards's view, since none of them could make them out, they assumed that these were of no value and only collected three or four as souvenirs. About these, Edwards writes:

> We little dreamed that Dr. Birch, in his cheerless official room at the British Museum so many thousand miles away, was at this very time occupied in deciphering a collection of similar fragments, nearly all of which had been brought from this same spot. . . . Six months later, we lamented our ignorance and our lost opportunities.⁸⁴

Edwards is disappointed not only for the lost academic opportunity but because these would have been nice additions to her collection.

For Edwards, collecting was a means of preserving Egypt's cultural heritage, not a threat to it as understood by today's standards. The EEF, under her influence, used to fund excavations by rewarding donors with artifactual finds from the excavations.⁸⁵ Edwards's calls for the protection of Egyptian heritage should be seen as part of the process of the professionalization of the field. For she does not call for the end of collecting, only the end of collecting by non-specialists. She does not call for antiquities to be recognized as belonging to the people of modern Egypt. Rather, she articulates the argument that these remnants of ancient Egypt are part of a world history that is best curated by experts. She straddles the amateur–professional distinction; having little formal training herself, she managed to make a career out of Egyptology as a professional writer and lecturer and helped establish some of the infrastructure of professional modern Egyptology. The next chapter, in contrast, examines the works of other travellers, whose approaches have been rejected by Egyptologists, and are disparagingly referred to as 'pyramidiots' by professionals in the field.

---

82. Rees, *Traveller, Novelist and Egyptologist*, p. 91.
83. Eamonn Gearon, 'War and Peace and Travel and Writing: European Exploration in Egypt and the Sudan, 1798–1898', in *Souvenirs and New Ideas: Travel and Collecting in Egypt and the Near East* (ed., Diane Fortenberry; Oxford: ASTENE and Oxbow Books, 2013), pp. 44-54 (50).
84. Edwards, *Thousand Miles*, pp. 181-82.
85. Elaine Altman Evans, 'Edward Libbey: An American Glass Magnate Collects in Egypt', in *Souvenirs and New Ideas: Travel and Collecting in Egypt and the Near East* (ed. Diane Fortenberry; Oxford: ASTENE and Oxbow Books, 2013), pp. 24-38 (30).

9

Science Is Measurement: The First 'Pyramidiots'

> Thus, in the Great Pyramid we see the fountain head of all the ancient metrology subsequent to the Sacred Cubit and the coffer contents, which were used in its predecessor, the Ark of Noah, as well as in its successors, the Tabernacle and the Temple.
> —William Flinders Petrie, 1874[1]

For Egyptologists, amateur enthusiasts (and especially the media treatment of amateur enthusiasts) can be a frustrating distraction from their academic work, especially when the basic premises of amateur studies differ significantly from academic archaeology. Since the 1920s, curses have been used to explain a variety of phenomena, and since the 1970s, aliens have been increasingly argued to be the source of Egyptian technological achievements. The pyramids, however, have been most consistently subjected to idiosyncratic treatment. In the 1970s, for example, the idea that pyramids had some kind of innate power (such as the ability to sharpen dull razor blades through invisible energy) circulated widely, and periodically claims that the pyramids are some sort of power station are made in infotainment settings. It is surprisingly common for amateurs and professionals to hold substantially divergent beliefs in the function and origin of the pyramids. Metrological, mathematical and astronomical interpretations are the basis for many of these alternative interpretations, and the veneer of science seems to convince amateurs that these are legitimate readings. For Egyptologists, these amateurs are known disparagingly as 'pyramidiots'.[2] In the nineteenth century, however, the research strategies that these twentieth-century pyramidiots followed were relatively mainstream. Flinders Petrie

---

1. William Flinders Petrie, *Researches on the Great Pyramid, Or Fresh Connections, Being a Preliminary Notice of Some Facts and a Fuller Statement* (London: Dalton, 1874), p. 57.
2. For a popular account of the history of alternative approaches to understanding the pyramids, see Daniel J. Boorstin, 'Afterlives of the Great Pyramids', *Wilson Quarterly* 16 (1992), pp. 130-38.

(one of the first truly scientific archaeologists) was strongly influenced by his father, who was both a scientist and a lay preacher. His father was himself influenced by the works of Piazzi Smyth and John Taylor and was convinced that the Great Pyramid of Giza in some way manifested a message from God.[3] Petrie himself first visited Giza believing that coded within the structure were secrets about original forms of weights and measurements, and he even published an article on this in 1874. This chapter discusses the most influential of these fringe scholars and the intellectual climate in which their ideas emerged.

Most of these fringe interpretations of the pyramids that centre on measurement can be traced back to the work of Charles Piazzi Smyth (1819–1900). Smyth was a respected scientist at the time, Astronomer Royal of Scotland, who made important contributions to spectroscopy. He was also one of the true fathers of Egyptological pseudoscience. Using the best technology of his day, and basing his arguments off of complex measurements, mathematical calculations and research, Smyth argued that the Great Pyramid was a metrological monument to a divinely inspired measurement system. His books on the subject were immensely popular, and, although rarely read today, his arguments continue to be adapted to suit various pseudoscientific enterprises. Most noteworthy of these, certainly in terms of numbers and durative influence, is the emergence of the Jehovah's Witnesses, the theology of which is partially based upon Smyth's conclusions. Despite the fact that Smyth's contributions to Egyptology have been greatly minimized in Egyptologists' own accounts of their discipline, his influence on the reception of Egypt (especially in relation to the Bible) was quite extensive. Smyth's treatment has been further influential in pseudo-scholarly interpretations of pyramids as worldwide phenomena, although he believed the Great Pyramid was unique among these monuments.

John Taylor and Early Pyramidology

In the preface of his *Life and Work at the Great Pyramid*, Smyth explains that the task of investigating the pyramids at Giza was left to him as a dying request of John Taylor (1781–1864), author of *The Great Pyramid: Why Was It Built, and Who Built It?*[4] Taylor's work can be seen as part of a consistent tradition of thinking about the pyramids since Greek times. He was heavily influenced by Herodotus's description and speculations about

---

3. Dominic Montserrat, *Ancient Egypt: Digging for Dreams* (Glasgow: Glasgow City Council, Cultural and Leisure Services, 2000), p. 6.

4. Charles Piazzi Smyth, *Life and Work at the Great Pyramid; during the Months of January, February, March, and April, A.D. 1865; with a Discussion of the Facts Ascertained*, I (Edinburgh: Edmonston & Douglas, 1867), p. vii.

the pyramids at Giza, and Taylor fully adopted the Greek view that mathematical and other scientific wisdom emerged from Egypt. His familiarity with Renaissance scholarship, both hermetic and scientific, also helped him formulate his approach. One of his Renaissance predecessors, John Greaves (1602–1652), well read in hermetic literature, argued that the Great Pyramid held ancient Egyptian wisdom in the form of a primordial system of measurements. It was only necessary for the scholar to reconstruct the metrological system through calculations based on the dimensions of the pyramid. Isaac Newton used Greaves's measurements taken in Egypt and identified the 'ancient cubit'. From this, Newton hoped to reveal the exact dimensions of Solomon's Temple (but was never able to). So, the idea that the Great Pyramid held metrological secrets had a firm rooting in Renaissance science.

John Taylor never actually visited Giza himself. A poet, essayist and editor, Taylor was the typical man of letters who dabbled in a variety of subjects and interests and made his living through the burgeoning periodical press. He came to the study of the pyramids late in life, in his fifties, but once he started on this path, this became the dominant area of study for his remaining thirty years. His first studies were based on observations that there were considerable inconsistencies with measurements reported for the pyramids. This was explained, logically enough, through the difficulties of measurement at the time, and the fact that as more of the base of the pyramid was cleared, the measurements of area and the size of the base became more accurate.

However, where Taylor began to deviate from normative scientific practice was in his correlation of measurements of the pyramid with other mathematical properties. Taylor looked for coincidences in the measurements and manipulated those figures until patterns emerged. For example, when he divided the perimeter of the base of the pyramid by twice the height of the pyramid, the result was 3.144, which is quite close to π. Using similar types of logic, Taylor showed that the unit of measurement employed in the construction of the pyramid reflected a 366-day year and a knowledge of the circumference of the Earth (as well as knowledge that the Earth is a sphere). The circumference of the Earth was represented by a specific fraction of the actual dimensions of the pyramid. Here is the type of logic that has led people to claim that the size of the base of the pyramid proves that the Egyptians knew the circumference of the Earth or the distance between the Earth and the sun. This kind of approach is fundamental to numerological-pyramidical pseudo-science; one can find numerical correlations by applying various calculations until patterns seem to emerge. Those patterns then become proof of ancient metrological, cosmological or theological knowledge.

Taylor's familiarity with the classics and Renaissance-era science were, in some ways, the inspiration for his 'number-play' approach to the pyramids. Taylor determined that Newton's measurement (of the 'sacred cubit') was correct and that this corresponded with the British inch, which meant that the British inch was no arbitrary figure but an ancient measurement system that had survived from earliest times. Thus British metrology was not just functional; it was sacred and connected Britain directly to ancient Egypt. Britain may have been the home of one of the lost tribes of Israel, and the British inch was proof of that. Taylor was absolutely convinced of the sophistication of the pyramids' measurement systems and of the knowledge of the Earth and astronomy that these measurement systems reflected. The problem for him, a devoted Christian, was to make sense of this incredibly sophisticated structure within the context of an Earth that had only been created four thousand years ago. This meant that the pyramid could only be a few hundred years old at most. It was inconceivable to him that science had developed so quickly, so he postulated that God had given some of the early humans access to divine knowledge. Thus the Great Pyramid was in fact a monument to divine wisdom, and the measurements, as Newton had suggested, were sacred and universal.

For the most part, the Victorian scientific community ignored Taylor's findings. However, Piazzi Smyth, who had the engineering and astronomical background to make him part of the Victorian scientific establishment, was convinced by Taylor's reasoning and followed through with Taylor's work after his death. In the preface to *Our Inheritance*, he notes that Taylor's work was ignored and stated that he wanted to validate his mentor's arguments: 'But Academic Archaeology did not accept it; and meanwhile some portions of the new pathway were so little removed from much of my own scientific professional occupations, that I felt it something like a public duty to examine into the foundation of Mr. Taylor's theory as rigidly and as extensively as I could'.[5] It is Smyth's work that truly popularized these approaches to the pyramids and established much of the basis for later pseudo-scientific and esoteric approaches

Piazzi Smyth Measures the Pyramid

In 1864, Smyth and his wife travelled to Egypt, where they were received by the viceroy and granted twenty men to help with his investigations of the pyramid. He had requested significantly more assistance, but this was enough for him to start work in 1865. Much of the work involved emptying out the interior of the pyramid in order to accurately measure it. He used

---

5. Charles Piazzi Smyth, *Our Inheritance in the Great Pyramid* (London: W. Ibister & Co., new and enlarged edn, 1874), p. vii.

the best surveying and measuring equipment of the day, and gained fairly accurate results. Smyth's goal at Giza was straightforward. He wished to 'go out to the Pyramid and measure it in European fashion'.[6] His specific proposal, made to Auguste Mariette (the French scholar who founded the Egyptian Department of Antiquities, see Chapter III.3), was to clean the interior of the pyramid (to facilitate accurate measurement); to uncover the base of the pyramid; and to sink various shafts, observation passages and channels in order to allow for accurate calculations.[7] Smyth saw the Great Pyramid as a '*contemporary* record of the events of more than four thousand years ago' and 'that its interpretation can be approached directly, by the application of modern exact science alone'.[8] However, since he did not clear the base of the pyramid, all of his results were preliminary. Having booked his return trip in advance, Smyth and his wife were compelled to return home before finishing all of their measurements, although, before leaving, he arranged for others to complete these tasks for him. He analyzed his results at home and presented them in a number of extensive publications. These results were lauded at first, and he was awarded a gold medal by the Edinburgh Royal Society. However, upon the release of his massive three-volume *Life and Work at the Great Pyramid*, the scientific community realized that his analysis was scandalously bad. The measurements may have been fine (although not completely accurate), but the arguments he made from them and the claims he made about ancient Egyptian knowledge could not be upheld.

Piazzi Smyth's *Life and Work at the Great Pyramid* was well suited to a popular audience. The book is divided into three distinct volumes. The first volume is a typical Egyptian travel account, which differed from others of the time only in its emphasis on the kinds of work that Smyth and his team engaged in at the pyramids (and even in this regard, it bears similarities to parts of Belzoni's book). The second volume was a detailed presentation of the data. The third volume was his theoretical and analytical discussion, based on the results of his findings, which also included a brief discussion of Egyptian history. As the book progresses, it departs more and more from mainstream Egyptology. By the third volume, little within would commend itself to the twenty-first-century Egyptologist. However, twenty-first-century alternative theorists will find the 'empirical' basis of many of their own arguments in Smyth's work.

Generally volume I of *Life and Work at the Great Pyramid* is a fairly engaging, but standard, Victorian travel story, about the adventures of Europeans living in Egypt. The book is filled with curious incidents that befell

---

6. Smyth, *Life and Work*, I, p. 4.
7. Smyth, *Life and Work*, I, pp. 7-8.
8. Smyth, *Life and Work*, I, p. xiv.

them and discussions of the bizarre cultural practices of their hosts. Camping in the tombs nearby, Smyth and his wife lived and worked with local Arabs, and much of the humour of the book is typical 'fish out of water' material. There is a chapter, for example, discussing the problems associated with conducting work during Ramadan. Another section discusses what happens in response to a village murder. All of these stories, much more accessible than the many mathematical calculations included later, would have been of great interest to the general reader and likely were highly responsible for the popularity of the book.

One particular incident is indicative of the tone that Smyth uses for these stories of local Egyptian culture. He writes of the discovery of a very large snake that was taken back to camp to be photographed. By the time it was brought back, it was too late to take a photo so they waited until morning. However, upon awakening, Smyth discovers that one of the workers had thrown it into a seventy-foot-deep pit during the night, fearing that the snake's wife would come and kill everyone in camp in vengeance. Smyth concludes the chapter by commenting, 'we began to think that this was a land where, though "Allah" is worshipped by day, the serpent is the power that is feared at night'.[9] These kinds of expositions of 'Mohammedanism' as superstition are riddled throughout. Volume I ends with a comment on their encounters with the nineteenth-century Egyptians. In summing up their experiences, Smyth explains the benefits that his work had brought for the locals:

> But a higher testimony came afterwards from the same worthy American missionary, the Rev. Mr. Lancing, who had been of so much service to us at the beginning of our Egyptian experiences: for he, in returning from a tour among the churches of the Faioum, visited east Tombs within a very few days after we had left; and having had much conversation with the natives, reported subsequently, 'that there was a most perceptible improvement in the manners of the Pyramid Arabs'; and he only 'hoped it might continue'.[10]

Here, Smyth's expedition had performed a civilizing as well as a scientific function.

In retrospect, Smyth's work was obviously flawed, but this was an expedition that was sanctioned by the Egyptian government and Mariette. Smyth, in his first volume, describes the procedures of gaining governmental approval for his work and how the Egyptian authorities equipped his expedition. The acknowledgments at the beginning of the work reflect those of a well-connected lay person; there are few academic acknowledgments but numerous messages of thanks to government officials and wealthy

---

9. Smyth, *Life and Work*, I, p. 424.
10. Smyth, *Life and Work*, I, p. 563.

donors. At the time, though, this was not fringe science. This is the work of a skilled scientist who has genuinely attempted to understand the pyramid through measurement. To put Smyth's work in perspective, one needs to be cognizant of the level of understanding of the pyramids at the time. Knowledge was so minimal that he felt the need to rebut the theory put forward by Johann Vansleb (1635–1679) that the pyramid was merely a rock cut in the shape of a pyramid or that it was actually built atop two hills (which explains the curious interior).[11] Likewise, he, at times, treats classical sources as suspect, for example, arguing against the ancient legend that beneath the pyramid was a complex, underground structure.[12] This skeptical treatment of classical sources, however, was inconsistent.[13] In the book, Smyth evaluates the work and methods of past Egyptological explorers. He argued that Belzoni's approach to Egyptian antiquities was unacceptable, basically calling him a well-intentioned thief (the only difference Smyth saw between him and looters was Belzoni's recognition that it was not just gold that was valuable).[14] Smyth also argues that Colonel Howard Vyse's practice of quarrying into the pyramid at random in the hopes of discovering some clue to follow had left the pyramid permanently disfigured and that such activities should cease.[15]

Biblical Chronology, Archaeoastronomy, and Critical Rejection

What was convincing for many Victorian readers was the serious consideration that Smyth gave to biblical connections with the pyramids and his interest in a literal treatment of biblical chronology. Through Smyth's work, hermetic traditions that treated the Bible as infallible seemed to be supported through scientific analysis, and the Great Pyramid appeared to be a physical sign of God's power. Volume I opens with a quote from the book of Jeremiah (32.18-20): 'The Great, the Mighty God, the Lord of Hosts, is his name; great in counsel, and mighty in work:—which hast set signs and wonders in the land of Egypt, even unto this day'.[16] The implication is clear, that the Great Pyramid of Giza constitutes one of these signs established by the Lord. Indeed, he sees connections between the Great Pyramid and the religion of the early Hebrews. At the end of his preface, he states that

---

11. Smyth, *Life and Work*, I, p. 181.
12. Smyth, *Life and Work*, I, p. 309.
13. For example, he trusts Herodotus's argument that all Babylonian women were compelled to act as temple prostitutes at some point in their lives (Charles Piazzi Smyth, *On the Antiquity of Intellectual Man, from a Practical and Astronomical Point of View* [Edinburgh: Edmonston & Douglas, 1868], p. 77).
14. Smyth, *Life and Work*, I, pp. 9-10.
15. Smyth, *Life and Work*, I, pp. 189-90.
16. Smyth, *Life and Work*, I, facing page 1.

9. Science Is Measurement

the Great Pyramid exhibits 'some remarkable connexions with, as well as dependences on, the religion of Sacred Writ in the Patriarchal times of the world'.[17]

After the initial success of his *Life and Work*, Smyth published a study of archaeoastronomy called *On the Antiquity of Intellectual Man*. This is a comparative work, in which Smyth attempts to compare known examples of ancient architecture for the sake of chronologically related matters and, more importantly, for evidence of knowledge of astronomy and metrology. It is an attempt, he states, to apply the same principles that he used in his study of the Great Pyramid to other buildings of antiquity.[18] For the most part, Smyth merely analyzes buildings discussed in a book by Fergusson, and so the research is not as original (and much more mainstream) than his other works.

He presents some reactions to his critics in *Antiquity*, and here can be seen the first stirrings of controversy that his previous books created. The book begins with a dedication that reads as follows: 'To those few, but earnest, friends who are working with me for the elucidation of the important history and impressive teachings of the Great Pyramid, this book, is affectionately dedicated by Piazzi Smyth'.[19] His bitterness about attacks made on his research in *Life and Work* shows through in the book. In the preface, he talks of the 'vindictive opposition carried on before the Royal Society of Edinburgh'.[20] Later in *Antiquity*, Smyth recalls that meeting in more detail, prefacing this discussion with a comment that academics are afraid of the truth: 'Alas! They have been frightened'.[21] He later likens his treatment to that of a witch trial, writing:

> The fact that Professor Smyth was left alone before the Society, to bear the above torrent of invective—will, in a future day, be looked at in the same manner in which we now regard the records of those old courts of 'justice', where learned judges formally condemned both men and women for allegedly *proved* acts of necromancy, witchcraft, and other really impossible matters; and no one said a word against it.[22]

The scorn shown to his work by the scientific community would only increase.

Following the critical rejection but popular acceptance of *Life and Work*, Smyth produced a single-volume work titled *Our Inheritance in the Great Pyramid*. This book summarizes much of the data and analysis from the

17. Smyth, *Life and Work*, I, p. xiv.
18. Smyth, *Antiquity*, p. v.
19. Smyth, *Antiquity*, p. iii.
20. Smyth, *Antiquity*, p. vii.
21. Smyth, *Antiquity*, p. 355.
22. Smyth, *Antiquity*, p. 357.

previous study, removing the travel account of volume I and the extensive mathematical data of volume II. It is written in a defensive and anti-establishment tone, unlike *Life and Work*. In *Our Inheritance*, his Christian perspective is at the forefront. He also further develops theological arguments based on his data and rejects the criticisms that had been levied at him.

A Monument to Metrology

In all of his books, Smyth's main theory, which has had lasting influence on alternative views of the pyramids, regards their function, which basically follows Taylor. He lays this out in brief in the preface:

> In its [the Great Pyramid's] origin and before it was used for any sepulchral purposes,—a *Metrological* monument; or, a grand commemoration in stone of a truly cosmopolitan system of *weights and measures*: extending through nearly all subjects, such as length, weight, heat [sic], angle, and time; with a wealth too, as well as surpassing power, of exactness of reference to the great standards of Nature,—whether of the earth as a whole, or the processional movements of the starry heavens,—such as may worthily excite the attention, and claim the respect of all the educated amongst mankind.[23]

It is, in some ways, not surprising that a project devoted to measuring the pyramid would find, as its result, that the object being measured was in fact a monument to the act of measurement itself. It is more surprising that Smyth was not self-aware to see the almost tautological reasoning that lay behind this.

As with Taylor, Smyth followed hermetic and Renaissance notions that Egypt was the source of great and primitive wisdom. In this case, the antiquity of Egypt meant that certain primitive truths were known and the construction of the Great Pyramid was still within the timeframe in which God communicated directly with great men. Smyth states this outright, calling the Great Pyramid 'that most authentic book of primeval science'.[24] In *Our Inheritance* (the title itself referring to the divine message of the Great Pyramid), he calls it 'that stone-book of Revelation which stands on the Jeezah hill, open, though hitherto illegible, to all mankind'.[25] Placed in Egypt, at the centre of early civilizations, the wisdom built into its very design was available to anyone, if they had only known, the 'true sun-distance'.[26] Likewise, it is an anthropological monument, and in so far as its design *may* contain a message from heaven to man, touching closely on his personal

---

23. Smyth, *Life and Work*, I, p. xiii.
24. Smyth, *Life and Work*, I, p. 309.
25. Smyth, *Antiquity*, p. 223.
26. Smyth, *Our Inheritance*, p. 53.

welfare and future social and governmental condition upon the earth'.[27] For him, the real value of nineteenth-century science was to 'mainly prove to these latter scientific days of the earth that the building so designed has a right, a title, an authority to speak to men of these times, and even to the most scientific of them, on another and far higher subject'.[28] For Smyth, science is a tool of revelation. And the teaching of science through the Great Pyramid was not its final object either. The pyramid was intended to inform people about the Messiah.[29]

This primeval science is evident, according to Smyth, when one fully understands the significance of the measurements of the pyramids. Smyth elaborates on Taylor's numerological reasoning, and this is the basis of much of his logic. For example, Smyth writes:

> On summing up the whole of the numbers that night [the measurements of the Grand Gallery], they gave 26° 17′ 3″; showing, too, in their details, another illustration of the Great Pyramid having been carefully finished and admirably brought up to truth for final ends and purposes; or on and for the *whole*, rather than for *each* petty and unimportant intervening part;—because, although the differences in the course of the long run of the Gallery were often large, some one way and some another, yet the ends of the Gallery, and on either side, were extraordinarily close to the mean of the whole length.[30]

Here is the kind of 'number play' that fuels much twenty-first-century pseudoscience on the pyramids. Smyth has taken up Taylor's approach to manipulating numbers and uses these manipulations to find 'coincidences' with standard measurements or scales. By doing so, he demonstrates that these are not, in fact, coincidence, but Egyptian wisdom embodied materially. He offers various figures that show that the dimensions of the Great Pyramid reflect knowledge of the Earth and astronomy. The Great Pyramid was built at the exact centre of the Earth (Fig. 9.1). The diameter of the Earth described in Pyramid inches is 499,878,000 or 500,060,000, both figures too exact to be coincidence.[31] The sides of the Great Pyramid are oriented along the directions of the compass.[32]

It is too complex to get into the specific ways that metrology was monumentalized in the Great Pyramid, according to Smyth. Some examples will suffice. He derives time measurements from establishing that the base of the pyramid, in pyramid cubits, corresponds to the numbers of days in a

---

27. Smyth, *Our Inheritance*, p. 47.
28. Smyth, *Our Inheritance*, p. 54.
29. Smyth, *Our Inheritance*, p. 471.
30. Smyth, *Life and Work*, I, p. 310.
31. Smyth, *Our Inheritance*, p. 42.
32. Smyth, *Our Inheritance*, p. 55.

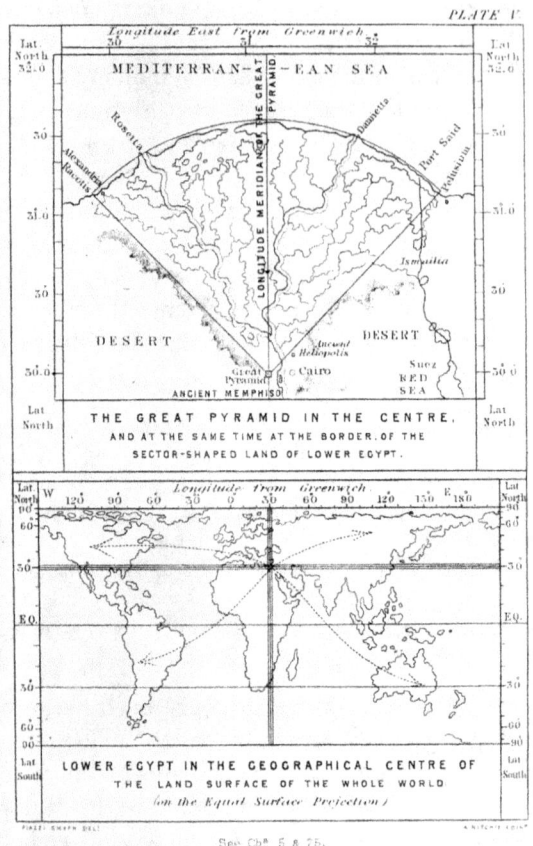

Fig. 9.1. The Great Pyramid in the centre of the world; Piazzi Smyth, *Our Inheritance in the Great Pyramid* (London: W. Ibister & Co., new and enlarged edn, 1874), plate V.

year (accounting for leap years).³³ Or, of even greater significance, and well illustrative of his logic, are his arguments about the relationship between the pyramid and the sun (Fig. 9.2):

> But a still grander time-measure is obtained by viewing the whole Pyramid's base periphery in the light of the equivalent circle, struck with a radius equal to the vertical height of the Pyramid, which by its sun-distance commensurability, symbolizes the sun in the centre of that circle; for then the interval of twenty-four solar hours, or the time elapsing between the sun apparently leaving the meridian of any place and returning to it again,

33. Smyth, *Our Inheritance,* p. 304.

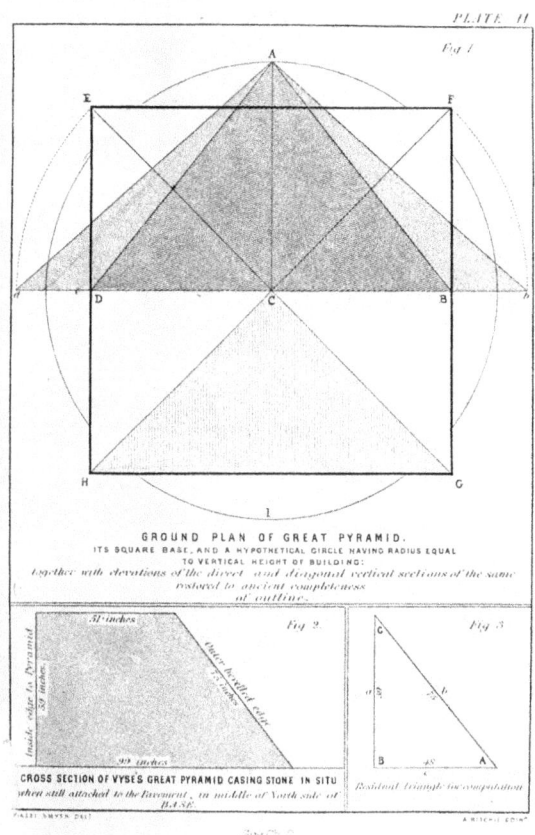

Fig. 9.2. Ground plan of the Great Pyramid; Piazzi Smyth, *Our Inheritance in the Great Pyramid* (London: W. Ibister & Co., new and enlarged edn, 1874), plate II.

by virtue of the rotation of the earth on its axis before the sun, *i.e.*, a mean solar day,—is measured off on that circle's circumference by 100 pyramid inches evenly.[34]

It is the manipulation of numbers to come up with even sums that lies as the basis of his discovery of the Pyramid measurement system. Even the sarcophagus in the King's Chamber is designed as a monument to metrology, being a standard of capacity in the Pyramid measurement scheme.[35] Perhaps most important is the further justification for the measurement of the week in seven days (in sabbatical terms), consistent with that system

34. Smyth, *Our Inheritance*, pp. 304-305.
35. Smyth, *Our Inheritance*, p. 225.

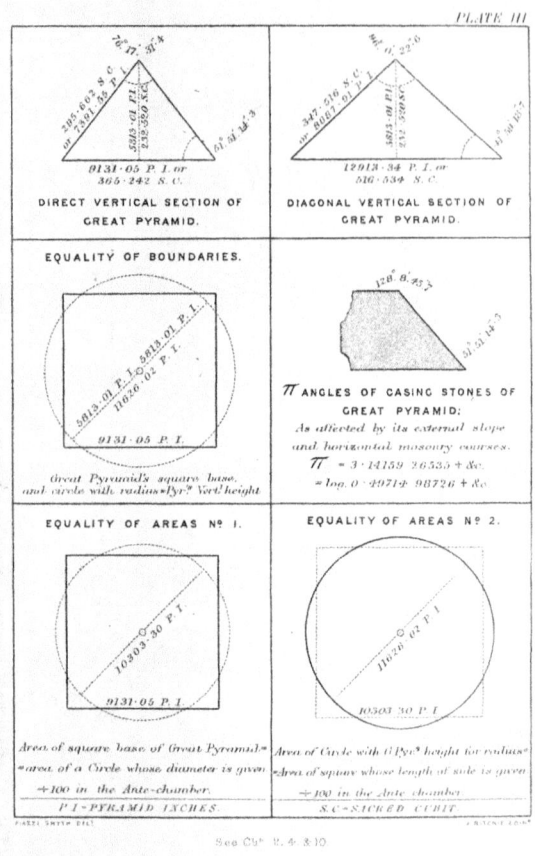

Fig. 9.3. Various measurements including the sacred cubit and the pyramid inch; Piazzi Smyth, *Our Inheritance in the Great Pyramid* (London: W. Ibister & Co., new and enlarged edn, 1874), plate III.

espoused in Genesis. As a calendar system without astronomical justification, this shows true evidence of the divine inspiration of the Great Pyramid. Smyth's demonstration of this is just as forced as most of the rest of his reasoning, but he 'proves' that there is 'sabbatical symbolism' associated with the passage leading to the Queen's Chamber.[36]

That sabbatical symbolism and other biblical connections are going to be a major part of his argument is signaled at the outset of the book. In *Antiquity*, he opens the book with a quote from Daniel, '*Mene, Mene, Tekel, Upharsin*', translating it as 'number, number, weight, division', interpreting

36. Smyth, *Our Inheritance*, pp. 376-78.

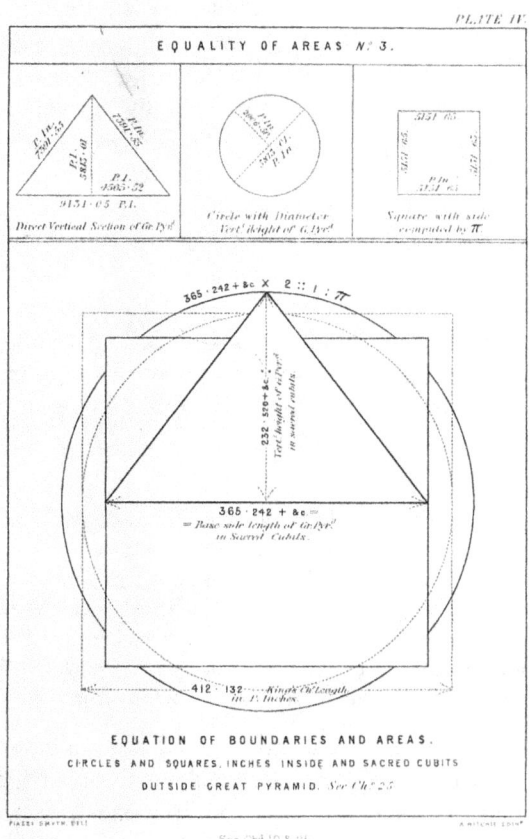

Fig. 9.4. Equality of areas demonstrating the sacred cubit; Piazzi Smyth, *Our Inheritance in the Great Pyramid* (London: W. Ibister & Co., new and enlarged edn, 1874), plate IV.

the writing on the wall literally, implying that the idiomatic interpretation given in the book of Daniel had missed the point of God's message.[37] It is the metrology of the Great Pyramid that is the most important argument in Smyth's work. To make this claim as a committed Christian, Smyth was compelled to make sense of the relationship between Old Testament measurements, ancient Egyptian measurements and the Pyramid measurements that he had 'discovered'. This part of the argument put forward by Smyth is as convoluted as the rest (Figs. 9.3 and 9.4). The Pyramid measurement scheme was essentially the same as that of the ancient Hebrews. However, it

---

37. Smyth, *Antiquity*, p. xx.

was radically different from the mainstream ancient Egyptian measurement system. The Hebrew system was divinely inspired; the Egyptian system was as corrupt as all of the rest of the idolatrous practices of the Egyptians. There is a long discussion of Hebrew metrology in volume II, in which he eventually concludes that the Ark of the Covenant was the divinely inspired standard.[38] Solomon's standardized measurements were based off of the Ark, which aligns with those represented by the Great Pyramid. Here, Smyth embraces Taylor's argument that there is a connection between Newton's sacred cubit and the pyramid inch.

Following Taylor, he also sees a remarkable resemblance between this Hebrew–Pyramid measure and the British inch.[39] This Hebrew system was transmitted to the Anglo-Saxons, and Smyth puts forward an argument about the various connections between the Anglo-Saxons and the Israelites. He summarizes his main argument (based on numerous other authors' suggestions):

> the Hebrew of the English language specially appertains to one tribe of Israel, who never belonged to the kingdom of Judah at all, and were never therefore to be termed Jews; a tribe, indeed, which formed the head of the historical opposition to Judah, viz., Ephraim,—with its capital city of Samaria, and the kings thereof, usually termed Kings of Israel. Hence the Hebraic portions of the Anglo-Saxon language may be called either Ephraimite or Israelite with historical truth, but never Jewish.[40]

Thus, those with Anglo-Saxon roots could claim a biblical and explicitly non-Jewish heritage. In keeping with the mainstream anti-Semitism of Victorian Britain, Israelite was not taken to mean Jewish. With Smyth's emphasis on the connections between Great Britain and the monotheistic, divinely inspired builders of the Great Pyramid, Smyth draws a direct connection between a subgroup within Egypt (and in good primitivist fashion, this is one of the oldest groups in Egypt), the ancient Israelites, and the Anglo-Saxons. Thus Great Britain is peculiarly connected to this ancient knowledge in a way that the rest of Europe is not.

Nationalism plays a role in another of Smyth's arguments. Smyth writes about the three major metrological systems (Egyptian; Hebrew–Pyramid; French):

> For now has it been discovered,—and mainly through the Pyramid investigations,—that not only does the ancient Hebrew standard possess all the earth-commensurabilities claimed for the French metre,—but it possesses

---

38. Smyth, *Life and Work*, II, p. 466.

39. Smyth provides a chart showing that the British measurement system is closest to that of the Pyramid. The French and Turkish systems are the most divergent (Smyth, *Life and Work*, III, p. 595).

40. Smyth, *Life and Work*, III, pp. 587-88.

them in a far higher spirit and of a purer kind: while the Egyptian has nothing whatever of the sort.[41]

Smyth explains that the British system is the closest to the sacred measurement system that was given as divine inspiration to the pyramid builders. But he warns that the British are in danger of abandoning this heritage. Those that accept the yard as an official unit of measurement (the legal unit) are adopting an invention of men, not of God.[42] Similarly, adoption of the French metrological system is a further erosion of British divine heritage.[43] Smyth writes of these dangers:

> How art thou fallen from heaven, O Lucifer, 'son of the morning!' might then indeed be addressed to England with melancholy truth! Or, more plainly, and in words seemingly almost intended for such a case, and uttered with depressing grief of heart, 'O Israel, thou hast destroyed thyself!'[44]

That Smyth should end his nearly 1,800-page, three-volume study on this issue speaks to his passionate concerns regarding the sacred British Pyramid inch.

Smyth continues his argument against the metric system in *Our Inheritance*. Unfortunately (from Smyth's persepctive), no British politician had taken the study of the Pyramid measurement scheme seriously, and so it was not considered in policy discussions.[45] He argues that those that seek profit above all else and are not allowing the British population to have a voice in this destruction of their heritage are pushing through the adoption of the French system.[46] The French system is particularly abhorrent because:

> simultaneously with the elevation of the metrical system in Paris, the French nation . . . did for themselves formally abolish Christianity, burn the Bible, declare God to be a non-existence, a mere invention of the priests, and institute a worship of humanity, or of themselves, under the title of the Goddess of Reason; while they also ceased to reckon time by the Christian era, trod on the Sabbath and its week of seven days and began a new reckoning of time for human history in years of their then new French Republic, and in *decades* of days so as to conform in everything to their own decimal system, rather than to revelation.[47]

---

41. Smyth, *Life and Work*, III, p. 580.
42. Smyth, *Life and Work*, III, p. 597.
43. Smyth, *Life and Work*, III, p. 599.
44. Smyth, *Life and Work*, III, p. 598.
45. Smyth, *Our Inheritance*, p. 445.
46. Smyth, *Our Inheritance*, p. 209.
47. Smyth, *Our Inheritance*, p. 218.

Later, Smyth goes so far as to describe the metric system as a 'nationally suicidal scheme over all the nations of the world'.[48]

Smyth's open disdain for the standardization of the metrical system is based on his idea that metrology is hereditary. As different languages assist in the 'keeping up of the heaven-appointed institution of *nations*;—the chief characteristic of all mankind from the days of the dispersion', so do different measurement systems.[49] The deluge and the destruction of the Tower of Babel were God's answers to earlier attempts at such standardization, and the metric system itself may result in a similar catastrophe.[50] It is difficult to reconcile these arguments with Smyth's argument that the Great Pyramid is a divine monument to standardized metrology available to any who view it properly. It is the fact that the metric system is a human invention that is so appalling to him: 'Neither is it in the power of any scientific men, with all their science up to its very latest developments, to invent a truly national set of weights and measures any more than they can make a national language and a national people'.[51] Luckily enough, the British system is based on the Pyramid system, so retaining the status quo is the safest approach.

The Stirrings of Pseudoscience

What is remarkable in reading Smyth's book today is how similar his work is to what was to come with twenty-first-century popular investigations of the pyramids. He seems to establish some of the major tropes of 'scientific' investigation that are now reserved for documentary makers, journalists and scientists from other disciplines (especially geography and astronomy). The technology that he uses to study the pyramids is presented in greater detail than the results of his work. He writes at length about 'the Playfair', an astronomical instrument that he brought to Egypt to take observations with.[52] Likewise, an entire chapter is devoted to his work on photographing the interior of the pyramid through magnesium photography.[53] Here, European technological heroism is at the forefront of the presentation; scientific instruments facilitate new understandings of the past. The main difference between Smyth's interpretation and twenty-first-century pseudo-scholarship is that God's hand in constructing the pyramids has been replaced by New Age spiritualism, aliens or other esoteric (but non-Christian) forces.

Smyth's activities likewise reflect the kinds of concerns that twenty-first-century non-specialists have with the pyramids. Most of his work involves

48. Smyth, *Our Inheritance*, p. 448.
49. Smyth, *Our Inheritance*, p. 446.
50. Smyth, *Inheritance*, pp. 217, 446.
51. Smyth, *Inheritance*, p. 217.
52. Smyth, *Life and Work*, I, pp. 425ff.
53. Smyth, *Life and Work*, I, pp. 469ff.

measurement, and much of the presentation explains how these are the most sophisticated measurements yet taken. He tries to take the temperature of the interior of the pyramid by dripping water through the air-channels.[54] This does not work, so he concludes that the air-channel is blocked and, as many will do later, approaches the study of these air-chambers through various technologies (to little avail). Smyth is also concerned with the astronomical alignment of the pyramids (which makes sense given his background in astronomy), but, unlike past and later pyramidical astronomers, argues that these were not ancient astronomical observatories.[55]

Of greatest interest to Smyth (and those that followed in his footsteps) was the engineering behind the pyramids. Smyth rhapsodizes about the advanced engineering techniques, marveling at the abilities of the ancient Egyptians. For example, he discusses the entrance passage into the Great Pyramid:

> [E]nter within the actual walls of the passage, and then, see how fine and straight the joints of the masonry courses are there; so straight that no modern optical instrument-maker could work better straight edges, and so close, after four thousand years of wear and tear, expansion and contractions, lightning and earthquake, as to compete with the best of recent work in stone anywhere.[56]

Here is a standard Victorian response to the discoveries of the ancient world—that these cultures were significantly more technologically advanced than was previously thought. For the Victorian scholar and audience, this was also a moral judgment, for technology was seen as virtuous. However, the level of technological skill cannot be explained by human ingenuity alone. As he states:

> Those original plans [of the Great Pyramid], we say, must have been based on a knowledge of astronomy, geography, and physics, so vastly beyond the powers of unaided man in the day when the Pyramid was built, or indeed within several thousand years therefrom,—that scientifically there is no resource for us, but to allow the planners of the building must have been assisted by Divine inspiration.'[57]

In the post-Victorian world, comments such as these were taken up by the pseudo-scholars and the alternative theorists, and claims about the technological skills of the ancients are recontextualized as questions about whether or not these cultures could have been responsible for them (and postulating Atlantean or alien engineers in their stead). Smyth's comments

---

54. Smyth, *Life and Work*, I, p. 414.
55. Smyth, *Life and Work*, I, p. 447.
56. Smyth, *Life and Work*, I, p. 146.
57. Smyth, *Life and Work*, I, p. 570.

in *Our Inheritance* could be taken directly from a twenty-first-century 'ancient aliens' argument:

> For, besides coming forth suddenly in primeval history without any childhood, or known preparation, or long-acknowledged duration and slowly growing senility afterwards . . . the actual results at the Great Pyramid, in the shape of numerical knowledge of grand cosmical phenomena of both earth and heavens, not only rise above, the extremely limited and almost infantine knowledge of science possessed by any of the Gentile nations of 4,000, 3,000, 2,000, nay, 1,000 years ago, but they are also, in whatever they chiefly apply to, very essentially above any scientific knowledge of any man up to our own time as well.[58]

However, Smyth's claims are not consistent. In places, he gives full credit to the skills of the ancient engineers and, if anything, attempts to draw similarities between the nineteenth-century European and the ancient Egyptian. These claims are subtle, but there is a sense in which Smyth minimizes the 'otherness' of the Egyptian. For example, in his study of the wall joints of the Great Pyramid, he compares the accuracy of his own engineering skills with the ancient builders:

> the errors of the ancient joints from a perpendicular to the axis of the passage, were smaller than the error of my laboured piece of carpentry [a wooden square that he built]; or rather, I may perhaps be allowed to say, for it had stood some close tests before leaving the tomb, smaller than the errors induced in it by the sunshine, as it was being carried to the Pyramid [due to the drying effects of the heat on wood]. But when after many days spent in this one particular passage,—I discovered a line on either wall, ruled apparently by a master hand as a guide to the original working masons,—and applied and reapplied the square to that,—the mean of all the readings for error, came out to 0.[59]

Here, in finding the master mason's mark, Smyth both marvels at the skill and evokes the builders as real, working people, comrades in engineering. Interestingly, he immediately follows this up by showing the mark to a local and then describes how nineteenth-century Egyptians explain any idiosyncrasy in the pyramids as the marks left by travellers.[60] Thus the Europeans and ancient Egyptians are connected by their technological skills, and both are disconnected from the nineteenth-century Egyptian for the same reason. Nevertheless, there is an inconsistency in the presentation, since Smyth's perspective also presumes a lack of sophistication on the part of the ancients. It is fundamental to his argument that this metrological knowledge

---

58. Smyth, *Our Inheritance*, p. 11.
59. Smyth, *Life and Work*, I, p. 150.
60. Smyth, *Life and Work*, I, p. 151.

had to be divinely inspired, given that ancients could not have been at that stage of development.

Throughout Smyth's marveling at the skills of the ancient builders, he also comments enough on the mysteries of the pyramids to evoke a sense of wonder in the reader. Despite being filled with scientific maps of the interior, the narrative reads as though the pyramid is filled with secret passages, hidden chambers, and that many more may still be left to be revealed. For Smyth, the sense of mystery is more pragmatic, but many readers, not familiar with engineering, likely read these passages in a different manner. Take, for example, the following discussion:

> Were these unusual joints then two secret key-marks? and if so, what for? And what purpose can indeed be sufficient to account for all the pains connected with them? for they have no structural necessity practically, architecturally, or aesthetically.[61]

Smyth goes on to explain what these 'unusual joints' were—part of the 'rectangular stone' that blocked a secret entrance to the tomb in antiquity. The actual explanation that he gives is relatively blasé, but he emphasizes that he has solved a mystery that has baffled explorers since Graeco-Roman times. Here his description hints at a gothic-style mystery presented in somewhat scientific prose.

In other instances, he is not able to identify the utility of certain ancient engineering choices. For example, he talks of a curious niche in the Queen's Chamber. He remarks that he is unable to identify its function and describes older interpretations: the 'Arabs of old' thought it was to conceal treasure; the 'mediaeval Europeans' thought it was an opening to an underground passage to the sphinx; and the 'modern sepulchral theorists' believed that it was a mummy pit.[62] Now Smyth does not follow any of these approaches, but, of course, these are the romantic ideas that would have excited the Victorian imagination.

The Egyptian Monotheists

Yet there are limits to Smyth's own presentation of the pyramids as gothic space. Because of his own belief in the biblical connections implicit in the pyramid, he goes to great pains to make this non-sacrilegious space. This is made very apparent in Smyth's digression on Cheops's religious views, arguing against the belief that Cheops was an atheist (a view that had been proposed to account for the striking lack of religious iconography associated with the pyramid in comparison to other Egyptian architecture). Following John Taylor, Smyth explains:

61. Smyth, *Life and Work*, I, p. 154.
62. Smyth, *Life and Work*, I, p. 200.

> King Cheops, being no atheist, but on the contrary, a zealous, and Elijah-like worshipper of the one true God in spirit and in truth,—took every method which was open to him, for trying to wean his besotted subjects from their degrading animal-worship; and for showing them practically that their gods, in whom they trusted, were no gods.[63]

In *Our Inheritance*, Smyth argues that since the Egyptians preserved stories of the wickedness of Cheops, and that they were wicked themselves, by extension, Cheops was likely *not* wicked.[64] It was not uncommon for Victorian scholars to attempt to portray early advanced civilizations as monotheistic, since polytheism was not easily harmonized with contemporary notions of progress (see Chapter I.4). This argument is essential for Smyth since he is claiming that the metrology of the Great Pyramid was divinely inspired.

Smyth pushes this presumed monotheism much further than the typical Victorian scholar, however. For the most part, he sees the Egyptian culture as idolatrous and abhorrent. The Great Pyramid, however, is distinct from all other Egyptian architecture, despite the ubiquity of the pyramid shape in Egyptian material culture to the contrary. In his words, 'The Great Pyramid, an entirely prehistoric monument, is found, though in Egypt, not to be *of* Egypt' [original italics]. The lack of iconography in the Great Pyramid is his primary evidence. Toward the end of *Our Inheritance* he summarizes the other main reasons why the Great Pyramid should be understood as 'antagonistic' to Egyptian architecture, although most boil down to the same argument in regards to the lack of hieroglyphs and images of animal-headed gods.[65]

In *Life and Work*, Smyth notes that he was completely unimpressed with the sphinx, stating that he and his companions 'could hardly believe in its paltriness and complete distinction from the Pyramids'.[66] He compared it to 'any trifling modern tomb!'[67] By the time he writes *Our Inheritance*, his dislike of the monument has grown, commenting, 'that monster, an idol in itself, with symptoms typifying the lowest mental organization, positively reeks with anti-Great Pyramid idolatry throughout its substance'.[68] He continues, 'As a rule, it is Frenchmen and Roman Catholics . . . who get up the most outrageous enthusiasm for the Sphinx', then launches into an attack on Auguste Mariette, who argued that the Sphinx dates to the same dynasty as the Great Pyramid builders.[69] This is quite different from the Great Pyra-

---

63. Smyth, *Life and Work*, I, p. 468.
64. Smyth, *Our Inheritance*, p. 9.
65. Smyth, *Our Inheritance*, pp. 460-63.
66. Smyth, *Life and Work*, I, p. 57.
67. Smyth, *Life and Work*, I, p. 58.
68. Smyth, *Our Inheritance*, p. 414.
69. Smyth, *Our Inheritance*, p. 414.

mid, of which Smyth states, 'we find in all its *finished* parts not a vestige of heathenism, nor the smallest indulgence in anything approaching to idolatry; not even the most distant allusion to Sabaism, or to the worship of sun or moon, or any of the starry host of heaven'.[70]

Smyth reads Scripture as demonstrating that inspiration was granted only to pious individuals who stood above their fellows as role models and were usually from the line of Shem (as opposed to the idolatrous line of Ham, from whom Egypt descended).[71] Egypt's latitude and position as a crossroads of three continents made it an ideal location for the divine monument to metrology, and so the Egyptians were the necessary vehicle for God's message, despite their idolatrous practices.[72] Smyth also notes the monotheism of some Egyptians and the original Egyptian setting of Mosaic religion. However, he makes a point to argue that the influence on Moses should be seen as divine inspiration undermining and supplanting Moses's Egyptian education.[73] Smyth explains, 'Moses, then, in that inimitable work, instead of copying anything from the profane Egyptians of his day, was rather anticipating the march of science in the Christian ages of the world', and was not shy to depart from Egyptian practices.[74]

Taylor had assumed that Noah was the builder of the pyramid, and his understanding of the dating of the deluge allowed this, as the Great Pyramid could have been built during Noah's lifetime. Smyth's own dating of the Great Pyramid ruled Noah out.[75] A more likely candidate was a contemporary of Abraham's, Melchizedek, King of Salem (which Smyth equates to Jerusalem). Smyth dates Melchizedek's reign to around 2170, the same date that he gives for the construction of the Great Pyramid.[76] Since little is said of Melchizedek in the Bible, Smyth has much room for interpretation, and he uses the silence of the text to help build his argument in favour of this king (noting that the Great Pyramid was likely built in his early years, of which nothing is reported by Scripture). Toward the end of *Our Inheritance*, Smyth answers the question of who built the Great Pyramid, stating that Cheops 'plodded at fulfilling in masonry the orders given to

---

70. Smyth, *Our Inheritance*, p. 5.
71. Smyth, *Life and Work*, I, p. 511.
72. Smyth, *Life and Work*, I, p. 520.
73. Smyth, *Our Inheritance*, p. 328.
74. Smyth, *Our Inheritance*, p. 336.
75. He provides a summary of different views of dates of the deluge, and continues with a discussion of deluge stories as a worldwide phenomenon, but ends up dating the Great Pyramid between Noah's Ark and the Ark of the Covenant (Smyth, *Life and Work*, III, pp. 489-95).
76. Smyth, *Our Inheritance*, p. 433.

[him]', but that Melchizedek 'furnished the design of the building and saw to its being realized'.[77]

Smyth predicts the problems that his fellow scientists will have with his theory of divine inspiration. He writes:

> But the mere naming of it [a wisdom higher than man's], in the present day, before scientific men in a scientific subject, and connected with practical facts,—is greeted immediately with a storm of clamour, reproaches, regrets, objections, and the most determined opposition. Not without some reason too,—because the attribution of a Divine origin, when men find anything either in science or early history, above their immediate power to explain on simple principles of human learning,—has been hitherto generally, if not always, a sign of weakness in the science of those employing it: so that the progress of natural philosophy in recent years, contains not a few cases of phenomena, once thought supernatural, yet now shown to be amenable to mechanical principles, as well as following implicitly the regular order of nature.[78]

These comments were written with no sense of irony. Smyth dispenses with what he feels are the potential objections to a divine explanation here. To the argument that it could have been a single human genius, Smyth responds, quoting Renan, 'there was never a particle of genius in the whole land of Egypt'.[79] Yet even if there was a genius, this was an achievement of theory and practice, requiring knowledge of the entire globe, impossible to have achieved 'confined as they were in their narrow valley'.[80] It could not have been another civilization that we do not have record of because the quarry marks prove that it was built by Egyptians of the Fourth Dynasty. Presuming the criticism that *'no number of coincidences make a proof'* [original italics]', Smyth used the 'watchmaker' argument (still used by twenty-first-century creation scientists) to explain that the coincidences are meaningful—'all the numerous coincidences of the watch's wheel and pinions working exactly into each other . . . forms *no proof* [original italics] that there has been any intention on the part of an intelligent watchmaker to produce such coincidence!'.[81] Smyth's most common complaint, however, is that his fellow scientists refused to consider his view at all. In all his rebuttals, Smyth is establishing the 'logic' of counter-arguments that are still used in the twenty-first-century by pseudo-scientists in relation to archaeological (and more broadly scientific) arguments.

77. Smyth, *Our Inheritance*, p. 463.
78. Smyth, *Life and Work*, I, pp. 470-71.
79. Smyth, *Life and Work*, III, pp. 472.
80. Smyth, *Life and Work*, I, p. 473.
81. Smyth, *Life and Work*, I, pp. 474-75.

9. *Science Is Measurement* 373

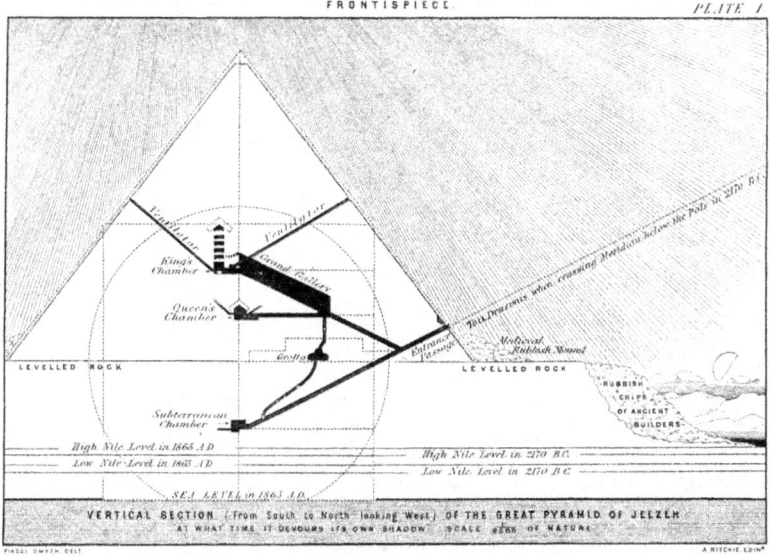

Fig. 9.5. Section drawing of the Great Pyramid; Piazzi Smyth, *Our Inheritance in the Great Pyramid* (London: W. Ibister & Co., new and enlarged edn, 1874), plate I (frontispiece).

The Messages Hidden in the Pyramid

In his later books, Smyth describes the positive impact of his studies on the works of other scholars. Perhaps the first 'scholar' to build on Smyth's work was his good friend Robert Menzies. Menzies believed his last name was a simplified form of Manasseh, prompting Smyth to refer to him as '[t]his Israelite, then, but no Jew', and was influential enough on Smyth to warrant reference in *Our Inheritance*.[82] Menzies defended Smyth against the mainstream scientific community who rejected the pyramid as a divinely inspired monument to metrology. Menzies fully embraced Smyth's argument and pushed it even further. He claimed that it was not just a monument to metrology but literally God's prophecy of human history. Predictions about all of the major events in world history were recorded in the internal passages of the pyramids (Fig. 9.5), and it was only up to humans to translate these messages in order to predict future events, leading right up to the return of Christ. Of central importance was the Grand Gallery, its importance signaled by its immense height. Smyth describes this interpretation of the Great Pyramid in detail:

82. Smyth, *Our Inheritance*, p. 387.

> From the north beginning of the Grand Gallery floor, said Robert Menzies, there in southward procession, begin the years of the Saviour's earthly life, expressed at the rate of a Pyramid inch to a year. Three-and-thirty inch-years therefore, or thereabout, bring us right over against the mouth of the well, the type of His death, and His glorious resurrection too; while the long lofty Grand Gallery shows the dominating rule in the world of the blessed religion which he established thereby, over-spanned above by the 36 stones of His months of ministry on earth, and defined by the floor-length in inches, as to its exact period.[83]

In a subsection of *Our Inheritance*, called 'The Floor Roll of Human History', Smyth discusses some further interpretations of Menzies's basic concept, which is worth quoting at length:

> Beginning at its upper and northern end, it starts at the rate of a Pyramid inch to a year, from the Dispersion of mankind, or from the period when men declined any longer to live the patriarchal life of Divine instruction, and insisted on going off upon their own inventions; when they immediately began to experience that universal *'facilis descensus Averni'* of all idolaters; and which is so sensibly represented to the very life or death, in the long-continued descent of the entrance-passage of the Great Pyramid, more than 4,000 inch-years long, until it ends in the symbol of the bottomless pit, a chamber deep in the rock, well finished as to its ceiling and top of its walls, but without any attempt at a floor.[84]

Smyth interprets the relationship between the various chambers of the Great Pyramid as symbolic of various elements of Christian history. This is reinforced by the correlation of the lengths of the gallery in Pyramid inches and dates of significant events. He gives as an example of this proof: 'Measuring along the passages backward from the north beginning of the Grand Gallery, you find the exodus at either 1483 or 1542 B.C., and the dispersion of mankind in 2528 B.C., up at the beginning of the entrance passage'.[85] The pyramid is a physical model of history; the exodus is represented by one of the passages. Smyth explains:

> One escape, indeed, there was in that long and mournful history of human decline; but for a few only, when the Exodus took place in the first-ascending passage, which leads on into the Grand Gallery; showing Hebraism ending in its original prophetic destination—Christianity. But another escape was also eventually provided, to prevent any immortal soul being necessarily lost in the bottomless pit; for before reaching that dismal abyss, there is a possible entrance, though it may be a strait and narrow way, to the one and only gate of salvation through the death of Christ—viz., the well representing his descent into Hades: not the bottomless pit of idolaters and the wicked at the lowest point to which the entrance-passage

---

83. Smyth, *Our Inheritance*, p. 388.
84. Smyth, *Our Inheritance*, pp. 389-90.
85. Smyth, *Our Inheritance*, p. 390.

subterraneously descends, but a natural grotto rather than artificial chamber in the course of the well's further progress to the other place; while the stone which once covered that well's upper mouth is blown outwards into the Grand Gallery with excessive force (and was once so thrown out, and is now annihilated), carrying part of the wall with it, and indicating how totally unable was the grave to hold Him beyond the appointed time.[86]

Christ's resurrection was also predicted in the architecture of the pyramid. Smyth elaborates further on various tests that he made to corroborate this reading, demonstrating that it is accurate, even though he had not been aware of it when he published *Life and Work*.

The Comparative Method

Another pseudoscientific argument that appears, especially in volume II of *Life and Work*, is a comparative method, which looks for universal practices among primitive cultures and is modeled on nineteenth-century anthropology. But here the comparisons are treated with little rigour. Smyth follows scholars such as R.G. Haliburton in positing similarities among world calendars, as well as similarities in festivals and treatments of the dead.[87] Most important for the later theosophists (see Chapter III.8), who read Smyth's work with great interest, was his argument about the direct connections between ancient Egypt and India. He follows Edward Greswell in seeing similarities in calendar and worship (equating Isis with Durga) between the two regions and posits a connection.[88]

However, his comparative method is more fully realized in *Antiquity*. Most of the comparison is dedicated to other buildings or material culture from Egypt, but there are extended discussions of Mesopotamia and briefer notices about henge monuments and other Neolithic structures from Europe (although he does not describe them as such). He also discusses the 'residual architecture' of the Hebrews, Greeks, Romans and early Buddhists. In this context he makes a statement about the primacy of archaeological materials over textual sources, the first stirrings in a debate that is still present in the discipline:

> Now, when we look around for any such contemporary remains of the earliest possible ages,—it is not books or rolls of writing, but something more or less in the shape of *buildings*, which answer to our call. No doubt Hindoos may boast of the 20,000 years of age of some of their sacred hymns, and Egyptians of the 30,000 years of their books of Hermes; but they cannot show *contemporary* copies either of that time or of its mere twentieth part. Yet are there buildings in the world, still standing open

---

86. Smyth, *Our Inheritance*, pp. 389-90.
87. See, for example, Smyth, *Life and Work*, II, p. 375.
88. Smyth, *Life and Work*, II, pp. 410-11.

to examination, which were erected several thousand years before any known copy of any of those books was transcribed.[89]

Archaeology provides direct evidence in a way that textual sources do not (according to Smyth), and thus the meaningful comparison is of different buildings that have survived. In an atypically critical fashion, Smyth even rejects any discussion of the Tower of Babel, since our knowledge of this oldest building is based on 'belief alone'.[90]

Generally his comparative studies uphold his belief that the Great Pyramid is a singularly unique monument. In his discussion of Chaldean (meaning Sumerian), Assyrian and Babylonian architecture, he admits that the buildings do seem to be astronomically aligned. However, Smyth has to engage in some sophistry to minimize the meaningfulness of this:

> they [scholars of Mesopotamia such as Loftus and Rawlinson] would seem to have overlooked the impossibility of *all* the corners of a long rectangular building being directed truly to the four cardinal points, and to there being a difference of many degrees to be disposed of somewhere, as error on two corners, if other two had been set true, as above indicated, from one central point, on a ground-plan of the very long rectangular proportions which they give.[91]

In other words, Assyriologists have made a mathematical error in their descriptions of the monuments. He continues:

> The better practical method of proceeding would probably have been, for our explorers to have recorded the direction of the *sides* of a structure (eliminating the buttresses); and then, in stating that *they* (the sides) point half-way between all the four cardinal directions, there would have cropped out more prominently the astronomical antithesis of these Chaldaean buildings to all Egyptian Pyramids; viz., that instead of being oriented, as those are *to* or *upon* the cardinal points, they are as *far from* them, angularly, as they possibly can be.[92]

Following this convoluted logic, the buildings of the 'Chaldaeans' (and the rest of Mesopotamia is similarly treated) illustrate a significantly lower level of engineering, metrological and astronomical skills than the Great Pyramid.

Smyth's scorn for Mesopotamia grows as his argument develops. This is exemplified in his attack on those that see the Borsippa ziggurat as exemplifying Babylonian astronomical skills. He writes:

89. Smyth, *Antiquity*, p. 4.
90. Smyth, *Antiquity*, p. 45.
91. Smyth, *Antiquity*, p. 56.
92. Smyth, *Antiquity*, p. 56.

> But they [the admirers of Babylon] do say for the Borsippa building, that, being dedicated to the seven planets of Chaldaean astronomy, each stage was appropriately *coloured*.
>
> Appropriately coloured! a surface demonstration only; but of what nature and with what object?
>
> Why, the lowest stage, we are told, was coloured black, as symbolical for Saturn; the next orange, for Jupiter; the third red, for Mars; the fourth yellow, for the Sun; the fifth green, for Venus; the sixth blue, for Mercury; and the seventh white, for the Moon.
>
> A very ill-assorted list of so-called planets surely, and extremely deficient without Uranus and Neptune and the Planetoids,—especially for a people supposed, by their friends, to have discovered the vastly fainter 6th and 7th satellites of Saturn. But, accepting the planets as given above in their diverse-coloured stages, what learning were these colours intended to typify?
>
> And then comes the sorry confession, that each hue was supposed to be symbolical of such planet's influence on human well-being, both moral and physical; and therefore was superstitious, astrological, and nonsensical, rather than astronomical.[93]

Clearly Smyth did not hold Chaldaean astronomy in as high regard as the ancient Greeks did. It is curious that Smyth is keen to prove Egyptian astronomical knowledge (even if divinely inspired) with meagre evidence and minimize evidence relating to Mesopotamian science.

Smyth similarly criticizes, though with less vehemence, Babylonian metrology. He states that the system is very similar to the Egyptian system (not the divinely inspired Pyramid system), and is thus:

> utterly unscientific, so far as regards any known earth appropriate commensurability; entirely unlike, therefore, and totally inferior, to the system of the Great Pyramid.... Modern science therefore can say nothing in favour of the Nebuchadnezzarian standards,—while she abhors the employment of their favourite sexagesimal division, in any case where decimals can be used.[94]

For Smyth, this comparative study of ancient architecture (and by extension metrology and astronomy) 'has merely landed us in a quagmire of too evidently human idolatrous follies, scientific absurdities, and general mental childishness'.[95] The Great Pyramid, in comparison, 'is a pearl of great price both in the cause of truth, and for the development of primeval history'.[96] At first, his hostility toward Mesopotamia may seem puzzling,

---

93. Smyth, *Antiquity*, pp. 339-40.
94. Smyth, *Antiquity*, p. 342.
95. Smyth, *Antiquity*, p. 343.
96. Smyth, *Antiquity*, p. 348.

but it is essential for his argument. The Great Pyramid needs to be absolutely unique within the context of ancient science in order to be considered divinely inspired.

As has already been noted, the academic response to *Life and Work* was almost uniformly negative, despite the positive response to his initial presentation of his raw data. By the time of writing *Our Inheritance*, Smyth had become comfortable attacking Egyptology and nineteenth-century academia more broadly. Whether these were beliefs held in check earlier or whether they reflect a response to the ready dismissal of his ideas is not clear (but I suspect the latter). His criticisms of Egyptology are interesting, stemming mostly from his Christian perspective. He describes the pitfalls of this approach at length:

> To learn indeed; but not from our many modern Egyptologists, as they proudly call themselves. For surely by this time we should have acquired a wholesome fear of those who, instead of studying the Great Pyramid from a truly religious and Christian, or any, point of view, have rushed headlong into a Cainite desire to know about the sacrificial bulls and cats, crocodiles and ibises, snake and beetle gods, and all the other unholy holies of that impure Egyptian nation. . . . A people who changed the truth of God into a lie, and worshipped and served the creature more than the Creator, who is blessed forever. Amen.[97]

According to Smyth, there is little of merit to be learned from reading hieroglyphs. He paraphrases Sir George Cornewall Lewis, stating, 'that there is nothing worthy of being known remaining to be interpreted in all the rest of the hieroglyphics of the reputedly *wise* land of Egypt'.[98] Of sole interest to Smyth are matters relating to chronology. And despite his extensive work documenting the Great Pyramid, Smyth implies, in an off-hand comment, that it is immoral to document other elements of Egyptian civilization:

> the Egyptian system bases on Cainite assertions and re-assertions of self-righteousness, and a multitude of gods, half animal and half man—some of them, too, not a little obscene (to an extent which makes us wonder at several modern European governments reproducing their portraits one after another in costly folios and large-sized plates, for the information of the public of the present day). . . .[99]

No doubt reproductions of the ithyphallic deity Min were especially troubling to Smyth.

---

97. Smyth, *Our Inheritance*, p. 301.
98. Smyth, *Our Inheritance*, p. 409.
99. Smyth, *Our Inheritance*, p. 330.

Millenarianism and the Jehovah's Witnesses

While Egyptology and academia more broadly rejected Smyth's claims, his work had an impact on other areas of Victorian life and continues to resonate with people today. Hargrave Jennings, for example, was inspired by Piazzi Smyth but disagreed with his interpretation of the function of the Great Pyramid, believing it to be an altar to a fire divinity worshipped throughout Europe and Asia.[100] While the pseudoarchaeological community is obviously indebted to him, there are other communities who were profoundly influenced by his analysis, especially within new nineteenth-century religious movements. The obvious implications of his integration of scientific measurements with Menzies's pyramid prophecies were millenarian, and Smyth became an important participant in this movement in the late nineteenth century. Smyth, using his pyramidological measurements, predicted the second coming of Christ to be in 1882, and was able to muster much seemingly empirical, scientific data (especially mathematical) to prove this. When the second coming did not occur, Smyth modified the dates, and continued to do so each time he was proven incorrect. His predicted dates ranged between 1892 and 1911, moving further into the future with each forecast. Passing away in 1900, he did not live to see that his predictions never came true.

The mantle of the millenarian theological aspects of Smyth's works was picked up by Charles Taze Russel (1852–1916). The founder of the journal *Zion's Watch Tower* (now published by the Jehovah's Witnesses as *The Watchtower Announcing Jehovah's Kingdom*), Russel was a restorationist preacher from Pittsburgh, Pennsylvania. He was the founder of the Bible Student Movement, the movement out of which the Jehovah's Witness church emerged. Although the twenty-first-century Jehovah's Witness Church rejects pyramidological studies, this was an important influence in its early development and differentiated it from other millenarian groups of the time. Unlike many of his nineteenth-century American colleagues, Russel did not claim to be privy to any special revelation from God. He was, however, a prolific writer, author of six volumes, originally titled *Millennial Dawn* but reissued as *Studies in the Scriptures.* Russel's approach to the Bible differed from typical Protestant exegesis of the time by dispensing with a verse-by-verse approach. Rather, theological matters are dealt with topically. It is the third volume that incorporates the works of Piazzi Smyth. Published in 1891, *The Kingdom Come* describes how the Great Pyramid

---

100. The evidence that Jennings cites is difficult to follow. If one replaces the 'p' with 'an 'f' in 'pyramid' (since those sounds are interchangeable in many languages) the corrected word suggests a meaning of 'fire begotten' (Hargrave Jennings, *The Rosicrucians: Their Rites and Mysteries* [London: George Routledge & Sons, 2nd edn, 1879], pp. 199-200), pp. 93-94.

reflects divine inspiration. Of particular influence was the correspondence between Smyth and Russel paraphrased in the book. There, Russel agreed that Smyth's identification of the beginning of the end times was accurate. The actual date presented in Russel's book has been updated subsequently, but the Jehovah Witness Church still accepts one of these dates as the beginning of the time of troubles, which members believe that we are currently experiencing.

Smyth's popular success and academic failures point to a major transformation of the field in the latter half of the nineteenth century. By the 1860s, enough was known of Egypt, Mesopotamia and the Holy Land based on archaeological explorations and philological breakthroughs that a scholarly community could emerge. Lone scholars, using only their ingenuity, biblical and classical sources, and the results of ad hoc expeditions, could no longer enact the study of the ancient Near East. They needed to work within established frameworks, according to increasingly more rigorous scholarly norms, and base their conclusions on academic criteria. The next chapter explores the professionalization of the field, and illustrates how enthusiasts such as Piazzi Smyth came to be excluded from Near Eastern studies and how the study of Egypt, Mesopotamia and biblical archaeology came to be formally adopted by the academy.

10

From Gentleman Scholars to Scholarly Societies: Legitimating the Socially Marginal and Excluding Marginal Readings

> Criticism achieved security by committing political suicide; its moment of academic institutionalization is also the moment of its effective demise as a socially active force. —Terry Eagleton

As Eagleton has suggested for literary criticism, so it was for Near Eastern studies; when it was institutionalized as a formal academic discipline, it began to lose its relevance in the social discourse of British and American society. Stephen Bann similarly argues that as history writing was established as a profession distinct from other types of writing, it 'forfeited the right to speak directly to a mass audience, and to justify its products by the simple measure of market demand'.[1] No longer was it possible for a non-professional but learned gentlemen to be fully engaged with the discipline. Formal training, degrees and language instruction were all requirements that came to mean more than a convenient diplomatic posting overseas. As politicians and diplomats ceased to participate in archaeological excavations, they ceased to use Near Eastern civilization as a talking point in public lectures and democratic debates. The Near East was no longer the site of adventuring for future politicians, such as Austen Henry Layard (with notable exceptions like T.E. Lawrence). The study of Near Eastern antiquity stopped being part of the biographical background that could be called upon by the public figure as a signal of aristocratic pedigree, and the past was less used as a safe staging ground for discussing the controversial social and economic issues of the day. Once claimed by the university, Near Eastern studies advanced in methods and practices but declined in public relevance, other than as an area of curiosity (the exotic Holy Land) or a trendy news item (King Tutankhamun's tomb).

1. Stephen Bann, *The Inventions of History: Essays on the Representation of the Past* (Manchester: Manchester University Press, 1990), p. 13.

Philippa Levine and Eitan Bar-Yosef have both argued that the engagement with the Near East in the nineteenth century was practiced through an 'invisible college'. For Levine, the invisible college involved 'informal networks within a specific area of study . . . collaboration, citation of one another's works and informal communication. . . .'[2] Both scholars argue that this kind of informal grouping of scholars, writers, artists, travellers and elites was not just about inclusion but was as equally about establishing exclusionary boundaries, both philosophically and practically. As Billie Melman has argued, the ambiguity of Oriental studies as a discipline facilitated women's participation, although much of that participation manifested itself through travel (see Chapter I.7).[3] The formalization of scholarly networks and programs worked to exclude women to a significant degree (with some notable exceptions).[4] The voluntary association (scholarly society) became one key access point for women interested in academic study of the Near East.

Men of Letters

In the first half of the nineteenth century, the practitioner of Near Eastern studies was most typically a 'man of letters'. The Near Eastern scholars who were most widely read by Victorians were the same individuals who reported, summarized and editorialized other public events of the day. Inextricably interwoven with the explosion of print material in Victorian England, the man of letters was neither a scholar nor a writer nor a journalist but a combination of all of these figures. Only mathematics was exempt from the unofficial curriculum of the learned gentleman, being a subject that had been recognized since the eighteenth century as requiring advanced training. More importantly, the activities surrounding mathematics did not lend themselves well to social ventures.[5] Eagleton characterizes this figure:

---

2. Philippa Levine, *The Amateur and the Professional: Antiquarians, Historians, and Archaeologists in Victorian England, 1838–1886* (Cambridge: Cambridge University Press, 1986), pp. 36-37. See also Eitan Bar-Yosef, *The Holy Land in English Culture 1799–1917: Palestine and the Question of Orientalism* (Oxford: Clarendon Press, 2005), pp. 70-72.

3. Billie Melman, *Women's Orients: English Women and the Middle East, 1718–1918* (London: Macmillan, 1992), p. 255.

4. An example of this is Samuel Birch's antagonism toward Amelia Edwards. From his position of authority at the British Museum, he worked against Edwards's attempts to form the Egypt Exploration Fund, both to keep outsiders from gaining access to the discipline and to prevent a woman from founding such a prominent organization. See Melman, *Women's Orients*, p. 258.

5. Mary Terrall, 'Natural Philosophy for Fashionable Readers', in *Books and the Sciences in History* (ed. Marina Frasca-Spada and Nick Jardine; Cambridge: Cambridge University Press, 2000), pp. 239-54 (249).

> Like the eighteenth-century periodicalists, the man of letters is the bearer and dispenser of a generalized ideological wisdom rather than the exponent of a specialist intellectual skill, one whose synoptic vision, undimmed by any narrow technical interest, is able to survey the whole cultural and intellectual landscape of his age. . . . The man of letters knows as much as he does because he cannot make a living out of only one intellectual specialism. . . . The man of letters is in this sense a hack; but he is a figure of sagelike ideological authority too, and in the Victorian Period one can observe this unsettling coexistence as often as not within the same individuals.[6]

In class as well as profession, the man of letters was conceptually complex, not easily fitting into any of the established categories. As often as not a member of the middle class, middle-class values would not do. The man of letters posed as an aristocrat for whom noblesse oblige masquerading as social welfare compelled him to publish his studies in periodicals (which thrived off of middle-class purchasing power) for public edification. This middle class, not wanting to 'feel' middle class, would sympathize with a privileged view of the world, especially as mediated through discourse on such arcane topics as the ancient Babylonians.

Intellectualism functioned almost as an alternative status that, while not exempting one from class boundaries, allowed some degree of circumvention of established roles and access to elite circles. Samuel Coleridge called these intellectual public figures the clerisy (the later term intelligentsia is now more common). The clerisy was a group, like the clergy, who upheld and preserved the national culture. How important this group was in defining national culture was debatable. Thorstein Veblen, for example, jokingly wrote that the study of ancient languages exemplified conspicuous consumption since the work was both time consuming and useless.[7] In Victorian times, offering intellectual commentary for public edification was a successful means of earning social capital. It is worth comparing some examples of these men of letters who contributed to Near Eastern studies.

John Gardner Wilkinson: Britain's Victorian Expert on Egypt

The embodiment of the gentleman scholar, John Gardner Wilkinson (1797–1875) was a foundational figure in the development of Egyptology as a professional discipline (Fig. 10.1).[8] While he himself had no formal Egyptological training, as none was available when he began his work, his

---

6. Terry Eagleton, *The Function of Criticism* (London: Verso, 1984), pp. 45-46.
7. Thorstein Veblen, *The Theory of the Leisure Class* (New York: Penguin, 1994 [1899]), p. 45.
8. For biographies on Wilkinson, see Sarah J.A. Flynn, *Sir John Gardner Wilkinson, Traveller and Egyptologist (1797–1875)* (Oxford: Bodleian Library, 1997); and John

Fig. 10.1. John Gardner Wilkinson. Wikimedia Commons.

1837 *Manners and Customs of the Ancient Egyptians* was one of the most important Egyptological texts of the nineteenth century. Its reception led to his knighthood as well as Victorian acknowledgment that he was the pre-eminent British expert on Egypt until his death in 1875. As Fagan comments, this book was not superseded until James Breasted's 1905 *History of Egypt* and Wilkinson's expertise not surpassed until William Flinders Petrie entered the field.[9]

Wilkinson's career in Egyptology began during his Grand Tour. Not intending a career in archaeology or history, Wilkinson, who supported himself through an inheritance, had planned on a military career. However, stopping in Rome on his tour, he met Sir William Gell (1777–1836), a classicist and expert archaeological illustrator. Gell was an archetypal man of letters, and his talent for scientific illustration was already well established when he met Wilkinson. Gell had recently become interested in Egypt and introduced Wilkinson to the basics of Egyptology as known at the time (1820), and trained him in scientific illustration. He also arranged for Wilkinson to be introduced to Salt and other major figures in British Egyptology, and when Wilkinson arrived in Alexandria in 1821, those expatriates welcomed him.

For the next twelve years, Wilkinson immersed himself in Egyptian life. Dressing as a Turkish aristocrat right from the outset, he would, while in Egypt, pass himself off as a Turk, acquire a slave to be his mistress and

Jason Thompson, *Sir Gardner Wilkinson and his Circle* (Austin, TX: University of Texas Press, 1992).

9. Brian Fagan, *The Rape of the Nile: Tomb Robbers, Tourists, and Archaeologists in Egypt* (Oxford: Westview Press, rev. and updated edn, 2004), p. 177.

travel throughout the land, sometimes in the company of fellow artists and sometimes alone.[10] At the time of his travels, the process of the decipherment of hieroglyphs was well under way by Champollion and others, and Wilkinson developed a rudimentary knowledge of the writing system. More important than his translations were his accurate copies of hieroglyphs and monuments; these, when eventually made available to others, along with the images from Napoleon's *Description* provided the empirical basis for early Egyptian philology.

It was not just in philology that Wilkinson made his contributions. He made one of the first systematic attempts to better understand chronology in light of newly found inscriptional materials. He travelled throughout Egypt, identifying numerous sites. One of these was Amarna, the capital city of the heretic king Akhenaten. Wilkinson sent copies of the strange images of Akhenaten to Gell, who misidentified them as depictions of pregnant women making offerings.[11] From 1827 to 1833, Wilkinson was based in Thebes. There he moved into the tomb of a New Kingdom noble and 'renovated' it to make it more appropriate for the living quarters of a Turkish aristocrat. Burning mummy coffins and welcoming guests, Wilkinson lived a 'gentlemanly' life while he worked his way through the Theban tombs, copying the paintings and studying the scenes of daily life.

In 1833 he returned to England and began work on various publications related to his scholarly work. The most influential of these was his *Manners and Customs of the Ancient Egyptians*, which was published by John Murray a year after Murray published Lanes's *An Account of the Manners and Customs of the Modern Egyptians* (1836). Wilkinson's book set the standard and established the research trajectory of Egyptology as a professional discipline. The book deals with issues of chronology and history but was more novel in that it greatly emphasized the daily life of ancient Egypt. Now this kind of work would be considered social history or historical anthropology, but at the time of its publication, this was an unusual approach to a historical subject. By using scenes of daily life from the nobles' tombs, Wilkinson was able to reconstruct much of ancient Egyptian life, developing a methodology that integrated philology and art history for social-historical ends—an approach that came to be typical of Egyptology and atypical of other archaeological regional studies. The book was a scholarly book but was not overly technical, and thus it reached a wide readership. The emphasis on daily life and the rich illustrations (by Joseph Bonomi, who had visited him in Egypt and would later become one of the designers of the Egyptian Court at the Crystal Palace—see Chapter II.7) also helped make this work accessible; and most popular writers on Egypt in the mid- to late-Victorian

---

10. Fagan, *Rape of the Nile*, p. 172.
11. Fagan, *Rape of the Nile*, p. 172.

period used this book as their main source. For those wishing to know what the Victorians knew about Egypt, this book encapsulates that knowledge.

Despite the fact that beyond these early projects Wilkinson did not continue much further research into Egypt, he was acknowledged as the British authority on Egypt for the rest of his life. He assisted the British Museum occasionally, although his interest in Egyptology was later replaced by that of the archaeology of Cornwall and zoology. In popular presentations of Egypt, references to Wilkinson acted as proof of historical authenticity. For example, he wrote the guidebook for the Egyptian Court at the Crystal Palace, which worked to establish that exhibition as academically accurate. In fact, critics complained that he was not consulted enough in its production. He returned to Egypt in 1841 at the request of John Murray to research a handbook for tourists to Egypt (see Chapter I.7). Its first publication in 1847 (and the continued popularity of *Manners and Customs*) meant that most nineteenth-century English speakers interested in Egypt learned about it through Wilkinson's prose.

Samuel Sharpe: Finding Unitarianism in the Ancient Near East

Samuel Sharpe (1799–1881) also exemplifies the nineteenth-century man of letters, although he was more of a writer than a traveler. He was a non-professional scholar, son of a brewer and a member of a family of Dissenters (Unitarians) on his mother's side, himself breaking away from his early Anglican upbringing formally in 1821. Most of his income derived from his work as a banker. After his retirement, he was able to devote himself full-time to the study of the ancient world, especially the study of Egypt and the translation of the Bible. It was not just curiosity about the past that drove him but the conviction that the Bible needed to be better translated and that Egyptian trinitarian ideas had had a profound, negative influence on early Christianity. For the most part, his academic positions have not withstood the test of time, but his theological arguments were an important part of mid-nineteenth-century public discourse. His self-description, 'I am a heretic in everything, even among Unitarians', is widely quoted in reference to his work.

Although mostly ignored in contemporary accounts of the history of Egyptology, Sharpe was one of those diligent non-professionals who began working on Egypt's history in the immediate aftermath of the decipherment of hieroglyphs. His first book was published in 1836—*The Early History of Egypt*—and by the end of his life he had published numerous works on the subject, including technical works on the ancient Egyptian and Coptic languages. From 1837 to 1855 he published Egyptian materials from the British Museum, and while his translations were often quite speculative (given the state of knowledge at the time), these were legitimately important works in the early establishment of British Egyptology.

The Early History of Egypt is an interesting example of the kinds of scholarship that were practiced in the immediate aftermath of the decipherment of hieroglyphs. The full title, *The Early History of Egypt, from the Old Testament, Herodotus, Manetho, and the Hieroglyphical Inscriptions*, indicates its reliance on the same sources that had been most important prior to the Napoleonic expedition but which were now supplemented with the first translated Egyptian texts. The biblical and classical texts are still the foundations for the historical narrative, but a new level of critical approach is emerging here. In his preface, Sharpe writes:

> The extracts from each historian are placed separately, so that, in the words of Herodotus quoted in the title page, 'each person may use those which he thinks may be relied upon'; and the remarks which are added, with a view to explain the extracts, and to show how far the account of one historian is consistent with that of another, are also kept distinct, so that the value of the quotations may not be lessened by the errors of the criticisms.[12]

The first half of the book, then, is structured according to source. What marks this as the start of a new approach is that Sharpe is able to compare these classical accounts with Egyptian sources. This is most readily apparent in his comparison of Manetho's chronology with the Abydos king list. Drawing heavily on the works of Banks and Wilkinson, Sharpe compares the names in the various dynasties presented in the two sources in order to determine the level of agreement and attempts to explain discrepancies. Similar approaches to other texts are taken, and Sharpe uses a diverse variety of Egyptian sources for comparative purposes. What this book represents is a first step in a synthetic approach to Egyptian history, integrating recent archaeological and linguistic discoveries with more traditional biblical and classical scholarship.

The latter half of the book is devoted to more general comments on aspects of Egyptian civilization. These comments vary. Sharpe uses art–historical evidence to explain that the Egyptians and the Ethiopians were not 'Negroes'; he describes various deities (mostly through recourse to classical sources); and makes various comments on Egyptian languages (including Coptic). Throughout the entire book, many of Sharpe's general comments on ancient Egypt reflect a belief in parallels between ancient Egypt and nineteenth-century Britain. For example, on Egyptian government, he writes:

> it was monarchical, but very far from despotic in the bad meaning of the word; for a king surrounded by an hereditary order of soldiers and an

12. Samuel Sharpe, *The Early History of Egypt, from the Old Testament, Herodotus, Manetho, and the Hieroglyphical Inscriptions* (London: Edward Moxon, 1836).

hereditary order of priests, and these possessed of civil power, must have felt himself a good deal checked by his aristocracy. And, without supposing the assembly of elected judges to have possessed the important privileges of legislation and control of the monarch which we now annex to the idea of a representative chamber, it can hardly have been of less importance in those respects than the old French parliaments, which were not elected. But the few facts which we possess, respecting the limitation of the royal power, are strengthened by their adoption of the English constitutional axiom, and exactly in the sense in which we now use it, that the king could do no wrong: his advisors bore the blame.[13]

Here then, Sharpe has described ancient Egypt as monarchy kept in check by a hereditary aristocracy, which would have been seen as an ideal form of governance within conservative British circles in the 1830s. At times, however, Sharpe's more radical tendencies are presented, as when he states that the Egyptians 'exceeded the politeness of moderns' in their allowance for female leadership and in placing female names first in lists (such as Isis and Osiris).[14]

At the same time that Sharpe was participating in early Egyptology, he was also working on new translations of the Bible, and these endeavours were, in fact, linked.[15] His first published translation was an 1840 edition of the New Testament, which he revised through eight editions. His first attempt at the Old Testament was published in 1865, and this was revised three further times. One of his concerns with revising Bible translations was to remove archaic approaches to the treatment of the text and format it according to modern conventions. His Bibles are broken into paragraphs, dialogue indicated, and tables used to break up lists. His translations are also markedly Unitarian, and when possible he made minor translation choices to be consistent with Unitarian ideas.

Sharpe's biblical translations were informed by archaeological materials. His 1874 *Short Notes to Accompany a Revised Translation of the Hebrew Scriptures* is an almost line-by-line commentary of the Old Testament in translation. As he states in the introduction, it was meant to be entirely 'geographical and antiquarian' as well as to provide notes on difficulties in the text and suggestions on matters of textual production.[16] Basic source-critical comments are given, mostly following the discoveries of the German

---

13. Sharpe, *Early History of Egypt*, p. 6.
14. Sharpe, *Early History of Egypt*, p. 6.
15. Beyond this scholarly work, although most certainly influenced by it, Sharpe was a voluminous writer of religious tracts, signed by his initials (S.S.) as was common for periodicals of the time. Many of these works appeared in the *Christian Reformer* from 1834 to 1863, or in *Christian Life* from 1876 to 1881.
16. Samuel Sharpe, *Short Notes to Accompany a Revised Translation of the Hebrew Scriptures* (London: J. Russel Smith, 1874), p. iii.

school. After very brief introductions to each book of the Old Testament, Sharpe provides line-by-line commentary, mostly related to explaining the verse from within the context of ancient Near Eastern studies, especially Egyptology, Assyriology and archaeology. This is not a theological commentary; for the most part it remains committed to a historical exposition of the text, and in many ways may be considered one of the first biblical commentaries rooted in the archaeological study of the Near East.

A good example of his approach is found in Genesis 3 (the Garden of Eden). Sharpe explains at the outset of the chapter, 'This is the only part of the Hebrew Scriptures in which an attempt is made to explain the origin of moral evil. The inquiry is foreign from the Hebrew mind, which looked upon God as the sole author of everything, whether we call it good or evil. Much in the account of the Garden of Eden is Egyptian in character.'[17] Sharpe then proceeds to illustrate what is Egyptian in character, much of which seems suspect to a twenty-first-century reader. For example, he translates Gen. 3.15 as follows: 'I will put enmity between thee and the woman'.[18] Sharpe comments, 'In the Egyptian sculptures we have the goddess Isis piercing the head of the serpent with a spear, and numerous representations of men fighting the wicked enemy of the human race'.[19] The exact relationship that he perceives between Gen. 3.15 and Isis is unclear, but this is typical of the kind of illustration of verse that Sharpe provides.

Sharpe takes a similar approach, but using illustrations as well, in his *Texts from the Holy Bible Explained by the Help of the Ancient Monuments with a Few Plans and Views* (1866). The book contains around 160 woodcarvings, mostly by Joseph Bonomi, who had also illustrated Wilkinson's book. As with his later *Short Notes*, the book is mostly organized on a verse-by-verse basis, although significantly fewer verses are dealt with and there is less discussion of translation problems. As regards Gen. 3.15, Sharpe provides the same comments as in *Short Notes*. Here, however, he offers Bonomi's woodcarving of a scene from an Egyptian sarcophagus in the Louvre, with the following label: 'The Egyptian goddess Isis standing in a boat, and piercing through the head of the Serpent of Wickedness, which has been brought to her in chains, after having received numerous stabs'.[20] As in *Short Notes*, no further explanation of the relation between this verse and this Egyptian scene is offered.

Assyrian remains are used similarly in Sharpe's work. Genesis 10.9 (referencing Nimrod the mighty hunter before the Lord) is illustrated with

---

17. Sharpe, *Short Notes*, p. 3.
18. Sharpe, *Short Notes*, p. 3.
19. Sharpe, *Short Notes*, p. 3.
20. Samuel Sharpe, *Texts from the Holy Bible Explained by the Help of the Ancient Monuments with a Few Plans and Views* (London: Day & Son, 1866), p. 6.

Bonomi's woodcarving of the Assyrian sculpture from Khorsabad, identified here as an 'imaginary portrait of Nimrod, the Assyrian hero, killing the lion'.[21] Sharpe is more thorough in his explanation of the relationship between this image and the verse:

> The sculptor has represented him, not as a man who would fight with a sword or spear, but as a giant, or demi-god, who has no need of such weapons. The ancient city of Nineveh is now called by its yet more ancient name of Nimroud. The hero was probably named after the city. Lion-hunting was one of the favourite amusements of the Assyrian kings. It is represented in a variety of ways on the sculptures in the British Museum...[22]

Most of these comments are incorrect, as is typical of Sharpe's work, in part due to his willingness to speculate but mostly due to the immaturity of the field. However, the basic methodology that he helped establish here, to some degree still perpetuated in popular biblical archaeology, is that biblical verses can be illustrated by the artifacts of archaeology. This type of one-to-one comparison was thought to be theologically meaningful.

Arguably Sharpe's most novel contribution is his 1863 work *Egyptian Mythology and Egyptian Christianity, with their Influence on the Opinions of Modern Christendom*. This is a historical description of Egyptian religion detailing the religions of Upper and Lower Egypt separately and then describing transformations under later conquerors, from the Persians to the Byzantine emperors. What makes the book peculiar is his emphasis on how nineteenth-century Christian practices had adopted numerous elements of Egyptian religion. His goal, with this work, was to identify these practices and beliefs so that they could be removed from the modern church. Sharpe explains in the first line of his preface that 'The study of error is often only a little less important than the study of truth'.[23] Later, he continues:

> When Christians shall at length acknowledge that many of those doctrines which together now make up orthodoxy, or the religion of the majority, as distinguished from the simple religion which Jesus taught and practiced, when they shall acknowledge that many of them are so many sad and lamentable errors, then, and not till then, will they seek to know their origin, and enquire from which of the several branches of Paganism they sprung. They will then see that most of the so called Christian doctrines, that have no place in the New Testament, reached Europe from Egypt, via Alexandria.[24]

---

21. Sharpe, *Texts from the Holy Bible*, pp. 9-10.
22. Sharpe, *Texts from the Holy Bible*, p. 10.
23. Samuel Sharpe, *Egyptian Mythology and Egyptian Christianity, with their Influence on the Opinions of Modern Christendom* (London: John Russel Smith, 1863), p. vii.
24. Sharpe, *Egyptian Mythology*, pp. vii-viii.

10. *From Gentleman Scholars to Scholarly Societies*

By the end of his preface, Sharpe has outlined various of these practices, and there can be no doubt that the author is arguing a Unitarian case (that Jesus is divine but is not consubstantial with God, his father). His final comments, before launching into the body of the work, read:

> These fanciful customs and foolish opinions and traditions of art, help to show that although the old Egyptian race has ceased to be a nation for more than twelve hundred years, during which its history has been neglected, and its very existence often forgotten, yet the Egyptian mind still has a most important influence upon our modern civilization. Protestant Europe is even now struggling to throw off the gravest errors of the Nicene Creed and the Atonement, which Rome received from Egypt fifteen centuries ago.[25]

Sharpe's explicit reference to the Nicene Creed (321 CE, revised 381) is an attack on the orthodoxy of the Trinity, since this is the creed that affirmed the divinity of the Father, Son and Holy Spirit, in reaction to the Arian controversy (which saw Jesus as divine but subordinate to his father). For Sharpe, who saw this creed as essentially polytheistic, this was the most significant problem that the church had inherited from Egyptian beliefs.

Other elements of his reconstruction of Egyptian religion better reflect Unitarian theology. Sharpe lays out the 'principle doctrines' that emerged from Egyptian mythology in the preface.[26] The first, of course, is 'That the creation and government of the world is not the work of one simple and undivided being, but of God, made up of several persons. This is the doctrine of Plurality in Unity.'[27] Other observations about Egyptian theological notions that were adapted by Christianity include beliefs that sacrifice to an intermediary being could result in favour from the divine being; that a god could suffer pain and die; and that god could be born of a human mother without a human father. Each of these arguments reflects disagreements or concerns that Unitarians had/have with the church. By 'proving' that these were actually Egyptian beliefs, and not held by the early church, Sharpe justified Unitarian stances.

Other Christian practices and beliefs that Sharpe points out as originally Egyptian are less intrinsic to Unitarian theology but are further indicative of the Egyptian flavor of European Christianity. He explains that wedding rings originated as an Egyptian custom. Various Christmas practices and feast events are, according to Sharpe, rooted in Egyptian practice. Certain clothing and accoutrements of priests and clergymen are based in Egyptian not Christian understandings, such as the reading of liturgy in robes of linen. Various Christian art motifs are based on the iconography of Isis and

---

25. Sharpe, *Egyptian Mythology*, p. xii.
26. Sharpe, *Egyptian Mythology*, pp. ix-xii.
27. Sharpe, *Egyptian Mythology*, p. ix.

Horus, and the triangle of the Trinity references the pyramid shape. Various astrological and magical practices are also Egyptian. For Sharpe, the study of Egyptian religion facilitated his strong arguments for Unitarianism. These are, in some ways, fundamentally Protestant arguments in that they are rooted in a notion that a return to the original church was preferable to the practice of the faith through seemingly later traditions. Yet this is a particularly novel approach to that kind of argument in that it does not come from the study of the New Testament or early church writings but from a comparative approach to ancient Near Eastern studies.

Social Climbing through the Ancient Near East

Wilkinson held an independent source of income, and Sharpe was a professional whose major contributions to the field came after his retirement. Ancient Near Eastern studies, to some extent, provided an outlet for talented middle-class and otherwise marginalized figures to enter into the civil service, through diplomatic or museum posts. What emerged was no longer a completely class-based system in which birth determined the ability to participate. More so, the community of Near Eastern scholars came to be a meritocracy wherein men, with natural talents (especially in languages), and the ability to make connections with society figures came to dominate the field. On a more abstract level, archaeology legitimized 'curiosity' and the questioning of the status quo. Barbara Benedict has shown that various forms of the establishment in the Early Modern Period resisted this kind of questioning and that those who expressed curiosity were seen as social climbers, attempting to escape their station or create new stations.[28] During the Enlightenment, this changed somewhat, and connoisseurship was seen as a means of improving oneself and allowed some transgression of social boundaries.[29] The archaeologically curious of the nineteenth century in many ways were culturally or socially ambitious and did use their academic skills to subvert class boundaries (or at least to operate more freely within them). For in the Victorian era, and unlike the Early Modern Period, academic and scientific findings were seen as culturally useful if not essential, and so rather than discouraging this behavior, the scientific work of the skilled was supported and encouraged. That did not mean that all who wanted to could pursue historical study. Levine has argued that whereas participation in the sciences allowed significant social and economic mobility, participation in the fields of history, archaeology and antiquarian stud-

---

28. Barbara M. Benedict, *Curiosity: A Cultural History of the Early Modern Period* (Chicago: University of Chicago Press, 2001), pp. 22-23.

29. Benedict, *Curiosity*, p. 158.

Fig. 10.2. George Smith in an 1875 engraving from *The Illustrated London News*. Wikimedia Commons.

ies required some degree of established economic comfort.[30] She explains that they 'read for degrees at ancient universities, earned their living in the professions and worshipped in Anglican congregations meanwhile pursuing all manner of studies'.[31] Especially for those scholars who were deemed antiquarians, this lack of devotion to full-time study meant that this was a fundamentally amateur occupation. Only after one's professional activities were finished for the day or week could one engage in studies, and often antiquarians operated with little formal background in the specific area of study.[32]

George Smith (1840–1876) was one of these major figures who came from an obscure, non-aristocratic background, but managed to secure himself a position in the British Museum (Fig. 10.2). At the age of fourteen, Smith was apprenticed to a bank-note engraver, where he learned that trade. Smith's real interests, however, lay in the translations of ancient cuneiform texts, where he had an unusual aptitude. As Seton Lloyd describes, Smith 'devoted every minute of his spare time to reading about Assyrian excavations, and his dinner-hours to studying the sculptures and inscriptions exhibited in the British Museum'.[33] Smith first started working at the museum as a volunteer, cataloging and reading tablets, especially those from Ashurba-

---

30. Levine, *Amateur and the Professional*, p. 11.
31. Levine, *Amateur and the Professional*, p. 11.
32. Levine, *Amateur and the Professional*, pp. 22-23.
33. Seton Lloyd, *Foundations in the Dust: The Story of Mesopotamian Exploration* (New York: Thames & Hudson, 1947), p. 146.

Fig. 10.3. Tablet XI of the Gilgamesh Epic. AN00372371_001. © Trustees of the British Museum.

nipal's library.[34] Henry Rawlinson, to whom Smith was introduced by the paid museum staff, provided the patronage that was essential for securing Smith a permanent position. After their initial introduction, Smith's work on the Black Obelisk convinced Rawlinson of Smith's talents.[35] Rawlinson made the argument to the museum trustees that Smith should be given a paid position.

Smith's particular skills lay in identifying tablets and their fragments and making 'joins' of broken ones. It was his project in classifying the tablets

---

34. Ashurbanipal's library is one of the most substantial collections of cuneiform tablets ever discovered, unearthed by Layard and Rassam at Koyunjik and now held by the British Museum. Ashurbanipal was a Neo-Assyrian king who was an avid collector of tablets and sent scribes around the empire to gather materials for his library.

35. The Black Obelisk is a monumental inscription that describes and depicts King Jehu of Israel paying tribute to Shalmanezer III. Smith's reading provided an important extrabiblical correlation of a biblical event. At the time, when the accounts of the books of Kings were taken as straightforwardly historical, the importance of this discovery was seen more for its establishment of the exact date of the event rather than as actual proof that the event had occurred.

from Kuyunjik that led to one of the most sensational discoveries of the nineteenth century, already discussed in Chapter I.4. On December 3, 1872, Smith announced at a meeting of the Society of Biblical Archaeology, that he had discovered the Mesopotamian version of the biblical deluge story.[36] By piecing together fragments from two different copies, Smith had managed to reconstruct most of the story, but there was still a considerable missing section (Fig. 10.3). Shortly after this announcement, the *Daily Telegraph* (a London newspaper) offered to fund Smith's return to Kuyunjik to search for the remaining part of the flood story, providing £1,000. By May of 1873 Smith was at the site, and five days into his excavations discovered the missing portion of the story. The *Daily Telegraph* brought him back to London almost immediately and did not support further excavations. However, the British Museum did send him out again, and on this last expedition, Smith died of dysentery in the field.

Here, then, can be seen the origins of one of the major themes of Assyriological work in its early years as a discipline—the comparison of cuneiform documents with the Hebrew Bible. Whereas Smith's attempts at drawing connections between cuneiform and biblical culture proved to be productive, many of these early efforts at connecting the discoveries of ancient Near Eastern studies with biblical ideas were not successful. An interesting, and somewhat parallel, figure is Gerald Massey (1828–1907). Massey (Fig. 10.4) came from an impoverished family, and much of his childhood was spent eking out a living in silk and straw factories. Despite the fact that formal education could not be a priority, he managed to teach himself, and as an adult was able to support himself as a writer and poet, publishing his first book of poems at the age of twenty-two. Massey was a devoted spiritualist, and he used his 'psychic' abilities to better understand Egyptian civilization.

It was in the 1870s, around the same time that Smith made his discoveries, that Massey began to study Egyptology seriously. For Massey, there were significant parallels between the Gospel stories and Egyptian mythology, most especially in the tales surrounding Osiris and Horus. He wrote three books on the subject: *The Book of the Beginning, The Natural Genesis,* and *Ancient Egypt: The Light of the World.* It is in *The Natural Genesis* that Massey spells out his most significant argument—that there are significant parallels in the stories of the life of Jesus and the life of Horus. Most of these perceived similarities bear little actual resemblance to the stories of Horus (death by crucifixion, river baptism, born of virgins on December 25, etc.). They require significant leaps of logic to follow and very charitable readings of the Egyptian stories to identify the similarities. Nevertheless, his books were popular and are still cited in fringe and non-scholarly circles

---

36. The text of this address can be found in George Smith, 'The Chaldean Account of the Deluge', *Transactions of the Society of Biblical Archaeology* 2 (1873), pp. 213-34.

Fig. 10.4. Image of Gerald Massey, dated to 1856. Wikimedia Commons.

as evidence that Christian traditions merely usurped and transformed earlier pagan practices.[37] Massey's views are summarized in a poem at the front of his *The Book of the Beginning*:

> Egypt! how I have dwelt with you in dreams,
> So long, so intimately, that it seems
> As if you had borne me; though I could not know
> It was so many thousand years ago!
> And in my gropings darkly underground
> The long-lost memory at last is found
> Of motherhood—you Mother of us all!
> And to my fellow-men I must recall
> The memory too; that common motherhood
> May help to make the common brotherhood.
>
> Egypt! it lies there in the far-off past,
> Opening with depths profound and growths as vast
> As the great valley of Yosemité;
> The birthplace out of darkness into day;
> The shaping matrix of the human mind;
> The Cradle and the Nursery of our kind.
> This was the land created from the flood,
> The land of Atum, made of the red mud,
> Where Num sat in his Teba throned on high,
> And saw the deluge once a year go by,
> Each brimming with the blessing that it brought,

---

37. See, for example, Tom Harpur, *The Pagan Christ: Recovering the Lost Light* (Toronto: Thomas Allen Publishers, 2004). For a response to this work and commentary on Harpur's reliance on Massey and similar authors with dubious Egyptological credentials, see W. Ward Gasque, 'The Leading Religion Writer in Canada... Does He Know What He's Talking About?', *George Mason University's History News Network*, Tuesday, August 17, 2004.

And by that water-way, in Egypt's thought,
The gods descended; but they never hurled
The Deluge that should desolate the world.

There the vast hewers of the early time
Built, as if that way they would surely climb
The heavens, and left their labours without name–
Colossal as their carelessness of fame–
Sole likeness of themselves—that heavenward
Forever look with statuesque regard,

As if some Vision of the Eternal grown
Petrific, was forever fixed in stone!
They watched the Moon re-orb, the Stars go round,
And drew the Circle; Thought's primordial bound.
The Heavens looked into them with living eyes
To kindle starry thoughts in other skies,
For us reflected in the image-scroll,
That night by night the stars for aye unroll.

The Royal Heads of Language bow them down
To lay in Egypt's lap each borrowed crown.
The glory of Greece was but the After-glow
Of her forgotten greatness lying low;
Her Hieroglyphics buried dark as night,
Or coal-deposits filled with future light,
Are mines of meaning; by their light we see
Thro' many an overshadowing mystery.

The nursing Nile is living Egypt still,
And as her low-lands with its freshness fill,
And heave with double-breasted bounteousness,
So doth the old Hidden Source of mind yet bless
The nations; secretly she brought to birth,
And Egypt still enriches all the earth.

Egypt, in Massey's view, is the mother culture for most subsequent cultures, and other religions are mostly just modified versions of Egyptian beliefs. Massey's attempts to connect Horus with Christ were not unique in late-Victorian times, and, in fact, the Keeper of Egyptian and Assyrian Antiquities of the British Museum, E.A. Wallis Budge, made similar claims.

E.A. Wallis Budge was one of the most contentious figures in Near Eastern studies in the latter half of the nineteenth century. Here is another figure who saw strong connections between Egyptian and Christian theology. These theories have likewise been abandoned in mainstream scholarship, but, unlike Massey, Budge's ability to secure a position at the British Museum meant that he had a much more significant impact on Near Eastern studies. Budge's 1934 obituary in the *Daily Telegraph* (dated November 24) is strange and gives no hint as to the influence he had at the British Museum and over ancient Near Eastern studies as a whole:

> Budge's extraordinary cubical figure, with its squareness accentuated by a flat-topped hat, was familiar for over half a century to the museum's visitors, for he retired in 1924 to a house overlooking the museum in Bloomsbury Street, and continued to feed the pigeons in the museum courtyard. For many years, even during the war, he had devoted to them four bushels of maize a day . . . he was also the devoted protector and eventually the biographer of the museum cat, Mike, and he had not a few human pensions as well. Visitors to his home he treated to the Indian cheroots which he had begun to smoke in order to keep off the Mesopotamian flies, and he was an excellent, if occasionally an imaginative, raconteur.

The picture painted by this obituary is of a gentle, elderly and portly man who loved animals and entertaining guests. This is not how he has been remembered. Egyptologists generally revile Budge today because of his generally poor scholarship, especially in terms of his philology, interpretations and ill-conceived attempts at preserving papyrus. Budge's 'extra-legal' efforts to acquire texts and artifacts for the British Museum have not been held in high esteem by historians of the discipline, although Seton Lloyd commends Budge for retrieving tablets excavated by the British Museum that had leaked onto the black market.[38] Assyriologists tend to revile him for his driving role in the Balawat gates controversy and his campaigns against Hormuzd Rassam at the British Museum.[39] Budge's contemporaries seem to have either loved or hated him. Rawlinson supported Budge in the early stages of his career and clearly held him in high esteem. Layard, however, hated Budge with a passion.[40] The non-specialist public seems to have been enamored with Budge. Edith Nesbit dedicated her children's

---

38. Lloyd, *Foundations*, pp. 165-70. This was particularly controversial as Budge claimed to be only recovering tablets that had been looted from excavations that were improperly conducted. Budge blamed Hormuzd Rassam for not taking care to secure his excavation sites or to properly account for the materials excavated. Rassam responded by suing Budge, bringing figures such as his friend, Austen Henry Layard, to testify on his behalf, and eventually winning the suit against Budge. Budge's animosity toward Rassam only increased, in response to this public spectacle.

39. Lloyd, *Foundations*, pp. 153-55. The Balawat Gates controversy began with Budge's claims that Rassam did not discover the gates where he said that he did. Budge visited the site and argued that Rassam had been tricked by the 'natives' and sold these gates. Although no one questions the accuracy of Rassam's description of their provenance today, it was not until 1942 that Seton Lloyd formally set the record straight within the museum administration.

40. Mogens Trolle Larsen, *The Conquest of Assyria: Excavations in an Antique Land 1840–1860* (New York: Routledge, 1996), p. 355.

novel, *The Amulet* (1906), to him.[41] Probably due to the cheap editions of his books available through Dover and editions published through New Age presses such as Arkana, Budge's work is widely read today. Despite the relatively poor quality of Budge's books, they have become fundamental to 'alternative' interpretations of ancient Egypt.

How Budge came to wield so much influence at the British Museum is an interesting subject that sheds light on how ancient Near Eastern studies provided opportunities for the socially marginal to enter Victorian high society. Budge was an illegitimate child born in Cornwall to the daughter of a hotel waiter. He eventually moved to London, where he lived with his grandmother (Jane Thompson Wallis) and worked as a clerk for W.H. Smith & Co., a not uncommon type of work for a literate lower-middle-class individual. In his spare time, he took up the study of ancient languages and spent much of his time at the British Museum working with the collection and studying with a volunteer tutor. There, Samuel Birch took Budge under his wing, introducing him to Rawlinson and other major figures in Near Eastern studies. Budge spent his lunch hours (while working at W.H. Smith) studying at St Paul's Cathedral. The organist noticed the studious Budge and took the case of this poor, but seemingly talented, youth to Budge's employer W.H. Smith. Smith and others raised a fund for Budge to study at Cambridge. When finally enrolled at Cambridge, Budge consciously re-imagined himself. He pretended that his grandfather's name was also his father's (he actually believed that his father was a Mr Vyuyuan) and passed himself off as an orphan rather than an illegitimate child. He adopted the name E.A. Wallis Budge, a combination of different family names.

One of the contributors to Budge's study fund was William Gladstone, who provided a tremendous amount of support to Budge. The two corresponded for the remainder of Gladstone's life. Some have speculated that Gladstone may have been Budge's father because of the tone of some of the surviving correspondence and the level of financial support provided, but this is unlikely. Gladstone was himself a classicist and had a tremendous interest in Mediterranean archaeology, often attending scholarly meetings and participating to some extent in scholarly discourse. Thus it is not surprising that Gladstone should act as a patron to a burgeoning scholar of antiquity.

---

41. The two seem to have had quite a close relationship, and some have speculated that they may have had an affair. Whatever the case may be, Budge helped her with the historical details in *The Amulet*. See Kevin McGeough and Elizabeth Galway, '"Working Egyptians of the World Unite!": How Edith Nesbit Used Near Eastern Archaeology and Children's Literature to Effect Social Change', in *World of Women in the Ancient and Classical Near East* (ed. Beth Alpert Nakhai; Newcastle upon Tyne: Cambridge Scholars, 2009), pp. 181-202.

Budge's letters to Gladstone have been preserved at the British Library. These letters are instructive on the relationship between a patron and student in the nineteenth century, especially a student from outside of Victorian high society. The first correspondence between the two men takes place between Gladstone's first two terms as prime minister (at this time Benjamin Disraeli was prime minister).

A letter by Budge (addressed to 'Sir') dated February 25, 1878, and written on British Museum stationary reads:

> I have had an introduction to Dr. Newton of the British Museum and have shown him my work with which he appears to be satisfied. M.F. Leourmant of Paris, has written a paper:—'Les noms de l'aurais et du cuivre dans les deux langues des inscriptions cuneiformes de la Chaldée et de l'Assyrie'. I have been asked to translate it, make a Précis for printing, and to read it at the Society of Biblical Archaeology next Tuesday (March 5). I am afraid I ask too much, but I should so like to show the translation to you. I have been to your house several times, but have not been able to see you. I remain Sir, Your Obedient Servant, Ernest A. Budge.

Here, the young Budge is using this translation assignment as an excuse to meet with Gladstone in person. He probably hoped to impress Gladstone with his work and demonstrate that he would be a good candidate for financial support.

A letter dated March 8 implies that the two had finally met and that Gladstone had offered Budge some form of support (most likely money to purchase books with) along with a letter of reference. The tone of the letter is somewhat peculiar and shows how Budge further attempted to cement the two men's relationship:

> I thank you very, very much for your great kindness to me. I think you will understand what I mean when I say 'I thank'. Your kindness has shown such a bright light over the dark past years, and gives me energy to work for the future, which I will do God giving me health and strength. But 'my feet had well-nigh slipped', and I had almost lost heart. And again I thank you. Your letter will always remind me of your interview with me, but I should very much like to have your photograph. But I am afraid I ask too much, and such kindness is rare.

Budge's request for Gladstone's photograph seems strange here, and this particular letter has been the source of speculation that Gladstone was, in fact, Budge's father. There is no reason to assume this based on this evidence. Here, instead, is a letter from an admiring young man, genuinely thankful for an opportunity that has been granted him. A letter sent on March 11 thanks Gladstone for the photograph and reports about Budge's visit to the Schliemann collection. He drew two patterns that he noticed on the Trojan pottery that he thought would be of interest to Gladstone, mentions that he 'liked the style of the necklaces' and ends by stating, 'I hope

10. *From Gentleman Scholars to Scholarly Societies* 401

to read Dr. Schliemann's book carefully now'. Thus, the student kept his patron updated on his studies.

By March 21 of that same year, Budge's demands of Gladstone had increased. Now Budge was angling for a formal position within the British Museum, and his efforts were resulting in frustration. Budge writes:

> Yesterday the Speaker [of Parliament] sent a letter to me saying 'Please to call at the BMuseum and see M. Newton, etc. and I shall better be able to consider your claim'. I called today, and saw M. Newton, and he told me that the place would be filled up very shortly by the appointment of Mr. Pinches. I understand him to be a candidate for the vacancy, but Assyrian is his only knowledge, and I should be prepared to compete in an examination with him. Now, I see there is no chance of my getting what I have worked so hard for. And sir, I am disappointed thoroughly. I love Assyria and will still work and make the Semitic languages my study according to the time and appointment that I get, but from appearances I am afraid these have now passed out of my reach, seeming that I shall still have to work at a business which takes the best part of my time and strength. I think my application was the first and I believe it is the oldest, and it seems strange that he has got the appointment. I have been enabled through your liberality to get the other two volumes of Cuneiform Inscriptions, Delitsches Assyrien Studien, and a free Arabic Bible, and have still a surplus. This kindness I shall never forget. The only thing I now want is time. May I ask you Sir, if you should hear of any place that I could fill and which would give me more opportunities for study, will you please remember me? All I can do is to work, which I will. I cannot plead my own cause to the trustees, but I wish all really knew how I have struggled, and that I am willing to devote my life to Cuneiform. Will you tell me Sir if the Speaker has already signed the appointment? I sent Sir H.C. Rawlinson a Précis and told him of your kindness to me, and asked him to speak for me (being the cuneiform scholar) now he is trustee. I enclose his answer. May I trouble you to read and please return. Again, thanking you for your great kindness. I remain Dear Sir, Your Obedient Servant, Ernest A. Budge. Ps. I understand from the Speaker's letter that I had to tell M. Newton something, on particulars, but I was not asked.

In this letter, Budge's competitiveness and drive are apparent—personality traits that became much more apparent as he gradually promoted himself at the British Museum. The means for his self-promotion, at least at first, was to curry favour with important personages, both within the field (Rawlinson) and in the government (who, to some extent, exercised control over appointments at the British Museum).

It eventually became clear to Budge that without a formal education, he would not be able to further his career. He wrote to Gladstone to discuss the matter on April 27, 1878:

> I am sorry indeed to trouble you again, but a misfortune has befallen me. My annual rise in salary has been due a month, and as was usual, I men-

tioned it to our manager, who spoke to the head of our Department and I have been told that they cannot give me any more money and if a position offered itself, I should not have it, and they would be glad to see me better myself. I know it is the custom to treat anyone and everyone in that manner, but it virtually leaves me without a situation in the trade elsewhere, I should not get as much money, and have to begin at the bottom again, and you will guess what that means. [I have] done my work there in every respect like anyone else, and have been shown no leniency. M. Poole, Dr. Stainer and others all say that an university degree is the thing to try and get, but I have no means to get the necessary learning . . . and have scarcely now a situation. Do you know if Mr. Layard or M. Rassam want anyone out with them, who has a knowledge of the Assyrian Cuneiform writing? Mr. Sayce tells me that to get anything at Oxford I should have to know a certain amount of Latin & Greek, and that would he says necessitate residence. I believe if I had a chance I should come off all right in it. But now, I have told you all I can about it Sir; I am sorry to waste your time, but I can do nothing now. I told my employers about myself, that I might not appear dishonourable. I have this week finished the Sennacherib text containing 489 lines of Cuneiform and it is the first time I believe that it has been completely translated. M. Fox Talbot gave 4 and a half columns of it, and many of his readings are different to mine, and some lines that he has left untranslated I have made out.

Other letters around this time are similar. Budge asks Gladstone to find him a position at parliament with more flexible hours, or to send him off with Layard and Rassam to Assyria. He emphasizes how much a degree at Oxford would help him and how the study of Latin and Greek are essential for his future studies. In a letter dated April 9, 1878, Budge asserts his desire to work hard ('I am anxious to have an object, I don't care how hard I have to work, as long as there is a goal') and describes how he is at an impasse and cannot proceed without Gladstone's help ('I have kept awake several hours of the night wondering what plan or course to take, and as yet cannot see any'). By May 28, Budge has started to think that Cambridge would be a better fit for him (on the advice of Sayce) and has started asking for annual contributions to his education fund and suggests that an article of his on incantations be used by Gladstone as evidence of his scholarly promise.

Through May and June of 1878, under Gladstone's guidance, Budge had a fund formally set up for himself. A circular, with the names of patrons, was sent to potential donors, along with letters from the museum on his behalf. Dr Stainer (the organist at St Paul's who initially suggested this course of action) acted as treasurer of the fund. Tuition fees, household expenses and book costs (Budge enumerated these by price and title for Gladstone) were all covered by the fund. In the preparation of the circular, lists of amounts donated by each individual are mentioned and discussed in the letters.[42]

---

42. In a letter dated June 21, 1878, Budge calculates his yearly expenses as £106.

Budge also sent Gladstone samples of the Assyrian dictionary that he was working on—words listed on flashcards with transliteration, English translation and ancient Hebrew equivalent. Budge also discussed with Gladstone the particulars of his proposed course of study at Cambridge and the subject of his examinations. The question of how long Budge needed to study at Cambridge was worked out at this time as well.

Once completed, the circular was typed and sent along with handwritten letters to those who may have been interested in contributing. The circular reads:

> We, the undersigned, having inquired into the case of Mr. E.A. Budge, are desirous to obtain for him the means of repairing to one of the universities, and taking his degree. While employed as a Boy and as a Book-Collector during eight-and-a-half years under Messrs. W.H. Smith & Son, he has by economy and diligence found time and means to prosecute the study of languages—especially of Eastern languages,—and has acquired a knowledge of cuneiform inscriptions, which is deemed competent by authorities of high promise. We desire for him the means of prosecuting his studies and improving his gifts by a full Academical Education.
>
> We find that the time required for this purpose would be about three and a-half years and the probable expense about £450. Towards this sum, Mr. Smith has munificently promised a contribution of £150.
>
> Those qualified and willing have promised to assist Mr. Budge with their advice from time to time; and Dr. Stainer will act as treasurer, and will receive contributions, which we heartily solicit from those who deem the object worthy of their aid.
>
> A note of the promises already made is subjoined, should the sum received exceed the amount which has been named, it will be laid out to assist the future studies of Mr. Budge.
> (signed) W.E. Gladstone
> A.H. Sayce

Right Hon W.E. Gladstone, M.P.	20
W.H. Smith, M.P.	150
Rev. A.H. Sayce, M.A.	30
Dr. Stainer, M.A.	30
Sir W.C. James	20
Lord Wolverton	20
W.S.W. Vaux eq	5
Mrs Birks	5
A. Morrison esq.	30
Marquis of Alisbury	10

> Cheques may be made payable to Dr. Stainer, or may be paid direct to the account standing in the joint names of John Stainer and Ernest Budge of the Holburn Branch of the London and County Bank.

Budge succeeded in gaining enough funding to support his studies at Cambridge, which lasted from 1878 until 1883, where he worked closely with the Semitics scholar William Wright. Before leaving for Cambridge, Budge requested letters of introduction from Gladstone for 'any gentleman you think fit', and requested addresses of individuals that he should visit in Cambridge. Throughout his time at Cambridge, Budge kept Gladstone posted about his progress, about the courses that he was taking, about his examinations and other day-to-day matters. During this time, Budge attempted to gain notice from Rawlinson and periodically requested that Gladstone intervene on his behalf with Rawlinson. Here though, it is evident how talented individuals of the wrong class could be supported by elites and how elite patronage in tandem with Near Eastern studies could help individuals circumvent the strict class boundaries of Victorian times.

Budge's later correspondence with Gladstone has a decidedly different tone. After Budge has become an established figure in Near Eastern studies, his correspondence with Gladstone is less deferent and usually consists of responses to Gladstone's own questions about the ancient world. In a number of letters dated to 1892, Budge answers Gladstone's queries about various Egyptological finds and especially about the word 'Akausha' (mentioned in cuneiform and hieroglyphs), which may be related to the Greek 'Achaean' and thus of great interest to Gladstone, who was deeply interested in the Trojan War. Budge also thanks Gladstone for an evening get together, which indicates that the two socialized. Here the patronage is still apparent, but now Budge is an established figure in Victorian society.

Partially due to the fact that Budge worked in one of the foremost establishments of academic Near Eastern scholarship, Budge's writings have had a long-lasting effect on fringe interpretations of ancient Egypt. As Hornung has noted, Budge's Egyptological studies are frequently the basis for New Age and occult understandings of Egypt—mediums supposedly channeling ancient Egyptians use language surprisingly akin to Budge's incorrect or outdated readings of Egyptian.[43] His books remain popular today and are among the most widely distributed Egyptological books due to their cheap reissues. Although of great popular appeal, his work is mostly ignored by academics today. Given its importance in the popular imagination of Egypt, a few of his key ideas are worth surveying.

Budge's take on ancient Egyptian religion is very peculiar and is not really coherent. He argues that the Egyptians were monotheists (or at least tended toward monotheism) and that much of their belief system seems to

---

43. Erik Hornung, *The Secret Lore of Egypt: Its Impact on the West* (trans. D. Lorton; Ithaca, NY: Cornell University Press, 2001), p. 199.

have prefigured Christianity.⁴⁴ He states this clearly at the beginning of his 1899 survey of Egyptian religion: 'A study of ancient Egyptian religious texts will convince the reader that the Egyptians believed in One God, who was self-existent, immortal, invisible, eternal, omniscient, almighty. . . .'⁴⁵ Budge goes on to describe how this was the foundation of Egyptian theology, from very early periods until the end of Egyptian civilization. He concedes that the religion of the Egyptians before their 'complex social system' developed may have been 'little better than those of the savage tribes now living'.⁴⁶ According to Budge, early, less advanced superstitions were perpetuated in Egyptian religion because of a certain reverence for inherited tradition, 'not because they themselves believed in them. . . .'⁴⁷ He further states, 'the educated classes in Egypt at all times never placed the "gods" on the same high level as God, and they never imagined that their views on this point could be mistaken'.⁴⁸ For the most part, however, Budge seems to suggest that the Egyptians conceived of a God that is recognizable to Christians. Budge frequently conflates nineteenth-century conceptions of God with Egyptian gods, making for some odd commentary. For example, he states, 'The epithets which the Egyptians applied to their gods also bear valuable testimony concerning the ideas which they held about God . . . the "gods' are only forms, manifestations, and phases of Ra. . . .'⁴⁹

Budge's view of Egyptian religion is certainly colored by an evolutionary perspective (see Chapter I.4), in which religion advances toward monotheism as a society advances toward civilization. He writes:

> Many writers on the Egyptian religion have somewhat blinked the fact that it had two sides; on the one it closely resembles in many respects the Christian religion of to-day, and on the other the religion of many sects which flourished in the first three or four centuries of our era, and which may be said to have held beliefs which were part Christian and part non-Christian. In its non-Christian aspect it represents a collection of ideas and superstitions which belong to a savage or semi-savage state of existence, and which maintained their hold in a degree upon the minds of the Egyptians long after they had advanced to a high state of civilization. We may think that such ideas and beliefs are both childish and foolish, but there is no possible reason for doubting that they were very real things to those who held them. . . .⁵⁰

---

44. E.A. Wallis Budge, *Egyptian Religion: Egyptian Ideas of the Future Life* (New York: Arkana, 1987 [1899]), p. 14.
45. Budge, *Egyptian Religion*, p. 1.
46. Budge, *Egyptian Religion*, p. 7.
47. Budge, *Egyptian Religion*, p. 39.
48. Budge, *Egyptian Religion*, p. 84.
49. Budge, *Egyptian Religion*, p. 17.
50. Budge, *Egyptian Religion*, pp. 1-2.

Here, Budge lays out (although in a somewhat inconsistent fashion) a set of criteria for mapping out which components of Egyptian religion were civilized and which were not. That this is the introduction to a book on Egyptian magic suggests that here is an apology to his audience on behalf of the Egyptians for believing in the type of magic he is about to discuss. This book itself comes to play an important role in New Age adoptions of 'Egyptian' practices in that it lays out various ideas about the practice of the 'occult' arts.

In a number of works, Budge explains his take on Osiris, in which he speaks of the Egyptian conceptions of Osiris as prefiguring Christian understandings of Christ. He writes, 'they [the Egyptians] had certain hope of the resurrection in an immortal, eternal, and spiritual body, because Osiris had risen in a transformed spiritual body, and had ascended into heaven, where he had become the king and the judge of the dead, and had attained unto everlasting life therein'.[51] Budge discusses how these ideas about Osiris well prepared the Egyptians to embrace Christianity. He states, 'Never did Christianity find elsewhere in the world a people whose minds were so thoroughly well prepared to receive its doctrines as the Egyptians'.[52] The Egyptian anticipation of Christianity is apparent in his treatment of the Papyrus of Ani (a copy of the *Book of the Dead*), which continues to be one of the best-selling versions of the Egyptian text (and most popular among non-specialist audiences).

The Professionalization of Near Eastern Studies

As knowledge of the Near East progressed, especially understandings of the languages (which required more dedicated study), the norms of the field were established, and the study of the Near East became a professionalized discipline: first through the British Museum, second through professional societies and third, and really after the nineteenth century, through university teaching positions. The professional societies, however, did not function entirely as exclusionary bodies. While setting normative practices for the field (both in terms of archaeological methods and reporting standards) their dependence on subscriptions required participation from a wider cross-section of the public. Yet as Jonathan Rose has argued, following Mary Douglas, 'the drive to maintain differentials of information is present in all societies'.[53] To make Near Eastern studies a viable career option, or in Rose's words, 'to have exchange value in the marketplace', monopolies

---

51. Budge, *Egyptian Religion*, p. 80.
52. Budge, *Egyptian Religion*, p. 81.
53. Jonathan Rose, *The Intellectual Life of the British Working Class* (New Haven, CT: Yale University Press, 2nd edn, 2010), p. 394.

or other limitations on that knowledge need to be fostered.[54] Néstor García Canclini has noted, in the context of Latin American modernization, that artifacts of the past may seem to belong to everyone but they really do not.[55] As history is brought into the modernist project, the kind of knowledge that was once held by everyone (or in the case here by any man of letters) becomes less valuable than the knowledge generated by those individuals with specialist training who then become arbiters of that knowledge.

The types of materials available by the latter half of the nineteenth century made it possible for Egyptologists and Assyriologists to work much as historians of other periods were working at the time. The discovery of cuneiform records, and to some limited extent Egyptian papyri, allowed Near Eastern studies to begin to adopt some of the practices of the new 'records' history that emerged in the Victorian academy. The recognition of state records as an important source in the writing of history (for non-classical time periods) transformed the historical profession in the mid-nineteenth century and meant that by the end of the Victorian era, a professional historian was most likely someone who worked with archival documents as opposed to the formal narrative accounts of past times that had been typical of historical research at the beginning of the century.[56] While the actual practice of this kind of history reached only very basic levels during the nineteenth century, the recognition of the importance of these kinds of sources by professional historians likely played a role in the collection of these tablets from the field. By the time Akkadian and other languages were understood well enough for this kind of research, records history had become normative in professional practice.

The university, however, was not the major source of support for Near Eastern studies until after the Victorian age. While this is, without a doubt, the major institution of Near Eastern studies in the twenty-first century, it was slow to be adopted by nineteenth-century universities. Classical studies was already an established field in the academy by the beginning of the nineteenth century, and the early orientalists attempted to emulate this field to some extent, though often in schools of theology and especially in the context of biblical studies.[57] Secular studies of the Near East were slower to become institutionalized. The Disney Chair of Archaeology at Cambridge was endowed in 1851, but this was not devoted to the Near East. History more broadly was incorporated at Cambridge and Oxford over the course

---

54. Rose, *Intellectual Life*, p. 394.
55. Néstor García Canclini, *Hybrid Cultures: Strategies for Entering and Leaving Modernity* (trans. Christopher Chiappari and Sylvia López; Minneapolis, MN: University of Minnesota Press, 1995), pp. 135-36.
56. Levine, *Amateur and the Professional*, p. 75.
57. Suzanne L. Marchand, *German Orientalism in the Age of Empire: Religion, Race, and Scholarship* (Cambridge: Cambridge University Press, 2009), pp. 78-79.

of the 1850s to 1870s.[58] Active historians did have university posts before, but often these were not posts in history per se; the historical work was more of a side-line unrelated to the paid position.[59] The latter half of the century saw history become a discipline in its own right that was taught as a university subject, independent of classics and theology. The early establishment of history within the university (as opposed to archaeology or antiquarianism) meant that both of these enterprises were seen as subsidiary to the more legitimate work of writing 'History'.[60] Narrative presentations of the past superseded representations of the past mediated by objects.[61] Over the long term, this distinction between history and archaeology has been maintained in the academy, in part due to the kinds of evidence and training required but also in part because of disciplinary prejudices. By the end of the nineteenth century, the communities of Near Eastern archaeological practice had established enough normative practices within the discipline to be able to mount legitimate university programs with some degree of agreed-upon academic rigour. Likewise, full-time professionalization led to increased specialization of knowledge; as more became known, it became impossible to master all of the material and even less possible to participate as a non-specialist.[62] However, as Levine has noted, by the end of the nineteenth century, Near Eastern studies had developed all of the traits that David Allen has argued are necessary to support a scientific field: 'popularity, a common social code, standardisation of techniques and the existence of an overseeing institution'.[63] After 1870, specialist journals had begun to proliferate.[64] Popular studies of archaeology could readily be differentiated from scholarly studies, and the institutions of the academy had gained the power to dictate the 'true' past of the ancient Near East.

What distinguished archaeologists from antiquarians in the nineteenth century was the growing specificity of archaeological interests—interests limited to artifacts and excavation.[65] Antiquarians could be interested in anything and apply any method to whatever they felt inclined to study.[66] Archaeologists were defined by their method (excavation) and by their subject of study (material culture). While many antiquarians were interested in

58. Levine, *Amateur and the Professional*, p. 2.
59. Levine, *Amateur and the Professional*, p. 23.
60. See Levine, *Amateur and the Professional*, p. 29.
61. Bann, *Inventions of History*, p. 131.
62. Levine, *Amateur and the Professional*, p. 38.
63. Levine, *Amateur and the Professional*, p. 54.
64. Suzanne Marchand notes that in 1898, the Assyriologist F.E. Peiser was already complaining that there were too many specialist journals in the field (*German Orientalism*, p. 165).
65. Levine, *Amateur and the Professional*, p. 31.
66. Levine, *Amateur and the Professional*, p. 71.

archaeology, the reverse was not really true, at least in the academic manifestations of the enterprises. Archaeologists, to some extent, retained some of the romantic manifestations of antiquarianism, especially notions of rescuing the past.[67] However, the antiquarian affection for ruin and decay (and its preservation) was transformed into a more active practice of excavation. By the end of the nineteenth century, archaeology had become a professional activity, distinct from the hobby of antiquarianism and as such, antiquarians, who were unable to devote their full time (and interests) to the study of one subject, had become marginal figures in the construction of knowledge about the ancient Near East. Local history could still be the work of the amateur, but the study of Egypt or Mesopotamia could not.[68]

For scholars of the Near East, the physical distance of travel (and the difficulties involved) further distinguished their work from the dabbling of other types of enthusiasts (especially classicists, who never actually had to visit Greece or Italy if they did not wish to), and the expatriate communities that formed in the Near East brought these scholars into close association with one another. This facilitated a kind of networking that was reinforced by gatherings at home as well as in the field. This community was fundamental to the construction of disciplinary practices and boundaries. As Levine has noted, the early archaeologists were seen as 'travellers' first and foremost, and, as has been argued here earlier, the first archaeological reports fall within the genre of travel literature.[69] At the same time, it was the act of travel that lent authority to the early archaeologists. They had little formal training, if any (perhaps some background in Hebrew, Greek, or Latin and the classics more broadly), and even Petrie, one of the first truly professional archaeologists, was home schooled.[70]

For those who engaged in archaeological research, most found some way to support the work as a full-time occupation.[71] Though these were not usually lifelong occupations (take Layard, for example), during the excavation, at least, there was no way to 'moonlight' as an archaeologist. Other Near Eastern scholars could work on their studies in their spare time, but archaeologists needed to be in the field to do their work, away from other possible occupations. As Levine has noted, Petrie's training consisted of self-education, through working at the British Museum and viewing sales at Sotheby's.[72] After Petrie, archaeologists would be trained in his methods. However, until the archaeological methodological revolutions of Petrie, and the development of field schools under Wheeler and others, the most secure

67. Bann, *Inventions of History*, p. 130.
68. Levine, *Amateur and the Professional*, p. 174.
69. Levine, *Amateur and the Professional*, p. 31.
70. Levine, *Amateur and the Professional*, p. 32.
71. Levine, *Amateur and the Professional*, p. 32.
72. Levine, *Amateur and the Professional*, p. 92.

institutional support for archaeologists was through the museum. Thus, some of the most influential figures in shaping the trajectory of Near Eastern studies in the nineteenth century were people like E.A. Budge, who, as an employee of the British Museum, was also, effectively, a civil servant.[73] Thus the academic works of Budge, based on rigorous self-study but shaky theoretical and methodological grounds, have not had nearly the same influence as the professional practices that he established for the discipline.

The Role of Scholarly Societies

By the mid-nineteenth century, scholarly societies became important institutions for the support of Near Eastern studies and for the formalization of professional standards. Earlier efforts had not met with much success; the Palestine Association (founded in 1804 and again in 1840) and the Syro-Egyptian Society, which eventually merged into the Biblical Archaeology Society, achieved little traction in British intellectual life.[74] In the United States, the American Oriental Society, founded in 1842, was more successful and is still a thriving academic society today. However, other American efforts, such as the American Palestine Exploration Society, were less fruitful.[75] By the 1860s, scholarly societies in Britain were in a better position to achieve their goals of fostering Near Eastern exploration and scholarship, although their successes varied. Part of that work was to standardize methods of enquiry, as had been the goal in other sciences of organization like the Royal Society, which sought to create rules for establishing 'truth'.[76] The scholarly societies that supported ancient Near Eastern scholarship were regionally focused and topic specific. Unlike other historical societies, the organizations through which Near Eastern scholars operated were specific and helped further articulate distinct disciplinary boundaries in ways that were not true of other historical disciplines. Whereas a historian of mediaeval Europe may find herself today in a department with American historians, Early Modern historians, etc., departments of Near Eastern studies (or other means of regional constitution) keep the field methodologically insulated to some degree.

---

73. Levine, *Amateur and the Professional*, p. 175.

74. Yehoshua Ben-Arieh, *The Rediscovery of the Holy Land in the Nineteenth Century* (Jerusalem: Sefer Ve Sefel Publishing, 2007 [1979]), p. 195.

75. The American Palestine Exploration Society (1870–1880) was founded as an American correlate of the British Palestine Exploration Fund, but never managed to establish itself. For an interesting account of the failed APES and its survey endeavors, see Rachel Hallote, Felicity Cobbing and Jeffrey B. Spur, *The Photographs of the American Palestine Exploration Society* (Annual of the American Schools of Oriental Research, 66; Boston: American Schools of Oriental Research, 2012).

76. Benedict, *Curiosity*, p. 12.

10. *From Gentleman Scholars to Scholarly Societies* 411

Whereas professional historians tended to distance themselves from non-professionals, archaeologists sought public outreach, especially through academic societies.[77] This was fundamental to the fund-raising practices of early archaeologists, who required public donations (in the absence of governmental or institutional support). This meant that there was a significant social element to the early archaeological societies—dinners, parties and other non-academic activities were important events that facilitated interactions between professional and non-professional and allowed the people to participate in an intellectual life without having to devote themselves full time to the enterprise.[78] As Moscrop points out, voluntary and self-regulating societies were a common form of middle-class leisure as the standard of living increased in the nineteenth century.[79] Since these societies were charitable and educational, the social, entertainment and networking values of participation could be framed as improving and dutiful. These voluntary societies also welcomed women (unlike organizations such as the Royal Geographic Society), who were able to play prominent roles in the governance and activities of these groups and participate through 'informal' work.[80]

In 1870, Samuel Birch (Fig. 10.5) founded the Society of Biblical Archaeology, a society that existed as an independent entity until 1919 when it was incorporated into the Royal Asiatic Society of Great Britain and Ireland.[81] That an Egyptologist would found a society for biblical archaeology would be unlikely in twenty-first-century Egyptology, but this well reflects the nineteenth-century relationship between these disciplines. Likewise, that the British Museum would be connected to the foundation of at least one Near Eastern archaeological society should not be surprising. Others involved in the early stages of the society were drawn from a wide background.[82] The first meeting was held in the house of Joseph Bonomi, by that time the curator of the Soane Museum. Rawlinson, Sayce and Wilson were among the early active members in the field. Gladstone was also a member and attended meetings. At first simply meeting in members' homes, the society was able to open its headquarters in 1872 and by 1891 had estab-

---

77. Levine, *Amateur and the Professional*, p. 35.
78. Levine, *Amateur and the Professional*, p. 64.
79. John James Moscrop, *Measuring Jerusalem: The Palestine Exploration Fund and British Interests in the Holy Land* (London: Leicester University Press, 2000), p. 49.
80. Melman, *Women's Orients*, pp. 8-9.
81. For a description of the institutional and membership history of the society, see F. Legge, 'The Society of Biblical Archæology', *Journal of the Royal Asiatic Society of Great Britain and Ireland* 51 (January 1919), pp. 25-36.
82. As Levine has noted, 59 percent of the membership at first came from London, which makes sense given that non-residents would not have easily been able to take advantage of the classes and lectures (Levine, *Amateur and the Professional*, p. 52).

Fig. 10.5. Samuel Birch. Wikimedia Commons.

lished offices across the street from the British Museum. It kept a research library and held lectures and classes (including instruction in Akkadian and Egyptian language) that were open to the public.

In the late Victorian period, this was one of the most important organizations for the public dissemination of information about the ancient Near East. The first volume of *Transactions of the Society of Biblical Archaeology* explains the justification for establishing the society:

> to collect from the fast perishing monuments of the Semitic and cognate races illustrations of their history and peculiarities; to investigate and systematize the Antiquities of the ancient and mighty empires and primeval peoples whose records are centered around the venerable pages of the Bible. In other words, an Association to bring into connexion the labours of individual scholars, and to utilize the results of private enterprize and national munificence—to accumulate data, and to preserve facts—to give a voice to the past, a new life to the future, and assistance, publicity, and permanence to the efforts of all students in Biblical Archaeology.[83]

The formation of the group was rooted in the recognition that something that could be called biblical archaeology had emerged as a discipline in its own right. As a multidisciplinary field of study, the field was of sufficient depth to now require its own specialization, although there were numerous other fields that could host elements of biblical archaeology. In many ways

---

83. N.A., 'Introduction', *Transactions of the Society of Biblical Archaeology* 1 (1872), part 1, pp. i-iv (i-ii).

these sentiments, especially the claims to multidisciplinarity, prefigure W.F. Albright's later American multidisciplinary model of biblical archaeology. For here, the goal was to create a forum for scholars who were otherwise members of the 'Asiatic, Geographic, Literary, and Palestinian Societies' in which they could treat the subject of biblical archaeology 'as a whole'.[84] Specifically, the mandated topics of study were:

> the Archaeology, Chronology, Geography, and History, of Ancient and Modern Assyria, Arabia, Egypt, Palestine, and other Biblical Lands, the promotion of the study of the Antiquities of those countries, and the preservation of a continuous record of discoveries, now or hereafter to be in progress.[85]

The birth, then, of formal biblical archaeology involved the study of the past and present, through archaeology and other means, of the Near East, from Arabia to Egypt.

In the next article in the first issue of the *Transactions of the Society of Biblical Archaeology*, Birch explains how recent progress in Near Eastern studies has led to the emergence of biblical archaeology as a maturing discipline.[86] He argues that the first stage in the development of the discipline came with archaeological investigations of Egypt and that the two disciplines (biblical studies and Egyptology) will be forever linked. Following that, the discoveries of Mesopotamia were particularly prominent. Less influential were explorations of Phoenician regions and the Eastern Mediterranean, especially Cyprus. He notes that the exploration of Palestine is still a desiderata, having only been investigated to a minor extent. It should be noted that most of Birch's discussion focuses on textual discoveries, and there seems to be little distinction between archaeological and historical study as there comes to be in the twentieth century. Birch concludes with the following quasi-secular statement:

> Its [the society's] scope is Archaeology, not Theology; but to Theology it will prove an important aid. To all those it must be attractive who are interested in the primitive and early history of mankind; that history which is not written in books nor on paper, but upon rocks and stones, deep in the soil, far away in the desert; that history which is not to be found in the library or the mart, but which must be dug up in the valley of the Nile, or exhumed from the plains of Mesopotamia.[87]

---

84. N.A., 'Introduction', *Transactions,* p. ii.
85. N.A., 'Introduction', *Transactions,* p. ii.
86. Samuel Birch, 'The Progress of Biblical Archaeology: An Address', *Transactions of the Society of Biblical Archaeology* 1 (January 1872), part 1, pp. 1-12.
87. Birch, 'Progress of Biblical Archaeology', p. 12.

Biblical archaeology then, became the study of the ancient Near East more broadly with the hopes that it would benefit theology but not be subordinate to it.

The society itself remained a semi-popular society. The major European figures of Mesopotamian and Egyptian studies were members and presented their work in this forum. Yet the publications themselves were intended to be understandable to the lay person. Legge suggests that this may have contributed to its decline just before World War I; the complexity of academic work had increased so greatly that a semi-popular forum was no longer a suitable location for the dissemination of results.[88] Given that there were significantly more technical periodicals available for dissemination, the society eventually became a less relevant force in the field. The war itself dramatically reduced the membership (especially the non-specialist and foreign membership), and by 1919, the society was absorbed by the Royal Asiatic Society.

Arguably more influential than the Society for Biblical Archaeology was the Palestine Exploration Fund (PEF), which in the twenty-first century remains one of the foremost institutions for facilitating British work in the region. Of critical early importance was the success of its mapping projects; as Ben-Arieh notes, the foundation produced the first large-scale map of the Holy Land—greatly facilitating future work in the region.[89] On June 22, 1865, in Willis's Rooms, St James, His Grace the Archbishop of York chaired a proceedings in which the Palestine Exploration Fund was brought into being. The minutes of the proceedings were recorded, and the speeches given by various founding members give ample evidence for the (at least) public rationale for the creation of such a scholarly society.[90] As John Moscrop describes, this was not really an attempt to get new members to join the committee and create a fund—this had essentially already been done.[91] Rather, Moscrop describes this as a public relations exercise, an attempt at raising subscriptions. In some ways that makes this particular event more interesting for this study since the minutes illustrate how the society members felt that the public could best be convinced to support the organization. By the time of this meeting, the organization had an established membership of mostly middle-class citizens, from a variety of occupations.[92] Some key elite public figures acted as the celebrity endorsers, and these figures dominated the opening meeting. Two men, however,

---

88. Legge, 'Society of Biblical Archæology', p. 34.

89. Ben-Arieh, *Rediscovery*, p. 13.

90. These proceedings are preserved in the PEF archive in London, in a pamphlet entitled 'Report of the Proceedings at a Public Meeting' (PEF/1865/2/8).

91. Moscrop, *Measuring Jerusalem*, p. 69.

92. The reason that the society had such a substantial middle-class membership was that it emerged from the Jerusalem Water Relief and those subscribers were targeted for

were truly responsible for the creation of the fund. George Grove, the secretary of the Crystal Palace Company (discussed in Chapter II.7), was an evangelical Christian and devoted to the idea of educating the public about ancient scriptural history. Walter Morrison was a wealthy patriot, who was also, in Moscrop's words, 'a fervent imperialist'; his wealth was the basis of the society's finances until 1912 and the only reason it remained viable given its lackluster financial management.[93] Another important figure in the early years of the Fund was Walter Besant, the brother of Frank Besant, the husband of the prominent theosophist Annie Besant (discussed in Chapter III.8).

Right from the outset, the archbishop (as chair) was explicit in describing the goals and purposes of this organization. He stated:

> we are about to-day to embody ourselves into a society, to be called the Palestine Exploration Fund, having this object in view,—the exploration of the Holy Land; but in order to bind together persons differing in important points of opinion, and in order to work together for this one common object, we mean to lay down and vigorously adhere to this principle—that our object is strictly an inductive inquiry. We are not to be a religious society; we are not about to launch into any controversy; we are about to apply the rules of science, which are so well understood by us in other branches, to an investigation into the facts concerning the Holy Land.[94]

The archbishop makes clear the scientific basis of the organization. It is intended to approach the study of the Holy Land in a manner divorced from religion and apply scientific reasoning, as developed in other disciplines, to the exploration of Palestine. (That being said, he did open the meeting with a prayer.)

It is not just scientific, however, in the archbishop's view, but explicitly colonialist. And in fact, almost immediately upon asserting the scientific approach of the society, the archbishop invokes Scripture. He continues in his opening remarks:

> This country of Palestine belongs to *you* and *me* [original italics], it is essentially ours. It was given to the Father of Israel in the words: 'Walk through the land in the length of it, and in the breadth of it, for I will give it unto thee'. *We* mean to walk through Palestine in the length and in the breadth of it, because that land has been given to us. It is the land from which comes the news of our Redemption. It is the land towards which we may look with as true patriotism as we do to this dear old England, which we love so much. (Cheers.)[95]

---

subscriptions before the formal formation of the society (Moscrop, *Measuring Jerusalem*, pp. 66-67).

93. Moscrop, *Measuring Jerusalem*, p. 65.
94. 'Report of the Proceedings at a Public Meeting' (PEF/1865/2/8).
95. 'Report of the Proceedings at a Public Meeting' (PEF/1865/2/8).

Thus the scientific approach does not undermine scriptural truth. Rather, it seems that the archbishop is concerned that the society not involve itself in theological controversies; the general validity of Scripture is not questioned. In fact, it is this reading of Scripture that justifies the claims made to the land, as the archbishop equates the covenant with Abraham with a covenant with England. Moscrop put its well: 'The parallel was clear and simple. The Chosen People of old, the Israelites, had been succeeded by the new Chosen People, the English.'[96] Barbara Tuchman argues that the PEF, in some ways, combined nostalgia for the biblical past with imperialist motivations.[97] Eitan Bar-Yosef complicates the issue a bit further and sees in this statement a challenge for understanding the PEF through a strictly Saidian model, for here, there is no strict binary between self and other.[98] According to Bar-Yosef, this does not fit with Said's model of orientalism, in which knowledge leads to a desire to conquer. Rather, in this case there is already a claim for the land, and the PEF seeks to gain the knowledge that will help further establish the claim. Thus scholarship is not the initial driving force of imperialism, it is the later manifestation and support structure of the colonialist–Christian enterprise.

Here is the nineteenth-century version of the crusades. Rather than conquer the land militarily, the land will be conquered scientifically, through measurement. It is a Christian crusade but justified and manifest through scientific method. This is made explicit in the archbishop's final comments:

> I think we are giving ourselves a great pleasure in being banded together for this purpose; but I also think it is a sacred duty which we now undertake to endeavor, by a new crusade, to rescue from darkness and oblivion much of the history of that country, in which we all take so dear an interest (Cheers.).[99]

There is no attempt to disguise the use of crusader language here. Unlike other scholarly societies, the PEF is associated with the military right from the outset, with expeditions organized roughly along military lines and military rank titles used by members who had earned them. This was an organization that, in Bar-Yosef's words, 'saw clergymen work alongside military officials'.[100] No figure perhaps greater reflects the militarism of the early PEF better than Lord Kitchener. Kitchener, while still a lieutenant, was assigned to the PEF in 1874, well before he earned fame at the Battle of Omdurman, to participate in the survey of western Palestine. Perhaps it is

---

96. Moscrop, *Measuring Jerusalem*, p. 2.
97. Barbara W. Tuchman, *Bible and Sword: England and Palestine from the Bronze Age to Balfour* (New York: Ballantine Books, 1984 [1956]), pp. 239-40.
98. Bar-Yosef, *Holy Land*, p. 8.
99. 'Report of the Proceedings at a Public Meeting' (PEF/1865/2/8).
100. Bar-Yosef, *Holy Land*, p. 3.

this militaristic–imperialist approach that led Gladstone to refuse membership in the organization, given his own anti-imperialist stance.[101] Although some were uncomfortable with the imperialism, in general, Moscrop explains, 'The appearance of a group of military Christian heroes fighting for and working for God, the Empire and the commercial and military prosperity of Britain matched well the mood of age that saw Britain, her Empire and her armies almost as divinely blessed'.[102] Barbara Tuchman sees this combined military and religious role as quintessentially English, writing, 'Here are Bible and Sword working together unmistakably'.[103] This military role would remain key to the functioning of the PEF on and off; sometimes it was devoted entirely to archaeology, other times it was a front for British military interests, and often it was a mix of both.

The bishop of London, in his preamble to the motion to form the society, seems, however, to dispense entirely with reference to the secular study of the Holy Land. He explains the importance of the society as follows:

> We feel that of all the departments of sacred learning there is none in which the present age is more interested than the interpretation of the Bible; that exegetical theology seems to be the theology of this age, and that this enterprise must greatly assist and strengthen the hands of students of exegetical theology. Moreover we are desirous to strengthen the faith of our people, and nothing is so likely to strengthen a man's faith as an intimate acquaintance with the scenes in which the great events occurred on which our teaching depends. Having learned by our own experience that the light which has of late been thrown upon these scenes has strengthened our own faith, we feel confident that such an effort must strengthen the faith of our people. (Hear, hear).[104]

Here is an explicitly proselytizing justification. The real benefit of the exploration of the Holy Land is to give exegetical theologians more material to work with, and subsequently they would be better able to contextualize the Bible in their public outreach.

On behalf of the archaeological interests of the PEF, Austen Henry Layard, now in his position as a member of parliament, moved a second resolution to explicitly incorporate archaeological research. In particular, Layard comments that archaeological work of this nature will shed light on the early history of the Jewish people and help better understand connections with Assyria and Egypt at the time. Layard testifies that there are significant discoveries to be made in Palestine, first describing finds made

---

101. Moscrop, *Measuring Jerusalem*, p. 68. The Prince of Wales also refused membership, but Queen Victoria became a patron.
102. Moscrop, *Measuring Jerusalem*, p. 2.
103. Tuchman, *Bible and Sword*, p. 239.
104. 'Report of the Proceedings at a Public Meeting' (PEF/1865/2/8).

by French archaeologists in Tyre and Sidon and then more generally in relation to the area of interest to the PEF:

> There is scarcely a plain in Syria, whether to the east or west of Jordan, in which ancient mounds are not seen; what may be buried beneath them no one can tell.... Even if they should not contain monuments as important as those in Assyria, you will probably agree with me in thinking that we ought to endeavor to ascertain what they really do contain.[105]

There is a wealth of archaeological materials to be pillaged from Palestine, and Layard's successes in Assyria provide the proof of that.

Layard is not shy about his disdain for the lack of government support for this kind of exploration and juxtaposes this with French government support of its archaeologists (an argument he made in numerous venues). That the lack of government support for archaeology is a mistake is evident by the interest that 'the working man' shows in archaeological discoveries. Layard explains his own successes in this kind of outreach:

> A great deal has been said of late of the working man. Let me say this, that if there is any subject in which the working man takes an interest, it is one connected with the illustration of the Holy Scriptures. I speak this after some experience. I am in the habit of giving lectures and discourses to working men—my constituents in Southwark amongst others—and I have generally chosen some such subject,—for instance, my own journeys in the East, with incidents illustrating Eastern life, manners, and art as bearing upon the Bible,—and I have always found that such subjects command the largest audiences of working men, and excite the greatest attention; and I know that nothing in the British Museum ever created greater interest amongst the working classes than the remains of Nineveh. Therefore, though Government may not be inclined to help us,—leaving such things, as usual, to private enterprise,—I think upon the score of public utility, and the interest which the people at large take in researches of this kind, we might almost fairly appeal to it for its sympathy, aid, and support.[106]

Layard's motion is seconded by the French Count de Vogüé, who, apologizing for his lack of skill in English, compliments the English aristocracy, 'I cannot help adding that, if in this country by private researches and private efforts you can do what can only be done in France by the support of the government, in the parallel you have the best share and we must envy you'. Here the importance of private research initiative has been made clear, justifying the foundation of such an organization. The Count de Vogüé concludes by summing up the value that the archaeology of Palestine can bring to European society:

---

105. 'Report of the Proceedings at a Public Meeting' (PEF/1865/2/8).
106. 'Report of the Proceedings at a Public Meeting' (PEF/1865/2/8).

10. *From Gentleman Scholars to Scholarly Societies* 419

> It has been justly repeated that the best way of conducting this business is to put aside all exaggerated, or national, or ecclesiastical feeling—to collect facts and leave others to come to a conclusion. That is what this society has to do; in that liberal and independent line she must act, and she will obtain a result worthy of the free country of which I am happy to breathe, for the first time, the vivifying atmosphere. (Cheers).[107]

The PEF then, will gather archaeological data. Others will interpret it. In practice, the PEF was forced to focus on Old Testament sites. This was not out of any particular interest in the Old Testament (over the New Testament). Rather it was because the known New Testament sites of the day (the Church of the Holy Sepulchre, for example) were all under the control of non-Protestant organizations.[108]

During this foundational meeting, the geographical, geological and ethnographical aspects of the PEF's work were also mandated. As Moscrop argues, Protestant scholars who had been deeply influenced by Robinson dominated this organization.[109] The creation of the fund was a professionalization of Robinson's approach, and thus geography and cartography were at the forefront of its intended activities. In explaining the important geological discoveries that are to be made in Palestine, special reference is made by Sir Frederick Murchison and W. Gifford Palgrave to the Dead Sea and how its study will lead to a better understanding of catastrophism. The destruction of Sodom and Gomorrah is referenced, and it is clear that, in spite of it being 1865, geology is still dependent on Scripture in some circles. Ethnographically, the interests of the PEF, at least as mandated here, were to understand connections between the past and present peoples of Palestine. After seconding Murchison's comments on the Dead Sea, Palgrave turns to this matter:

> And to consider, in the first place, the Jewish race itself, there is a main question yet to be solved, namely how we might discover in Palestine . . . any ethnological links between those days and our own in the existing races of the country; any living relics of that vigorous Jewish race which may have in some degree escaped the great catastrophes of time and the strange reversals which befell that fated people. There are reasons for believing that much of this nature remains yet to be discovered, and that among the inhabitants of Palestine, and its immediate neighborhood, there may be found not only those who immigrated at a later period into the country, but some traces of those who were the original inhabitants of the land.[110]

---

107. 'Report of the Proceedings at a Public Meeting' (PEF/1865/2/8).
108. Moscrop, *Measuring Jerusalem*, p. 2.
109. Moscrop, *Measuring Jerusalem*, p. 68.
110. 'Report of the Proceedings at a Public Meeting' (PEF/1865/2/8).

Thus there are two main ethnographic goals: to see which contemporary practices may reflect ancient practices and to identify the potential biological–racial connections between the nineteenth-century inhabitants and the ancient Jews.

The early success of the PEF is somewhat debated. Certainly the financial management of the organization remained on shaky ground for many years, and thus its ability to support projects was limited. Bar-Yosef argues that this was in part due to its lack of ability to encourage support from the more general public: 'despite their fervent efforts to mobilize support for the exploration of Palestine, the Fund's leaders found it extremely difficult to make their work known to the public, or to attract public interest; consequently, the Fund remained on the brink of financial collapse until the First World War'.[111] Bar-Yosef further argues that there was a significant disjuncture between the rhetoric of public outreach and the actual ability to convince the public to become patrons.[112] A display of biblical objects at the Egyptian Hall in 1869 was not able to attract many visitors.[113] It is unclear how many readers of *Cook's Tourist Handbook for Palestine and Syria* took the guidebook's advice to read the PEF's reports and help fund the organization through subscriptions, but it could not have been many.[114] Despite the fact that the general public did not necessarily support the organization financially, the popularity of lectures given by PEF members suggests that it was able to disseminate the results of its research program somewhat. The reality, however, was that this was a society for academics, even if academic Syro-Palestinian archaeologists did not completely exist yet. Its real success was scholarly; it established the foundations for the academic study of ancient Palestine.

The closing of the ranks and the professionalization of the discipline, both through the university and the civil service, began the process of limiting the ability of non-specialists to interpret and make meaning of the results of ancient Near Eastern studies. As Stephen Bann notes about historians specifically (but can be applied to Near Eastern studies as well), 'the self-defining profession provides a paradigm for the nascent political class, and in the end reveals itself to be symmetrical with state power in its offering of a knowledge to which no adequate response can be made by the private citizen'.[115] Following Mark Ferro, Bann argues that the 'docility' of the public in relation to the specialist and the specialist's claims is a fundamental, though rhetorically hidden, outcome of professionaliza-

---

111. Bar-Yosef, *Holy Land*, pp. 14-15.
112. Bar-Yosef, *Holy Land*, p. 171.
113. Bar-Yosef, *Holy Land*, pp. 174-75.
114. N.A., *Cook's Tourist Handbook for Palestine and Syria* (London: Thomas Cook & Son, 1876), pp. 56-57.
115. Bann, *Inventions of History*, p. 16.

tion; the historian creates the same relationship to the public as the medical doctor or lawyer.[116] One mechanism that remained (and continued in practice) for the non-specialist was the voluntary society. Participation in organizations like the PEF allows the non-specialist to make an active contribution (especially through financial aid and organizational service). The other approach for non-specialists is to eschew professional approaches altogether. Although less common in Assyriology (with noteworthy exceptions), amateur approaches that embrace alternative interpretations of ancient history are quite common in biblical archaeology and Egyptology. The end of the nineteenth century brought the beginnings of professionalized Near Eastern studies and the divergence between specialist and non-specialist interpretations.

---

116. Bann, *Inventions of History*, p. 18.

Conclusion to Volume I

> King Consul [referring to the British Consul in Jerusalem] rules supreme, not over the natives of the city, but over strangers; but yet these strangers for the most part are the rightful owners; the natives for the most part, are usurper.
> —Charles Warren, excavator of Jerusalem, 1876[1]

Punch published yet another satire of Egyptian travel in 1848—'Punch's Cheap Excursion up and down the Nile.'[2] It was printed over the course of three weeks and advertised that it would save readers the expense and hassle of having to go to Egypt themselves. The itinerary, however, is actually an itinerary through London and well illustrates how the Near East acted as a mirror for nineteenth-century British life. The 'journey' begins by putting the reader in the midst of the tour:

> You start from Piccadilly. It has long been a matter of doubt which was the real source of the Nile. That doubt is for ever set at rest,—it is the umbrella-stand of the Egyptian Hall. Never mind about band-boxes, carpetbags, or trunks—travel for once without luggage. Go up that dirty staircase on your right, enter that dark room and you are on the steamboat which is starting for the Nile. Be quick, or else you will be too late.

The source of *Punch*'s Nile is Bullock's Egyptian Hall, where Belzoni exhibited his reconstruction of Seti's tomb (Chapter I.3 and Chapter II.2) and likely where many Londoners had their first experience of Egypt. The tour, then, is written in the mocking style of a panorama show (see Chapter II.2) in which visitors are guided through a series of pictorial images of a distant locale. The next few 'stages' on the tour present puns typical of *Punch*. Cairo is said to be 'well off for soap' because of all of its baths,

---

1. Charles Warren, *Underground Jerusalem: An Account of Some of the Difficulties Encountered in its Exploration and the Results Obtained* (London: Richard Bentley & Son, 1876), p. 82.

2. The three installments were printed as 'Punch's Cheap Excursion up and down the Nile', *Punch* 17 (1849), p. 70; 'Punch's Cheap Excursion up and down the Nile', *Punch* 17 (1849), p. 79; and 'Punch's Cheap Excursion up and down the Nile', *Punch* 17 (1849), p. 91.

which is not surprising since this was 'the land where the pail of civilisation was first discovered'. Minarets are said to 'give the city the heavy, sombre look' since 'there is "the weight of Care (oh!) on its brow"'. The Mosque of Sultan Tooloon[3] is claimed to have been based on the design of the Lyceum Theatre. Further puns are made, and various Egyptian buildings and institutions are comically shown to have been based on London prototypes. One final pun, referencing John Gardiner Wilkinson, ends the first instalment of the tour:

> As we are now approaching the Desert, you had better run out to Farrance's, and get an Ice,—you know that Ices generally come in with the Desert! Besides you cannot be far wrong, for if Wilkinson and Gunter tell us rightly, the tutelar deity of Egypt was Isis.

The humour here may not be all that sophisticated, but in order to make sense of the joke, the reader in 1849 had to be familiar with Egyptologists and with the deity Isis.

The second instalment continues with the same kind of puns. The 'tour' has left Cairo and has begun to travel down the Nile, about which *Punch* provides travel-guide-like commentary:

> You have just come back in time to see the Nile change its bed. The lazy thing does not do this with one good vigorous plunge, but after a series of leaps, as if it were stretching its arms, and a number of whirlpools, that look like so many yawns,—all proving what a sluggish river the Nile is—and how difficult it is to get up.

After hearing about the 'Midland Counties of Africa' and crocodiles who have valets, enjoy a 'rubber of whist' and were tamed by Cleopatra, the tour arrives at the Egyptian town named This, which of course lends itself well to puns:

> We have now reached This. This This is an invisible town, so it is useless looking for it. It is sunk to the top in sand, and it must be, we should say, a most highly-polished town. By-the-by, since nothing now exists of it but a chimney-top or two, we suggest that This should be called That, for it is absurd to speak of a town in the present tense, that has been dead and buried for years, and probably is a mummy by this time. But if This does not like That, it may take a French title, and write over its remains the following appropriate inscription, '*Immediatement, sous presse, les Outrages complètes de* Sand'.

The reader is then shown a palm tree, said to be the source of 'our Palm oil and Palmer's candles'. The real produce of Egypt, however, is its antiquities, at least as explained to the *Punch* tourist:

---

3. This is the mosque of ibn Tulun, built in Cairo in 879 CE.

> Right and left, up and down, look in any direction you please, the ground seems sown with thick crops of Temples. It is true that many of these crops have been shamefully trodden down by the heavy foot of Time, but still there is an immense field of them left standing, more than sufficient to yield to the archaeologist, who knows how to separate the Egyptian chaff from the Egyptian corn, a most bountiful harvest. Here he may read not only 'sermons in stones', but histories, whole encyclopaedias, and, aided by the new light which the Fonetic Nuz has lately thrown upon the dark study of hieroglyphics, he may yet discover in the mouth of some colossal statue the recipe for the long lost 'black sauce' of the Lacedaemonians,[4] or accidentally find in the granite ear of some monster Sphinx the tunes which Old Memnon most delighted to sing.

The 'Fonetic Nuz' is a reference to an 1840s movement in England toward the phoneticization of spelling. The new ability to read hieroglyphs, it is explained, can lead to all sorts of relatively mundane discoveries, as described here. The second instalment of the tour then draws to a close with a comparison of the banks of the Nile with the financial banks on Threadneedle Street.

The third and final instalment begins, like the others, with a series of puns:

> The traveller now begins to have the Second Cataract in his eye. He will be pleased doubtlessly to learn that the cliffs on this bank are composed of an extremely friable material. We never knew ourselves that stones were subjected to the same process as liver-and-bacon, but we suppose, when taken out of the frying-pan, they make a very good stony-batter. Old Saturn, that tremendous lapidary, must have been the inventor of this dish.

Cataracts are the rapids on the Nile found in its southern portion (the Second Cataract is now submerged under Lake Nasser). Immediately following the play on the term 'friable' and the typical guide-like explanation, the text digresses to a discussion of Egyptian names:

> The Egyptian towns are very hard to recollect. Their names seem to be a happy mixture of the Welsh and Hungarian. If they had been called upon, like the Spanish towns in the time of Don Carlos, to have pronounced, they must have been completely dumb-founded, for it is not so easy to pronounce a name that scarcely has a vowel, or a liquid running through it. But probably the Egyptians wisely thought as their principal towns were only cemeteries, with a large floating population of mummies, that they were best described by mutes?

Here, then, *Punch* plays on the nature of the Egyptian writing system, expecting much from its readers in the way of linguistic knowledge.

---

4. Another term for Spartan.

The tour continues with what is a typical discussion of the seeming Egyptian fixation on death:

> A curious race of people these Egyptians must have been! Their great end of life was Death. They were no sooner born than they thought about dying. The whole nation seemed to live in a sort of forcing Pyramid. An Egyptian did not care so much where he lodged so long as he knew where he was to be buried. His greatest comfort was the idea of being made a nice mummy of. His card was an epitaph. He was walking about with a tombstone continually in his hand. In fact, the largeness of the Pyramids is a standing proof, if proof be wanting, what, a set of tremendous undertakers the Egyptians were! Their Present was the Future. This may partly account for their being so much in advance of other nations. To speak extravagantly, they seemed to calculate Time with a death-watch, which they wound up with a skeleton-key! They made themselves in fact so familiar with Death, that they invited him to all their feasts, and put him at the head of the table at all their weddings, anniversaries, pic-nics, and grand dinners. It is but right to mention, however, one glorious exception to the above rule! and that is the Egyptian Hall at the Mansion House.

Mansion House is the official residence of the Lord Mayor of London. A columned entrance hall is named the Egyptian Hall but is not actually Egyptianizing in appearance. It is merely named as such because the Roman architect Vitruvius declared this type of column to be Egyptian.

Much of the rest of the tour is devoted to the sphinx, which is said to better resemble the stage actor and comedian Robert Keeley (1793–1869) than Ramses. It is also suggested that phrenologists should be sent to evaluate the bumps on the sphinx's head. After these suggestions about the sphinx are offered, the singing of the Colossi of Memnon is referred to. There was a tradition that when the wind blew in a certain manner, the colossi seemed to sing. For *Punch*, it was only logical that the song should be '*I Dreamt That I Dwelt in Marble Halls*'. Leaving the colossi aside, the scale of monuments found in Egypt are marveled at and *Punch* wishes, 'Oh! if the Great Pyramid could, like Chateaubriand, publish its "*Mémoires d'outretombe!*"' Here the scale of Egyptian monuments and of Chateaubriand's monumental memoir is commensurate, although only the first volume had been released by the time this article was written in *Punch*.

For *Punch*, the parodying of an Egyptian travel guide by substituting London for the Near East was very much in keeping with its typical approaches to satirizing British life. Much of the humour here is not very scathing; playful puns and jokes about Egyptian materials in London abound. The familiar is made unfamiliar, highlighting different ways to think about the urban environment experienced, but not consciously thought about, every day. The unfamiliarity of the city is also highlighted, playing on the Victorian trend to see the urban environment as something else to be explored, as a site of teeming otherness that inhabits the same physical space but is separated by numerous invisible social boundaries. Here the imperialist gaze is reversed, in an almost Lacanian sense, for it points to the possibility that London can be viewed just as Egypt is. The humour is destabilizing. The trivializing that is enacted through the imperial gaze works as well to trivialize the culture that is used to being the viewer. (Of course, many readers would have simply enjoyed the puns.)

Much of this book has been devoted to understanding how the ancient Near East was used in the nineteenth century to make sense of the European and, to some degree, American self. What seems readily apparent is that at least in terms of public reception, Egypt and Mesopotamia were invoked for reasons beyond just the historical. This is most readily apparent in surveying the various ways that people thought about progress and decline, topics for which the newly rediscovered cultures of antiquity presented direct evidence. It is also apparent in the treatment of the artifacts themselves, which were subjected to what were framed as heroic feats of transportation and industry in order to remove them from what came to be seen as undeserving hands.

The willingness to use the 'other' (in such an explicit manner) to think about the self has declined substantially since the nineteenth century. For twenty-first-century scholars and commentators, the kind of one-to-one correlations that *Punch* offers in its 'Cheap Excursion up the Nile' are naïve, misleading, potentially racist, and otherwise problematic in any number of ways. For sociologists and anthropologists, ancient Egypt and Mesopotamia are simply not as important as they were in the nineteenth century for generating social theory about the human condition. Even for those scholars from other disciplines who are interested, the increasing specialization of Near Eastern studies has meant that it is very difficult for non-specialists to gain access to the data that would be necessary to generate such theory. European and North American archaeologists themselves are less comfortable in the twenty-first century in allowing their results to be used in nationalist contexts, much of which stems out of a rejection of 'culture–historical' models of archaeological theorizing. This is not to say that archaeological work is no longer nationalistic, only that archaeological practitioners are not as comfortable advertising this. Antiquities have played important roles in the construction of Near Eastern national identities in the twentieth century, especially in Israel, Iraq and Egypt, and they continue to be the subject of contested political readings. Various stakeholders and participants have different understandings of how the past fits into the thinking about the contemporary state.

For Europeans and North Americans, debates about the role of Near Eastern antiquities in their own polities began in earnest in the nineteenth century. This issue is explored in greater detail in the context of the British Museum in the next volume in this study, but suffice it to say, this is the period in which the Near East is adopted into the canon of the Western heritage. The Old Testament had already been part of that tradition, to some extent, but by the end of the nineteenth century, the cultures of the ancient Near East were seen as the first civilizations, the origin points for the history of progress of which Britain (or France, Italy, Germany or the United States) was now the pinnacle. Archaeology became a formal element of the colonial and imperial systems, enacted by diplomats and, by the end of the century, beginning to be integrated into formal colonial governance. Right from the outset, Napoleon's savants, Giovanni Belzoni, Austen Henry Layard and many others 'proved' that antiquities were better off in Europe than in Africa or Asia and that they were the true inheritors of the past, not the people who lived near them because of what were seen as accidents of history or the unavoidable decline that all great civilizations are fated to experience. For Edward Robinson and other explicitly Christian travellers, Palestine had long been the patrimony of the West, and visits to the region were infused with nostalgia more than discovery. Less explicit, but no less influential over the long term, was the opening of the region for middle-class travel and the adoption of the Near East (focussed on the experience of its antiquities) as a form of European and North American middle-class tourism. Especially for Egypt and what is now Israel, this claiming of the space by the middle class for their leisure activities has become a driving force of local economies.

On an individual level, interest in the ancient Near East has probably increased since the nineteenth century. That is to say, more people are better able to learn about the ancient world than was the case in the nineteenth century. On a larger social and public level, however, this is not the case, and Near Eastern studies as an intellectual endeavour is now less rooted in ideas about the public good. Participation in the field usually is not framed as a virtuous service to the church, nation or community at large. The declining social relevance of Near Eastern studies has also been mirrored in the changing theologies of the twentieth century. The challenges that biblical archaeology, Egyptology and to a lesser extent Assyriology brought to the question of the historicity of the Bible did not mean that the Bible lost its value for people as a means of understanding the world. But it did mean that that value could no longer be unquestionably taken as straightforwardly historical, and the archaeological interpretations of the Bible had to be either reconsidered in terms of literary analysis, recontextualized within different historical situations or the whole apparatus of historical-critical scholarship had to be ignored. The direct experience of the Holy Land and ancient material culture became less significant for theology more broadly, although on the personal level those experiences continued to vary from individual to individual. This was a slow and uneven process that occurred over the course of the twentieth century as the idea of 'biblical archaeology' was replaced with approaches to that discipline more grounded in anthropology and regional studies.

Throughout this book, most of the interpreters of the ancient Near East that have been surveyed were non-specialists and non-professionals. At the outset of the period, the primary means of reporting about Near Eastern discoveries was through travel literature, a specifically amateur form of academic work. This gave way, eventually, to a professionalized variation on travel literature, the site report, where a purposefully scientific veneer replaces the personal elements of travel. The two genres are not really as distinct as they seem; it is just that the balance between narrative and description has shifted dramatically. Visually, the first stirrings of professionalization came with the scientific illustrations of the Napoleonic expedition. While tourists continued to draw, paint and perhaps even measure Egyptian monuments, the techniques of the savants set a standard for professional archaeological work.

By the end of the nineteenth century, the beginnings of professionalization were established; the arbiters of ancient Near Eastern culture required the authority of the academy or state institutions (such as museums or antiquities authorities), and the practices of individuals were regulated by scholarly societies. To a great extent this reflects the explosion of complex data that is available regarding the ancient cultures, far beyond that which can easily be controlled by a non-specialist 'man of letters'. Partially it is related to the formation of disciplinary boundaries, many of which are especially necessary in archaeology to prevent the wanton destruction of sites. Certainly Layard's excavation methods can no longer be encouraged, and field excavators need to use the most up-to-date techniques. There are also many more people able to participate in this venture professionally who can make a living through ancient Near Eastern studies. Throughout the book, the same names are returned to over and over again, for it was really a small club that made up British Near Eastern studies in the nineteenth century. That is not the case now—with many people actively engaging in the practice. Although the community may feel small to those who are in it, much of this is due to the nature of field research, which makes archaeologists more familiar with one another than is typical of other scholarly disciplines. Yet this increased professionalization has also meant that Near Eastern studies is less consequential in non-specialists' lives, and there is little perceived urgency in Near Eastern discoveries for the greater community.

That being said, academic experiences of the ancient Near East are not the only experiences available. If anything, the ability to travel to the Near East and experience sites directly has only increased (although it is subject to the political instability of the region). Now the professional archaeologist and the tourist are distinct; an enterprising tourist could not just excavate a site as Amelia Edwards did during her first journey up the Nile. Non-professional experiences are more passive now (although the occasional Piazzi Smyth figure is able to gain access to a site), but that does not mean that the experiences are not meaningful. Volumes II and III of this study survey different types of non-academic encounters with ancient Egypt, Mesopotamia and Syria-Palestine.

Volume II is a study of how the materiality of the ancient Near East was experienced in the nineteenth century, first through the exhibition of objects brought back from the Near East and second through the manufacture of new material culture inspired by ancient examples. Belzoni's application of his own circus-sideshow background to exhibit (and profit from) his Egyptological discoveries established one of the main forms through which the public has come to experience the ancient world, and numerous other types of exhibition (mummy unwrappings, panoramas, travelling Bible carnivals, to name a few) followed. The museum emerged as the state-sanctioned form of this exhibit as it was transformed from a consulting repository to a mechanism for public outreach. The new manufacturing of the nineteenth century was influenced by the ancient materials made newly available for European and North American consideration, and Egyptian styles especially came to be adopted in design and architecture. This new manufacturing and new means through which history was presented merged in the hyperreal spectacles of the Victorian era, first in the Crystal Palace at Sydenham and later in the cultural pavilions that came to be a feature of world expositions.

Volume III is a study of how the ancient Near East was imagined in different media and explores just how important fictional readings of the ancient world were in its public reception. The first half of Volume III explores fantasy forms according to genre, including painting, fiction, theatre and opera. The second half of the volume is a discussion of esoteric societies that emerged over the course of the century that articulated distinct relationships with Egypt, ancient Israel, Phoenicia and Mesopotamia. These include Rosicrucian groups, the Hermetic Order of the Golden Dawn, the Mormons, Freemasons and Theosophists. It ends with a consideration of this kind of reception in the early twentieth century, using the fiction of H.P. Lovecraft and the scholarly works of Sigmund Freud as examples. There is still much more to be said about nineteenth-century experiences of the ancient Near East.

It is difficult to sum up what the experiences of rediscovering 'meant' to nineteenth-century Europeans and North Americans. In fact, any attempt at a monolithizing conclusion would be inappropriate, since it is apparent that there were so many ways that these discoveries were made meaningful to people, and it is likely that, at the individual level, feelings were multiple and contradictory, conscious and unconscious. What does seem to have been common is that these discoveries were part of a larger project of making sense of Europe's place within the global present and past. While the binary thinking of East and West was one framework through which the ancient Near East was understood, it was not the only one. The ancient Near East was claimed as the self and the other (and perhaps a bit of both); it seemed to mirror European life and subvert it. Technology helped to mark these differences. For non-specialists (including academics and journalists), progress and decline were the messages of the material culture. For archaeologists, material culture was more literally a marker of changing time, as the Three-Age system was adopted; Petrie's seriation made this scientific. For all, transportation and scientific technology were what allowed the past to be 'rescued' from the oblivion of time or the seeming carelessness of the Ottoman Empire. Perhaps Blake's Satanic Mills (of industrial technology) did not obscure England's biblical past so much as help construct a new relationship to it in which the English claimed the role of protector and arbiter of that heritage.

BIBLIOGRAPHY FOR VOLUME I

N.A., *The Industry of Nations, as Exemplified in the Great Exhibition of 1851: The Materials of Industry.* (London: Society for Promoting Christian Knowledge, 1852).

N.A., 'Introduction', *Transactions of the Society of Biblical Archaeology* 1 (January, 1872), Part 1, pp. i-iv.

N.A., *Cook's Tourist Handbook for Palestine and Syria* (London: Thomas Cook & Son, 1876).

N.A., *Complete History of the Romantic Life and Tragic Death of the Beautiful Egyptian Queen Cleopatra; and All about her Needle, 3,000 Years Old! And the Events That Led to its Arrival in England; with an Interpretation of its Curious Hieroglyphic Inscriptions* (London: W. Sutton, 1878).

Albright, W.F., *From the Stone Age to Christianity: Monotheism and the Historical Process* (Baltimore, MD: Johns Hopkins University Press, 1940).

Altick, Richard D., *The English Common Reader: A Social History of the Mass Reading Public, 1800–1900* (Chicago: University of Chicago Press, 1957).

—'Nineteenth-Century English Best-Sellers: A Third List', *Studies in Bibliography* 39 (1986), pp. 235-41.

Anderson, Patricia, *The Printed Image and the Transformation of Popular Culture, 1790–1860* (Oxford: Clarendon Press, 1991).

Arnold, Bill T., and David Weisberg, 'Delitzch in Context', in *God's Word for our World, Volume II: Theological and Cultural Studies in Honor of Simon John De Vries* (ed. J. Harold Ellens, Deborah L. Ellens, Rolf P. Knierim and Isaac Kalimi; Journal for the Study of the Old Testament Supplement Series, 389; Sheffield: JSOT, 2004), pp. 37-45

Asher-Greve, Julia M., 'From "Semiramis of Babylon" to "Semiramis of Hammersmith"', in *Orientalism, Assyriology and the Bible* (ed. Steven W. Holloway; Hebrew Bible Monographs, 10; Sheffield: Sheffield Phoenix Press, 2007), pp. 322-73.

Baedeker, Karl, *Egypt: Handbook for Travellers. Part 1* (Leipzig: Karl Baedeker, 2nd edn, 1885).

Bailey, Peter, *Popular Culture and Performance in the Victorian City* (Cambridge: Cambridge University Press, 1998).

Bann, Stephen, *The Inventions of History: Essays on the Representation of the Past* (Manchester: Manchester University Press, 1990).

Bar-Yosef, Eitan, *The Holy Land in English Culture 1799–1917: Palestine and the Question of Orientalism* (Oxford: Clarendon Press, 2005).

Barrell, John, 'Death on the Nile: Fantasy and the Literature of Tourism 1840–1860', *Essays in Criticism* 41 (April 1991), pp. 97-127.

Baucom, Ian, *Out of Place: Englishness, Empire, and the Locations of Identity* (Princeton, NJ: Princeton University Press, 1999).

Bednarski, Andrew, *Holding Egypt: Tracing the Reception of the* Description de l'Égypte *in Nineteenth Century Great Britain* (Egyptology, 3; London: Golden House Publication, 2005).
Belzoni, Giovanni, *Travels in Egypt and Nubia* (Vercelli, Italy: White Star Publishers, 2007 [1820]).
Ben-Arieh, Yehoshua, *The Rediscovery of the Holy Land in the Nineteenth Century* (Jerusalem: Sefer Ve Sefel Publishing, 2007 [1979]).
Benedict, Barbara M., *Curiosity: A Cultural History of the Early Modern Period* (Chicago: University of Chicago Press, 2001).
Birch, Samuel, 'The Progress of Biblical Archaeology: An Address', *Transactions of the Society of Biblical Archaeology* 1 (January 1872), Part 1, pp. 1-12.
Bohlman, Philip V., and Ruth F. Davis, '*Mizrakh*, Jewish Music and the Journey to the East', in *Music and Orientalism in the British Empire, 1780s–1940s: Portrayal of the East* (ed. Martin Clayton and Bennett Zon; Music in Nineteenth-Century Britain; Hampshire: Ashgate, 2007), pp. 95-125.
Bohrer, Frederick, *Orientalism and Visual Culture: Imagining Mesopotamia in Nineteenth-Century Europe* (Cambridge: Cambridge University Press, 2003).
Bonald, Louis de, *Sur les premiers objets des connaissances morales* (Paris: D'Adrien Le Clere, 1826).
Boorstin, Daniel, *The Image or What Happened to the American Dream* (London: Penguin Books, 1961).
Boorstin, Daniel J., 'Afterlives of the Great Pyramids', *Wilson Quarterly* 16.3 (1992), pp. 130-38.
Booth, Marilyn, 'Insistent Localism in a Satiric World: Shaykh Naggār's 'Reed-Pipe' in the 1890s Cairene Press', in *Asian Punches: A Transcultural Affair* (ed. Hans Harder and Barbara Mittler; Heidelberg: Springer, 2103), pp. 187-218.
Breed, Benjamin, 'Nomadology of the Bible: A Processual Approach to Biblical Reception History', *Biblical Reception* 1 (2012), pp. 299-322.
Brendon, Piers, *Thomas Cook: 150 Years of Popular Tourism* (London: Secker & Warburg, 1991).
Brier, Bob, *Egyptomania* (Middlesex, NJ: Hillwood Art Museum, 1992).
Budge, E.A. Wallis, *Egyptian Religion: Egyptian Ideas of the Future Life* (New York: Arkana, 1987 [1899]).
Burckhardt, Jacob, *Force and Freedom: Reflections on History* (ed. James Hastings Nichols; Boston: Beacon Press, 1943).
Burgin, Victor, *In/Different Spaces: Place and Memory in Visual Culture* (Berkeley, CA: University of California Press, 1996).
—*The Remembered Film* (London: Reaction, 2004).
Buzard, James, *The Beaten Track: European Tourism, Literature, and the Ways to Culture, 1800–1918* (Oxford: Clarendon Press, 1993).
Canclini, Néstor García, *Hybrid Cultures: Strategies for Entering and Leaving Modernity* (trans. Christopher Chiappari and Sylvia López; Minneapolis: University of Minnesota Press, 1995).
Cannadine, David, *Ornamentalism: How the British Saw their Empire* (Oxford: Oxford University Press, 2001).
Carneiro, Robert L., 'Herbert Spencer as an Anthropologist', *Journal of Libertarian Studies* 5 (Spring 1981), pp. 153-210.
Chard, Chloe, *Pleasure and Guilt on the Grand Tour: Travel Writing and Imaginative Geography 1600–1830* (Manchester: Manchester University Press, 1999).

Colla, Elliott, *Conflicted Antiquities: Egyptology, Egyptomania, Egyptian Modernity* (Durham, NC: Duke University Press, 2007).
Shepherd, Naomi, *The Zealous Intruders: The Western Rediscovery of Palestine* (London: Collins, 1987).
Comte, Auguste, *Cours de philosophie positive,* I (Paris: Bachelier, 1830–1842).
Cowan, Edward J., 'Myth and Identity in Early Medieval Scotland', *Scottish Historical Review* 63.176, part 2 (October 1984), pp. 111-35.
Crolley, George, 'Review of *Nineveh and its Remains*, by Austen Henry Layard', *Dublin Review* 28 (1850), pp. 354-98.
Curl, James Stevens, *The Art and Architecture of Freemasonry* (New York: Overlook Press, 1991).
Dalley, Stephanie, 'Semiramis in History and Legend: A Case Study in Interpretation of an Assyriological Historical Tradition, with Observations on Archetypes in Ancient Historiography, on Euhemerism before Euhemerus, and on the So-Called Greek Ethnographic Style', in *Cultural Borrowings and Ethnic Appropriations in Antiquity: Oriens et occidens* (ed. Erich S. Gruen; Sudien zu antiken Kulturkontakten und ihrem Nachleben, 8; Stuttgart: Franz Steiner Verlag, 2005), pp. 11-22.
Damiani, Anita, *Enlightened Observers: British Travellers to the Near East, 1715–1850* (Lebanon: American University of Beirut, 1978).
Davis, John, 'Holy Land, Holy People? Photography, Semitic Wannabes, and Chautauqua's Palestine Park', *Prospects* 17 (1992), pp. 241-71.
—*The Landscape of Belief: Encountering the Holy Land in Nineteenth-Century American Art and Culture* (Princeton, NJ: Princeton University Press, 1996).
Delitzsch, Friedrich, *Babel and Bible: Three Lectures on the Significance of Assyriological Research for Religion, Embodying the Most Important Criticisms and the Author's Replies* (Chicago: Open Court Publishing Company, 1906).
Denon, Dominique Vivant, *Voyage dans la Basse et la Haute Égypte* (Paris: Éditions Gallimard, 1998 [1802]).
—*Egypt Delineated* (London: Charles Taylor, 1819).
Diodorus Siculus, *Library of History* (trans. C.H. Oldfather; Loeb Classical Library, 303; Cambridge, MA: Harvard University Press, 1961).
Dobrizhoffer, M., *An Account of the Abipones*, II (London: J. Murray, 1822 [1783]).
Doyon, Wendy, 'The Poetics of Egyptian Museum Practice', *British Museum Studies in Ancient Egypt and Sudan* 10 (2008), pp. 1-37.
Eagleton, Terry, *The Function of Criticism* (London: Verso, 1984).
Ebeling, Florian, *The Secret History of Hermes Trismegistus: Hermeticism from Ancient to Modern Times* (trans. David Lorton; Ithaca, NY: Cornell University Press, 2007).
Edwards, Amelia, *A Thousand Miles up the Nile* (London: George Routledge & Sons, 1899 [1881]).
—'The Story of Tanis', *Harper's New Monthly Magazine* 73 (1886), pp. 710-38.
—*Pharaohs, Fellahs, and Explorers* (London: Harper & Brothers, 1891).
Ellis, Kirsten, *Star of the Morning, The Extraordinary Life of Lady Hester Stanhope* (New York: HarperPress, 2008).
Evans, Elaine Altman, *Scholars, Scoundrels, and the Sphinx: A Photographic and Archaeological Adventure up the Nile* (Knoxville, TN: University of Tennessee, Frank H. Clung Museum, 2000).
—'Edward Libbey: An American Glass Magnate Collects in Egypt', in *Souvenirs and New Ideas: Travel and Collecting in Egypt and the Near East* (ed. Diane Fortenberry; Oxford: ASTENE and Oxbow Books, 2013), pp. 24-38.

Fabian, Ann, 'The Curious Cabinet of Dr Morton', in *Acts of Possession: Collecting in America* (ed. Leah Dilworth; New Brunswick, NJ: Rutgers University Press, 2003), pp. 112-37.
Fagan, Brian, *The Rape of the Nile: Tomb Robbers, Tourists, and Archaeologists in Egypt* (Cambridge, MA: Westview Press, rev. edn, 2004).
Fahim, Hussein M., 'European Travellers in Egypt: The Representation of the Host Culture', in *Travellers in Egypt* (ed. Paul Starkey and Janet Starkey; London: I.B. Tauris Publishers, 1998), pp. 7-11.
Finkel, I.L., and M.J. Seymour (ed.), *Babylon: Myth and Reality* (London: British Museum Press, 2008).
Flynn, Sarah J.A., *Sir John Gardner Wilkinson, Traveller and Egyptologist (1797–1875)* (Oxford: Bodleian Library, 1997).
Frahm, Eckart, 'Images of Assyria in Nineteenth- and Twentieth-Century Western Scholarship', in *Orientalism, Assyriology and the Bible.* (ed. Steven W. Holloway; Hebrew Bible Monographs, 10; Sheffield: Sheffield Phoenix Press, 2007), pp. 74-93.
Frazer, James, *The Golden Bough: A Study in Comparative Religion*, I (London: Macmillan, 1894).
Gaehtgens, Thomas, Jörg Ebeling and Ulrich Leben, 'Eugène de Beauharnais: *Honneur et fidélité* at the Hôtel Beauharnais', in *Symbols of Power: Napoleon and the Art of the Empire Style: 1800–1815* (ed. Odile Nouvel and Anne Dion-Tenenbaum; NewYork: Abrams, 2007), pp. 78-87.
Gasque, W. Ward, 'The Leading Religion Writer in Canada . . . Does He Know What He's Talking About?', *George Mason University's History News Network*, Tuesday, August 17, 2004.
Gearon, Eamonn, 'War and Peace and Travel and Writing: European Exploration in Egypt and the Sudan, 1798–1898', in *Souvenirs and New Ideas: Travel and Collecting in Egypt and the Near East* (ed. Diane Fortenberry; Oxford: ASTENE and Oxbow Books, 2013), pp. 44-54.
Gibb, Lorna, *Lady Hester: Queen of the East* (London: Faber & Faber, 2005).
Gillooly, Eileen, 'Historical Remedies for Taxonomic Troubles: Reading the Great Exhibition', in *Victorian Prism: Refractions of the Crystal Palace* (ed. J. Buzzard, J. Childers and E. Gillolly; Charlottesville, VA: University of Virginia Press, 2007), pp. 23-39.
Gindy, Nadia, '"While I Was in Egypt, I Finished *Dr Thorne"'*, in *Interpreting the Orient: Travellers in Egypt and the Near East* (ed. Paul and Janet Starkey; Reading: Ithaca Press, 2001), pp. 139-51.
Gordon, Lucie Duff, *Letters from Egypt* (London: Virago Press, 1983).
Gould, Stephen Jay, 'Morton's Ranking of Races by Cranial Capacity: Unconscious Manipulation of Data May be a Scientific Norm', *Science* 200 (May 5, 1978), pp. 503-509.
Gregory, Derek, *The Colonial Present: Afghanistan, Palestine, Iraq* (New York: Blackwell, 2004).
Grewal, Inderpal, *Home and Harem: Nation, Gender, Empire and the Cultures of Travel* (London: Duke University Press, 1996).
Hackford-Jones, Jocelyn, and Mary Roberts (eds.), *Edges of Empire: Orientalism and Visual Culture* (New Interventions in Art History; Malden, MA: Blackwell Publishing, 2005).
Hallote, Rachel, *Bible, Map, and Spade: The American Palestine Exploration Society,*

Frederick Jones Bliss, and the Forgotten Story of Early American Archaeology (Piscataway, NJ: Gorgias Press, 2006).

—'Jacob H. Schiff and the Beginning of Biblical Archaeology in the United States', *American Jewish History* 95 (2009), pp. 225-47.

Hallote, Rachel, Felicity Cobbing and Jeffrey B. Spur, *The Photographs of the American Palestine Exploration Society* (Annual of the American Schools of Oriental Research, 66; Boston: American Schools of Oriental Research, 2012).

Hamann, Byron Ellsworth, 'Drawing Glyphs Together', in *Past Presented: Archaeological Illustration and the Ancient Americas* (ed. Joanne Pillsbury; Washington, DC: Dumbarton Oaks, 2012), pp. 231-81.

Harder, Hans, 'Prologue: Late Nineteenth and Twentieth Century Asian *Punch* Versions and Related Satirical Journals', in *Asian Punches: A Transcultural Affair* (ed. Hans Harder and Barbara Mittler; Heidelberg: Springer, 2103), pp. 1-11.

Harpur, Tom, *The Pagan Christ: Recovering the Lost Light* (Toronto: Thomas Allen Publishers, 2004).

Harris, Marvin, *The Rise of Anthropological Theory* (Walnut Creek, CA: Altamira Press, updated edn, 2001).

Harvey, John, *The Bible as Visual Culture: When Text Becomes Image* (The Bible in the Modern World, 57; Oxford: Sheffield Phoenix Press, 2013).

Hasinoff, Erin, 'Faith in Objects: American Indian Object Lessons of the World in Boston', in *Archaeologies of Materiality* (Malden, MA: Blackwell, 2005), pp. 96-125.

Hegel, Georg W.F., *The Philosophy of History* (trans. J. Sibee; London: Allen & Unwin, 1856 [1837]).

Heitmann, Sine, 'Authenticity in Tourism', in *Research Themes for Tourism* (ed. Peter Robinson, Sine Heitmann, Peter U.C. Dieke; Oxfordshire: CABI, 2011), pp. 45-58.

Hibbert, Christopher, *The Illustrated London News: Social History of Victorian Britain* (London: Angus & Robertson Publishers, 1975).

Holloway, Steven W., 'Introduction: Orientalism, Assyriology, and the Bible', in *Orientalism, Assyriology and the Bible* (ed. Steven W. Holloway; Hebrew Bible Monographs, 10; Sheffield: Sheffield Phoenix Press, 2007), pp. 1-41.

Hornung, Erik, *The Secret Lore of Egypt: Its Impact on the West* (trans. D. Lorton; Ithaca, NY: Cornell University Press, 2001).

Houston, Stephen D., 'Telling It Slant: Imaginative Reconstructions of Classic Maya Life', in *Past Presented: Archaeological Illustration and the Ancient Americas* (ed. Joanne Pillsbury; Washington, DC: Dumbarton Oaks, 2012), pp. 387-411.

Humbert, Jean-Marcel, 'Denon and the Discovery of Egypt', in *Egyptomania: Egypt in Western Art 1730–1930* (ed. Jean-Marcel Humbert *et al.*; Ottawa: National Gallery of Canada, 1994), pp. 202-49.

Jackson, Emmet, 'An Irish Woman in Egypt: The Travels of Lady Harriett Kavanagh', in *Souvenirs and New Ideas: Travel and Collecting in Egypt and the Near East* (ed. Diane Fortenberry; Oxford: ASTENE and Oxbow Books, 2013), pp. 55-67.

Jacobs, Jennifer, and Benjamin Porter, 'Excavating *Turath*: Documenting Local and National Heritage Discourses in Jordan', in *Ethnographies and Archaeologies: Iterations of the Past* (ed. Lena Mortensen and Julie Hollowell; Gainesville, FL: University Press of Florida, 2009), pp. 71-88.

Jacobsen, Thorkild, *The Treasures of Darkness: A History of Mesopotamian Religion* (New Haven, CT: Yale University Press, 1976).

Jenkins, Ian, *Archaeologists and Aesthetes in the Sculpture Galleries of the British Museum 1800–1939* (London: British Museum Press, 1992).

Jenkyns, Richard, *The Victorians and Ancient Greece* (Oxford: Basil Blackwell, 1980).
Jennings, Hargrave, *The Rosicrucians: Their Rites and Mysteries* (London: George Routledge & Sons, 2nd edn, 1879).
Jerrold, W. Blanchard, *How to See the British Museum in Four Visits* (London: Project Gutenberg E-Book, 2004 [1852]).
Kabbani, Rana, *Europe's Myths of Orient* (Bloomington, IN: Indiana University Press, 1986).
Kark, Ruth, 'From Pilgrimage to Budding Tourism: the Role of Thomas Cook in the Rediscovery of the Holy Land in the Nineteenth Century', in *Travellers in the Levant: Voyagers and Visionaries* (ed. Sarah Searight and Malcolm Wagstaff; Durham: University of Durham, 2001), pp. 155-74.
Katz, David, *God's Last Words: Reading the English Bible from the Reformation to Fundamentalism* (New Haven, CT: Yale University Press, 2004).
Keith, Alexander, *Evidence of the Truth of the Christian Religion Derived from the Literal Fulfilment of Prophecy; Particularly as Illustrated by the History of the Jews, and by the Discoveries of Recent Travellers* (New York: Harper & Brothers, 6th edn, 1850).
Kholy, Nadia el, 'Romances and Realities of Travellers', in *Unfolding the Orient: Travellers in Egypt and the Near East* (ed. Paul Starkey and Janet Starkey; Reading: Ithaca Press, 2001), pp. 261-75.
Kinglake, A.W., *Eothen: Traces of Travel Brought Home from the East* (London: J. Oliver, 1844).
Kirschenblatt-Gimblett, Barbara, 'A Place in the World: Jews and the Holy Land at World's Fairs', in *Encounters with the 'Holy Land': Place, Past, and Future in American Jewish Culture* (ed. Jeffrey Shandler and Beth S. Wenger; Hanover, NH: University Press of New England, 1997), pp. 60-82.
Klemm, Gustav, *Allgemeine Cultur-Geschichte der Menschheit* (Leipzig: Leubner, 1843).
Kuklick, Bruce, *Puritans in Babylon: The Ancient Near East and American Intellectual Life 1890–1930* (Princeton, NJ: Princeton University Press, 1996).
Laquer, Thomas, *Religion and Respectability: Sunday Schools and Working-Class Culture, 1780–1850* (New Haven, CT: Yale University Press, 1976).
Larsen, Mogens Trolle, *The Conquest of Assyria* (New York: Routledge, 1996).
—'The "Babel/Bible" Controversy and its Aftermath', in *Civilizations of the Ancient Near East* (ed. Jack M. Sasson; Peabody, MA: Hendrickson Publishers, 2000 [1995]), I, pp. 95-106.
Larsen, Timothy, *The People of One Book: The Bible and the Victorians* (Oxford: Oxford University Press, 2011).
Layard, Austen Henry, *Nineveh and its Remains* (London: John Murray, 1849).
Lefkowitz, Mary, *Not Out of Africa: How Afrocentrism Became an Excuse to Teach Myth as History* (New York: BasicBooks, 1997).
Legge, F., 'The Society of Biblical Archæology', *Journal of the Royal Asiatic Society of Great Britain and Ireland* (January 1919), pp. 25-36.
Levine, Philippa, *The Amateur and the Professional: Antiquarians, Historians, and Archaeologists in Victorian England, 1838–1886* (Cambridge: Cambridge University Press, 1986).
Livingstone, David, *Adam's Ancestors: Race, Religion, and the Politics of Human Origins* (Baltimore, MD: Johns Hopkins University Press, 2008).
Long, Burke O., *Imagining the Holy Land: Maps, Models, and Fantasy Travels* (Bloomington, IN: Indiana University Press, 2003).

Lloyd, Seton, *Foundations in the Dust: The Story of Mesopotamian Exploration* (New York: Thames & Hudson, 1947).

Lubbock, John, *Prehistoric Times, as Illustrated by Ancient Remains, and the Manners and Customs of Modern Savages* (London: Williams & Norgate, 1865).

MacCannell, Dean, *The Tourist: A New Theory of the Leisure Class* (Berkeley, CA: University of California Press, 1999).

Maggiolini, Paolo, 'Studies and Souvenirs of Palestine and Transjordan: The Revival of the Latin Patriarchate of Jerusalem and the Rediscovery of the Holy Land during the Nineteenth Century', in *Orientalism Revisited: Art, Land and Voyage* (ed. Ian Richard Netton; New York: Routledge, 2013), pp. 165-75.

Maidment, Brian, 'The Presence of *Punch* in the Nineteenth Century', in *Asian Punches: A Transcultural Affair* (ed. Hans Harder and Barbara Mittler; Heidelberg: Springer, 2103), pp. 15-44.

Malley, Shawn, 'Austen Henry Layard and the Periodical Press: Middle Eastern Archaeology and the Excavation of Cultural Identity in Mid-Nineteenth Century Britain', *Victorian Review* 22.2 (1996), pp. 152-70.

—'Shipping the Bull: Staging Assyria in the British Museum', *Nineteenth-Century Contexts* 26 (2004), pp. 1-27.

—*From Archaeology to Spectacle in Victorian Britain* (Surrey: Ashgate, 2012).

Manley, Deborah, and Peta Rée, *Henry Salt: Artist, Traveller, Diplomat, Egyptologist* (London: Libri, 2001).

Manley, Deborah, and Sahar Abdel-Hakim (eds.), *Egypt through Writers' Eyes* (London: Eland, 2007).

Mansel, Philip, 'The Grand Tour in the Ottoman Empire, 1699–1826', in *Unfolding the Orient: Travellers in Egypt and the Near East.* (Reading: Ithaca Press, 2001), pp. 41-64.

Marchand, Suzanne L., *German Orientalism in the Age of Empire: Religion, Race, and Scholarship* (Cambridge: Cambridge University Press, 2009).

Marson, Duncan, 'From Mass Tourism to Niche Tourism', in *Research Themes for Tourism* (ed. Peter Robinson, Sine Heitmann, Peter U.C. Dieke; Oxfordshire: CABI, 2011), pp. 1-15.

Matthews, William, 'The Egyptians in Scotland: The Political History of a Myth', *Viator* 1 (1970), pp. 289-306.

McGeough, Kevin M., *Exchange Relationships at Ugarit* (Ancient Near Eastern Studies Supplement, 26; Leuven: Peeters, 2007).

—'Imagining Ancient Egypt as the Idealized Self in 18th Century Europe', in *Eighteenth-Century Thing Theory in a Global Context: From Consumerism to Celebrity Culture* (ed. Christine Ionescu and Ileana Baird; Surrey: Ashgate Press, 2013), pp. 89-110.

McGeough, Kevin M., and Elizabeth A. Galway, '"Working Egyptians of the World Unite!": How Edith Nesbit Used Near Eastern Archaeology and Children's Literature to Effect Social Change', in *World of Women in the Ancient and Classical Near East* (ed. Beth Alpert Nakhai; Newcastle upon Tyne: Cambridge Scholars, 2009), pp. 181-202.

Meisel, Martin, *Realizations: Narrative, Pictorial, and Theatrical Arts in Nineteenth-Century England* (Princeton, NJ: Princeton University Press, 1983).

Melman, Billie, *Women's Orients: English Women and the Middle East, 1718–1918* (London: Macmillan, 1992).

Miliband, Ralph, 'Marx and the State', *The Socialist Register* 2 (1965), pp. 278-96.

Mills, Sarah, *Discourses of Differences: An Analysis of Women's Travel Writing and Colonialism* (London: Routledge, 1991).

Mitchell, Timothy, *Colonising Egypt* (Cambridge: Cambridge University Press, 1988).

Monad, Paul Kléber, *Solomon's Secret Arts: The Occult in the Age of Enlightenment* (New Haven, CT: Yale University Press, 2013).

Montserrat, Dominic, *Ancient Egypt: Digging for Dreams* (Glasgow: Glasgow City Council, Cultural and Leisure Services, 2000).

Moon, Brenda, *More Usefully Employed: Amelia B. Edwards, Writer, Traveller, and Campaigner for Ancient Egypt* (Egypt Exploration Society Occasional Publication, 15; London: Egypt Exploration Society, 2006).

Moore, Abigail Harrison, '*Voyage*: Dominique-Vivant Denon and the Transference of Images of Egypt', *Art History* 25 (2002), pp. 531-49.

Morris, Robert, *Freemasonry in the Holy Land. Or, Handmarks of Hiram's Builders: Embracing Notes Made during a Series of Masonic Researches, in 1868, in Asia Minor, Syria, Palestine, Egypt and Europe, and the Results of Much Correspondence with Freemasons in Those Countries* (Chicago: Knight & Leonard Printers, 10th edn, 1876).

Morton, Samuel George, *Crania Americana; or, A Comparative View of the Skulls of Various Aboriginal Nations of North and South America* (Philadelphia: J. Dobson, 1839).

Moscrop, John James, *Measuring Jerusalem: The Palestine Exploration Fund and British Interests in the Holy Land* (London: Leicester University Press, 2000).

Moser, Stephanie, *Designing Antiquity: Owen Jones, Ancient Egypt and the Crystal Palace* (Paul Mellon Centre for Studies in British Art; New Haven, CT: Yale University Press, 2012).

Mostyn, Trevor, *Egypt's Belle Epoque: Cairo 1869–1952* (London: Quartet Books, 1989).

Nowhickey, Judith, *Baron Dominique Vivant Denon (1747–1825): Hedonist and Scholar in a Period of Transition* (Cranbury, NJ: Associated University Presses, 1970).

O'Connor, Ralph, *The Earth on Show: Fossils and the Poetics of Popular Science, 1802–1856* (Chicago: University of Chicago Press, 2007).

O'Neill, Patricia, 'Amelia Edwards: From Novelist to Egyptologist', in *Interpreting the Orient: Travellers in Egypt and the Near East* (ed. Paul Starkey and Janet Starkey; Reading: Ithaca Press, 2001), pp. 165-73.

Owen, A.L., *The Famous Druids: A Survey of Three Centuries of English Literature on the Druids* (Westport, CT: Greenwood Press, 1962).

Ozouf, Mona, *Festivals and the French Revolution* (trans. Alan Sheridan; Cambridge, MA: Harvard University Press, 1988).

Pearce, Ian, 'Waynman Dixon: In the Shadow of the Needle', in *Souvenirs and New Ideas: Travel and Collecting in Egypt and the Near East* (ed. Diane Fortenberry; Oxford: ASTENE and Oxbow Books, 2013), pp. 129-41.

Petrie, William Flinders, *Researches on the Great Pyramid, or Fresh Connections, Being a Preliminary Notice of Some Facts and a Fuller Statement* (London: Dalton, 1874).

—*Descriptive Sociology; or, Groups of Facts, Classified and Arranged by Herbert Spencer. Ancient Egyptians*, XI (London: Williams & Norgate, 1925).

Phillips, James, *The Past and the Public: Archaeology and the Periodical Press in Nineteenth Century Britain* (PhD thesis, University of Southampton, 2004).

Pillsbury, Joanne, 'Perspectives: Representing the Pre-Columbian Past', in *Past*

Presented: Archaeological Illustration and the Ancient Americas (ed. Joanne Pillsbury; Washington, DC: Dumbarton Oaks, 2012), pp. 1-46.

Porter, Bernard, '"Empire, What Empire?" Or, Why 80% of Early- and Mid-Victorians Were Deliberately Kept in Ignorance of It', *Victorian Studies* 46, Papers from the Inaugural Conference of the North American Victorian Studies Association (2004), pp. 256-63.

Porter, Dennis, *Haunted Journeys: Desire and Transgression in European Travel Writing* (Princeton, NJ: Princeton University Press, 1991).

Quynn, Dorothy Mackay, 'The Art Confiscations of the Napoleonic Wars', *American Historical Review* 50 (1945), pp. 437-460.

Reade, Julian E., 'Tablets at Babylon and the British Museum', in *Babylon: Myth and Reality* (ed. I.L. Finkel and M.J. Seymour; London: British Museum Press, 2008), pp. 74-80.

Rees, Joan, *Amelia Edwards: Traveller, Novelist and Egyptologist* (London: Rubicon Press, 1998).

—'Preparing to Be an Egyptologist: Amelia Edwards before 1873', in *Egypt through the Eyes of Travellers* (ed. Paul Starkey and Nadia el Kholy; Durham: ASTENE, 2002), pp. 39-44.

Reid, Donald Malcolm, *Whose Pharaohs?: Archaeology, Museums, and Egyptian National Identity from Napoleon to World War I* (Berkeley, CA: University of California Press, 2002).

Robinson, Edward, *Biblical Researches in Palestine, Mount Sinai and Arabia Petræa: A Journal of Travels in the Year 1838 by E. Robinson and E. Smith*, II (Boston: Crocker & Brewster, 1841).

Rodenbeck, John, 'Dressing Native', in *Unfolding the Orient: Travellers in Egypt and the Near East* (Durham: Ithaca Press, 2001), pp. 65-100.

Rose, Jonathan, *The Intellectual Life of the British Working Class* (New Haven, CT: Yale University Press, 2nd edn, 2010).

Rumney, Jay, *Herbert Spencer's Sociology* (New York: Atherton Books, 1966).

Russel, John Malcolm, *From Nineveh to New York: The Strange Story of the Assyrian Reliefs in the Metropolitan Museum and the Hidden Masterpiece at Canford School* (with contributions by Judith McKenzie and Stephanie Dalley; in association with the Metropolitan Museum of Art; New Haven, CT: Yale University Press, 1997).

Russel, Terrence M., *The Discovery of Egypt: Vivant Denon's Travels with Napoleon's Army* (Gloucestershire: Sutton Publishing, 2005).

Said, Edward, *Orientalism* (New York: Vintage Books, 25th anniversary edn, 2003 [1978]).

—*Culture and Imperialism* (New York: Vintage Books, 1993).

Scheppig, Richard (ed.), *Descriptive Sociology; or, Groups of Facts, Classified and Arranged by Herbert Spencer. Hebrews and Phoenicians*, VII (London: Williams & Norgate, 1880).

Searight, Sarah, *The British in the Middle East* (London: East-West Publications, 1979).

—*Steaming East: The Forging of Steamship and Rail Links between Europe and Asia* (London: Bodley Head, 1991).

Secord, James A., *Victorian Sensation: The Extraordinary Publication, Reception, and Secret Authorship of* Vestiges of the Natural History of Creation (Chicago: University of Chicago Press, 2000).

Shandler, Jeffrey, and Beth S. Wenger, '"The Site of Paradise": The Holy Land in American Jewish Imagination', in *Encounters with the 'Holy Land': Place, Past,* and *Future in American Jewish Culture* (ed. Jeffrey Shandler and Beth S. Wenger; Hanover, NH: University Press of New England, 1997), pp. 11-40.

Sharpe, Samuel, *The Early History of Egypt, from the Old Testament, Herodotus, Manetho, and the Hieroglyphical Inscriptions* (London: Edward Moxon, 1836).

—*Egyptian Mythology and Egyptian Christianity, with their Influence on the Opinions of Modern Christendom* (London: John Russel Smith, 1863).

—*Texts from the Holy Bible Explained by the Help of the Ancient Monuments with a Few Plans and Views* (London: Day & Son, 1866).

—*Short Notes to Accompany a Revised Translation of the Hebrew Scriptures* (London: J. Russel Smith, 1874).

Silberman, Neil Asher, *Digging for God and Country: Exploration, Archeology, and the Secret Struggle for the Holy Land 1799–1917* (New York: Alfred A. Knopf, 1982).

—*Between Past and Present: Archaeology, Ideology, and Nationalism in the Modern Middle East* (New York: Anchor Books, 1989).

Sinnema, Peter W., *Dynamics of the Pictured Page: Representing the Nation in the Illustrated London News* (Aldershot: Ashgate, 1998).

Sketchely, Arthur, *Mrs Brown up the Nile* (London: George Routledge & Sons, 1869).

—*Mrs Brown on Cleopatra's Needle* (London: George Routledge & Sons, 1878).

Smith, George, 'The Chaldean Account of the Deluge', *Transactions of the Society of Biblical Archaeology* 2 (1873), pp. 213-34.

Smyth, Charles Piazzi, *Life and Work at the Great Pyramid; during the Months of January, February, March, and April, A.D. 1865; with a Discussion of the Facts Ascertained* (3 vols.; Edinburgh: Edmonston & Douglas, 1867).

—*On the Antiquity of Intellectual Man, from a Practical and Astronomical Point of View* (Edinburgh: Edmonston & Douglas, 1868).

—*Our Inheritance in the Great Pyramid* (London: W. Ibister & Co., new and enlarged edn, 1874).

Starkey, Janet, 'James Rennell and his Scientific World of Observation', in *Knowledge Is Light: Travellers in the Near East* (Oxford: ASTENE and Oxbow Books, 2011), pp. 38-58 (42-43).

Syson, Luke, 'The Ordering of the Artificial World: Collecting, Classification, and Progress', in *Enlightenment: Discovering the World in the Eighteenth Century* (ed. K. Sloan; London: British Museum Press, 2003), pp. 108-21.

Taylor, W. Cooke, *The Natural History of Society: The Barbarian and the Civilized State*, I (London: Orme, Brown, 1840).

Terrall, Mary, 'Natural Philosophy for Fashionable Readers', in *Books and the Sciences in History* (ed. Marina Frasca-Spada and Nick Jardine; Cambridge: Cambridge University Press, 2000), pp. 239-54.

Terrasson, Jean, *The Life of Sethos: Taken from Private Memoirs of the Ancient Egyptians, Translated from the Greek Manuscript into French*, I (trans. Mr Lediard; London: J. Walthoe, 1732).

Thompson, John Jason, *Sir Gardner Wilkinson and his Circle* (Austin, TX: University of Texas Press, 1992).

Trafton, Scott, *Egypt Land: Race and Nineteenth-Century American Egyptomania* (Durham, NC: Duke University Press, 2004).

Tuchman, Barbara W., *Bible and Sword: England and Palestine from the Bronze Age to Balfour* (New York: Ballantine Books, 1984 [1956]).

Urry, John, *The Tourist Gaze* (London: Sage, 1990).

Usick, Patricia, 'The Reverend Joliffe's Advice to Travellers', in *Unfolding the Orient: Travellers in Egypt and the Near East* (Reading: Ithaca Press, 2001), pp. 219-24.

Vaczek, Louisa, and Gail Buckland, *Travelers in Ancient Lands: A Portrait of the Middle East, 1839–1919* (Boston: New York Graphic Company, 1981).

Varisco, Daniel Martin, 'Orientalism and Bibliolatry: Framing the Holy Land in Nineteenth-Century Protestant Bible Customs Texts', in *Orientalism Revisited: Art, Land and Voyage* (ed. Ian Richard Netton; New York: Routledge, 2013), pp. 187-204.

Veblen, Thorstein, *The Theory of the Leisure Class* (New York: Penguin, 1994 [1899]).

Verbrugghe, Gerald P., and John M. Wickersham, *Berossos and Manetho, Introduced and Translated: Native Traditions in Ancient Mesopotamia and Egypt* (Ann Arbor, MI: University of Michigan Press, 1996).

Vögel, M., *On Beer: A Statistical Account* (London: Trübner & Co., 1874).

Warburton, Eliot, 'Dedicatory Preface to the 8th edition', in *The Crescent and the Cross; or, Romance and Realities of Eastern Travel* (London: Hurst & Blackett Publishers, 16th edn, 1860 [1854]).

Warner, Nicholas (ed.), *An Egyptian Panorama: Reports from the 19th Century British Press* (Cairo: Zeitouna, 1994).

Warren, Charles, *Underground Jerusalem: An Account of Some of the Difficulties Encountered in its Exploration and the Results Obtained* (London: Richard Bentley & Son, 1876).

Waterfield, Gordon, *Layard of Nineveh* (London: John Murray & Sons, 1963).

Werner, Alex, 'Egypt in London—Public and Private Displays in the 19th Century Metropolis', in *Imhotep Today: Egyptianizing Architecture* (ed. Jean-Marcel Humbert and Clifford Price; Encounters with Ancient Egypt; London: UCL Press, 2003), pp. 75-104.

White, Hayden, *Metahistory: The Historical Imagination in Nineteenth-Century Europe* (Baltimore, MD: Johns Hopkins University Press, 1974).

Williams, S.C., *Religious Belief and Popular Culture in Southwark, c. 1830–1939* (Oxford: Oxford University Press, 1999).

Winslow, William Copley, 'The Queen of Egyptology', *American Antiquarian* 14 (1892).

Wittfogel, Karl A., *Oriental Despotism: A Comparative Study of Total Power* (New Haven, CT: Yale University Press, 1957).

Wolfe, S.J., with Robert Singerman, *Mummies in Nineteenth-Century America* (Jefferson, NC: McFarland & Co., 2009).

Wood, Gillen D'Arcy, *The Shock of the Real: Romanticism and Visual Culture, 1760–1860* (New York: Palgrave, 2001).

Ziter, Edward, *The Orient on the Victorian Stage* (Cambridge: Cambridge University Press, 2003).

Index of Biblical References and Other Ancient Texts

Hebrew Bible/Old Testament

Genesis	2, 56, 142, 149-50, 255, 362
3.15	389
10.9	389-90

Exodus 257-64

Deuteronomy	
11.10	118-19

Judges	
21.19-23	109

Ruth 118

1 and 2 Samuel 146

1 Samuel	
14.4-5	111

1 and 2 Kings 146, 394

Nehemiah	
3.5	307

Isaiah	104-105, 230-31
8.6	307
65.3-4	171
66.3	171
66.17	171

Jeremiah	
32.18-20	356

Daniel	56, 201, 362-64
5.25	
6.16-24	256

Jonah 56-57

Nahum 56

Zephaniah 56

New Testament

Matthew	
22.11	118

Mark	
2.23	118

Luke	
6.1	118
13.4	307

John	
9.6-7	307

Egyptian

Abydos king list 387

Papyrus Ani (*Book of the Dead*) 406

Papyrus Sallier 259

'The Tale of Two Brothers' 171

Classical

Aegyptiaca 59

Vergil	
Aeneid	167

Corpus hermeticum	71-72

Diodorus Siculus 65, 66-70, 151, 170, 179-80, 234-35

Apuleius	
The Golden Ass	76

Herodotus	59-66, 102, 151, 170, 351, 356
Histories	59-66

Josephus 55, 307

Manetho 59, 387

Pliny	32
Natural History	32

Plutarch	70-71, 170
Moralia	70-71

Pythagoras 67

Strabo 102, 334

INDEX OF AUTHORS

Aguirre, R. 134
Allen, D. 408
Altick, R. 84, 185-86
Anderson, P. 8, 185-88, 190, 196-97
Arnold, B. 173
Asher-Greve, J. 60, 327

Bailey, P. 7-8, 10-11
Bann, S. 381, 408, 409, 420
Bar-Yosef, E. 2, 4, 14-16, 19, 56, 108, 289, 382, 416, 420
Barrell, J. 23, 165
Baucom, I. 24
Bednarski, A. 50
Ben-Arieh, Y. 4, 24, 30, 107-108, 112, 119, 288, 410, 414
Benedict, B. 20, 23, 187, 392, 410
Bohrer, F. 12-14, 129, 189-90, 198
Bohlman, P. 3-4
Boorstin, D. 279, 350
Booth, M. 226, 242
Breed, B. 9
Brendon, P. 284, 287, 289, 291, 293-95
Brier, B. 244-45
Buckland, G. 292, 311, 316
Burgin, V. 24-25
Buzard, J. 279-80, 303, 317

Canclini, N. 407
Cannadine, D. 16-17
Carneiro, R. 158
Chloe, C. 18-20, 316
Cobbing, F. 410
Colla, E. 25, 95, 98, 101, 178, 315-16
Cowan, E. 3

Damiani, A. 282
Davis, J. 15, 16, 103-104
Davis, R. 3, 4
Douglas, M. 406

Eagleton, T. 381-83
Ebeling, J. 52
Ellis, K. 328-29
Evans, E. 349

Fabian, A. 152
Fagan, B. 50, 384-85
Fahim, H. 282
Finkel, I. 59
Flynn, S. 383-84
Frahm, E. 174
Fussel, P. 279

Gaehtgens, T. 52
Galway, E. 399
Gasque, W.W. 396
Gearon, E. 38, 349
Gibb, L. 329
Gillooly, E. 177
Gindy, N. 318-19, 321
Gould, S.J. 154
Gregory, D. 36, 108
Grewal, I. 279-81, 303, 304

Hackford-Jones, J. 25
Hallote R. 15, 112, 114, 119, 155, 173, 410
Hamann, B.E. 32, 33
Harpur, T. 396
Harris, M. 155-56, 159, 161, 165, 172
Harvey, J. 34
Hasinoff, E. 326
Heitmann, S. 283
Hibbert, C. 188
Holloway, S. 17, 174, 316
Hornung, E. 53, 71, 404
Houston, S. 33-34
Humbert, J. 41, 47

Jacobs, J. 99

Jackson, E. 281, 328
Jenkins, I. 209
Jenkyns, R. 5-6

Kabbani, R. 18-19, 21-23, 171
Kark, R. 289
Katz, D. 156, 166-67
Keel, O. 53
Kholy, N. el 282
Kirschenblatt-Gimblett, B. 175
Kuklick, B. 149

Landor, W.S. 137
Laqueur, T. 55-56
Larsen, M.T. 121, 125, 127-28, 137, 175, 398
Larsen, T. 56, 58
Leben, U. 52
Lefkowitz, M. 72, 74, 76-77, 80
Legge, F. 411, 414
Levine, P. 182, 382, 392-93, 407-11
Livingstone, D. 149-50, 152, 154
Lloyd, S. 121, 124, 393, 398
Long, B.O. 104, 114-15
Longfellow, H.W. 54

MacKenzie, J. 281
Maggiolini, P. 286
Malley, S. 122-23, 129, 132, 134, 197-203
Mandel, P. 284
Manley, D. 120
Marchand, S. 58, 148, 173-74, 407, 408
Marson, D. 293
McCannel, D. 280, 316
McGeough, K. 29, 52, 161, 399
Meisel, M. 13
Melman, B. 281, 325, 327, 336-37, 340, 348, 382, 411
Michaelis, J.D. 12
Miliband, R. 162
Mills, S. 325-28, 337, 340
Mitchell, T. 282
Monad, P.K. 57
Moon, B. 330-31, 333-34, 337, 341
Moore, A. 32, 34, 38, 50-51
Moscrop, J. 105, 114, 411, 414-17, 419
Moser, S. 9
Mostyn, T. 293, 295

Nichols, J.H. 160
Nowhickey, J. 39

O'Connor, R. 10, 191
O'Neil, P. 325, 336, 340, 348
Owen, A.L. 2
Ozouf, M. 29

Pearce, I. 206-207
Phillips, J. 185, 187-88, 190, 209, 212-13
Pillsbury, J. 32-34
Porter, B. 8
Porter, B.W. 99
Porter, D. 18-20, 23, 279, 284, 309, 317

Quynn, D.M. 30

Reade, J. 135
Rée, P. 120
Rees, J. 331, 336-37, 339-40, 349
Reid, D.M. 25, 299, 300-301, 310
Roberts, M. 25
Rose, J. 4, 9, 56, 186, 406-407
Russel, J.M. 56
Russel, T. 40, 49

Said, E. 13-15, 21-22, 30-31, 34-35, 38
Saltus Saltus, F. 28
Searight, S. 286-287
Secord, J. 9, 83, 137, 184-86
Seymour, M.J. 59
Shandler, J. 280
Shapira, Y. xvii
Shepherd, N. 24, 30, 87, 155, 163, 294, 298
Silberman, N. 25, 103, 109, 112, 120, 329-30
Singerman, R. 235
Sinnema, P. 5, 187-89, 204, 207
Spencer, H. 140
Spur, J. 410
Starkey, J. 107
Syson, L. 164-65

Terral, M. 382
Thompson, J. 383-84
Trafton, S. 16
Tuchman, B. 53, 330, 416-17

Urry, J. 310
Usick, P. 303-304

Vaczek, L. 292, 311, 316
Varisco, D.M. 12
Verbrugghe, G.P. 59

Warburton, E. 83
Warner, N. 188
Waterfield, G. 121-22, 128, 133

Weisberg, D. 173
Wenger, B. 280
White, H. 145
Wickersham, J.M. 59
Williams, S. 55
Wittfogel, K. 162
Wolfe, S.J. 235
Wood, G. 12

Ziter, E. 39

Index of Subjects

Abraham 57, 173
  as a Druid 2
Abu Simbel 86-87, 332-33
*An Account of the Manners and
    Customs of the Modern Egyptians*
  385
Achaeans 404
Adam 149
Adler, Cyrus 175
Adonis 170
Aedile of London 133
Aeneas 167
Afrocentrism 16, 80
Akausha 404
Akhenaten 385
Akkadian 81-82
Albert (prince consort) 60
Albright, W.F. 120, 175
Alchemy 55, 72
Alexander II (tsar) 261-64
Alexandria 35, 44-45, 206-207, 384
  as travel destination 270, 277, 285,
    300, 314
Ali, Muhammed 86, 205, 235, 294
Aliens 350
Alison, Charles 199-200
Allegory of 18 Brumaire 53
Amarna 385
American Palestine Exploration Society
  410
The Amulet 398-99
Ancient Egypt (1844) 152
*Ancient Egypt: The Light of the
  World* 395
Ancient Society (1877) 159
Animism 172
Anti-Semitism 257-58, 261-64
Antiquarianism 408-409
On the Antiquity of Intellectual Man 357-
  58, 363, 376-77

Antiquity of Man (1863) 155
Antony and Cleopatra 216-17, 250
Aphrodite 170
  temple of 65
Apis 61-62, 67, 77, 171, 242, 244, 334
Apollo 230-31
*An Appeal to the Antiquaries of Europe
    on the Destruction of the Monu-
    ments of Egypt* 314-15
Apuleius 76
Aramaic 57, 66, 81
Arnold, Matthew 230
Art
  Assyrian 189, 202-203, 343-45
  Egyptian 102, 202-203, 343-45
  Christian 391-92
  classical 102, 202-203, 343-45
  Western canon 100-101, 202-203,
    343-45
Ascent of Man 230
Asclepius 71
Ashkelon 68, 329-30
Ashurbanipal 69, 393-94
Ashurnasirpal II 123, 126
Asiatic mode of production 162-63
Association for the Study of Travel
    in Egypt and the Near East
    (ASTENE) 279
Assyrian (language) 81, 403
Assyrian sculpture 14, 191-98, 200, 202-
    203, 389-90
  bull 129-31, 135-36, 198-99, 231
Astrology 55
Astronomy 356-60, 376-78
Avatar 343
Azeth, the Egyptian; Amymone
    (1848) 230

Baal 65
Babel, Tower of 65, 142-43, 366, 376

Index of Subjects

Babylon 4-5, 57, 59
   excavation of 126
   founding of 69
   Herodotus's description 64
   Hanging Gardens of 64, 69
   in *Punch* 230
Babylonian (language) 81
Babylonian marriage market 65
Backsheesh 98, 269, 306
Baden-Powell, Robert 171
Baedeker, Karl 294-95, 304, 308
Baedeker's Egypt: Handbook for Travellers (1885) 304, 307-309
Balawat 195, 398
Balkan Rebellion (1875) 134
Banks, William John 303
Baptism 395
Bastille 28-29
The Battle of Aboukir 53
Battle of Omdurman 224, 416-17
Bedouin 12, 157, 163, 165, 283, 304-305, 329
   food production 118
Beer 234-34
On Beer: A Statistical Account 234-35
Behistun Inscription 81
Bell, Gertrude 286, 328
Belus 69
Belzoni, Giovanni 20-21, 84-103, 120, 138, 151, 179, 328, 333, 336, 339-40, 354 356, 422
Belzoni, Sarah 85-87, 89, 328
Benjamin, Walter 13
Berenice 87
Berossos 59
Berthollet, Claude-Louis 32
Besant, Annie 415
Besant, Walter 415
Bhaba, Homi 13
Bibel-und-Babel 172-76
Biblical Archaeology Review 7
Biblical Archaeology Society 410
Biblical conception of history 56-58
Biblical criticism, German 56
Biblical literacy 55-56
Biblical translation 388-89
Bibliotheca historica 66-70
Biblical Researches in Palestine, Mount Sinai and Arabia Petræa 103-20

Birch, Samuel 333-34, 341, 349, 382, 399, 411-14
The Birth of Osiris (ballet) 72
Black Hand Group 5
Black Obelisk 394
'Black orientalism' 16
Black plague 287
Blake, William 1-4
   Jerusalem 1-4
   Jerusalem: The Emanation of the Giant Albion 2
   Milton: A Poem 2
Blind, Mathilde 211-12
Blyden, Edward Wilmot 16
Bonald, Louis de 142
Bonomi, Joseph 385, 389, 411
The Book of the Beginning 395-97
Bordeaux, Place de la Bourse 266
Borsippa 376-77
Botta, Paul Émile 81, 121, 125, 127, 134, 195, 200
Boy Scouts 171
Bradbury, K. 348-49
Bradlaugh, Charles 58
Breasted, James Henry 384
Bridges, Robert 1
Bright, John (politician) 222-23, 247
'Brit Abroad' 273
British Archaeological Association 190
British Museum 100, 123, 125-26, 176-77, 179, 193, 195, 197, 200, 208-209, 252, 336, 341, 386-88, 393-94, 397-402, 409-10
British occupation of Egypt 290-91
Bruno, Giordino 72
Budge, E.A. 6, 333, 397-406, 410
Buddhism 151, 375
Bulak Museum 313-15, 341
Bulgarian Horrors 134
Bullock's Egyptian Hall 422
Burckhardt, Jacob 160-61
Burckhardt, Johann Ludwig 86-87, 329
Burrel, George 207
Byblos 170
Byron, Lord 304, 329

Cairo
   antiquities trade 152
   compared to London 422-23

Cairo (*continued*)
    'Englishman's playground' 293
    travel destination 88, 229, 233, 238, 277, 284, 290, 294-96, 301, 314, 319-20
Canaanite, migration to Africa 151
Calah 126
Callet, Antoine-François 53
Cambridge University 182, 402-404, 407-408
Canning, Stratford 122, 125, 134, 195-96
Carthage, origin of 78
Cartouche 80-81
Cataracts 424
Catastrophism 419
Celtic culture, supposed Egyptian origins 3, 64
Chaldaean, definition 57, 66, 70, 82, 202
Chamberlain, Joseph 255-56
Champollion, Jean-François 81, 264-65, 385
Chateaubriand, François-René 425
Cheops 227, 235-36, 260, 324, 369-72
    Herodotus's account 63
Cherbourg–Paris railway line 250
Child sacrifice 170-71
China 144-46
Cholera 287
Christian Life 388
Christian Reformer 388
Chronology 56, 356-58, 373-75, 378, 387
Church of England 2
Church of the Holy Sepulchre 134
Church of the Nativity 134
Cingrus 3
Clarke, Edward 163
Classical studies 6, 55, 58-59
    and education 58-59
Clavicula Salomonis 57
Cleopatra 205, 210-11, 216, 230, 232, 250, 266, 277, 311, 423
Cleopatra (pontoon) 206-208, 267
Cleopatra (by Rider Haggard) 227
Cleopatra's Needle 35, 47, 49, 204-212, 250, 264-68
Cleopatra's Needle (New York) 49, 205
Clerisy 383
Coleridge, Mary Elizabeth 181-82

Coleridge, Samuel Taylor 383
Collecting 348-49
Collier, James 156
Colossi of Memnon 255-56, 425
commedia dell'arte 215
commodification (of ancient culture) 7, 237-38, 283, 323
Comte, Auguste 143-44
Comte de Volney 22
Condor, Claude 119-20, 307
Constantinople 284-85
Cook, John 290-91
Cook, Thomas 268-69, 289-91, 294, 297, 304
Cook's Tourist Handbook for Palestine and Syria 276, 298, 304-307, 420
Copperplates 37
Corn Laws 246
Cosmology 75
Country Party 237
Cranborne, Lord 247
Crania americana 150-52
Crania egyptica 152-54
Cranial measurements 15-16, 150-54
Crimean War 132, 134, 251,253
The Critique of Political Economy (1859) 162-63
Crolley, George 202
Crystal Palace 128, 208-209, 385-86, 415
Ctesias the Cnidian 69
Cubit, sacred 350, 352, 358-66
Cuneiform, decipherment of 55, 80-82
Curiosity 20
Curses 350
Cuvier, Georges 151-52

Dahabiyya 300-301, 332
Daily Telegraph 195, 395, 397-98
Darwin, Charles 20, 154
David, Jacques Louis 29-30, 40, 53
Dead Sea 155, 419
The Decline of the West 149
Degenerationism 142-43
Delitzsch, Friedrich 173-75
Deluge 140, 173, 366, 394-95
Denderah (Tentyra) 45-47, 315
    Temple of Hathor 338-39, 341
Denon, Vivant 32-51, 54-55, 151

Index of Subjects

Derby, Lord 238-39, 247
Derceto 68
Desaix, Louis Charles Antoine, monument to 52
Description d'Egypte 32-38, 47-48, 50-51, 129, 150, 385
  bookshelf 38
Descriptive Sociology 156-58
Dickens, Charles 84
Diderot, Denis 35
Diffusion 159-60, 166, 175
Dimitrijević, Dragutin 5
Disney Chair of Archaeology at Cambridge 407
Disraeli, Benjamin 122, 132, 215, 219, 247-48, 400
  in satire 246-50, 268
  purchase of Suez Canal shares 247-48
Dissenters (*see* Unitarianism)
Divided monarchy 57
Divine revelation 58
Dixon, Waynman 206-207, 267
Dixon, John 206-207, 267
Djed pillar 169
Djinn 99
Dobrizhoffer, Martin 142
Dragoman 293-94, 297-98, 311, 322
Drovetti, Bernardino 90-93
Drug tourism 284
Druids 2
Drummond, Henry 230-31
Duncan, David 156
Dunraven, SS 260-61
Dupuis, Charles 166
Durga 375
Dying-and-rising gods 168-70
'The Dying Gladiator' 190

The Early History of Egypt 386-88
Early modern scholarship 72
Eastern question 133-34, 247
Ebers, Georg 308-309
Ecclesiastical tradition 112
Eden 2, 389
  expulsion from 142
Edfu, Temple of Horus 98
Edinburgh Royal Society 354, 357
Edomites 151

Edward (prince of Wales), visit to Egypt 231-34, 301
Edwards, Amelia 13, 276, 291-95, 297, 299, 301-302, 310-14, 315-17, 327, 330-49, 382, 428-29
Egypt Exploration Fund 340-42
'Egypt Unvisited (Suggested by Mr David Roberts' Egyptian Sketches)' 317-18
Egyptian Department of Antiquities 354
Egyptian Hall, Bullock's 422
Egyptian Hall, Mansion House 425
Egyptian language, decipherment of hieroglyphs 55, 80-81
Egyptian Mythology and Egyptian Christianity, with their Influence on the Opinions of Modern Christendom 390-92
The Egyptian Red Book 220-24
Egyptomania 102
'Egypt's Might Is Tumbled Down' 181-82
Elephantine 349
Elgin Marbles 14
Encyclopaedia 35
Engels, Friedrich 161-63
Ephesus 190
Esarhaddon 123
Ethics, archaeological 271
Eunuchs 93, 193
Evidence of the Truth of the Christian Religion Derived from the Literal Fulfilment of Prophecy 177-78
Exodus 57, 58, 336, 374-75
  route of 116-17
Expositions universelles 45
Ezekiel 211

Fayûm portraits 344-46
Ficino, Marsilio 72
Fellah 292-93
Female authority figures, ancient 60
Fénelon, François 74
Ferdinand, Franz (archduke) 5
Fergusson, James 307, 357
Festival of Unity 28-29
Film studies 24-25
Fire deities 379
Flaubert, Gustave 294-95, 317

Fontaine de la Régénération 28-29
Forbin, Count de 92, 97, 100
Fountain of the Fellah (rue de Sèvres) 52
Fountain of Victory (Place du Châtelet) 52
Frazer, James G. 167-71
Freemasonry 72-73, 276
Freemasonry in the Holy Land 276
French army, at Thebes 42-43
French navy, defeat 37
French Revolution 28-30

Gael 3
Gell, Sir William 384-85
George III 37
George V 1
'George Walker at Suez' 319
The German Ideology (1846) 162
German Oriental Society 173
Geschichte des Altertums 148
Geytholos (Gathelus) 3
Gibraltar, Ishmael 85-86
Gilder, Richard Watson 212
Gilrastes 179
Gladstone, William 132-35, 141, 215, 220-24, 247-48, 250, 399-404, 411, 416-17
Gliddon, George 152, 154, 294, 314-15
Gnosticism 71
God Save the Queen 1
Golden Age 142, 155
The Golden Bough 167-71
Gomorrah 119, 419
Gordon, General Charles (Chinese) 220-24, 291
Gordon, Lucie Duff 287
Goschen, George 260
Gospels, compared to Egyptian mythology 395-97
Government Commission for the Research of Artistic and Scientific Objects in Conquered Countries 30
Graeco-Roman view of the Near East 58-72
graffiti 311, 332-33
Grand Tour 280-81, 283-85, 288-89, 384
Grande Armée, monument to (Pont Neuf) 52

Granville, Lord 132, 222-24
Great Exhibition 177
Great Pyramid: Why Was It Built, and Who Built It?, The 351-53
Greaves, John 352
Greek relations with Persia 64
Gros, Jean 53
Grove, George 415
Guidebooks, tourist 270, 290, 299-309, 386

Hades 167
Haggard, H. Rider 8, 227
Haliburton, R.G. 375
Ham 371
Hart, Solomon 255
Harvard University 175
Hatshepsut 342, 348
Hauss, Hans-Robert 13
Hebrew (language) 81
Hegel, Georg 144-49, 161-62
Hercules 67
Herder, Johann 31, 57-58
Hermes 67, 71
Hermes Trismegistus 71-72, 375
'Hermes Trismegistus' (poem) 54
Hincks, Edward 82
Hislop, Alexander 65
History of Egypt 384
History of Mesopotamia 59
Horus 70-71, 79, 169, 391-92, 395
Hotels and accommodations 290, 294-99
  Coulomb's Hôtel de l'Orient 295
  Hill's Hôtel de l'Europe (Rey's Hôtel de l'Europe) 294-95
  Hotel du Nil 294-95
  meals served 298-99
  Shepheard's (Hôtel de l'Orient) 294-97, 320-21
  tent-camps (Palestine) 297-99
Hume, David 166
Hussein, Saddam 5

Ibis mummies 33, 61
Illustrated London News (*ILN*) 187-210
  circulation figures 188
Illustration, scientific 32-34, 428
Imhotep 71

India 144-46, 375
  British in 292-93
Initiation rituals 76-79
The Innocents Abroad 311
Institute of Egypt 40-41
Irish nationalism 3
Isaiah 211
Ishtar 170
Isis 28-30, 51-52, 66, 70-71, 75, 79, 169, 375, 389, 391-92
  priesthood of 76
Islam 308-309, 355
Ismail, Khedive 260
'Israel in Egypt' 246-47
Israeli nationalism 5

Jacobovici, Simcha 7
Jacobsen, Thorkild 176
Jehovah's Witnesses 351, 379-80
Jehu 394
Jennings, Hargrave 379
Jeremiah 211
Jericho 119
Jerome, St, commentaries of 56
Jerrold, W. Blanchard 177
Jerusalem 286, 306-307, 371-72
Jerusalem Water Relief 414-15
Jesus 391, 395
  and Osiris 406
John Bull 131-32, 231, 242, 244, 250-52
Johns Hopkins University 175
Joliffe, Thomas 304
Jonathan (book of Samuel) 111
Jones, Indiana 90
Joseph 218, 255-56
Joshua 57
Journalism, archaeological 184-213
Jupiter Ammon
  oracle of 69
  temple of 75, 102

Kavanaugh, Lady Harriet 281
Keith, Alexander 177-78
Kent, Charles Foster 119
Khartoum, siege of 220-24, 291
Khorsobad 195, 200, 390
King, Stephen 84
Kingdom Come, The 379-80
Kinglake, Alexander 283, 329

Kitchener, Lord Herbert 224, 416-17
Klemm, Gustav 148
Klima 31
Kuyunjik 123, 125-26, 395

Labyrinth 64
Landscape illustration 34
Lane, Edward 385
Lane, Jenny 332
Lang, Andrew 172
La Peyrère, Isaac 149-50
Latin Patriarchate 286
Lawrence, T.E. 283, 381
Layard, Austen Henry 20-21, 84, 96, 120-38, 140, 188, 190, 195-96, 198-200, 203-204, 328, 333, 336, 339-40, 343, 381, 394, 402, 409, 417-18
  political career 131-37, 428
  political satire 131, 135-36, 251-55, 268
Lebolo, Antonio 92
Leisure culture 10-11
Levy, Reuben 157-58
Lewis, Sir George Cornewall 378
Les Liaisons dangereuses 40
Liberia 16
Life and Work at the Great Pyramid 354-59, 364-72, 375
The Life of Sethos 55, 72-80
  and Afrocentrism 80
Limp cover 308
Linton, Lynn 230-31
Lion's den 256
Literacy 185, 194
'Little Key of Solomon' 57
Locke, John 166
Louis XIV 39
Louis Philippe 53
Louvre 41
Lubbock, John 160
Luxor 43-44, 302
  as health resort 287
  hotels 290
  inhabitants of (nineteenth century) 44
  Karnak 48-49, 287
Lyell, Charles 155-56
Lynch, William Francis 155

MacCullum, Andrew 332
Madden, Richard 151
Magic 57, 406
Mahdi 220-24
The Making of Religion 172
Malthus, Thomas 154
Mammon 260-61
Manners and Customs of the Ancient Egyptians 331-32, 384-86
Mansion House 425
Marchands de l'eau 51
Mariette, Auguste 314, 334, 354, 370-71
Marsyas 230-31
Martin, John 178
Marx, Karl 161-63
Masada 5
Maspero, Gaston 170-71, 341
Massey, Gerald 395-97
May Laws 261
Mediaeval scholarship 3, 55, 71-72
Medical tourism 286-87
Medinet Habu 338
Melchizedek 371-72
Memphis, founding of 62
'men of letters' 382-83, 428
Menes 68
Menon 68-69
Menou, Abdallas Jacques-François de 36
Menzies, Robert 373-75
Metrology 358-66, 370, 374
    Anglo-Saxon 364-66
    Babylonian 377-78
    Israelite 364-66
    metric system 364-66
    Pyramid 358-66, 370, 374
    Solomonic 364
Meyer, Eduard 148
Michmash, passage of 111
Middle class, emergence of 10-11
Mill, John Stuart 162
Millenarianism 379-80
Millennial Dawn 379-80
Milton, John 307
Min 62, 378
Missionaries 286
Mitford, Charles 122
Mnevis 67
Monotheism 346-47, 369-72, 404-406

Moralia 70-71
Morgan, Lewis Henry 159
Morgan, Thomas 190
Morris, Robert 276, 291-92
Morrison, Walter 415
Morton, Samuel George 150-54, 345
'Mosé in Egitto' (opera) 248
Moses 3, 173, 371
Mount Sinai 115
    Saint Catherine Monastery 112, 138
Mrs Brown
    Mrs Brown on Cleopatra's Needle 214-20, 264
    Mrs Brown up the Nile 268-73
Müller, Max 172
Mummies and mummification 60, 61, 95, 151-52, 385
    ethics 271
    as paper source 235-38
Murchison, Sir Frederick 419
Murray, John 88-89, 127-29, 304-305, 386
Mystery religions 67, 76

The Naked Archaeologist 7
Napoleon III 5, 250-51
Napoleon Bonaparte 30-53, 179
Nast, Thomas 244-46
Native Americans 15
The Natural Genesis 395-96
Nature worship 61
Naumann, Johann Gottlieb 72
Nelson, Horatio 37, 205
Nemes-headdress 30, 53, 227, 241
Nesbit, Edith 398-99
Nestorians 202
New Age 366, 406
New England theological movements 103
New Woman 230
Newton, Isaac 352
Niebuhr, Hermann 151
Nightingale, Florence 22
Nile
    cruise 290
    flooding of 66
    Nilocentrism 61
    source of 66
Nimrod 389-90

Nimrud 192, 194-95, 199, 231, 390
excavation of 122-26, 136-37
Nineveh
fall of 70, 178
founding of 68-69
misidentification 124-25, 390
Nineveh and its Remains 120-21, 127-31
Ninus 68-69
Ninyas 69-70
Nippur 126
Nitocris (Egypt) 62
Nitokris (Babylon) 64-65
Niul 3
Noah 371
ark of 256, 350
Noblesse oblige 182

Obelisks 30, 35, 43-44, 49, 52, 92, 204-212, 214, 217-19, 250, 264-68
in Ramsgate Harbour 266
'The Obelisk' 212
Oedipus tyrannus 230
L'oeuvre priapique 40
Olga 206-208
Ophir 200-201
Ophthalmia 93
Opium 284
Oriental despotism 162-63
Orientalists' Congress in Vienna 341-42
Ornamentalism 16-17
Orpheus 77
Osiris 67-68, 70-71, 75, 79, 168-69, 234-35, 334, 406
Osiris (opera) 72
Ottoman Empire, dissolution of 134
Our Inheritance in the Great Pyramid 353, 358-62, 366, 368, 370-75, 378
The Outline of History 148-49
Outlines of a Critique of Political Economy 162-63
Oxford University 402, 407-408
Ozymandias 68
'Ozymandias' (poem) 179-81
'Ozymandias or on a Stupendous Leg of Granite, Discovered Standing by Itself in the Deserts of Egypt, with the Inscription Inserted Below' 180

Palestine Association 410
Palestine Exploration Fund (PEF) 119-20, 197, 410, 414-22
Palgrave, W. Gifford 419-20
Pan-Africanism 16
Paper, manufactured from mummies 235-38
Paris 28-29
coat of arms 51-52
etymology 51
Parthians 126
Pasha, Tewfik 260
Peel, Robert 246
Peiser, F.E. 408
Pentaour 259, 261
Père Lachaise cemetery 52
Periodical press
circulation 186, 188, 225
education 186-87
finances of 186
leisure 186
rise of 185-86
values 187, 225-26
Perseus 67
Persians 64, 145-46, 148
relations with Greeks 64
Petra 86, 151
Petrie, W.F. 6, 157-58, 338, 341-43, 348-49, 350-51, 384, 409-10
Pettigrew, Thomas 236-37
Pharaohs, Fellâhs, and Explorers 341-48
Philae 91
Philistine, as insult 230, 255
Phoenicians 145-47
Phoneticization 424
Photography 309-10
Phrygian language 60
Pilgrimage 112, 280-81, 290, 306
Platonism 71
Playfair 366
Pogroms, Russian 261-64
Point de lendemain: Conte dédiée à la reine 402
Political cartoons 131, 135-36, 220-24, 238-55
Polygamy 67
Polygenesis 149-50

Pompadour, Madame de (Jeanne Poisson) 39
Pompeii 40
Popular culture, definition 7-8
Positivism 143-44
Poynter, John 246-47
Pre-Adamites 149-50
Primitive Culture (1871) 156, 166
Professionalization (of Near Eastern studies) 182, 406-10
Prophets 57, 146
Protestant work ethic 288-89
Psammetichos 60
Ptah 334
Publishing practices 83-84
  best-sellers 84
Punch 131-33, 135-36, 214, 224-68, 276-78, 422-26
  biblical comedy 255-64
Punch-and-Judy 224-25
Puritans 15-16
'pyramidiots' 350-80
Pyramids 350-80
  air-channels 366-67
  emperor of Austria's visit 312
  engineering 366-69
  Great Pyramid 76-77, 97, 270-71, 316-17
  and Hebrew slaves 58
  Khafre's 84-86, 97-98
  tourism 311-14, 322-24

Quatermain, Allan 90
Quern, Scottish 118

Ra 405
Race 150-54, 272, 345-48, 387-88
Rachel's tomb 111
Raiders of the Lost Ark 90
Railroad 287
Rameau, Jean-Philippe 72
Ramesseum 86-87
Ramsay, Andrew Michael 74
Ramses II 86-87, 179-80, 259, 335-36, 425
Ramses III 338
Rassam, Christian 123
Rassam, Horzmud 126, 135, 195, 394, 398, 402

Rawlinson, Henry 81, 122, 124, 127-28, 199, 394, 398-99, 404, 411
Receptive fallacy 9
'Records history' 407
Red Sea parting 117-18
Reform Bill of 1867 247
Rehoboth 110-11
Religion of the Semites (1889) 166-67
Renaissance
  magical texts 57
  scholarship 55, 57, 71, 352-53, 358
Renan, Ernest 372
Rennel, James 107
Researches into the Early History of Mankind 155-56
Revolutionary Cult of Reason 29-30
Rhampsinitos 62-63
Riebau, George 5
Rifaud's Guidebook 310
The River Jordan Company 256
Roberts, David 178
Robespierre, Maximilien de 40
Robinson, Edward 84, 103-20, 138, 285, 287-89, 294, 304, 307, 333, 336, 419, 427
  itinerary of 107
  site identification criteria 110-11
Rosetta Stone 36-37, 80-81
Ross, H.J. 311-12
Rothschild family 247
Rouet, M. 122-23
Royal Asiatic Society of Great Britain 81, 411-14
Royal Geographic Society 411
la Ruffiana 215
Russel, Charles Taze 379-80
Russo-Turkish War 133-34, 219

Sabbatical calendars 361-64
The Sacred Books of the East 172
Sacred king 167-68
Saint Simon, Claude Henry 143
Salt, Henry 87, 90, 92-93, 120, 384
Saphon 78-79
Saqqarah 312-13, 334-35
Sardanapalus 69-70
Sargon I 173
Sargon II 69-70
Sayce, A.H. 170, 402, 411
Scarab(s) 102, 310-11

Index of Subjects

Scheppig, Richard 156-57
Scientific and Artistic Commission 30, 32, 40
Schliemann, Heinrich 110, 132, 343, 400-401
Scholarly societies 410-21
Scota (Scotia) 3
Scottish nationalism 3
Scythic 82
Séchelles, Marie-Jean Hérault de 28
second coming of Christ 379-80
Semiramis 64-65, 68-69
Sennacherib 104-105, 246
Serapeum 334
Sesostris 63-64, 68
Seth 67-68, 70-71, 169
Seti I, tomb of 87-88, 99-100
Sex tourism 284
Shalmanezer III 394
Shammuramat 64-65
Sharpe, Samuel 386-92
She 8
Shelley, Percy Bysshe 179-81, 230
Shiloh 109
Short Notes to Accompany a Revised Translation of the Hebrew Scriptures 388
Sibyl 167
Sinai and Palestine in Connection with their History 234
Site report, genre 137
'site sacralization' 316
Sketchley, Arthur (George Rose) 215
Slavery
    Egypt 271, 284, 384-85
    United States 15-16, 152-54
Smith, Eli 105, 108-109
Smith, George 38, 140-41, 173, 393-95
Smith, Horace 180-81
Smith, Robertson 166-67
Smyth, Charles Piazzi 152, 312, 350-80
Soane Museum 411
Social evolution (see unilinear cultural evolution)
Society of Biblical Archaeology 395, 411-14
Society for the Preservation of the Monuments of Ancient Egypt (SPMAE) 315

Sodom 119, 419
Solomon 57, 105, 255, 276
    wisdom of 57, 255
Spencer, Herbert 156-59
Spengler, Oswald 149
Speos 333-34
Sphinx (Giza) 47-48, 147-48, 370-71
    in *Punch* 227-30, 246-50
    as symbol of Egypt 246, 316-17
'The Sphinx Speaks' 28
The Spirit of Man 1
Stainer, John 402-403
Stanhope, Lady Hester 327, 328-30
Stanley, Canon Arthur 234
Steamship 287, 288
From the Stone Age to Christianity: Monotheism and the Historical Process 175
Stone of Destiny (Stone of Scone) 3
Studies in the Scriptures 379-80
Sudan 220-24, 291
Suez Canal
    construction of 241
    and Disraeli 247-48
Sumerian (language) 81-82
Sunday School 55
Survey of western Palestine 416-17
sweating system 257-58
Swedenborgians 5

Tabernacle 350
Tait, Archibald 417
Tammuz 170
Tanis 338
Taylor, John 351-53, 358, 369-71
Taylor, W. Cooke 143
Telemachus (*Les aventures de Télémaque*) 74
Temple of Solomon 57, 350, 352
Temple prostitution 65, 356
Terrasson, Jean 55, 72-80
Texts from the Holy Bible Explained by the Help of the Ancient Monuments with a Few Plans and Views 389
Thackeray, W.M. 140, 276-78
Thames Embankment 49, 205, 209-10
Theosophy 375
Thiele, C.P. 168

Thomas Cook & Son 287, 289-91, 294, 297, 306-307
Thompson, E.P. 8
Thomsen, C.J. 164
Thomson, William 414-16
Thoth 71
A Thousand Miles up the Nile (*see* Edwards, Amelia)
Three Age System 164
Thutmoses III 205, 210
Tilden, Samuel 244-45
'To the Obelisk during the Great Frost, 1881' 211-12
Totemism 346-47
Tourist, definition 278-80
'Tourist gaze' 310
Toynbee, Arnold 149
Transactions of the Society of Biblical Archaeology 412-13
Travel
   authenticity 283
   clothing 299, 305, 326, 329, 384-85
   commodification 279, 283, 317, 323
   equipment 299-300
   health concerns 287
   souvenirs 309-11
Travel literature 17-21, 83-84
Traveller, definition 278-80
Travels in Egypt and Nubia 88-103
The Travels of Cyrus 74
The Treasures of Darkness 176
Treaty of Alexandria 36
Treaty of Paris 134
Treaty of San Stefano 135
Treaty of Versailles 134
Trojan War 404
Trollope, Anthony 318-24
Twain, Mark 295, 311
Tylor, Edward 155-56, 159, 165-67, 172
Typhon 67-68, 70, 75, 79

Unilinear cultural evolution 155-61, 165, 175, 182-83, 293, 343-48, 405-406
   and religion 165-72, 405-406
Unitarianism 386-92
United monarchy 57
University of Pennsylvania 175
'An Unprotected Female at the Pyramids' 319-24

Valley of the Kings 50, 88, 102, 385
Vandalism of antiquities 91, 311, 314-16, 329-30, 332-33, 341, 385
Vansleb, Johann 356
Veblen, Thorstein 383
Vico, Giambattista 166
Victoria, Alexandrina (queen) 60, 348
Vitruvius 425
Vögel, M. 234-35
Vogüé, Count Melchior de 418-19
Volksgeister 144-45
Volney, Count de 151, 163
Voyage dans la Basse et la Haute Egypte 32, 38-50, 54
Voyage en Sicile 39
Voyage en Syrie et en Égypte pendant les années 1783, 1784, et 1785 22
The Voyage of the Beagle 20
Vulcan 75
Vyse, Colonel Howard 356

Wadi Bahariyah 102
Wadi er-Ruhaibeh 109-11
Wallace, Alfred 154
Warren, Charles 304, 307, 422
The Watchtower Announcing Jehovah's Kingdom 379-80
Watts, Aleric Alexander 317-18
Weber, Max 159
Wellhausen, Julius 6
Wells, H.G. 148-49, 183
Weltgeist 144-45, 148, 182-83
Wheeler, Mortimer 409-10
Wilhelm II (kaiser) 173-75, 291
Wilkinson, John Gardiner 50, 151, 259, 331-32, 383-87, 392, 423
Wilson, Erasmus 205-206, 209, 266-67
Winckler, Hugo 174
wisdom, secret 57, 71-72, 372
   of Egyptian priests 60, 67, 72, 352-53, 358-59
women's participation in politics 60, 67, 348
Wright, William 404

Young, Thomas 80-81
Younger Memnon 86-87, 91, 95-96, 179-80

Zeus-Belos 65
Zias, Joe 7
Ziggurat 376-77
Zimbabwe 200-201
Zion 2

Zionism 24
   'Anglo-Zionism' 56
Zion's Watch Tower 379-80
Zoolatry 148
Zoroastrianism 57

www.ingramcontent.com/pod-product-compliance
Lightning Source LLC
Chambersburg PA
CBHW071056230426
43666CB00009B/1727